Online Accounting Information Systems

LABORATORY TEXT

using RealWorld
PRACTICAL ACCOUNTING SYSTEM

and fully integrated
LOTUS 1–2–3 SPREADSHEETS

Alan L. Eliason
Ronald O. Waite

Library of Congress Cataloging-in-Publication Data

Eliason, Alan L.
Online accounting information systems : laboratory text / Alan L.
Eliason, Ronald O. Waite.
p. cm.
"Using RealWorld practical accounting system and fully-integrated
Lotus 1-2-3 spreadsheets."
Includes bibliographical references.
ISBN 0-13-064957-0
1. Practical accounting system. 2. Small business--Accounting-
-Computer programs. 3. Electronic spreadsheets. I. Waite, Ronald
O. II. Title.
HF5679.E47 1994
657'.0285--dc20 93-24647
CIP

Production Editor: *Penelope Linskey*
Acquisitions Editor: *Frank Burrows*
Prepress Buyer: *Ilene Sanford*
Manufacturing Buyer: *Ed O'Dougherty*
Cover Design: *Marianne Frasco*
Cover Photo: *RealWorld Corporation*
Editorial Assistant: *Scott Montgomery*

Printed in the United States of America

10 9 8 7 6 5 4 3 2 1

ISBN 0-13-064957-0

Prentice-Hall International (UK) Limited, *London*
Prentice-Hall of Australia Pty. Limited, *Sydney*
Prentice-Hall Canada Inc., *Toronto*
Prentice-Hall Hispanoamericana, S.A., *Mexico*
Prentice-Hall of India Private Limited, *New Delhi*
Prentice-Hall of Japan, Inc., *Tokyo*
Simon & Schuster Asia Pte. Ltd., *Singapore*
Editora Prentice-Hall do Brasil, Ltda., *Rio de Janeiro*

TABLE OF CONTENTS

DAILY OPERATIONS

DAILY OPERATIONS (continued)

MONTHLY OPERATIONS

MONTHLY OPERATIONS (continued)

SPREADSHEET APPLICATIONS

SPREADSHEET APPLICATIONS (continued)

PRACTICE EXERCISES

INTRODUCTION

START–UP OPERATIONS

DAILY OPERATIONS

DAILY OPERATIONS (continued)

MONTHLY OPERATIONS

MONTHLY OPERATIONS (continued)

SPREADSHEET APPLICATIONS

SPREADSHEET APPLICATIONS (continued)

REFERENCE MATERIAL

APPENDIX

PREFACE

Online Accounting Information Systems was written to introduce students of business to computer–based accounting. A key objective was to provide a practical, "hands on" method of learning about receivables, payables, general ledger, payroll and inventory management processing. Toward this end, the text materials contain a series of laboratory exercises designed for the hands–on use of the Practical Accounting System (PAS), a multifunctional, integrated software system written specifically for small businesses by the RealWorld Corporation.

Simulating an Accounting System in the Computing Laboratory

In writing this text, a key objective was to remove much of the mystery regarding how and why computers are utilized in managing today's stream of accounting data. What we attempted to do was simulate in the computing laboratory a set of tasks which might be found in the "real world." This simulation consists of a series of hands–on exercises, with each exercise dedicated to a single topic such as the processing of customer invoices. While in the laboratory, you are asked to use the computer to complete a series of exercise steps that will replicate a set of output reports which are appended to the exercise. In this way, you can confirm the accuracy of your work.

A Beginning Assumption

We assumed that all users of the text and the software would have some basic background in accounting. This assumption removes the need to write about such topics as the difference between debits and credits, and assets compared to liabilities. The danger with this assumption is that some of you might not remember certain aspects of accounting called for by an exercise. When this occurs, read the reference material placed at the end of the text. When this is not enough, return to your accounting concepts text to review particular topics.

Text Expectations

What might you expect on completion of all text materials? This is perhaps the key question to ask. Our expectations are this: on completion, you should have an excellent understanding of how to start–up and implement a computer–based system of accounting for a small business. Does this actually occur? Our test results are positive. In class testing of the material, students were able to set up and implement PAS for a small, simulated business, and quickly noted this important fact on their resumes.

Organization of the Text

The organization of the text is important because it starts slow and gradually builds momentum. It begins with three exercises which describe what companies must do to get ready for computer–based processing. Entitled Start–up Operations, you will be asked to load the PAS software, to review and modify the general ledger, and to review and set accounting controls. These exercises are quite easy to complete and are designed to "get you going." The second section, entitled Daily Operations, features five exercises which deal with accounting functions performed every day by many businesses. In this section you will be asked to load customer and vendor files, and to process customer invoices, sales without customer invoices, cash receipts, and accounts payable. The third section, called Monthly Operations, consists of four exercises which depict accounting functions once (or more) each month, rather than daily. You will be asked to produce customer (monthly) statements, process the company payroll, process the physical inventory, and produce month–end reports. The final section, termed Spreadsheet Applications, extends the use of accounting data for management analysis and interpretation. The two exercises for this section ask you to export data from PAS, and to import it into the Lotus 1–2–3 spreadsheet software.

Besides this initial set of fourteen laboratory exercises, there is a second, fourteen–exercise practice set. The difference between the first set and the practice set is important. The first set asks you to become acquainted with the PAS software, while the second set asks you to practice what you have learned. You will find the practice set more difficult to complete. For this set we have assumed that you now know both accounting and PAS concepts.

Organization of Each Laboratory Exercise

The organization of each exercise is the same. Each exercise begins with a brief introduction and a set of objectives which indicate what you should be able to do on completion of the exercise. Case study materials then follow. These materials are written to help you visualize some of the "human" fears and misgivings that often accompany the implementation of computer–based processing procedures. Hands–on computer work comes next. Each exercise contains several things you must do with the PAS software. Most require you to produce formal business documents and reports. At the end of each exercise you will then find two additional sections, one entitled Questions About the Software, and the other simply called Management Issues. These sections ask you questions about what you have done and how computer–based processing affects the management of a business. You will find it helpful to read both sets of questions before beginning an exercise.

Organization of Each Practice Set Exercise

The organization of each practice set exercise is much more abbreviated than each laboratory exercise. For each practice set exercise, you are presented with a list of things to do. Following this, you are given the data needed to accomplish each "thing to do." However, you are not instructed step–by–step on how to accomplish each task. We expect you to be able to produce documents and reports without assistance. Most exercises also include a section entitled More Things to Explore. In this section you are asked to use the software in order to answer specific questions about the results of processing. For example, you are often asked to switch from the application you are working on (such as customer invoices) to another application (such as general ledger) to determine how computer–based processing in one area affects account totals in another area. What is somewhat chilling is that these changes occur automatically whenever you decide to post financial transactions. Consequently, you need to explore these changes to understand the true power of a computer–based accounting system.

Reference Material

A special section of the text provides reference material drawn from the RealWorld PAS Getting Started Manual and the RealWorld PAS User Manual. These reference materials explain in more detail the meaning of the various fields found on data entry screens. A glossary of terms for each accounting function is also placed in this section of the text. How should you use this section of the text? We advise that you refer to these materials whenever data entry requirements are not clear. For example, when working with the general ledger, suppose you find the words "fin statement type" confusing. The Maintain Chart of Accounts reference materials tells you that "fin statement type" stands for financial statement type and, further, that the types are limited to B for balance sheet and P for profit and loss (or income) statement.

Appendix Materials

The materials placed in the appendix of the text include computer requirements, the installation procedure for the PAS software, steps important to using the educational version of the PAS software, steps needed in backing up and restoring PAS data files, and steps important to exporting data from PAS for Lotus 1–2–3 use. Of these five sections, read "How to use the educational version" before you begin. You will discover how to recover if you make a severe error, miss an exercise, or decide to skip one or more exercises. This section tells you that you can begin anywhere in the text by reading in the data to begin the exercise. Why is this helpful? Suppose you are ill and miss an exercise. With starting data for each exercise, it becomes possible to skip to where you want to begin, and to return to the exercise you missed because of illness at a later time. As another example, suppose you want to run through an exercise more than once. Since you will always have the data needed to begin an exercise, you can repeat any set of exercises as often as needed.

Supplements for the Instructor

A Solutions Manual and Teaching Guide is available for the instructor. It contains answers to all of the questions asked at the end of each exercise and throughout the practice set, and provides a copy of all printed output. Helpful suggestions are also included which describe various options for setting up and using the students' starting data sets. The instructor will also be provided with a copy of RealWorld's educational version of the Practical Accounting System software, along with appropriate manuals.

Acknowledgments

This text could not have been written without the direct assistance of the staff at the RealWorld Corporation, the excellent editorial and production staff at Regents/Prentice Hall, and the students and faculty at Gordon College.

When the design of the text was little more than an abstract set of ideas, we called on Tammy Emond, Communications Director at the RealWorld Corporation, seeking her advice on whether or not to go ahead with the text. Her positive response to our ideas helped clear the way for the subsequent writing of exercise materials. Cathy Burmeister, Training Director at RealWorld, also deserves special thanks. She field tested the laboratory exercises, noting both errors and omissions.

When it was time to test this text in an actual computer laboratory setting, a very important group of individuals became involved in helping refine the final product. These individuals, senior business and information systems students at Gordon College, tested and retested each exercise to assure the accuracy of the exercises' keystrokes and smooth flow of the designated activities. The following students provided many valuable comments and suggestions:

David Alley, Andrea Bingham, James Bingham, Francine Cyganiewicz,
Richard Klein, David McCulley and Eric Mollenhauer.

Special recognition also must be given to Theodore Wood, Accounting and Finance professor at Gordon College. Ted's accounting expertise and management perspective contributed to the quality of the text, and helped establish it at a level above the purely systems or procedural orientation often observed in similar texts.

Last, but certainly not least, we wish to thank the staff at Regents/Prentice Hall and, in particular, our editor Frank Burrows, the invisible hand which served to guide the organization and layout of the materials; and his assistant, Scott Montgomery, the person who steered the text from its initial draft stage to this final manuscript. We also wish to thank

... our reviewers who provided many helpful suggestions

Jean Gutmann
University of Southern Maine

Frank Korman
Mountain View College

Phil Landers
Pennsylvania College of Technology

Kathy Perdue
De Vry Institute of Technology

Ron Strittmater
Accounting & Computer Services

Theodore Wood
Gordon College

... the Regents / Prentice Hall production staff

Mary Carnis
Production Manager

Patrick Walsh
Production Manager

Penny Linskey
Production Editor

Ilene Sanford
Pre–press Buyer

Ed O'Dougherty
Manufacturing Buyer

Cindy Harford
Supplements Editor

Julie Hildebrandt
Director of Marketing, Regents/PH

Debbie Sunderland
Marketing Manager, Regents/PH

Marianne Frasco
Art Director

Paula Maylahn
Creative Director

BACKGROUND

RealWorld Corporation

RealWorld Corporation has been a leading manufacturer of accounting and business software for over ten years. Established as Micro Business Software, Inc., the company name was changed in 1983 to align with its popular RealWorld Software brand.

RealWorld's recognition in the accounting and business software industry also continues to grow. RealWorld Software was voted #1 in the general accounting category in a poll of UnixWorld readers, #1 in the vertical market category in an extensive survey of Reseller Management magazine readers, and #1 by resellers in the accounting software category by VAR Business' 1989 State of the Market Survey, to name a few.

A 1990 Computer Reseller News study found that RealWorld accounting software was recommended by more resellers than any other brand. Resellers also rated RealWorld #1 in the September 1990 VAR Business Accounting Report Card on accounting software.

There are currently over 300,000 packages of RealWorld Accounting and Business Software installed worldwide. RealWorld is also becoming a key player in the international marketplace; the software has been translated into seven different languages, and major distributors are located on six continents.

Over 150 staff members are employed at RealWorld's corporate headquarters in Concord, New Hampshire and research and development offices located in Clearwater, Florida.

Practical Accounting System

RealWorld Practical Accounting System (PAS) is a computerized accounting and control system for small businesses. It is especially appropriate for businesses with under $2 million in annual revenues (up to $10 million maximum). PAS incorporates sound accounting practices and comprehensive security in an easy–to–tailor package.

The diagram on the next page shows the seven functions that can be performed within the PAS package. Following is a summary of the data flow.

General Ledger
This is the area of accounting where the records from other accounting areas are brought together for categorization and summarization, thereby creating a picture of the overall condition of the company's finances.

Accounts Receivable
This is the accounting area dealing with sales made by a company and with the monies it is owed. It stores customer data and prints customer statements.

Inventory management
The management of inventory includes being able to regulate or know what goes into inventory and what comes out of inventory. This includes knowing the value of what is in inventory at any time. It tracks inventory items and prints inventory management reports.

Sales Invoicing
This is the accounting process of making a complete record of a sales transaction for the buyer and the seller at the time of the sale.

Payroll
This is the accounting area dealing with compensation an employer pays his employees. It stores employee information, prints payroll checks, and prints quarterly and year–end reports.

Accounts Payable
This is the accounting area dealing with purchases and disbursements made by a company and the monies it owes. It holds vendor information and prints vendor reports.

Check Reconciliation
This is the process of bringing into agreement the balance of your checkbook and the balance shown on your bank statement. It substantially reduces the time needed for reconciling the two.

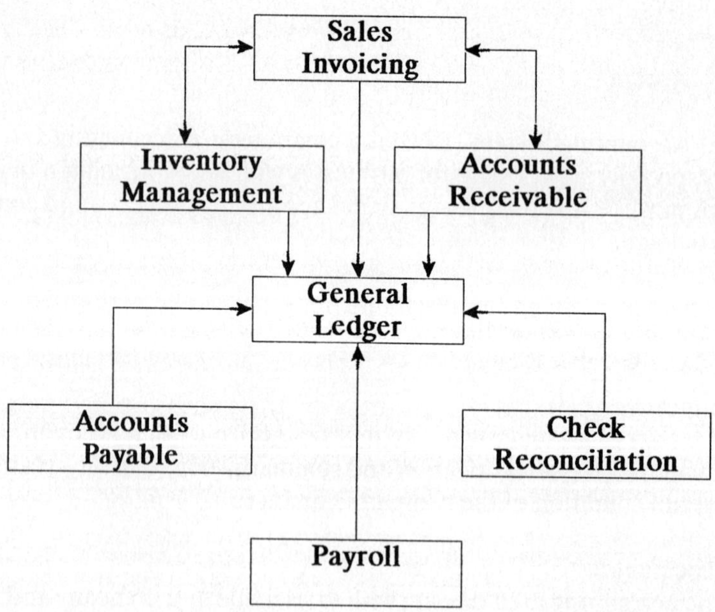

INTRODUCTION

Case Study

Lyons–Garten Lawn and Garden, Inc.

Daniel Lyons mutters, "We have to do something about our bookkeeping. It's too expensive, for what we get. Our month–to–month comparisons are always late. They are much too late for us to take any kind of corrective action."

Rose Garten, Daniel's partner, could not help overhearing Daniel's complaint. She states, "Dandy (Daniel's nickname), I realize you had trouble with computers in the past, but have you ever considered switching over to a computer–based method of processing our books. Some marvelous advances have been made in this area in the past few years. Why, with some training, I would bet that Rich could help automate our company books. After all, he keeps our inventory records current, and can tell us things about our store's inventory that our company books never reveal. Besides, Rich is interested in computers and always wants to keep abreast of changes in technology. He'll also be willing to give Jen a hand."

"I don't know about a computer," responds Dandy. "I remember my experiences at the university. It seemed that most of the time the software we used had 'bugs.' We have enough 'bugs' to worry about, being in the lawn and garden business."

Rose adds, "But your experience was from ten years ago. That was before computer companies were able to supply low–cost, high–quality software to businesses our size. Better yet, today's software is more reasonably priced and includes clear, user tutorials to help folks like us quickly understand how to implement the software. The better companies also provide their own training and service. You don't have to hire a consultant if you can't figure out what to do."

"I realize that improvements have been made with computers and business software, but what about Jen in accounting?" Dandy counters.

"What's the problem with Jen this time?" Rose asks, showing some impatience.

"Jen always claims that our bookkeeping is too complex as it is," claims Dandy. "She just can't find enough time to keep all our records straight."

"That's exactly why we need a computer," emphasizes Rose. "Jen is too busy because she is forced to do everything by hand. In my opinion, Jen is going to have to step up to the modern world or our business will suffer. We can't continue to grow if we can't keep ahead of the paperwork."

Dandy admits, "Rose, you're so right on that score. Perhaps I have been spending too much of my time attending to increasing our sales, without concentrating on the needed office support. Let's ask Jen to attend the next operations meeting to discuss the feasibility of acquiring a computer and a practical business accounting system. Will you brief Jen about our thinking? She'll play an important role if we decide to move ahead on this."

Rose responds, "Good suggestion. I'll talk to Jen and add the topic to our next agenda."

Company Organization

Lyons–Garten Lawn and Garden, Inc. was formed in the early 1980's by Daniel ("Dandy") Lyons and Rose Garten. Initially, the company limited itself to the repair of lawns and installing new lawns. Gradually, the company expanded it's base of operations to include landscape consulting and wholesale and retail sales of lawn and garden products and nursery stock.

The company is organized into four departments, with department heads reporting either to President Lyons or Vice–President Garten. Daniel is responsible for providing overall direction to the operations of the business and for supervising the work contracted by the landscape consulting and lawn installation departments. Rose shares in the responsibility of providing overall direction and supervises lawn and garden product sales and nursery stock sales.

Besides the four departments, Jenny (Jen) Ledger, the company bookkeeper, occupies a staff position. She reports to both Dandy and Rose ... which leads to problems now and then.

Landscape & Consulting Department

The Landscape & Consulting Department at Lyons–Garten was one of the smaller units as measured in terms of monthly sales volume and sales transactions. However, each job, if bid properly, was quite profit–able. Roy Sodenlayer, the supervisor of this unit comments:

"We tend to bid for most of our jobs. When a customer needs something done, we typically prepare a bid, broken down by land preparation, plantings and follow–up. We guarantee all of our plantings to last a full season."

"We have some need for a computer," Roy states with emotion, "primarily in helping us to track the profitability of this department. Quite frankly, we think we are profitable, but we might be flat out wrong. I've spoken to Jen about our need for an income statement for our department, but without much success. She is just too darn busy. Doing normal bookkeeping takes all her time."

"How do I get along with others in the company? I work more with Thatcher than with Rich or Daisy. Thatcher is still a bit green, but we get along. It's nice to have him as a backup when we have too much work."

Lawn Installation Department

The Lawn Installation Department is much like Landscape & Consulting in terms of how it operates. Thatcher Wellbe, head of this unit comments:

"Generally, we bid on all jobs, including those that involve maintaining outdoor lawn and garden dis–plays for several business accounts. If we bid on a new lawn installation, our bid includes the cost of preparing the ground (the landscape folks help us on this one), usually installing some type of sprinkler system, laying sod (or planting seed), and placing the lawn on maintenance until we know the new grass will take. I tip my hat to Roy, the way he trained me. He taught me what I need to know about repairing lawns as well as growing and laying sod."

"We could use a computer to help us track expenses," Thatcher continues. "It's not clear at the end of the month how we did. And, the reports are always late. Dandy gives us trouble during periods of weak sales.

Thank goodness our sales are strong when Landscape/Consulting sales are slack. This allows us to borrow personnel and equipment, and share some of the cost of overhead."

Lawn and Garden Sales Department

The largest sales unit at Lyons–Garten was the Lawn and Garden Sales Department. Richard (Rich) Grower, head of the department comments:

"We tend to run somewhat of a seasonable business, but all–in–all, considering everything, the peaks and valleys are not too great. In the spring and fall, we sell a variety of garden products, like fertilizers, grass seed, and bug and pest sprays. In the winter, we continue to sell seed, tools, and home and garden repair items. Gardening is a major hobby for so many of our customers. I'm surprised by the number of "hot–house–kits" (heated greenhouse kits) we sell during the colder months."

"We could use a computer for many of our areas," Rich continues. "Why take inventory! We just have to have a better way of keeping track of what we have in stock. Why, I'm the only person who really knows what's going on down here. I'm afraid to be sick or even take vacation. I worry that the department won't survive."

"Invoicing is another area," Rich notes. "The number of customer complaints tells me that something goes wrong upstairs now and then. Busy periods, in particular, lead to mass confusion in our bookkeeping area."

Nursery Sales Department

Like the Lawn and Garden Department, the Nursery Sales Department was also quite large. Headed by Daisy Stalker, the unit has experienced sizeable growth during the last three years. Daisy explains her area:

"We tend to run a more seasonable business than the other three areas. In the spring, for example, we have to bring in most of our new stock and get ready for the 'rush'. Each year there seems to be a two–week period when we do 20 percent of our annual sales. It is really something! Everyone decides to plant on the same day, it seems."

"During other periods," Daisy adds, "we tend to work closely with Landscape/Consulting and the Lawn Installation folks. The landscape designer, for example, will give us a list, telling us what plantings they need, and by when. We usually have enough time to meet their requirements. Lawn Installation staff order less from us, but frequently they are called in to repair both lawn and landscaping. This is especially so after a year with several weeks of freezing temperatures."

"We probably need computer systems for inventory more than for any other purpose," claims Daisy. "We need to have a much better handle of cost–of–goods–sold by department. Although, come to think of it, invoicing is another problem area. Sometimes a customer will call and ask if we sent out a bill for the goods delivered the month before. I relay this request to Jen. Even so, this type of call is strange to my mind. Whenever I buy something, businesses are sure quick to bill me."

Office Support and Bookkeeping

The Office Support and Bookkeeping Department was managed by Jenny (Jen) Ledger. She was responsible for all accounts receivable (A/R), accounts payable (A/P), employee payroll, and general ledger (G/L) activity. Jen indicates:

"Receivables, payables, payroll and general ledger keep me busy all month long. During periods of strong sales, I nearly go crazy getting payroll out on time and bills sent within 48 hours. I only wish Dandy and Rose would allow me to hire more staff. I can't keep doing more and more without some help."

"Do we need a computer?" questions Jen. "Only if it saves me time and the accounting system is easy for me to work with. What good is a computer if it confuses more than it helps. Friends of mine swear by the results they get using a computer, but I'm not certain if I would achieve the same results, considering my weak background in computing."

MANAGEMENT ISSUES

1. Do the people at Lyons–Garten remind you of people that you know? How would you advise them on the need for an online accounting information system?

2. Does the climate in this organization suggest that the time is "right" for a computer? Explain your reasoning.

3. Because of his experience 10 years ago, Dandy has little confidence in the computer. Do you agree with how Rose attempted to deal with Dandy's fears? What else would you do to make Dandy more eager to move to the implementation of an online accounting information system?

4. Jen is a key person in the successful implementation of the computer system. However, she expresses some reservations about her ability to achieve the desired results. What advice would you give Rose in helping Jen adjust to the idea of installing a computer system?

5. Sketch out a chart of organization at Lyons–Garten. This will help you remember the names and responsibilities of these people as you work through the various chapters in this text.

6. Review the introductory information about Lyons–Garten. List the problems described which various people in the company think will be solved with a computer system. Briefly state why you agree or disagree with their assessment.

LABORATORY EXERCISES

When working through the exercises you should be mindful of the importance of the setup and proc–essing files, and the key role played by the registers that are produced by the various application modules.

The Data Files Needed for Setup and Processing

Several types of data are required before PAS is able to do anything. You might call these "Getting Started Files." As shown below, getting started data include two types: (1) required setup files, and (2) processing files.

The **setup files** include information about the company (name, address, and so forth), accounting controls (PAS provides 47 different controls for you to use in processing), accounting periods (which month and year you will be working in), invoicing controls (PAS provides 40 controls to help control customer billing), and company checkbooks (you can have multiple checkbooks).

The **processing files** include chart of accounts, customer, vendor, item, and employee information. Before you can do anything, you must design a chart of accounts. As discussed in Chapter 2, this chart shows how you want sales, expenses, assets and liabilities reported. Files about customers and vendors are needed before you can bill customers (customer invoicing) or pay vendors for items you buy (process accounts payable). The two remaining files, the item file and the employee file, are required before you can add items to inventory or pay employees.

Setup files:

Company Data	Accounting Control	Accounting Periods	Invoicing Controls	Company Checkbooks

Processing files:

Maintain Chart of Accounts	Maintain Customer File	Maintain Vendor File	Maintain Item File	Maintain Employee File

The Role of Registers

As you work through the maze of details placed in this text, you might feel lost at times, trying to figure out where you are and where it all leads to. Within an application, the document to key on is called a **register** -- a report which indicates how sales, expenses, assets and liabilities are debited and credited. Carefully review the debits and credits shown in the following model. In working with PAS, you will be asked to examine these seven types of registers when working with financial information: Payroll, Disbursements, Bills Payable, Invoice, Sales, Cash Receipts and General Journal registers.

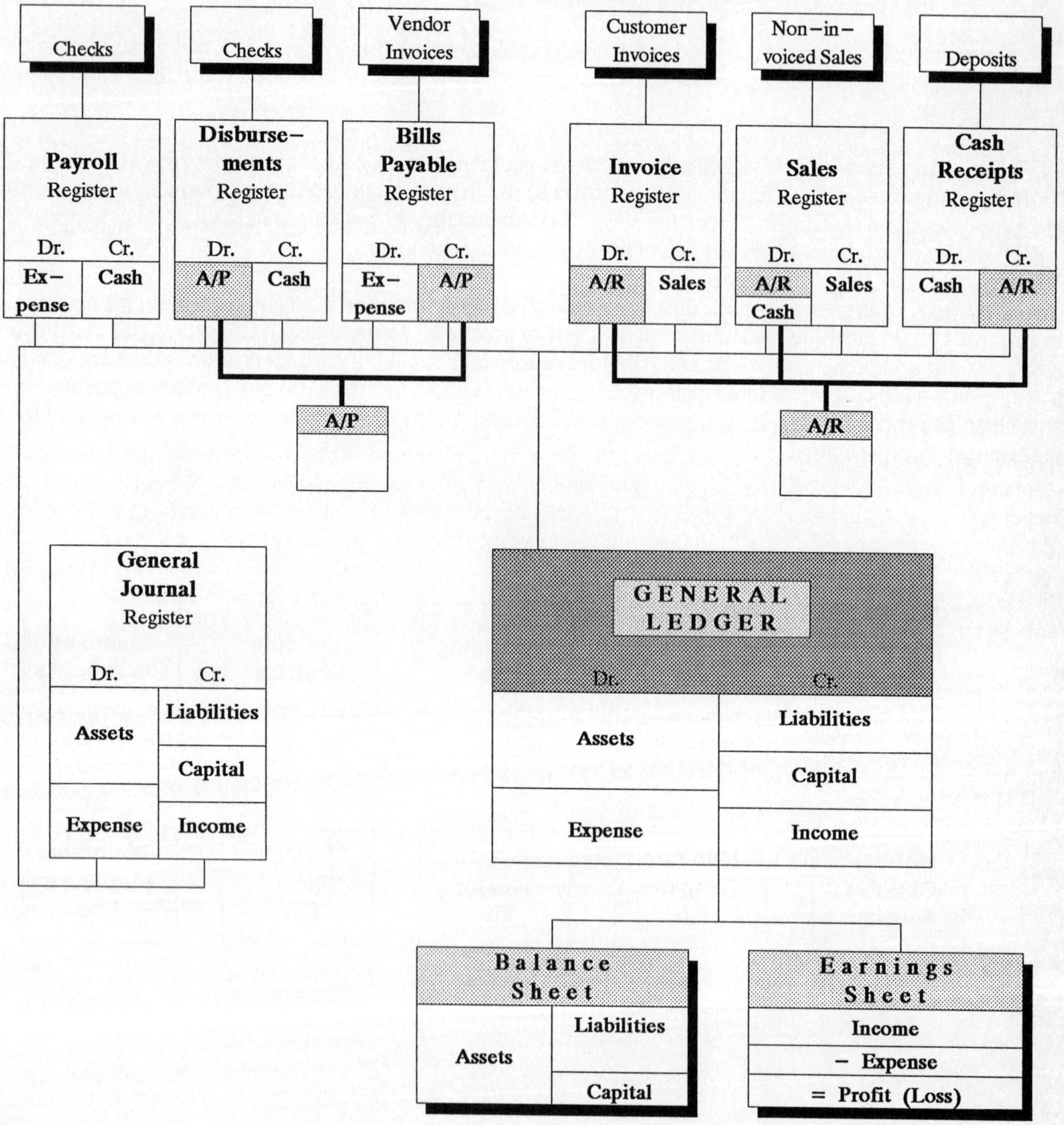

To simplify, try grouping the registers as follows:

* **The accounts receivable (A/R) and sales registers.** The customer invoice, sales, and cash receipts registers indicate debits and credits to a company's receivables. With invoices, A/R is debited and sales is credited. The increase in the amount customers owe you is shown on the **Invoice Register.** A decrease in this A/R amount is provided by a second register, the **Cash Receipts Register.** The receipts register credits A/R and debits cash (which adds to the dollar amount in your checking account). When sales are not invoiced, e.g., non-invoiced sales, the **Sales Register** shows the amounts debited to A/R or to cash, and the sales amounts. Typically, a company uses the sales register for cash sales (no A/R). However, this is not always the case. As discussed in the text, non-invoiced sales also include such things as recurring monthly charges. For example, most of us who pay rent or a mortgage are not presented with a monthly bill. Each month, we simply pay the amount due and outstanding.

* **The accounts payable (A/P) and expense registers.** The **Bills Payable Register** and the **Disbursements Register** serve to debit and credit A/P. When a bill is received, it is recorded as a payable. When a bill is paid, the payable amount is debited. Payroll does not change vendor payable amounts. Instead, the **Payroll Register** shows the amount paid to employees and the different types of payroll expenses.

When comparing the A/R side of processing to the A/P and payroll side, observe that the right-hand side adds cash to a business, while the left-hand side takes cash away. In running a business, there is a constant struggle keeping the side charged with adding cash always ahead of the side subtracting cash.

* **The general journal register.** The most flexible register shown by the model is called the **General Journal Register.** This register can be used to debit assets and expenses and to credit liabilities, capital and income. In fact, if you wanted to record all business transactions one at a time, the general register would be the only register needed. Typically, the general journal and its corresponding register are needed for correcting mistakes and for handling sales and expenditures which fall outside A/R and A/P. For example, a company might sell a piece of property. This type of transaction would normally be recorded on the general journal register.

Two important reports follow from these registers. Since information flows from all seven into the general ledger (G/L), the G/L can be used directly to produce the **balance sheet** (a report which compares assets to liabilities and capital) and the **earnings sheet** (a report which compares income to expenses and determines whether a company has earned a profit or incurred a loss during a period).

When working through the chapters in the text, plan to refer back to this model. It should help to visualize what is occurring within the PAS computerized accounting system.

Exercise 1 – START–UP AND OVERVIEW

Introduction

In this initial exercise, you are asked to personalize the Practical Accounting System (PAS) software by adding the name, address and telephone number of your company. If you do not personalize the software, you will not be able to use it. The name you select will depend on what your instructor requires. For example, your instructor may ask you to type your name, or allow you to enter a unique name such as "Dr. YardCare", instead of the suggested name of Lyons–Garten Lawn and Garden, Inc.

A second objective of this exercise is to ask you to become familiar with the way in which Main Menu choices work. PAS is a "menu–driven system." This means you must navigate your way through the software by making a number of menu choices. If you want to back up to an earlier menu, press the END or TAB key on your keyboard.

A third objective is to ask you to become familiar with the built–in, online Help function provided by PAS. This function is designed to provide you with a clear description of a term, or a brief "how to" explanation of what action is permitted or required (for example, how to enter company address information using three data input lines).

Before you begin, however, you should know that PAS contains several types of computer programs. These include (1):

* **Edit programs** to check on the accuracy of data entered into processing and print these data before they are posted (that is, written) to computer files.
* **Update programs** to create or modify records stored on computer files.
* **Display programs** to extract records from computer files and to display them on the computer monitor.
* **Register programs** to list the information stored on a computer file.
* **Summary programs** to extract data from computer files and print a summary report, such as a financial statement.
* **Action–document programs** to produce formal business documents such as customer invoices.
* **Change–report programs** to show information changed by an update program.

In PAS, an edit and update function are sometimes combined into a single program. For example, if an amount is entered and "posted to" (or added to) a file by the same program, this represents a combined edit–update program. When working through this initial exercise, think about the function provided by each PAS program. You will be asked questions about program functions at the end of the exercise.

---

1 These seven types of programs are more fully described in Eliason, A. L., Online Business Computer Applications (Third Edition), MacMillan Publishing Co., 1991.

Objectives

When you complete this exercise you should be able to:

- load the PAS software and sample data (optional; see note above)
- navigate your way through the PAS software
- add company set–up information
- use the online Help facility

Case Study

With the arrival of the computer and the PAS software, the first decision Dandy and Rose must make is where to physically place the machine.

Rose suggests, "I think the computer should be placed in Jen's office. While she is somewhat afraid to take on more work, she seems willing to give the computer a try. She also feels that unless something is done, we will have to hire a new bookkeeper. This would also require her to take on more work."

"Can we move ahead slowly," cautions Dandy. "I don't want to get 'burned.' I keep reading about companies where the computer did this or that."

"We definitely will move ahead slowly," assures Rose. "We need to set up the software before we can use it. Even this will take some time. We also want the staff to feel comfortable working with a computer. Unless they see the benefits, they will resist any attempt at networking together several computers at a future date."

"I'm glad we agree on this one," concludes Dandy.

While Dandy and Rose are talking, Jen Ledger is thinking about what initial steps she should take. "First, I'll load the software and review all the application menus. The Table of Contents indicates that the software will allow us to bill our customers (process customer invoices), record cash payments (process cash receipts), manage our accounts receivable (what customers owe us) and accounts payable (what we owe our suppliers), record our inventory (showing what is available and product prices), and prepare our month–end financial reports (the balance sheet and income statements)."

"What I really need to examine," Jen continues, "are the functions designed for each application, so I can distinguish the programs designed to enter data for processing (input) from those written to process the entered data (process) or to print the results of processing (output). Input–processing–output (IPO); that's what it's all about."

Load the PAS Software and Exercise Data

Your instructor may not choose to have you perform the PAS installation procedure. The PAS software and sample data may have already been installed on your computer.

However, if your instructor chooses to have you become familiar with the installation procedure, there are automated installation procedures on the INSTALLATION DISKETTE. These procedures will perform all of the steps needed to install the software and sample data on your computer. The installation instructions are detailed in Appendices B and C. There is no multi–company capability in PAS, which would allow you to keep separate books for a number of different companies.

Start–up Procedure

After PAS is installed, you can activate it by following these steps.

☐ 1. Turn your computer on, and change to the PAS directory by typing **CD PAS.**

☐ 2. At the subsequent prompt, type PAS and press ENTER to load the software.

Review the Menus

The successful loading of the software into your computer will lead to the display of the title and copyright screen. Do the following to advance to the Main Menu.

☐ 3. Press ENTER to remove the title and copyright screen. The PAS Main Menu will appear as follows:

MAIN MENU

```
RealWorld Practical Accounting System                          XYZ Co.
Version 1.0

                    Please select
                       1. Sales Invoicing
                       2. Inventory Management
                       3. Accounts Receivable
                       4. Accounts Payable
                       5. Payroll
                       6. General Ledger
                       7. Check Reconciliation
                       8. Setup Functions

Press F10 for help at any time
```

☐ 4. If passwords have been set up to control access to PAS functions, enter your password when requested, and press ENTER. Otherwise, ignore this step.

☐ 5. Press the F10 key, and follow instructions by pressing ENTER and using the ARROW keys to acquaint yourself with the HELP function.

☐ 6. Press the TAB or END key to return to the Main Menu.

☐ 7. With the Main Menu facing you, type 1 (Sales Invoicing), and press ENTER. Write down the seven sub–menu choices for Sales Invoicing on the PAS Menu page at the end of this exercise.

NOTE: Do not change, add or delete any data already in your data base. This will be done in subsequent exercises.

☐ 8. Press the END or TAB key to return to the Main Menu.

☐ 9. Make other menu choices from the Main Menu to explore the remaining functions provided by the software. Each time, record the observed sub–menus for each selection on the PAS Menu page at the end of the exercise. Once again, do NOT change, add or delete data at this time.

Set Up Company Data

Now that you've explored the menu system and PAS parts, we must enter some preliminary company, user, control and computing configuration data.

☐ 10. Type 8 (Setup Functions) from the Main Menu, and press ENTER.

```
RealWorld Practical Accounting System                          XYZ Co.
Setup Functions

                         Please select
                          1. Maintain company data
                          2. Maintain chart of accounts
                          3. Maintain accounting control data
                          4. Maintain accounting periods
                          5. Maintain invoicing control data
```

☐ 11. Type 1 (Maintain Company Data) from the above Setup Functions menu, and press ENTER. Examine the list of 12 data items displayed on the next pagc. If you have questions about the terms displayed, use the HELP function (press F10) or refer to "Setup Functions, Maintain Company Data" in the Reference Section found at the back of this text.

☐ 12. Select the appropriate field numbers (1–6) and enter the following information in upper or lower case letters.

Company Name (long):	LYONS–GARTEN LAWN AND GARDEN, INC.
Company Name (short):	L–G LAWN AND GARDEN
Address:	1169 Greenbelt Way Nice Valley, OR 97000
Phone Number:	503–686–5000

The limits on length of each field are: Company Name (long): 50 characters
Company Name (short): 30 characters

NOTE: Optionally, your instructor may suggest that you use long and short company names that incorporate your individual name or group name so that the printed output of these exercises will be uniquely identified. However, if you follow the start–up procedure outlined in Appendix C for loading each exercise's data, the above step #12 should be repeated each time after loading the data. Otherwise, the standard Lyons–Garten company name will appear on all printed reports.

Maintain company data

1. Company name (long)		XYZ Company	
2. Company name (short)		XYZ Co.	
3. Address line 1	500 W. Lincoln Blvd.		
4. Address line 2	Anytown, Texas 12345		
5. Address line 3			
6. Phone number	123/456-7890		
7. Are G/L profit centers used?	N	10. Printer	LPT1
8. Allow protected changes?	Y	11. Compressed?	Y
9. Use passwords?	N	12. Printer type	Epson

------------------- Printer types -------------------

1. Tandy DMP-300	5. IBM & Compatibles	09. C. Itoh
2. Tandy DMP-107/133	6. Epson	10. NEC
3. Tandy DMP-442	7. Okidata	11. Other
4. Tandy DMP-2102/21 20	8. Toshiba	

Field number to change?

☐ 13. Enter the following for fields 7 to 12. (NOTE: Your instructor may provide different information for field numbers 7–12.)

Field number		
7	Are G/L profit centers used?	Type Y, for yes.
8	Allow protected changes?	Type N, for no.
9	Use passwords?	Leave as N, for no, and read the warning in the Reference Section.
10	Printer?	Leave as LPT1.
11	Compressed?	Leave as Y for 8.5" paper, or type N for 14" wide paper. (Check your printer.)
12	Printer Type?	If you answered Y to "Compressed?" print, enter the number representing your printer. (Ask your instructor if you don't know your "Printer type".)

☐ 14. After you have completed the above step,

- ➟ press ENTER at "Field number to change?" to save your company data and return to the Setup Functions menu,
- ➟ press END to return to the Main Menu, and
- ➟ press END to exit the software.

Backup Your Data Files

☐ 15. Follow the instructions in Appendix D to:

- ➡ format and label three backup data disks, and
- ➡ backup your PAS data files onto the first (PAS Backup Series A) of these three data disks.

NOTE: It is very important that you develop the habit of backing up your data files each time you complete an exercise or merely change one data item.

QUESTIONS ABOUT THE SOFTWARE

1. How can you tell that the Practical Accounting System is a menu–driven system?

2. What is the purpose of the F10 function key?

3. What would happen if you decided to use passwords BEFORE any have been provided for? (Hint: Find the answer in the Reference Section, page R–3.)

MANAGEMENT ISSUES

4. Suppose you are an accountant for a small, but growing, candy manufacturer. By browsing through PAS, how might EACH of the seven functions (shown on the Main Menu) help you to manage the company books? For example, how do you think Sales Invoicing will help you in managing the company books? How would Inventory Management help you?

   Save your answers to these questions. Later on, we will ask you to return to revise your initial impressions.

5. Managers in today's fast–paced environment need accurate information prepared in a timely manner. For example, they might require a display showing the number of units shipped yesterday. How can a computer–based system such as PAS help managers to realize "accurate information prepared in a timely manner"?

   Again, save your written response to this initial impression.

THINGS TO DO

6. With the Main menu facing you, type 6 (General Ledger). When the submenu appears, type 1 (Maintain Chart of Accounts). Press F10 to answer the following question: What is a "chart of accounts"?

   Exit from Help and answer the following question: Of the seven types of computer programs that were explained at the beginning of this exercise, what types of programs are: Add accounts? Change accounts? Delete accounts?

   Press END a sufficient number of times to return to the Main menu.

7. With the Main menu facing you, type 1 (Sales Invoicing). When the submenu appears, type 3 (View Invoices). Press F10 and answer the following: What is the purpose of the View Invoices selection? Which one of the seven types of computer programs is the View Invoices program?

   Return to the Main menu.

8. With the Main menu facing you, type 5 (Payroll). When the submenu appears, type 9 (Print Quarterly Payroll Report). What is the purpose of this report (press F10)? Which of the seven types of computer programs is needed to produce the quarterly payroll report?

   Return to the Main menu.

9. With the Main menu facing you, type 3 (Accounts Receivable). When the submenu appears, type 8 (Print Customer Statements). What does this program accomplish (press F10)? What type of computer program is the Print Customer Statements program?

   Return to the Main menu.

10. With the Main menu facing you, type 4 (Accounts Payable). When the submenu appears, type 3 (Process Disbursements). What is a disbursement (press F10)? What is a recurring transaction (press F10)? What type of computer program is required to:

    a. Add Transaction ______________________

    b. Change Transaction ______________________

    c. Delete Transaction ______________________

    d. Print Transaction Edit List ______________________

    e. Print Disbursement Checks ______________________

    f. Post Transactions ______________________

PAS Menus

1 Sales Invoicing

1
2
3
4
5
6
7

2 Inventory Management

1
2
3
4
5
6
7
8

3 Accounts Receivable

1
2
3
4
5
6
7
8
9

4 Accounts Payable

1
2
3
4
5

5 Payroll

1
2
3
4
5
6
7
8
9
10
11

6 General Ledger

1
2
3
4
5
6
7
8

7 Check Reconciliation

1
2
3
4

8 Setup Functions

1
2
3
4
5

Exercise 2 – MODIFY GENERAL LEDGER ACCOUNTS

Introduction

Before the LYONS–GARTEN LAWN AND GARDEN company can really get started, it must modify the chart of accounts provided in the PAS start–up data, and establish certain account balances. The modified chart of accounts should reflect the way in which the company wants to have its sales, expenses, assets and liabilities reported. (NOTE: Experience shows that it is easier to start with the PAS–supplied chart of accounts than to create one from nothing.)

Objective

In this exercise, you are initially asked to print the PAS predefined chart of accounts list. Following this, you are asked to change and delete general ledger (G/L) accounts and to print the revised chart of accounts lists. When you complete this exercise, you should be able to:

- ➡ tell how the LYONS–GARTEN chart of accounts is organized.
- ➡ change the chart of accounts by adding, deleting and revising codes
- ➡ print the chart of accounts list

Case Study

Dandy Lyons remarks, "Some of the entries in the chart of accounts supplied by the software don't meet our needs. For example, we need to label our cash accounts differently. Don't we use one cash account for payroll and another for payables?"

"Yes we do use our two accounts in this way," Jen Ledger replies. "However, the name of any account is very easy to change using the PAS software."

"Well, what about the deletion of an account?", continues Dandy. "That must be more difficult to handle."

"Quite the opposite," states Jen. "Deleting an account is almost too easy. Because of its simplicity, it's very important that we back up our computer files every day and tightly control access to the computer."

"What do you mean by control access?", questions Dandy.

"We have to treat the computer much like we treat a cash register," Jen clarifies. "No one should be allowed to access the computer unless they are authorized to do so."

"And knows what they are doing," Dandy adds.

"Correct," Jen states.

"Jen, can we set up a new set of sales and cost of goods sold (COGS) accounts; one for each department?", questions Dandy.

"I don't know why not," responds Jen. "We can track sales and cost of goods sold in any way we want. The only difficulty is that the more complexity we add, the more difficult it will be to enter the data correctly."

"Well, I think we should post sales and COGS by department to begin. This will help us determine how well our departments are performing."

"I'll do it," states Jen. "And while I'm labeling our cash accounts, I'll also enter and post our current cash balances.

Set Transaction Date

Before you start this exercise, set today's date at April 2, 1997 using the MS-DOS 'DATE' command. At the C: prompt, type: **DATE** and press ENTER. At a subsequent prompting, type the date in requested format as: **4-2-97** and press ENTER.

Print the Predefined Chart of Accounts

PAS provides a predefined chart of accounts for a business. Do the following to review and print this chart of accounts:

☐ 1. Log on using the instructions in Exercise 1. The Main menu will appear on your screen.

MAIN MENU

```
RealWorld Practical Accounting System                L-G LAWN AND GARDEN
Version 1.0

                     Please select
                        1.  Sales Invoicing
                        2.  Inventory Management
                        3.  Accounts Receivable
                        4.  Accounts Payable
                        5.  Payroll
                        6.  General Ledger
                        7.  Check Reconciliation
                        8.  Setup Functions

Press F10 for help at any time
```

☐ 2. Type 8 (Setup Functions) from the Main menu, and press ENTER.

```
RealWorld Practical Accounting System                L-G LAWN AND GARDEN
Setup Functions

                 Please select
                    1.  Maintain company data
                    2.  Maintain chart of accounts
                    3.  Maintain accounting control data
                    4.  Maintain accounting periods
                    5.  Maintain invoicing control data
```

☐ 3. Type 2 (Maintain Chart of Accounts) from the above Setup Functions menu, and press ENTER.

```
Maintain chart of accounts                           L-G LAWN AND GARDEN

                 Please select
                    1.  Add accounts
                    2.  Change accounts
                    3.  Delete accounts
                    4.  Print out accounts
```

☐ 4. Type 4 (Print Out Accounts) from the above Maintain Chart of Accounts menu, and press ENTER.

☐ 5. At the following Print Out Accounts menu, press F1 (the function key) twice to indicate that you want to begin printing with the "first" account, and end printing with the "last" account.

```
Maintain chart of accounts                           L-G LAWN AND GARDEN
Print out accounts

              Please enter
                 Starting account     "First"
                 Ending account       "Last"

Any change?   N
```

☐ 6. Press ENTER (N) at "Any change?" to indicate that the above was done correctly.

☐ 7. Type Y when asked, "Display this report?", and press ENTER. The entire report will be scrolled on the screen. Experiment with different speeds of scrolling by typing two or three numbers between 1 and 9, where 1 = slow and 9 = fast. (NOTE: You should not press ENTER after selecting a number.) At the end of the report, press ENTER to continue.

☐ 8. To print the report (see Figure 2–1), repeat steps 4 through 6, and press ENTER (N) at "Display this report?". If you experience problems in printing, press the F1 key.

Change General Ledger (G/L) Accounts

PAS allows you to add, change or delete a G/L account from the predefined chart of accounts. In this way, you can tailor account numbers for specific types of businesses. Do the following to change an account:

☐ 9. From the Maintain Chart of Accounts menu, type 2 (Change Accounts), and press ENTER.

☐ 10. From the Change Accounts menu, type 1010 for the Account #, and press ENTER twice. Your screen will appear as follows:

```
Maintain chart of accounts                              L-G LAWN AND GARDEN
Change accounts

        1.   Account #                 1010-000
        2.   Description               Cash in bank - #1
        3.   Fin statement type        B
        4.   Paren control code        C
        5.   Compression code          D

Make changes, or press F1 for next account
Field number to change?
```

☐ 11. Type 2 when asked "Field number to change?", and press ENTER.

☐ 12. Type **Cash #1 – Payables** and press ENTER.

☐ 13. Repeat the above steps to modify the following account descriptions: (NOTE: To enter the desired account number, you may press ENTER and type in the account number, or press F1 as many times as needed to advance to the next G/L account.)

account #	from	to
1020	Cash in bank – #2	Cash #2 – Payroll
1900	Goodwill	Organization
4010	Sales – merchandise	Sales – Lawn Installation
5010	Cost of goods sold	COGS – Lawn Installation

NOTE: If you accidently go past an account number when pressing F1, you have two recovery options:
a) Keep pressing the F1 key until you come to the end of the Chart of Accounts file. Then press ENTER and key in the desired account number; or
b) Press ENTER at "Field number to change?"; then key in the desired number.

☐ 14. Press ENTER at "Field number to change?"; then press END to exit the Change Accounts menu, returning to the Maintain Chart of Accounts menu.

Delete G/L Accounts

Deleting an account is easier than modifying one as long as there are no transactions on file for the account you wish to delete. (There are built–in precautions which prevent you from deleting accounts with recorded activity.)

Do the following to remove accounts from the G/L:

☐ 15. From the Maintain Chart of Accounts menu, type 3 (Delete Accounts), and press ENTER. You will see that the Delete Accounts menu is identical to the Change Accounts menu.

☐ 16. Type 2370 when asked to enter the account number, and press ENTER twice. The account number for Local Income Tax Withheld will be displayed.

☐ 17. Local withholding taxes are not required by our business. Therefore, answer Y when asked, "Ok to delete account?", and press ENTER. PAS will indicate that you have successfully deleted account number 2370. Press ENTER to continue.

☐ 18. Repeat the above steps to delete accounts:

1030	Cash in bank – #3
6210	Salaries – bonuses
4020	Sales – services

☐ 19. After deleting the above accounts, press END to exit the Delete Accounts menu and return to the Maintain Chart of Acounts menu.

Add G/L Accounts

Adding a G/L account is similar to changing a G/L account. In this instance, the data for all fields must be key–entered. To add an account to the G/L, do the following:

☐ 20. From the Maintain Chart of Accounts menu, type 1 (Add Accounts), and press ENTER. You will see that the Add Accounts menu is also identical to the Change Accounts menu.

☐ 21. Type 4000 and press ENTER twice to indicate the new account number you wish to add.

☐ 22. Type "Sales – Landscape/Consult" to add a field description to the new account. In later exercises you will be asked to group sales by department.

☐ 23. Type P to indicate that this account is to be printed on the Profit and Loss financial statement.

☐ 24. Type D to indicate that parentheses are to be displayed when this account holds a Debit balance. (Sales accounts, of course, typically have a credit balance.) NOTE: Refer to Reference Material R–4 at the end of the text for a description of the Paren Control Code.

☐ 25. Type P to indicate that you would like to compress transactions for this account number. By com–pressing transactions, the result is a single transaction for each Period when there is activity for this G/L account. NOTE: Refer to Reference Material R–5 for a description of the Compression Code.

After entering the above data, your Add Accounts menu should appear as shown on the following page.

Maintain chart of accounts Add accounts		L–G LAWN AND GARDEN
1. Account #	4000–000	
2. Description	Sales – Landscape/Consult	
3. Fin statement type	P	
4. Paren control code	D	
5. Compression code	P	
Field number to change?		

☐ 26. Press ENTER when asked "Field number to change?". This will add the new account to the chart of accounts.

☐ 27. Repeat the above steps to add the following accounts. In the process, enter the same codes for item numbers 3, 4 and 5 entered in steps 23–25.

4020 Sales – Lawn and Garden
4030 Sales – Nursery

☐ 28. Repeat the above steps to add the following accounts. In this case, though, type C at Paren Control Code to indicate that parentheses are to be shown when these accounts have a Credit balance.

5000 COGS – Lawn and Garden
5005 COGS – Landscape/Consult
5015 COGS – Nursery

☐ 29. Press ENTER when asked "Field number to change?". Press END at the Add Accounts menu to return to the Maintain Chart of Accounts menu.

Print the Revised G/L

☐ 30. Print the Modified Chart of Accounts (see Figure 2–2) to verify and document the changes you have made. To do so, repeat steps 4 to 8 at the beginning of this exercise.

☐ 31. Press END twice to return to the Main menu.

Examine the Checkbook Balance

One of the first steps to take in setting up a computer–based accounting system is to determine if the checkbook balances agree with the G/L cash account balances. If not, either the checkbook balances or the G/L account balances must be adjusted.

☐ 32. Type 6 (General Ledger) from the Main menu, and press ENTER.

```
RealWorld Practical Accounting System                    L-G LAWN AND GARDEN
General Ledger

              Please select
                  1.    Maintain chart of accounts
                  2.    Process general journal
                  3.    View G/L account activity
                  4.    Print trial balance
                  5.    Print financial statements
                  6.    Compress G/L transactions
                  7.    Calculate a loan payment
                  8.    Close accounting year
```

☐ 33. Type 3 (View G/L Account Activity) from the General Ledger menu, and press ENTER.

☐ 34. Type 1010 and press ENTER twice for Cash #1 – Payables.

☐ 35. Press F1 for "Earliest."

☐ 36. Press F1 for "Latest."

After making the above entries, your screen should look like the following:

```
G/L account activity                                  L-G LAWN AND GARDEN
                                               Cur prd: 4/01/97 to 4/30/97
              Please enter:
                1.  Account #        1010-000 Cash #1-Payables
                2.  Starting date    "Earliest"
                3.  Ending date      "Latest"

Field number to change?
```

☐ 37. Press ENTER at "Field Number to Change?", and press F1 to move to the second screen shown on the next page. Observe that the last General Ledger (G/L) entry was on 3/15/97 and the Ending Balance in Account #1010 (Cash #1 – Payables) is $0.00.

View G/L account activity — L–G LAWN AND GARDEN

Account: 1010–000 Cash #1 – Payables — Cur prd: 4/01/97 to 4/30/97

Trans–date	Source	DR–amount	CR–amount	Reference
02/15/97	DB0062		846.94	Hanson Manufacturing Co.
02/15/97	DB0062		301.15	South–Western Bell
02/15/97	GJ0066	3,801.42		Add cash from R/E
03/15/97	DB0062		1,150.00	Jones Property Management
03/15/97	DB0062		859.72	Reynolds Tool Company
03/15/97	DB0062		270.10	South–Western Bell

Begin–bal	Total–DR	Total–CR	Net–change	Ending–bal
.00	15,271.56	15,271.56	.00	.00

Press F2 to see previous page or press END to make another selection

☐ 38. Press END three times to return to the Main menu.

☐ 39. Type 7 (Check Reconciliation) from the Main menu, and press ENTER.

RealWorld Practical Accounting System — L–G LAWN AND GARDEN

Check Reconciliation

Please select
1. Record checking account transfers
2. Process checking account adjustments
3. Reconcile a checking account
4. Print a checkbook

☐ 40. Type 4 (Print a Checkbook) from the above Check Reconciliation menu, and press ENTER.

☐ 41. Type 1 for checking account number, and press ENTER.

☐ 42. Answer N (press ENTER) for "Purge cleared items?".

NOTE: You will learn how to mark the items in your checkbook that have cleared the bank in a later exercise. Purging (removing) cleared items from your checkbook should be done at least once a year. A good time to do it is after you have finalized your tax return for the previous year (in which case you should purge only through the end of the previous year).

After making the above entries, your screen should appear as shown on the following:

```
Print a checkbook                                   L-G LAWN AND GARDEN

                  Please enter:
                    1. Checking account #      1  8765-432-19876
                    2. Purge cleared items?    N

Field number to change?
```

☐ 43. Press ENTER when asked "Field number to change?".

☐ 44. Type Y when asked "Display the report?", and press ENTER.

☐ 45. Observe that the Current checkbook balance is also $0.00. This means (thank goodness!) that the checkbook now balances with the cash in the bank.

☐ 46. Press ENTER to continue, followed by END (twice) to return to the Main menu.

Enter Cash Account Balances

Next we ask you to add some money to the checking account you will be working with. Remember, you often need considerable funds (cash) just to open the doors of a business such as Lyons–Garten.

☐ 47. Type 6 (General Ledger) from the Main menu, and press ENTER.

☐ 48. Type 2 (Process General Journal) from the G/L menu, and press ENTER.

```
Process general journal                             L-G LAWN AND GARDEN

                  Please select
                    1.   Add transactions
                    2.   Change transactions
                    3.   Delete transactions
                    4.   Print transaction edit list
                    5.   Post transactions
```

☐ 49. Type 1 (Add Transactions) from the above Process General Journal menu, and press ENTER. The screen on the next page will appear first to confirm the current period dates.

```
Process general journal                                L-G LAWN AND GARDEN
Add transactions

        ---Current period---          --Accounting periods--
         4/01/97  to  4/30/97

                                       1 - 1/01/97   to  1/31/97
                                       2 - 2/01/97   to  2/28/97
                                       3 - 3/01/97   to  3/31/97
                                       4 - 4/01/97   to  4/30/97
                                       5 - 5/01/97   to  5/31/97
                                       6 - 6/01/97   to  6/30/97
                                       7 - 7/01/97   to  7/31/97
                                       8 - 8/01/97   to  8/31/97
                                       9 - 9/01/97   to  9/30/97
                                      10 - 10/01/97 to 10/31/97
                                      11 - 11/01/97 to 11/30/97
                                      12 - 12/01/97 to 12/31/97

Any change to current period?   N
```

☐ 50. Enter N(no) at "Any change to current period?".

☐ 51. Enter the following transaction information for Checking Account #1.

Account #	1010–000 (press ENTER twice)
Trans Date	40297
DEBIT Amount	25000
Reference	Set up cash account

If the above data has been entered correctly, your screen should look like the following:

```
Process general journal                             L-G LAWN AND GARDEN
Add transactions                            Current period: 4/01/97 to 4/30/97

        1. Account #        1010-000   Cash #1 - Payables
        2. Trans date       4/02/97
        3. Debit amount     25,000.00      Credit amount
        4. Reference        Set up cash account

                    Running balance:        .00

Field number to change?
```

☐ 52. Press ENTER when asked, "Field number to change?".

☐ 53. Enter the following information to Long Term Debt to indicate the source of the above funds.

Account #	2530–000
Trans Date	40297
CREDIT Amount	25000
Reference	Set up cash account

☐ 54. Press ENTER when asked, "Field number to change?".

☐ 55. Press END to return to the Process General Journal menu.

☐ 56. Type 4 (Print Transaction Edit List) from the Process General Journal menu, and press ENTER.

☐ 57. Press ENTER (N) when asked, "Display this report?". This choice produces the General Journal Transaction Edit List (see Figure 2–3), showing changes to accounts 1010 and 2530.

☐ 58. Type 5 (Post Transactions) from the Process General Journal menu, and press ENTER.

☐ 59. Type Y and press ENTER when asked, "Are General Journal transactions OK to post?". This prints the General Journal Transaction Register (see Figure 2–4).

☐ 60. Press END twice to return to the Main menu.

Bring the Checkbook Up To Date

A cash infusion from long–term debt, such as the one just processed, does not automatically update the PAS checkbooks. Special adjustments are required. In this section we bring one checkbook up to date. We will add funds to the second checkbook later in the text.

☐ 61. Type 7 (Check Reconciliation) from the Main menu, and press ENTER.

```
RealWorld Practical Accounting System                L-G LAWN AND GARDEN
Check Reconciliation

            Please select
               1.   Record checking account transfers
               2.   Process checking account adjustments
               3.   Reconcile a checking account
               4.   Print a checkbook
```

☐ 62. Type 2 (Process Checking Account Adjustments) from the above menu, and press ENTER.

☐ 63. Type 1 and press ENTER for Checking Account # 8765–432–19876.

☐ 64. Answer N at "Any change?". The Process Checking Account Adjustments menu will appear as shown on the next page.

```
Process checking account adjustments                      L-G LAWN AND GARDEN

            Checking account: 8765-432-19876              4400998877

                      Please select
                          1.  Add transactions
                          2.  Change transactions
                          3.  Delete transactions
                          4.  Print transaction edit list
                          5.  Post transactions
```

☐ 65. Type 1 (Add Transactions) from the above menu, and press ENTER.

☐ 66. Enter the following transaction information for Checking Account #1.

Adjustment date:	040297
CREDIT amount:	25000
Reference:	Set up cash balance
G/L account #:	1010–000 (Cash #1 – Payables)

☐ 67. Press ENTER at "Field number to change?", and press END to return to the Process Checking Account Adjustments menu.

☐ 68. Type 4 (Print Transaction Edit List) from the Process Checking Account Adjustments menu, and press ENTER.

☐ 69. Answer Y when asked, "Display this report?" to verify your entry.

☐ 70. Press ENTER to remove the display.

☐ 71. Type 5 (Post transactions) from the Process Checking Account Adjustments menu, and press ENTER.

☐ 72. Answer Y when asked, "Are checking account adjustment transactions OK to post?", and press ENTER. The Checking Account Adjustment Register will be printed (see Figure 2–5). The checkbook balance now matches the cash in the bank. Press END to return to the Check Reconciliation menu.

Check the Checkbook Balance

☐ 73. Type 4 (Print a Checkbook) from the Check Reconciliation menu, and press ENTER to determine what the new checkbook balance is.

☐ 74. Type 1 (Checking account #), and press ENTER.

☐ 75. Press ENTER (N) at "Purge cleared items?" to indicate that you do NOT want to purge cleared checks at this time.

☐ 76. Press ENTER when asked, "Field number to change?".

☐ 77. Press ENTER (N) when asked, "Display this report?". Figure 2–6 shows the revised checkbook balance.

☐ 78. This completes the exercise. Press END a sufficient number of times to leave PAS.

QUESTIONS ABOUT THE SOFTWARE

1. How many G/L account numbers have been predefined for you by PAS?
2. Why is it important to be able to add, change and delete G/L account numbers?
3. Suppose you wanted to collect sales data on 24 different products. What changes to the chart of accounts are required?
4. For this exercise, all outstanding checks had been cleared, but not purged. What is meant by cleared? What is meant by purged? How often should checks be purged?
5. What are the implications of cash in the bank being LESS THAN cash in your PAS checkbook? What are the implications of cash in the bank being GREATER THAN cash in your checkbook?
6. Why is the maintaining of the G/L accounts called a setup function?
7. What do you think would happen if you tried to delete an account that contained a dollar balance?

MANAGEMENT ISSUES

8. Most of us realize that the cash in the bank should balance to the amount we show in our checkbooks. This is why we sit down each month (or so) to reconcile our checkbook. In a company like Lyons–Garten, the issue whether the company books are in balance is more difficult to determine. With a computer–based system like PAS, how do managers like Dandy and Rose determine that the company's cash is in balance? Explain a procedure to keep Dandy and Rose informed using PAS.
9. Why would a company such as Lyons–Garten, have two checking accounts rather than one? Why are different accounts important to management?
10. Why do you think Dandy Lyons wants sales and cost of goods sold entered by department? Why is this breakdown of information important to management?
11. Some people believe that once a chart of accounts is set, it should never be changed. Do you agree or disagree with this statement? Why might management want to change an account (add, change, delete)?

THINGS TO DO

12. From the Maintain Chart of Accounts menu (via Setup Functions), display the accounts starting with 4000 and ending with 5000. How many accounts are displayed? What is the value in being able to display a range of accounts?

13. From the G/L menu, try to view account number 2370 (one of the accounts you deleted). What message is displayed?

14. Check the G/L to determine if the long–term debt was processed correctly. The account number is 2530. How many transactions are displayed for the long–term debt account? What is the ending balance for long–term debt?

15. With PAS it is possible to print financial statements as needed to determine if amounts have been processed correctly. To print a balance sheet, do the following:

    a. Select: General Ledger

    b. Select: Print Financial Statements

    c. Select: 2 (Print Statements)

    d. Enter for

Layout number:	1
Show ratios:	N
Starting period date:	"Earliest"
Ending period date:	43097
Profit center:	0
Number of copies:	1

    e. Press ENTER at "Field number to change?".

    f. Type Y and press ENTER at "Display the report?". Press F1 to stop the display in order to answer the following:

    i. What dollar total represents Total Current Assets?
    ii. What dollar total represents Total Assets?
    iii. What dollar total represents Total Liabilities?
    iv. What dollar total represents Total Liabilities and Equities?
    v. What can you conclude from this information?

Date 04/02/97 LYONS–GARTEN LAWN AND GARDEN, INC. #0001 Page 0001

Figure 2–1 – PREDEFINED CHART OF ACCOUNTS LIST

Accounts: "First" thru "Last"
Financial statement types: P = profit and loss B = balance sheet
Parenthesis control codes: D = enclose when debit C = enclose when credit
Compression codes: N = no compression D = by date P = by period

Account–#	Description	Fin–stmnt type	Paren code	Compress code
1010 – 000	Cash in bank – #1	B	C	D
1020 – 000	Cash in bank – #2	B	C	D
1030 – 000	Cash in bank – #3	B	C	D
1040 – 000	Credit card deposits	B	C	D
1050 – 000	Petty cash	B	C	D
1100 – 000	Accts Receivable – Trade	B	C	D
1110 – 000	Accts Recvble – Employee	B	C	D
1200 – 000	Notes receivable	B	C	D
1210 – 000	Interest receivable	B	C	D
1300 – 000	Prepaid expenses	B	C	D
1400 – 000	Inventory	B	C	D
1600 – 000	Furniture and fixtures	B	C	D
1610 – 000	Office equipment	B	C	D
1620 – 000	Automobiles and trucks	B	C	D
1630 – 000	Building	B	C	D
1640 – 000	Leasehold improvements	B	C	D
1650 – 000	Land	B	C	D
1700 – 000	Accum depr – furn & fixt	B	C	D
1710 – 000	Accum depr – office equip	B	C	D
1720 – 000	Accum depr – auto & truck	B	C	D
1730 – 000	Accum depr – building	B	C	D
1740 – 000	Accum depr – lease improv	B	C	D
1800 – 000	Deposits	B	C	D
1810 – 000	Investments	B	C	D
1900 – 000	Goodwill	B	C	D
1910 – 000	Other intangibles	B	C	D
2100 – 000	Accounts Payable – Trade	B	D	D
2110 – 000	Uninvoiced receivings	B	D	D
2200 – 000	Accrued expenses	B	D	D
2310 – 000	Fed income tax withheld	B	D	D
2320 – 000	EIC advances paid	B	D	D
2330 – 000	Emp Social Sec Payable	B	D	D
2335 – 000	Emp Medicare Payable	B	D	D
2340 – 000	Empr Social Sec Payable	B	D	D

Date 04/02/97 LYONS–GARTEN LAWN AND GARDEN, INC. #0001 Page 0002

Figure 2–1 – PREDEFINED CHART OF ACCOUNTS LIST

Account–#	Description	Fin–stmnt type	Paren code	Compress code
2345 – 000	Empr Medicare Payable	B	D	D
2350 – 000	State income tax withheld	B	D	D
2360 – 000	Other state tax withheld	B	D	D
2370 – 000	Local income tax withheld	B	D	D
2380 – 000	Pension contrib withheld	B	D	D
2390 – 000	Charity contrib withheld	B	D	D
2410 – 000	Accrued fed income tax	B	D	D
2420 – 000	Accrued state income tax	B	D	D
2430 – 000	Accrued state sales tax	B	D	D
2440 – 000	Accrued local sales tax	B	D	D
2450 – 000	Accrued fed unemp tax	B	D	D
2460 – 000	Accrued state unemp tax	B	D	D
2510 – 000	Deposits received	B	D	D
2520 – 000	Notes and loans payable	B	D	D
2530 – 000	Long term debt	B	D	D
3000 – 000	Common stock	B	D	D
3100 – 000	Paid in capital	B	D	D
3200 – 000	Treasury stock	B	D	D
3300 – 000	Retained earnings	B	D	D
4010 – 000	Sales – merchandise	P	D	P
4020 – 000	Sales – services	P	D	P
4510 – 000	Sales discounts	P	D	P
4520 – 000	Sales retrns & allowances	P	D	P
4910 – 000	Finance charges	P	D	P
4920 – 000	Freight charges	P	D	P
4930 – 000	Miscellaneous charges	P	D	P
4940 – 000	Deposits forfeited	P	D	P
4950 – 000	Other misc income	P	D	P
5010 – 000	Cost of goods sold	P	C	P
5020 – 000	Inventory adjustments	P	C	P
5030 – 000	Purchase discounts	P	C	P
5040 – 000	Cost corrections	P	C	P
6010 – 000	Advertising	P	C	P
6020 – 000	Auto and truck	P	C	P
6030 – 000	Bad debt expense	P	C	P
6040 – 000	Bank charges and fees	P	C	P
6050 – 000	Cash over or short	P	C	P
6060 – 000	Charitable contributions	P	C	P
6070 – 000	Commissions	P	C	P

Date 04/02/97 LYONS–GARTEN LAWN AND GARDEN, INC. #0001 Page 0003

Figure 2–1 – PREDEFINED CHART OF ACCOUNTS LIST

Account–#	Description	Fin–stmnt type	Paren code	Compress code
6080 – 000	Depreciation	P	C	P
6090 – 000	Insurance	P	C	P
6100 – 000	Interest	P	C	P
6110 – 000	Legal & accounting fees	P	C	P
6120 – 000	Licenses and fees	P	C	P
6130 – 000	Merchant credit card fees	P	C	P
6140 – 000	Miscellaneous	P	C	P
6150 – 000	Office expense	P	C	P
6160 – 000	Rents & utilities	P	C	P
6170 – 000	Repairs and maintenance	P	C	P
6180 – 000	Salaries – administrative	P	C	P
6190 – 000	Salaries – floor sales	P	C	P
6200 – 000	Salaries – officers	P	C	P
6210 – 000	Salaries – bonuses	P	C	P
6220 – 000	Sales and promotions exp	P	C	P
6230 – 000	Supplies	P	C	P
6240 – 000	Taxes – other	P	C	P
6250 – 000	Taxes – payroll	P	C	P
6260 – 000	Taxes – sales tax	P	C	P
6270 – 000	Telephone	P	C	P
6280 – 000	Travel & entertainment	P	C	P
7110 – 000	Taxes – federal income	P	C	P
7120 – 000	Taxes – state income	P	C	P
9110 – 000	Interest income	P	D	P
9120 – 000	Gain/loss sale of assets	P	D	P
9999 – 000	Transfer/suspense Account	P	D	D

99 Accounts printed

-- End of report --

Date 04/02/97 LYONS–GARTEN LAWN AND GARDEN, INC. #0002 Page 0001

Figure 2–2 – MODIFIED CHART OF ACCOUNTS LIST

Accounts: "First" thru "Last"
Financial statement types: P = profit and loss B = balance sheet
Parenthesis control codes: D = enclose when debit C = enclose when credit
Compression codes: N = no compression D = by date P = by period

Account–#	Description	Fin–stmnt type	Paren code	Compress code
1010 – 000	Cash #1 – Payables	B	C	D
1020 – 000	Cash #2 – Payroll	B	C	D
1040 – 000	Credit card deposits	B	C	D
1050 – 000	Petty cash	B	C	D
1100 – 000	Accts Receivable – Trade	B	C	D
1110 – 000	Accts Recvble – Employee	B	C	D
1200 – 000	Notes receivable	B	C	D
1210 – 000	Interest receivable	B	C	D
1300 – 000	Prepaid expenses	B	C	D
1400 – 000	Inventory	B	C	D
1600 – 000	Furniture and fixtures	B	C	D
1610 – 000	Office equipment	B	C	D
1620 – 000	Automobiles and trucks	B	C	D
1630 – 000	Building	B	C	D
1640 – 000	Leasehold improvements	B	C	D
1650 – 000	Land	B	C	D
1700 – 000	Accum depr – furn & fixt	B	C	D
1710 – 000	Accum depr – office equip	B	C	D
1720 – 000	Accum depr – auto & truck	B	C	D
1730 – 000	Accum depr – building	B	C	D
1740 – 000	Accum depr – lease improv	B	C	D
1800 – 000	Deposits	B	C	D
1810 – 000	Investments	B	C	D
1900 – 000	Organization	B	C	D
1910 – 000	Other intangibles	B	C	D
2100 – 000	Accounts Payable – Trade	B	D	D
2110 – 000	Uninvoiced receivings	B	D	D
2200 – 000	Accrued expenses	B	D	D
2310 – 000	Fed income tax withheld	B	D	D
2320 – 000	EIC advances paid	B	D	D
2330 – 000	Emp Social Sec Payable	B	D	D
2335 – 000	Emp Medicare Payable	B	D	D
2340 – 000	Empr Social Sec Payable	B	D	D
2345 – 000	Empr Medicare Payable	B	D	D

Date 04/02/97 LYONS–GARTEN LAWN AND GARDEN, INC. #0002 Page 0002

Figure 2–2 – MODIFIED CHART OF ACCOUNTS LIST

Account–#	Description	Fin–stmnt type	Paren code	Compress code
2350 – 000	State income tax withheld	B	D	D
2360 – 000	Other state tax withheld	B	D	D
2380 – 000	Pension contrib withheld	B	D	D
2390 – 000	Charity contrib withheld	B	D	D
2410 – 000	Accrued fed income tax	B	D	D
2420 – 000	Accrued state income tax	B	D	D
2430 – 000	Accrued state sales tax	B	D	D
2440 – 000	Accrued local sales tax	B	D	D
2450 – 000	Accrued fed unemp tax	B	D	D
2460 – 000	Accrued state unemp tax	B	D	D
2510 – 000	Deposits received	B	D	D
2520 – 000	Notes and loans payable	B	D	D
2530 – 000	Long term debt	B	D	D
3000 – 000	Common stock	B	D	D
3100 – 000	Paid in capital	B	D	D
3200 – 000	Treasury stock	B	D	D
3300 – 000	Retained earnings	B	D	D
4000 – 000	Sales – Landscape/Consult	P	D	P
4010 – 000	Sales – Lawn Installation	P	D	P
4020 – 000	Sales – Lawn and Garden	P	D	P
4030 – 000	Sales – Nursery	P	D	P
4510 – 000	Sales discounts	P	D	P
4520 – 000	Sales retrns & allowances	P	D	P
4910 – 000	Finance charges	P	D	P
4920 – 000	Freight charges	P	D	P
4930 – 000	Miscellaneous charges	P	D	P
4940 – 000	Deposits forfeited	P	D	P
4950 – 000	Other misc income	P	D	P
5005 – 000	COGS – Landscape/Consult	P	C	P
5010 – 000	COGS – Lawn Installation	P	C	P
5000 – 000	COGS – Lawn and Garden	P	C	P
5015 – 000	COGS – Nursery	P	C	P
5020 – 000	Inventory adjustments	P	C	P
5030 – 000	Purchase discounts	P	C	P
5040 – 000	Cost corrections	P	C	P
6010 – 000	Advertising	P	C	P
6020 – 000	Auto and truck	P	C	P
6030 – 000	Bad debt expense	P	C	P
6040 – 000	Bank charges and fees	P	C	P

Date 04/02/97 LYONS–GARTEN LAWN AND GARDEN, INC. #0002 Page 0003

Figure 2–2 – MODIFIED CHART OF ACCOUNTS LIST

Account–#	Description	Fin–stmnt type	Paren code	Compress code
6050 – 000	Cash over or short	P	C	P
6060 – 000	Charitable contributions	P	C	P
6070 – 000	Commissions	P	C	P
6080 – 000	Depreciation	P	C	P
6090 – 000	Insurance	P	C	P
6100 – 000	Interest	P	C	P
6110 – 000	Legal & accounting fees	P	C	P
6120 – 000	Licenses and fees	P	C	P
6130 – 000	Merchant credit card fees	P	C	P
6140 – 000	Miscellaneous	P	C	P
6150 – 000	Office expense	P	C	P
6160 – 000	Rents & utilities	P	C	P
6170 – 000	Repairs and maintenance	P	C	P
6180 – 000	Salaries – administrative	P	C	P
6190 – 000	Salaries – floor sales	P	C	P
6200 – 000	Salaries – officers	P	C	P
6220 – 000	Sales and promotions exp	P	C	P
6230 – 000	Supplies	P	C	P
6240 – 000	Taxes – other	P	C	P
6250 – 000	Taxes – payroll	P	C	P
6260 – 000	Taxes – sales tax	P	C	P
6270 – 000	Telephone	P	C	P
6280 – 000	Travel & entertainment	P	C	P
7110 – 000	Taxes – federal income	P	C	P
7120 – 000	Taxes – state income	P	C	P
9110 – 000	Interest income	P	D	P
9120 – 000	Gain/loss sale of assets	P	D	P
9999 – 000	Transfer/suspense Account	P	D	D

101 Accounts printed

-- End of report --

Date 04/02/97 LYONS–GARTEN LAWN AND GARDEN, INC. #0003 Page 0001

Figure 2–3 – GENERAL JOURNAL TRANSACTION EDIT LIST

Period: 04/01/97 to 04/30/97

Account: 1010–000 Cash #1 – Payables

Trans–date	Debit–amt	Credit–amt	Reference
04/02/97	25,000.00		Set up cash account

Account: 2530–000 Long term debt

Trans–date	Debit–amt	Credit–amt	Reference
04/02/97		25,000.00	Set up cash account

Grand totals:	25,000.00	25,000.00	2 Transactions

–– End of report ––

Date 04/02/97 LYONS-GARTEN LAWN AND GARDEN, INC. #0004 Page 0001

Figure 2-4 - GENERAL JOURNAL TRANSACTION REGISTER

Period: 04/01/97 to 04/30/97

Account: 1010-000 Cash #1 - Payables

Trans-date	Debit-amt	Credit-amt	Reference
04/02/97	25,000.00		Set up cash account

Account: 2530-000 Long term debt

Trans-date	Debit-amt	Credit-amt	Reference
04/02/97		25,000.00	Set up cash account

Grand totals:	25,000.00	25,000.00	2 Transactions

-- End of report --

Date 04/02/97 LYONS-GARTEN LAWN AND GARDEN, INC. #0005 Page 0001

Figure 2-5a – CHECKING ACCOUNT ADJUSTMENT REGISTER

Checking account #: 1 8765-432-19876 4400998877

Adjustment date	Reference Acct-#	Account-description	Payment/DR	Deposit/CR
04/02/97	Set up cash balance			25,000.00
	1010-000	Cash #1 – Payables		
1 Adjustment transaction		Totals:	.00	25,000.00

Date 04/02/97 LYONS-GARTEN LAWN AND GARDEN, INC. #0005 Page 0002

Figure 2-5b – CHECKING ACCOUNT ADJUSTMENT REGISTER

---------- G/L account distribution totals ----------

25,000.00 Distributed to 1010-000 Cash #1 – Payables

-- End of report --

Date 04/02/97 LYONS–GARTEN LAWN AND GARDEN, INC. #0006 Page 0001

Figure 2–6 – CHECKBOOK

Checking account #: 1 8765–432–19876 4400998877
Cleared items have "*" next to them

Item		Date	Reference	Amount	Balance
Adjustmnt		01/01/97	BBF	7,482.62CR	7,482.62
Deposit		01/03/97		306.32CR	7,788.94
CK#	1072	01/15/97	Acme Office Supplies	137.52	7,651.42
CK#	1073	01/15/97	Hill Equipment & Supply	400.00	7,251.42
CK#	1074	01/15/97	Jones Property Management	1,150.00	6,101.42
CK#	1075	01/15/97	South–Western Bell	352.51	5,748.91
CK#	1149	02/15/97	Hill Equipment & Supply	200.00	5,548.91
CK#	1150	02/15/97	Jones Property Management	1,150.00	4,398.91
CK#	1151	02/15/97	Reynolds Tool Company	500.00	3,898.91
CK#	1152	02/15/97	South–Western Bell	315.80	3,583.11
CK#	1223	02/15/97	Acme Office Supplies	155.20	3,427.91
CK#	1224	02/15/97	Hanson Manufacturing Co.	846.94	2,580.97
CK#	1225	02/15/97	South–Western Bell	301.15	2,279.82
CK#	1234	03/15/97	Jones Property Management	1,150.00	1,129.82
CK#	1235	03/15/97	Reynolds Tool Company	859.72	270.10
CK#	1236	03/15/97	South–Western Bell	270.10	.00
Adjustmnt		04/02/97	Set up cash balance	25,000.00CR	25,000.00

Current checkbook balance: 25,000.00

-- End of report --

Exercise 3 – ESTABLISH ACCOUNTING CONTROL DATA

Introduction

This exercise introduces you to three types of control built into the PAS software: accounting controls, accounting period controls, and invoicing (customer billing) controls. "Accounting controls" include default G/L account numbers, such as the G/L account number used when entering a sales discount. "Accounting period controls" define the accounting year for the company and the current period. "Invoicing controls" provide information pertinent to the billing of customers. These controls allow such specifics as the number of "days allowed" on an open invoice before finance charges are assessed.

You can do this exercise only if you have defined your company information using the Maintain Company Data function in Exercise 1 and have set up your general ledger accounts using the new information found in Exercise 2. This exercise asks you to reference these accounts.

Objective

In this exercise, you are asked to change a limited number of predefined accounting controls, the accounting period, and a limited number of invoicing controls. When you complete this exercise, you will:

- ➡ be familiar with the accounting, accounting period, and invoicing controls provided by the PAS software, and know how to
- ➡ review and change accounting, accounting period, and invoicing controls when necessary.

Case Study

After inspecting the Maintain Accounting Control Data function, Jen Ledger is thinking. "Very interesting. The maintain accounting control data section is extensive. Good! By tying G/L accounts to specific types of business transactions, it simplifies the posting of charges and helps to ensure that posting is correct."

Rose Garten stops by and asks Jen, "How are things going with the new accounting software? Any problems?"

Jen responds, "So far so good. But, I'm trying to decide which account numbers to use as the default for sales and cost of goods sold, given that we are going to post charges by department."

"How many transactions per day are there for the four departments," questions Rose.

"Oh, probably less than 20 for Landscaping and less than 20 for Lawn Installation. Nursery runs higher. We probably experience 100 on a normal day and 400 on a busy day. Lawn and Garden is probably the highest, year round. We normally experience 200 on a normal day."

"Well then," quips Rose. "You have answered your question on which department should contain the defaults, given that Lawn and Garden averages the highest number of transactions per day".

Smiling, Jen concludes, "You're absolutely right. Thanks, Rose."

Maintain Accounting Control Data

☐ 1. From the Main Menu, type 8 (Setup Functions) and press ENTER.

☐ 2. From the Setup Functions menu, type 3 (Maintain Accounting Control Data) and press ENTER. NOTE: If you make a mistake at any time during this exercise and want to start over, press the ESCape key on the keyboard and follow the directions displayed.

☐ 3. From Screen 1 (see below) of the Maintain Accounting Control Data menu, select the following field numbers and change as follows:

		From	To
10.	Default sales acct #	4010	4020
11.	Default COGS acct #	5010	5000
12.	Default returns acct #	4010	4520

SCREEN 1

```
Maintain accounting control data                         L-G LAWN AND GARDEN

   1. Accts receivable acct #          1100-000 Accts Receivable - Trade
   2. Discount allowance acct #        4510-000 Sales discounts
   3. Accts payable acct #             2100-000 Accounts Payable - Trade
   4. Discounts taken acct #           5030-000 Purchase discounts
   5. Check acct transfer acct #       9999-000 Transfer/suspense Account
   6. Check acct adjustment acct #     6040-000 Bank charges and fees

   7. Summarize G/L distributions ?    N
   8. Print company name on stmts ?    Y

   9. Default profit center            000
  10. Default sales acct #             4010
  11. Default cost of goods acct #     5010
  12. Default returns acct #           4010
  13. Default adjustment acct #        5020
  14. Default inventory acct #         1400-000 Inventory
  15. Uninvoiced receivings acct #     2110-000 Uninvoiced receivings
  16. Cost correction acct #           5040-000 Cost corrections
  17. Price to 3 decimal places ?      N
  18. Stock to 3 decimal places ?      N

Field number to change?
```

☐ 4. Press ENTER at "Field number to change?" to advance to Screen 2 (see next page), and change field numbers 19–21 as follows:

19.	Employer name	L-G LAWN AND GARDEN, INC.
20.	Address–1	1169 Greenbelt Way
21.	Address–2	Nice Valley, OR 97000

NOTE: Use the same employer name (up to 25 characters) and address that you used in Exercise 1.

SCREEN 2

Maintain accounting control data	L–G LAWN AND GARDEN
19. Employer name	XYZ Company
20. Address–1	500 W. Lincoln Blvd.
21. Address–2	Anytown, Texas 12345
22. Address–3	
23. Hours in day	8.00
24. Hours in week	40.00
25. Hours in bi–week	80.00
26. Hours in semi–mon	86.67
27. Hours in month	173.33
28. Yearly days	260
29. Yearly weeks	52
30. Yearly bi–weeks	26
31. Yearly semi–mons	24
32. Yearly months	12
33. Overtime pay factor	1.50
34. Special pay factor	2.00
35. Distribute wages ?	Selective
36. Use meals and tips	Y
Field number to change?	

☐ 5. Review the remaining contents of Screen 2, and press ENTER at "Field number to change?" to advance to Screen 3 shown below.

SCREEN 3

Maintain accounting control data	L–G LAWN AND GARDEN
37. Print A/P check # on	Both
38. Print comp name on A/P checks ?	Y
39. Print PR check # on	Both
40. Print comp name on PR checks ?	Y
41. Checking account # 1	8765–432–19876
Bank account #	4400998877
G/L account #	1010–000 Cash #1 – Payables
42. Checking account # 2	9983–321–87651
Bank account #	551183457
G/L account #	1020–000 Cash #2 – Payroll
43. Checking account # 3	
Bank account #	
G/L account #	
44. Payroll checking account	2
45. Last PR check # used	3000
46. Current payroll year	97
47. Payroll is in setup mode ?	N
Field number to change?	

☐ 6. Review the contents of Screen 3.

☐ 7. Press ENTER at "Field number to change?" to return to the Setup Functions menu.

Establish Accounting Periods

☐ 8. From the Setup Functions menu, type 4 (Maintain Accounting Periods) and press ENTER. Observe the established accounting periods. The Current Period should be indicated as Period #4 ..... 4/1/97 to 4/30/97. If it isn't, press ENTER and type '14' at "Field number to change?"; then type '4' to change to the correct period.

☐ 9. Press ENTER at "Field number to change?" to return to the Setup Functions menu.

Modify Invoicing Control Data

☐ 10. From the Setup Functions menu, type 5 (Maintain Invoicing Control Data) and press ENTER.

☐ 11. From Screen 1 (see below) of the Maintain Invoicing Control Data menu, select field number 6 and press F10 to read about this Yes/No switch. Answer Y (yes) to the question "Print invoices immed?". Review the remaining control data on Screen 1.

SCREEN 1

Maintain invoicing control data — L-G LAWN AND GARDEN

1. Next bill ref #	2	12. Dflt misc chgs acct #	4930-000
2. Next invoice #	1	13. Dflt freight acct #	4920-000
3. Use pre-printed invoices ?	N	14. Dflt scrap acct #	5020-000
4. Print comp data on invc ?	Y		
5. Invoice line item form	Fmt 1	15. Cust hist class 1 desc	Products
6. Print invoices immed ?	N	16. Cust hist class 2 desc	Services
7. Multiple profit centers ?	N	17. Cust hist class 3 desc	Repair
		18. Cust hist class 4 desc	Other
8. Default payment terms			
		19. Fin chg pct - level 1	.00
NET 30		20. Level 1 cut-off amt	0
		21. Fin chg pct - level 2	(N/A)
		22. No. days for fin charge	
9. Default shipping methods		23. Minimum finance charge	.00
		24. Calc F/C on F/C ?	N
USPO PARCELPOST	USPO 1ST CLASS	25. Finance charges acct #	4910-000
UPS GROUND	UPS NXT DAY AIR		
		26. Period end date	4/30/97
10. Calc sls tax on misc chgs ?	N	27. Year end date	12/31/97
11. Calc sls tax on freight ?	N		

Field number to change?

☐ 12. Select the following field numbers and change as follows:

		From	To
15.	Cust hist class 1 desc	Products	Landscape
16.	Cust hist class 2 desc	Services	Lawn Instl
17.	Cust hist class 3 desc	Repair	Lawn/Gardn
18.	Cust hist class 4 desc	Other	Nursery

☐ 13. Press ENTER at "Field number to change?" to advance to Screen 2 (see below) of the Maintain Invoicing Control Data menu.

SCREEN 2

```
Maintain invoicing control data                                    L-G LAWN AND GARDEN

               ------------- Invoicing Stations --------------
                   Code    Description      Nxt-invc-#      Printer
               28.
               29.
               30.
               31.
               32.

     --------------------- Tax Codes ----------------------
               Code   Description   Rate    Acct
          33.  TEX    Texas tax     5.000   2430-000  Accrued state sales tax
          34.  CNT    County tax    7.000   2440-000  Accrued local sales tax
          35.
          36.
          37.
          38.
          39.
          40.

Field number to change?
```

☐ 14. Select field #28 and complete the fields as follows:

Code	(your initials – 2 or 3 letters)
Description	(your name – up to 15 letters)
Nxt–invc–#	1
Printer	(Press F1 to default to standard printer LPT1.)

NOTE: In the future, when using Enter Invoices, press F1 to indicate your station code (initials and name) or type your initials in order to print invoices immediately.

☐ 15. Modify the Tax Codes in field numbers 33 – 40 as follows:

33	NM	New Mexico	4.75	2430–000	Accrued state sales tax

NOTE: Be sure to delete the 'X' in TEX; otherwise the Tax Code for New Mexico will be entered as NMX.

35	NE	Nebraska	4.0	2430–000	Accrued state sales tax
36	ID	Idaho	5.0	2430–000	Accrued state sales tax
37	CA	California	4.75	2430–000	Accrued state sales tax
38	NJ	New Jersey	6.0	2430–000	Accrued state sales tax
39	MA	Mass	5.0	2430–000	Accrued state sales tax
40	AZ	Arizona	5.0	2430–000	Accrued state sales tax

NOTE: These sales tax rates are ficticious. For those of you who live in states such as California, you would be delighted if the sales tax were reduced to only 4.75%. We assumed that by 1997, sales tax rates would be different. We also assumed that if you purchased goods from another state, you would have to pay that state's sales tax.

☐ 16. Press ENTER at "Field number to change?" to save the new Tax Codes.

☐ 17. This completes the exercise. Press END a sufficient number of times to exit PAS.

QUESTIONS ABOUT THE SOFTWARE

1. Why did Jen select the Lawn and Garden department as the default, rather than one of the other three departments? NOTE: 'Default' is defined in this context as the value or action taken by a computer program in the absence of any specific choice entered by the person using the program.

2. What purpose is served by assigning a default account number?

3. Why are 13 accounting periods provided by the software (see Step #8)? What purpose is served by the 13th period?

4. Describe what would happen if you answered N to print invoices immediately.

MANAGEMENT ISSUES

5. Suppose you are Jen Ledger and schedule a meeting with Rose Garten at Lyons–Garten. Explain specifically what Jen should tell Rose about the accounting and the invoicing controls built into PAS. Why should Rose care about these two types of controls?

6. Both the accounting and invoicing controls tie to G/L accounts. What does this tell you about the design of the general ledger? Why should the senior managers of a business help in the design of the general ledger?

THINGS TO DO

Explore the Maintain Invoicing Control settings using online help (press F10). To answer each of the following questions, type the indicated field number and press ENTER; then press the F10 key. After reviewing the explanations here and in the appropriate Reference Material at the end of your text, press END to return to the Maintain Invoicing Control Data menu and then press ENTER.

7. What is a pre–printed invoice? (see Invoicing Control Item #3)

8. What is a profit center? (see Invoicing Control Item #7) How are profit centers affected by the processing of customer invoices?

9. What is the purpose of a Customer History Class? (see Invoicing Control Item #15)

10. What is a two–level finance charge? (see Invoicing Control Item #19 and applicable Reference Material)

11. What is meant by F/C on F/C? (see Invoicing Control Item #24)

Exercise 4 – LOAD CUSTOMER & VENDOR FILES

Introduction

Now that you have a better understanding of what PAS is all about, it's time to begin creating master files. "Master files" are those which contain relatively permanent records, where a "record" describes the details of an event, person, or object. An important rule to remember is that master files are created in advance, to allow their use in transaction processing. For example, a customer master file is created in advance of processing customer orders, bills or payments. Why is this? Because you can't process an order, bill or payment unless you know the name of the responsible party, and that name has been added to the computer files.

Objectives

The main purpose of this exercise is to ask you to add additional customers and vendors to the customer and vendor master files respectively. This is a major first step in designing the integrated receivables and payables systems provided by PAS. When you complete this exercise, you should be able to:

- ➡ describe the contents of the customer and vendor master files
- ➡ know how to add, change and delete records stored on the customer and vendor master files
- ➡ explain how sales can be analyzed using the customer master file
- ➡ display and print the contents of the customer and vendor master files

Case Study

Jen asks Dandy and Rose if she can meet with them briefly. Dandy and Rose agree and quickly schedule a time.

Jen opens the meeting. She comments, "Thanks for agreeing to meet with me so quickly. I need help in deciding what to do next with the PAS software."

"Why don't you explain," remarks Rose.

"Now that we have installed PAS and have the chart of accounts set, my concern is what to implement first," Jen begins. "Do we start with payroll, inventory, invoicing, receivables or payables? We can't do all of these areas at once. Can you give me some guidance on which area to pick first?"

Dandy is the first to speak. "Roy (in Landscaping/Consulting) and Thatcher (in Lawn Installation) want sales invoicing, payroll and accounts payable implemented as quickly as possible. They have less interest in inventory or accounts receivable."

"What do you think, Rose?", questions Dandy.

"Rich (in Lawn and Garden) and Daisy (in Nursery) have different needs," she explains. "They want sales invoicing, inventory and accounts receivable implemented first. They have much less interest in payroll and accounts payable."

Jen enters the conversation again by asking, "What needs do the two of you have? They also have to be added to the list."

After thinking for a few moments, Dandy states: "We need quick access to customers and vendors, timely financial statements, and the capability to analyze the financial "wellness" of the company."

"Now, do you understand my problem?", states Jen. "PAS provides a number of important functions, but different people have different needs. How can we decide where to begin?"

Rose jumps in. "Jen," she asks. "In your judgment, where would you start?"

"OK, let me try," responds Jen. "First, I would enter data into the General Ledger to ensure that current consolidated financial totals are correct and in balance. Following this, I advise implementing accounts receivable, which begins with the creation of files of all our customers. With the customer file complete, this leads directly to sales invoicing. If we can invoice our customers faster, we can eliminate the three–four day delay in sending out bills. We can also eliminate the time and expense of typing invoices. This is so inefficient. With the customer file complete, we can then quickly proceed to accounts payable to set up our vendors."

"Let me tell you more about why a file of customers is so important," continues Jen. "Besides storing valuable customer information, this file will store sales information, once we begin the processing of invoices. We can use this file to determine how much each customer buys from us this month compared to last month, or this year compared to last year."

"Wow," exclaims Dandy. "Let's implement the customer file first!"

"Quite agree," seconds Rose.

Set Transaction Date

Before you start this exercise, set today's date at April 2, 1997 using the MS–DOS 'DATE' command. At the PAS prompt, type: **DATE** and press ENTER. At the next prompt, type the date in requested format as: **4–2–97** and press ENTER.

Add Customer Master File Information

Information must be added to the customer master file before customers can be processed. To add customer data to PAS, do the following:

☐ 1. Log on using the instructions in Exercise 1. The Main menu will appear on your screen as shown on the following page.

MAIN MENU

RealWorld Practical Accounting System	L–G LAWN AND GARDEN
Version 1.0	

Please select
1. Sales Invoicing
2. Inventory Management
3. Accounts Receivable
4. Accounts Payable
5. Payroll
6. General Ledger
7. Check Reconciliation
8. Setup Functions

Press F10 for help at any time

☐ 2. Type 3 (Accounts Receivable) from the above Main menu, and press ENTER.

RealWorld Practical Accounting System	L–G LAWN AND GARDEN
Accounts Receivable	

Please select
1. Maintain customer data
2. Process sales and DR/CR memos
3. Process cash receipts
4. Print A/R aging report
5. Change apply–to number
6. View customer accounts
7. Process finance charges
8. Print customer statements
9. Purge customer accounts

☐ 3. Type 1 (Maintain Customer Data) from the above Accounts Receivable menu, and press ENTER.

Maintain customer data	L–G LAWN AND GARDEN

Please select
1. Add customers
2. Change customers
3. Delete customers
4. Print customer list
5. Print customer labels
6. Purge inactive customers

☐ 4. Type 1 (Add Customers) from the above Maintain Customer Data menu, and press ENTER.

5. Your Customer file has already been set up. However, several new customers must be added to update the file. Using the customer data on the two screens shown below and on the next page, follow steps 5a–g. If you make a mistake, you can use the ARROW keys on your keyboard to change fields.

- [ ] a. Type the first business name shown, and press ENTER. Use only capital letters in typing this name.
- [ ] b. Enter the address next. Place the street number and name on one line, the city on the second line, and the state and zip code on the third line.
- [ ] c. Enter the remaining information requested on Screen 1.
- [ ] d. When you complete the last field for each customer, the screen displays "Field number to change?". Press ENTER to go to the second "Add customers" screen shown on the next page.
- [ ] e. Press ENTER or type 40297 for item #14 (1st activity date), and press ENTER three times to set all remaining date fields (#15,16,17) to "None". Press F1 to set all quantity fields to zero.
- [ ] f. At "Field number to change?", press ENTER to add the new customer to the customer master file.
- [ ] g. Add the other new customers to the file using the same procedure (steps 5a–f).
- [ ] h. Press TAB or END to return to the Maintain Customer Data menu.

SCREEN 1

Maintain customer data — L–G LAWN AND GARDEN

Add customers — New Customer List

1. Name	MOUNTAIN GARDEN SUPPLY	LAWNS–ARE–GREEN	FARMERS CO–OP
2. Address–1	484 Berry St.	1225 Fairview Lane	P.O. Box 35
3. Address–2	Moscow	Prettyville	Crown Point
4. Address–3	ID 83843	CA 95000	NM 87313
5. Contact	Deb Weber	Mary Rogers	Mark Survene
6. Phone #	208–234–3552	408–777–9999	505–786–9999
7. Comment	Landscaping	Good potential customer	Navajo project
8. Cust type	WSL	RET	RET
9. Sales rep	AW	JPR	JPR
10. Tax code	ID	CA	NM
11. Bal method	O	B	B
12. Statement frequency	M	M	M
13. Fin Chg ?	Y	N	N

Field number to change?

SCREEN 2

Maintain customer data — L-G LAWN AND GARDEN
Add customers — New Customer List

Name:	MOUNTAIN GARDEN SUPPLY		LAWNS-ARE-GREEN		FARMERS CO-OP	
14. 1st activity date	40297		40297		40297	
15. Last sale date	None		None		None	
16. Last payment date	None		None		None	
17. Last fin chg date	None		None		None	
18. Last fin chg amt	.00		.00		.00	
19. Fin charges YTD	.00		.00		.00	
20. Sales this period	.00		.00		.00	
21. Sales last period	.00		.00		.00	
22. Sales this year	.00		.00		.00	
23. Sales last year	.00		.00		.00	
	This-year	Last-year	This-year	Last-year	This-year	Last-year
24. Landscape sales	.00	.00	.00	.00	.00	.00
25. Lawn Instl sales	.00	.00	.00	.00	.00	.00
26. Lawn/Garden sales	.00	.00	.00	.00	.00	.00
27. Nursery sales	.00	.00	.00	.00	.00	.00

Field number to change?

Change Customer Master File Information

After adding customer information to a file, you can review and change it, if necessary, using the change function. Do the following:

☐ 6. Type 2 (Change Customers) from the Maintain Customer Data menu, and press ENTER.

Make the following changes to two of your accounts. (The modified account information is shown on the next page.)

☐ 7. Type LAWNS and press ENTER to display the LAWNS-ARE-GREEN account information.
Type 6 when asked "Field number to change?", and press ENTER.
Type the new telephone number 408-787-9999, and press ENTER.
Press ENTER twice when asked "Field number to change?" to return to Screen 1 of the Change Customers menu.

☐ 8. Type '21st' (lower case 'st') and press ENTER to display the 21st Century Construction account information.
Type 4 when asked "Field number to change?", and press ENTER.
Correct the zip code (75204), and press ENTER.
Press ENTER twice when asked "Field number to change?" to return to Screen 1 of the Change Customers menu.

☐ 9. Press TAB or END to return to the Maintain Customer Data menu.

Maintain customer data Change customers		L–G LAWN AND GARDEN
1. Name	LAWNS–ARE–GREEN	21st Century Construction
2. Address–1	1225 Fairview Lane	P.O. Box 4545
3. Address–2	Prettyville	670 Mason Street
4. Address–3	CA 95000	Dallas, TX 75204
5. Contact	Mary Rogers	Herbert Mandel
6. Phone #	408–787–9999	555–7844
7. Comment	Good potential customer	
8. Cust type	RET	WSL
9. Sales rep	JPR	JAK
10. Tax code	CA California	CNT County tax
11. Bal method	Bal fwd	Bal fwd
12. Statement frequency	M	M
13. Fin Chg ?	N	N
Make changes, or press F1 for next customer		

Print the Contents of the Customer Master File

Once all accounts have been added to the customer master file, its contents can be printed. To print the customer master file register, do the following:

☐ 10. Type 4 (Print Customer List) from the Maintain Customer Data menu, and press ENTER.

☐ 11. At the Print Customer List menu, press F1 for item numbers 1–4, and enter N at "Show sales detail?" as shown on the following screen.

Maintain customer data Print customer list	L–G LAWN AND GARDEN
Please enter:	
1. Starting customer	"First"
2. Ending customer	"Last"
3. Customer type	"All"
4. Last sale date	"Earliest"
5. Show sales detail ?	N
Field number to change?	

☐ 12. Press ENTER at "Field number to change?".

☐ 13. Press ENTER (N) at "Display this report?". NOTE: You may need to adjust your printer to compressed mode in order to print all of the data. Ask your instructor if you need assistance.

☐ 14. After the report is printed (see Figure 4–1), press TAB or END twice to return to the Main menu.

Add Supplier (Vendor) Master File Information

Vendors (companies that supply goods to your company) must be added to the vendor master file before goods and services can be ordered. To add vendor information to PAS, do the following:

☐ 15. Type 4 (Accounts Payable) from the Main menu, and press ENTER.

```
RealWorld Practical Accounting System                    L-G LAWN AND GARDEN
Accounts Payable

                     Please select
                        1.  Maintain vendor data
                        2.  Process bills payable
                        3.  Process disbursements
                        4.  View or print vendor accounts
                        5.  Aged accounts payable summary
```

☐ 16. Type 1 (Maintain Vendor Data) from the above Accounts Payable menu, and press ENTER.

```
Maintain vendor data                                     L-G LAWN AND GARDEN

                     Please select
                        1.  Add vendors
                        2.  Change vendors
                        3.  Delete vendors
                        4.  Print vendor list
                        5.  Print vendor labels
```

☐ 17. Type 1 (Add Vendors) from the above Maintain Vendor Data menu, and press ENTER.

18. Using the vendor data shown on the next page, do the following steps. If you make a mistake, you can use the ARROW keys on your keyboard to go back to change fields.

☐ a. Type the first vendor name, and press ENTER. Use only capital letters in typing this name.

☐ b. Enter the address next. Place the street name on one line, the city on the second line, and the state and zip code on the third line.

- [ ] c. Type the name of the person to contact at the vendor's location.
- [ ] d. Type the phone number of the vendor.
- [ ] e. Type the date when you first started doing business with the vendor.
- [ ] f. Enter additional information about the vendor (up to 25 characters) in the comment field.
- [ ] g. Enter the G/L number to automate the assignment of purchases from this vendor to this account at the time purchases enter processing. Type the first 4 digits and press ENTER; then press ENTER again.
- [ ] h. After the G/L number is keyed, the message "Field number to change?" will appear. If there are no changes to be made, press ENTER to add the new vendor to the Vendor Master File.

Maintain vendor data		L-G LAWN AND GARDEN
Add vendors	New Vendor List	
1. Name	A AND P CHEMICALS	JXX TOOLS AND SUPPLIES
2. Address-1	1662 Route 66	Franklin Building
3. Address-2	Carsonville	Daysroad
4. Address-3	NH 03000	NJ 07600
5. Contact	Mary Ford	Joan Fairday
6. Phone #	603-224-9999	201-590-9999
7. First date	010197	010197
8. Comment	Solid supplier	Temporary supplier
9. Default exp acct	5000-000	5015-000
Field number to change?		

- [ ] 19. Add the other new vendor to the file using the same procedure.
- [ ] 20. Press TAB or END to return to the Maintain Vendor Data menu.

Print the Contents of the Vendor Master File

Once all accounts have been added to the Vendor Master File, its contents can be printed. To print the vendor master file, do the following:

- [ ] 21. Type 4 (Print Vendor List) from the Maintain Vendor Data menu, and press ENTER.

☐ 22. At the Print Vendor List menu shown on the next page, press F1 (the function key) twice to indicate that you want to begin printing with the "first" vendor, and end printing with the "last" vendor.

```
Maintain vendor data                              L-G LAWN AND GARDEN

                    Please enter:
                      1.  Starting vendor     "First"
                      2.  Ending vendor        "Last"

Any change ?  N
```

☐ 23. Press ENTER (N) at "Any change?".

☐ 24. Press ENTER (N) at "Display this report?". NOTE: You may need to put your printer in compressed mode to print all of the data. The Vendor List is printed (see Figure 4–2).

☐ 25. This completes the exercise. Press END a sufficient number of times to exit PAS.

QUESTIONS ABOUT THE SOFTWARE

1. Compare the Add Customer Data 'procedure' to the Add Vendor Data 'procedure'. In what ways are the procedures similar? How do they differ? Why do you think that they differ?

2. Why are master files important to the design of an accounting system? Why is it important to create these files in advance of processing?

3. Suppose you need to change a vendor's record. What procedure is required?

4. Examine the chart of accounts printed in Exercise 2. Why were accounts 5010 and 5015 selected as the G/L accounts for the two suppliers? What would happen if there were 50 suppliers?

5. Both "customer type" and "sales rep" fields are contained on the Add Customer display. What is the purpose of each field? How might each field be used in the analysis of customer sales?

MANAGEMENT ISSUES

6. A manager states the following: "Once we have placed a customer on file, that customer remains there forever. It's just too much work to acquire a customer in the first place. Why should we ever remove this valuable customer information from the file?" Do you agree or disagree with this statement? Explain your reasoning.

7. Dandy and Rose were told that customer information would be important to analyzing the company sales. Why is it important to be able to analyze sales to begin with? What decisions might you make, having this information?

8. Dandy and Rose were not told how vendor information could be used by management. Explain the importance of keeping vendor information.

9. Suppose a company has over 50,000 active customers and 40,000 active suppliers. All information about customers and suppliers is kept on cards, stored in manual files. How would you justify to management the cost of converting these 90,000 records so they could be processed by a computer?

THINGS TO DO

10. Test the Print Customer Labels function (A/R, Maintain Customer Data). Enter:

1. Labels per customer	"Count only"
2. Starting customer	"First"
3. Ending customer	"Last"
4. Customer type	"All"
5. Last sale date	"Earliest"
6. Select by sales volume?	N

Do not print the labels. How many labels would be printed?

11. Suppose you decide to purge customers from the master file. Using the Purge Inactive Customer function and the F10 Help key, answer the following:

    "Under what conditions can and should a customer be purged from the customer master file?"

12. From the Accounts Receivable menu, select View Customer Accounts. When the display screen appears,

    a. type **lawns** in lowercase rather than uppercase. What happens?

    b. Next, type **LAWNS.** What happens this time?

    c. What can you determine from this test?

NOTE:
If PAS does not allow you to END, press ESCape and then END to return to a previous menu or end the session.

Date: 04/02/97 Time: 16:16:07 LYONS–GARTEN LAWN AND GARDEN, INC. #0006 Page 0001

Figure 4–1 – MODIFIED CUSTOMER LIST

Starting customer: "First"
Ending customer: "Last"
Customer type: "All"
Last sale date: "Earliest"

Cust–name	Phone–#	Cust–typ	Stmt–freq	1st–actv–dat	Lst–fin–chg–dat		Comment
Address	Contact	Bal–meth	Fin–chg?	Lst–sls–dat	Lst–fin–chg–amt		
	Sales–rep	Tax–code		Lst–pmt–dat	Fin–chg–YTD		
21st Century Construction	555–7844	WSL	M	1/01/97	(None)		
P.O. Box 4545	Herbert Mandel	Bal fwd	N	3/05/97		.00	
670 Mason Street	JAK	CNT		1/03/97		.00	
Dallas, TX 75204							
Allied Plumbing Co.	221–8520	WSL	M	1/01/97	(None)		
555 N. Grand Blvd.	M. J. Thorpe	Bal fwd	N	(None)		.00	
Mesquite, TX 75882	JAK	TEX		(None)		.00	
Baker, Richard C.	478–9090	WSL	M	(None)	(None)		
2554 Broad Street	Richard Baker	Bal fwd	N	3/15/97		.00	
Irving, TX 75103	TJF	CNT		(None)		.00	
Elliot Enterprises	779–6010	WSL	M	1/01/97	(None)		
123 Broadway	Paul Elliot	Bal fwd	N	(None)		.00	
Glendale, TX 75155	TJF	TEX		(None)		.00	
FARMERS COOP	505–786–9999	RET	M	4/02/97	(None)		Navajo project
P.O. Box 35	Mark Survene	Bal fwd	N	(None)		.00	
Crown Point	JPR	NM		(None)		.00	
NM 87313							
Harris, Goldberg, & Jones	554–4300	RET	M	1/01/97	(None)		
1 Commerce Square	Michael Jones	Bal fwd	N	(None)		.00	
Dallas, TX 75201	JAK	CNT		(None)		.00	
Holcomb Industrial Supply	722–2233	WSL	M	1/01/97	(None)		
2323 Holcomb Way	Jim Ewing	Open item	N	3/10/97		.00	
Dallas, TX 75205	JAK	CNT		(None)		.00	
LAWNS–ARE–GREEN	408–787–9999	RET	M	4/02/97	(None)		Good potential customer
1225 Fairview Lane	Mary Rodgers	Bal fwd	N	(None)		.00	
Prettyville	JPR	CA		(None)		.00	
CA 95000							

Date: 04/02/97 Time: 16:16:07 LYONS–GARTEN LAWN AND GARDEN, INC. #0006 Page 0002

Figure 4–1 – MODIFIED CUSTOMER LIST

Cust–name / Address	Phone–# / Contact / Sales–rep	Cust–typ / Bal–meth / Tax–code	Stmt–freq / Fin–chg?	1st–actv–dat / Lst–sls–dat / Lst–pmt–dat	Lst–fin–chg–dat / Lst–fin–chg–amt / Fin–chg–YTD	Comment
MOUNTAIN GARDEN SUPPLY	208–234–3552	WSL	M	4/02/97	(None)	Landscaping
484 Berry St.	Deb Weber	Open item	Y	(None)	.00	
Moscow	AW	ID		(None)	.00	
ID 83843						
Neptune Underwater Supply	736–1102	RET	M	1/01/97	(None)	
345 Lewisville Rd.	Sam Johnston	Bal Fwd	N	3/05/97	.00	
Lewisville, TX 75540	TJF	TEX		1/03/97	.00	
Newton, Boyd, & Co.	886–7722	WSL	M	1/01/97	(None)	
1024 Marble Avenue	Bob Newton	Bal fwd	N	(None)	.00	
Dallas, TX 75050	JAK	CNT		(None)	.00	
Washington, Mrs. Thomas	444–7780	RET	M	1/01/97	(None)	
350 Hillcrest Circle	Ann Washington	Bal fwd	N	(None)	.00	
Dallas, TX 75201	TJF	CNT		(None)	.00	

12 customers 10 balance forward 2 open item

– – End of report – –

Date: 04/02/97 LYONS–GARTEN LAWN AND GARDEN, INC. #0007 Page 0001

Figure 4–2 – MODIFIED VENDOR LIST

Starting vendor: "First"
Ending vendor: "Last"

Name	Address–1 Address–2 Address–3	Contact Phone Comment	First–date Exp–acct
A AND P CHEMICALS	1662 Route 66 Carsonville NH 03000	Marty Ford 603–224–9999 Solid supplier	01/01/97 5000–000
Acme Office Supplies	456 N. Broadway Dallas, TX 75201	B. Caldwell 999–9765	01/01/97 6230–000
Hanson Manufacturing Co.	65 Industrial Circle Chicago, IL 60655	Don Barber 413–669–8560	01/01/97 2110–000
Hill Equipment & Supply	3507 Oak Rd. Denver, CO 85366	Carl Rawlings 412–968–7650	01/01/97 2110–000
JXX TOOLS AND SUPPLIES	Franklin Building Daysroad NJ 07600	Joan Fairday 201–590–9999 Temporary supplier	01/01/97 5015–000
Jones Property Management	11056 E. Commercial Dallas, TX 75330	Robert Jones 774–6700	01/01/97 6160–000
Reynolds Tool Company	3922 Frontier Pkwy. Austin, TX 79811	Bill Ryan 512–447–8900	01/01/97 2110–000
South–Western Bell	Irving Office 500 S. Central Irving, TX 75021	721–1213	01/01/97 6270–000

8 vendors

–– End of report ––

Exercise 5 – PROCESS CUSTOMER INVOICES

Introduction

Once master files have been created, they can be used for several types of business computer applications. The customer master file, for example, is required in support of sales (customer) invoicing, accounts receivable, and order–entry processing (the processing of customer orders). The vendor master file is required in support of purchasing and receiving, accounts payable and, in some instances, inventory control. In this exercise, it is demonstrated how the customer master file is utilized in preparing customer invoices and posting outstanding charges to the LYONS–GARTEN accounts receivable file.

Figure 5–1 illustrates the flow of information when entering an invoice.

Figure 5–1 – SALES INVOICING OVERVIEW

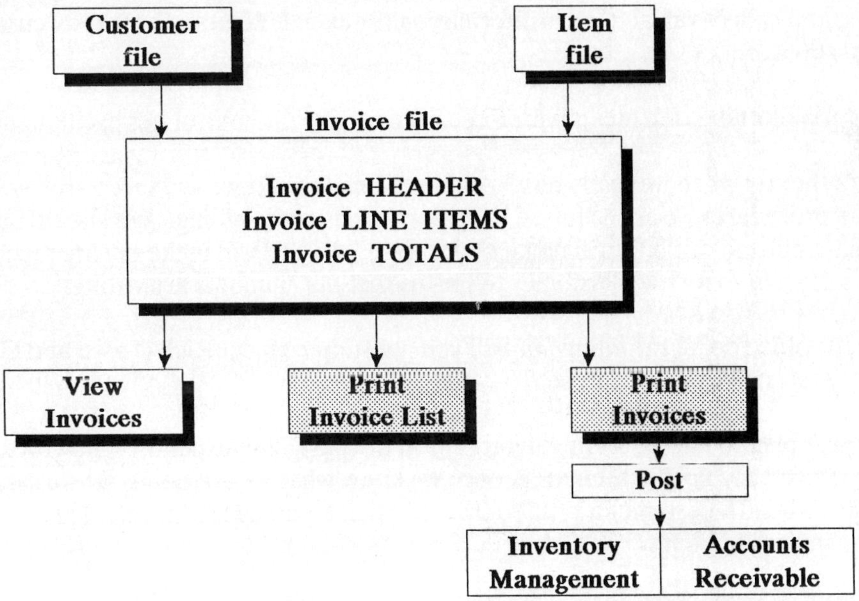

As indicated, two master files, the customer and the item files, are required in support of processing. The invoice file itself consists of a "header" for each invoice, one or more "line items" for each invoice, and an "invoice totals" section. The functions built into PAS allow a user to view an invoice stored in the invoice file, to print an invoice list (or register), and to print invoices. Once invoices are printed, invoice totals are posted to the inventory management file and the accounts receivable file.

In this exercise, you will be asked to modify a third master file, the product master file. The changes you are asked to make are limited to a change in product name and the general ledger sales account number.

Objectives

In this exercise we turn our attention to processing sales (customer) invoices. This business computer application serves a number of vital purposes. It is used to collect and organize sales information and terms of sales, to produce a formal bill to be sent to the customer, to post sales totals to accounts receivable, and to collect and store sales dollar totals for each LYONS–GARTEN account. When you complete this exercise, you should be able to do a number of things, including:

- ➡ making minor changes to the product master file
- ➡ processing several sales transactions
- ➡ printing invoice transaction registers
- ➡ viewing and printing customer invoices
- ➡ posting invoice transaction totals

Case Study

Jen is excited. Today she will begin to enter sales information, produce computer–printed invoices for customers, and collect valuable sales information for each LYONS–GARTEN customer that is invoiced for goods and services.

In the early morning, Jen meets with Rose. Jen can hardly control her excitement.

"Today's the day when we really test PAS," exclaims Jen. "If we are successful, we should be able to streamline the procedures we are required to follow for customer billing. We should be able to shorten the time to get out a bill and our bills will be more accurate. All this will make my life much less hectic. I just hate to get a call from some irate customer telling us that our numbers are wrong."

"Will your office do all the billing, or will you get support from Rich (Lawn and Garden sales) and Daisy (Nursery sales)?", questions Rose.

"For now, I plan to handle all the invoices as in the past," Jen explains. "However, Rich and Daisy would like to process invoices in their area, once we know what we are doing. If we can decentralize billing, we will be able to hand a customer a printed invoice when a purchase is made. This will eliminate up to 40 percent of our invoice mailings."

"Sweet!", purred Rose. "Let me know how today's test goes."

Set Transaction Date

☐ Before you start this exercise, set today's date at 4/20/97 using the MS–DOS 'DATE' command.

Change the Product Master File

Before entering sales information, you are asked to make several changes to the item (product) master file.

MAIN MENU

```
RealWorld Practical Accounting System          L-G LAWN AND GARDEN
Version 1.0

          Please select
             1.  Sales Invoicing
             2.  Inventory Management
             3.  Accounts Receivable
             4.  Accounts Payable
             5.  Payroll
             6.  General Ledger
             7.  Check Reconciliation
             8.  Setup Functions

Press F10 for help at any time
```

☐ 1. Type 2 (Inventory Management) from the above Main Menu, and press ENTER.

```
RealWorld Practical Accounting System          L-G LAWN AND GARDEN
Inventory Management

          Please select
             1.  Maintain item data
             2.  Maintain item prices
             3.  Process Inventory
             4.  Process purchases
             5.  Process physical inventory
             6.  Print inventory status report
             7.  Print inventory valuation report
             8.  Print inventory analysis report
```

☐ 2. Type 1 (Maintain Item Data) from the above Inventory Management menu, and press ENTER.

```
Maintain item data                             L-G LAWN AND GARDEN

          Please select
             1.  Add items
             2.  Change items
             3.  Delete items
             4.  Print item list
             5.  Purge inactive items
```

☐ 3. Type 2 (Change Items) from the Maintain Item Data menu, and press ENTER.

Customer Class: **LANDSCAPE / CONSULT**

☐ 4. Press F1 to reach product 1091, as displayed below on the Change Items display.

```
Maintain item data                                          L-G LAWN AND GARDEN
Change items

   1. Item number        1091
   2. Description        GAUGE, HI-PRESSURE
   3. Bar code                                 15. List price        17.95
   4. Substitute item #                        16. Discount by       Customer type
                                               17. Better price      15.75
   5. Item type          Inventory                 For cust type     WSL
   6. Department         PARTS                 18. Best price        .00
   7. Cust hist class    1  Landscape

   8. Stocking unit      EACH                  19. Alt sell unit 1
   9. Qty on hand        1
  10. Qty committed      0
  11. Qty on order       23                    20. Alt sell unit 2
  12. Average cost       9.72
  13. Last cost          9.72
  14. Purchase unit                            21. Preferred unit

Make changes, or press F1 for next item
Field number to change?
```

☐ 5. When product 1091 is displayed, you are asked the field number you wish to change. Type 2 and press ENTER to change the description of the product.

☐ 6. Type HI–PRESSURE HOSE and press the spacebar to the end of the field to replace GAUGE,. HI–PRESSURE; then press ENTER twice.

☐ 7. Press ENTER at "Field number to change?" to advance to the second screen (field numbers 22–48) shown on the next page.

```
Maintain item data                                          L-G LAWN AND GARDEN
Change items
  Item #: 1091                    HI-PRESSURE HOSE

  22. Vendor                      Hill Equipment & Supply
  23. Notes
  24. Inventory acct #            1400-000
      Inventory                                 37. Qty sold this prd    0
  25. Sales acct #                4010          38. Qty sold last prd    0
  26. Cost of goods acct #        5010          39. Qty sold this yr     0
  27. Returns acct #              5010          40. Qty sold last yr     0
  28. Taxable ?                   Y
  29. Bin location                              41. Sales this period    .00
                                                42. Sales last period    .00
  30. Min qty on hand             10            43. Sales this year      .00
  31. Min order qty               0             44. Sales last year      .00
  32. Max qty on hand             30
  33. First receipt date          None          45. Cost this period     .00
  34. Last receipt date           None          46. Cost last period     .00
  35. Last order date             None          47. Cost this year       .00
  36. Last sale date              None          48. Cost last year       .00

 Field number to change?
```

☐ 8. Modify selected fields as follows:

Field No.	Field Name	From	To
25	Sales acct #	4010	4000
26	Cost of goods acct #	5010	5005
27	Returns acct #	5010	4520

☐ 9. Press ENTER at "Field number to change?" to save the changes and return to the first screen (field numbers 1–21).

Customer Class: **LAWN AND GARDEN**

☐ 10. Press F1 to advance to item number 1100.

☐ 11. Repeat the above steps, making the following changes to screens 1 and 2.

Field No.	Field Name	From	To
2	Description	DRILL, POWER HAND	LAWN EDGER
7	Cust hist class	1 Landscape	3 Lawn/Gardn
25	Sales acct #	4010	4020
26	Cost of goods acct #	5010	5000
27	Returns acct #	5010	4520

☐ 12. Press F1 to advance to item number 1105.

☐ 13. Repeat the above steps, making the following changes to screens 1 and 2.

Field No.	Field Name	From	To
25	Sales acct #	4010	4020
26	Cost of goods acct #	5010	5000
27	Returns acct #	5010	4520

Customer Class: **LAWN INSTALLATION**

☐ 14. Press F1 to advance to item number 2200.

☐ 15. Make the following changes:

Field No.	Field Name	From	To
2	Description	HAMMER, 16 OZ. CLAW	LAWN HAMMER
7	Cust hist class	1 Landscape	2 Lawn Instal
27	Returns acct #	5010	4520

Customer Class: **NURSERY**

☐ 16. Press F1 to advance to item number 5770.

☐ 17. Make the following changes:

Field No.	Field Name	From	To
2	Description	CHISEL, 5 PC SET	NURSERY STAKES–30 PC SET
7	Cust hist class	1 Landscape	4 Nursery
25	Sales acct #	4010	4030
26	Cost of goods acct #	5010	5015
27	Returns acct #	5010	4520

☐ 18. Press F1 to advance to item named LABOR.

☐ 19. Make the following changes:

Field No.	Field Name	From	To
27	Returns acct #	5010	4520

☐ 20. Press F1 to advance to item named PARTS.

☐ 21. Make the following changes:

Field No.	Field Name	From	To
2	Description	MISCELLANEOUS PARTS	MISCELLANEOUS PLANTS
6	Department	PARTS	PLANT
25	Sales acct #	4010	4030
26	Cost of goods acct #	5010	5015
27	Returns acct #	5010	4520

☐ 22. Press ENTER at "Field number to change?", and press TAB or END as needed to return to the Main menu.

Process an Invoice (Sales) Transaction

To ready an invoice transaction, do the following:

☐ 23. Type 1 (Sales Invoicing) from the Main menu, and press ENTER.

```
RealWorld Practical Accounting System                 L-G LAWN AND GARDEN
Sales Invoicing

                  Please select
                     1.  Enter invoices
                     2.  Print invoice list
                     3.  View invoices
                     4.  Print invoices
                     5.  Post invoices
                     6.  Print sales tax report
                     7.  Close sales period
```

☐ 24. Type 1 (Enter Invoices) from the above Sales Invoicing menu, and press ENTER.

```
Enter invoices                                        L-G LAWN AND GARDEN

                       Please enter invoicing station

F1 = next station code, blank = no immediate printing
```

☐ 25. Press F1 to indicate your station code (your initials and name) or type your initials. Press ENTER (Y) at "Right station?", and press ENTER (N) at "Any change?".

26. There are three different invoicing screens on which you enter information about an invoice. The FIRST of these three screens contains the HEADER INFORMATION shown below.

☐ a. Press F2 to use the next available Bill ref # as specified earlier in the Invoicing Control file.

☐ b. Press ENTER for Bill Type I (Invoice).

☐ c. Press ENTER to indicate that you want the Invoice Date to be assigned at the time the invoice is printed.

☐ d. Press F1 to select 21st Century Construction, and press ENTER (Y) to the question "Right customer?". (If you know the customer's name, you may enter the full or partial [e.g., 21st] name of the customer instead.)

☐ e. Press ENTER to indicate that the Deliver–to Address is the same as the customer's billing address.

☐ f. Type '100' and press ENTER to indicate the customer's purchase order #.

☐ g. Press F1 repeatedly to scroll through the payment terms. NOTE: Since NET 30 is the only terms you entered in your Invoicing Control Data, simply press F1 once and press ENTER (Y) when asked "Right terms?" to select it.

☐ h. Press F1 repeatedly until you scroll to Ship via UPS GROUND. Press ENTER(Y) when asked "Right method?".

☐ i. Press ENTER to default to 21st Century's normal Tax Code (CNT County tax) as specified earlier in Setup Functions / Maintain Invoicing Control Data.

☐ j. Press ENTER once to skip Bill Group and Profit ctr.

HEADER INFORMATION

```
Enter invoices                                      L-G LAWN AND GARDEN

     1. Bill ref #     2                     6. P.O. #      100
     2. Bill type      Invoice               7. Terms       NET 30
     3. Invoice date                         8. Ship via    UPS GROUND
        (Assigned at print time)
     4. Customer                             9. Tax code    CNT   County tax
        21st Century Construction           10. Bill group
        P.O. Box 4545                       11. Profit ctr  (Not applicable)
        670 Mason Street
        Dallas, TX 75204
     5. Deliver to:
        (same as above)

Field number to change?
```

☐ k. Press ENTER at "Field number to change?" to proceed to the second screen.

27. The SECOND of three entry screens contains LINE ITEM INFORMATION.

☐ a. Press F2 to default to the predetermined Sequence of line items that will be printed on the invoice.

☐ b. Press F1 to Select Item #1091 – HI–PRESSURE HOSE; press ENTER (Y) to the question "Right item?".

☐ c. Press ENTER twice to accept the Description, Unit and Item Type that normally would be pre–assigned by you in Inventory Management / Maintain Item Data.

☐ d. Type '10' to indicate Quantity ordered, and press ENTER. In answer to the warning that "Quantity exceeds qty available", press ENTER and then the UP ARROW to return to menu selection "Quantity". Select the quantity of '01' for this order, and press ENTER.

☐ e. Press F1 to use the pre–determined price of $15.75.

☐ f. Press ENTER to indicate no discount. The remainder of the Line Item Information will be auto–matically filled. Closely review its contents shown below.

☐ g. If there are no fields to be changed, press ENTER to proceed to the third screen.

LINE ITEM INFORMATION

```
Enter invoices                                          L-G LAWN AND GARDEN

            Bill ref #:   2                 Customer:  21st Century Construction
            Bill type:    Invoice

      1.    Sequence      10
                                                 Unit:  EACH
      2.    Item #        1091                          Item type:   Inventory
      3.    Description   HI-PRESSURE HOSE
      4.    Quantity      1             EACH       Qty available:            0

      5.    Unit price    15.75         EACH       Extended price:       15.75
      6.    Discount %    .00                      Line disc amt:          .00
      7.    Avg cost      9.72          EACH                             -----
      8.    Rtrn to inv   (Not applicable)         Line item net:        15.75
      9.    Taxable ?     Y

     10.    G/L acct #    4000-000   Sales - Landscape/Consult

                 0  line items                     Invoice total:        15.75

 Field number to change?
```

☐ h. Add the following second and third items to this invoice by assigning sequence #20 (press F2) to the second line item and #30 (press F2) to the third.

Sequence #	Item #	Item Description	Qty	Unit Price	Discount
20	1100	LAWN EDGER	1	25.95	No (press ENTER)
30	2200	LAWN HAMMER	1	13.50	No (press ENTER)

☐ i. After entering the above line items for invoicing, press ENTER at the question "Field number to change?" to save the screen–2 Line Item Information.

☐ j. Press TAB or END to advance to the third invoicing screen.

28. The THIRD of three invoicing screens contains INVOICE TOTALS INFORMATION.

21st Century Construction is a preferred customer who receives a 5% discount on all orders. You are shipping their most recent order for which you have received a $10.00 cash deposit. Use the information shown below to complete the Totals Screen.

INVOICE TOTALS INFORMATION

Enter invoices			LYONS–GARTEN LAWN AND GARDEN, INC.
Bill ref #:	**2**	Customer:	**21st Century Construction**
Invoice tot:	**55.20**	Taxable total:	**52.44**
Invoice disc:	**.00**		
1. Invc disc %	**5**	Discounted net:	**52.44**
2. Misc charges	**(press ENTER) .00**		
3. Freight	**2.05**	Acct **4920–000**	Freight charges
4. Sales tax	**3.67**	Billed total:	**58.16**
5. Payment recd	**10**	7. Bank rte #	**25–16238**
6. Check #	**4662**	8. Chk acct #	**(press ENTER) 1**
9. Comment	**Thank you for your business!**		

☐ a. Press F2 after entering the comment line.

☐ b. Press ENTER at "Field number to change?" to save the screen–3 Invoice Totals Information for this customer.

☐ c. Press ENTER(Y) to indicate that you wish to print the invoice immediately (see Figure 5–2).

```
Enter invoices                                          L-G LAWN AND GARDEN

   Bill ref #:       1                Customer:       21st Century Construction
   Invoice tot:      57.40            Taxable total:  54.53
   Invoice disc:     2.87

 1. Invc disc %      5.00           Discounted net:   54.53
 2. Misc charges     .00
 3. Freight          2.05        Acct  4920-000   Freight charges
 4. Sales tax
 5. Payment rec    ┌──────────────────────────────────────────────┐
 6. Check #        │          Immediate invoice printing          │
 9. Comment        │                                              │
                   │   Invoice station:    ROW  Ronald O. Waite   │
                   │           Printer:    LPT1                   │
                   │   Invoice number:     1                      │
                   │                                              │
                   │          Print this invoice now ?     Y      │
                   │                                              │
                   │   Select:  Y = Yes   N = No   I = change Invoice #  │
                   └──────────────────────────────────────────────┘
```

☐ d. Review the invoice closely for any errors and, if none, type Y at "Is the invoice just printed OK?", and press ENTER.

```
Enter invoices                                          L-G LAWN AND GARDEN

   Bill ref #:       2                Customer:       21st Century Construction
   Invoice tot:      55.20            Taxable total:  52.44
   Invoice disc:     2.76

 1. Invc disc %      5.00           Discounted net:   52.44
 2. Misc charges     .00
 3. Freight          2.05        Acct  4920-000   Freight charges
 4. Sales tax
 5. Payment rec    ┌──────────────────────────────────────────────┐
 6. Check #        │          Immediate invoice printing          │
 9. Comment        │                                              │
                   │   Invoice station:    ROW  Ronald O. Walte   │
                   │           Printer:    LPT1                   │
                   │   Invoice number:     1                      │
                   │                                              │
                   │      Is the invoice just printed OK ?   Y    │
                   └──────────────────────────────────────────────┘
```

☐ 29. Use the following information to create another invoice (next bill reference #).

HEADERS	Invoice Date:	(when invoice printed)	P.O. #:	243–2342
	Customer:	Baker, Richard C.	Terms:	NET 30
	Deliver to:	(same)	Ship via:	UPS GROUND
			Tax code:	CNT
			Bill group:	(your station code)

LINE ITEMS (start with sequence 10)

Item #	Qty	Description	Unit Price	Unit Cost
5770	1	NURSERY STAKES–30 PC SET	27.75	–
PARTS	1	MISCELLANEOUS PLANTS	32.50	20.00
W30	1	30 DAY WARRANTY–NO REFUND	–	–

No line item discounts are given.

TOTALS Freight: 3.25 Invoice discount: 5% Payment received: 0
Comment: (your own wording)

DO NOT PRINT THIS INVOICE NOW.

☐ 30. Press TAB or END to return to the Sales Invoicing menu.

View Invoices

☐ 31. From the Sales Invoicing menu, type 3 (View Invoices) and press ENTER to view the invoices you have entered.

☐ 32. From the View Invoices screen, press F1 at the "Starting bill ref #" field to choose "First". NOTICE that no date is shown for Bill ref #3. This is because you asked that the date be assigned when it is printed.

View invoices L–G LAWN AND GARDEN

Starting bill ref # **"First"** Starting customer

	Bill–ref–#	Customer–name	Grp	Date	Cust–P.O.#	Terms
1)	2	21st Century Construction		4/20/97	100	NET 30
2)	3	Baker, Richard C.	ROW		243–2342	NET 30

Select screen line # for detailed inquiry

☐ 33. Select the line number of an invoice you entered, and use the F1 and F2 keys to view the line items and totals section of the invoice.

☐ 34. Press TAB or END an appropriate number of times to return to the Sales Invoicing menu.

Print the Invoice List (Register)

Invoices are generally printed as a batch, rather than one at a time. Before printing a batch of invoices on expensive, custom forms, it is advised that a register of all invoices be printed and reviewed.

☐ 35. From the Sales Invoicing menu, type 2 (Print Invoice List), and press ENTER. Use the following information to print this list.

```
Print invoice list                                    L-G LAWN AND GARDEN

        Please enter

            1. Print in order by:        B (bill reference number)
            2. Starting bill ref #:      "first"        (press F1)
            3. Ending bill ref #:        "last"         (press F1)

            4. Starting invoice date     "Earliest"     (press F1)
            5. Ending invoice date       "Latest"       (press F1)

            6. What to print:

               # of header lines         "All"          (press F1)
               # lines per line item     "All"          (press F1)
               Bill totals ?             Yes
               Report totals ?           Yes

Field number to change?
```

☐ 36. Press ENTER at "Field number to change?", and press ENTER (N) at "Display this report?" to print the invoice list (see Figure 5–3).

☐ 37. Press TAB or END to return to the Sales Invoicing menu.

Print Invoices

☐ 38. From the Sales Invoicing menu, type 4 (Print Invoices) and press ENTER. Press F1 for your invoicing station, and press ENTER. Use the following information to PRINT the invoice that you prepared earlier but delayed printing (see Figure 5–4).

a. Print in order by: B (Bill reference number)
Default invoice date: (press ENTER for today's date of 4/20/97)
Starting bill ref #: "first" (press F1)
Ending bill ref #: "last" (press F1)
Default comments: (press F2 to use any comments previously entered on invoice)

b. Do NOT print invoices already printed (Bill ref #2 was previously printed.)

c. Press ENTER at "Field number to change?".

d. Before printing, make sure the paper in your printer is properly aligned. Press ENTER (N) to indicate you do not need to print an alignment test pattern. NOTE: Starting invoice will be #2. Press ENTER (N) at "Any change?".

☐ 39. Review the invoice (see Figure 5–4) closely for any errors and, if none, type Y at "Are invoices just printed OK?" and press ENTER.

☐ 40. Press TAB or END to return to the Sales Invoicing menu.

Post Invoices

This function posts invoices to the accounts receivable (A/R) and inventory management (I/M) files. You MUST print invoices, as you just did, before they can be posted. As will become evident on the exercise dealing with inventory management, invoices cannot be posted if physical inventory transactions have not been posted. Observe the priority here. Inventory transactions must be posted before invoices can be posted, and invoices must also be printed before they can be posted.

It is VERY IMPORTANT to also note that the posting process results in the printing of several reports. These reports require a wide–carriage printer with 14" paper. If your printer can only print on standard–sized 8 1/2" x 11" paper, be sure to adjust your printer to compress the report.

☐ 41. From the Sales Invoicing menu, type 5 (Post Invoices) and press ENTER to post the invoices you have printed.

☐ 42. Use the following information to post your invoices.

a.

Cut–off invoice date to post:	(press F1 – "Latest")
Cut–off invoice # to post:	(press F1 – "Last")
Bill group to post:	(press F1 – "All")
Deposit date for pmts rcvd:	(press ENTER – 4/20/97)
Print deposit slips?	N

☐ 43. Press ENTER at "Field number to change?". The following reports will be printed.

➡ Services / Non–inventory–Item Register	(see Figure 5–5)
➡ Inventory Transaction Register	(see Figure 5–6)
➡ Sales Register (2 pages)	(see Figure 5–7)
➡ Cash Receipts Register (2 pages)	(see Figure 5–8)

The posting process ends by indicating that it is processing the $10.00 deposit check #4662 for customer 21st Century Construction.

☐ 44. This completes the exercise. Press END a sufficient number of times to exit PAS.

QUESTIONS ABOUT THE SOFTWARE

1. Why must all customer and product master file information be current before starting to process customer invoices?

2. Why is it important to print the invoice list before printing a batch of invoices? What if you discover an error?

3. Different customer history class numbers were assigned to different products. What will these class numbers be used for?

4. Why must invoices be printed before they can be posted to the A/R and the I/M files?

5. What information is provided by the
   a. Services / non–inventory–item Register?
   b. Inventory Transaction Register?
   c. Sales Register?
   d. Cash Receipts Register?

MANAGEMENT ISSUES

6. A manager states: "We used to print invoices once a week when we first started using the computer, but we were recently informed that invoices should be printed daily, and no longer than eight hours following a shipment." Discuss the importance in being able to bill customers on a more timely basis.

7. "Customer billing is not very expensive when the computer is used." Based on your very recent experience, would you agree or disagree with this statement? Why or why not?

8. Suppose customers pay in advance, using credit cards to make their payments. Should the customer invoice continue to be prepared and printed? Should it be mailed or be placed with the shipment? Explain your answers.

9. What is management's overall role in supervising the processing of customer invoices? As a case in point, what actions should Rose take to make sure that all invoices are processed accurately and completely?

10. What controls would L–G Lawn and Garden have in place to assure that goods shipped are billed?

11. What advantages are there to updating the inventory file at the time that invoices are printed?

12. Why is it important that the Accounts Receivable file be updated when printing invoices?

THINGS TO DO

When you decided to post invoices, several events took place. To examine these events, we ask you to do the following:

☐ 13. From the Main Menu, select General Ledger, followed by View G/L account activity. Enter a starting date of 4/01/97 and ending date of 4/30/97. What are the account names and ending balances?

After you have recorded the information, press END to return to the Main menu.

Account Number	Account Name	Ending Balance
4000		
5005		
4010		
5010		
4020		
5000		
4030		
5015		
2440		
4920		

How did customer invoicing change these account balances? Be specific.

What is the value of posting sales and COGS to different accounts?

14. From the Main menu, select Check Reconciliation; then, do the following:

☐ a. Select 4 (Print a Checkbook).

☐ b. Enter 1 for Checking account #.

☐ c. Press ENTER (N) when asked "Purge cleared items?".

☐ d. Type Y and press ENTER to display the report.

☐ e. Answer the questions below and press END to return to the Main menu.

What is the new checkbook balance?

How did invoicing change this balance?

Figure 5–2 – SALES INVOICE TO 21ST CENTURY CONSTRUCTION

INVOICE

L–G LAWN AND GARDEN
1169 Greenbelt Way
Nice Valley, OR 97000

Date: 4/20/97 Page: 1
Invoice #: 1

Sold to:

21st Century Construction
P.O. Box 4545
670 Mason Street
Dallas, TX 75204

Ship to:

21st Century Construction
P.O. Box 4545
670 Mason Street
Dallas, TX 75204

Ref–#	P.O.–#	Terms	Ship–via
2	100	NET 30	UPS GROUND

Item–#	Description	Quantity	Unit	Unit–price	Ext–price
1091	HI–PRESSURE HOSE	1	EACH	15.75	15.75
1100	LAWN EDGER	1	EACH	25.95	25.95
2200	LAWN HAMMER	1	EACH	13.50	13.50

Invoice discount:	2.76
Sale total:	52.44
Misc. charges:	0.00
Sales tax:	3.67
Shipping:	2.05
Invoice total:	58.16
Deposit:	10.00
Balance due:	48.16

Thank you for your business!

Date: 04/20/97 Time: 17:09:46 LYONS–GARTEN LAWN AND GARDEN, INC. Report #0015 Page #0001

Figure 5–3 – I N V O I C E L I S T

Costs shown were current at the time the invoice was entered.

For inventory items, actual costs are exactly determined during posting of invoices.

Bill–ref–#: 2	Invc–date: 04/20/97	Cust:	21st Century Construction	Deliver to:	* SAME AS BILL ADDRESS *
Bill–group:	Profit–ctr: 000		P.O. Box 4545		
Bill–type: INVOICE			670 Mason Street		
Invoice–#: 1	** ALREADY PRINTED **		Dallas, TX 75204		

Cust–PO–#: 100 Invc–disc–%: 5.000

Terms: NET 30 Tax code: CNT County Tax

Ship–via: UPS GROUND

Seq#	Type	Quantity / Unit	–––––––––––Item/Service/Text–––––––––––		Unit price / Unit cost	Line–item–net / Line–disc–%	G/L acct / Ret–to–inv	Txbl?
10	Inventory	1 EACH	1091	HI–PRESSURE HOSE	15.75 / EACH 9.720 / EACH	15.75	4000–000	Y
20	Inventory	1 EACH	1100	LAWN EDGER	25.95 / EACH 12.830 / EACH	25.95	4020–000	Y
30	Inventory	1 EACH	2200	LAWN HAMMER	13.50 / EACH 7.310 / EACH	13.50	4010–000	Y

3 line items	Invoice total :	55.20	Comment: Thank you for your business!
	Invoice disc :	2.76	
	Misc charges :	.00	
	Freight :	2.05	Dist–to: 4920–000 (not taxbl)
	Sales tax :	3.67	Taxable: 52.44
	Total billed :	58.16	
	Payment rec'd:	10.00	Check–#: 4662 Bank–rte–#: 25–16238 Chk–acct–#: 1 8765–432–19876

Date: 04/20/97 Time: 17:09:49 LYONS–GARTEN LAWN AND GARDEN, INC. Report #0015 Page #0002

Figure 5–3 – INVOICE LIST

Bill–ref–#: 3 Invc–date: NONE YET Cust: Baker, Richard C. Deliver to: * SAME AS BILL ADDRESS *
Bill–group: ROW Profit–ctr: 000 2554 Broad Street
Bill–type: INVOICE Irving, TX 75103

Cust–PO–#: 243–2342 Invc–disc–%: 5.000
Terms: NET 30 Tax code: CNT County Tax
Ship–via: UPS GROUND

Seq#	Type	Quantity Unit	———Item/Service/Text———		Unit price Unit cost	Line–item–net Line–disc–%	G/L acct Ret–to–inv	Txbl?
10	Inventory	1 SET	5770	NURSERY STAKES–30 PC SET	27.75 / SET 18.200 / SET	27.75	4030–000	Y
20	Non–inv	1 EACH	PARTS	MISCELLANEOUS PLANTS	32.50 / EACH 20.000 / EACH	32.50	4030–000	Y
30	Text		30 DAY WARRANTY–NO REFUND					

2 line items Invoice total : 60.25 Comment: Thank you for your business!
Invoice disc : 3.01
Misc charges : .00
Freight : 3.25 Dist–to: 4920–000 (not taxbl)
Sales tax : 4.01 Taxable: 57.24
Total billed : 64.50

Date: 04/20/97 Time: 17:09:52 LYONS–GARTEN LAWN AND GARDEN, INC. Report #0015 Page #0003

Figure 5–3 – INVOICE LIST

2 Invoices with 5 line items Total amount of Invoices: 115.45
Discounts: 5.77
Freight: 5.30
Sales tax: 7.68 Taxable: 109.68

Total amount Billed: 122.66
Received: 10.00

–– End of report ––

Figure 5–4 – SALES INVOICE TO RICHARD C. BAKER

INVOICE

L–G LAWN AND GARDEN
1169 Greenbelt Way
Nice Valley, OR 97000

Date: 4/20/97 Page: 1
Invoice #: 2

Sold to:

Baker, Richard C.
2554 Broad Street
Irving, TX 75103

Ship to:

Baker, Richard C.
2554 Broad Street
Irving, TX 75103

Ref–#	P.O.–#	Terms	Ship–via
2	243–2342	NET 30	UPS GROUND

Item–#	Description	Quantity	Unit	Unit–price	Ext–price
5770	NURSERY STAKES–30 PC SET	1	SET	27.75	27.75
PARTS	MISCELLANEOUS PLANTS	1	EACH	32.50	32.50

30 DAY WARRANTY–NO REFUND

Invoice discount: 3.01

Sale total: 57.24

Thanks for your business!

Misc. charges: 0.00
Sales tax: 4.01
Shipping: 3.25

Invoice total: 64.50

Date 04/20/97 Time 17:26:47 LYONS-GARTEN LAWN AND GARDEN, INC. Report #0016 Page 0001

Figure 5-5 – SERVICES/NON-INVENTORY-ITEM REGISTER

Type Item/Svc-#	Customer Item/Service-description	Invc-#	Invc-dat	Invc-typ	Bill-# Unit	Quantity Sell-unit	Lin-dsc Invc-dsc	Unit-cost Ext-cost	Unit-price Lin-item-net
Non-inv-item	Baker, Richard C.	2	4/20/97	Invoice	3	1		20.00 EACH	32.50 /EACH
PARTS	MISCELLANEOUS PLANTS				EACH	EACH	5.000	20.00	30.87
1 items					Total non-inventory items:			20.00	30.87
						Total services:		.00	.00

-- End of report --

Date 04/20/97 Time 17:26:51 LYONS–GARTEN LAWN AND GARDEN, INC. Report #0017 Page 0001

Figure 5–6 – INVENTORY TRANSACTION REGISTER

Current period ending date: 4/30/97

G/L account is shown for up and down adjustments; Profit center is shown for sales and credit memos

List, better, best, and alternate prices are only shown if modified by the transaction

Cost correction is only shown if applicable to the transaction

Date	Type	Doc–#	Trans–qty / Running–qty–oh	Unit	Unit–cost	Tot–actual–cost / New–avg–cost	Comment / G/L–acct	Price–per–unit
Item: 1091		HI–PRESSURE HOSE				Stocking unit:	EACH	
4/20/97	Sale	000001	1	EACH	9.720	9.72	From invoice: 000001	14.960
			0	EACH		9.72000	000	
Item: 1100		LAWN EDGER				Stocking unit:	EACH	
4/20/97	Sale	000001	1	EACH	12.830	12.83	From invoice: 000001	24.650
			0	EACH		12.83000	000	
Item: 2200		LAWN HAMMER				Stocking unit:	EACH Alt–unit–1: DOZ	
4/20/97	Sale	000001	1	EACH	7.310	7.31	From invoice: 000001	12.820
			0	EACH		7.31000	000	
Item: 5770		NURSERY STAKES–30 PC SET				Stocking unit:	SET	
4/20/97	Sale	000002	1	SET	18.200	18.20	From invoice: 000002	26.360
			0	SET		18.20000	000	

Grand totals:						
	Receiving entries:	0	Qty received:	0	Cost:	.00
	Credit memo entries:	0	Qty credited:	0	Cost:	.00
	Up adj entries:	0	Qty adjusted:	0	Cost:	.00
	Down adj entries:	0	Qty adjusted:	0	Cost:	.00
	Sale entries:	4	Qty sold:	4	Cost:	48.06

–– End of report ––

Date 04/20/97 LYONS–GARTEN LAWN AND GARDEN, INC. #0018 Page 0001

Figure 5–7 – SALES REGISTER

Customer–name / Trans–type		Trans–dat / Reference	Doc–#	Terms	Apply–to	Trans–amt
21st Century Construction		04/20/97	1	NET 30		58.16
Sale		Ref #: 000002				
Distributions:	4920–000	Freight charges			2.06	
	2440–000	Accrued local sales tax			3.67	
	4000–000	Sales–Landscape/Consult			14.96	
	4020–000	Sales–Lawn and Garden			24.65	
	4010–000	Sales–Lawn Installation			12.82	
Baker, Richard C.		04/20/97	2	NET 30		64.50
Sale		Ref #: 000003				
Distributions:	4920–000	Freight charges			3.26	
	2440–000	Accrued local sales tax			4.01	
	4030–000	Sales–Nursery			57.23	

2 Sales transactions Grand total: 122.66

Date 04/20/97 LYONS–GARTEN LAWN AND GARDEN, INC. #0018 Page 0002

SALES REGISTER

------------G/L account distribution totals------------

7.68	credited to 2440–000	Accrued local sales tax
14.96	credited to 4000–000	Sales–Landscape/Consult
12.82	credited to 4010–000	Sales–Lawn Installation
24.65	credited to 4020–000	Sales–Lawn and Garden
57.23	credited to 4030–000	Sales–Nursery
5.32	credited to 4920–000	Freight charges

122.66	Total credited	
122.66	debited to 1100–000	Accts Receivable – Trade

-- End of report --

Date 04/20/97 Time 17:27:09 LYONS-GARTEN LAWN AND GARDEN, INC. Report #0019 Page 0001

Figure 5-8 – CASH RECEIPTS REGISTER

Customer-name	Bal-meth	Rect-dat	Check-#	Amount-recd	Cash-acct	Bank-rte-#/Ref	Discount
21st Century Construction	BAL-FORWD	4/20/97	4662	10.00	1010-000	25-16238	.00
						Total credited:	10.00

Date 04/20/97 Time 17:27:10 LYONS-GARTEN LAWN AND GARDEN, INC. Report #0019 Page 0002

Figure 5-8 – CASH RECEIPTS REGISTER

Customer-name	Bal-meth	Rect-dat	Check-#	Amount-recd	Cash-acct	Bank-rte-#/Ref	Discount

Total recd: 10.00
Total disc: .00
------
1 cash receipt transactions Total credited: 10.00

-----------G/L account distribution totals------------

10.00 credited to 1100-000 Accts Receivable – Trade

10.00 debited to 1010-000 Cash #1 – Payables
.00 debited to 4510-000 Sales discounts

10.00 Total debited

-- End of report --

Exercise 6 – PROCESS NON–INVOICED SALES & DR/CR MEMOS

Introduction

Besides billing customers for goods that are sold, organizations must have procedures for keeping accurate records of bills to be paid, processing cash payments, and keeping accurate records of bills that have been paid. In PAS, these important functions are handled by the accounts receivable computer application. As shown in this exercise, this application is complex. In addition to keeping track of amounts owed by customers, the application must be able to debit (DR) or credit (CR) dollar amounts in error, post dollar amounts to be paid in the absence of an invoice, and process recurring transactions, namely those that are supposed to occur from one period to another, such as from month to month.

Figure 6–1 illustrates the flow of information when processing accounts receivable data.

Figure 6–1 – ACCOUNTS RECEIVABLE OVERVIEW

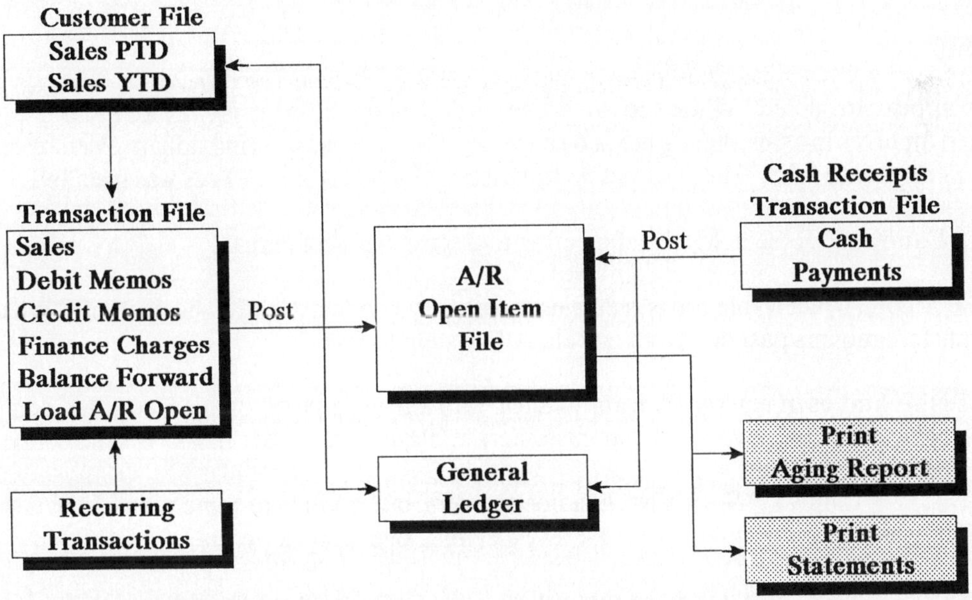

The various types of sales transactions and operations to be performed are indicated by the Transaction File shown above. The following types of transactions are posted to the A/R Open Item File: invoiced sales, debit memos, and credit memos. Finance charges are also posted to accounts for late payment of amounts due. "Balance Forward" ages as a single lump sum the amounts owed by customers. For example, suppose a customer orders $100 of merchandise this month and owes $400 from previous months. If no additional purchases or payments are made by a designated cutoff point ... say month–end, a balance–forward system would age the account, showing $100 as current charges and $400 as dollars owed from previous months. Finally, "Load A/R Open" is used ONLY to enter beginning customer balances when initially setting up PAS. Entries made using this function do not generate debits or credits in the general ledger.

Besides processing various types of transactions, the A/R application must be able to process cash payments received from customers and to post these to the A/R Open–Item File. If payments do not offset outstanding charges, a second bill (shown as a statement) must be mailed to the customer. A second important output of this system is the Aging Report ... a report showing the age of dollar amounts owed by customers.

Objectives

Much like the last exercise, this one asks you to perform a number of processing activities. When you complete this exercise, you should be able to:

- ➟ post a non–invoiced sale to the A/R open–item file
- ➟ enter a credit memo transaction
- ➟ print an A/R transaction edit list
- ➟ post A/R transactions
- ➟ view customer accounts
- ➟ add and activate a recurring sale

Case Study

Jen appears troubled. While she can process sales, as she thought she could, she is not quite sure what to do when an error in a customer's bill is discovered. She also has to bring dollars owed by customers from previous periods into PAS. These would be transactions incurred before PAS was installed.

Jen, Dandy and Rose hold a brief meeting to discuss Jen's concerns.

"The accounts receivable file is really just another type of master file," begins Jen. "What I failed to do was to transfer amounts past due from our old A/R system to PAS."

"Will this hurt us in any way?", Dandy states, with a troubled look on his face. "We don't ever want to reach the point where we have to tell our customers ... 'Please excuse our mess. It's the computer's fault.'"

Jen assures Dandy ... "No, it's not a major problem, but it will take some time. Conversion to a computer system simply takes a lot of time. We can't do everything over a week–end."

Rose questions, "Does this mean that we can't use the computer to analyze sales?"

"For now," Jen responds, "our concern should not be with the analysis of sales. A far more important issue lies in our ability to analyze what customers owe and how old their bills are. Once this area is controlled, and only then, will it be safe to move ahead to flashier types of analyses."

"I understand," concludes Rose. "I just get caught up with the hype that goes along with computers. I agree that we must have receivables in control."

"Actually, we might save more dollars by controlling receivables, than by undertaking a critical look at sales patterns," Dandy quips.

"What do you mean?", Rose and Jen ask.

"If we can reduce the average time of collection for receivables, it will more than pay for the computer," explains Dandy. "For example, if we can reduce receivables by $50,000, we will save the bank interest expense on this amount. With interest rates right around 10 percent, we'll save $5,000 per year."

Set Transaction Date

☐ Before you start this exercise, set today's date at 4/23/97 using the MS–DOS 'DATE' command.

Process Non–Invoiced Sales

Typically a sale is entered using the sales invoicing function, with accompanying updates to A/R, G/L and I/M, and production of an invoice. However, occasionally you may not present an invoice to a customer who makes a purchase. The customer makes a payment at the time of sale, or sometimes, as in the case of Lyons–Garten, when a project is complete. In this case, the non–invoiced sale only updates A/R and G/L. Inventories are not adjusted using this function. Later, you will learn how to adjust the affected inventories for non–invoiced sales when you process inventory in exercise 11.

MAIN MENU

```
RealWorld Practical Accounting System                L-G LAWN AND GARDEN
Version 1.0

              Please select
                 1. Sales Invoicing
                 2. Inventory Management
                 3. Accounts Receivable
                 4. Accounts Payable
                 5. Payroll
                 6. General Ledger
                 7. Check Reconciliation
                 8. Setup Functions

Press F10 for help at any time
```

☐ 1. Type 3 (Accounts Receivable) from the above Main menu, and press ENTER.

```
RealWorld Practical Accounting System                L-G LAWN AND GARDEN
Accounts Receivable

              Please select
                 1. Maintain customer data
                 2. Process sales and DR/CR memos
                 3. Process cash receipts
                 4. Print A/R aging report
                 5. Change apply-to number
                 6. View customer accounts
                 7. Process finance charges
                 8. Print customer statements
                 9. Purge customer accounts
```

NOTE: You have already updated the Customer File using the Maintain Customer Data menu in Exercise 4. Therefore, we will not perform any customer data maintenance in this exercise.

☐ 2. Type 2 (Process Sales and DR/CR Memos) from the above Accounts Receivable menu, and press ENTER.

```
Process sales and DR/CR memos                              L-G LAWN AND GARDEN

                         Please select
                            1. Add transactions
                            2. Change transactions
                            3. Delete transactions
                            4. Print transaction edit list
                            5. Post transactions
```

☐ 3. Type 1 (Add Transactions) from the above Process Sales and DR/CR Memos menu, and press ENTER.

☐ 4. Mountain Garden Supply has an outstanding project agreement with Lyons–Garten for $400 of landscape work and $55 for plants. They want the two amounts kept separate. Since they are an Open–item customer, they can decide which bill they want to pay rather than to make a "payment on account." Therefore, they may make a payment of $100, with the expressed desire to apply all of the payment to landscape work rather than for plants.

Use the information on the following two screens to post this sales information to accounts receivable. In these screens, observe that one transaction is referenced as document # INV1, while the second is referenced as document # INV2.

☐ 5. Type abbreviation MOU to access customer Mountain Garden Supply. In the process of recording each of the two transactions, press ENTER at "Field number to change?" to save the transaction information, press ENTER (N) at "Any change?", and press END to finish the transaction.

```
Process sales and DR/CR memos                              L-G LAWN AND GARDEN
Add transactions

     1. Customer        MOUNTAIN GARDEN SUPPLY        484 Berry St.
                        (enter abbreviation 'MOU')    Moscow
     2. Trans type      S   Sale                      ID 83843
     3. Trans date      4/23/97
     4. Document #      INV1
     5. Amount          55.00
     6. Terms           NET 30
     7. Reference       Plants

       Acct #          ----Description----        Distrib amt
      4030-000         Sales - Nursery              55.00

                       Amount to distribute:  .00
Any change?  N
```

```
Process sales and DR/CR memos                              L-G LAWN AND GARDEN
Add transactions

     1. Customer        MOUNTAIN GARDEN SUPPLY        484 Berry St.
                        (enter abbreviation 'MOU')    Moscow
     2. Trans type      S   Sale                      ID 83843
     3. Trans date      4/23/97
     4. Document #      INV2
     5. Amount          400.00
     6. Terms           NET 30
     7. Reference       Project completed

        Acct #          ----Description----           Distrib amt
       4010-000         Sales - Lawn Installation      400.00

                        Amount to distribute:  .00
Any change?  N
```

☐ 6. Use the following information to record another NON-INVOICED SALE. In the process of recording this transaction, press ENTER at "Field number to change?" to save the transaction, press ENTER (N) at "Any change?", and press END to finish the transaction.

Allied Plumbing Co. purchased landscape drills from Lyons-Garten, Inc.

```
Process sales and DR/CR memos                              L-G LAWN AND GARDEN
Add transactions

     1. Customer        Allied Plumbing Co.           555 N. Grand Blvd.
                        (enter abbreviaiton 'All')    Mesquite, TX 75882
     2. Trans type      S   Sale
     3. Trans date      4/23/97
     4. Document #      7843
     5. Amount          373.75
     6. Terms           NET 30
     7. Reference       Sprinkler Supplies

        Acct #          ----Description----           Distrib amt
       4020-000         Sales - Lawn and Garden        373.75

                        Amount to distribute:  .00
Any change?  N
```

☐ 7. Use the following information on the next page to enter a CREDIT MEMO transaction. In the process of recording this transaction, press ENTER at "Field number to change?" to save the transaction, and press ENTER (N) at "Any change?".

Harris, Goldberg & Jones recently received a statement from Lyons–Garten, Inc. indicating they owe $48.99. In January, Harris purchased tulip bulbs which turned out to be the wrong colored flowers as indicated on their boxes. Therefore, Lyons–Garten shipped new ones. Harris should not have been charged for the replacements.

```
Process sales and DR/CR memos                              L-G LAWN AND GARDEN
Add transactions

     1. Customer       Harris, Goldberg, & Jones     1 Commerce Square
                       (enter 'Har')                 Dallas, TX 75201
     2. Trans type     C   CR memo
     3. Trans date     4/23/97
     4. Document #     3573
     5. Amount         48.99
     6. Terms          CREDIT MEMO  (type in)
     7. Reference      Defective bulbs - color

        Acct #         ----Description----           Distrib amt
      4020-000         Sales - Lawn and Garden       48.99

                       Amount to distribute:  .00
Any change?  N
```

☐ 8. Press END twice to return to the Process Sales and DR/CR Memos menu.

Print Sales Edit List

☐ 9. Type 4 (Print Transaction Edit List) from the Process Sales and DR/CR Memos menu, and press ENTER. Answer N to "Display this report?". (See Figure 6–2 for the printed report.)

Post Sales and Credit Transactions

☐ 10. Type 5 (Post Transactions) from the Process Sales and DR/CR Memos menu, and press ENTER. Answer Y to "Are sales transactions OK to post?". After the Sales Register is printed (see Figure 6–3), press END to return to the Accounts Receivable Menu.

View Customer Accounts

☐ 11. Type 6 (View Customer Accounts) from the Accounts Receivable menu, and press ENTER. Enter "MOU" to select Mountain Garden Supply. When "Mountain Garden Supply" is displayed, answer Y to "Right customer?". Press F1 for a start date of "Earliest". Mountain's account will be displayed as shown on the next page.

```
View customer accounts                                        L-G LAWN AND GARDEN

Customer     MOUNTAIN GARDEN SUPPLY          Contact:     Deb Weber
             484 Berry St.                   Phone #:     208-234-3552
             Moscow                          First date:  4/02/97
             ID  83843                       Comment:     Landscaping

Start date   "Earliest"

Doc-#   Type   Doc-dte    Apply-to    Amount-1    Amount-2    Doc-total
INV1    Sale   04/23/97   INV1           55.00         .00        55.00
INV2    Sale   04/23/97   INV2          400.00         .00       400.00

Sales:       455.00     CR-M:     .00     DR-M:     .00     Total:   455.00
Bfwd:           .00     Fchg:     .00     Pmnt:     .00
End of account - press ENTER for more information, END for new account
```

☐ 12. Press ENTER to view Terms and Reference information; Press END twice to return to the Accounts Receivable menu.

```
Terms        Reference
NET 30       Plants
NET 30       Project completed
```

Add and Activate a Recurring Sale

Recurring transactions are those transactions that occur over and over again, either for an indefinite length of time or for a fixed period of time. Instead of entering these types of transactions each period, you need only enter them once as recurring transactions. Then, when they become due, all you need to do is activate them and enter any data that is specific to the current activation (such as the amount of a bill).

☐ 13. Type 2 (Process Sales and DR/CR Memos) from the Accounts Receivable menu, and press ENTER.

☐ 14. Type 6 (Process Recurring Sales) from the Process Sales and DR/CR Memos menu, and press ENTER.
NOTE: If selection 6 does not appear, press F1. Then type 6, and press ENTER.

```
Process sales and DR/CR memos                           L-G LAWN AND GARDEN
Process recurring sales

                  Please select
                     1. Add recurring sales
                     2. Change recurring sales
                     3. Delete recurring sales
                     4. Print recurring sales list
                     5. Activate recurring sales
```

☐ 15. Type 1 (Add Recurring Sales) from the Process Recurring Sales menu, and enter the following recurring transaction:

Customer	Elliot Enterprises (abbrev 'E')	Amount	75.00
Trans type	S sale	Terms	NET 30 (press F1)
Frequency	M (monthly)	Reference	Lawn service contract
Next due date	50197		

☐ 16. Press ENTER at "Field number to change"?.

☐ 17. Distribute the full amount to Acct # 4010–000 Sales – Lawn Installation.

After you add the recurring sale, your screen should look like this:

```
Process sales and DR/CR memos                                L-G LAWN AND GARDEN
Add transactions

    1. Customer        Elliot Enterprises                    123 Broadway
                                                             Glendale, TX 75155
    2. Trans type      S   Sale
    3. Frequency       M
    4. Next due date   5/01/97
    5. Amount          75.00
    6. Terms           NET 30
    7. Reference       Lawn service contract

      Acct #           ----Description----                   Distrib amt
    4010-000           Sales - Lawn Installation             75.00

                       Amount to distribute:  .00
Any change?  N
```

☐ 18. Press ENTER (N) at "Any change?"

☐ 19. Press END twice to save the transaction and return to the Process Recurring Sales menu.

☐ 20. Type 5 (Activate Recurring Sales) from the Process Recurring Sales menu, and press ENTER.

```
Process sales and DR/CR memos                                L-G LAWN AND GARDEN
Activate recurring sales

                 Please select
                      1. Activate individual sales
                      2. Automatically activate thru a date
```

☐ 21. Type 2 and press ENTER to Automatically Activate Thru a Date. Use the following information to complete the exercise.

```
Process sales and DR/CR memos                              L-G LAWN AND GARDEN
Activate recurring sales

                    Please enter:
                         Starting document #          SC3820
                         Cut-off activation date      123197

         All recurring sales transactions with next due date on
          or before this cut-off date having a non-zero amount
                    will automatically be activated.

Any change?  N
```

☐ 22. Press ENTER (N) at "Any change?".

☐ 23. Press END a sufficient number of times to return to the Process Sales and DR/CR Memos menu.

View Transaction Edit List

☐ 24. Type 4 (Print Transaction Edit List) from the Process Sales and DR/CR Memos menu, and press ENTER. Answer Y to "Display this report?" rather than printing it. You should see the recurring service contract that you activated. If there is an error, return to Process Sales and DR/CR Memos menu, and select option 2 (Change Transactions).

☐ 25. Press ENTER to continue.

Post Sales Transactions to the G/L

☐ 26. Type 5 (Post Transactions) from the Process Sales and DR/CR Memos menu, and answer Yes at "Are sales transactions OK to post?". The sales transactions will be posted and the Sales Register (see Figure 6–4) printed.

☐ 27. This completes the exercise. Press END a sufficient number of times to exit PAS.

QUESTIONS ABOUT THE SOFTWARE

1. Why would you NOT want option 6 (Process Recurring Sales) of the Process Sales and DR/CR Memos menu to be automatically visible to a user?

2. What purpose is served by an invoice credit memo? What purpose would be served by an invoice debit memo? Is there a simpler method for correcting an invoice error than issuing a credit memo and creating a new invoice?

3. Is there a simpler method for correcting an invoice error than processing a credit memo and creating a new invoice?

4. Explain the credits and debits associated with the sale to Applied Plumbing Company. What would happen if debits and credits were not in balance?

5. How does a recurring sale differ from a non–recurring sale? Give an example of each.

MANAGEMENT ISSUES

6. Many managers strive to obtain as many recurring sales as possible for a business. Why are recurring sales of such importance?

7. Compare and contrast non–invoiced sales with invoiced sales. Since with non–invoiced sales, an invoice is never printed and sent to the customer, how would the customer know what amount to pay? Think of several businesses that might prefer to use a non–invoiced method of billing compared to those which use invoices.

8. If 1,000 customers were processed using this non–invoiced sales and credit memos module, the sales register would become massive. Which members of management would ever need to use this register? (Or is it printed without any real purpose?) Explain your response.

9. Compare the non–invoiced sales procedures to cash register sales procedures used, for example, by your local grocery store. Does a cash register provide the same information as that shown on the PAS sales register? If not, how does the recorded information differ?

10. Why is it important to separate the approval process for credit memos from Jen Ledger's bookkeeping function.

11. From L–G Lawn and Garden's perspective, what is an advantage of designating a particular customer as an "open item" customer?

12. How might Dandy and Rose sustain Jen's motivation during the difficult transition from their manual accounting system to PAS?

THINGS TO DO

This exercise asked you to perform a variety of tasks which may appear somewhat unrelated. Do the following to better appreciate what was done.

13. Determine if accounts receivables are in balance.

☐ a. From the Main Menu, type 3 (Accounts Receivable).

☐ b. Type 4 (Print A/R Aging Report).

This report will age all outstanding receiving accounts, telling you the approximate age of each outstanding amount.

☐ c. Complete the following screen.

Print A/R aging report	L–G LAWN AND GARDEN
Please enter:	
1. Aging date	4/23/97
2. Include items after aging date ?	N
3. Starting customer	"First"
4. Ending customer	"Last"
5. Sales rep	"All"
6. Print DR/CR bal customers	Both DR and CR accounts
7. Print zero bal customers ?	Y
8. Cut–off balance due	No cut–off (press ENTER)
9. Detail or summary	Summary
10. Print on separate pages ?	(Not applicable)
11. Age open item customers like bal forward customers ?	Y
Field number to change?	

☐ d. Print the report. **What is the total A/R account balance?**

☐ e. Return to the Main Menu and type 6 (General Ledger).

☐ f. Type 3 (View G/L Account Activity).

☐ g. Type 1100 to reveal the Trade Account.

☐ h. Use a beginning date of 4–01–97 and an ending date of 4–23–97.

What is the total A/R account balance? Are the accounts in balance?

14. Review the sale and credit transactions for Applied Plumbing and Harris, Goldberg & Jones, and compare the amounts to those on the Aged Accounts Receivable report.

☐ a. From the Main Menu select Accounts Receivable, followed by View Customer Accounts.

☐ b. Type "All" for customer.

☐ c. Enter 040197 for Start Date.

How much is now owed by Allied Plumbing and Company?

☐ d. Press END to review another account.

☐ e. Type "Harris" to view the Harris, Goldberg & Jones account.

☐ f. Again, enter 040197 for Start Date.

How much is now owed by Harris, Goldberg & Jones?

What conclusions can you draw from the processing of a sale and a credit outside of customer invoicing?

☐ g. Compare these totals to those shown on the Aged Accounts Receivable report that you printed in step 1d.

Are these amounts shown in the current period?

15. Finally, let's review the recurring sales transaction for Elliot Enterprises.

☐ a. From the Accounts Receivable menu, select Process Sales and DR/CR Memos menu.

☐ b. Select Process Recurring Sales.

☐ c. Activate Recurring Sales.

☐ d. Activate Individual Sales.

☐ e. Press F1. **What name appears?**

☐ f. Type Y to activate this account. **What happens? Explain this message.**

☐ g. Press ENTER (N) ... do not continue.

☐ h. Press F1 for the next transaction. **What happens?**

☐ i. Press ENTER, and then press END several times to exit PAS.

What is the value of entering and storing recurring sales transactions?

Date 04/23/97 LYONS-GARTEN LAWN AND GARDEN, INC. #0020 Page 0001

Figure 6-2a – SALES EDIT LIST

Customer-name Trans-type	Trans-dat Reference	Doc-#	Terms	Apply-to	Trans-amt
Allied Plumbing Co.	04/23/97	7843	NET 30		373.75
Sale	Sprinkler Supplies				
Distributions: 4020-000	Sales - Lawn and Garden			373.75	
Harris, Goldberg, & Jones	04/23/97	3573	CREDIT MEMO		48.99 CR
CR memo	Defective bulbs - color				
Distributions: 4020-000	Sales - Lawn and Garden			48.99	
MOUNTAIN GARDEN SUPPLY	04/23/97	INV1	NET 30		55.00
Sale	Plants				
Distributions: 4030-000	Sales - Nursery			55.00	
MOUNTAIN GARDEN SUPPLY	04/23/97	INV2	NET 30		400.00
Sale	Project completed				
Distributions: 4010-000	Sales - Lawn Installation			400.00	
4 Sales transactions			Grand total:	779.76	

Date 04/23/97 LYONS-GARTEN LAWN AND GARDEN, INC. #0020 Page 0002

Figure 6-2b – SALES EDIT LIST

-----------G/L account distribution totals-----------

48.99	credited to 1100-000	Accts Receivable - Trade
400.00	credited to 4010-000	Sales - Lawn Installation
373.75	credited to 4020-000	Sales - Lawn and Garden
55.00	credited to 4030-000	Sales - Nursery

877.74	Total credited	
828.75	debited to 1100-000	Accts Receivable - Trade
48.99	debited to 4020-000	Sales - Lawn and Garden

877.74	Total debited	

-- End of report --

Date 04/23/97 LYONS–GARTEN LAWN AND GARDEN, INC. #0021 Page 0001

Figure 6–3a – SALES REGISTER

Customer–name Trans–type	Trans–dat Reference	Doc–#	Terms	Apply–to	Trans–amt
Allied Plumbing Co.	04/23/97	7843	NET 30		373.75
Sale	Sprinkler Supplies				
Distributions: 4020–000	Sales – Lawn and Garden			373.75	
Harris, Goldberg, & Jones	04/23/97	3573	CREDIT MEMO		48.99 CR
CR memo	Defective bulbs – color				
Distributions: 4020–000	Sales – Lawn and Garden			48.99	
MOUNTAIN GARDEN SUPPLY	04/23/97	INV1	NET 30		55.00
Sale	Plants				
Distributions: 4030–000	Sales – Nursery			55.00	
MOUNTAIN GARDEN SUPPLY	04/23/97	INV2	NET 30		400.00
Sale	Project completed				
Distributions: 4010–000	Sales – Lawn Installation			400.00	
4 Sales transactions			Grand total:	779.76	

Date 04/23/97 LYONS–GARTEN LAWN AND GARDEN, INC. #0021 Page 0002

Figure 6–3b – SALES REGISTER

-----------G/L account distribution totals-----------

48.99	credited to 1100–000	Accts Receivable – Trade
400.00	credited to 4010–000	Sales – Lawn Installation
373.75	credited to 4020–000	Sales – Lawn and Garden
55.00	credited to 4030–000	Sales – Nursery

877.74	Total credited	
828.75	debited to 1100–000	Accts Receivable – Trade
48.99	debited to 4020–000	Sales – Lawn and Garden

877.74	Total debited	

-- End of report --

Date 04/23/97 LYONS–GARTEN LAWN AND GARDEN, INC. #0022 Page 0001

Figure 6–4a – SALES REGISTER

Customer–name	Trans–dat	Doc–#	Terms	Apply–to	Trans–amt
Trans–type	Reference				
Elliot Enterprises	04/23/97	SC3820	NET 30		75.00
Sale	Lawn service contract				
Distributions: 4010–000	Sales – Lawn Installation			75.00	

1 Sales transaction

Date 04/23/97 LYONS–GARTEN LAWN AND GARDEN, INC. #0022 Page 0002

Figure 6–4b – SALES REGISTER

-----------G/L account distribution totals-----------

75.00 credited to 4010–000 Sales – Lawn Installation

75.00 debited to 1100–000 Accts Receivable – Trade

–– End of report ––

Exercise 7 – PROCESS CASH RECEIPTS

Introduction

As indicated in the last exercise, the PAS A/R component allows for the entry of sales information, the billing of customers, the record–keeping needed to show amounts owed and paid by customers, and the processing of cash payments. Thus far, we have asked you to perform the first two of these functions. In this exercise, we ask you to process cash receipts.

The PAS software allows cash receipts to be applied in different ways, depending on the type of A/R account selected for a customer. When adding a new customer to the customer master file, the A/R balance method must be chosen. (Review Exercise 4, screen 1 of Maintain Customer Data, if you do not remember where you had to choose.) The choices are: O for "open item", or B for "balance forward". PAS treats an open–item invoice as "open" until it is paid in its entirety. Any "open" invoice remains on file until it is paid or offset by a credit. When a cash payment is received, it is applied to a specific invoice.

The balance–forward method is much less complex. This method does not continue to keep an invoice open if it is from a previous period (such as last month). Instead, only current charges are itemized; past–due charges are shown as a total past–due amount. When a cash payment is made with this method, the first dollar is applied, first, to the past–due amount. Any remainder is applied against current charges.

Objectives

In this exercise, you are asked to perform a variety of tasks important to recording payments from customers. When you complete this exercise, you should be able to:

- print an aged A/R report
- process customer cash receipts
- print a receipts transaction edit list and produce a bank deposit slip
- post cash receipts to the general ledger and print a cash receipts register

In working through these tasks, compare the similarities and differences between the processing of cash receipts to the processing of customer invoices and credit/debit memos experienced in Exercise 6.

Case Study

Jen is so completely satisfied with how she is able to process sales information and credit and debit receivables that she assumes that the processing of cash receipts will be a simple operation. She says to her–self, "Why, I bet Rich (Lawn and Garden Sales) and Daisy (Nursery Sales) could process customer invoices and customer payments for their walk–in trade. We should be able to hand an invoice to a customer at the time of sale, if the customer is in one of the yards. Likewise, Rich and Daisy should be able to query A/R when a customer asks how much is owed and to take payments to offset an outstanding balance."

Rich Grower and Daisy Stalker meet with Jen to discuss the possibility of entering sales and payment information into PAS.

Rich states: "I would like to be able to do more than simply query a customer's account. When the customer is in the store and a sale is made, I need to be able to hand the customer an invoice."

"I agree with Rich's position," adds Daisy. "If we can improve our point–of–sale billing procedures, our customers will be impressed."

"What about handling cash payments?", questions Jen.

"There are times when a customer drops by and hands me a check," Rich states. "He then will ask, 'After this payment, how much do I owe?'" "If I tell him one dollar amount, based on my manual calculations, and I send the check to you, Jen, for processing, and it takes even a day to process the payment, we might be embarrassed. For example, if a payment is made today and processed tomorrow, but monthly statements are processed this afternoon, the paid amount won't be reflected on the statement and the customer will be ..... (angry)."

"I understand," exclaims Jen. "Let me work with PAS to determine how we should set it up so that you and Daisy can enter sales and payments for our customers on file, with satisfactory payment histories."

Set Transaction Date

☐ Before you start this exercise, set today's date at 4/27/97 using the MS–DOS 'DATE' command.

Print Aged Accounts Receivables Report

Before asking you to process cash receipts, we ask you to print the A/R aging report. This report shows what each customer owes, as well as the age of all unpaid amounts. It reveals that several sales transactions and A/R balances were included in the sample PAS database. For example, the Neptune Underwater Supply Company has a balance showing charges from an earlier period.

MAIN MENU

```
RealWorld Practical Accounting System                L–G LAWN AND GARDEN
Version 1.0

                    Please select
                         1. Sales Invoicing
                         2. Inventory Management
                         3. Accounts Receivable
                         4. Accounts Payable
                         5. Payroll
                         6. General Ledger
                         7. Check Reconciliation
                         8. Setup Functions

Press F10 for help at any time
```

☐ 1. Type 3 (Accounts Receivable) from the above Main Menu, and press ENTER.

```
RealWorld Practical Accounting System                L-G LAWN AND GARDEN
Accounts Receivable

                 Please select
                        1. Maintain customer data
                        2. Process sales and DR/CR memos
                        3. Process cash receipts
                        4. Print A/R aging report
                        5. Change apply-to number
                        6. View customer accounts
                        7. Process finance charges
                        8. Print customer statements
                        9. Purge customer accounts
```

- [ ] 2. Type 4 (Print A/R Aging Report) from the Accounts Receivable menu, and press ENTER.
- [ ] 3. Make the choices shown in the following aging report selection screen.

```
Print A/R aging report                               L-G LAWN AND GARDEN

  Please enter:
    1. Aging date                               04/27/97
    2. Include items after aging date?          N
    3. Starting customer                        "First"  (press F1)
    4. Ending customer                          "Last"   (press F1)
    5. Sales rep                                "All"    (press F1)
    6. Print DR/CR bal customers                Both DR and CR accounts
    7. Print zero bal customers?                Y
    8. Cut-off balance due                      No cut-off  (press ENTER)
    9. Detail or summary                        Summary
   10. Print on separate pages?                 (Not applicable)
   11. Age open item customers
         like bal forward customers?            N

Field number to change?
```

- [ ] 4. Press ENTER at "Field number to change?".
- [ ] 5. Answer 'N' at "Display this report?". (See Figure 7–1 for the printed report.)

Process Payments on Balance–forward Accounts

As shown by the Aged A/R Report, most of Lyons–Garten's customers have balance–forward accounts. Two accounts, Holcomb Industrial Supply and Mountain Garden Supply, are the only open–item accounts.

To process a cash receipt to a balance–forward account, do the following:

☐ 6. Type 3 (Process Cash Receipts) from the Accounts Receivable menu, and press ENTER.

```
Process cash receipts                                   L-G LAWN AND GARDEN

                      Please select
                          1. Add transactions
                          2. Change transactions
                          3. Delete transactions
                          4. Print transaction edit list
                          5. Print deposit slips
                          6. Post transactions
```

☐ 7. Type 1 (Add Transactions) from the above Process Cash Receipts menu, and press ENTER.

8. Do the procedure outlined below to enter the following cash receipt from the Neptune Underwater Supply Company.

```
NEPTUNE UNDERWATER SUPPLY                                          4851
345 Lewisville Rd.
Lewisville, TX 75540                              April 19   1997

PAY TO THE                                                      67-3/621
ORDER OF    LYONS-GARTEN LAWN AND GARDEN, INC.                  $ 50.00
Fifty and ---------------------------------------- 00/100 DOLLARS
     SOUTH PLAINS COOPERATIVE BANK
     Morehouse, Tx 75286
Memo ____________________
     561604063    6487219  5
```

☐ a. Type 'Neptune' for Customer (Neptune Underwater Supply), and press ENTER.

☐ b. Enter '4851' for Check #.

☐ c. Enter '42797' (today's date) for Receipt date.

☐ d. Enter 50.00 for Amount recd.

☐ e. Press ENTER to indicate that you will be depositing this receipt in Checking Account #1.

☐ f. Enter '67–3/621' for the Bank route #. **Note the location of this number on the check.**

☐ g. "Credit A/R" means "Credit this transaction to the accounts receivable G/L account specified in the Accounting Control file?". Enter Y(yes) to accomplish this.

☐ h. Since Neptune is a balance–forward customer, and you answered Y for field 7, "CREDIT A/R?", another field, Discount, appears on the screen. Press ENTER to indicate zero discount for ALL cash transactions in this exercise.

The following shows your completed screen.

```
Process cash receipts                                L-G LAWN AND GARDEN
Add

        1. Customer          Neptune Underwater Supply   Bal forward
        2. Check #           4851
        3. Receipt date      4/27/97
        4. Amount recd       50.00
        5. Chk acct code     1  1010-000  Cash #1 - Payables
        6. Bank route #      67-3/621
        7. Credit A/R ?      Y
        8. Discount          .00              Total credit: 50.00

Field number to change?
```

☐ i. Press ENTER when asked "Field number to change?" to save the transaction data and proceed to the next customer.

Add Additional Cash Receipts to Balance–forward Customers

☐ 9. Repeat the above procedure for each of the following two cash receipts received today.

```
BAKER, RICHARD C.                                              143
2554 Broad Street
Irving, TX 75103                           April 23  1997

PAY TO THE                                                     13-7/586
ORDER OF   LYONS-GARTEN LAWN AND GARDEN, INC.                  $ 100.00
One hundred and ---------------------------- 00/100            DOLLARS
     FIRST SAVINGS BANK
     Taco, Tx 75107
Memo ______________                        ____________________
     001400072   1234567   8
```

```
21st CENTURY CONSTRUCTION                                      10234
P.O. Box 4545
Dallas, TX 75204                           April 24  1997

PAY TO THE                                                     64-5/295
ORDER OF   LYONS-GARTEN LAWN AND GARDEN, INC.                  $ 25.00
Twenty five and ---------------------------- 00/100            DOLLARS
     DALLAS SAVINGS AND LOAN
     Dallas, TX 75206
Memo ______________                        ____________________
     005401232   6520053   2
```

Process Payments on Open–item Accounts

☐ 10. Repeat the above procedure to add the following cash receipt to an open–item account.

MOUNTAIN GARDEN SUPPLY 812
484 Berry Street
Moscow, ID 83843 April 21 1997

PAY TO THE 52–7/014
ORDER OF LYONS–GARTEN LAWN AND GARDEN, INC. $ 455.00
Four hundred fifty five -------------------------- 00/100 DOLLARS
MOSCOW NATIONAL BANK
Moscow, ID 83847
Memo ____________
001459728 1128432 4

☐ 11. After you have added the above cash receipt information, press ENTER at "Field number to change?" Since Mountain Garden Supply is an open–item customer, and you answered Y to the question "CREDIT A/R?", you now have an opportunity to apply this cash receipt to one or more specific unpaid invoices of Mountain Garden Supply.

The application choices are displayed at the bottom of the screen. As you enter the requested information, you will notice that the screen will show the amount remaining to be applied.

☐ 12. Press F1 for Apply–to document INV1, and press ENTER (Y) at "Right document?". The resulting screen will appear as follows:

```
Process cash receipts                                L-G LAWN AND GARDEN
Add
          1. Customer        MOUNTAIN GARDEN SUPPLY    Open item
          2. Check #         812
          3. Receipt date    4/27/97
          4. Amount recd     455.00
          5. Chk acct code   1  1010-000  Cash #1 - Payables
          6. Bank route #    52-7/014
          7. Credit A/R ?    Y     Amt remaining: 455.00

     Apply-to   Type  Doc date   Orig amt      Balance

     INV1       SLS   4/23/97      55.00         55.00

          Terms:      NET 30

       8. Amt paid
       9. Discount
      10. Reference
```

☐ 13. Type 55 at "Amt paid" to apply part of the $455.00 cash receipt to the $55.00 invoice that Mountain Garden Supply has on account, and press ENTER.

☐ 14. Press ENTER for zero Discount, and type 'full payment on invoice' for future Reference to this transaction.

☐ 15. Press ENTER at "Field number to change?".

☐ 16. Press F1 to show Mountain's other outstanding invoice balance (INV2) of $400.00. Press ENTER (Y) at "Right document?".

☐ 17. Type 400 to apply the remaining part of the $455.00 cash receipt to the outstanding balance, and press ENTER.

☐ 18. Press ENTER for zero discount, and type 'full payment on invoice' for Reference.

☐ 19. Press ENTER at "Field number to change?"

☐ 20. Press F1 to determine if Mountain has any other outstanding invoices.

☐ 21. Since PAS indicates there are "no more open items for this customer", press ENTER to continue, and press TAB or END to return to a new Add screen.

Add an Additional Cash Receipt to an Open–item Account

☐ 22. Repeat the above procedure on the following cash receipt received today.

HOLCOMB INDUSTRIAL SUPPLY 8406
2323 Holcomb Way
Dallas, TX 75205 April 25 1997

PAY TO THE 99–3/385
ORDER OF LYONS–GARTEN LAWN AND GARDEN, INC. $ 43.34
Forty three and ------------------------------ 34/100 DOLLARS
INSTITUTION FOR SAVINGS
Dallas, TX 75187
Memo
435704699 3475100 8

☐ 23. Apply the full amount of the receipt to document number SL022 (press F1), and reference it as 'full payment on invoice'.

Your completed screen is shown on the next page.

```
Process cash receipts                                L-G LAWN AND GARDEN
Add
            1. Customer        Holcomb Industrial Supply        Open item
            2. Check #         8406
            3. Receipt date    4/27/97
            4. Amount recd     43.34
            5. Chk acct code   1  1010-000  Cash #1 - Payables
            6. Bank route #    99-3/385
            7. Credit A/R ?    Y     Amt remaining:     .00

      Apply-to    Type   Doc date    Orig amt        Balance

      SL022       SLS    3/10/97       43.34             .00

            Terms:       NET 30

          8. Amt paid     43.34
          9. Discount     .00
         10. Reference    full payment on invoice

Field number to change?
```

☐ 24. Press ENTER when asked "Field number to change?". Press TAB or END to return to the Add menu.

Process Cash Receipts – Non–A/R Cash

Non–A/R cash refers to cash receipts that will not be credited to A/R. For example, if a customer pays for an item with cash at the time of a purchase, the transaction should not affect the A/R account. Instead, you can specify up to three different accounts to which this cash receipt will be credited.

If you answer N to "Credit A/R?", the non–A/R cash distribution information will display at the bottom of the screen.

☐ 25. Enter the following non–A/R cash transaction. **Answer N to the question "Credit A/R?".**

```
MOUNTAIN GARDEN SUPPLY                                            835
484 Berry Street
Moscow, ID 83843                          April 27  1997

PAY TO THE                                                    52-7/014
ORDER OF   LYONS-GARTEN LAWN AND GARDEN, INC.                 $ 586.25
Five hundred sixty and ------------------------- 00/100      DOLLARS
    MOSCOW NATIONAL BANK
    Moscow, ID 83847
Memo ______________________
    001459728    1128432  4
```

☐ 26. Distribute the cash receipt as follows:

```
              *** Non-A/R cash distribution ***

     Acct-#                                        Amount
  8. 4000-000       Sales - Landscape/Consult      377.00
  9. 4010-000       Sales - Lawn Installation      209.25
 10.                                              -------
                                   Remaining:         .00

Field number to change?
```

☐ 27. Press ENTER when asked "Field number to change?". Press TAB or END to return to the Process Cash Receipts menu.

Print Cash Receipts Edit List

☐ 28. Type 4 (Print Transaction Edit List) from the Process Cash Receipts menu, and press ENTER.

☐ 29. Answer N when asked "Display this report?". (See Figure 7–2 for the printed report.)

> **NOTE:** You may need to put your printer in compressed mode to print all of the data.

Print the Bank Deposit Slip

☐ 30. Type 5 (Print Deposit Slips) from the Process Cash Receipts menu, and press ENTER.

☐ 31. Enter '42797' as the deposit date.

☐ 32. Press ENTER (N) to indicate no change. (See Figure 7–3 for the printed deposit slips.)

Post Cash Receipt Transactions to the G/L

☐ 33. Type 6 (Post Transactions) from the Process Cash Receipts menu, and press ENTER.

☐ 34. Type Y and press ENTER to answer the question "Are cash transactions OK to post?".

☐ 35. Enter '42797' as the deposit date.

☐ 36. Press ENTER (N) to indicate no change. (See Figure 7–4 for the printed register.)

☐ 37. This completes the exercise. Press END a sufficient number of times to exit PAS.

QUESTIONS ABOUT THE SOFTWARE

1. What information does the Aged Accounts Receivable provide?

2. Compare the Cash Receipts Register in this exercise to the Sales Register in Exercise 5. In what ways are the two registers similar? How do they differ?

3. What would happen if $300 were received, with $25 applied to INV1 and $250 to INV2?

MANAGEMENT ISSUES

4. PAS provides for two types of accounts receivable systems: balance–forward and open item. Based on your knowledge gained from this exercise, how does a balance–forward system differ from an open item receivables system?

5. Cash sales in companies are typically processed by cash registers. Using cash registers, it is possible to post to an account, such as 4000 and 4010, as in the Lyons–Garten case. Explain how this is done.

6. Speculate on how the management of Lyons–Garten would utilize the aged accounts receivable report.

7. Suppose a customer owes $455.54 and submits $455.45 in payment. Since this is only a $0.09 difference, should the cash receipt be recorded as $455.54 to show the outstanding bill paid in full? If not, should the customer be billed for $0.09? Which application should be used, if not cash receipts, to handle "messy little details" such as this?

8. Some managers contend that invoicing tells them very little about how their company is doing, in contrast to cash receipts. Do you agree or disagree with this statement? What information does cash receipts provide that invoicing does not? What information does invoicing provide that cash receipts does not?

9. What controls should Lyons–Garten have in place to insure that all cash is accounted for on a daily basis?

10. What cash management problems occur if a customer's account is not kept up–to–date?

THINGS TO DO

In this section, we ask you explore different ways of analyzing accounts receivables and to understand how cash is applied to general ledger and checking accounts (debited) and against accounts receivables (credited).

11. Initially, we ask you to take another look at the A/R Aging report.

    a. Type 3 (Accounts Receivable) from the Main menu.
    b. Type 4 (Print A/R Aging Report).
    c. Make the following choices:

1. Aging date	04/27/97
2. Include items after aging date?	N
3. Starting customer	"First"
4. Ending customer	"Last"
5. Sales rep **(this one is essential)**	JAK
6. Print DR/CR bal customers	Both DR and CR accounts
7. Print zero bal customers	Y
8. Cut–off point	No cut–off
9. Detail or summary	Summary
10. Print on separate pages	(Not applicable)
11. Age open item customers like bal forward customers?	N

d. Answer Y when asked, "Display this report?".

Which customer is the slowest in payment of its outstanding bills?
Should the Sales rep, JAK, know this information? Why or why not?

e. Return to the Main menu.

12. Next, investigate how the cash deposit was applied.

a. Type 6 (General Ledger) from the Main menu.
b. Type 3 (View G/L accounts).
c. Press F1 to view account 1010.
d. Use a beginning date of 042797.
e. Use an ending date of 043097.

How much cash was added to Cash #1?
How many transactions were processed?
Are these counts and amounts the same as those appearing on the deposit slip? Yes or No?

f. Return to the Main menu.

g. Type 7 (Check Reconciliation) from the Main menu.
h. Type 4 (Print a Checkbook).
i. Type 1 for the checking account number.
j. Press ENTER. (Do NOT purge.)

What dollar deposit was made on 4/27/97?

k. Return to the Main menu.

What does this exercise tell you about how cash receipts are applied to Lyons–Garten accounts?

13. Finally, examine how a cash receipt changes customer A/R accounts.

    a. Type 3 (Accounts Receivable) from the Main menu.
    b. Type 6 (View Customer Accounts).
    c. Press F1 to advance to Neptune Underwater Supply.
    d. Press F1 for "Start Date."

    Examine this account. Is it possible to tell how the $50.00 was applied to any one outstanding invoice? Yes or No.
    Explain how the payment is applied to this balance–only account.

    e. Press END to view a second account.
    f. Type 'MOU' to view the MOUNTAIN GARDEN SUPPLY account.

    Examine this account. Is it possible to tell how the $455.00 payment was applied to any one outstanding invoice? Yes or no?
    Explain how the payment is applied to this open–item account.

Date: 04/27/97 Time: 14:50:32 LYONS-GARTEN LAWN AND GARDEN, INC. Report #0024 Page #0001

Figure 7-1 – AGED ACCOUNTS RECEIVABLE

Aging date: 4/27/97

Customer-name Sls-rep	Phone-# Contact	Last-pmt-dat Bal-meth	Balance	Current	31-60 days	61-90 days	Over 90 days
21st Century Construction JAK	555-7844 Herbert Mandel	4/20/97 BAL-FWD	176.56	58.16	67.41	50.99	.00
Allied Plumbing Co. JAK	221-8520 M. J. Thorpe	None BAL-FWD	373.75	373.75	.00	.00	.00
Baker, Richard C. TJF	478-9090 Richard Baker	None BAL-FWD	186.48	64.50	121.98	.00	.00
Elliot Enterprises TJF	779-6010 Paul Elliot	None BAL-FWD	75.00	75.00	.00	.00	.00
Harris, Goldberg, & Jones JAK	554-4300 Michael Jones	None BAL-FWD	48.99CR	48.99CR	.00	.00	.00
Holcomb Industrial Supply JAK	722-2233 Jim Ewing	None OPN-ITM	43.34	.00	43.34	.00	.00
MOUNTAIN GARDEN SUPPLY AW	208-234-3552 Deb Weber	None OPN-ITM	455.00	455.00	.00	.00	.00
Neptune Underwater Supply TJF	736-1102 Sam Johnston	1/03/97 BAL-FWD	113.09	.00	18.85	94.24	.00

Grand totals for 8 customers printed; aging date 4/27/97

DR Lines show totals for customers with debit balances as of the aging date
CR Lines show totals for customers with credit balances as of the aging date

	Balance	Current	31-60 days	61-90 days	Over 90 days
DR bal cust totals:	1,423.22	1,026.41	251.58	145.23	.00
CR bal cust totals:	48.99CR	48.99CR	.00	.00	.00
Net totals:	1,374.23	977.42	251.58	145.23	.00

-- End of report --

Date 04/27/97 Time 14:57:46 LYONS–GARTEN LAWN AND GARDEN, INC. Report #0027 0001

Figure 7–2a – CASH RECEIPTS EDIT LIST

Customer–name	Bal–meth	Rect–dat	Check–#	Amount–recd	Cash–acct	Bank–rte–#/Ref	Discount
21st Century Construction	BAL–FORWD	4/27/97	10234	25.00	1010–000	64–5/295	.00
						Total credited:	25.00
Baker, Richard D.	BAL–FORWD	4/27/97	143	100.00	1010–000	13–7/586	.00
						Total credited:	100.00
Holcomb Industrial Supply	OPEN–ITEM	4/27/97	8406	43.34	1010–000	99–3/385	

Apply–to	Amt–paid	Discount	Total–applied	Reference
SL022	43.34	.00	43.34	full payment on invoice
Chk totals:	43.34	.00	43.34	

Customer–name	Bal–meth	Rect–dat	Check–#	Amount–recd	Cash–acct	Bank–rte–#/Ref	Discount
MOUNTAIN GARDEN SUPPLY	OPEN–ITEM	4/27/97	812	455.00	1010–000	52–7/014	

Apply–to	Amt–paid	Discount	Total–applied	Reference
INV1	55.00	.00	55.00	full payment on invoice
INV2	400.00	.00	400.00	full payment on invoice
Chk totals:	455.00	.00	455.00	

Customer–name	Bal–meth	Rect–dat	Check–#	Amount–recd	Cash–acct	Bank–rte–#/Ref	Discount
MOUNTAIN GARDEN SUPPLY	OPEN–ITEM	4/27/97	835	586.25	1010–000	52–7/014	

Amt–credited	Acct–#	
377.00	4000–000	Sales – Landscape/Consult
209.25	4010–000	Sales – Lawn Installation

Customer–name	Bal–meth	Rect–dat	Check–#	Amount–recd	Cash–acct	Bank–rte–#/Ref	Discount
Neptune Underwater Supply	BAL–FORWD	4/27/97	4851	50.00	1010–000	67–3/621	.00
						Total credited:	50.00

Date 04/27/97 Time 14:57:49 LYONS–GARTEN LAWN AND GARDEN, INC. Report #0027 0002

Figure 7–2b – CASH RECEIPTS EDIT LIST

Customer–name	Bal–meth	Rect–dat	Check–#	Amount–recd	Cash–acct	Bank–rte–#/Ref	Discount

Total recd: 1,259.59
Total disc: .00

6 cash receipt transactions Total credited: 1,259.59

--------- G/L account distribution totals ---------

Amount		Account	Description
673.34	credited to	1100–000	Accts Receivable – Trade
377.00	credited to	4000–000	Sales – Landscape/Consult
209.25	credited to	4010–000	Sales – Lawn Installation
1,259.59	Total credited		
1,259.59	debited to	1010–000	Cash #1 – Payables
.00	debited to	4510–000	Sales discounts
1,259.59	Total debited		

-- End of report --

Figure 7–3 – DEPOSIT SLIP

L–G LAWN AND GARDEN
1169 Greenbelt Way
Nice Valley, OR 97000

8765–432–19876
Acct #: 4400998877

Deposit date: 04/27/97

Bank #	Amount	Check #
64–5/295	25.00	10234
13–7/586	100.00	143
99–3/385	43.34	8406
52–7/014	455.00	812
52–7/014	586.25	835
67–3/621	50.00	4851
Total deposit:	1,259.59	

Date 04/27/97 Time 15:02:03 LYONS–GARTEN LAWN AND GARDEN, INC. Report #0028 0001

Figure 7–4a – CASH RECEIPTS REGISTER

Customer–name	Bal–meth	Rect–dat	Check–#	Amount–recd	Cash–acct	Bank–rte–#/Ref	Discount
21st Century Construction	BAL–FORWD	4/27/97	10234	25.00	1010–000	64–5/295	.00
						Total credited:	25.00
Baker, Richard D.	BAL–FORWD	4/27/97	143	100.00	1010–000	13–7/586	.00
						Total credited:	100.00
Holcomb Industrial Supply	OPEN–ITEM	4/27/97	8406	43.34	1010–000	99–3/385	

Apply–to	Amt–paid	Discount	Total–applied	Reference
SL022	43.34	.00	43.34	full payment on invoice
Chk totals:	43.34	.00	43.34	

Customer–name	Bal–meth	Rect–dat	Check–#	Amount–recd	Cash–acct	Bank–rte–#/Ref	Discount
MOUNTAIN GARDEN SUPPLY	OPEN–ITEM	4/27/97	812	455.00	1010–000	52–7/014	

Apply–to	Amt–paid	Discount	Total–applied	Reference
INV1	55.00	.00	55.00	full payment on invoice
INV2	400.00	.00	400.00	full payment on invoice
Chk totals:	455.00	.00	455.00	

Customer–name	Bal–meth	Rect–dat	Check–#	Amount–recd	Cash–acct	Bank–rte–#/Ref	Discount
MOUNTAIN GARDEN SUPPLY	OPEN–ITEM	4/27/97	835	586.25	1010–000	52–7/014	

Amt–credited	Acct–#	
377.00	4000–000	Sales – Landscape/Consult
209.25	4010–000	Sales – Lawn Installation

Customer–name	Bal–meth	Rect–dat	Check–#	Amount–recd	Cash–acct	Bank–rte–#/Ref	Discount
Neptune Underwater Supply	BAL–FORWD	4/27/97	4851	50.00	1010–000	67–3/621	.00
						Total credited:	50.00

Date 04/27/97 Time 15:02:06 LYONS–GARTEN LAWN AND GARDEN, INC. Report #0028 0002

Figure 7–4b – CASH RECEIPTS REGISTER

Customer–name	Bal–meth	Rect–dat	Check–#	Amount–recd	Cash–acct	Bank–rte–#/Ref	Discount

	Total recd:	1,259.59
	Total disc:	.00
6 cash receipt transactions	Total credited:	1,259.59

--------- G/L account distribution totals ---------

673.34	credited to 1100–000	Accts Receivable – Trade
377.00	credited to 4000–000	Sales – Landscape/Consult
209.25	credited to 4010–000	Sales – Lawn Installation
1,259.59	Total credited	
1,259.59	debited to 1010–000	Cash #1 – Payables
.00	debited to 4510–000	Sales discounts
1,259.59	Total debited	

–– End of report ––

Exercise 8 – PROCESS ACCOUNTS PAYABLE

Introduction

The reverse of accounts receivable is accounts payable. In this instance, vendors bill the organization for goods shipped and received. As a direct consequence, organizations must have procedures for keeping track of items purchased from vendors, where no bill has been received to–date; bills received, but not paid; bills paid, but the cancelled check has not been returned by the bank; and bills paid, where the cancelled check has been returned and reconciled. In PAS, these important functions are handled by two applications ..... the accounts payable application and the check reconciliation application. Before any activity can be undertaken, a "vendor master file" is required. As discussed in Exercise 4, this file stores the names, addresses and financial summary information for each vendor of the organization.

Figure 8–1 illustrates the flow of information when processing accounts payable data.

Figure 8–1 – ACCOUNTS PAYABLE OVERVIEW

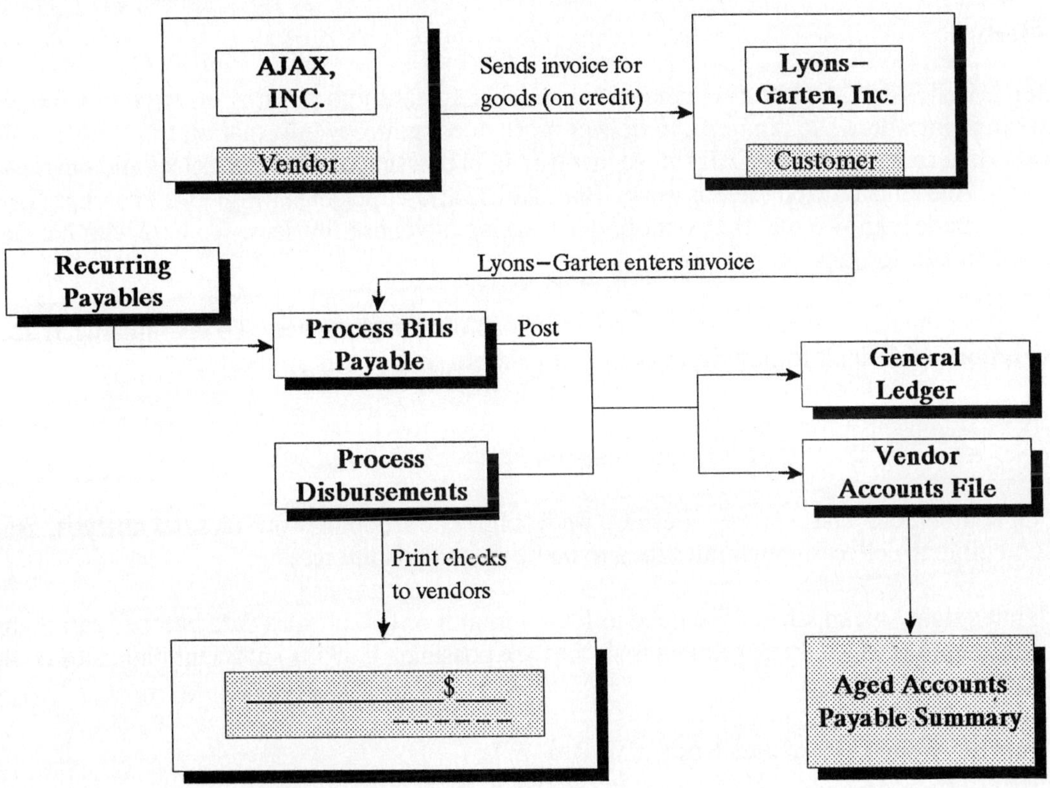

As shown, the process begins when Ajax, Inc. sends an invoice to the Lyons–Garten, Inc. company. This, and invoices received from other vendors, are combined with "recurring payables" .... payments that are due on a regular interval. The first activity to be performed is to process all bills payable, determining which bills to pay and the amount to pay. Following this step, allocated payments are disbursed. The output of this function is printed checks which must be mailed to vendors. Two other outputs from processing are postings to the general ledger and to the vendor accounts file. This latter file is used in printing the aged accounts payable summary.

Objective

The objectives of this exercise parallel those of accounts receivable. When you complete this exercise, you should be able to:

- ➡ Record the bills that are received
- ➡ Add and activate a recurring payable
- ➡ Print a recurring bills payable list
- ➡ Post payables transactions
- ➡ Process and post disbursements
- ➡ Print an edit list, vendor checks, and vendor labels

Case Study

Jen is undecided. On the one hand, she would like to continue working on Accounts Receivable, at least to the point where she can begin to deliver more sales summary information to Dandy and Rose. She would also like to see Rich and Daisy more involved in processing customer invoices and payments. On the other hand, Accounts Payables needs work. Both Roy (Landscape/consulting) and Thatcher (Lawn install–ation) have made it known that they want better tracking of vendor invoices. To help with her personal dilemma, Jen asks for Rose's opinion.

Rose comments, "Sales analysis or accounts payable? Tough choice! To my thinking, if accounts payable is not too difficult to stabilize, we probably should shift to this application."

"If we do this, will you support me when Dandy, Rich and Daisy begin to complain about our office not moving ahead on sales analysis?," questions Jen.

"Of course, Jen," states Rose. "Besides, we wouldn't be stopping work on sales analysis. Rather, we need some time to collect enough sales data to make an analysis interesting."

"That's right," gleams Jen. "We need as least a month or two of sales data before I can do much more than guess on the types of 'real' sales analysis that are possible. Lacking sufficient data, all I could do would be to mock up some reports."

"Any more questions?," asks Rose.

"No, we begin payables tomorrow," responds Jen.

Set Transaction Date

☐ Before you start this exercise, set today's date at 4/29/97 using the MS–DOS 'DATE' command.

Determine How Much Is Currently Owed

One of the first steps in processing payables is determining the dollar amount currently owed.

MAIN MENU

```
RealWorld Practical Accounting System                    L-G LAWN AND GARDEN
Version 1.0

                    Please select
                         1. Sales Invoicing
                         2. Inventory Management
                         3. Accounts Receivable
                         4. Accounts Payable
                         5. Payroll
                         6. General Ledger
                         7. Check Reconciliation
                         8. Setup Functions

Press F10 for help at any time
```

☐ 1. Type 4 (Accounts Payable) from the above Main menu, and press ENTER.

```
RealWorld Practical Accounting System                    L-G LAWN AND GARDEN
Accounts Payable

                    Please select
                         1. Maintain vendor data
                         2. Process bills payable
                         3. Process disbursements
                         4. View or print vendor accounts
                         5. Aged accounts payable summary
```

☐ 2. Type 5 (Aged Accounts Payable Summary) from the Accounts Payable menu, and press ENTER.

☐ 3. Complete the Aged Accounts Payable Summary screen as follows:

```
Aged accounts payable summary                            L-G LAWN AND GARDEN

                    Please enter:
                         1. Starting vendor          "First"  (press F1)
                         2. Ending vendor            "Last"   (press F1)
                         3. Cut off date             4/29/97
                         4. Print zero balance?      N

Field number to change?
```

☐ 4. Press ENTER at "Field number to change?".

☐ 5. Press ENTER (N) when asked "Display the report?". Figure 8–2 shows the dollar amount currently owed by the company.

☐ 6. Press TAB or END to return to the Accounts Payable menu.

Record Bills Your Company Has Received

☐ 7. Type 2 (Process Bills Payable) from the Accounts Payable menu, and press ENTER.

```
Process bills payable                                L-G LAWN AND GARDEN

                    Please select
                        1. Add transactions
                        2. Change transactions
                        3. Delete transactions
                        4. Print transaction edit list
                        5. Post transactions
```

☐ 8. Type 1 (Add Transactions) from the Process Bills Payable menu, and press ENTER.

☐ 9. Enter the following invoice (B=bill) received from Hill Equipment & Supply. Use today's date (4/29/97) for the Transaction date. Reference the transaction as "Computer installation." Credit A/P, and debit account # 6150–000 Office Expense for the full amount.

INVOICE # 36355

HILL EQUIPMENT & SUPPLY
3507 Oak Rd.
Denver, CO 85366

AMOUNT DUE
$102.00

ACCOUNT NUMBER
014–448

INVOICE DATE
3/28/97

Lyons–Garten Lawn and Garden, Inc.
1169 Greenbelt Way
Nice Valley, OR 97000

PLEASE DETACH AND RETURN THIS PORTION WITH YOUR PAYMENT

DELIVERY ADDRESS	ACCOUNT NUMBER	INVOICE DATE	TERMS
123 Main Street **Contact: H. Whitman**	014–448	3/28/97	COD

Stock #	Item	Price per Unit	Total	Credit	Total Due
235	20 ft. Co–axial cable	1.50 ft	30.00		30.00
247	Parallel printer cable – 9 pin	36.00	72.00		72.00
					$ 102.00

TELEPHONE – IF YOU SHOULD HAVE ANY QUESTIONS ABOUT YOUR ACCOUNT, WE ENCOURAGE YOU TO CONTACT US AT 1–800–555–4484.

Your completed screen is shown below.

```
Process bills payable                                   L-G LAWN AND GARDEN
Add transactions

     1. Vendor          Hill Equipment & Supply    3507 Oak Rd.
                                                   Denver, CO  85366
     2. Trans type      B  Bill
     3. Trans date      4/29/97
     4. Invoice #       36355
     5. Reference       Computer installation
     6. Amount          102.00

     7. Credit A/P?     Y

          Acct #      ------Description-----        Distrib amt
          6150-000    Office expense                     102.00

                      Amount to distribute:   .00

Any change?  N
```

☐ 10. Answer N(no) at "Any change?", and press TAB or END twice to return to the Process Bills Payable menu.

Add and Activate a Recurring Bill

☐ 11. If option 6 (Process Recurring Bills) does not appear in the Process Bills Payable menu, press F1 to make it appear.

☐ 12. Type 6 (Process Recurring Bills) from the Process Bills Payable menu, and press ENTER.

```
Process bills payable                                   L-G LAWN AND GARDEN
Process recurring bills

                    Please select
                          1. Add recurring bills
                          2. Change recurring bills
                          3. Delete recurring bills
                          4. Print recurring bills list
                          5. Activate recurring bills
```

☐ 13. Type 1 (Add Recurring Bills) from the Process Recurring Bills menu, and press ENTER.

☐ 14. Add the recurring monthly bill shown on the next page:

```
Process bills payable                                L-G LAWN AND GARDEN
Add recurring bills

      1. Vendor          Jones Property Management   11056 E. Commercial
                                                      Dallas, TX 75330
      2. Trans type      B  Bill
      3. Frequency       M
      4. Next due date   4/29/97
      5. Reference       Rent on Main St.
      6. Amount          1,150.00
      7. Credit A/P?     Y

       Acct #        ------- Description -------        Distrib amt
       6160-000   Rents & Utilities                         1,150.00

                  Amount to distribute:  .00

Any change?  N
```

☐ 15. Press TAB or END twice to return to the Process Recurring Bills menu.

☐ 16. Type 5 (Activate Recurring Bills) from the Process Recurring Bills menu, and press ENTER.

☐ 17. In the "Vendor" field, press F1 to display the bill you have just entered. Answer Y (yes) to "activate this transaction".

☐ 18. Enter today's transaction date (4/29/97). Press ENTER to show the NEXT DUE DATE (5/29/97). (This is automatically calculated using the recurring bill's frequency. For example, if the bill's frequency is Monthly, the NEXT DUE DATE defaults automatically to the same day of the following month.)

☐ 19. Use '888' for your invoice number, and press ENTER at "Field number to change?".

☐ 20. Since, in this case, you do not desire to change the previously entered distribution, press TAB or END instead of entering a G/L account number. Press TAB or END again to return to the Process Recurring Bills menu.

Print Recurring Bills Payable List

☐ 21. Type 4 (Print Recurring Bills List) from the Process Recurring Bills menu, and press ENTER.

☐ 22. Answer N (no) at "Display this report?". The Recurring Bills Payable List (see Figure 8–3) will be printed.

☐ 23. Review the contents of this report. Any recurring bill with a NEXT DUE DATE today or earlier will be flagged with two asterisks beside the Nxt–due–date column.

☐ 24. Press TAB or END to return to the Process Bills Payable menu.

☐ 25. Press F1 to make option 6 (Process Recurring Bills) disappear.

NOTE: The processing of recurring payables may not receive as close a scrutiny as regular, non–recurring bills. Therefore, this feature helps you control the entry of a recurring transaction.

Post Transactions

☐ 26. Type 5 (Post Transactions) from the Process Bills Payable menu, and press ENTER.

☐ 27. Answer Y (yes) to "Are bills payable transactions OK to post?". A Bills Payable Register (see Figure 8–4) will be printed.

☐ 28. Press TAB or END to return to the Accounts Payable menu.

View Vendor Accounts

☐ 29. Type 4 (View or Print Vendor Accounts) from the Accounts Payable menu, and press ENTER.

```
View or print vendor accounts                     L-G LAWN AND GARDEN

                    Please select
                        1. View vendor accounts
                        2. Print vendor accounts
```

☐ 30. Type 1 and press ENTER to View Vendor Accounts.

☐ 31. Select vendor "Jones" to view the Jones Property Management account, as shown on the next page, and press ENTER (Y) at "Right vendor?".

☐ 32. In the START DATE field, press F1 for "Earliest". Review the transactions on file for Jones Property Management. Particularly note the transaction you have entered on 04/29/97.

```
View or print vendor accounts                                      L-G LAWN AND GARDEN

       Vendor:  Jones Property Management          Contact:   Robert Jones
                11056 E. Commercial                Phone #:   774-6700
                Dallas, TX  75330                  First date: 1/01/97
                                                   Comment:
Start date:  "Earliest"

 Date      Type    Doc-#   Reference                        Amount       Balance
 01/04/97  Bill                                            1,150.00     1,150.00
 01/15/97  Check   1074                                    1,150.00 CR       .00
 02/05/97  Bill                                            1,150.00     1,150.00
 02/15/97  Check   1150                                    1,150.00 CR       .00
 03/08/97  Bill                                            1,150.00     1,150.00
 03/15/97  Check   1234                                    1,150.00 CR       .00
 03/30/97  Bill                                            1,150.00     1,150.00
 04/29/97  Bill    888     Rent on Main St.                1,150.00     2,300.00

End of account - press F2 for totals, or press END for new account
```

☐ 33. Press F2 to view vendor totals. Note the current balance that L–G Lawn and Garden owes Jones Property Management.

```
View or print vendor accounts                                      L-G LAWN AND GARDEN

       Vendor:  Jones Property Management          Contact:   Robert Jones
                11056 E. Commercial                Phone #:   774-6700
                Dallas, TX  75330                  First date: 1/01/97
                                                   Comment:
Start date:  "Earliest"
                              Vendor totals

                       Beginning balance           .00
                      Total bills payable     5,750.00
                      Total disbursements     3,450.00 CR
                          Total discounts          .00
                                              --------
                          Current balance     2,300.00

Press END for new account
```

☐ 34. Follow the above procedure to review the previous transactions of one or more of your other vendors. Experiment with various START DATES.

☐ 35. Press TAB or END enough times to return to the Accounts Payable menu.

Process Disbursements

☐ 36. Type 3 (Process Disbursements) from the Accounts Payable menu, and press ENTER.

☐ 37. Type 1 (Add Transactions) from the Process Disbursements menu, and press ENTER.

☐ 38. Use the following information to process a disbursement to South–Western Bell to pay L–G's outstanding balance of $357.12. Enter 0 for DISCOUNT TAKEN, and press ENTER to default to CHECKING ACCOUNT #1.

```
Process disbursements                                        L–G LAWN AND GARDEN
Add transactions

      1. Payee                   South–Western Bell          Irving Office
      2. Transaction type        C  Computer check           500 S. Central
      3. Bill prev. entered?     Y                           Irving, TX  75021

      4. Transaction date        4/29/97
      5. Check #                 N/A
      6. Reference               Payment on inv bal
      7. Amount paid             357.12
      8. Discount taken          .00
      9. Checking account #      1    8765–432–19876
     10. Debit A/P?              Y

Field number to change?
```

☐ 39. Press ENTER at "Field number to change?". A second screen will appear which is used to input check information.

☐ 40. Enter the following check information to disburse the South–Western Bell payable. Press F2 until you reach the vendor invoice dated 3/08/97. Then enter the INVOICE # indicated below.

```
Disbursements processing                                     L–G LAWN AND GARDEN
Enter check information

                       Payee:   South–Western Bell
                                Irving Office
                                500 S. Central
                                Irving, TX  75021

  Check amount:  357.12          Discount:  .00          Total CR:  357.12
  ------------------------------------------------------------------------
  INVOICE#  INV–DATE  INV–AMOUNT  CASH–PAID   DISC–TAKEN   INV–AMT–CR
  46121     3/08/97   357.12      (press F1)  (press F1)   357.12

  ------------------------------------------------------------------------
    Check amt remaining:  .00                 Discount remaining:  .00

  Any change?  N
```

☐ 41. Answer N (no) to "Any change?". Press TAB or END to save the check information and return to the Add Transactions menu.

☐ 42. Jones Property Management sent someone over to collect April's rent payment. Since there was no time to produce a computer check, you 'wrote' a check.

Use the following information to enter that check into the system:

```
Process disbursements                                          L-G LAWN AND GARDEN
Add transactions

    1. Payee                  Jones Property Management      11056 E. Commercial
    2. Transaction type       H  Hand-written check          Dallas, TX  75330
    3. Bill prev entered ?    Y

    4. Transaction date       4/29/97
    5. Check #                1242
    6. Reference              April '97 rent payment
    7. Amount paid            1,150.00
    8. Discount taken         .00
    9. Checking account #     1     8765-432-19876
   10. Debit A/P ?            Y

Field number to change?
```

☐ 43. Press ENTER at "Field number to change?".

☐ 44. Press TAB or END to return to the Process Disbursements menu.

Print Edit List and Checks

☐ 45. Type 4 (Print Transaction Edit List) from the Process Disbursements menu, and press ENTER.

☐ 46. Print the transaction Edit List (see Figure 8–5) rather than display it.

Before you can post your disbursements, you must print the computer checks for those disbursements. (Note the warning on the Disbursement Edit List.)

☐ 47. Type 5 (Print Disbursement Checks) from the Process Disbursements menu, and press ENTER.

☐ 48. Enter the information shown on the next page to prepare for printing checks.

```
Process disbursements                                    L-G LAWN AND GARDEN
Print disbursement checks

     Please enter:

          1. Print list or actual checks ?     C
          2. For checking account #            1    8765-432-19876
          3. Starting check number             2050
          4. Starting name                     "First"  (press F1)
          5. Ending name                       "Last"  (press F1)

Field number to change?
```

☐ 49. Press ENTER at "Field number to change?".

☐ 50. Type the word 'DONE' as if you have now mounted 'check forms' on your printer, and press ENTER. Of course, in this exercise we are only simulating the printing of one check.

☐ 51. Press ENTER (N) at "Print form alignment?" to indicate that you do NOT wish to print a sample check to verify that the check forms are properly aligned on the printer. The check and stub will be printed. See Figure 8–6 as an example of what they might look like on a pre–printed form.

☐ 52. Press TAB or END once, and enter the word 'DONE' to indicate that you have replaced the check forms in the printer with your 'regular' printer paper. This will also return you to the Process Disbursements menu.

☐ 53. Press TAB of END again to return to the Accounts Payable menu.

Print Vendor Labels

An important responsibility of your Accounts Payable department is to assure that remittances are mailed to the vendor's correct address with attention drawn, if possible, to the individual responsible for processing your payment. PAS has the ability to print vendors' address labels using up–to–date information on the addressee. You can print up to 9 labels for each vendor you specify.

On a second screen, you can select the number of columns of labels to print (1 or 2), and can print an initial test label to check if your label stock is properly aligned in the printer.

☐ 54. Type 1 (Maintain Vendor Data) from the Accounts Payable menu, and press ENTER.

```
Maintain vendor data                                    L-G LAWN AND GARDEN

               Please select
                    1. Add vendors
                    2. Change vendors
                    3. Delete vendors
                    4. Print vendor list
                    5. Print vendor labels
```

☐ 55. Type 5 (Print Vendor Labels) from the Maintain Vendor Data menu, and press ENTER.

☐ 56. Enter the following information for printing the labels:

```
Maintain vendor data                                   L-G LAWN AND GARDEN
Print vendor labels

              Please enter:
                   1. Labels per vendor       1
                   2. Starting vendor         "First"  (press F1)
                   3. Ending vendor           "Last"  (press F1)

Field number to change?
```

☐ 57. Press ENTER at "Field number to change?".

☐ 58. Type the word DONE as if you have now mounted labels on your printer, and press ENTER. Of course, in this exercise, we are only simulating the printing of labels.

☐ 59. Select '2' columns for printing.

☐ 60. Answer N(no) at "Any change?".

☐ 61. Answer N(no) to not print an alignment test label. One label will be printed for each vendor (see Figure 8–7).

☐ 62. Enter the word DONE to indicate that you have replaced the labels in the printer with your usual printer paper. This will also return you to the Maintain Vendor Data menu.

☐ 63. Press TAB or END to return to the Accounts Payable menu.

Post Disbursements

☐ 64. Type 3 (Process Disbursements) from the Accounts Payable menu, and press ENTER.

☐ 65. Type 6 (Post Transactions) from the Process Disbursement menu, and press ENTER.

☐ 66. Answer Y (yes) to the question "Are disbursement transactions OK to post?". The transactions will be posted, and a Disbursements Register (see Figure 8–8) will be printed.

☐ 67. This completes the exercise. Press END a sufficient number of times to exit PAS.

QUESTIONS ABOUT THE SOFTWARE

1. Examine the Hill Equipment & Supply vendor account. What do the aged Accounts Payable sub–totals tell you? Why are aged sub–totals important for an organization?

2. What is the main purpose of the Process Bills Payable portion of the A/P application? What is the main purpose of the Process Disbursements portion?

3. What is the difference between a recurring and a non–recurring vendor invoice?

4. The two invoices processed in this exercise were posted to different G/L accounts. What types of accounts were they? What do postings such as these tell you about the relationship of the A/P application to the preparing of monthly financial statements?

MANAGEMENT ISSUES

5. Examine the Aged Accounts Payable Summary report once again. How might the top management, namely Dandy and Rose, use the information contained on this report?

6. Besides helping to remind the payables staff at Lyons–Garten to pay a recurring bill, what management information is provided by the Recurring Bills Payable List? Why is this type of information so important?

7. Would managers ever have a need to examine the disbursements register? Explain how this register should be used by managers.

8. Some bills should NOT be paid immediately. Suppose you are Rose Garten (or Dandy Lyons). Explain those conditions under which a bill should be held (and allowed to age) and not paid by the date printed on the vendor invoice.

THINGS TO DO

9. One of the first things to do following the processing of payables is to determine if the dollar totals are in balance. Determine the amounts in a–c using reports printed in this exercise. Use another Aged Accounts Payable Summary to determine the ending balance:

    a. **Dollar amount owed – beginning balance** ____________________
    b. **Dollar amount added to payables** ____________________
    c. **Amount paid (disbursed)** ____________________
    d. **Dollar amount owed – ending balance** ____________________

10. One bill continues to be older than 90 days.

    What is the name of the vendor and what amount is owed?

11. Examine the Jones Property Management account once again.

    How has it changed since the last time you looked at it?

12. Determine how payables processing has changed the accounts payable G/L account.

    a. Type 6 (General Ledger) from the Main menu.
    b. Type 3 (View G/L Account Activity).
    c. Type 2100 for the account number.
    d. Use a starting date of 040197, and an ending date of 043097.

    What do the totals for this account tell you?

13. Determine how the cash–in–bank balance has changed, again using the View G/L Account Activity menu.

    a. Type 1010 to view account 1010.
    b. Use a starting date of 040197, and an ending date of 043097.

    How has the cash balance been changed?
    What is the new cash balance?

14. Determine how the checking account balance has changed.

    a. Type 7 (Check Reconciliation) from the Main menu.
    b. Type 4 (Print a checkbook).
    c. Type 1 (Checking account number 1).
    d. Press ENTER (Do not purge the cleared items).
    e. Display the account.

    How has the checking account been changed?
    What is the new cash balance?

Date 04/29/97 LYONS–GARTEN LAWN AND GARDEN, INC. #0027 Page 0001

Figure 8–2 – AGED ACCOUNTS PAYABLE SUMMARY

Starting vendor: "First" Ending vendor: "Last"
Cut off date: 04/29/97

Vendor Contact	Phone	Current	31–60	61–90	Over 90
Hill Equipment & Supply Carl Rawlings	412–968–7650	.00	.00	.00	144.32
Jones Property Management Robert Jones	774–6700	1,150.00	.00	.00	.00
Reynolds Tool Company Bill Ryan	512–447–8900	.00	526.40	.00	.00
South–Western Bell	721–1213	.00	357.12	.00	.00
	Totals:	1,150.00	883.52	.00	144.32
	Grand total:	2,177.84			

–– End of report ––

Date 04/29/97 LYONS–GARTEN LAWN AND GARDEN, INC. #0028 Page 0001

Figure 8–3a – RECURRING BILLS PAYABLE LIST

'' next to date means the transaction is now due**

Vendor–name		Nxt–due–date	Credited–to	Trans–amt
Frequency	Trans–type	Reference		
Jones Property Management		05/29/97	A/P	1,150.00
Monthly	Bill	Rent on Main St.		
Distributions: 6160–000	Rents & utilities			1,150.00
1 Recurring transaction			Grand total:	1,150.00
			Now due:	.00

Date 04/29/97 LYONS–GARTEN LAWN AND GARDEN, INC. #0028 Page 0002

Figure 8–3b – RECURRING BILLS PAYABLE LIST

------------ G/L account distribution totals ------------

1,150.00	Credited to 2100–000	Accounts Payable – Trade
1,150.00	Debited to 6160–000	Rents & utilities

-- End of report --

Date 04/29/97 LYONS-GARTEN LAWN AND GARDEN, INC. #0029 Page 0001

Figure 8-4a - BILLS PAYABLE REGISTER

Vendor-name		Trans-date	Credited-to		Trans-amt
Invoice-#	Trans-type	Reference		Debited-to	
Hill Equipment & Supply		04/29/97	A/P		102.00
36355	Bill	Computer installation			
Distributions: 6150-000	Office expense			102.00	
Jones Property Management		04/29/97	A/P		1,150.00
888	Bill	Rent on Main St.			
Distributions: 6160-000	Rents & utilities			1,150.00	
2 Bills payable transactions			Grand total:		1,252.00

Date 04/29/97 LYONS-GARTEN LAWN AND GARDEN, INC. #0029 Page 0002

Figure 8-4b - BILLS PAYABLE REGISTER

------------ G/L account distribution totals ------------

1,252.00	Credited to	2100-000	Accounts Payable - Trade
102.00	Debited to	6150-000	Office expense
1,150.00	Debited to	6160-000	Rents & utilities
1,252.00	Total debited		

-- End of report --

Date 04/29/97 LYONS–GARTEN LAWN AND GARDEN, INC. #0030 Page 0001

Figure 8–5a – D I S B U R S E M E N T S   E D I T   L I S T

Payee Trans–type	Chk–#	Trans–date Credit–to	Amt–paid Disc–taken	Total–CR Reference	Debit–to
Jones Property Management **Hand wrt check**	1242	04/29/97 Chk acct 1	1,150.00 .00	1,150.00 April '97 rent payment	A/P
South–Western Bell **Computer check**		04/29/97 Chk acct 1	357.12 .00	357.12 Payment on inv bal	A/P

*** Check must be printed for this transaction before posting ***

2 Transactions

Date 04/29/97 LYONS–GARTEN LAWN AND GARDEN, INC. #0030 Page 0002

Figure 8–5b – D I S B U R S E M E N T S   E D I T   L I S T

	#–of–trans	Amt–paid	Disc–taken	Total–CR
Computer checks:	1	357.12	.00	357.12
Hand wrt checks:	1	1,150.00	.00	1,150.00
Grand totals:	2	1,507.12	.00	1,507.12

------------ G/L account distribution totals ------------

1,507.12 Credited to 1010–000 Cash #1 – Payables

1,507.12 Debited to 2100–000 Accounts Payable – Trade

** All checks must be printed before any posting will be allowed **

-- End of report --

Figure 8–6 – PRINTED CHECK AND STUB

VENDOR South–Western Bell CHECK NO. 002050

INVOICE NO.	INVOICE DATE	INVOICE AMOUNT	AMOUNT PAID	DISCOUNT TAKEN	NET CHECK AMOUNT
46121	03/08/97	357.12	357.12	.00	357.12
				Check total	357.12

LYONS–GARTEN LAWN AND GARDEN, INC.
1169 Greenbelt Way
Nice Valley, OR 97000

CHECK NO.	CHECK DATE
002050	04/29/97

CHECK AMOUNT
$*****357.12

THREE HUNDRED FIFTY–SEVEN AND 12/100 DOLLARS******

Pay to the order of

South–Western Bell
Irving Office
500 S. Central
Irving, TX 75021

Authorized Signature

Figure 8–7 – VENDOR LABELS

ATTN: Mary Ford A AND P CHEMICALS 1662 Route 66 Carsonville NH 03000	ATTN: B. Caldwell Acme Office Supplies 456 N. Broadway Dallas, TX 75201
ATTN: Don Barber Hanson Manufacturing Co. 65 Industrial Circle Chicago, IL 60655	ATTN: Carl Rawlings Hill Equipment & Supply 3507 Oak Rd. Denver, CO 85366
ATTN: Joan Fairday JXX TOOLS AND SUPPLIES Franklin Building Daysroad NJ 07600	ATTN: Robert Jones Jones Property Management 11056 E. Commercial Dallas, TX 75330
ATTN: Bill Ryan Reynolds Tool Company 3922 Frontier Pkwy. Austin, TX 79811	South–Western Bell Irving Office 500 S. Central Irving, TX 75021

Date 04/29/97 LYONS–GARTEN LAWN AND GARDEN, INC. #0031 Page 0001

Figure 8–8a – DISBURSEMENTS REGISTER

Payee / Trans–type	Chk–#	Trans–date / Credit–to	Amt–paid / Disc–taken	Total–CR / Reference	Debit–to
Jones Property Management		04/29/97	1,150.00	1,150.00	A/P
Hand wrt check	1242	Chk acct 1	.00	April '97 rent payment	
South–Western Bell		04/29/97	357.12	357.12	A/P
Computer check	2050	Chk acct 1	.00	Payment on inv bal	

2 Transactions

Date 04/29/97 LYONS–GARTEN LAWN AND GARDEN, INC. #0031 Page 0002

Figure 8–8b – DISBURSEMENTS REGISTER

	#–of–trans	Amt–paid	Disc–taken	Total CR
Computer checks:	1	357.12	.00	357.12
Hand wrt checks:	1	1,150.00	.00	1,150.00
Grand totals:	2	1,507.12	.00	1,507.12

------------ G/L account distribution totals ------------

1,507.12 Credited to 1010–000 Cash #1 – Payables

1,507.12 Debited to 2100–000 Accounts Payable – Trade

–– End of report ––

Exercise 9 – PRODUCE CUSTOMER STATEMENTS, COMPARE AGING REPORTS, RECONCILE CANCELLED CHECKS, AND TRANSFER BANK FUNDS

Introduction

At month–end, there are often a number of tasks to accomplish by a business, including the mailing of customer statements, the comparing of accounts receivable aging totals to accounts payable aging totals, and the reconciling of company checkbooks.

Of these tasks, the mailing of customer statements is perhaps the most obvious ... customers must be billed when they have not paid an outstanding invoice within the stated time. It is critical to release monthly statements close to the end of the month or mid–month, since many companies pay their outstanding bills much like we as individuals do at these two times of the month.

The comparison of accounts receivable to payables is undertaken to determine how the company's net trade balance is changing. The "net trade balance" is the difference between what customers owe (A/R) versus what a company owes its vendors (A/P). A growing net trade balance is troublesome. A business is much better off with a shrinking net trade balance.

Reconciliation of the company checkbook must also be done by month–end each month. Without such a reconciliation, a company cannot accurately balance month–end financial statements.

Objectives

The objectives of this exercise follow these three month–end activities. When you complete this exercise, you should be able to:

- ➡ Print monthly customer statements
- ➡ Print A/R and A/P aging reports and compare their differences
- ➡ Reconcile cancelled checks returned from the bank
- ➡ Make a transfer of funds

Case Study

"Before I take on anything more, I need some closure," Jen muttered. "Both accounts receivable and accounts payable require that I perform month–end activities. Thank goodness for the computer! In the past, I used to hole up in the office for most of the week trying to analyze data and get numbers to balance. Completing this work by computer should take much less time."

Rose Garten pops into Jen's office and asks: "How did accounts payable work out? Were there any glitches?"

"Not so far," comments Jen. "If I am able to reconcile checks, the application will work as described. Actually, it will save us considerable time when we reach the busy time of the year when lawn installation and landscaping crews are working six days a week."

Jen remembers an additional feature of PAS.

"Rose," Jen begins. "Both accounts receivable and payables feature aging reports. My plan is to print both reports at month–end and compare one to the other. This will provide us with a month–to–month look at our net trade balance to determine if it is improving or deteriorating."

"What happens if it deteriorates?," questions Rose.

"It means that we would have to secure additional short– or long–term financing to cover our payables," continues Jen. "We can delay the payment of vendor invoices somewhat, but we don't want to lose out on any vendor cash discounts. That's too expensive a way to finance the company."

A concerned Rose asks, "How is our cash position?"

"Not too bad," indicates Jen. "We have a working agreement with the bank to transfer $25,000 into checking accounts 1 and 2 while we are converting over to PAS. If you take a look at our checking accounts, as displayed by the computer, it looks as if we are writing checks without any money. This looks bad, but only in the short run. We aren't like some businesses who 'kite' their checks. Ours are always covered."

"Thanks for your words of explanation. Let's discuss our cash position once you have a clearer idea of where we stand," concludes Rose. "At least now I understand why aging information is so valuable."

Set Transaction Date

☐ Before you start this exercise, set today's date at 4/30/97 using the MS–DOS 'DATE' command.

Print Customer Statements

☐ 1. Type 3 (Accounts Receivable) from the following Main menu, and press ENTER.

MAIN MENU

```
RealWorld Practical Accounting System                    L–G LAWN AND GARDEN
Version 1.0

                       Please select
                            1. Sales Invoicing
                            2. Inventory Management
                            3. Accounts Receivable
                            4. Accounts Payable
                            5. Payroll
                            6. General Ledger
                            7. Check Reconciliation
                            8. Setup Functions

Press F10 for help at any time
```

```
RealWorld Practical Accounting System                    L-G LAWN AND GARDEN
Accounts Receivable

                    Please select
                         1. Maintain customer data
                         2. Process sales and DR/CR memos
                         3. Process cash receipts
                         4. Print A/R aging report
                         5. Change apply-to number
                         6. View customer accounts
                         7. Process finance charges
                         8. Print customer statements
                         9. Purge customer accounts
```

☐ 2. Type 8 (Print Customer Statements) from the Accounts Receivable menu, and press ENTER.

NOTE: All cash receipts should be entered and posted so that customer payments will be shown on statements.

☐ 3. Enter the data shown below to print statements for all customers in the period 4/1/97 to 4/30/97. For STATEMENT PERIOD, first type '40197' and press ENTER. Then type '43097' and press ENTER again. NOTE: In this exercise, you will ONLY print 21st Century Construction's statement.

```
Print customer statements                                L-G LAWN AND GARDEN

   Please enter:
    1. Statement period               4/01/97   to   4/30/97
    2. Starting customer              21st Century Construction   (type '21st')
    3. Ending customer                21st Century Construction   (press ENTER)
    4. Stmnt frequencies to print     "All"     (press F1)
    5. Print DR/CR bal customers      Both
    6. Print zero bal customers ?     N
    7. Print finance charges ?        N
    8. Print document reference
         for bal fwd customers ?      N
    9. Print open item customers
         by apply-to number ?         Y     Invc bal only ?  N
   10. Show fully paid items for
         open item customers ?        N

Field number to change?
```

☐ 4. Press ENTER at "Field number to change?".

☐ 5. Type the word 'DONE' as if you have now mounted pre-printed 'statement forms' on your printer, and press ENTER.

☐ 6. Press ENTER (N) at "Print alignment?". (See Figure 9–1 for the printed statement as it might look on a pre–printed statement form.)

☐ 7. Press TAB or END once, and enter the word 'DONE' to indicate that you have replaced the state–ment forms in the printer with your 'regular' printer paper. This will also return you to the Accounts Receivable menu.

Print Accounts Receivable Aging Report

The A/R Aging Report is a report showing each customer's account balance in each of four aging periods. The aging periods are preset at:

0 – 30 days (i.e. Current)
31 – 60 days
61 – 90 days
Over 90 days

☐ 8. Type 4 (Print A/R Aging Report) from the Accounts Receivable menu, and press ENTER.

☐ 9. Enter the data shown below to print the A/R aging report for 4/30/97.

Print A/R aging report	L–G LAWN AND GARDEN
Please enter:	
1. Aging date	4/30/97
2. Include items after aging date ?	N
3. Starting customer	"First" (press F1)
4. Ending customer	"Last" (press F1)
5. Sales rep	"All" (press F1)
6. Print DR/CR bal customers	Both DR and CR accounts
7. Print zero bal customers ?	N
8. Cut–off balance due	No cut–off (press ENTER)
9. Detail or summary	Detail
10. Print on separate pages ?	N
11. Age open item customers like bal forward customers ?	N Invc bal only ? N
Field number to change?	

☐ 10. Press ENTER at "Field number to change?".

☐ 11. Press ENTER (N) at "Display this report?". (See Figure 9–2 for the printed report.)

NOTE: You may need to put your printer in compressed mode to print all of the data. The aged accounts receivable report will be printed, and you will be returned to the Accounts Receivable menu.

☐ 12. Press TAB or END to return to the Main menu.

Print Accounts Payable Aging Summary

The Aged Accounts Payable Summary shows the aged totals that you owe each of your vendors.

☐ 13. Type 4 (Accounts Payable) from the Main menu, and press ENTER.

```
RealWorld Practical Accounting System                    L-G LAWN AND GARDEN
Accounts Payable

                Please select
                       1. Maintain vendor data
                       2. Process bills payable
                       3. Process disbursements
                       4. View or print vendor accounts
                       5. Aged accounts payable summary
```

☐ 14. Type 5 (Aged Accounts Payable Summary) from the Accounts Payable menu, and press ENTER.

☐ 15. Enter the data shown below to print the A/P aging report for 4/30/97.

```
Aged accounts payable summary                            L-G LAWN AND GARDEN

          Please select

               1. Starting vendor           "First"   (press F1)
               2. Ending vendor             "Last"    (press F1)
               3. Cut off date              4/30/97
               4. Print zero balance?       N

Field number to change?
```

☐ 16. Press ENTER at "Field number to change?".

☐ 17. Press ENTER (N) at "Display this report?". (See Figure 9–3 for the printed report.)

☐ 18. Press TAB or END twice to return to the Main menu.

Reconcile the Payables Checkbook

☐ 19. Type 7 (Check Reconciliation) from the Main menu, and press ENTER.

```
RealWorld Practical Accounting System                    L-G LAWN AND GARDEN
Check Reconciliation

                    Please select
                         1. Record checking account transfers
                         2. Process checking account adjustments
                         3. Reconcile a checking account
                         4. Print a checkbook
```

☐ 20. Type 3 (Reconcile A Checking Account) from the Check Reconciliation menu, and press ENTER.

☐ 21. Type 1 (Mark Cleared Items) from the Reconcile A Checking Account menu, and press ENTER.

☐ 22. Enter the data shown on the following screen:

```
Reconcile a checking account                             L-G LAWN AND GARDEN
Mark cleared items

   Please enter:

        Checking account #        1  8765-43219876        (type 1)
        Statement date            4/30/97                 (type 43097)
        Starting check date       "Earliest"              (press F1)

Any change?   N
```

☐ 23. Answer N at "Any change?".

Use the F1 key to clear a check, and the down-arrow key to move to the next checkbook entry.

☐ 24. Clear the checks and the deposits shown on the following screen (continued on the next page).

```
Reconcile a checking account                                         L-G LAWN AND GARDEN
Mark cleared items

   Checking account:  8765-432-19876                 4400998877
   Statement date:  04/30/97                         Actual starting date:  01/01/97

   Chk-#      Date      Reference                    Deposit/CR     Check/DR     Clr-date

           01/01/97   BBF                             7,482.62
           01/03/97   Deposit                           306.32                   (press F1)
     1072  01/15/97   Acme Office Supplies                             137.52    (press F1)
     1073  01/15/97   Hill Equipment & Supply                          400.00    (press F1)
     1074  01/15/97   Jones Property Management                      1,150.00    (press F1)
     1075  01/15/97   South-Western Bell                               352.51    (press F1)
     1149  02/15/97   Hill Equipment & Supply                          200.00    (press F1)
```

1150	02/15/97	Jones Property Management		1,150.00	(press F1)
1151	02/15/97	Reynolds Tool Company		500.00	(press F1)
1152	02/15/97	South–Western Bell		315.80	(press F1)
1223	02/15/97	Acme Office Supplies		155.20	(press F1)
1224	02/15/97	Hanson Manufacturing Co.		846.94	(press F1)
1225	02/15/97	South–Western Bell		301.15	(press F1)
1234	03/15/97	Jones Property Management		1,150.00	
1235	03/15/97	Reynolds tool Company		859.72	
1236	03/15/97	South–Western Bell		270.10	
	04/02/97	Set up cash balance	25,000.00		(press F1)
	04/20/97	Deposit	10.00		
	04/27/97	Deposit	1,233.34		
1242	04/29/97	Jones Property Management		1,150.00	
2050	04/29/97	South–Western Bell		357.12	

Press up– or down–arrow, PgUp or PgDn, press F1 to clear/unclear, or enter clear date

☐ 25. Press TAB or END to return to the Reconcile A Checking Account menu.

☐ 26. Type 2 (Print Reconciliation) from the Reconcile a Checking Account menu, and press ENTER.

☐ 27. Type 1 for Checking Account #1, and press ENTER.

☐ 28. Press ENTER (N) at "Any change?" and "Display this report?" to print the check Reconciliation Report (see Figure 9–4).

☐ 29. Press TAB or END twice to return to the Check Reconciliation menu.

Transfer Funds To Checking Account #2

The next set of steps illustrates how funds from one bank account are transferred to another bank account using the Record Checking Account Transfers function. A common practice is to transfer funds at month–end, moving over cash to cover payroll expenses from the Cash Receipts & Accounts Payable designated checking account.

```
RealWorld Practical Accounting System                L–G LAWN AND GARDEN
Check Reconciliation

                 Please select
                        1. Record checking account transfers
                        2. Process checking account adjustments
                        3. Reconcile a checking account
                        4. Print a checkbook
```

- [ ] 30. Type 1 (Record Checking Account Transfers) from the above Check Reconciliation menu, and press ENTER.

```
Record checking acct transfers                    L-G LAWN AND GARDEN

                 Please select
                     1. Add transfers
                     2. Change transfers
                     3. Delete transfers
                     4. Print edit list
```

- [ ] 31. Type 1 (Add Transfers) from the Record Checking Acct Transfers menu, and press ENTER.
- [ ] 32. Enter the transfer information shown on the following screen:

```
Record checking acct transfers                    L-G LAWN AND GARDEN
Add transfers

        1. From checking account #      1  8765-432-19876
        2. Check number                 1153
        3. Check date                   4/30/97
        4. To checking account #        2  9983-321-87651
        5. Amount transferred           10,000.00
        6. Reference                    Transfer of funds

Field number to change?
```

- [ ] 33. Press ENTER at "Field number to change?".
- [ ] 34. Press TAB or END to return to the Record Checking Acct Transfers menu.
- [ ] 35. Type 4 (Print Edit List) from the Record Checking Acct Transfers menu, and press ENTER.
- [ ] 36. Press ENTER (N) at "Display this report?" to print the report (see Figure 9–5).
- [ ] 37. Press TAB or END. You will be presented with the following display:

```
Record checking acct transfers                    L-G LAWN AND GARDEN

                Cash and disbursement transactions will
                now be made from the information you
                have entered. As these transactions
                are made, the cash transfer information
                will be automatically deleted for you.

Do you wish to do this now?  N
```

☐ 38. Type Y (yes) at "Do you wish to do this now?".

☐ 39. After the transfer, press END twice to return to the Main menu.

Post Transferred Funds

Transfers from one bank account to another are not reflected either by the General Ledger cash accounts or by the checking accounts until the next time cash receipts (using Process Cash Receipts) and cash disbursements (using Process Disbursements) are posted. The following T–accounts illustrate the complete cash–transfer process:

Checking Account	Payroll Cash		A/P Cash		Cash Transfer	
#1 – Payables				10,000	10,000	
#2 – Payroll	10,000					10,000

Since you have performed both of these processing functions in a previous exercise, the instructions for the next set of steps have been abbreviated.

Process Cash Receipts

☐ 40. Type 3 (Accounts Receivable) from the Main menu.

☐ 41. Type 3 (Process Cash Receipts).

☐ 42. Type 4 (Print Transaction Edit List) to print the Cash Receipts Edit List (see Figure 9–6). Observe that you do not have to enter a transaction. This was done earlier.

☐ 43. Type 6 (Post Transactions) using today's date (4/30/97) as the deposit date. The Cash Receipts Register (see Figure 9–7) will be printed. Return to the Main menu.

Process Disbursements

☐ 44. Type 4 (Accounts Payable) from the Main menu.

- [ ] 45. Type 3 (Process Disbursements).
- [ ] 46. Type 4 (Print Transaction Edit List) to print the Disbursements Edit List (see Figure 9–8).
- [ ] 47. Type 6 (Post Transactions). The Disbursements Register (see Figure 9–9) will be printed.
- [ ] 48. This completes the exercise. Press TAB or END a sufficient number of times to exit PAS.

QUESTIONS ABOUT THE SOFTWARE

1. Compare the format of the PAS monthly statement in this exercise to that of the PAS customer invoice in Exercise 5. How are the two documents similar? How do they differ?

2. Compare the aged A/R report to the aged A/P report. What is Lyons–Garten's net trade balance (the dollar difference between the two reports)? Why is it important to be able to determine the net trade balance? Who in Lyons–Garten would use this type of information?

3. Why is it important to be able to transfer funds from one account to another? In Lyons–Garten's case, will funds generally be transferred from checking account #1 (Payables) to account #2 (Payroll), or will the transfer from account #2 to account #1 occur with greater frequency? Explain why.

MANAGEMENT ISSUES

4. Why is it important for "top management" at Lyons–Garten to keep track of the company's net trade balance?

5. Explain why A/R and A/P aging information is important to the management of a company.

6. Explain why all transfer–of–funds between bank accounts in a business should be approved by a member of management. (Hint: What might happen if they were not approved in advance?)

7. Explain why the "kiting" of checks is a bad business practice.

8. Some individuals allow several months to pass before they decide to reconcile their checkbook. Explain why this would be an unacceptable practice in a company like Lyons–Garten.

THINGS TO DO

9. Investigate further how balance forward works by producing an earlier statement for the customer 21st Century Construction.

   a. Type 3 (Accounts Receivable) from the Main menu.
   b. Type 8 (Print Customer Statements).
   c. Enter the dates 03–01–97 to 03–31–97 and follow the steps shown earlier in producing the statement for 21st Century Construction.
   d. Compare the two statements.

   In general, how does the monthly statement produced on 04–30–97 differ from the monthly statement produced on 03–31–97?

10. If you haven't done so already, inspect the two general ledger accounts, 1010 and 1020.

    What is the new cash balance in account 1010?
    What is the new cash balance in account 1020?

    Next, inspect the two checking accounts.

    What is the balance in checking account #1?
    What is the balance in checking account #2?

    What conclusions can you draw about the transfers done in this exercise?

11. Print the contents of Checkbook #1. Do the following:

    a. Type 7 (Check reconciliation) from the Main menu.
    b. Type 4 (Print checkbook).
    c. Type 1 for checking account #1. Do NOT purge checks at this time.
    d. Print the checkbook.

    How can you tell if checks have been cleared?

12. Purge cleared items from a checkbook. This time you are asked to remove cleared items from the checkbook.

    a. Return to the Print A Checkbook menu.
    b. Type 1 for Checking Account #1.
    c. Type Y when asked if you wish to purge checks at this time.
    d. Type 30197 as the purge ending date.
    e. Print the checkbook.

    How does this checkbook differ from the one printed earlier?

    f. After the checkbook has been printed, return to the Print Checkbook menu, type 1 for Check Account #1, and do NOT purge checks at this time.
    g. Display the checkbook.

    How does this checkbook display differ from the one printed earlier?
    Explain why the 'printed' checkbook should differ from the 'displayed' checkbook.

Figure 9–1 – PRINTED CUSTOMER STATEMENT

L–G LAWN AND GARDEN
1169 Greenbelt Way
Nice Valley, OR 97000

Telephone 503–686–5000

STATEMENT

21st Century Construction
P.O. Box 4545
670 Mason Street
Dallas, TX 75204

STATEMENT DATE
4/30/97

DATE	CODE	REF.NO.	CHARGES	CREDITS	BALANCE
4/01/97	BF	Balfwd	128.40		128.40
4/20/97	I	1	58.16		186.56
4/20/97	P	4662		10.00–	176.56
4/27/97	P	10234		25.00–	151.56

TOTAL
151.56

PLEASE RETURN THIS STUB WITH PAYMENT

ACCOUNT NAME
21st Century Construct

STATEMENT DATE
4/30/97

AMOUNT
ENCLOSED $ ____________

REF.NO.	CODE	CHARGES
Balfwd	BF	128.40
1	I	58.16
4662	P	10.00CR
10234	P	25.00CR

TOTAL AMT DUE
151.56

Date: 04/30/97 Time: 10:45:23 LYONS–GARTEN LAWN AND GARDEN, INC. Report #0037 Page #0001

Figure 9–2 – AGED ACCOUNTS RECEIVABLE

Aging date: 4/30/97

Document types: S = Sale P = Payment C = Cr memo D = Dr memo B = Balance forward F = Finance charge

Customer–name Sls–rep	Phone–# Contact	Last–pmt–dat Bal–meth	Balance	Current	31–60 days	61–90 days	Over 90 days
21st Century Construction JAK	555–7844 Herbert Mandel	4/27/97 BAL–FWD	151.56	58.16	67.41	25.99	.00

Doc–#	Doc–date	typ	Apply–to	Reference	Doc–amount	Discount	Doc–total	Age	Terms
22222	1/03/97	P		310/6654	83.30CR	.00	83.30CR	117	
SL013	1/03/97	S			83.30	.00	83.30	117	
SL016	2/04/97	S			60.99	.00	60.99	85	
SL018	3/05/97	S			67.41	.00	67.41	56	
1	4/20/97	S		Ref #: 000002	58.16	.00	58.16	10	NET 30
4662	4/20/97	P		Inv #: 000001	10.00CR	.00	10.00CR	10	NET 30
10234	4/27/97	P		64–5/295	25.00CR	.00	25.00CR	3	

Customer–name Sls–rep	Phone–# Contact	Last–pmt–dat Bal–meth	Balance	Current	31–60 days	61–90 days	Over 90 days
Allied Plumbing Co. JAK	221–8520 M. J. Thorpe	None BAL–FWD	373.75	373.75	.00	.00	.00

Doc–#	Doc–date	typ	Apply–to	Reference	Doc–amount	Discount	Doc–total	Age	Terms
7843	4/23/97	S		Sprinkler Supplies	373.75	.00	373.75	7	NET 30

Customer–name Sls–rep	Phone–# Contact	Last–pmt–dat Bal–meth	Balance	Current	31–60 days	61–90 days	Over 90 days
Baker, Richard C. TJF	478–9090 Richard Baker	4/27/97 BAL–FWD	86.48	64.50	21.98	.00	.00

Doc–#	Doc–date	typ	Apply–to	Reference	Doc–amount	Discount	Doc–total	Age	Terms
SL020	3/15/97	S			121.98	.00	121.98	46	
2	4/20/97	S		Ref #: 000003	64.50	.00	64.50	10	NET 30
143	4/27/97	P		13–7/586	100.00CR	.00	100.00CR	3	

Customer–name Sls–rep	Phone–# Contact	Last–pmt–dat Bal–meth	Balance	Current	31–60 days	61–90 days	Over 90 days
Elliot Enterprises TJF	779–6010 Paul Elliot	None BAL–FWD	75.00	75.00	.00	.00	.00

Doc–#	Doc–date	typ	Apply–to	Reference	Doc–amount	Discount	Doc–total	Age	Terms
SC3820	4/23/97	S		Lawn service contract	75.00	.00	75.00	7	NET 30

Date: 04/30/97 Time: 10:45:28 LYONS-GARTEN LAWN AND GARDEN, INC. Report #0037 Page #0002

Figure 9-2 – AGED ACCOUNTS RECEIVABLE

Aging date: 4/30/97

Document types: S = Sale P = Payment C = Cr memo D = Dr memo B = Balance forward F = Finance charge

Customer-name Sls-rep	Phone-# Contact	Last-pmt-dat Bal-meth	Balance	Current	31-60 days	61-90 days	Over 90 days
Harris, Goldberg, & Jones JAK	554-4300 Michael Jones	None BAL-FWD	48.99CR	48.99CR	.00	.00	.00

Doc-#	Doc-date	typ	Apply-to	Reference	Doc-amount	Discount	Doc-total	Age	Terms
3573	4/23/97	C		Defective bulbs – color	48.99CR	.00	48.99CR	7	CREDIT MEMO

Customer-name Sls-rep	Phone-# Contact	Last-pmt-dat Bal-meth	Balance	Current	31-60 days	61-90 days	Over 90 days
Neptune Underwater Supply TJF	736-1102 Sam Johnston	4/27/97 BAL-FWD	63.09	.00	18.85	44.24	.00

Doc-#	Doc-date	typ	Apply-to	Reference	Doc-amount	Discount	Doc-total	Age	Terms
SL02	1/01/97	S			223.02	.00	223.02	119	
12345	1/03/97	P		3345/992	223.02CR	.00	223.02CR	117	
SL04	2/04/97	S			94.24	.00	94.24	85	
SL06	3/05/97	S			18.85	.00	18.85	56	
4851	4/27/97	P		67-3/621	50.00CR	.00	50.00CR	3	

Grand totals for 6 customers printed; aging date 4/30/97

DR Lines show totals for customers with debit balances as of the aging date
CR Lines show totals for customers with credit balances as of the aging date

	Balance	Current	31-60 days	61-90 days	Over 90 days
DR bal cust totals:	749.88	571.41	108.24	70.23	.00
CR bal cust totals:	48.99CR	48.99CR	.00	.00	.00
Net totals:	700.89	522.42	108.24	70.23	.00

-- End of report --

Date: 04/30/97 LYONS–GARTEN LAWN AND GARDEN, INC. #0038 Page 0001

Figure 9–3 – AGED ACCOUNTS PAYABLE SUMMARY

Starting vendor: "First" Ending vendor: "Last"
Cut off date: 04/30/97

Vendor Contact	Phone		Current	31–60	61–90	Over 90
Hill Equipment & Supply Carl Rawlings	412–968–7650		102.00	.00	.00	144.32
Jones Property Management Robert Jones	774–6700		1,150.00	.00	.00	.00
Reynolds Tool Company Bill Ryan	512–447–8900		.00	526.40	.00	.00
		Totals:	1,252.00	526.40	.00	144.32
		Grand total:	1,922.72			

-- End of report --

Date: 04/30/97 LYONS–GARTEN LAWN AND GARDEN, INC. #0039 Page 0001

Figure 9–4 – RECONCILIATION

Checking account #: 1 8765–432–19876 4400998877

Chk–#	Date	Reference	Clr–date	Amount	Balance
				Beginning bank balance:	.00
	01/01/97	BBF	04/30/97	7,482.62CR	7,482.62
	01/03/97	Deposit	04/30/97	306.32CR	7,788.94
1072	01/15/97	Acme Office Supplies	04/30/97	137.52	7,651.42
1073	01/15/97	Hill Equipment & Supply	04/30/97	400.00	7,251.42
1074	01/15/97	Jones Property Management	04/30/97	1,150.00	6,101.42
1075	01/15/97	South–Western Bell	04/30/97	352.51	5,748.91
1149	02/15/97	Hill Equipment & Supply	04/30/97	200.00	5,548.91
1150	02/15/97	Jones Property Management	04/30/97	1,150.00	4,398.91
1151	02/15/97	Reynolds Tool Company	04/30/97	500.00	3,898.91
1152	02/15/97	South–Western Bell	04/30/97	315.80	3,583.11
1223	02/15/97	Acme Office Supplies	04/30/97	155.20	3,427.91
1224	02/15/97	Hanson Manufacturing Co.	04/30/97	846.94	2,580.97
1225	02/15/97	South–Western Bell	04/30/97	301.15	2,279.82
	04/02/97	Set up cash balance	04/30/97	25.000.00CR	27,279.82
				Ending bank balance:	27,279.82

Total deposits/CR: 32,788.94 Total checks/DR: 5,509.12

–– End of report ––

Date: 04/30/97 LYONS–GARTEN LAWN AND GARDEN, INC. #0040 Page 0001

Figure 9–5 – CHECKING ACCOUNT TRANSFER EDIT LIST

Checking accounts: 1 = 8765–432–19876
2 = 9983–321–87651

From	Chk–#	Chk–date	To	Chk–amount	Reference
1	1153	04/30/97	2	10,000.00	Transfer of funds

1 transfer

–– End of report ––

Date: 04/30/97 Time 11:20:43 LYONS-GARTEN LAWN AND GARDEN, INC. #0041 Page 0001

Figure 9-6a – CASH RECEIPTS EDIT LIST

Customer-name	Bal-meth	Rect-dat	Check-#	Amount-recd	Cash-acct	Bank-rte-#/Ref	Discount
*Cash transfer		4/30/97	1153	10,000.00	1020-000	Transfer of funds	

Amt-credited	Acct-#
10,000.00	9999-000 Transfer/suspense Account

Date: 04/30/97 Time 11:20:44 LYONS-GARTEN LAWN AND GARDEN, INC. #0041 Page 0002

Figure 9-6b – CASH RECEIPTS EDIT LIST

Customer-name	Bal-meth	Rect-dat	Check-#	Amount-recd	Cash-acct	Bank-rte-#/Ref	Discount

	Total recd:	10,000.00
	Total disc:	.00
		----------
1 cash receipt transactions	Total credited:	10,000.00

---------------G/L account distribution totals---------------

10,000.00 credited to 9999-000 Transfer/suspense Account

10,000.00 debited to 1020-000 Cash #2 - Payroll

-- End of report --

Date: 04/30/97 Time 11:22:34 LYONS–GARTEN LAWN AND GARDEN, INC. #0042 Page 0001

Figure 9–7a – CASH RECEIPTS REGISTER

Customer–name	Bal–meth	Rect–dat	Check–#	Amount–recd	Cash–acct	Bank–rte–#/Ref	Discount
*Cash transfer		4/30/97	1153	10,000.00	1020–000	Transfer of funds	

Amt–credited	Acct–#
10,000.00	9999–000 Transfer/suspense Account

Date: 04/30/97 Time 11:22:35 LYONS–GARTEN LAWN AND GARDEN, INC. #0042 Page 0001

Figure 9–7b – CASH RECEIPTS REGISTER

Customer–name	Bal–meth	Rect–dat	Check–#	Amount–recd	Cash–acct	Bank–rte–#/Ref	Discount

Total recd: 10,000.00

Total disc: .00

1 cash receipt transactions Total credited: 10,000.00

---------------G/L account distribution totals---------------

10,000.00 credited to 9999–000 Transfer/suspense Account

10,000.00 debited to 1020–000 Cash #2 – Payroll

-- End of report --

Date: 04/30/97 LYONS–GARTEN LAWN AND GARDEN, INC. #0043 Page 0001

Figure 9–8a – DISBURSEMENTS EDIT LIST

Payee Trans–type	Chk–#	Trans–date Credit–to	Amt–paid Disc–taken	Total–CR Reference	Debit–to
*Cash transfer **Hand wrt check**	1153	04/30/97 Chk acct 1	10,000.00 .00	10,000.00 Transfer of funds	

Distributions: 9999–000 Transfer/suspense Account 10,000.00

1 Transaction

Date: 04/30/97 LYONS–GARTEN LAWN AND GARDEN, INC. #0043 Page 0002

Figure 9–8b – DISBURSEMENTS EDIT LIST

	#–of–trans	Amt–paid	Disc–taken	Total–CR
Hand wrt checks:	1	10,000.00	.00	10,000.00
Grand totals:	1	10,000.00	.00	10,000.00

---------------G/L account distribution totals---------------

10,000.00 Credited to 1010–000 Cash #1 – Payables

10,000.00 Debited to 9999–000 Transfer/suspense Account

-- End of report --

Date: 04/30/97 LYONS–GARTEN LAWN AND GARDEN, INC. #0044 Page 0001

Figure 9–9a – DISBURSEMENTS REGISTER

Payee		Trans–date	Amt–paid	Total–CR	Debit–to
Trans–type	Chk–#	Credit–to	Disc–taken	Reference	
*Cash transfer		04/30/97	10,000.00	10,000.00	
Hand wrt check	1150	Chk acct 1	.00	Transfer of funds	

Distributions: 9999–000 Transfer/suspense Account 10,000.00

1 Transaction

Date: 04/30/97 LYONS–GARTEN LAWN AND GARDEN, INC. #0044 Page 0002

Figure 9–9b – DISBURSEMENTS REGISTER

	#–of–trans	Amt–paid	Disc–taken	Total–CR
Hand wrt checks:	1	10,000.00	.00	10,000.00
Grand totals:	1	10,000.00	.00	10,000.00

---------------G/L account distribution totals---------------

10,000.00 Credited to 1010–000 Cash #1 – Payables

10,000.00 Debited to 9999–000 Transfer/suspense Account

–– End of report ––

Exercise 10 – PROCESS EMPLOYEE PAYROLL

Introduction

The employee payroll portion of PAS must produce payroll checks for an organization as well as quarterly reports and year-end reports, and print W-2 statements for all employees.

Figure 10-1 provides an overview of the payroll system.

Figure 10-1 – PAYROLL OVERVIEW

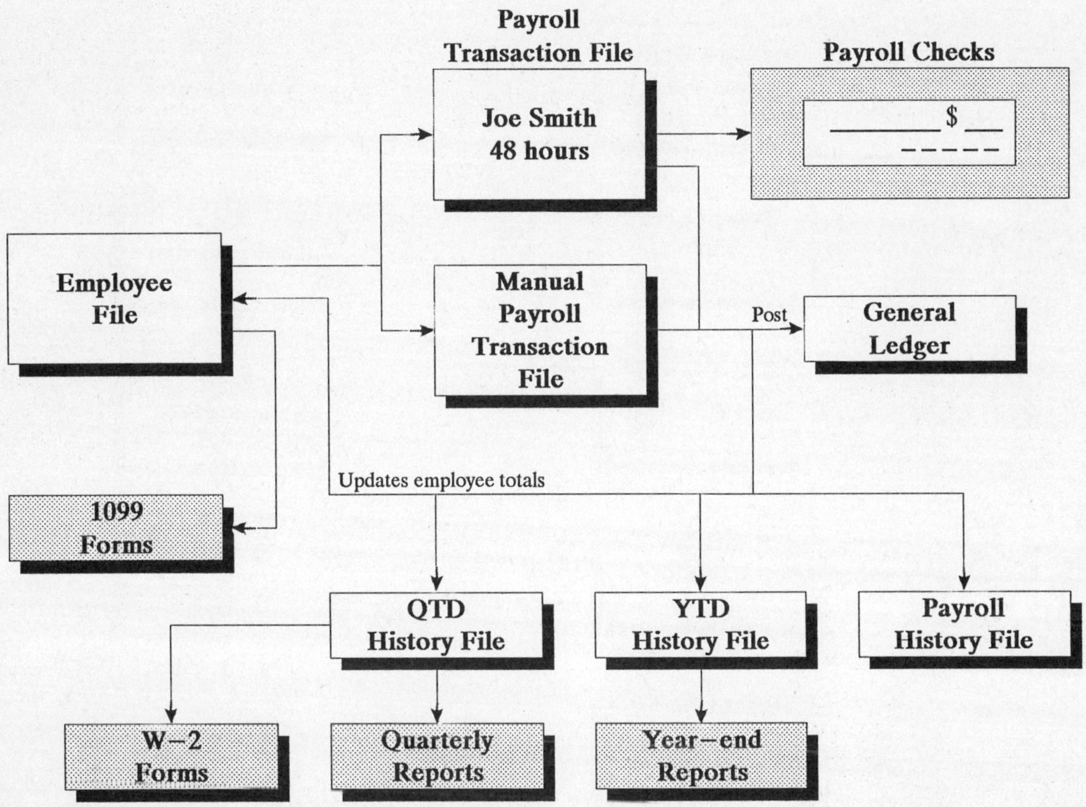

As shown, the employee file is central to this application. Not only does this file contain information needed for each payroll check printed; it also stores information required in printing quarter-to-date (QTD) and year-to-date (YTD) reports. Besides payroll checks and several types of reports, the application posts payroll totals to the general ledger.

Two transaction files are important in producing payroll checks. The Payroll Transaction File stores hours worked by employees. This file is used directly in producing Payroll Checks. The Manual Payroll

Transaction File is used in making irregular employee payments such as bonus payments and payroll adjustments.

W–2 forms (those required in reporting your personal federal and state income) are printed from information stored in the QTD History File. This file (and other history files) are updated when payroll transactions are posted following check–writing. When "setting up" the employee file, DO NOT change or add YTD figures on the fourth screen of the employee record. If YTD figures are changed, the history files will not be updated correctly by entries made to the employee record.

Figure 10–2 shows the steps important to processing payroll transactions.

Figure 10–2 – PAYROLL TRANSACTIONS OVERVIEW

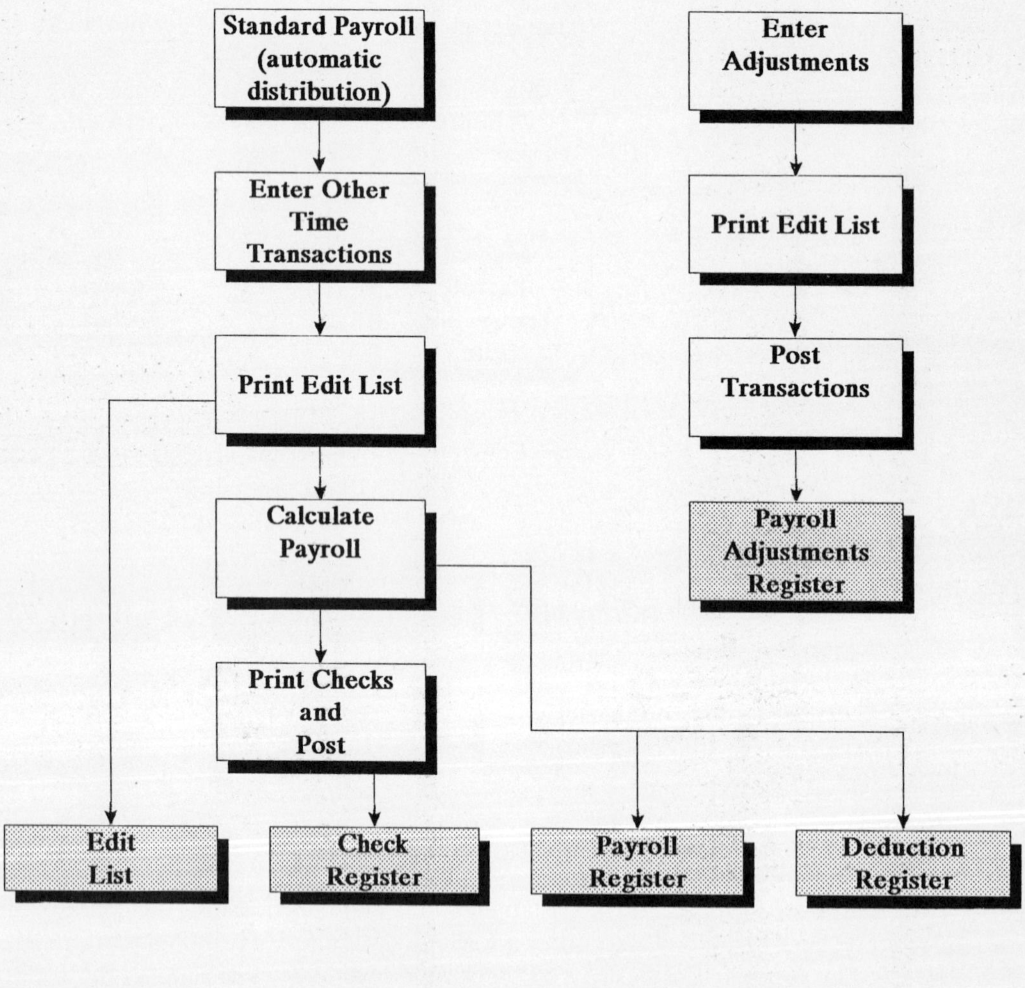

The left–hand side of the diagram shows the normal (customary) sequence for processing payroll. The first function which can be used is called Standard Payroll. If set up to do so, the software will create payroll transactions for employees whose payroll expense is always distributed to the same G/L account.

Once the standard payroll is complete, transactions are entered for employees whose wages are manually distributed (Step 3 on the left–hand side of Figure 10–2). Next, an Edit List is printed to show the hours–worked by employee, by wage account. After this list is approved, the Calculate Payroll step is executed. In this step, the software is accessing information in several data files and doing many calculations. It produces a payroll and deduction register which must be thoroughly reviewed before checks are printed and posted. If any changes need to be made ... as discovered on the payroll register or the deduction register ... payroll must be recalculated.

The right–hand side of Figure 10–2 represents the sequence followed in making adjustments for manual payroll transactions. Following the entry of adjustments, an Edit List is printed and, if accurate, transactions are posted. All posted adjustments are listed on the Payroll Adjustments Register.

Objectives

This exercise asks you to accomplish a number of tasks. You are asked to:

- set up deduction and earning codes
- review federal tax codes and tables
- ready the employee file
- process payroll transactions
- print payroll checks
- print the quarterly payroll report

Case Study

Jen continues to hold off on the analysis of sales. She concludes that the day–to–day activities of her area have to be more smooth before she has the time to think about how information ought to be analyzed. There are even some applications that tend to frighten Jen. Payroll, Inventory and General Ledger are complex applications. However, she knows she cannot side–step any of these important applications if she expects to regain some normalcy in her job.

In reviewing payroll processing, Jen makes note of the several requirements imposed by the software. She gives careful thought to the various documents to be processed.

"The deduction and earnings list (the D/E list) had better be correct before any check is printed. This list includes codes for bonuses, pension contributions, and charitable contributions. All codes must also map to another code contained on the G/L Chart of Accounts," Jen thought.

"A careful listing of all employee records is also required," Jen continues. "For example, each employee is either salaried, paid by the hour or, in some instances, is a non–employee. And, we can pay each person daily, weekly, bi–weekly, semi–monthly or monthly."

"Besides employee type and when paid, we need to know how much each person is to be paid, as well as tax information such as personal exemptions for federal and states taxes. Then, too, vacation, sick leave, and D/E (deduction from earnings) amounts must be correct."

"Fortunately, once the D/E codes and the employee file is set, processing the standard payroll is straight–forward. For each employee, we have to enter normal hours worked, plus any special hours such as holidays with pay, and accrue eligible vacation and sick leave time. Then, we have to distribute the employee's wages to general account code (for example, to 6180–000 – Salaries Administrative). Third, we can compute the employee's pay and print three registers: Payroll Time Register, Payroll Register, and Deductions Register. Fourth, we must check each register to determine if the totals printed are correct. Finally, we can print employee checks and post the pay totals to G/L accounts," Jen concluded.

Just then, Rose pops in and asks Jen how she is progressing. Jen responds, "Converting our payroll must be done with care. In this area I will need help from all of our departments."

"Oh," remarks Rose, with a look of surprise on her face. "What help do you need?"

"Let me explain first," Jen adds. "It tends to be confusing. Before checks are printed, three registers will be produced. These are the Payroll Time Register, the Payroll Register, and the Deductions Register."

"The Payroll Time Register records hours worked by employee type, pay frequency, and distribution type. All department heads should check this register for accuracy. For example, if Susan Levine is coded incorrectly as salaried, rather than hourly, we need to be informed of this."

"The Payroll Register is equally important. This register records department totals for all payroll amounts: gross pay, deductions from gross pay, and net pay amounts, divided into our wage and salary categories. It also lists our employer liability amounts: for Social Security, Medicare, Unemployment Insurance, and so on. Each department head will have to carefully review these payroll totals. I can't print paychecks until these dollar amounts are approved."

"The Deductions Register lists the amounts subtracted from an employee's pay that result from D/E entries. For example, if Jeffrey Scott decides to pay $5.00 each month to one of our authorized charity accounts, this $5.00 amount will be printed. This, too, should be checked by department heads."

"Sounds complex," states Rose. "What about training?"

"A walk–through of all reports will be needed," remarks Jen. "We will work with each department head, one–on–one, to make sure that these reports are understood. That's why payroll processing the first time around will take some time and a great deal of cooperation."

"Count on me to help," concludes Rose. "We can't make mistakes when it comes to payroll."

Background

Lyons–Garten's payroll clerk, Susan Moneychecker, processes payroll for all of the Lyons–Garten's departments. The following is a summary of the company's payroll control structure and practices:

- ➡ The employer name and address lines in the company and control files are:

  LYONS–GARTEN
  1169 Greenbelt Way
  Nice Valley, OR 97000

- ➡ Lyons–Garten's payroll is based on 8–hour work days, 40–hour work weeks, and a standard number of pay periods. (When you enter hours in the Payroll exercises, start with 8–hour days and accept all defaults. You can also accept the defaults for the number of yearly pay periods.)

- ➡ Employees who work more than 40 hours per week are entitled to an overtime rate of time and one–half (1 1/2 times the regular rate). Typically, employees who receive special pay for unusual circumstances, such as working both Saturday and Sunday, will receive double–time pay (two times the regular rate).
- ➡ Meals and tips are not included in Lyons–Garten's payroll set of codes.
- ➡ Lyons–Garten uses checks that do not have their company name pre–printed. To control each pay document, a check number, assigned by the company, is printed on the employee's check and check stub. The first check number to be used in this exercise is #3001.

Set Transaction Date

☐ Before you start this exercise, set today's date at 4/30/97 using the MS–DOS 'DATE' command.

Set Up and Print Deduction / Earning Codes

Deduction and earning codes define deductions and earnings that affect an employee's wages. Codes for all possible employee deductions and earnings (except wages and withholding taxes) are entered here. Examples of deductions are insurance, charitable donations, and savings bonds. Earnings include enter–tainment allowances, travel subsidies, commissions, meals, tips, bonuses, etc.

MAIN MENU

```
Real World Practical Accounting System                L-G LAWN AND GARDEN
Version 1.0

              Please select
                    1. Sales Invoicing
                    2. Inventory Management
                    3. Accounts Receivable
                    4. Accounts Payable
                    5. Payroll
                    6. General Ledger
                    7. Check Reconciliation
                    8. Setup Functions

Press F10 for help at any time
```

☐ 1. Type 5 (Payroll) from the Main menu, and press ENTER.

☐ 2. Type 7 (Maintain Deduction/Earning Codes) from the Payroll menu shown on the following page, and press ENTER.

```
RealWorld Practical Accounting System                    L-G LAWN AND GARDEN
Payroll

                    Please select
                         1. Maintain employee data
                         2. Process payroll time transactions
                         3. Calculate payroll
                         4. Print payroll checks
                         5. Process manual payroll transactions
                         6. Print payroll history report
                         7. Maintain deduction/earning codes
                         8. Maintain tax codes and tables
                         9. Print quarterly payroll report
                        10. Print year-end payroll reports
                        11. Close payroll for calendar year
```

☐ 3. Type 1 (Add Codes) from the Maintain Deduction/Earning Codes menu, and press ENTER.

```
Maintain deduction/earning codes                         L-G LAWN AND GARDEN

                    Please select
                         1. Add codes
                         2. Change/Inquire codes
                         3. Delete codes
                         4. Print out codes
```

☐ 4. Enter '123' in the code field and 'deduct' in the description field as shown below.

```
Maintain deduction/earning codes                         L-G LAWN AND GARDEN
Add

                    1. Code           123
                    2. Description    deduct
                    3. Type
                                       D = deduction
                                       B = before tax deduction
                                       E = earning
                                       S = supplemental earning
                                       X = special tax
                                       M = meals
                                       T = tips
```

☐ 5. The list of Code Types will automatically be displayed. Do NOT enter TYPE at this time. Merely review the Code Types as described on the next page.

Code Types

D = Deduction from employee net pay after tax calculations.
B = Deduction from employee gross pay before tax calculations.
E = Earning added to employee pay that may or may not be taxable, as defined.
S = Supplemental earning, such as a bonus or commission, that is added to the employee's pay. If taxed, supplemental earnings are taxed at a flat percentage rate specified in the Federal, state and city tax table records. If the rate in the tax code record is set to zero, then supplemental earnings are added to the regular earnings and the sum is taxed at the regular rate.
X = Special tax, such as State Unemployment Insurance (SUI), where part of these taxes come out of the employee's pay.
M (Meals) and T (Tips) are not used in this exercise.

- [ ] 6. Press ESCape, and then ENTER to return to the Add menu.

- [ ] 7. Use the following information to set up an earning code for commissions that are paid to salespeople.

Code:	ET2	**Type:**	E (earning)
Description:	Phone	**G/L acct #:**	6280–000 Travel & entertainment

NOTE: This travel subsidy is exempt from all taxes, so answer Y (yes) to all remaining fields, as shown on the following screen.

```
Maintain deduction/earning codes                       L-G LAWN AND GARDEN

            1. code                       ET2
            2. Description                Phone
            3. Type                       Earning
            4. G/L acct #                 6280-000   Travel & entertainment

            5. Exempt from fed w/h?       Y
            6. Exempt from emp SS?        Y         Medicare?   Y
            7. Exempt from empr SS?       Y         Medicare?   Y
            8. Exempt from FUI?           Y
            9. Exempt from EIC?           Y

           10. Exempt from state w/h?     Y
           11. Exempt from SUI?           Y
           12. Exempt from OST?           Y
           13. Exempt from suppl ben?     Y

           14. Exempt from city w/h?      Y

Field number to change?
```

- [ ] 8. Press ENTER at "Field number to change?" to save the new earning code.

☐ 9. Use the following information to set up a deduction code for gifts to a charity.

Code:	D2	**Type:**	D (deduction)
Description:	UntFund	**G/L acct #:**	2390−000 Charity contrib withheld

☐ 10. Press ENTER at "Field number to change?" to save the new deduction code.

☐ 11. Press TAB or END to return to the Maintain Deduction/Earning Codes menu.

☐ 12. Type 3 (Delete Codes) from the Maintain Deduction/Earning Codes menu, and press ENTER. Delete the following two codes:

Code:	EB1	**Code:**	EC1
Description:	Bonus	**Description:**	Commissn

☐ 13. Press TAB or END to return to the Maintain Deduction/Earning Codes menu.

☐ 14. Type 4 (Print Out Codes) from the Maintain Deduction/Earning Codes menu, and press ENTER.

☐ 15. Press F1 twice ("First" and "Last") for the STARTING and ENDING CODES to be printed.

☐ 16. Press ENTER (N) at "Any change?" and at "Display this report?". The updated Deduction and Earning Code List (see Figure 10−3) will be printed. Note the new entries you made.

☐ 17. Press TAB or END to return to the Payroll menu.

Review Federal Tax Codes & Tables

☐ 18. Type 8 (Maintain Tax Codes and Tables) from the Payroll menu, and press ENTER.

```
Maintain tax codes and tables                         L-G LAWN AND GARDEN

                    Please select
                         1. Add tax codes/tables
                         2. Change/Inquire tax codes/tables
                         3. Delete tax codes/tables
                         4. Print out tax codes/tables
```

☐ 19. Type 2 (Change/Inquire Tax Codes/Tables) from the Maintain Tax Codes and Tables menu, and press ENTER.

☐ 20. Type 'F' for Federal Tax Authority, and press ENTER.

NOTE: You will see the first of four data entry screens that include all federal tax information. Review the field definitions in the Reference Section to understand the content of each field on these screens.

☐ 21. Change the minimum wage from $3.80 to $4.75.

SCREEN 1

```
Maintain tax codes and tables                              L-G LAWN AND GARDEN
Change

     * 1. Tax authority           Federal
     * 2. Tax code                (Not applicable)

       3. Description             Federal Tax Tables
       4. Tax rpt ID #            99-9999999
       5. Tax liab acct #         2310-000   Fed income tax withheld
       6. Suppl earn w/h %        20.00
       7. Minimum wage            4.75
                                   ---Employee--   ---Employer--
   Define exemptions:  Fed-w/h  Soc-sec  Medicare  Soc-sec  Medicare  FUI  EIC

       8. Regular pay?    N        N        N         N        N       N    N
       9. Overtime pay?   N        N        N         N        N       N    N
      10. Special pay?    N        N        N         N        N       N    N
      11. Holiday pay?    N        N        N         N        N       N    N
      12. Sick pay?       N        N        N         N        N       N    N
      13. Vacation pay?   N        N        N         N        N       N    N

Make changes, or press F1 for next tax code
Field number to change?
```

☐ 22. Press ENTER at "Field number to change?" to view the second screen (fields 14–25).

SCREEN 2

```
Maintain tax codes and tables                              L-G LAWN AND GARDEN
Change

      14. Employer soc sec pct           6.20
      15. Employee soc sec pct           6.20
      16. Maximum soc sec wages          53,400.00

      17. Employer soc sec exp acct      6250-000   Taxes - payroll
      18. Employer soc sec liab acct     2340-000   Empr Social Sec Payable
      19. Employee soc sec liab acct     2330-000   Emp Social Sec Payable

      20. Employer medicare pct          1.45
      21. Employee medicare pct          1.45
      22. Maximum medicare wages         125,000.00

      23. Employer medicare exp acct     6250-000   Taxes - payroll
      24. Employer medicare liab acct    2345-000   Empr Medicare Payable
      25. Employee medicare liab acct    2335-000   Emp Medicare Payable

Field number to change?
```

☐ 23. Press ENTER at "Field number to change?" to view the third screen (fields 26–33).

SCREEN 3

```
Maintain tax codes and tables                              L-G LAWN AND GARDEN
Change

        26. Federal unemployment %       .80
        27. Federal unemp max wages      7,000.00

        28. FUI expense account #        6250-000  Taxes - payroll
        29. FUI liability account #      2450-000  Accrued fed unemp tax

        30. Vacation pay exp acct #      6190-000  Salaries - floor sales
        31. Holiday pay exp acct #       6190-000  Salaries - floor sales
        32. Sick pay exp acct #          6190-000  Salaries - floor sales

        33. EIC advance acct #           2320-000  EIC advances paid

Field number to change?
```

☐ 24. Press ENTER at "Field number to change?" to view the fourth screen (fields 34–49).

SCREEN 4

```
Maintain tax codes and tables                              L-G LAWN AND GARDEN
Change

   34. Fed w/h allowance amt  2,150.00

   -----Single-w/h-tables-----          ----Married-w/h-tables---
      $-amt      %-amt  On-amt-over        $-amt      %-amt  On-amt-over
   35. .00         15.00    1,250       41. .00          15.00   3,550
   36. 3,052.50    28.00   21,600       42. 5,100.00     28.00  37,550
   37. 11,158.50   31.00   50,550       43. 18,582.00    31.00  85,700
   38. .00           .00        0       44. .00            .00       0
   39. .00           .00        0       45. .00            .00       0
   40. .00           .00        0       46. .00            .00       0

   -------EIC-tables-------
      $-amt      %-amt  On-amt-over
   47. .00        14.00        0
   48. 953.00       .00    6,807
   49. 953.00    10.00-   10,734
```

NOTE: Your instructor may obtain up-to-date information about tax percentages and amounts from an IRS Circular E pamphlet, and ask you to make selected changes to one or more of these fields. The Single and Married withholding information displayed on this screen was obtained from Table 7 of a recent Circular E (see excerpt on next page).

TABLE 7 – If the Payroll Period With Respect to an Employee is Annual

(a) SINGLE person – including head of household:				**(b) MARRIED person –**			
If the amount of wages (after subtracting withholding allowances) is:		The amount of income tax to be withheld shall be:		If the amount of wages (after subtracting withholding allowances) is:		The amount of income tax to be withheld shall be:	
Not over $1,250 0				Not over $3,550 0			
Over–	**But not over–**		**of excess over–**	**Over–**	**But not over–**		**of excess over–**
$1,250	–$21,600	15%	–$1,250	$3,550	–$37,550	15%	–$3,550
$21,600	–$50,550	$3,052.50 plus 28%	–$21,600	$37,550	–$85,700	$5,100.00 plus 28%	–$37,550
$50,550		$11,158.50 plus 31%	–$50,550	$85,700		$18,582.00 plus 31%	–$85,700

☐ 25. Press ENTER at "Field number to change?" to return to the Change menu.

☐ 26. Press TAB or END twice to return to the Payroll menu.

Review Employee Data Menus

☐ 27. Type 1 (Maintain Employee Data) from the Payroll menu, and press ENTER.

```
Maintain employee data                              L-G LAWN AND GARDEN

                Please select
                     1. Add employees
                     2. Change/Inquire employees
                     3. Delete employees
                     4. Print numeric employee list
                     5. Print alphabetic employee list
                     6. Print labels by employee #
                     7. Print labels by employee name
```

☐ 28. Type 2 (Change/Inquire Employees) from the Maintain Employee Data menu, and press ENTER.

> **NOTE:** You will see the first of four data entry screens that include all employee payroll information. These screens contain the same fields that you will fill to add an employee. By using the Change/Inquire Employees function, you can review the DATA and FIELD NAMES (see Reference Section for field definitions) without having to enter data.

☐ 29. In the EMPLOYEE NUMBER field, press F1 to bring up the first employee, **Palmer, Edward W.**

☐ 30. Press ENTER at "Field number to change?", then press ENTER (Y) when asked "Do you wish to see the next screen?" to view the second screen (fields 29–47).

☐ 31. Repeat step 30 to view the third screen (fields 48–55).

☐ 32. Repeat step 30 to view the fourth screen (fields 56–75).

NOTE: You would NEVER change any YTD fields directly on the fourth screen. These fields are all updated when you post time transactions or manual payroll transactions.

☐ 33. Press ENTER at "Field number to change?" to return to the Change/Inquire Employees menu, and press TAB or END once to return to the Maintain Employee Data menu.

Add a New Employee

☐ 34. Type 1 (Add Employees) from the Maintain Employee Data menu, and press ENTER.

☐ 35. Use the information on the following screens to add a new employee, Jeffrey Scott.

NOTE: Dates must be entered without slashes (/). The educational version of PAS also limits dates to the years 1997, 1998 and 1999. In the case of field 8, Birth Date, this constraint will obviously create an unrealistic age for your new employee.

SCREEN 1

Maintain employee data — L–G LAWN AND GARDEN

Add employees

1. Employee number: 4
2. Employee name: Scott, Jeffrey
3. Street address: 120 Pine St.
4. City: Winoga Falls
5. State: CA
6. Zip code: 91055

7. Soc sec #	104–36–2911	18. Salary	(Not applicable)
8. Birth date	11597	19. Regular rate	8.50
9. Marital status	H (Head of household)	20. Overtime rate	12.75 (press F1)
10. Hire date	22097	21. Special rate	17.00 (press F1)
11. Last raise	(press ENTER)		
12. Review date	82097	22. Vac hours due	.00
13. Terminate date	(press ENTER)	23. Vac hours paid	.00
14. Emp type	H (Hourly)	24. Sick hours due	.00
15. Pay frequency	B (bi–weekly)	25. Pension plan?	N
16. Home department	0000 (press ENTER)	26. Distrib wages?	Y
17. Wage account #	6180–000	27. W–2 ins prem?	.00
Salaries – administrative		28. Can get tip CR?	N

Field number to change?

☐ 36. Press ENTER at "Field number to change?" to advance to the next screen.

SCREEN 2

Maintain employee data			L–G LAWN AND GARDEN
Add employees		Employee: 4	Scott, Jeffrey

***** TAX INFORMATION *****

29. State tax code	CA–H (Type 'CA', press ENTER and type H)		
30. City tax code	(press ENTER)		
31. # FWT exemptions	1	40. Added FWT	10.00 **amount**
32. $ FWT exemptions	.00	41. Added SWT	.00
		42. Added CWT	.00
33. # SWT exemptions	1		
34. $ SWT exemptions	.00	43. Soc sec exempt?	N
		44. Medicare exempt?	N
35. # OST exemptions	0	45. FUI exempt?	N
36. $ OST exemptions	.00	46. SUI exempt?	N
37. # CWT exemptions	0	47. # of EIC certs	0
38. $ CWT exemptions	.00		
39. State tax credit	.00		

Field number to change?

☐ 37. Press ENTER at "Field number to change?" to advance to the next screen.

SCREEN 3

Maintain employee data			L–G LAWN AND GARDEN
Add employees		Employee: 4	Scott, Jeffrey

48. Vac due date	22098	52. D/E code–3	
Hrs per pay freq	2.00	Amt/rate/pct	.00
Max vac hrs	Unlimited	Frequency	
49. Sick hrs due date	22098	53. D/E code–4	
Hrs per pay freq	2.00	Amt/rate/pct	.00
Max sick hrs	Unlimited	Frequency	
50. D/E code–1	D1 Charity	54. D/E code–4	
Amt/rate/pct	5.00 per prd	Amt/rate/pct	.00
Frequency	bi–weekly	Frequency	
51. D/E code–2	(press END)	55. D/E code–5	
Amt/rate/pct	.00	Amt/rate/pct	.00
Frequency		Frequency	

Field number to change?

☐ 38. Press ENTER at "Field number to change?" to advance to the next screen.

SCREEN 4

```
Maintain employee data                                   L-G LAWN AND GARDEN
Add employees                              Employee:  4    Scott, Jeffrey

----------------- Employee Year-to-date Totals -----------------

   56.  YTD gross                 (press END)    66.  YTD empr soc sec     .00
   57.  YTD FWT gross                .00         67.  YTD emp medicare     .00
   58.  YTD emp soc sec gross        .00         68.  YTD empr medicare    .00
   59.  YTD empr soc sec gross       .00         69.  YTD FWT              .00
   60.  YTD emp medicare gross       .00         70.  YTD EIC              .00
   61.  YTD empr medicare gross      .00         71.  YTD SWI              .00
   62.  YTD FUI gross                .00         72.  YTD OST              .00
   63.  YTD suppl ben gross          .00         73.  YTD CWT              .00
   64.  YTD SUI gross                .00         74.  YTD other taxes      .00
   65.  YTD emp soc sec gross        .00         75.  YTD tip credit       N/A

Field number to change?
```

☐ 39. Press END to set all fields to zero, and press ENTER at "Field number to change?". Press TAB or END to return to the Maintain Employee Data menu.

Print Employee List

☐ 40. Type 4 (Print Numeric Employee List) from the Maintain Employee Data menu, and press ENTER.

☐ 41. Enter the data shown below to print the Numeric Employee List.

```
Print numeric employee list                              L-G LAWN AND GARDEN

     Please enter:
          1.  Starting employee #          "First"    (press F1)
          2.  Ending employee #            "Last"     (press F1)
          3.  Department                   "All"      (press F1)
          4.  Show detail ?                   N
          5.  Include non-terminated ?        Y
          6.  Include terminated ?            N

Field number to change?
```

☐ 42. Press ENTER at "Field number to change?".

NOTE: You may need to put your printer in compressed mode to print all of the data.

☐ 43. Press ENTER (N) at "Display this report?". The Numeric Employee List (see Figure 10–4) will be printed. Note the new employee, Jeffrey Scott, that you entered.

☐ 44. Press TAB or END twice to return to the Payroll menu.

Process Manual Payroll Transactions

This function is used to enter manual payrolls and to correct erroneous prior entries. A positive adjustment would cause fields to increase. A negative adjustment would cause fields to decrease. All field adjustments should take place through this function to assure that all files are updated accordingly.

Over the next few pages, you will process a manual payroll transaction that will bring Jeffrey Scott up to date for the year. Start by reading the following information:

- ➡ The current date is 4/30/97 (already set at the beginning of this exercise).
- ➡ Jeffrey Scott is paid Bi–weekly. He has had 4 pay periods since being hired on 2/20/97.
- ➡ Lyons–Garten, Inc. has been recording payroll information on employee record sheets. Jeffrey Scott's PAYROLL RECORD SHEET is shown on the next page. This information is used in the manual payroll transaction described thereafter.

☐ 45. Type 5 (Process Manual Payroll Transactions) from the Payroll menu, and press ENTER.

☐ 46. Type 1 (Add Transactions) from the Process Manual Payroll Transactions menu, and press ENTER. The first of four data entry screens will be displayed into which you will enter the manual payroll transaction.

☐ 47. Referring to the Manual Payroll Record Sheet TOTALS shown on the next page for Jeffrey Scott's four previous pay periods, complete the four data screens as shown on the subsequent pages to bring his payroll record up to date through 4/17/97.

NOTE: After completing this procedure, you will process his first Payroll Time Transaction using PAS for the period 4/18/97 to 4/30/97.

Manual Payroll Record Sheet

EMPLOYEE #	4	SOC. SEC. #	104-36-2911	MARRIED	
				SINGLE	X
EMP. NAME	Scott, Jeffrey				
ADDRESS	120 Pine St.	# EXEMPT	1	BIRTH DATE	1/15/97
	Winoga Falls, CA 91055	WAGE	8.50/hr	DATE OF EMPLOY	2/20/97
PHONE	592-862-1408	HOME DEPT	0000	DISTR. ACCT #	6180
VAC HRS DUE	8	SICK HRS	0	PENSION PLAN?	N

PERIOD ENDING	HRS WORKED REG	HRS WORKED OT	EARNINGS ($) REG	EARNINGS ($) OT	EARNINGS ($) OTHER	EARNINGS ($) TOTAL	DEDUCTIONS ($) FICA	DEDUCTIONS ($) Mdicare	DEDUCTIONS ($) FED	DEDUCTIONS ($) State	DEDUCTIONS ($) A *	NET PAY	CK #
3/ 3	64/16*	–	544/136	–	–	680	42.16	9.86	88.75	4.08	5.00	530.15	650
3/17	80	8	680	102	–	782	48.48	11.34	102.05	4.69	5.00	610.44	673
4/ 3	80	–	680	–	–	680	42.16	9.86	88.75	4.08	5.00	530.15	706
4/17	80	–	680	–	–	680	42.16	9.86	88.75	4.08	5.00	530.15	738
TOTALS													
Regular	304	8	2584	102	–	2822	174.96	40.92	368.30	16.93	20.00	2200.89	
Holiday	16	–	136	–	–	136							

NOTES: * 2/21 – 2/22 Washington's birthday holiday week-end – 16 holiday hrs.
Deduction 'A' = charity

SCREEN 1

Process manual payroll transactions — L–G LAWN AND GARDEN
Add transactions

1. Employee: 4 Scott, Jeffrey Hourly

2.	Check #	111	17.	Oth D/E 1	(press ENTER)
3.	Check date	4/17/97	18.	Oth D/E 2	(press ENTER)
4.	Pay prd date	4/17/97	19.	Oth D/E 3	(press ENTER)
5.	Regular pay	2584	20.	Charity	20.00
6.	Regular hrs	304	21.	*No D/E*	
7.	Overtime pay	102	22.	*No D/E*	
8.	Overtime hrs	8	23.	*No D/E*	
9.	Vacation pay	0	24.	*No D/E*	
10.	Vacation hrs	0	25.	*No D/E*	
11.	Holiday pay	136			
12.	Holiday hrs	16	26.	Vac accrued	2
13.	Sick pay	0	27.	Sick accrued	2
14.	Sick hrs	0	28.	Weeks worked	8
15.	Special pay	0	29.	Work units	(Not applicable)
16.	Special hrs	0	30.	Fed tip cr	0
			31.	State tip cr	0

Field number to change?

☐ 48. Press ENTER at "Field number to change?" to advance to the next screen.

SCREEN 2

Process manual payroll transactions — L–G LAWN AND GARDEN
Add transactions

Employee: 4 Scott, Jeffrey Check #: 111
Calculated gross: 2,822.00

32.	Gross pay	2,822	44.	Emp soc sec	174.96
33.	Soc sec wages	2,822			
34.	Soc sec tips	0	45.	Emp medicare	40.92
35.	Medicare wages	2,822			
36.	Medicare tips	0	46.	FWT	368.30
37.	FWT gross	2,822	47.	EIC	0
38.	EIC gross	0			
			48.	Empr soc sec	174.96
39.	Empr soc sec wgs	2,822			
40.	Empr soc sec tips	0	49.	Empr medicare	40.92
41.	Empr medicare wages	2,822			
42.	Empr medicare tips	0	50.	FUI	22.58
43.	FUI gross	2,822			
	FUI wages	2,822			

Field number to change?

☐ 49. Press ENTER at "Field number to change?" to advance to the next screen.

The third entry screen contains state withholding and state unemployment tax information.

NOTE: The net pay amount must equal the value of the check. If not, you may have entered a deduction field incorrectly.

SCREEN 3

```
Process manual payroll transactions                          L-G LAWN AND GARDEN
Add transactions

        Employee:         4     Scott, Jeffrey                  Check #:  111
        Calculated gross:    2,822.00                        Gross Pay:  2,822.00

        51.  SWT gross               2,822            56.  SWT            16.93
        52.  OST gross               (press ENTER)    57.  OST            0
        53.  CWT gross               0                58.  CWT            0
        54.  SUI gross               2,822            59.  SUI            0
             SUI wages               2,822            60.  Empr OST       (N/A)
        55.  Supp ben gross          0                61.  Supp ben       0

                         62.  Net pay       2,200.89

Field number to change?
```

☐ 50. Press ENTER at "Field number to change?" to save the data and advance to the next screen.

The last entry screen contains distributions for the Manual Payroll Transaction. Because you have answered Y (yes) to "Distribute wages?" in Jeffrey Scott's employee record, you must make manual distributions for both regular and overtime pay.

SCREEN 4

```
Process manual payroll transactions                          L-G LAWN AND GARDEN
Add transactions

        Employee:      4    Scott, Jeffrey                    Hourly

              -------- Distribution --------
        Type     Account                             Hours     Rate    Amount
        *
        R     6180   Salaries - administrative      304.00    8.500   2,584.00
        O     6180   Salaries - administrative        8.00   12.750     102.00

        Reg hrs remaining:   .00                 Reg pay remaining:   .00
        Ovt hrs remaining:   .00                 Ovt pay remaining:   .00
       Spec hrs remaining:   .00                Spec pay remaining:   .00

        R = regular      O = overtime      X = special
```

☐ 51. You cannot exit this screen until all of the amounts remaining are shown to be zero. To end your entry of distributions, press END for the "Type".

☐ 52. Press TAB or END to return to the Process Manual Payroll Transactions menu.

☐ 53. Type 4 (Print Transaction Edit List) from the Process Manual Transactions menu, and press ENTER. Display this report to determine if the changes you made are correct.

☐ 54. Press ENTER to return to the Process Manual Payroll Transactions menu.

☐ 55. Type 2 (Change/Inquire Employees) from the Process Manual Payroll Transactions menu, and press ENTER.

☐ 56. Review the four screens for employee #4, Jeffrey Scott, to assure that the data has been entered as desired. To do this, press F1 to display the first screen, and then press ENTER at "Field number to change?" to move to each of the next three screens.

☐ 57. Press TAB or END to return to the Process Manual Payroll Transactions menu.

☐ 58. Type 5 (Post Transactions to PR Files) from the Process Manual Payroll Transactions menu, and press ENTER.

☐ 59. Type Y (yes) at "Are manual PR transactions OK to post?" The Manual Payroll Register (see Figure 10–5) will be printed.

☐ 60. Press TAB or END to return to the Payroll menu.

Generate Standard Payroll

Standard payroll generates time transactions for employees who do not have their pay manually distributed. If any payroll time transactions (hours, etc.) are on file, Generate Standard Payroll cannot be run, and the program will display a message advising you of the existing time entries.

☐ 61. Type 2 (Process Payroll Time Transactions) from the Payroll menu, and press ENTER.

☐ 62. Type 5 (Generate Standard Payroll) from the Process Payroll Time Transactions menu, and press ENTER.

☐ 63. Run the Generate Standard Payroll function using the information below.

```
Process manual payroll transactions                         L-G LAWN AND GARDEN
Generate standard payroll

              Please enter:
                 1. Pay period starting date                 41897
                 2. Pay period ending date                   43097
                 3. Pay employees with pay frequencies       B
                 4. Number of holiday hours to take          0

Field number to change?
```

☐ 64. Press ENTER at "Field number to change?" and enter Y at "Are you sure?". The payroll will be generated.

☐ 65. Following generation of the payroll, press TAB or END to return to the Process Payroll Time Transactions menu.

Process Payroll Time Transactions

The Standard Payroll transactions that are handled automatically by the above function can be modified as needed for overtime and special pay, as well as holiday and sick hours.

☐ 66. Type 1 (Add Transactions) from the Process Payroll Time Transactions menu, and press ENTER.

☐ 67. Run the Add Transactions function using the information below:

```
Process payroll time transactions                        L-G LAWN AND GARDEN
Add
            Please enter:
                1. Pay period starting date                  41897
                2. Pay period ending date                    43097
                3. Pay employees with pay frequencies        B
                4. Number of holiday hours to take           0

Field number to change?
```

☐ 68. Press ENTER at "Field number to change?" to advance to the next screen.

NOTE: Initially, your entry screen displayed below will show field #2 without a field name. When you enter the employee number in field #1, a field name will appear for field #2. If the employee is set up as Salaried, then field #2 will display "Pay salary?". For an Hourly employee, such as Jeffrey Scott, field #2 displays "Regular hours".

☐ 69. Use the information below to process a time transaction for Jeffrey Scott (employee #4).

```
Process payroll time transactions                        L-G LAWN AND GARDEN
Add
        1. Employee #    4           Scott, Jeffrey      Hourly     Bi-weekly

        2. Regular hrs    80     8. Temp D/E 1     (press ENTER)
        3. Overtime hrs    4     9. Temp D/E 2     (press ENTER)
        4. Special hrs     0    10. Temp D/E 3     (press ENTER)
        5. Holiday hrs     0    11. Vac accrued    2
        6. Sick hrs        0    12. Sick accrued   2
        7. Vacation hrs    0    13. Wks worked     2   Pay prd start 04/18/97
                                14. Work units     (Not applicable)

Field number to change?
```

☐ 70. Press ENTER at "Field number to change?" to advance to an expanded screen.

☐ 71. Since you have specified that Jeffrey is to have his wages distributed, you are asked to distribute the transactions.

Enter these distributions:

Type	Account		Hrs/%	Rate
R	6180–000	Salaries – administrative	80.00	8.500
O	6180–000	Salaries – administrative	4.00	12.750

NOTE: Press F1 where the desired data is indicated.
Press ENTER (N) at "Any change?" after each entry.

☐ 72. Press TAB or END three times to return to the Payroll menu.

Calculate Payroll

After time transactions have been entered, payroll must be calculated based on those transactions. Under Calculate Payroll, you determine what frequencies of permanent deductions or earnings will be taken on this run. If the frequency entered on the Calculate Payroll screen matches a deductions/earnings frequency you entered in the Employee File, the deduction will be taken or the earning will be given on this payroll run.

☐ 73. Type 3 (Calculate Payroll) from the Payroll menu, and press ENTER. Calculate the payroll for the transactions you have previously entered by completing the following screen.

```
Calculate payroll                                          L-G LAWN AND GARDEN

          Enter the frequencies of employee permanent
          deductions/earnings to be taken on this run       B

          Enter the payment date for this payroll run       43097

Any change?   N
```

☐ 74. Answer N (no) at "Any change?".

Expect to produce several pages of output; one page for each department. Sample pages of three registers are shown as:

Payroll Time Register	(see Figure 10–6)
Payroll Register	(see Figure 10–7)
Deductions Register	(see Figure 10–8)

☐ 75. Press END to return to the Payroll menu.

Print Payroll Checks

- [ ] 76. Type 4 (Print Payroll Checks) from the Payroll menu, and press ENTER.

- [ ] 77. Type "DONE" on the first entry screen, and press ENTER.

- [ ] 78. Press ENTER (N) to "Print alignment form?".

- [ ] 79. Use the following information to print payroll checks on the time transactions and calculations you have already entered.

```
Print payroll checks                                  L-G LAWN AND GARDEN

          Please enter:

               1. Starting check #          3001     (press ENTER)
               2. Starting department #     "First"  (press F1)
               3. Ending department #       "Last"   (press F1)
               4. Starting employee #       (Not applicable)
               5. Ending employee #         (Not applicable)

Field number to change ?
```

- [ ] 80. Press ENTER at "Field number to change?".

- [ ] 81. Answer 'Y' to "Is this date OK?". (i.e., 4/30/97) The payroll checks for your three bi–weekly payroll employees will be printed. (See Jeffrey Scott's example in Figure 10–9.)

- [ ] 82. Answer 'Y' to "Are payroll checks just printed OK?".

- [ ] 83. Press TAB or END once. Type "DONE" and press ENTER. The Payroll Check Register (see Figure 10–10) will be printed.

- [ ] 84. This completes the exercise. Press TAB or END as needed to exit PAS.

QUESTIONS ABOUT THE SOFTWARE

1. Explain the meaning of the following payroll abbreviations:

   a. w/h
   b. SS
   c. FUI
   d. EIC
   e. SUI
   f. OST
   g. suppl ben

2. The deduction/earnings codes contain D and B types, where D is a deduction from employee net pay after tax calculations, and B is a deduction from employee gross pay before tax calculations. Why are the two codes needed?

3. What five types of pay frequencies are provided by the software? Why are different pay frequencies required?

4. What is meant by "Social security tips?" Why is this option provided by the software?

5. What is meant by "maximum social security wages?"

6. Why is it necessary to make additions to all of the payroll codes BEFORE beginning to process Payroll Time Transactions?

7. Suppose you want to have salaries and wages distributed to Lyons–Garten departments ..... Lawn and Garden, Lawn Installation, Nursery, Landscape/Consulting, or some combination. What changes would you make to implement this request?

8. Why are terminated employees still kept on the employee file? When are they removed from the file?

9. Compare the payroll computations for Jeffrey Scott on the payroll time register, the payroll register, and the deductions register.

   a. How can the payroll time register be used to determine the accuracy of the payroll register?
   b. How can the deductions register be used to determine the accuracy of the payroll register?

10. Examine the printed sample payroll check. What purpose is served by the check voucher? What is the advantage of not having the check supplier preprint a check number on each Payroll check and voucher?

MANAGEMENT ISSUES

11. Suppose you are Rose Garten at Lyons–Garten. Explain how you might audit employee payroll to determine if the amounts to be paid are correct?

12. Why is it important to be able to write payroll checks by hand when, for the majority of employees, payroll checks are processed and printed by the computer?

13. Payroll, to some, means nothing more than an automated method of printing company checks. Suppose you take issue with this position. What management information is provided by this application?

14. Why would it be important to distribute wages paid to employees by department at Lyons– Garten? How would management use this information?

15. Some managers insist that payroll be automated before any other computer application, such as customer invoicing and receivables. Do you agree with this point of view? Explain why or why not?

THINGS TO DO

16. You have just received information that the Federal income tax rate is to be reduced (impossible you say), from 28% to 26% for single persons earning over $21,600, but not over $50,550.

    What display screen and fields on that screen must be changed to implement this change?

17. From the Main menu, select General Ledger and View G/L Account Activity. Enter account 6190 and press F1 twice for "earliest" and "latest".

    How has standard payroll processing changed this G/L account?

    Next, enter account 6180 and press F1 twice.

    How has payroll processing changed this account?
    What does this inspection of two G/L accounts tell you about how payroll processing occurs?

18. While still in View G/L Accounts, enter account 1020 and press F1 twice.

    What is the Total–DR amount?
    What is the Total–CR amount?
    What is the Ending–Balance?
    Explain how payroll processing changes this account.

19. From the Main menu, select Check Reconciliation, followed by 4 (Print a Checkbook). Enter 2 for the Checking Account # and N for "Purge Cleared Items?".

    What is the current checkbook balance?
    How does this balance compare to the ending balance for G/L account 1020?
    Explain the processing procedure used to arrive at these totals.

20. From the Main menu, select Payroll followed by Maintain Employee Data. Choose 2 (Change/ Inquire Employees). Press F1 to inspect Edward Palmer's account. Advance to the last screen (Employee year–to–date Totals).

    How has payroll processing changed the last screen for Edward Palmer's employee record?
    What printed payroll report shows this information?

21. Use the Payroll menu to select 6 (Print Payroll History Report). Enter the following:

a. Starting date	**"Earliest"**	
b. Ending date	**"Latest"**	
c. Starting employee	**4**	
d. Ending employee	**(press ENTER)**	
e. By what date?	**P**	(pay period date)
f. Purge file?	**N**	(no)
g. Format	**F**	(full without ded/earn detail)

What is the purpose of this report?
Why didn't PAS print check #111?

22. Use the Payroll menu to select 9 (Print Quarterly Payroll Report). Enter the following:

a. Report format	**B (brief)**	
b. Which quarter?	**2**	**Ending 063097**
c. Summary or detail?		(Not applicable)
d. In order by		(Not applicable)
e. Print last name first?		(Not applicable)
f. Show employees with no wages for quarter?	**Y (yes)**	
g. Show sub–totals after how many employees?		(Not applicable)

What is the purpose of this report?
Based on this report, how much is owed by Lyons–Garten for the following:

i. State unemployment insurance
ii. State income tax
iii. Other state tax
iv. Federal income tax
v. Social security
vi. Medicare
vii. Federal unemployment insurance

23. Use the Payroll menu to select 10 (Print Year–end Payroll Reports).

What three types of year–end material can be printed?

Select 1 (Print Year–End Payroll Report), and enter the following:

a. Print grand totals only?	**N (No)**	
b. Employee to print	**4**	
c. State to print		(Not applicable)

What is the purpose of this report?
How does the year–end report differ from the quarterly report?

Date: 04/30/97 Time: 16:48:45 LYONS–GARTEN LAWN AND GARDEN, INC. Report #0049 Page 0001

Figure 10–3 – DEDUCTION AND EARNING CODE LIST

Starting code: "First" Ending code: "Last"

Ded/Earn types: D=after tax ded B=before tax ded E=earning S=supplemental pay M=meals T=tips X=special tax

Rate basis: P = percent on subject wages W = work units

Type of earnings: 1 = FWT gross 4 = fed unemp gross 5 = state unemp gross 7 = Emp soc sec gross
8 = Emp medicare gross 9 = Empr soc sec gross 10 = Empr medicare gross

SoSc = Social security MdCr = Medicare

Code	Desc	Typ	G/L–acct	G/L–acct–desc Rate–basis	Rate	FWT	–Emp– SoSc	MdCr	–Empr– SoSc	MdCr	FUI	EIC	SWT	SUI	OST	Suppl– ben	CWT
						YTD–earn–limit			Current–limit		Wrk–unit–desc			Type–of–earn			
B1	Pension	B	2380–000	Pension contrib withheld		N	N	N	N	N	N	N	N	N	N	N	N
D1	Charity	D	2390–000	Charity contrib withheld													
D2	UntFund	D	2390–000	Charity contrib withheld													
ET1	Travel	E	6280–000	Travel & entertainment		Y	Y	Y	Y	Y	Y	Y	Y	Y	Y	Y	Y
ET2	Phone	E	6280–000	Travel & entertainment		Y	Y	Y	Y	Y	Y	Y	Y	Y	Y	Y	Y
M1	Meals	M				Y	N	N	N	N	N	N	Y	N	N	N	N
S1	Sls com	S	6070–000	Commissions		N	N	N	N	N	N	N	N	N	N	N	N
T1	Tips	T				N	N	N	Y	Y	Y	N	N	Y	N	Y	N

8 codes on file: 2 after tax ded 1 before tax ded 2 earnings 1 supplement pay 1 meals 1 tips 0 spec tax

–– End of report ––

Date: 04/30/97 Time: 17:22:33 LYONS–GARTEN LAWN AND GARDEN, INC. Report #0050 Page 0001

Figure 10–4 – NUMERIC EMPLOYEE LIST

Starting employee #: "First" Ending employee #: "Last"

Employee types: H = hourly S = salary N = non–employee

Pay frequencies: D = daily W = weekly B = bi–weekly S = semi–monthly M = monthly

Emp#	Name	Street	City	St	Zip	Soc–sec–#	Emp type	Pay freq
1	Palmer, Edward W	225 Vista Boulevard	Orchard City	CA	90701	415–59–6091	S	B
2	Levine, Susan M	5097 Windward Ave.	Woodland Hills	CA	91002	234–56–7891	H	B
3	Lopez, Felicia J.	4600 E. 17th St. Apt. 5b	Pasadena	CA	90555	345–67–8912	N	S
4	Scott, Jeffrey	120 Pine St.	Winoga Falls	CA	91055	104–36–2911	H	B

–– End of report ––

Date: 04/30/97 Time: 17:22:33 LYONS–GARTEN LAWN AND GARDEN, INC. Report #0051 Page 0001

Figure 10–5a – MANUAL PAYROLL REGISTER

Employee types: H = hourly S = salaried N = non–emp
Distribution types: R = regular S = salary O = overtime X = special

---

Emp#	Name	Typ	Check#	Chk–date	Ppd–date	Reg–pay/sal	Ovt–pay	Vac–pay	Hol–pay	Sic–pay	Spec–pay
4	Scott, Jeffrey	H	111	4/30/97	4/30/97	2,584.00	102.00		136.00		

Reg–hrs	Ovt–hrs	Vac–hrs	Hol–hrs	Sck–hrs	Spc–hrs	Charity
304.00	8.00		16.00			20.00

Vac–accr	Sck–accr	Wks–wrk	Wrk–units	Fed–tip–cr	State–tip–cr	Gross–pay	SoSc–wages	Mdcr–wages	SoSc–tips
2.000	2.000	8.00				2,822.00	2,822.00	2,822.00	

Mdcr–tips	FWT–gross	EIC–gross	SWT–gross	OST–gross	CST–gross	Empr–SoSc–wgs	Empr–SoSc–tips	Empr–Mdcr–wgs	Empr–Mdcr–tips
	2,822.00		2,822.00			2,822.00		2,822.00	

FUI–gross	FUI–wages	SUI–gross	SUI–wages	Sup–ben–gr	Soc–sec	Medicare	FWT	EIC	SWT	OST
2,822.00	2,822.00	2,822.00	2,822.00		174.96	40.92	368.30		16.93	

CWT	Empr–SoSc	Empr–Mdcr	FUI	SUI	Empr–OST	Supp–ben	Net pay
	174.96	40.92	22.58				2,200.89

Distribution:	Type	Acct–#	Description	Hrs/%	Rate	Amount
	O	6180–000	Salaries – administrative	8.00	12.750	102.00
	R	6180–000	Salaries – administrative	304.00	8.500	2,584.00

Date: 04/30/97 Time: 17:22:36 LYONS–GARTEN LAWN AND GARDEN, INC. Report #0051 Page 0002

Figure 10–5b – MANUAL PAYROLL REGISTER

1 transactions

Totals:

Sal/Reg–pay:	2,584.00	Gross pay:	2,822.00
Ovt–pay:	102.00	Social security:	174.96
Vac–pay:	.00	Medicare:	40.92
Hol–pay:	136.00	FWT:	368.30
Sick–pay:	.00	EIC:	.00
Spec–pay:	.00	SWT:	16.93
Other–earns:	.00	OST:	.00
Net:	2,200.89	CWT:	.00
		Other–deds:	20.00
		Other–taxes:	.00

FWT gross:	2,822.00	Empr soc sec tips:	.00
Soc sec tips:	.00	Empr soc sec wages:	2,822.00
Soc sec wages:	2,822.00	Empr medicare tips:	.00
Medicare tips:	.00	Empr medicare wages:	2,822.00
Medicare wages:	2,822.00	FUI gross:	2,822.00
SWT gross:	2,822.00	FUI wages:	2,822.00
OST gross:	.00	SUI gross:	2,822.00
CWT gross:	.00	SUI wages:	2,822.00
EIC gross:	.00	Supp ben gross:	.00

Employer liability totals:

Social security:	174.96
Medicare:	40.92
FUI:	22.58
SUI:	.00
Supp–ben:	.00

–– End of report ––

Date: 04/30/97 Time: 18:12:23 LYONS–GARTEN LAWN AND GARDEN, INC. Report #0052 Page 0001

Figure 10–6 – PAYROLL TIME REGISTER

For the pay period ending 04/30/97

Employee types: H = hourly S = salary N = non–employee
Pay frequencies: D = daily W = weekly B = bi–weekly S = semi–monthly M = monthly
Distribution types: S = salary % R = regular hours O = overtime hours X = special hours

```
---------------------------------------------------------------------------------------------------------
                                                     -----Hours-----                          -Accrued-
Dept  Emp#   Name                              Salary  Regular  Special  Sick   Temp-ded/earn  Vacation  Wks  Work
             Soc-sec-#     Typ Wage-acct Frq           Overtime Holiday  Vac    Desc Type Amt  Sick-tim  wrk  units
---------------------------------------------------------------------------------------------------------

0000   4     Scott, Jeffrey                       .00    80.00     .00     .00                  2.000   2.00
             104-36-2911    H  6180-000  B                4.00     .00     .00                  2.000

      Distribution:  Type  Acct-#                              Hrs/%      Rate
                      O    6180-000 Salaries - administrative   4.00     12.750
                      R    6180-000 Salaries - administrative  80.00      8.500

      1 entries                    Department totals:  80.00             .00      Actual:  2.000
      1 hourly                                                  .00
      0 salary                                          4.00             .00      Actual:  2.000
      0 non-employee                                            .00


0247   1     Palmer, Edward W                 1,500.00   80.00     .00     .00                  6.154   2.00
             415-59-6091    S  6190-000  B                 .00     .00     .00                  3.077

      1 entries                    Department totals:  80.00             .00      Actual:  6.154
      0 hourly                                                  .00
      1 salary                                           .00             .00      Actual:  3.077
      0 non-employee                                            .00


0501   2     Levine, Susan M                      .00    80.00     .00     .00                  6.154   2.00
             234-56-7891    H  6190-000  B                 .00     .00     .00                  3.077

      1 entries                    Department totals:  80.00             .00      Actual:  6.154
      1 hourly                                                  .00
      0 salary                                           .00             .00      Actual:  3.077
      0 non-employee                                            .00

                                   Grand totals:      240.00             .00      Actual: 14.308
                                                                .00
                                                        4.00             .00      Actual:  8.154
                                                                .00

                                   -- End of report --
```

Date: 04/30/97 Time: 18:12:30 LYONS–GARTEN LAWN AND GARDEN, INC. Report #0053 Page 0001

Figure 10–7a – PAYROLL REGISTER

For department: 0000

For the pay period ending 04/30/97

Frequencies used on this run: B

Dept	Emp#	Employee–name		Salary	Reg–pay	Hol–pay	Gross	YTD–gross	Medicare	YTD–mdcr	Oth–ded
		Soc–sec–#	Emp–typ	Wks–wrk	Ovt–pay	Vac–pay	FWT–gross	YTD–FWT–grs	SWT	YTD–SWT	
		Net–pay		Prd–start	Spec–pay	Sick–pay	FWT	YTD–FWT	OST	YTD–OST	
							Soc–sec	YTD–soc–sec	CWT	YTD–CWT	
0000	4	**Scott, Jeffrey**			680.00		731.00	3,553.00	10.60	51.52	5.00
		104–36–2911	Hourly	2.00	51.00		731.00	3,553.00	17.53	34.46	
		548.13		4/18/97			100.03	468.33	4.39	4.39	
							45.32	220.28			

Date: 04/30/97 Time: 18:12:31 LYONS–GARTEN LAWN AND GARDEN, INC. Report #0053 Page 0002

Figure 10–7b – PAYROLL REGISTER

For department: 0000

For the pay period ending 04/30/97

Frequencies used on this run: B

1 checks to be printed

Department totals:

			YTD–in	This–period	YTD–out
Sal–pay:	.00	Gross:	2,822.00	731.00	3,553.00
Reg–pay:	680.00	FWT–grs:	2,822.00	731.00	3,553.00
Ovt–pay:	51.00	Soc–sec:	174.96	45.32	220.28
Vac–pay:	.00	Medicare:	40.92	10.60	51.52
Hol–pay:	.00	FWT:	368.30	100.03	468.33
Sick–pay:	.00	EIC:	.00	.00	.00
Spec–pay:	.00	SWT:	16.93	17.53	34.46
		OST:	.00	4.39	4.39
		CWT:	.00	.00	.00
		Spec–tax:	.00	.00	.00
		Oth–ded:		5.00	
		Net:		548.13	

Department employer liability totals:

	YTD–in	This–period	YTD–out
Soc–sec:	174.96	45.32	220.28
Medicare:	40.92	10.60	51.52
FUI:	22.58	5.85	28.43
SUI:	25.40	6.58	31.98
Supp–ben:	.00	.00	.00
EMPR–OST:	.00	.00	.00

Date: 04/30/97 Time: 18:12:43 LYONS–GARTEN LAWN AND GARDEN, INC. Report #0054 Page 0001

Figure 10–8a – DEDUCTIONS REGISTER

For department: 0000
For the pay period ending 04/30/97

Frequencies used on this run: B

Emp–# Name	Soc–sec–#	Emp–typ	D/E–1	D/E–2	D/E–3	D/E–4	D/E–5	D/E–6	TD/E–1	TD/E–2	TD/E–3	Total deductions
			Other deductions									
4 Scott, Jeffrey	104–36–2911	H	5.00 Charity									5.00

Date: 04/30/97 Time: 18:12:45 LYONS–GARTEN LAWN AND GARDEN, INC. Report #0054 Page 0002

Figure 10–8b – DEDUCTIONS REGISTER

For department: 0000
For the pay period ending 04/30/97

Frequencies used on this run: B

Department totals:

	Totals:		Acct–#	Description
1 checks				
1 with deductions	Charity	5.00	2390–000	Charity contrib withheld

Figure 10–9 – PAYROLL CHECK

Scott, Jeffrey

CHECK NO. 003001

EMPLOYEE NO.	HOURS				EARNINGS				
	REGULAR	OVERTIME	HOLIDAY	SPECIAL	REGULAR	VACATION	SICK		
4	80.00	4.00	.00	.00	680.00	.00	.00	.00	.00
SOCIAL SECURITY NO.	VACATION	SICK	TOTAL HRS		OVERTIME	HOLIDAY	SPECIAL		GROSS PAY
104–36–2911			84.00		51.00				731.00

TAXES / WITHHOLDINGS			VOLUNTARY DEDUCTIONS					
FICA	STATE W/H TAX	CITY W/H TAX	CHARITY					TOTAL TAXES W/H
55.92	17.53	.00	5.00	.00	.00	.00	.00	177.87
FEDRL W/H TAX	OTHER ST. W/h							TOTAL VOL. DED.
100.03	4.39		.00	.00	.00	.00		5.00

YEAR–TO–DATE						PAY PERD	NET PAY
GROSS	FICA	FEDRL W/H TAX	STATE W/H TAX	OTHER ST. W/H	CITY W/H TAX	04/18/97	
3,553.00	271.80	468.33	34.46	4.39	.00	04/30/97	548.13

Regular rate: 8.500

PLEASE DETACH AND RETAIN THIS STUB FOR YOUR RECORDS

L–G LAWN AND GARDEN
1169 Greenbelt Way
Nice Valley, OR 97000

CHECK DATE	CHECK NO.
04/30/97	003001

CHECK AMOUNT
$*****548.13

FIVE HUNDRED FORTY–EIGHT AND 13/100 DOLLARS******

PAY
TO THE
ORDER OF Jeffrey Scott
120 Pine St.
Winoga Falls CA 91055

Authorized Signature

Date: 04/30/97 Time: 18:12:43 LYONS–GARTEN LAWN AND GARDEN, INC. Report #0055 Page 0001

Figure 10–10 – PAYROLL CHECK REGISTER

For the pay period ending 04/30/97

Check–#	Check–date	Check–amt	Emp–#	Name
3001	04/30/97	548.13	4	Jeffrey Scott
3002	04/30/97	1,195.57	1	Edward W Palmer
3003	04/30/97	527.87	2	Susan M Levine

3 checks Total: 2,271.57

–– End of report ––

Exercise 11 – PROCESS PHYSICAL INVENTORY

Introduction

The Inventory application designed for PAS contains many features required by businesses to monitor their inventory. The menu for this application contains the following eight options: (1) maintain item data, (2) maintain item prices, (3) process inventory, (4) process purchases, (5) process physical inventory, (6) print inventory status report, (7) print inventory valuation report, (8) print inventory analysis report. By working your way through these options you will learn how to keep the inventory file current, add and subtract items carried in inventory, decide when to purchase new items, and print a variety of reports showing the status of inventory. Why all this "fuss" about inventory? Some business firms have as much as 90 percent of their money invested in inventory. Unless they can "turn over inventory" (sell it in order to purchase more) within a reasonable time period, they will not remain in business very long.

Figure 11–1 illustrates the flow of information when processing inventory data.

Figure 11–1 – INVENTORY MANAGEMENT OVERVIEW

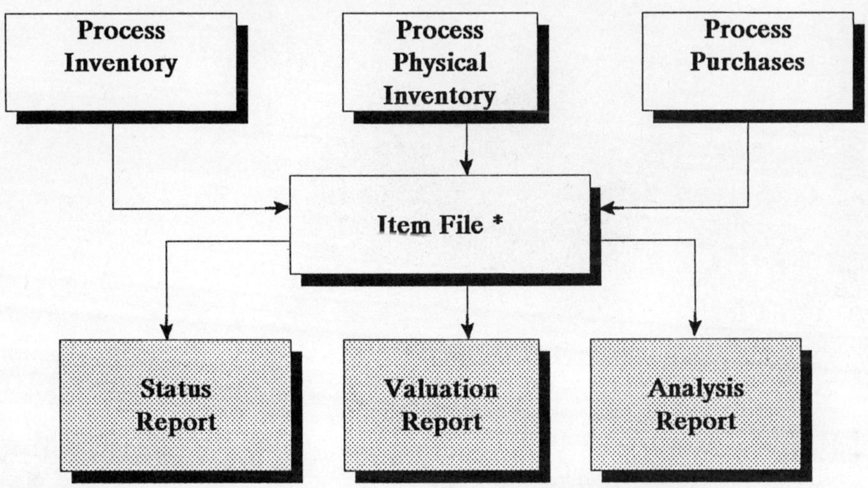

* Set up through the functions: Maintain Item Data
Maintain Item Prices

The center of the design is the Item File, the file containing specific information about each product carried in inventory. The three main inventory activities illustrated are: process inventory, process physical inventory, and process purchases.

Process inventory – records products received into inventory (what you buy), and any adjustments to inventory (what disappears, spoils, becomes damaged, and so on).

Process physical inventory – the process of comparing inventory count–sheet totals to counts stored on the item file to show "shorts" (we should have more stock than we do) or "longs" (we have more stock than we should).

Process purchases – the process of using the computer to advise the user on what new items to add to inventory and the generation of purchase orders.

Besides these processing functions, three main types of reports are available: the inventory status report (the number of units carried in stock and their age), the inventory valuation report (the dollar value of inventory), and the inventory analysis report (the degree to which the management of inventory is successful).

Objectives

This exercise asks you to work through all of the inventory processing functions. You are asked to:

- ➡ Review the contents of the inventory file and add a new item.
- ➡ Change the price of an item, change the price for a group of items, and set sale prices.
- ➡ Process inventory to add items to inventory following the receipt of a shipment from vendors and the return of items by a customer, to remove items from inventory following the sale of items to a customer, and to correct the count of the number of items on hand following the results of a physical count.
- ➡ Process purchases, to show what items need to be purchased.
- ➡ Process a physical count, to allow a manual count of inventory to be compared against the count stored on file.
- ➡ Print the Inventory Status Report, to show the current status of inventory.
- ➡ Print the Inventory Valuation Report to show the current value of all inventory items.
- ➡ Print the Inventory Analysis Report, to show changes in planned versus forecasted performance for items carried in inventory.

Case Study

Richard Grower and Daisy Stalker are excited. "Inventory management, by computer!" Daisy exclaims. "I never thought I would see the day."

"Two thumbs up!" adds Rich. "If the inventory system works as it's described, we should finally be able to get a handle on what we're understocking and what we're overstocking."

Meanwhile Jen is worried again. "I just hope I didn't oversell the inventory application," she whispers to Rose. "The application has loads of potential, but it will take considerable time to 'fine tune'."

Jen explains. "One way of making them aware of the problems with this application is to make them part of it. There is no way our accounting staff can enter in all product information; record purchases, sales, and adjustments; set regular and sale prices; and the most difficult tasks of all ..... decide when to buy stock, from whom, when, and in what quantity. This has to be done by departmental staff."

"What will your office do?" Rose asks.

Jen responds quickly, but her voice still holds an edge of uncertainty.

"We will provide training to each department, showing how the application works, check the printed output of all reports to verify their accuracy, and play a major role in the taking of physical inventory. We will hire independent checkers to count the number of units on hand and compare this count to the number we show on file. We can't have a department do this. If there is any kind of theft or mismanagement, we can't have the chicken in the henhouse (a dishonest department employee, for example) controlling the situation."

"I see," smiles Rose.

Rose, sensing the uncertainty in Jen, concludes with a mild warning. "Jen, I have no doubt your plan will work, but I want you to keep me abreast of our week–to–week progress in this area. I think our weekly operations meeting should include an agenda item devoted to improved inventory management. What do you think?"

"Great idea!" Jen adds without reservation. "Cooperation, not competition between departments is what we need to make better inventory management a success."

Set Transaction Date

☐ Before you start this exercise, set today's date at 4/30/97 using the MS–DOS 'DATE' command.

Review Contents of Inventory Item File

☐ 1. Type 2 (Inventory Management) from the following Main Menu, and press ENTER.

MAIN MENU

```
RealWorld Practical Accounting System                 L-G LAWN AND GARDEN
Version 1.0

                    Please select
                        1. Sales Invoicing
                        2. Inventory Management
                        3. Accounts Receivable
                        4. Accounts Payable
                        5. Payroll
                        6. General Ledger
                        7. Check Reconciliation
                        8. Setup Functions

Press F10 for help at any time
```

☐ 2. Type 1 (Maintain Item Data) from the Inventory Management menu shown on the next page, and press ENTER. Information on each item in inventory is kept under this function.

```
RealWorld Practical Accounting System                     L-G LAWN AND GARDEN
Inventory Management

                     Please select
                        1. Maintain item data
                        2. Maintain item prices
                        3. Process inventory
                        4. Process purchases
                        5. Process physical inventory
                        6. Print inventory status report
                        7. Print inventory valuation report
                        8. Print inventory analysis report
```

- [ ] 3. Type 2 (Change Items) from the following Maintain Item Data menu, and press ENTER.

```
Maintain item data                                        L-G LAWN AND GARDEN

                     Please select
                        1. Add items
                        2. Change items
                        3. Delete items
                        4. Print item list
                        5. Purge inactive items
```

- [ ] 4. Press F1 to familiarize yourself with the items currently in inventory. The inventory data for each item can be viewed in two different screens. Each time you press F1, you are presented with the contents of screen 1 (field numbers 1–21). To view the contents of screen 2 (field numbers 22–48), press ENTER at "Field number to change?". To view the next item, press ENTER again at "Field number to change?", and then press F1.

- [ ] 5. When you receive the message "No more items on file", press ENTER to continue.

- [ ] 6. Press TAB or END at the Change Items menu to return to the Maintain Item Data menu.

Add an Inventory Item

When items were originally entered, one item was missed.

- [ ] 7. Type 1 (Add Items) at the Maintain Item Data menu, and press ENTER.

- [ ] 8. Enter the information shown on the following page into screen 1.

SCREEN 1

Maintain item data | L–G LAWN AND GARDEN
Add items

1. Item number	5014		
2. Description	TREE STAKE – 5 FT.		
3. Bar code	74345	15. List price	1.10
4. Substitute item #	(press ENTER)	16. Discount by	Q (Quantity)
5. Item type	I (Inventory)	17. Better price	.95
6. Department	PARTS	Minimum qty of	100
7. Cust hist class	1 (Landscape)	18. Best price	.88
8. Stocking unit	EACH	Minimum qty of	500
9. Qty on hand	0	19. Alt sell unit 1	DOZ
10. Qty committed	(will be set to 0)	EACH per DOZ	12.00
11. Qty on order	0	Price per DOZ	11.88
12. Average cost	.45	20. Alt sell unit 2	(press Enter)
13. Last cost	.45		
14. Purchase unit	DOZ		
EACH PER DOZ	12.00	21. Preferred unit	EACH

Field number to change?

☐ 9. Press ENTER at "Field number to change?" to advance to screen 2.

☐ 10. On the second screen, press F1 to show Hanson Manufacturing Co. as the vendor. Enter the acct #s in fields 24–27, and enter the quantity totals in fields 30–32. Press ENTER to set all dates to "None" in fields 33–36, and press F1 to set amounts to zero for the remaining fields (37–48).

SCREEN 2

Maintain item data | L–G LAWN AND GARDEN
Add items
Item #: 5014 TREE STAKE – 5 FT.

22. Vendor	Hanson Manufacturing Co.		
23. Notes			
24. Inventory acct #	1400–000		
Inventory		37. Qty sold this prd	0
25. Sales acct #	4020	38. Qty sold last prd	0
26. Cost of goods acct #	5000	39. Qty sold this year	0
27. Returns acct #	4520	40. Qty sold last year	0
28. Taxable ?	Y		
29. Bin location		41. Sales this period	.00
30. Minimum qty on hand	24	42. Sales last period	.00
31. Minimum order qty	24	43. Sales this year	.00
32. Maximum qty on hand	240	44. Sales last year	.00
33. First receipt date	None	45. Cost this period	.00
34. Last receipt date	None	46. Cost last period	.00
35. Last order date	None	47. Cost this year	.00
36. Last sale date	None	48. Cost last year	.00

Field number to change?

☐ 11. Press ENTER at "Field number to change?" to save the entry.

☐ 12. Press TAB or END twice to return to the Inventory Management menu.

Change Item Prices

Due to additional storage costs, you need to increase the prices of two items.

☐ 13. Type 2 (Maintain Item Prices) from the Inventory Management menu, and press ENTER.

☐ 14. Type 2 (Change Individual Prices) from the following Maintain Item Prices menu, and press ENTER.

```
Maintain item prices                                L-G LAWN AND GARDEN

                  Please select
                     1. Print price list
                     2. Change individual prices
                     3. Change group prices
                     4. Set sale prices
                     5. Purge sale prices
```

☐ 15. The first price to change is for item # 2200 (LAWN HAMMER). Press F1 until you see this item in the Item Number field. Change the following fields:

List price	13.95	Best price	12.35
Better price	13.10	Price per DOZ	144.00

☐ 16. Press ENTER at "Field number to change?" to advance to the next screen.

☐ 17. The second set of prices to change is for item # 5770 (NURSERY STAKES–30 PC SET). Press F1 until you see this item in the Item Number field. Change the following fields:

List price	29.95
Better price	29.20

☐ 18. Press ENTER at "Field number to change?" and press TAB or END to return to the Maintain Item Prices menu.

Change Group Prices

One of your vendors, Hill Equipment and Supply, has just increased the prices on all of its items by 5%.

☐ 19. Type 3 (Change Group Prices) from the Maintain Item Prices menu, and press ENTER.

☐ 20. Use the information on the following page to change the prices on all of Hill's goods.

```
Maintain item prices                                    L-G LAWN AND GARDEN
Change group prices

   1. Starting item #        "First"    (press F1)
   2. Ending item #          "Last"     (press F1)
   3. Department             "All"      (press F1)
   4. Vendor                 Hill Equipment & Supply   (Type 'Hill' and press ENTER)
   5. Change price by        P  (Percentage)
                                        Basis for
                             Pct (+/-)  new price
   6. List price             5.00       O  (Old price)
   7. Better price           5.00       O
   8. Best price             5.00       O
   9. Alternate price 1      No change  (press ENTER)
  10. Alternate price 2      No change  (press ENTER)
  11. Change or print?       3  (Print and change)

 Field number to change?
```

☐ 21. Press ENTER at "Field number to change?" and type Y to "Are you sure you want to do this?". The Group Price Changes Log (see Figure 11–2) will be printed.

☐ 22. Press TAB or END twice to return to the Maintain Item Prices menu.

Set Sale Prices

Lyons–Garten will be running a sale on several items for the month of May.

☐ 23. Type 4 (Set Sales Prices) from the Maintain Item Prices menu, and press ENTER.

```
Maintain item prices                                    L-G LAWN AND GARDEN
Set sale prices

   1. Item number

      Item type:                        Department:
      Qty on hand:                      Last sold:
      Qty on order:                     Last recd:
      Average cost:                     Last cost:

   2. Start sale date
   3. End sale date
                                 Gross                             Gross
                     Sale-price  pft %               Reg-price     pft %
   4. Price per                                List:

Enter item #, press F1 for next item, or leave blank to look up by description
```

24. Using the Set Sale Prices menu shown on the previous page, set sale prices and sale dates for the following items:

Item Number	Start Sale Date	End Sale Date	Sale price
1091 HI-PRESSURE HOSE	50197	53197	15.95
1100 LAWN EDGER	50197	53197	21.95
1105 DRILL, YANKEE	50197	53197	12.75

25. Press ENTER at "Field number to change?" and press TAB or END twice to return to the Inventory Management menu.

Process Inventory

The Process Inventory function is used to enter, change or inquire into, delete, or print an edit list of receivings and adjustments for your inventory. NOTE: You cannot use this function if you have physical inventory transactions on file.

26. Type 3 (Process Inventory) from the Inventory Management menu, and press ENTER.

27. Type 1 (Add Transactions) from the following Process Inventory menu, and press ENTER.

```
Process inventory                                   L-G LAWN AND GARDEN

                        Please select
                          1. Add transactions
                          2. Change transactions
                          3. Delete transactions
                          4. Print transaction edit list
                          5. Post transactions
```

For each of the following examples, complete the proper inventory transaction.

28. On 4/28/97, you received (RECEIVING) 240 EACH of Item # 5014 costing $0.45 EACH. The document number is 042897. Comment the transaction as "received from vendor". The completed menu should appear as displayed on the next page.

NOTE: Be sure that you press F2 at line #5 to indicate EACH as the stocking unit.

Process inventory Add transactions		L–G LAWN AND GARDEN	
1. Item number	5014	TREE STAKE – 5 FT.	Stk–unit EACH
2. Transaction type	Receiving	Qty available: 0 Qty on order: 0	
3. Transaction date	4/28/97	Average cost: .45	
4. Document #	042897	Last cost: .45	
5. Qty received (EACH)	240	New qty avail: 240	
6. Cost per EACH	.45	New avg cost: .45	
	New–price	old–price	
7. List price (EACH)	(No change)	1.10	
8. Better price (EACH)	(No change)	.95	
9. Best price (EACH)	(No change)	.88	
10. Price per DOZ	(No change)	11.88	
11. Comment	received from vendor		
Field number to change?			

☐ 29. On 4/29/97, a customer returned (CREDIT MEMO) 10 units of Item # 2200, priced at $13.95. This transaction was NOT processed through Sales/Invoicing. The document number is 2832. The actual cost was $7.31. Comment the transaction as "customer returns". The completed menu should appear as follows:

Process inventory Add transactions		L–G LAWN AND GARDEN	
1. Item number	2200	LAWN HAMMER	Stk–unit EACH
2. Transaction type	Credit memo	Qty available: 0 Qty on order: 60	
3. Transaction date	4/29/97	Average cost: 7.31	
4. Document #	2832	Last cost: 7.31	
5. # of EACH credited	10	New qty avail: 10 New avg cost: 7.31	
6. Price per EACH	13.95	Ext price: 139.50	
7. Actual cost per EACH	7.31	Gross margin: 66.40	
8. Comment	customer returns		
9. Profit center	000		
Field number to change?			

☐ 30. On 4/30/97, a customer (SALE) ordered 5 of Item # 1105. Enter a date of 043097, a Document # of 62120, a price per EACH of $14.95. Comment the adjustment as "RUSH order". The completed menu should appear as follows:

```
Process inventory                                        L-G LAWN AND GARDEN
Add transactions

   1. Item number            1105         DRILL, YANKEE              Stk-unit
                                                                     EACH
   2. Transaction type       Sale         Qty available:   0
                                          Qty on order:    0
   3. Transaction date       4/30/97      Average cost:    8.51
   4. Document #             62120        Last cost:       8.72

   5. # of EACH sold         5            New qty avail:   5-
                                          New avg cost:    8.51

   6. Price per EACH         14.95        Ext price:       74.75
   7. Actual cost per EACH   8.51         Gross margin:    32.20

   8. Comment                RUSH order
   9. Profit center          000

Field number to change?
```

☐ 31. Add the following transactions dealing with quantities of products RECEIVED earlier. Accept the default for "Cost per EACH" and comment as "received from vendor".

Item No.	Qty Recd	Date	Document #
1091	23 EACH	4/20/97	62000
1100	11 EACH	4/20/97	62201
1105	15 EACH	4/20/97	62100
2200	25 EACH *	4/20/97	62101
5770	9 SET	4/20/97	62202

* Press F2 to indicate that stocking units are EACH.

☐ 32. Add the following SALE transactions to adjust the inventories of non–invoiced sales recorded in exercise 6. (Recall that PAS does not adjust inventories for non–invoiced sales transactions.) Accept the default for "Price and Cost per EACH". Comment as "non–invoiced sale".

Item No.	Qty Recd	Date	Document #
1105	25 EACH	4/23/97	7843
1091	20 EACH	4/27/97	835
2200	15 EACH	4/27/97	835

☐ 33. Press TAB or END to return to the Process Inventory menu.

☐ 34. Type 4 (Print Transaction Edit List) from the Process Inventory menu, and press ENTER.

```
Process inventory                                    L-G LAWN AND GARDEN
Print transaction edit list

                  Please enter:
                       Starting item number      "First"
                       Ending item number        "Last"

Any change?
```

☐ 35. Press F1 twice to indicate that the "First" through the "Last" item numbers are to be printed. View the Inventory Transaction Edit List on the screen. (Do not print it.)

☐ 36. If the transactions are correct, "Post" the transactions, selecting #5 (Post Transactions) from the Process Inventory menu. An Inventory Transaction Register (see Figure 11–3) will be printed.

☐ 37. Press TAB or END to return to the Inventory Management menu.

Process Purchases

The Process Purchases function shows what needs to be purchased, and automatically generates purchase transactions. It also allows you to manually add, change, view or delete purchase transactions, print an edit list of transactions, and post the transactions. When purchase transactions are posted, the quantity on order and optional notes for an item are updated.

☐ 38. Type 4 (Process Purchases) from the Inventory Management menu, and press ENTER.

```
Process purchases                                    L-G LAWN AND GARDEN

               Please select
                    1. Print purchasing advice report
                    2. Add transactions
                    3. Change transactions
                    4. Delete transactions
                    5. Print transaction edit list
                    6. Post transactions
```

☐ 39. Type 1 (Print Purchasing Advice Report) from the Process Purchases menu, and press ENTER.

☐ 40. Use the information on the next screen to print the Purchasing Advice Report.

```
Process purchases                                   L-G LAWN AND GARDEN
Print purchasing advice report

                Please enter:
                     1. Print in order by       3 (item-#)
                     2. Starting item #         "First"    (press F1)
                     3. Ending item #           "Last"     (press F1)
                     4. Starting vendor         "First"    (press F1)
                     5. Ending vendor           "Last"     (press F1)
                     6. Department              "All"      (press F1)
                     7. Print or generate?      3 (Print and generate)
                     8. Default order date      43097      (press F1)
                     9. Default item notes      April order

Field number to change?
```

NOTE: When "print and generate" or "generate transactions only" is selected, purchasing transactions are automatically generated for the inventory items that match the fields on this screen and that are also below minimum quantity on hand.

☐ 41. Press ENTER at "Field number to change?" and answer Y at "Are you sure you want to do this?". The Purchasing Advice Report (see Figure 11–4) will be printed.

☐ 42. Press TAB or END twice to return to the Process Purchases menu.

☐ 43. Type 5 (Print Transaction Edit List) from the Process Purchases menu, and press ENTER. Display a complete report for all departments in full format as indicated in the following completed screen. Review the purchase transactions (DRILL, YANKEE / HI–PRESSURE HOSE) that were generated.

```
Process purchases                                   L-G LAWN AND GARDEN
Print transaction edit list

                Please enter:
                     1. Starting vendor           "First"
                     2. Ending vendor             "Last"
                     3. Starting item number      "First"
                     4. Ending item number        "Last"
                     5. Department                "All"
                     6. Report format             Full
                     7. One vendor per page?      N

Field number to change?
```

☐ 44. Press ENTER to continue, and press TAB or END to return to the Process Purchases menu.

☐ 45. Type 6 (Post Transactions) from the Process Purchases menu, and press ENTER. This posting will update the Item File with quantity on order figures. The Purchase Transaction Register (see Figure 11–5) will be printed.

☐ 46. Press TAB or END to return to the Inventory Management menu.

☐ 47. Type 1 (Maintain Item Data) from the Inventory Management menu, and press ENTER.

☐ 48. Type 2 (Change Items) from the Maintain Item Data menu, and press ENTER. Use this function to view Item # 2200 (LAWN HAMMER). Notice that the quantity in field #9 has been updated to 20 units (ref., credits of 25 and 10 units, and sale of 15 units in the previous steps – see Figure 11–3).

```
Maintain item data                                  L-G LAWN AND GARDEN

              Please select
                  1. Add items
                  2. Change items
                  3. Delete items
                  4. Print item list
                  5. Purge inactive items
```

☐ 49. Press ENTER twice at "Field number to change?" and press TAB or END twice to return to the Inventory Management menu.

Performing a Physical Count

When performing a physical count of all or part of your inventory, each step must be done in the proper order to maintain the accuracy of your computer records.

The steps for performing a physical inventory count are:

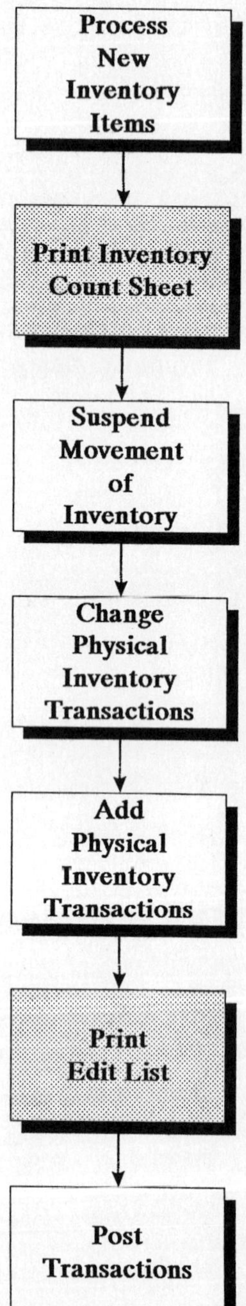

1. Enter and post any receiving and adjustment transactions for inventory items, using the Process Inventory function. This step is necessary if the new quantities are to be included in the count. (Step 3 cannot be performed if unposted receiving or adjustment transactions are on file.)

2. Print the Inventory Count Sheet for all items that you intend to count. (When initially setting up your data, you should select Balance Forward transactions.) Use the Print Inventory Count Sheet function on the Process Physical Inventory menu.

3. Suspend the movement of inventory items in your stocking areas long enough to count the quantity on hand for each item. Record the counted quantities on the Inventory Count Sheet. You can also record quantities for items which do not appear on the sheet; manual transactions can be entered later for these items.

4. Use the Change function on the Process Physical Inventory menu to enter counted quantities appearing on the count sheet.

5. Use the Add function to enter transactions for items that were not originally printed on the count sheet.

6. Print a transaction edit list to verify the entries, using the Print Transaction Edit List function on the Process Physical Inventory menu.

7. Post the transactions to update the on–hand quantity for each item and, for Count transactions only, to record any cost variance to the General Ledger.

Process Physical Inventory

The Process Physical Inventory function prints an Inventory Count Sheet for recording counted inventory items, and automatically generates inventory count transactions. This function also allows you to manually add, change, inquire into and delete the transactions.

You can also print an edit list of inventory count transactions, and post the transactions. When inventory count transactions are posted, the quantity on hand for an item is updated and the transactions are removed from the Transaction File.

You can use this function to load initial quantities on hand into the Item File. Therefore, before we proceed in this exercise to do a physical count of our inventory, we will transfer our manual records of inventory quantities into PAS using this function.

☐ 50. Type 5 (Process Physical Inventory) from the Inventory Management menu, and press ENTER.

☐ 51. Type 2 (Add Transactions) from the Process Physical Inventory menu, and press ENTER.

☐ 52. Enter the current non–computerized record of inventory quantities **(Balance Forward)** from the following list using today's date (43097) and no document #. Comment as you choose.

Item Number	Qty counted	
1091	23	(Enter the first line, and press ENTER at the second line. Use defaults for the other values.
1100	11	
1105	0	
2200	10	
5014	240	(in stocking units of EACH)
5770	9	

☐ 53. Press TAB or END to return to the Process Physical Inventory menu.

☐ 54. Type 6 (Post Transactions) from the Process Physical Inventory menu, and press ENTER.

☐ 55. Post with today's date (43097). Do NOT adjust non–counted items to zero. Continue on to post the transactions and print the Physical Inventory Transaction Register (see Figure 11–6).

☐ 56. Press TAB or END to return to the Inventory Management menu.

☐ 57. Type 5 (Process Physical Inventory) from the Inventory Management menu, and press ENTER.

☐ 58. Type 1 (Print Inventory Count Sheet) from the Process Physical Inventory menu, and press ENTER.

☐ 59. Use the information on the next page to process a physical count for all items in the TOOLS department. For each entry field, note the options from which you can choose.

```
Process physical inventory                          L-G LAWN AND GARDEN
Print inventory count sheet

        Please enter:
           1. Print in order by          1 (Bin location/description)
           2. Starting bin location      "First"  (press F1)
           3. Ending bin location        "Last"   (press F1)

           4. Starting item              "First"  (press F1)
           5. Ending item                "Last"   (press F1)

           6. Department                 TOOLS
           7. Vendor                     "All"    (press F1)

           8. Print quantity on hand?    Y

           9. Print or generate?         3 (print & generate)
          10. Transaction type           C (Count)
          11. Transaction date           43097    (press F1)
          12. Default comments           April physical count

Field number to change?
```

☐ 60. Press ENTER at "Field number to change?" and answer Y at "Are you sure you want to do this?". The Inventory Count Sheet (see Figure 11–7) will be printed.

☐ 61. Press TAB or END to return to the Process Physical Inventory menu.

☐ 62. Type 3 (Change Transactions) from the Process Physical Inventory menu, and press ENTER.

☐ 63. Enter the physical inventory counts that you made as shown below. **NOTE:** In the "Change" mode, the "qty counted" field allows you to enter two counts because a product might be located in more than one location in the warehouse. For this exercise, use only the first "qty counted" field.

Item Number	Qty counted
1105	0
1100	10
2200	12
5770	9

☐ 64. Press ENTER at "Field number to change?" and press TAB or END to return to the Process Physical Inventory menu.

☐ 65. Type 5 (Print Transaction Edit List) from the Process Physical Inventory menu, and press ENTER.

☐ 66. Select all bin locations by pressing F1 twice. Display the report to the screen, noticing the counted quantities with their variances.

☐ 67. Press ENTER to continue, and type 6 (Post Transactions) from the Process Physical Inventory menu, and press ENTER.

☐ 68. Enter the following information to post the inventory changes and continue on your own. The Physical Inventory Transaction Register (see Figure 11–8) will be printed.

Posting date	**43097**
Adjustment acct #	**(press F1) 5020–000 Inventory adjustments**
Adjust non–counted items to zero?	**N**

☐ 69. Press TAB or END to return to the Inventory Management menu.

Print Inventory Status Report

The purpose of this report is to show the current status of some or all of your inventory items. In the "stat(us)" column (far right), the report identifies items which are overstocked, understocked or out of stock. The current value is also included on the report, along with the projected cost of achieving the desired min–imum and maximum inventory stock levels.

☐ 70. Type 6 (Print Inventory Status Report) from the Inventory Management menu, and press ENTER.

☐ 71. Enter the following information to print the status of all items for all vendors. The Inventory Status Report (see Figure 11–9) will be printed.

```
Print inventory status report                          L-G LAWN AND GARDEN

          Please enter:
              1. Print in order by              I (Item number)
              2. Starting item number           "First"   (press F1)
              3. Ending item number             "Last"    (press F1)
              4. Department                     "All"     (press F1)
              5. Vendor                         "All"     (press F1)
              6. Print out of stock items?      Y
              7. Report format                  F (Full)
              8. Print single spaced?           N

Field number to change?
```

Print Inventory Valuation Report

The purpose of this report is to detail the current value of some or all of your inventory items. The current value is based on average cost, retail value, and replacement value.

☐ 72. Type 7 (Print Inventory Valuation Report) from the Inventory Management menu, and press ENTER.

☐ 73. Enter the information on the following page to print the current value of all items for all vendors. The Inventory Valuation Report (see Figure 11–10) will be printed.

```
Print inventory valuation sheet                          L-G LAWN AND GARDEN

                Please enter:
                     1. Print in order by          I (Item #)
                     2. Starting item #            "First"   (press F1)
                     3. Ending item #              "Last"    (press F1)
                     4. Department                 "All"     (press F1)
                     5. Vendor                     "All"     (press F1)

Field number to change?
```

Print Inventory Analysis Report

The purpose of this report is to show both historical and forecasted performance for items. The report allows you to focus on fast or slow moving items and forecasted inventory overages and shortages in order to make merchandising and purchasing decisions. The report can be printed in order by item department or by rank. Several ranking methods are available, such as inventory value, this period sales, and quantity sold this year.

☐ 74. Type 8 (Print Inventory Analysis Report) from the Inventory Management menu, and press ENTER.

☐ 75. Enter the following information to display an overall analysis of all items for all vendors, ranked by sales this period. The Inventory Analysis Report will be printed. (See Figure 11–11.)

```
Print inventory analysis report                          L-G LAWN AND GARDEN

          Please enter:
                 1. Starting item number               "First"   (press F1)
                 2. Ending item number                 "Last"    (press F1)
                 3. Department                         "All"     (press F1)
                 4. Vendor                             "All"     (press F1)
                 5. Print in order by                  R (Rank)
                 6. Ranking method                     S (Sales)
                    Ranking basis                      P (This period)
                 7. Top or bottom rankings?            "All"     (press F1)
                 8. Surplus or not enough items?       "All"     (press F1)
                 9. Fast or slow turning items?        "All"     (press F1)

Field number to change?
```

☐ 76. This completes the exercise. Press TAB or END as needed to exit PAS.

QUESTIONS ABOUT THE SOFTWARE

1. Most inventory reports can be prepared by Item Number or by Description. What is the difference between the two types of listings?

2. Four types of entries are possible when adding an inventory transaction to PAS. What is the difference between the following four types of transactions: receiving, sale, credit memo, and adjustment?

3. Examine the Group Price Changes Log. Why does it only list two of the six products carried in inventory?

4. Examine the "resultant" quantity on the purchasing advise report. What is meant by the quantity on hand? The quantity on order? The quantity committed? The order quantity? Why are all four quantities important when computing the resultant quantity?

5. Compare the Physical Inventory Transaction Register before and after the physical count of stock. How do the on–hand quantities of stock differ?

6. Examine the Inventory Status Report. What is an "overstocked" condition? What is an "under–stocked" condition? What is an "out–of–stock" condition?

MANAGEMENT ISSUES

7. The reports produced by Inventory Management vary in terms of their importance to different types of managers. For example, in Lyons–Garten, which manager(s) would most likely use the following reports:

    a. The purchasing advise report?
    b. The inventory status report?
    c. The inventory valuation report?
    d. The inventory analysis report?

    In your analysis, explain the major purpose of each report.

8. In step #29, a customer returned 10 units; however, this transaction was not processed through sales/invoicing. Is this a good management practice? Explain your position. Under what conditions might a return such as this take place?

9. Some companies never think about the maximum or the minimum quantities of inventory that should be on hand at any time. How would management decide on the minimum amount of stock to carry? How would they decide on the maximum amount of stock to carry? How might management quantify these decisions, given the information supplied to them by PAS?

10. Compare changing the price of a single item to changing the price for an entire group of items. When would group price changes be used by the management of a company? Cite more than one reason.

11. Suppose you are the manager of a Lyons–Garten department. If all products carried in inventory by your department are analyzed and listed on the inventory analysis report, how would the information help you to better manage inventory?

THINGS TO DO

12. From the View G/L Activities menu (via the General Ledger Main menu selection), enter account # 1400. Press F1 twice for starting and ending dates.

    Has this inventory account been changed by the receipt of goods to add to inventory?

    If it has not been changed, explain why?

13. While still in the View G/L activities, enter account #5020 and press F1 for the starting and ending dates.

    How has this account been changed by the inventory management module?

    Explain where the dollar figure came from.

    Where is the offsetting debit found?

14. Conduct maintenance on data item # 1105 (via the Inventory Management menu). Do the following:

    a. Change the maximum qty on hand to 25 (field 32).
    b. Change the minimum qty on hand to 10 (field 30).
    c. Following this, exit and return to the main inventory management menu.
    d. Move to the Process Purchases submenu.
    e. Select Print Purchasing Advise Report.
    f. Print in order by item number.
    g. Press F1 for starting and ending item number, starting and ending vendor, and dept.
    h. Select print only and display the report.

    What is the suggested order quantity?

    How was the quantity computed?

15. Work with item #1105 some more. Select Process Inventory from the Inventory Management menu and do the following:

    a. Select Add Transactions.
    b. Enter item number 1105.
    c. Enter transaction type R.
    d. Enter the receiving date as 4/30/97.
    e. Enter 5 as the quantity received.
    f. Press ENTER at Cost per Each.
    g. Type "quick shipment" for Comment.
    h. Exit and Post this transaction.

    Next print a revised inventory status report as follows:

    a. Select Print Inventory Status Report.
    b. Print in order by Item number.

c. Select a Beginning item number of 1105 and an Ending number of 1106.
d. Press F1 for department and vendor.
e. Type Y to print out of stock items.
f. Type F for a full report format.
g. Press ENTER at "Field number to change?". Print the report.

Compare the new stock status to the report printed earlier and answer the following:

How did the quantity–on–order change as a result of the new receipt of inventory?

Why was the quantity–on–order not increased as a result of the purchase advise?

Even though new units were received, the costs to replenish are now higher than before. Why is this?

Why is there one understocked condition reported this time, rather than one out–of–stock condition, as reported earlier?

16. Press TAB or END as needed to exit PAS.

Date: 04/30/97 Time: 16:48:45 LYONS-GARTEN LAWN AND GARDEN, INC. Report #0022 Page 0001

Figure 11-2 - GROUP PRICE CHANGES LOG

Starting item #: "First" Ending item #: "Last"
Department: "All" Vendor: Hill Equipment & Supply
List price: Add 5.00% to old price
Better price: Add 5.00% to old price
Best price: Add 5.00% to old price
Alt-1 price: No change
Alt-2 price: No change
Item types: I = Inventory N = Non-inventory S = Service

Item-#	Description	Type Dept	Qty-on-hand Last-cost		List Price	Better Price	Best Price	Alternate Price-1	Alternate Price-2
1091	**HI-PRESSURE HOSE**	I	0	Old:	17.95	15.75			
		PARTS	9.720	New:	18.85	16.54			
5770	**NURSERY STAKES - 30 PC**	I	0	Old:	29.95	29.20			
		TOOLS	18.200	New:	31.45	30.66			

Old retail value: $.00
New retail value: $.00
Net change: $.00

2 items printed

-- End of report --

Date: 04/30/97 Time: 17:22:33 LYONS–GARTEN LAWN AND GARDEN, INC. Report #0023 Page 0001

Figure 11–3 – INVENTORY TRANSACTION REGISTER

Current period ending date: 4/30/97

G/L account is shown for up and down adjustments; Profit center is shown for sales and credit memos
List, better, best, and alternate prices are only shown if modified by the transaction
Cost correction is only shown if applicable to the transaction

Date	Type	Doc–#	Trans–qty Unit Running–qty–oh	Unit–cost	Tot–actual–cost New–avg–cost	Comment G/L–acct	Price–per–unit
Item: **1091**		**HI–PRESSURE HOSE**			Stocking unit: EACH		
4/20/97	Receiving	62000	23 EACH	9.720	223.56	received from vendor	
			23 EACH		9.72000		
			(23 EACH	9.720)			
4/27/97	Sale	835	20 EACH	9.720	194.40	non–invoiced sale	18.850
			3 EACH	13.140	9.72000		
Item: **1100**		**LAWN EDGER**			Stocking unit: EACH		
4/20/97	Receiving	62201	11 EACH	13.140	144.54	received from vendor	
			11 EACH		13.14000		
			(11 EACH	13.140)			
Item: **1105**		**DRILL, YANKEE**			Stocking unit: EACH		
4/20/97	Receiving	62100	15 EACH	8.720	130.80	received from vendor	
			15 EACH		8.72000		
			(15 EACH	8.720)			
4/23/97	Sale	7843	25 EACH	8.510	212.75	non–invoiced sale	14.950
			10–EACH		8.58875	000	
4/30/97	Sale	62120	5 EACH	8.510	42.55	RUSH order	14.950
			15–EACH		8.58875	000	
Item: **2200**		**LAWN HAMMER**			Stocking unit: EACH	Alt–unit–1: DOZ	
4/20/97	Receiving	62101	25 EACH	7.310	182.75	received from vendor	
			25 EACH		7.31000		
			(25 EACH	7.310)			
4/27/97	Sale	835	15 EACH	7.310	109.65	non–invoiced sale	13.950
			10–EACH		7.31000	000	

Date: 04/30/97 Time: 17:22:35 LYONS-GARTEN LAWN AND GARDEN, INC. Report #0023 Page 0002

Figure 11-3 - INVENTORY TRANSACTION REGISTER (cont.)

Date	Type	Doc-#	Trans-qty Running-qty-oh	Unit	Unit-cost	Tot-actual-cost New-avg-cost	Comment G/L-acct	Price-per-unit
4/29/97	Credit memo	2832	10	EACH	7.310	73.10	Customer returns	13.950
			20	EACH		7.31000	000	
Item: **5014**		**TREE STAKE - 5 FT.**				Stocking unit: EACH	Alt-unit-1: DOZ	
4/28/97	Receiving	042897	240	EACH	.450	108.00	received from vendor	
			240	EACH		.45000		
			(240	EACH	.450)			
Item: **5770**		**NURSERY STAKES-30 PC SET**				Stocking unit: SET		
4/20/97	Receiving	62202	9	SET	18.200	163.80	received from vendor	
			9	SET		18.20000		
			(9	SET	18.200)			

Grand totals:						
	Receiving entries:	6	Qty received:	323	Cost:	953.45
	Credit memo entries:	1	Qty credited:	10	Cost:	73.10
	Up adj entries:	0	Qty adjusted:	0	Cost:	.00
	Down adj entries:	0	Qty adjusted:	0	Cost:	.00
	Sale entries:	4	Qty sold:	65	Cost:	559.35

-- End of report --

Date: 04/30/97 Time: 18:12:23 LYONS-GARTEN LAWN AND GARDEN, INC. Report #0025 Page 0001

Figure 11-4 - PURCHASING ADVICE REPORT

Item # range: "First" to "Last"
Vendor range: "First" to "Last"
Department: "All"
Default notes: April order Default order date: 4/30/97
Order-cost = Order-qty x Last-cost Retail-value = Order-qty x List-price

Item-#	Description / Vendor	Stk-unit / Pur-unit / Dept	Last-cost / Avg-cost / List-price	Min-qty-OH / Max-qty-OH / Min-ord-qty	Qty-on-hand / Qty-commit / Qty-on-ord	-Qty-sold- This-perod / Last-period / This-year	-Suggested-Order- Order-cost / Retail-val	Order-qty
1091	**HI-PRESSURE HOSE**	EACH	9.720	10	3	21	262.44	27 EACH
			9.720	30	0	0	508.95	
	Hill Equipment & Supply	PARTS	18.85	0	0	21		
1105	**DRILL, YANKEE**	EACH	8.720	0	15-	30	130.80	15 EACH
			8.720	0	0	0	224.25	
	Reynolds Tool Company	TOOLS	14.95	0	0	30	** Out of stock **	
				Totals:	12-	51	393.24	42
					0	0	733.20	
					0	51		

2 items printed 1 items are out of stock

-- End of report --

Date: 04/30/97 Time: 18:12:30 LYONS–GARTEN LAWN AND GARDEN, INC. Report #0025 Page 0001

Figure 11–5 – PURCHASE TRANSACTION REGISTER

Suggested–qty = Calculated order quantity based on min/max
Resultant–qty = Qty–on–hand + Qty–on–order – Qty–committed + Order–qty
Extended–cost = Order–qty x Unit–cost

Replacement–cost = Order–qty x Last–cost
Retail–value = Order–qty x List–price

Item–#	Description	Dept	Ord–date Min–qty–OH Max–qty–OH	Order–qty Suggest–qty Result–qty	Unit	Unit–cost Last–cost List–price	Extend–cost Replace–cost Retail–value	Notes Reference
Vendor: Hill Equipment & Supply								
1091	**HI–PRESSURE HOSE**	PARTS	4/30/97	27	EACH	9.720	262.44	April order
			10	27	EACH	9.720	262.44	
			30	30	EACH	18.85	508.95	
	Vendor totals:		1 items	27			262.44	
				27			262.44	
				30			508.95	
Vendor: Reynolds Tool Company								
1105	**DRILL, YANKEE**	TOOLS	4/30/97	15	EACH	8.720	130.80	April order
			0	15	EACH	8.720	130.80	
			0	0	EACH	14.95	224.25	
	Vendor totals:		1 items	15			130.80	
				15			130.80	
				0			224.25	
	Grand totals:	2 vendors	2 items	42			393.24	
				42			393.24	
				30			733.20	

-- End of report --

Date: 04/30/97 Time: 18:12:31 LYONS-GARTEN LAWN AND GARDEN, INC. Report #0026 Page 0001

Figure 11-6 - PHYSICAL INVENTORY TRANSACTION REGISTER

Current period ending date: 4/30/97

Retail-value = Transaction-qty x List-price
Transactions are printed in item number order

Item-number	Description	Type Doc-#	Date	Trans-qty New-qty-OH	Unit	Unit-cost	Total-cost New-avg-cost	List-price Retail-val
1091	**HI-PRESSURE HOSE**	Bfwd	4/30/97	23	EACH	9.720	223.56	18.85
				23	EACH		9.72000	433.55
							Comment: transfer manual records	
1100	**LAWN EDGER**	Bfwd	4/30/97	11	EACH	13.140	144.54	25.95
				11	EACH		13.14000	285.45
							Comment: transfer manual records	
1105	**DRILL, YANKEE**	Bfwd	4/30/97	0	EACH	8.720	.00	14.95
				0	EACH		8.72000	.00
							Comment: transfer manual records	
2200	**LAWN HAMMER**	Bfwd	4/30/97	10	EACH	7.310	73.10	13.95
				10	EACH		7.31000	139.50
							Comment: transfer manual records	
5014	**TREE STAKE - 5 FT.**	Bfwd	4/30/97	240	EACH	.450	108.00	1.10
				240	EACH		.45000	264.00
							Comment: transfer manual records	
5770	**NURSERY STAKES-30 PC**	Bfwd	4/30/97	9	SET	18.200	163.80	31.45
				9	SET		18.20000	283.05
							Comment: transfer manual records	

Grand totals: Balance entries: 6 Qty counted: 293 Cost: 713.00 Retail: 1,405.55

-- End of report --

Date: 04/30/97 Time: 18:12:43 LYONS–GARTEN LAWN AND GARDEN, INC. Report #0027 Page 0001

Figure 11–7 – INVENTORY COUNT SHEET

Bin location range: "First" to "Last"
Item range: "First" to "Last"
Department: TOOLS Vendor: "All"

Bin	Item–#	Description	Unit / Dept	On–hand	Count
	1105	**DRILL, YANKEE**	EACH TOOLS	0	________
	1100	**LAWN EDGER**	EACH TOOLS	11	________
	2200	**LAWN HAMMER**	EACH TOOLS	10	________
	5770	**NURSERY STAKES–30 PC**	SET TOOLS	9	________
			Total:	30	

4 items printed

–– End of report ––

Date: 04/30/97 Time: 18:12:55 LYONS–GARTEN LAWN AND GARDEN, INC. Report #0028 Page 0001

Figure 11–8 – PHYSICAL INVENTORY TRANSACTION REGISTER

Current period ending date: 4/30/97 Posting date: 4/30/97
Adjustment account: 5020–000

Retail–value = Transaction–qty x List–price
Variance–quantity = Transaction–qty – Qty–on–hand
Variance–inventory–value = New–value – Old–value
Transactions are printed in Location/item description order

Item–number	Description	Type Doc–#	Date	Trans–qty New–qty–OH	Unit	Unit–cost	Total–cost New–avg–cost	List–price Retail–val	–––Variance––– Quantity	 Inv–value
1105	**DRILL, YANKEE**	Cnt	4/30/97	0	EACH	8.720	.00	14.95	0	.00
		Phys–count		0	EACH		8.72000	.00		
							Comment: April physical count			
1100	**LAWN EDGER**	Cnt	4/30/97	10	EACH	13.140	131.40	25.95	1–	13.14–
		Phys–count		10	EACH		13.14000	259.50		
							Comment: April physical count			
2200	**LAWN HAMMER**	Cnt	4/30/97	12	EACH	7.310	87.72	13.95	2	14.62
		Phys–count		12	EACH		7.31000	167.40		
							Comment: April physical count			
5770	**NURSERY STAKES–30 PC**	Cnt	4/30/97	9	SET	18.200	163.80	31.45	0	.00
		Phys–count		9	SET		18.20000	283.05		
							Comment: April physical count			

Location totals:	Count entries:	4	Qty counted:	31	Cost:	382.92	Retail:	709.95
			Variance:	1	Cost:	1.48	Retail:	1.95
Grand totals:	Count entries:	4	Qty counted:	31	Cost:	382.92	Retail:	709.95
			Variance:	1	Cost:	1.48	Retail:	1.95

–– End of report ––

Date: 04/30/97 Time: 18:13:28 LYONS-GARTEN LAWN AND GARDEN, INC. Report #0029 Page 0001

Figure 11-9 - INVENTORY STATUS REPORT

Item # range: "First" to "Last"
Department: "All" Vendor: "All"
Report includes out of stock items

Inventory-value = Qty-on-hand x Average-cost Retail-value = Qty-on-hand x List-price
Out = Out of stock Understocked = Qty-on-hand is below Minimum-qty-on-hand Overstocked = Qyt-on-hand is above Maximum-qty-on-hand

Item-#	Description	Dept Loc	Unit Lst-rcvd	List-prc Lst-sold	Qty-on-hand qty-commit	Qty-on-ord Min-qty-OH	Avg-cost Max-qty-OH	Inv-value	Ret-value	Stat
1091	**HI-PRESSURE HOSE**	PARTS	EACH 4/20/97	18.85 4/27/97	23	27 10	9.720 30	223.56	433.55	
1100	**LAWN EDGER**	TOOLS	EACH 4/20/97	25.95 4/20/97	10	0 5	13.140 15	131.40	259.50	
1105	**DRILL, YANKEE**	TOOLS	EACH 4/20/97	14.95 4/30/97	0	15	8.720	.00	.00	Out
2200	**LAWN HAMMER**	TOOLS	EACH 4/20/97	13.95 4/27/97	12	25 20	7.310 40	87.72	167.40	Undr
5014	**TREE STAKE - 5 FT.**	PARTS	EACH 4/28/97	1.10	240	0 24	.450 240	108.00	264.00	
5770	**NURSERY STAKES-30**	TOOLS	SET 4/20/97	31.45 4/20/97	9	0 5	18.200 12	163.80	283.05	
Totals:					294	67 64	337	714.48	1,407.50	

64 is the minimum stock level - cost of minimum inventory: $410.90 (at avg-cost). Retail-value: $780.90
337 is the maximum stock level - cost of maximum inventory: $1,107.50 (at avg-cost). Retail-value: $2,154.15

1 items are out of stock - cost to replenish to minimum: $0.00 (at last-cost). Retail-value: $0.00
cost to replenish to maximum: $0.00 (at last-cost). Retail-value: $0.00

1 items are understocked - cost to replenish to minimum: $58.48 (at last-cost). Retail-value: $111.60
cost to replenish to maximum: $204.68 (at last-cost). Retail-value: $390.60

0 items are overstocked - value in excess of maximum: $0.00 (at avg-cost). Retail-value: $0.00

4 items are stocked ok - cost to replenish to maximum: $188.34 (at last-cost). Retail-value: $356.05

6 items printed

-- End of report --

Date: 04/30/97 Time: 18:14:16 LYONS-GARTEN LAWN AND GARDEN, INC. Report #0030 Page #0001

Figure 11-10 - INVENTORY VALUATION REPORT

Starting item #: "First"
Ending item #: "Last"
Department: "All"
Vendor: "All"

Retail-value = Qty-on-hand x List-price
Replacement-value = Qty-on-hand x Last-cost
Inventory-value = Qty-on-hand x Average-cost

Item-#	Description	Dept Loc	Stock Unit	Qty-on-hand Qty-avail	List-price Last-cost	Retail-value Replace-value	Average-cost	Inv-value
1091	**HI-PRESSURE HOSE**	PARTS	EACH	23 23	18.85 9.72	433.55 223.56	9.72000	223.56
1100	**LAWN EDGER**	TOOLS	EACH	10 10	25.95 13.14	259.50 131.40	13.14000	131.40
2200	**LAWN HAMMER**	TOOLS	EACH	12 12	13.95 7.31	167.40 87.72	7.31000	87.72
5014	**TREE STAKE - 5 FT.**	PARTS	EACH	240 240	1.10 .45	264.00 108.00	.45000	108.00
5770	**NURSERY STAKES-30**	TOOLS	SET	9 9	31.45 18.20	283.05 163.80	18.20000	163.80

Retail value:	1,407.50
Replacement value:	714.48
Inventory value:	714.48

5 items printed

-- End of report --

Date: 04/30/97 Time: 18:14:43 LYONS–GARTEN LAWN AND GARDEN, INC. Report #0031 Page 0001

Figure 11–11 – INVENTORY ANALYSIS REPORT

Item range: "First" to "Last" **DETAIL BY RANK**

Department: "All"

Vendor: "All"

Ranking is based on sales this period.

Turn rates are based on 30 of 30 days completed for this period and 120 of 365 days completed for this year.

This report includes: All stock levels
All turn rates
All ranks

Dept	Item–Number / Description	Rank / Rank–Val	Qty–on–hnd / This–prd: Qty–sold / This–yr: Qty–sold	Qty–commit / Disc–amt / Disc–amt	Qty–on–ord / Disc–% / Disc–%	Retail–val / Sales / Sales	Profit–val / Profit / Profit	Pft–% / Pft–% / Pft–%	Prds of Supply	Turn Rate
TOOLS	**1105**	1	0	0	15	0	0	.0		
	DRILL, YANKEE	449	30	0	.0	449	193	43.0	.0	.0
			30	0	.0	449	193	43.0	.0	.0
PARTS	**1091**	2	23	0	27	434	210	48.4		
	HI–PRESSURE HOSE	392	21	4	1.0	392	188	48.0	1.1	25.2
			21	4	1.0	392	188	48.0	4.3	6.4
TOOLS	**2200**	3	12	0	25	167	80	47.9		
	LAWN HAMMER	83	14	113	57.9	83	39	47.0	.9	8.4
			6	1	1.1	83	39	47.0	7.9	.9
TOOLS	**5770**	4	9	0	0	283	119	42.0		
	NURSERY STAKES–30 PC	26	1	5	16.1	26	8	30.8	9.0	1.9
			1	5	16.1	26	8	30.8	35.5	.5
TOOLS	**1100**	5	10	0	0	260	128	49.2		
	LAWN EDGER	25	1	1	3.8	25	12	48.0	10.0	2.4
			1	1	3.8	25	12	48.0	39.5	.6
PARTS	**5014**	6	240	0	0	264	156	59.1		
	TREE STAKE – 5 FT.	0	0	0	.0	0	0	.0	.0	.0
			0	0	.0	0	0	.0	.0	.0
Grand totals:			294	0	67	1,408	693	49.2		
			67	123	11.2	975	440	45.1		16.5
			59	11	1.1	975	440	45.1		3.8

Records Read 9

Records Processed 6

Records Printed 6

–– End of report ––

Exercise 12 – PROCESS GENERAL LEDGER ENTRIES; PRINT TRIAL BALANCE & FINANCIAL STATEMENTS

Introduction

Way back, in Exercise 2, you were introduced to the General Ledger (G/L) by way of preparing the Chart of Accounts and adding funds to selected accounts. In subsequent exercises, you were asked to assign dollar totals to G/L account codes and to post these totals. In this exercise, we take a closer look at the General Ledger application.

Figure 12–1 illustrates the flow of information through the general ledger.

Figure 12–1 – GENERAL LEDGER OVERVIEW

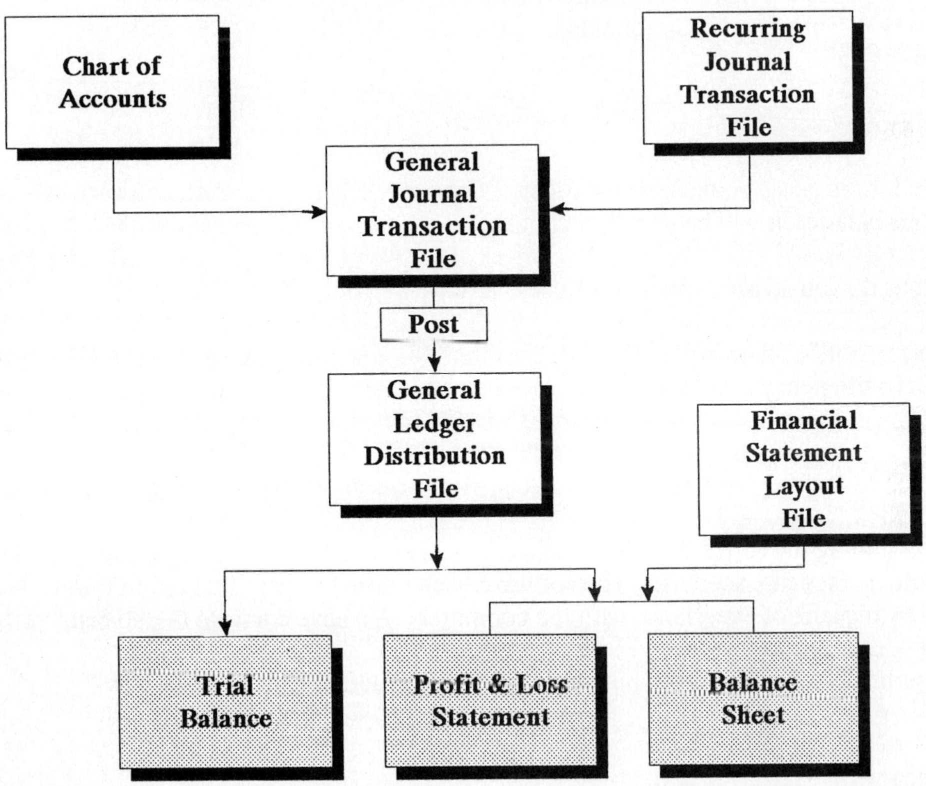

As shown by Figure 12–1, the two initial inputs to processing are the Chart of Accounts and a Recurring Journal Transaction File. These lead to the General Journal Transaction File. When the entries in this file are posted, a new file, the General Ledger Distribution File is the result. Why so many files? The first step in G/L processing, as previous exercises have demonstrated, is to validate a G/L account using the Chart of Accounts. A transaction is blocked from entry into the G/L until a "valid" account code is specified. Once validated, dollar totals are stored in the General Journal Transaction File until the decision is made to "post" these transactions. For example, the General Journal Transaction File might hold transactions for a day, or a week at most, before posting is undertaken. However, once the decision to "post" is made, transactions from the General Journal Transaction File are written to the G/L Distribution File, in Chart of Accounts sequence. Then later, the "distribution file" is used to prepare month–end financial statements (namely, the Trial Balance, the Profit and Loss Statement, and the Balance Sheet). Once posting is complete, the General Journal Transaction File is cleared. This means you CANNOT GO BACK. Once cleared, the General Journal Transaction File is ready to accept new, verified G/L transactions for later posting to the G/L Distribution File.

Objectives

The objectives of this exercise will help you understand the functions important to G/L processing. You are asked to:

- ➠ Process regular and recurring G/L transactions
- ➠ Print the trial balance
- ➠ Modify financial statement layouts
- ➠ Print financial statements

Case Study

"Well, here goes," remarks Jen Ledger. "Time to really test the PAS software and our work thus far. If our totals balance, it will be some small miracle."

"What do you mean?" questions Rose. "Are we in trouble?"

"I hope not!" exclaims Jen. "It's just that the G/L is so unforgiving. Unless all debits and credits balance ... to the penny ... we will be out–of–balance. And if assets fail to equal our liabilities plus equity, we are really in for it. Dandy will have fits if we give him an inaccurate financial accounting of the firm."

Rose interrupts. "So might I," she states. "Are you so positive we will be out–of–balance?"

Jen, reading the concern on Rose's face, quickly indicates: "I'm sorry Rose. You know I always imagine the worst–case scenario. The software hasn't failed us yet. It shouldn't now. However, I'm still bothered by my lack of experience with the computer. We have come so far, so fast."

"I quite agree," adds Rose, "but we're almost there, Jen. Don't give in now."

Set Transaction Date

☐ Before you start this exercise, set today's date at 4/30/97 using the MS–DOS 'DATE' command.

Review Functions in General Ledger

☐ 1. Type 6 (General Ledger) from the Main Menu, and press ENTER.

```
RealWorld Practical Accounting System              L-G LAWN AND GARDEN
Version 1.0

                Please select
                  1. Sales Invoicing
                  2. Inventory Management
                  3. Accounts Receivable
                  4. Accounts Payable
                  5. Payroll
                  6. General Ledger
                  7. Check Reconciliation
                  8. Setup Functions

Press F10 for help at any time
```

☐ 2. Review the General Ledger Reference Material in the back of this text to familiarize yourself with the functions, displayed below, that are available in the General Ledger portion of PAS.

```
RealWorld Practical Accounting System              L-G LAWN AND GARDEN
General Ledger

                Please select
                  1. Maintain chart of accounts
                  2. Process general journal
                  3. View G/L account activity
                  4. Print trial balance
                  5. Print financial statements
                  6. Compress G/L transactions
                  7. Calculate a loan payment
                  8. Close accounting year
```

☐ 3. Type 1 (Maintain Chart of Accounts) from the General Ledger menu, and press ENTER. Note that the G/L Maintain Chart of Accounts function, shown below, has the same options as those already seen in the Setup Functions' Maintain Chart of Accounts (ref. exercise 2).

```
Maintain chart of accounts                         L-G LAWN AND GARDEN

                Please select
                  1. Add accounts
                  2. Change accounts
                  3. Delete accounts
                  4. Print out accounts
```

☐ 4. Press TAB or END to return to the General Ledger menu.

Process General Journal Entries

The Process General Journal function is used to add, change, inquire into, delete and print an edit list of general journal transactions. Once you have verified them as correct, you can post them to the General Ledger Distribution file.

This function handles two types of general journal transactions ... regular and recurring.

"Regular" transactions become effective at once. This is the usual kind of transaction.

"Recurring" transactions occur over and over again. For example, monthly depreciation entries are recurring general journal transactions. You enter this kind of transaction once and store it on the Recurring Journal Transaction File. You then periodically "activate" it. This causes a new regular transaction to be created, based on the information stored in the recurring one.

☐ 5. Type 2 (Process General Journal) from the General Ledger menu, and press ENTER.

☐ 6. If field #6 (Process Recurring Transactions) is not displayed on the Process General Journal Menu shown below, press F1. The F1 key acts as a toggle to display/hide this menu choice.

```
Process general journal                         L-G LAWN AND GARDEN

                  Please select
                      1. Add transactions
                      2. Change transactions
                      3. Delete transactions
                      4. Print transaction edit list
                      5. Post transactions
                      6. Process recurring transactions
```

☐ 7. Type 1 (Add Transactions) from the Process General Journal menu, and press ENTER. The twelve "accounting periods" for the year 1997 are displayed, as well as the "current period", 4/01/97 to 4/30/97.

When you select "Add Transactions", you have the option of changing the current period. You would change the period only if the current period shown on the screen were incorrect, or if you needed to add many transactions for a previous or future period, and did not want to be continually warned that the date was out of the current period.

☐ 8. Answer N at "Any change to current period?".

On the following screen (next page), the "Trans date" you enter will be checked against the "current period". If you make a journal entry that does not fall within the current period, you will see the message "Date is out of the current period". Check your entry to be sure it is dated correctly.

NOTE: In the "Change Transactions" mode, neither the account number nor the transaction date can be changed. If the account number or date of a previously–entered transaction needs to be changed, you must delete the entire transaction, and then enter a new transaction.

```
Process general journal                              L-G LAWN AND GARDEN
Add transactions                          Current period: 4/01/97 to 4/30/97

            1. Account #
            2. Trans date
            3. Debit amount                   Credit amount
            4. Reference

               Running balance:          .00

Enter account #, or press F1 for next account
```

Lyons–Garten purchased a truck on 4/14/97 for $35,000. It was paid for with a bank note from Nice Valley National Bank. Enter the following two transactions using the above Add Transactions screen.

☐ 9. Account # 1620–000 Automobiles and trucks
Trans date 41497
DEBIT amount 35000
Reference 1997 delivery truck

Press ENTER at "Field number to change?".

☐ 10. Account # 2520–000 Notes and loans payable
Trans date 41497
CREDIT amount 35000
Reference 1997 delivery truck

Press ENTER at "Field number to change?".

☐ 11. Press TAB or END at the Add Transactions menu to return to the Process General Journal menu.

☐ 12. Type 4 (Print Transaction Edit List) from the Process General Journal menu, and press ENTER. DISPLAY the General Journal Transaction Edit List on your screen.

☐ 13. Review the edit list and make corrections, if necessary, under menu selection "Change Transactions". If no corrections are necessary, press ENTER to continue.

☐ 14. Type 5 (Post Transactions) from the Process General Journal menu, and press ENTER.

☐ 15. Type Y at "Are general journal transactions OK to post?" and press ENTER. The General Journal Transaction Register (see Figure 12–2) will be printed.

☐ 16. Press TAB or END to return to the General Ledger menu.

View G/L Account Activity

☐ 17. Type 3 (View G/L Account Activity) from the General Ledger menu, and press ENTER.

```
View G/L account activity                              L-G LAWN AND GARDEN
                                               Cur prd: 4/01/97 to 4/30/97

                    Please enter:
                        1. Account #
                        2. Starting date
                        3. Ending date

Enter account #, or press F1 for next account
```

☐ 18. View your activity on account #'s 1620 and 2520 for the period 040197 to 043097 by making the appropriate entries to the above screen. Press ENTER at "Field number to change?" and press END to return to the View G/L Account Activity menu.

The following chart summarizes the possible journal codes that can appear on each different transaction. For example, "GJ039" would represent a General Journal transaction, report number 39.

PACKAGE	ENTRY SOURCE	CODE
General Ledger	General Journal	GJ
Accounts Receivable	Sales Register Cash Receipts Register	SL CR
Accounts Payable	Bills Payable Register Disbursements Register	BP DB
Payroll	Payroll Register	PR
Check Reconciliation	Checking Account Adjustment Register	CA
Sales/Invoicing	Services/Non-inventory Item Register	SV

☐ 19. Repeat Step 18 to re-view the transaction for account #1620. Notice the Source code that shows "GJxxxx" with the report number previously printed on the General Journal Transaction Register.

☐ 20. View your full month's activity on account #1010 Cash #1 – Payables. You will use this information to answer one of the questions at the end of this exercise. (See Figure 12-5 for a printed copy.)

☐ 21. Press TAB or END at the View G/L Account Activity menu to return to the General Ledger menu.

Process Recurring Transactions

You can set up journal entries for transactions that occur on a regular basis. Recurring transactions for General Ledger operate on the same principle as recurring bills in A/P and recurring sales in A/R.

☐ 22. Type 2 (Process General Journal) from the General Ledger menu, and press ENTER.

☐ 23. If selection #6 in the Process General Journal menu is not showing, press F1 to make it appear.

☐ 24. Type 6 (Process Recurring Transactions) from the Process General Journal menu, and press ENTER.

```
Process general journal                                   L-G LAWN AND GARDEN
Process recurring transactions

                     Please select
                        1. Add recurring transactions
                        2. Change recurring transactions
                        3. Delete recurring transactions
                        4. Print recurring transaction list
                        5. Activate recurring transactions
```

☐ 25. Type 1 (Add Recurring Transactions) from the Process Recurring Transactions menu, and press ENTER.

```
Process general journal                                   L-G LAWN AND GARDEN
Add recurring transactions

                  1. Account #
                  2. Frequency                    Next date
                  3. Debit amount                 Credit amount
                  4. Reference

Enter account #, or press F1 for next account
```

Using the Add Recurring Transactions screen shown above, set up the following recurring transaction for the depreciation of Lyons–Garten's new truck.

☐ 26. Account # 1720–000 Accum depr – auto & truck
Frequency M (monthly)
Next date 43097
CREDIT amount 400 (first press ENTER to move to the credit field)
Reference truck depreciation

Press ENTER at "Field number to change?".

☐ 27. Account # 6080–000 Depreciation
Frequency M (monthly)
Next date 43097
DEBIT amount 400
Reference truck depreciation

Press ENTER at "Field number to change?".

☐ 28. Press TAB or END at the Add Recurring Transactions menu to return to the Process Recurring Transactions menu.

☐ 29. Type 5 (Activate Recurring Transactions) from the Process Recurring Transactions menu, and press ENTER.

☐ 30. Enter a cut–off date of 50197.

☐ 31. Answer N at "Any change?".

☐ 32. Press F1 to bring up the first depreciation transaction, shown below.

```
Process general journal                                L–G LAWN AND GARDEN
Activate recurring transactions              Current period: 4/01/97 to 4/30/97

        1. Account #        1720–000  Accum depr – auto & truck
        2. Frequency        M                 Next date        4/30/97
        3. Debit amount                       Credit amount   400.00
        4. Reference        truck depreciation

        Running balance:              .00

Answer Y or N, or press F1 for next transaction
Activate this transaction?
```

☐ 33. Answer Y at "Activate this transaction?".

☐ 34. Enter 43097 as the transaction date. Note that the "Next date" will be incremented to the same day of the next month, given a frequency of monthly.

☐ 35. Press ENTER at Next Date.

☐ 36. Press ENTER at "Field number to change?".

☐ 37. Press F1 to bring up the second depreciation transaction (account #6080), and repeat Steps 33–36 for this transaction.

☐ 38. Press TAB or END twice to return to the Process General Journal menu.

☐ 39. Type 4 (Print Transaction Edit List) from the Process General Journal menu and press ENTER. DISPLAY the General Journal Transaction Edit List on your screen. Press ENTER to continue.

☐ 40. If the edit is correct, type 5 (Post Transactions) from the Process General Journal menu, and press ENTER.

☐ 41. Type Y at "Are general journal transactions OK to post?" and press ENTER. The General Journal Transaction Register (see Figure 12–3) will be printed.

☐ 42. Press TAB or END to return to the General Ledger menu.

Print Trial Balance

This report shows the balance of each selected account. Two formats of the report are available: detail and summary. The "detailed" report shows all transactions for each account printed. The "summary" report shows the following for each account:

- Beginning balance
- Total debits and credits
- Net change for the period
- Ending balance

You can run a trial balance at any time. However, you will usually run it after all transactions have been entered and posted for a specified period.

☐ 43. Type 4 (Print Trial Balance) from the General Ledger menu, and press ENTER.

☐ 44. Press F1 to indicate your desire to print all of the accounts ("First" through the "Last"). Press ENTER to print account activity between the dates 4/01/97 and 4/30/97. Do NOT show the detail at this time. Press F1 to show "All" profit centers. Your screen should appear as follows:

```
Print trial balance                                  L-G LAWN AND GARDEN
                                          Current period: 4/01/97 to 4/30/97

                    Please enter:
                        1. Starting account        "First"
                        2. Ending account          "Last"
                        3. Starting date           4/01/97
                        4. Ending date             4/30/97
                        5. Show detail?            N
                        6. Profit center           "All"

Field number to change?
```

☐ 45. Press ENTER at "Field number to change?" and answer N at "Display this report?". The General Ledger Trial Balance report (see Figure 12–4) will be printed.

☐ 46. Print the Trial Balance report again, but only for account #1010 (Starting and Ending account). Show detail for the same time period and all profit centers as in the previous step. (See Figure 12–5 for the resulting report.) Compare the totals for account #1010 in this detail report to those in the previous summary report.

☐ 47. Press TAB or END at the Print Trial Balance menu to return to the General Ledger menu.

The same Trial Balancc detail report for a single account # can also be viewed by doing the following:

☐ 48. Type 3 (View G/L Account Activity) from the General Ledger menu, and press ENTER.

☐ 49. Enter the appropriate information to view the transactions posted in the month of April, 1997, for account # 1010.

☐ 50. Press ENTER at "Field number to change?" to view the report. Compare the contents of the screen with the printed detail report for account #1010 (see Figure 12–5).

☐ 51. Press TAB or END twice to return to the General Ledger menu.

Modify Financial Statement Layouts

Two standard types of financial statements can be produced by PAS. These are:

- The Income Statement (showing total revenue and expenses).
- The Balance Sheet (showing assets, liabilities and owner's equity).

PAS provides some flexibility in the layout of these statements. A layout number controls what information is printed on a financial statement, and how it is arranged.

☐ 52. Type 5 (Print Financial Statements) from the General Ledger menu, and press ENTER.

```
Print financial statements                              L-G LAWN AND GARDEN

                       Please select
                          1. Financial statement layout
                          2. Print statements
```

☐ 53. Type 1 (Financial Statement Layout) from the Print Financial Statements menu, and press ENTER.

```
Financial statement layout                              L-G LAWN AND GARDEN

                       Please select
                          1. Add layouts
                          2. Change layouts
                          3. Delete layouts
                          4. Print layouts
                          5. Test layouts
```

☐ 54. Type 2 (Change Layouts) from the Financial Statement Layout menu, and press ENTER.

☐ 55. Select Layout # 2 (Income Statement). Your screen should appear as shown on the next page.

Financial statement layout		L–G LAWN AND GARDEN
Change layouts		
	1. Layout #	2
	2. Type of statement	P
	3. Description	Income Statement (P & L)
		--Retailer--

☐ 56. Press ENTER at "Field number to change?".

☐ 57. Press F2; then enter "120" and press ENTER to go to sequence line #120.

☐ 58. Press F1 several times to view the remaining pages of the Income Statement layout.

☐ 59. Press F2; then enter "10" and press ENTER to return to the first page.

☐ 60. Type 10 and press ENTER to prepare for entering your company's name.

☐ 61. Answer Y at "Any change?".

☐ 62. Type "TXT" for the function code and press ENTER. Type "LYONS–GARTEN LAWN AND GARDEN, INC." and press ENTER.

☐ 63. Answer N at "Any change?".

> **NOTE:** You may want to repeat Steps 60–63 to center the company name. This can be done by skipping 8 spaces with the space bar before entering your company name.

You are required to make several changes to the Income Statement to make the accounts consistent with the Lyons–Garten chart of accounts. Do the following for the sequence numbers shown below.

☐ 64. First type the "sequence #" and answer Y (yes) when asked if you want to make a change. Then type the new account number and press ENTER. Third, type P (print) at "Prt/Accum" and press ENTER. Finally, press ENTER (N) when asked "Any change?". When making these changes, press F1 as needed to display the affected statement page on the screen.

Seq #	Function code (account)	Prt/Accum
50	4000	P
52	4010	P
55	4020	P
60	4030	P

After making the above changes, your screen should appear as shown on the following page.

```
Financial statement layout                              L-G LAWN AND GARDEN
Change layouts
Layout #: 2  Income Statement  (P & L)
                    --Retailer--
Seq      Function
 #         code

 0010    TXT          LYONS-GARTEN LAWN AND GARDEN, INC.
 0020    TXT                      Income Statement
 0030    BL
 0040    DAT
 0041    TXT          SALES
 0042    BL
 0045    SRB
 0050    4000-000   Sales - Landscape/Consult      Prt/Accum    P
 0052    4010-000   Sales - Lawn Installation      Prt/Accum    P
 0055    4020-000   Sales - Lawn and Garden        Prt/Accum    P
 0060    4030-000   Sales - Nursery                Prt/Accum    P
 0070    BL

Press F1 for next page or F2 + seq # to see a page from a specific position
```

☐ 65. Press F1 twice to advance two pages, and repeat step 64 to make the following changes.

Seq #	Function code (account)	Prt/Accum
250	5005	P
252	5010	P
255	5000	P
257	5015	P
258	BL (blank line)	

A few changes are also required to bring the Balance Sheet layout in line with the Lyons–Garten chart of accounts.

☐ 66. Press TAB or END to return to the Change Layouts menu.

☐ 67. Select Layout #1 (Balance Sheet).

☐ 68. Press ENTER at "Field number to change?".

☐ 69. Repeat steps 60–63 to enter Lyons–Garten's company name on the Balance Sheet.

☐ 70. Make the following additional changes to the Balance Sheet sequence #s shown below.

Seq #	Function code (account)	Prt/Accum	Print column
90	1010 (title change)	P	1
120	1020 (title change)	P	1
130	(press ENTER to delete this line)		

☐ 71. Press TAB or END twice to return to the Financial Statement Layout menu.

☐ 72. Type 1 (Add Layouts) from the Financial Statement Layout menu, and press ENTER.

You will not be asked to create a new, completely different, statement layout in this exercise. However, do the following to familiarize yourself with the flexibility of this important PAS function.

☐ 73. Enter the following information into the Add Layouts menu.

Layout #	**5**
Type of statement	**P**
Description	**Income Schedule**

Press ENTER at "Field number to change?".

☐ 74. Review the Layout Function Codes listed at the bottom of the screen by pressing F10 for Help, and scanning their descriptions, or by referring to the Reference Material in the back of this text. Particularly note the description of the SUBn subtotals function.

☐ 75. Press TAB or END until the Print Financial Statements menu appears.

Print Financial Statements

☐ 76. Type 2 (Print Statements) from the Print Financial Statements menu, and press ENTER.

☐ 77. Enter the information from the following two screens to print both the **Balance Sheet** (see Figure 12–6) and **Income Statement** statement (see Figure 12–7).

```
Print statements                                   L-G LAWN AND GARDEN
                                       Current period: 4/01/97 to 4/30/97
          Please enter:
             1. Layout number             1  Sample Balance Sheet
                                                  --Retailer--
             2. Show ratios ?             N
             3. Starting period date      "Earliest"
             4. Ending period date        4/30/97
             5. Profit center             "All" (press F1)
             6. Number of copies          1

Field number to change?    (press ENTER)
```

```
Print statements                                      L-G LAWN AND GARDEN
                                            Current period: 4/01/97 to 4/30/97
          Please enter:
             1. Layout number             2   Income Statement (P & L)
                                                  --Retailer--
             2. Show ratios ?             Y
             3. Starting period date      4/01/97
             4. Ending period date        4/30/97
             5. Profit center             "All"  (press F1)
             6. Number of copies          1

Field number to change?     (press ENTER)
```

☐ 78. This completes the exercise. Press TAB or END as needed to exit PAS.

QUESTIONS ABOUT THE SOFTWARE

1. In reviewing account 1010, what entry source codes were provided by the software? What do these codes signify? How do they help in checking the accuracy of the dollar totals listed?

2. Why must a recurring transaction be activated?

3. In the financial statement layout, what does the code SUBn designate? Where should it be used in the layout of a statement?

4. Examine the General Ledger Trial Balance. How can you determine if you are in–balance or out–of–balance?

5. Compare both the brief and complete general ledger reports for account 1010. Why is it important for the software to produce both types of reports for an account?

6. A loss of $6,828.74 was reported for the period 4/1/97 to 4/30/97. How is this loss reflected on the balance sheet?

7. The balance sheet reveals a number of employee payroll expenses such as Fed Income Tax Withheld, Emp Medicare Payable, and so forth. When and how are these expenses removed from the balance sheet?

MANAGEMENT ISSUES

8. Is it surprising that Lyons–Garten's lawn and garden business shows a year–to–date loss? What conclusions might Dan and Rose draw from this loss, and how did they arrive at their conclusions?

9. Some G/L accounts have no activity (no transactions are reported for an account). Is it a wise practice to include these accounts on the chart of accounts when dollar transactions are only expected in some future period?

10. Of what value to upper–level managers is the balance sheet? The income statement?

11. Would top managers ever be interested in examining a copy of the General Ledger Trial Balance? Explain your position.

THINGS TO DO

12. Select View G/L Account Activity and enter account 1050 (Petty cash). Use a starting date of 40197 and an ending date of 43097.

    Explain what you observe.
    Why does the $28.17 amount appear on the balance sheet?

13. Suppose you want to print a balance sheet for the periods 4/01/97 to 4/30/97. Return to Print Financial Statements and select layout #1. Use an ending date of 43097 and print 1 copy. When asked "Field number to change?", type 3 with the intention of entering 40197 in the Starting Period Date field.

    What happens?
    Explain why the software reacted this way.

14. Examine the Lyons–Garten Balance Sheet.

    Using PAS, describe the steps you would take to verify that the Accounts Payable–Trade dollar total is accurate.

15. Examine the Lyons–Garten Income Statement. Using PAS (and a calculator),

    How would you verify that the Total Product Sales amount is correct?
    That the Total Cost of Goods Sold amount is correct?

Date: 04/30/97 LYONS–GARTEN LAWN AND GARDEN, INC. #0119 Page 0001

Figure 12–2 – GENERAL JOURNAL TRANSACTION REGISTER

Period: 04/01/97 to 04/30/97

Account: 1620–000 Automobiles and trucks

Trans–date	Debit–amt	Credit–amt	Reference
04/14/97	35,000.00		1997 delivery truck

Account: 2520–000 Notes and loans payable

Trans–date	Debit–amt	Credit–amt	Reference
04/14/97		35,000.00	1997 delivery truck

Grand totals:	35,000.00	35,000.00	2 Transactions

–– End of report ––

Date: 04/30/97 LYONS–GARTEN LAWN AND GARDEN, INC. #0120 Page 0001

Figure 12–3 – GENERAL JOURNAL TRANSACTION REGISTER

Period: 04/01/97 to 04/30/97

Account: 1720–000 Accum depr – auto & truck

Trans–date	Debit–amt	Credit–amt	Reference
04/30/97		400.00	truck depreciation

Account: 6080–000 Depreciation

Trans–date	Debit–amt	Credit–amt	Reference
04/30/97	400.00		truck depreciation

Grand totals:	400.00	400.00	2 Transactions

–– End of report ––

Date: 04/30/97 LYONS–GARTEN LAWN AND GARDEN, INC. #0121 Page 0001

Figure 12–4 – GENERAL LEDGER TRIAL BALANCE

Starting account #: "First" Starting date: 04/01/97
Ending account #: "Last" Ending date: 04/30/97

Acct–#	Description / Begin–balance	Total–DR	Total–CR	Net–change	End–balance
1010–000	Cash #1 – Payables				
	.00	51,269.59	36,507.12	14,762.47	14,762.47
1020–000	Cash #2 – Payroll				
	.00	10,000.00	4,472.46	5,527.54	5,527.54
1050–000	Petty cash				
	28.17	.00	.00	.00	28.17
1100–000	Accts Receivable – Trade				
	406.81	1,026.41	732.33	294.08	700.89
1400–000	Inventory				
	2,826.80	1,028.03	607.41	420.62	3,247.42
1600–000	Furniture and fixtures				
	3,841.15	.00	.00	.00	3,841.15
1610–000	Office equipment				
	2,817.14	.00	.00	.00	2,817.14
1620–000	Automobiles and trucks				
	9,851.00	35,000.00	.00	35,000.00	44,851.00
1640–000	Leasehold improvements				
	2,180.45	.00	.00	.00	2,180.45
1700–000	Accum depr – furn & fixt				
	481.12CR	.00	.00	.00	481.12CR
1710–000	Accum depr – office equip				
	418.73CR	.00	.00	.00	418.73CR

Date: 04/30/97 LYONS-GARTEN LAWN AND GARDEN, INC. #0121 Page 0002

Figure 12-4 - GENERAL LEDGER TRIAL BALANCE

Acct-#	Description Begin-balance	Total-DR	Total-CR	Net-change	End-balance
1720-000	Accum depr - auto & truck 4,216.91CR	.00	400.00	400.00CR	4,616.91CR
1740-000	Accum depr - lease improv 281.00CR	.00	.00	.00	281.00CR
1810-000	Investments 150.00	.00	.00	.00	150.00
2100-000	Accounts Payable - Trade 2,177.84CR	1,507.12	1,252.00	255.12	1,922.72CR
2110-000	Uninvoiced receivings 408.76CR	.00	953.45	953.45CR	1,362.21CR
2310-000	Fed income tax withheld .00	.00	673.94	673.94CR	673.94CR
2330-000	Emp Social Sec Payable .00	.00	352.96	352.96CR	352.96CR
2335-000	Emp Medicare Payable .00	.00	82.55	82.55CR	82.55CR
2340-000	Empr Social Sec Payable .00	.00	352.96	352.96CR	352.96CR
2345-000	Empr Medicare Payable .00	.00	82.55	82.55CR	82.55CR
2350-000	State income tax withheld .00	.00	66.86	66.86CR	66.86CR
2360-000	Other state tax withheld .00	.00	17.23	17.23CR	17.23CR

Date: 04/30/97 LYONS-GARTEN LAWN AND GARDEN, INC. #0121 Page 0003

Figure 12-4 – GENERAL LEDGER TRIAL BALANCE

Acct-#	Description				
	Begin-balance	Total-DR	Total-CR	Net-change	End-balance
2390-000	Charity contrib withheld				
	.00	.00	27.00	27.00CR	27.00CR
2430-000	Accrued state sales tax				
	16.01CR	.00	.00	.00	16.01CR
2440-000	Accrued local sales tax				
	24.67CR	.00	7.68	7.68CR	32.35CR
2450-000	Accrued fed unemp tax				
	.00	.00	45.55	45.55CR	45.55CR
2460-000	Accrued state unemp tax				
	.00	.00	25.84	25.84CR	25.84CR
2520-000	Notes and loans payable				
	.00	.00	35,000.00	35,000.00CR	35,000.00CR
2530-000	Long term debt				
	.00	.00	25,000.00	25,000.00CR	25,000.00CR
3000-000	Common stock				
	1,000.00CR	.00	.00	.00	1,000.00CR
3300-000	Retained earnings				
	19,289.50CR	.00	.00	.00	19,289.50CR
4000-000	Sales-Landscape/Consult				
	.00	.00	391.96	391.96CR	391.96CR
4010-000	Sales-Lawn Installation				
	672.45CR	.00	697.07	697.07CR	1,369.52CR
4020-000	Sales-Lawn and Garden				
	.00	48.99	398.40	349.41CR	349.41CR

Date: 04/30/97 LYONS–GARTEN LAWN AND GARDEN, INC. #0121 Page 0004

Figure 12–4 – GENERAL LEDGER TRIAL BALANCE

Acct–#	Description / Begin–balance	Total–DR	Total–CR	Net–change	End–balance
4030–000	Sales–Nursery .00	.00	112.23	112.23CR	112.23CR
4520–000	Sales retrns & allowances .00	.00	73.10	73.10CR	73.10CR
4920–000	Freight charges .00	.00	5.32	5.32CR	5.32CR
5000–000	COGS – Lawn and Garden .00	268.13	.00	268.13	268.13
5005–000	COGS – Landscape/Consult .00	204.12	.00	204.12	204.12
5010–000	COGS – Lawn Installation 396.07	116.96	20.00	96.96	493.03
5015–000	COGS – Nursery .00	38.20	.00	38.20	38.20
5020–000	Inventory adjustments .00	.00	1.48	1.48CR	1.48CR
6080–000	Depreciation .00	400.00	.00	400.00	400.00
6150–000	Office expense .00	102.00	.00	102.00	102.00
6160–000	Rents & utilities 4,600.00	1,150.00	.00	1,150.00	5,750.00
6180–000	Salaries – administrative .00	3,417.00	.00	3,417.00	3,417.00

Date: 04/30/97 LYONS–GARTEN LAWN AND GARDEN, INC. #0121 Page 0005

Figure 12–4 – GENERAL LEDGER TRIAL BALANCE

Acct–#	Description				
	Begin–balance	Total–DR	Total–CR	Net–change	End–balance
6190–000	Salaries – floor sales				
	.00	2,276.00	.00	2,276.00	2,276.00
6230–000	Supplies				
	292.72	.00	.00	.00	292.72
6250–000	Taxes – payroll				
	.00	506.90	.00	506.90	506.90
6270–000	Telephone				
	1,596.68	.00	.00	.00	1,596.68
9999–000	Transfer/suspense Account				
	.00	10,000.00	10,000.00	.00	.00
Grand totals:					
	.00	118,359.45	118,359.45	.00	.00

–– End of report ––

Date: 04/30/97 LYONS–GARTEN LAWN AND GARDEN, INC. #0122 Page 0001

Figure 12–5 – GENERAL LEDGER TRIAL BALANCE

Starting account #: 1010–000 Starting date: 04/01/97
Ending account #: 1010–000 Ending date: 04/30/97

Profit center: "All"

Acct–#	Description				
	Begin–balance	Total–DR	Total–CR	Net–change	End–balance
1010–000	Cash #1 – Payables				
	.00	51,269.59	36,507.12	14,762.47	14,762.47

Dist–date	Source	DR–amount	CR–amount	Reference
04/02/97	CA0074	25,000.00		Set up cash balance
04/02/97	CA0074		25,000.00	Set up cash balance
04/02/97	GJ0073	25,000.00		Set up cash balance
04/20/97	CR0079	10.00		21st Century Construction
04/27/97	CR0086	25.00		21st Century Construction
04/27/97	CR0086	100.00		Baker, Richard C.
04/27/97	CR0086	50.00		Neptune Underwater Supply
04/27/97	CR0086	586.25		MOUNTAIN GARDEN SUPPLY
04/27/97	CR0086	55.00		MOUNTAIN GARDEN SUPPLY
04/27/97	CR0086	400.00		MOUNTAIN GARDEN SUPPLY
04/27/97	CR0086	43.34		Holcomb Industrial Supply
04/29/97	DB0091		1,150.00	Jones Property Management
04/29/97	DB0091		357.12	South–Western Bell
04/30/97	DB0100		10,000.00	*Cash transfer

Totals: *** Totals do not include all accounts ***

Begin–balance	Total–DR	Total–CR	Net–change	End–balance
.00	51,269.59	36,507.12	14,762.47	14,762.47

–– End of report ––

LYONS–GARTEN LAWN AND GARDEN, INC.

Figure 12–6 – BALANCE SHEET

As of 04/30/97

ASSETS				
CURRENT ASSETS				
Cash #1 – Payables	$	14,762.47		
Cash #2 – Payroll		5,527.54		
Petty cash		28.17		
Cash			$	20,318.18
Accts Receivable – Trade	$	700.89		
Inventory		3,247.42		

TOTAL CURRENT ASSETS			$	24,266.49
PROPERTY AND EQUIPMENT				
Furniture and fixtures	$	3,841.15		
Office equipment		2,817.14		
Automobiles and trucks		44,851.00		
Leasehold improvements		2,180.45		
Total property and equipment			$	53,689.74
Accum depr – furn & fixt	$	(481.12)		
Accum depr – office equip		(418.73)		
Accum depr – auto & truck		(4,616.91)		
Accum depr – lease improv		(281.00)		
Total accum depreciation			$	(5,797.76)

NET FIXED ASSETS			$	47,891.98
OTHER ASSETS				
Investments		150.00		

TOTAL OTHER ASSETS			$	150.00
TOTAL ASSETS			$	72,308.47
				===========

LIABILITIES AND STOCKHOLDERS' EQUITY

CURRENT LIABILITIES

Accounts Payable – Trade	$ 1,922.72		
Uninvoiced receivings	1,362.21		
Fed income tax withheld	673.94		
Emp Social Sec Payable	352.96		
Emp Medicare Payable	82.55		
Empr Social Sec Payable	352.96		
Empr Medicare Payable	82.55		
Accrued fed unemp tax	45.55		
State income tax withheld	66.86		
Other state tax withheld	17.23		
Accrued state unemp tax	25.84		
Other withholding	27.00		
Accrued state sales tax	16.01		
Accrued local sales tax	32.35		
Notes and loans payable	35,000.00		

TOTAL CURRENT LIABILITIES		$	40,060.73
LONG TERM DEBT			25,000.00

TOTAL LIABILITIES		$	65,060.73
STOCKHOLDERS' EQUITY			
Common stock	$ 1,000.00		
Retained earnings	19,289.50		
Current year income	(13,041.76)		

TOTAL STOCKHOLDERS' EQUITY		$	7,247.74

TOTAL LIAB AND EQUITY		$	72,308.47
			===========

LYONS-GARTEN LAWN AND GARDEN, INC.

Figure 12-7 – INCOME STATEMENT

For the period: 04/01/97 to 04/30/97

		Current-period Amount	Ratio		Year-to-date Amount	Ratio
SALES						
Sales – Landscape/Consult	$	391.96	24.06	$	391.96	17.03
Sales – Lawn Installation		697.07	42.79		1,369.52	59.50
Sales – Lawn and Garden		349.41	21.45		349.41	15.18
Sales – Nursery		112.23	6.89		112.23	4.88
Total product sales	$	1,550.67	95.19	$	2,223.12	96.59
Sales retrns & allowances	$	73.10	4.49	$	73.10	3.18
Freight charges		5.32	.33		5.32	.23
Total misc & other sales	$	78.42	4.81	$	78.42	3.41
		========			========	
TOTAL SALES	$	1,629.09	100.00	$	2,301.54	100.00
COST OF GOODS SOLD						
COGS – Landscape/Consult	$	204.12	12.53	$	204.12	8.87
COGS – Lawn Installation		96.96	5.95		493.03	21.42
COGS – Lawn and Garden		268.13	16.46		268.13	11.65
COGS – Nursery		38.20	2.34		38.20	1.66
Inventory adjustments		(1.48)	.09-		(1.48)	.06-
		========			========	
TOTAL COST OF GOODS SOLD	$	605.93	37.19	$	1,002.00	43.54
GROSS PROFIT ON SALES	$	1,023.16	62.81	$	1,299.54	56.46
OPERATING EXPENSES						
Depreciation	$	400.00	24.55	$	400.00	17.38
Office expense		102.00	6.26		102.00	4.43
Rents & utilities		1,150.00	70.59		5,750.00	249.83
Salaries – administrative		3,417.00	209.75		3,417.00	148.47
Salaries – floor sales		2,276.00	139.71		2,276.00	98.89
Supplies		.00	.00		292.72	12.72
Taxes – payroll		506.90	31.12		506.90	22.02
Telephone		.00	.00		1,596.68	69.37
		========			========	
TOTAL OPERATING EXPENSES	$	7,851.90	481.98	$	14,341.30	623.12

NON-OPERATING INCOME AND EXPENSES

		--------			--------	
Other income	$	.00	.00	$	.00	.00
		========			========	
NET INCOME BEFORE TAXES	$	(6,828.74)	419.18-	$	(13,041.76)	566.65-
		--------			--------	
Federal & state income tax	$	.00	.00	$	.00	.00
NET INCOME	$	(6,828.74)	419.18-	$	(13,041.76)	566.65-
		========			========	

Exercise 13 – SUMMARIZE SALES TAX COLLECTIONS USING A LOTUS 1–2–3 SPREADSHEET

Introduction

Often there are times when the user of an online accounting information system has a need to display a selection of data that is unique to their business and/or their colleagues' interests. In satisfying these information needs, the user should not be encumbered by the limited displays and formats that are built into the accounting system they are using.

In recognition of this desired flexibility, RealWorld has incorporated in PAS the ability to download data from one or more of its files in a format that is readily useable by the popular spreadsheet programs such as Lotus 1–2–3. PAS provides this capability through its File Utilities program. Using the PAS File Utilities program, you can export data files in ASCII format for later importing into Lotus 1–2–3.

ASCII stands for American Standard Code for Information Interchange. When you export a file, you are copying records from a data file to an "export" file in ASCII format. Lotus 1–2–3 can "import" ASCII–formatted data files. These data can then be manipulated and displayed in various spreadsheets.

Objectives

The objectives of this exercise are to acquaint you with the interface between Lotus 1–2–3 and PAS, and to provide an opportunity for you to practice building spreadsheets from raw, unformatted data.

This exercise asks you to work through all of the steps necessary to transfer data from PAS files into Lotus 1–2–3, and prepare an informative spreadsheet of the data. You are asked to:

- ➡ Export sales tax data from PAS
- ➡ Import sales tax data into Lotus 1–2–3
- ➡ Modify the sales tax data in preparation for spreadsheet development
- ➡ Develop a Lotus 1–2–3 spreadsheet

Case Study

Jen Ledger is contemplating the possibility of saving some of the accounting data captured each month for use in special types of management reports. Her thoughts run as follow:

"One of the problems with accounting systems is that valuable managerial information is often lost when we undertake month–end updates. What we need to be able to do is to export data from the PAS accounting system, and import it to another software package. In this way we can eliminate duplication of data entry and ensure consistency in our numbers. I think I should talk to Rose about how we might do this. She is used to working with electronic spreadsheet software, and I believe the latest versions of this type of software contain some type of import capability. And, I know for certain that PAS has an export data function."

Jen "pops into" Rose's office with a grin on her face. "Rose," she questions, "Is it possible for you to import data into your electronic spreadsheet software?"

Rose replies, "Well, yes, Jen. But what do you have in mind? I would like to export data from PAS to a file and have you try to import it into your spreadsheet software," Jen quickly states.

"Do you have some type of test in mind?" questions Rose in response.

"Come to think of it, yes," beams Jen. "Let's try to replicate the sales tax summary printed last month by PAS. Since this report is printed, we can easily compare the PAS output with the imported information and all totals."

"What is the value of such a test?" probes Rose.

Jen continues. "If we are able to replicate this report successfully, it means we can create a database of information useful for management analysis. For example, we could prepare reports showing month–by–month totals of various financial accounts, and create charts and graphs showing both growth and problem areas."

Rose begins to understand. "Are you telling me what I think you are? Is it possible to pick off totals processed by PAS and use these totals in building a database of vital management information? You mean I don't have to key in the data by hand anymore?"

"Yes, if the test works," encourages Jen.

"Well, if we can do this, it will save me hours of work each month," exclaims Rose. "I have always had to key in all data in the past. I didn't realize that the accounting and electronic spreadsheet software systems would be able to share information. But come to think of it, I never did understand the purpose of the import functions built into spreadsheet software. Let's look up the meaning of these two terms."

Rose grabs her software manual, finds the appropriate entries in the manual and reads the definitions to Jen.

"**File import** means to read data from a text file that is on disk, and write it into a current worksheet. **Data parse** works in conjunction with file import. It allows us to convert a column of long labels into several columns of data. Does this make sense?"

Jen responds. "I can provide you with a text file that will probably be treated as a set of long labels. We need to parse each long label ... remember this is text ... to convert it to a numerical format and to place each number into the appropriate cell on the worksheet."

Export Sales Tax Data from PAS

Follow these steps to export sales tax data to Lotus 1–2–3:

☐ 1. Change to your PAS top–level directory. For example: D:\PAS>

☐ 2. Type: **PASFU** and press ENTER. This starts the File Utility program. The following screen then appears:

```
Practical Accounting System file utilities              L-G LAWN AND GARDEN

                    Please select
                        1. Sales Invoicing
                        2. Inventory Management
                        3. Accounts Receivable
                        4. Accounts Payable
                        5. Payroll
                        6. General Ledger
                        7. Check Reconciliation
```

☐ 3. Type 1 (Sales Invoicing) from the above File Utilities menu, and press ENTER. The following screen appears. NOTE: Selection #5 only appears for Inventory Management.

```
Practical Accounting System file utilities              L-G LAWN AND GARDEN
Sales Invoicing

                    Please select
                        1. Rebuild a file
                        2. Export a file
                        3. Restore from an export file
                        4. Initialize files
                        5. Reset item commitments
```

☐ 4. Type 2 (Export a File) from the above Sales Invoicing menu, and press ENTER. The next screen appears as shown below:

```
Practical Accounting System file utilities              L-G LAWN AND GARDEN
Export a file

                    Please select
                        1. Invoice header file ..................... (TCHART)
                        2. Line items file ......................... (TCDIST)
                        3. Invoice auxiliary file .................. (TGJTRX)
                        4. Sales tax history file .................. (TAXHIS)
```

As the above screen shows, there are two names for each file: one in English, the other in computerese. For example, your computer recognizes the Sales Tax History file as TAXHIS.

☐ 5. Type 4 (Sales Tax History File) from the above Export a File menu, and press ENTER. The above screen will be expanded, as shown on the next page.

```
Practical Accounting System file utilities                    L-G LAWN AND GARDEN
Export a file

                    Please select
                        1. Invoice header file .................... (TCHART)
                        2. Line items file ........................ (TCDIST)
                        3. Invoice auxiliary file ................. (TGJTRX)
                        4. Sales tax history file ................. (TAXHIS)

                 Please enter device for export file  [D]

Any change?  N
```

☐ 6. Enter the hard disk device letter that Lotus 1–2–3 files are normally located on (e.g., D), or diskette drive A if you want to export the file to a diskette, and press ENTER. (Your instructor will indicate which device to use.)

☐ 7. Press ENTER (N) at "Any Change?".

```
Practical Accounting System file utilities                    L-G LAWN AND GARDEN
Export a file

                              Creating new export file for:
                                 DATAFILS\TAXHIS.DAT

            1. Starting file key   "First"
            2. Ending file key     "Last"

Field number to change?
```

☐ 8. Press F1 twice ("First" and "Last") to indicate that you want to export the whole file, and press ENTER at "Field number to change?". As the file is processed, a record count displays and increments by one for each record processed. NOTE: The export file has the same name as the original file, but the extension is .EXP.

☐ 9. When the export is complete, press TAB or END "to return to file selection menu."

☐ 10. Press END or TAB as needed to exit PAS.

Import Sales Tax Data into Lotus 1–2–3

☐ 11. Change to the directory in which your Lotus 1–2–3 system resides. For example, type C: and press ENTER.

☐ 12. At the resulting prompt (e.g., C:\>), type 123 and press ENTER. This starts the Lotus 1–2–3 program.

☐ 13. Select: / File Import Text **TAXHIS.EXP (type these letters).** The records that you previously "exported" from PAS now appear on your Lotus screen as shown in Figure 13–1. Figure 13–2 defines the sales tax (tax history) data that you are viewing.

☐ 14. Using your arrow keys, move the cell pointer around and observe that each complete record of sales tax data is located only in column A.

NOTE: Lotus 1–2–3 treats data you import with / File Import Text as long "labels." The labels are contained in one column even though the data may look like it extends across several columns. You can view or print imported data when it appears as long labels, but you cannot do calculations with the numbers each label contains, nor can you easily move any part of the label.

Save Imported File

When you are importing and modifying data, it is important to save your data at various points in this process. This will remove the burden of repeating any steps if you make an error, or the data somehow becomes corrupted.

☐ 15. Select: / File Save EXP_TAX (the new file name) to save the imported data to your disk.

Parse Imported Data

To be able to work with the imported data, you must separate the data within the long labels into individual cell entries using / Data Parse.

/ Data Parse works best with similarly structured data that can be separated into columns and rows easily, such as data from a database program or names and addresses from a word processing program.

When you select / Data Parse, Lotus 1–2–3 displays the Parse Settings dialog box. You can specify the input column range and the output range in the dialog box, or use the menu. The labels contained in the input column range are parsed using a format line. In a moment you will use / Data Parse Format–Line Create to create a format line.

A format line determines how Lotus 1–2–3 parses the label below the format line into individual entries. The pieces into which Lotus 1–2–3 breaks up the label are called data blocks. The format line is a label, preceded by the | (vertical bar) label prefix. (Some screens display a split vertical bar; others display an unbroken vertical bar.) The characters in the format line indicate the data type and the width of each data block in the long label below it. The data type is the type of data ... label, value, date or time ... within a data block.

Format lines can contain the symbols shown below and on the following page:

Symbol	Description
D	Represents the first character of a date block.
L	Represents the first character of a label block.
S	Skips the data block immediately below the symbol when parsing. Use this symbol when your labels include a data block you do not want Lotus 1–2–3 to parse.

Symbol	Description
T	Represents the first character of a time block.
V	Represents the first character of a value block.
>	Represents characters in a data block. For example, Lotus 1–2–3 displays a value block that is four characters wide as V>>>.
*	Represents blank space that can become part of a data block if that block in any label requires extra characters.

The above summary of parsing imported data was extracted from the Lotus USER'S GUIDE, Lotus 1–2–3 for DOS, Release 2.3. You are encouraged to review a complete description of parsing found in most Lotus 1–2–3 instructional texts.

Parse Sales Tax Data

☐ 16. Position the cell pointer in cell A1, the cell that contains the first long label to parse.

☐ 17. Select: / Data Parse Format–Line Create. Lotus 1–2–3 inserts a row, creates a format line in the current cell, and moves the range of data down one row.

The next step is to edit the newly created format line to correspond to the needed parsing.

☐ 18. With your cell pointer still in cell A1, select: Format–line Edit. Lotus 1–2–3 highlights the format line, places the cursor under the first character in the line, and enters OVR (overstrike) mode.

☐ 19. Using your left and right arrow keys, move the cursor across the format line, typing the parsing symbols as shown in Figure 13–3.

☐ 20. Press ENTER when you finish editing the format line to return to the Data Parse menu.

☐ 21. Enter the input and output settings shown below in the Parse Settings dialog box.

Parse Settings

Input column: [A1...A5.......]
Output range: [A10...J15....]

Press F2 (EDIT) to edit settings

☐ 22. Select: Go. Lotus 1–2–3 produces a parsed copy of the imported data in the output range by entering each data block as a value, date, time or label in a cell.

☐ 23. Move the cell pointer through the output range. Observe that EACH cell contains data in contrast to the pre–parsed condition in step 14.

Save Parsed File

☐ 24. Select: / File Save EXP_TAX Replace to save the parsed file.

Complete a Lotus 1–2–3 Spreadsheet

☐ 25. Using the newly parsed sales tax data, make the necessary changes in column widths and data formats, and provide appropriate arithmetic procedures, columnar headings and report title. The resulting spreadsheet should look similar to Figure 13–4.

Save Lotus 1–2–3 Spreadsheet

☐ 26. Select: / File Save EXP_TAX Replace to save the spreadsheet.

☐ 27. This completes the exercise. Select: / Quit Yes to exit Lotus 1–2–3.

QUESTIONS ABOUT THE SOFTWARE

1. What is meant by "parsing" and why is it necessary to parse the file exported from PAS and imported into Lotus 1–2–3? What is accomplished by parsing?

2. What would happen if the symbol S were omitted from the format line in parsing the sales tax file?

3. In undertaking a test to determine if data can be passed from PAS to other software, why is it helpful to begin with a very small file, such as the sales tax history file? What are the disadvantages associated with this type of test?

4. Parsing data is NOT a "fun" undertaking as this exercise demonstrates. If a sales tax report is to be imported into Lotus 1–2–3 next month, say from 5/1/97 to 5/31/97, would the same amount of work (on your part) be required? Why or why not?

MANAGEMENT ISSUES

5. Accounting packages such as PAS have only recently provided utility programs which allow data to be exported to a file and imported by other software such as Lotus 1–2–3.

Name several reasons for exporting data from PAS for use by spreadsheet software.
Explain why managers like this software feature.
From Rose Garten's view, what instructions would you pass on to Jen before she starts using Lotus 1–2–3 to analyze data produced by PAS?

THINGS TO DO

6. Select General Ledger, followed by Print Trial Balance. Enter the following and display the report.

Starting account	**2440–000**	
Ending account	**2440–000**	(press ENTER)
Starting date	**40197**	(press ENTER)
Ending date	**43097**	(press ENTER)
Show detail?	**Y(es)**	(press ENTER)
Profit center	**000**	(press ENTER)

What is the difference between this report and the one prepared using Lotus 1–2–3?

Enter the following and display the report.

Starting account	**2440–000**	
Ending account	**2440–000**	(press ENTER)
Starting date	**"Earliest"**	(press F1)
Ending date	**"Latest"**	(press F1)
Show detail?	**Y(es)**	(press ENTER)
Profit center	**000**	(press ENTER)

What does this display tell you about the report produced using Lotus 1–2–3?

7. Select Sales Invoicing and choose Print Sales Tax Report. Enter the following and display the report.

Tax code	**"All"**	(press F1)
Starting date	**40197**	
Ending date	**43097**	
Print detail?	**Y(es)**	
Print each tax code on separate page?	**N(o)**	(press ENTER)
Print only?	**1 (print only)**	

Compare the sales tax report to the Lotus 1–2–3 report. What does this comparison suggest?
What is meant by "purge?" How is a purge specified? Why must this file be purged periodically?
If records are purged from PAS at the end of each quarter of a year, what is the value of the report produced by using Lotus 1–2–3 (assuming exporting from PAS to Lotus 1–2–3 is performed each month and prior to any purging of sales tax records)?

Figure 13–1 – IMPORTED SALES TAX DATA

	A	B	C	D	E	F	G	H	I
1	CNT97042000000100021st Century ConstructionS00005816+00005244+00000205+0000367+								
2	CNT970420000002001Baker, Richard C. S00006450+00005724+00000325+0000401+								
3									

Figure 13–2 – TAX HISTORY FILE DEFINITION

PAS File: **TAXHIS (tax history file)**

Data Definition	# of Letters or Digits	Data Type
Tax Code	3	alphanumeric
Invoice Date	6	numeric
Invoice #	6	alphanumeric
Sequence #	3	numeric
Customer Name	25	alphanumeric
Tax History Type	1	alphanumeric
Invoice Total Amt	6	numeric, with 2 decimal pts
Invoice Taxable Amt	6	numeric, with 2 decimal pts
Invoice Non–Taxable Amt	6	numeric, with 2 decimal pts
Invoice Sales Tax	5	numeric, with 2 decimal pts

Figure 13–3 – IMPORTED DATA WITH FORMAT LINE

	A | B | C | D | E | F | G | H | I
1	`L>>D>>>>>V>>>>>S>>L>>>>>>>>>>>>>>>>>>>>>>>>SV>>>>>>>SV>>>>>>>SV>>>>>>>SV>>>>>>S`
2	`CNT97042000000100021st Century ConstructionS00005816+00005244+00000205+0000367+`
3	`CNT970420000002001Baker, Richard C.       S00006450+00005724+00000325+0000401+`

Figure 13–4 – LOTUS 1–2–3 SPREADSHEET OF SALES TAX DATA

LYONS–GARTEN LAWN AND GARDEN, INC.
SALES TAX SUMMARY
April, 1997

Tax Code	Doc Date (yymmdd)	Doc #	Customer Name	Sale Amount	Taxable	Non–Taxable	Sales Tax
County							
CNT	970420	1	21st Century Construction	$58.16	$52.44	$2.05	$3.67
CNT	970420	2	Baker, Richard C.	64.50	57.24	3.25	4.01
			TOTALS	$122.66	$109.68	$5.30	$7.68

Exercise 14 – SUMMARIZE CASH FLOW ACTIVITY USING A LOTUS 1–2–3 SPREADSHEET

Introduction

A statement of cash flows can take any number of forms and may cover any period of time deemed important by managers. Most firms "budget" cash on a monthly basis to make sure enough cash is available to meet short–term needs such as payroll and disbursements to suppliers. These short–term cash statements show the specific receipts and disbursements of cash expected, and highlight the sources and uses of these funds.

These same firms also need to regularly review the "actual" cash flow of their operations. This gives them the best picture of their cash needs, and enables them to more confidently plan their future cash requirements in light of expected changes in the nature and growth of their business.

Objectives

The objectives of this exercise are to further acquaint you with the interface between Lotus 1–2–3 and PAS, and to illustrate this interface using an important management information spreadsheet.

This exercise asks you to work through all of the steps necessary to transfer data from the PAS checkbook file into Lotus 1–2–3, and prepare an informative spreadsheet of the data. You are asked to:

- ➡ Export cash flow data from PAS
- ➡ Import cash flow data into Lotus 1–2–3
- ➡ Modify the cash flow data in preparation for spreadsheet development
- ➡ Develop a Lotus 1–2–3 spreadsheet

Case Study

This time Rose is excited. She describes to Jen her experiences in producing the Sales Tax Summary report.

"Working with PAS and Lotus 1–2–3 was easier than I expected. I was able to replicate the report with little difficulty, once I realized what parsing was all about."

"Can we run another test, creating a more useful report this time?" Rose continues. "Producing the Sales Tax Summary was interesting, but it's not the type of report I need in managing the areas that I'm responsible for."

"What type of report do you need?" questions Jen.

"Well, a month–to–month cash–flow report would be nice. A month–to–month payroll report is also something we should talk about, and a month–to–month sales analysis is just what we need at present."

"Can we start with the cash–flow report first?" asks Jen.

"Sure," responds Rose. "What do you have in mind?"

"Well, PAS provides us with a list of all cash outflows such as cash payments and payroll. If we add this listing to cash inflows, we can use your spreadsheet to compute cash–flow totals."

"Exactly what needs to be entered manually, and what can be supplied by PAS?" inquires Rose. "I'm not sure I understand."

Jen writes the following cash–flow report processing plan on a piece of paper and hands it to Rose.

BEGINNING CASH BALANCE:	***Enter manually***
Cash inflows:	
Sales and receivables	***Enter manually***
TOTAL INFLOWS:	(Computed by spreadsheet)
Cash outflows:	
Cash purchases	***Provided by PAS***
Other cash payments	***Provided by PAS***
Payroll cash payments	***Provided by PAS***
TOTAL OUTFLOWS:	(Computed by spreadsheet)
Change in cash from current activities:	(Computed by spreadsheet)
ENDING CASH BALANCE:	(Computed by spreadsheet)

After studying Jen's plan, Rose remarks. "If this works, it will provide us with incredible information. However, will it provide us with too much detail?" Rose wonders aloud.

"It may," explains Jen. "But you can create subtotals and then delete information you feel is irrelevant. Why don't you give it a try to find out what we are working with before starting to worry. I have to admit, this is as much an experiment for me as it is for you. Once we know more, we can make the necessary adjustments to store only the data that we need."

Rose agrees with Jen, and ends with the remark, "OK, let's try it. We just might learn something valuable."

Export Cash Flow Data from PAS

Follow these steps to export cash flow data to Lotus 1–2–3:

☐ 1. Change to your PAS top–level directory. For example: D:\PAS>

☐ 2. Type: **PASFU** and press ENTER. This starts the File Utility program. The following screen then appears:

```
Practical Accounting System file utilities          L-G LAWN AND GARDEN

                    Please select
                       1. Sales Invoicing
                       2. Inventory Management
                       3. Accounts Receivable
                       4. Accounts Payable
                       5. Payroll
                       6. General Ledger
                       7. Check Reconciliation
```

☐ 3. Type 7 (Check Reconciliation) from the above File Utilities menu, and press ENTER. The following screen appears. NOTE: Selection #5 only appears for Inventory Management.

```
Practical Accounting System file utilities          L-G LAWN AND GARDEN
Check Reconciliation

                    Please select
                       1. Rebuild a file
                       2. Export a file
                       3. Restore from an export file
                       4. Initialize files
                       5. Reset item commitments
```

☐ 4. Type 2 (Export a File) from the above Check Reconciliation menu, and press ENTER. The next screen appears as shown below:

```
Practical Accounting System file utilities          L-G LAWN AND GARDEN
Export a file

                    Please select
                       1. Checkbook file ..................... (YCHKBK)
                       2. Checking acct adjustment file .... (YCKADJ)
                       3. Check transfer file ..................... (XFRFIL)
```

As the above screen shows, there are two names for each file: one in English, the other in computerese. For example, your computer recognizes the Checkbook file as YCHKBK.

☐ 5. Type 1 (Checkbook File) from the above Export a File menu, and press ENTER. The above screen will be expanded, as shown on the next page.

```
Practical Accounting System file utilities                L-G LAWN AND GARDEN
Export a file

                    Please select
                        1. Checkbook file ............................ (YCHKBK)
                        2. Checking acct adjustment file .... (YCKADJ)
                        3. Check transfer file ....................... (XFRFIL)

                Please enter device for export file        [D]

Any change?  N
```

☐ 6. Enter the hard disk device letter that Lotus 1–2–3 files are normally located on (e.g., D), or diskette drive A if you want to export the file to a diskette, and press ENTER. (Your instructor will indicate which device to use.)

☐ 7. Press ENTER at "Any Change?". The following screen appears:

```
Practical Accounting System file utilities                L-G LAWN AND GARDEN
Export a file

                          Creating new export file for:
                           DATAFILS\YCHKBK.DAT

        1. Starting file key     [1970401000000000]
        2. Ending file key       [2970430999999999]

Field number to change?
```

☐ 8. Enter the Starting and Ending file keys, as shown, to indicate that you only want to export data from checking accounts 1 & 2 for the month of April 1997, and press ENTER at "Field number to change?". As the file is processed, a record count displays and increments by one for each record processed. NOTE: The export file has the same name as the original file, but the extension is .EXP.

☐ 9. When the export is complete, press TAB or END "to return to file selection menu."

☐ 10. Press END or TAB as needed to exit PAS.

Import Cash Flow Data into Lotus 1–2–3

☐ 11. Change to the directory in which your Lotus 1–2–3 system resides. For example, type C: and press ENTER.

☐ 12. At the resulting prompt (e.g., C:\>), type 123 and press ENTER. This starts the Lotus 1–2–3 program.

☐ 13. Select: / File Import Text **YCHKBK.EXP (type these letters).** The records that you previously "exported" from PAS now appear on your Lotus screen as shown in Figure 14–1. Figure 14–2 defines the cash flow (checkbook) data that you are viewing.

☐ 14. Using your arrow keys, move the cell pointer around and observe that each complete record of cash flow data is located only in column A.

NOTE: Lotus 1–2–3 treats data you import with / File Import Text as long "labels." The labels are contained in one column even though the data may look like it extends across several columns. You can view or print imported data when it appears as long labels, but you cannot do calculations with the numbers each label contains, nor can you easily move any part of the label.

Save Imported File

When you are importing and modifying data, it is important to save your data at various points in this process. This will remove the burden of repeating any steps if you make an error, or the data somehow becomes corrupted.

☐ 15. Select: / File Save EXPCASH (the new file name) to save the imported data to your disk.

To be able to work with the imported data, you must separate the data within the long labels into individual cell entries using / Data Parse.

Parse Imported Data

/ Data Parse works best with similarly structured data that can be separated into columns and rows easily, such as data from a database program or names and addresses from a word processing program.

When you select / Data Parse, Lotus 1–2–3 displays the Parse Settings dialog box. You can specify the input column range and the output range in the dialog box, or use the menu. The labels contained in the input column range are parsed using a format line. In a moment you will use / Data Parse Format–Line Create to create a format line.

A format line determines how Lotus 1–2–3 parses the label below the format line into individual entries. The pieces into which Lotus 1–2–3 breaks up the label are called data blocks. The format line is a label, preceded by the | (vertical bar) label prefix. (Some screens display a split vertical bar; others display an unbroken vertical bar.) The characters in the format line indicate the data type and the width of each data block in the long label below it. The data type is the type of data ... label, value, date or time ... within a data block.

Format lines can contain the following symbols:

Symbol	Description
D	Represents the first character of a date block.
L	Represents the first character of a label block.
S	Skips the data block immediately below the symbol when parsing. Use this symbol when your labels include a data block you do not want Lotus 1–2–3 to parse.

Symbol	Description
T	Represents the first character of a time block.
V	Represents the first character of a value block.
>	Represents characters in a data block. For example, Lotus 1–2–3 displays a value block that is four characters wide as V>>>.
*	Represents blank space that can become part of a data block if that block in any label requires extra characters.

The above summary of parsing imported data was extracted from the Lotus USER'S GUIDE, Lotus 1–2–3 for DOS, Release 2.3. You are encouraged to review a complete description of parsing found in most Lotus 1–2–3 instructional texts.

Parse Cash Flow Data

☐ 16. Position the cell pointer in cell A1, the cell that contains the first long label to parse.

☐ 17. Select: / Data Parse Format–Line Create. Lotus 1–2–3 inserts a row, creates a format line in the current cell, and moves the range of data down one row.

The next step is to edit the newly created format line to correspond to the needed parsing.

☐ 18. With your cell pointer still in cell A1, select: Format–line Edit. Lotus 1–2–3 highlights the format line, places the cursor under the first character in the line, and enters OVR (overstrike) mode.

☐ 19. Using your left and right arrow keys, move across the format line, entering the previously described parsing symbols as appropriate. The resulting format line is shown above the data in Figure 14–3.

☐ 20. Press ENTER when you finish editing the format line to return to the Parse Settings menu.

☐ 21. Enter the input and output settings shown below in the Parse Settings dialog box.

Parse Settings

Input column: [A1...A15......]
Output range: [J1....R15......]

Press F2 (EDIT) to edit settings

☐ 22. Select: Go. Lotus 1–2–3 produces a parsed copy of the imported data in the output range by entering each data block as a value, date, time or label in a cell.

☐ 23. Move the cell pointer through the output range. Observe that EACH cell contains data in contrast to the pre–parsed condition in step 14.

Save Parsed File

☐ 24. Select: / File Save EXPCASH Replace to save the parsed file.

Complete a Lotus 1–2–3 Spreadsheet

☐ 25. Using the newly parsed cash flow data, make the necessary changes in column widths and data formats, and provide appropriate arithmetic procedures, columnar headings and report title. The resulting spreadsheet should look similar to Figure 14–4.

Save Lotus 1–2–3 Spreadsheet

☐ 26. Select: / File Save EXPCASH Replace to save the spreadsheet.

☐ 27. Select: / Quit Yes to exit Lotus 1–2–3.

---------------- //////////////////////////// ----------------

QUESTIONS ABOUT THE SOFTWARE

1. How do credits differ from debits in the exported file? How do deposits differ from checks written?
2. How can you verify that the beginning and ending cash balances shown by the cash flow activity report are correct?

MANAGEMENT ISSUES

3. Why is it important to have a Cash–Flow report in addition to a Balance Sheet and an Income Statement? What does the Cash–Flow report tell a manager that the other reports might not?
4. On the Cash–Flow Report, change in cash from current activities can be positive or negative. If you were a manager at Lyons–Garten, which direction (positive or negative) would be the most important to you? Why is this direction important?

THINGS TO DO

5. Explore other PAS files that can be exported into spreadsheet software such as Lotus 1–2–3. Type **PASFU** and select Inventory Management, followed by Export a File.

   What three files can be exported?

   Select Accounts Receivable, followed by Export a File.

   What six files can be exported?

6. Select General Ledger, followed by Print Trial Balance. Enter the following and display the report.

Starting account	**1010–000**	
Ending account	**1020–000**	(press ENTER)
Starting date	**40197**	(press ENTER)
Ending date	**43097**	(press ENTER)
Show detail?	**Y(es)**	(press ENTER)
Profit center	**000**	(press ENTER)

The G/L display provides for more line entries than the exported file.

How does the exported file differ?

7. Repeat step 6 above, using a Starting and Ending date of 42797.

How does the exported file differ?

8. PAS can also be used to create a Cash–Flow Report. Design such a report, comparing it to the one shown on Figure 14–3.

What is the value of the report produced by PAS rather than by Lotus 1–2–3?
What is the value of the report produced by Lotus 1–2–3 rather than by PAS?

Figure 14–1 – IMPORTED CASH FLOW DATA

	A	B	C	D	E	F	G	H	I
1	1970402000000000ASet up cash balance					002500000+970430			
2	1970420000000000CDeposit					000001000+000000			
3	1970427000000000CDeposit					000125959+000000			
4	1970429001242000RJones Property Management000115000-000000								
5	1970429002050000RSouth-Western Bell					000035712-000000			
6	1970430001153000RTransfer of funds					001000000-000000			
7	2970417000111000RScott, Jeffrey					000220089-000000			
8	2970430000000000CDeposit					001000000+000000			
9	2970430003001000RScott, Jeffrey					000054813-000000			
10	2970430003002000RPalmer, Edward W					000119557-000000			
11	2970430003003000RLevine, Susan M					000052787-000000			
12									

Figure 14–2 – CHECKBOOK FILE DEFINITION

PAS File: **YCHKBK (checkbook file)**

Data Definition	# of Letters or Digits	Data Type
Checking Account #	1	alphanumeric
Check Date	6	numeric
Check #	6	numeric
Sequence #	3	numeric
* Check Type	1	alphanumeric
Check Reference	25	alphanumeric
Check Amount	9	numeric, with 2 decimal pts
Check Clearing Date	6	numeric

* Check Type:

B balance forward
R regular
A adjustment
C cash
O other

Figure 14–3 – IMPORTED DATA WITH FORMAT LINE

	A | B | C | D | E | F | G | H | I
1	`LD>>>>>V>>>>>V>>SL>>>>>>>>>>>>>>>>>>>>>>>>>V>>>>>>>>>S>>>>>>`
2	`1970402000000000ASet up cash balance        002500000+970430`
3	`197042000000000CDeposit                     000001000+000000`
4	`197042700000000CDeposit                     000125959+000000`
5	`197042900124200ORJones Property Management000115000-000000`
6	`1970429002050000RSouth-Western Bell         000035712-000000`
7	`1970430001153000RTransfer of funds          001000000-000000`
8	`2970417000111000RScott, Jeffrey             000220089-000000`
9	`2970430000000000CDeposit                    001000000+000000`
10	`2970430003001000RScott, Jeffrey            000054813-000000`
11	`2970430003002000RPalmer, Edward W          000119557-000000`
12	`2970430003003000RLevine, Susan M           000052787-000000`

Figure 14–4 – LOTUS 1–2–3 SPREADSHEET OF CASH FLOW ACTIVITY

LYONS–GARTEN LAWN AND GARDEN, INC.
CASH FLOW STATEMENT
April, 1997

BEGINNING CASH BALANCE:			$25,000.00
Cash inflows:			
Cash deposit		10.00	
Cash sales		1,259.59	
Cash receivables		0.00	
TOTAL INFLOWS:		1,269.59	
Cash outflows:			
Cash purchases		0.00	
Payments on rent – Jones Property Management		1,150.00	
Payments on payables – South–Western Bell		357.12	
Payroll – Scott, Jeffrey	548.13		
– Palmer, Edward W	1,195.57		
– Levine, Susan M	527.87		
Total Payroll		2,271.57	
TOTAL OUTFLOWS:		3,778.69	
Change in cash from current activities:		(2,509.10)	
ENDING CASH BALANCE:			$22,490.90

INTRODUCTION

Case Study

Acme Hardware Company

In this section of the text you are asked to work with a different company, named Acme Hardware. Much like Lyons–Garten, the general ledger for this company must be changed to allow sales and income to be received from more than one unit. More specifically, Acme derives it's income from store sales and from equipment repair (mowers, blowers) and rentals.

To begin, you are asked to enter company setup information and to add cash for financing purchases. You must modify the Acme chart of accounts, and establish setup controls. Like Lyons–Garten, you must maintain the customer, vendor, item and employee files.

The Acme Hardware materials allow you to explore more than you did with Lyons–Garten. For example, early on you are asked to observe how inventory is treated by sales. To do this, you must compare invoiced sales to non–invoiced sales to determine how each type changes inventory. To make them con–sistent (you will find out how they differ by working through the practice set), special postings are required.

In this practice set, you are asked to work more with the aged receivables and payables reports to ensure that they provide an accurate financial picture of Acme Hardware and can be reconciled with G/L account balances. Much like Lyons–Garten, the exercises are designed to make sure you completely understand how receivables differ from payables.

There are important extensions as well. While working with receivables, you are asked to calculate finance charges and to purge the customer file ... two activities not required of Lyons–Garten.

Payroll poses new challenges. You are asked to produce a bi–weekly payroll and to also print a wide variety of payroll reports, i.e. a payroll history, quarterly and year–end report.

The inventory exercise is expanded to ask questions about which items to order, and in what quantity. You are asked to set sale prices and to print a sales list. Before you leave this lesson you should have a good idea of what understocking represents.

Like Lyons–Garten, the last three practice sets ask you to prepare month–end financial statements and to export and import data. These sets provide more practice preparing financial reports and in parsing files of data.

Practice Set 1 – START–UP AND OVERVIEW

Introduction

In this short practice set, you are asked to:

- load the practice set data
- add company setup information

Load Practice Set Data

Load the starting practice set data (PSET01) into PAS using the procedure described in Appendix C. This step saves you considerable time. It avoids the need for you to enter start–up customer, product, employee, and vendor information. It provides needed setup data for a new company named the ACME HARDWARE COMPANY, and establishes a set of G/L codes and financial layouts for the Balance Sheet and Income Statement.

Set Up Company Data

As before, type 8 (Setup Functions) from the Main Menu to setup company data. Select the appropriate field numbers and enter the following information:

Company name (long):	**Acme Hardware Co.**
Company name (short):	**Acme Hardware**
Address line 1:	**123 Main St.**
Address line 2:	**Winoga Falls, MI 12345**
Address line 3:	
Phone number:	**213–443–1234**
Are G/L profit centers used:	**Y**
Allow protected changes:	**N**
Use passwords?	(This will depend on your class)
Printer	(usually LPT1)
Compressed	(This will depend on your printer)
Printer type	(Make the appropriate selection)

This completes Practice Set 1.

Practice Set 2 – MODIFY GENERAL LEDGER ACCOUNTS

Introduction

In this practice set, as in the original exercises, a General Ledger (G/L) has been provided for you. This G/L is similar, but not identical, to the one used by Lyons–Garten. You are asked to do the following:

- ➡ print the predefined chart of accounts
- ➡ change G/L accounts
- ➡ add G/L accounts
- ➡ print the revised chart of accounts
- ➡ examine the checkbook balances
- ➡ enter cash to checking
- ➡ bring the checkbook up to date

Set Transaction Date

Before starting this practice set, enter today's date as **06–01–97.**

Print the Predefined Chart of Accounts

Select Setup Functions once again, and type 2 (Maintain Chart of Accounts). Print the entire chart of accounts. The number of accounts that appear on this listing should total 108.

Change G/L Accounts

Exit Setup Functions, and move to the General Ledger menu. Select Maintain Chart of Accounts. You are asked to change the following accounts:

Account #	From	To
1010–000	Cash in bank–#1	Checking #1 – Payables
1020–000	Cash in bank–#2	Checking #2 – Payroll
6070–000	Commissions	Commissions – Store
6070–100	Commissions	Commissions – Repair

Next, delete the following accounts:

Account #	Name
1030–000	Cash in bank–#3
1740–000	Accum depr – lease improv
2440–000	Accrued local sales tax
4050–000	Rental Income

Add G/L Accounts

Using the old chart of accounts to determine the correct entries for item #s 3,4 and 5 in the Add Accounts screen, add the following G/L accounts:

Account #	Name			
4000–000	Sales – Main St. Store	P	D	P
4020–000	Sales – Services	P	D	P
4025–000	Income – Mower Repair	P	D	P
4026–000	Income – Blower Repair	P	D	P
4030–000	Income – Rentals	P	D	P

Print the Revised Chart of Accounts

After all these changes have been made, print the revised chart of accounts. Keep this chart in a handy place so you can refer to it from time to time.

Examine the Checkbook Balances

Exit Maintain Chart of Accounts, and move to View G/L Account Activity. Examine accounts 1010 and 1020, and record their Ending Cash Balances. Press F1 twice for earliest and latest balances.

Exit the General Ledger, and move to Check Reconciliation. Print checkbook #1 and checkbook #2, and record their Ending Cash Balances.

Enter Cash to Checking

Exit Check Reconciliation, and move to General Ledger once again. Type 2 (Process General Journal) and select Add. Verify that the current period is 6/01/97 to 6/30/97. Add the following cash amounts:

Account #	**1010–000**
Trans Date	**060197**
DEBIT amount	**50000**
Reference	**Cash transfer**

Account #	**2530–000**
Trans Date	**060197**
CREDIT amount	**50000**
Reference	**Debt to begin business**

Return to Process General Journal, and

* Display the Transaction Edit List. Verify that the processed G/L journal entries are correct.

* Post the transactions, printing the General Journal Transaction Register.

Bring the Checkbook Up to Date

Exit the G/L, and return to Check Reconciliation. Process the following checking account adjustment to add funds to checking account #1:

Adjustment date:	**060197**
CREDIT amount:	**50000**
Reference:	**Set up cash balance**
G/L account #:	**1010–000 (Checking #1 – Payables)**

Return to the Process Checking Account Adjustments menu, and

* Display the Transaction Edit List.

* After review, post the transaction, printing the Checking Account Adjustment Register.

* Return to the Check Reconciliation menu, and print the checkbook for Checking Account #1.

This completes Practice Set 2.

Date 06/01/97 | Acme Hardware Co. | #0096 Page 0001

PREDEFINED CHART OF ACCOUNTS LIST

Accounts: "First" thru "Last"
Financial statement types: P = profit and loss B = balance sheet
Parenthesis control codes: D = enclose when debit C = enclose when credit
Compression codes: N = no compression D = by date P = by period

Account-#	Description	Fin-stmnt type	Paren code	Compress code
1010 - 000	Cash in bank - #1	B	C	D
1020 - 000	Cash in bank - #2	B	C	D
1030 - 000	Cash in bank - #3	B	C	D
1040 - 000	Credit card deposits	B	C	D
1050 - 000	Petty cash	B	C	D
1100 - 000	Accts Receivable - Trade	B	C	D
1110 - 000	Accts Recvble - Employee	B	C	D
1200 - 000	Notes receivable	B	C	D
1210 - 000	Interest receivable	B	C	D
1300 - 000	Prepaid expenses	B	C	D
1400 - 000	Inventory	B	C	D
1410 - 000	Services	B	D	N
1600 - 000	Furniture and fixtures	B	C	D
1610 - 000	Office equipment	B	C	D
1620 - 000	Automobiles and trucks	B	C	D
1630 - 000	Building	B	C	D
1640 - 000	Leasehold improvements	B	C	D
1650 - 000	Land	B	C	D
1700 - 000	Accum depr - furn & fixt	B	C	D
1710 - 000	Accum depr - office equip	B	C	D
1720 - 000	Accum depr - auto & truck	B	C	D
1730 - 000	Accum depr - building	B	C	D
1740 - 000	Accum depr - lease improv	B	C	D
1800 - 000	Deposits	B	C	D
1810 - 000	Investments	B	C	D
1910 - 000	Other intangibles	B	C	D
2005 - 000	Uninvoiced Receivings	B	D	N
2025 - 000	Medical Ins. Deduct	B	D	N
2100 - 000	Accounts Payable - Trade	B	D	D
2110 - 000	Notes Payable - Main St.	B	D	N
2200 - 000	Accrued expenses	B	D	D
2310 - 000	Fed income tax withheld	B	D	D
2320 - 000	EIC advances paid	B	D	D
2330 - 000	Emp Social Sec Payable	B	D	D
2335 - 000	Emp Medicare Payable	B	D	D
2340 - 000	Empr Social Sec Payable	B	D	D

Date 06/01/97 Acme Hardware Co. #0096 Page 0002

PREDEFINED CHART OF ACCOUNTS LIST

Account–#	Description	Fin–stmnt type	Paren code	Compress code
2345 – 000	Empr Medicare Payable	B	D	D
2350 – 000	State income tax withheld	B	D	D
2360 – 000	Other state tax withheld	B	D	D
2370 – 000	Local income tax withheld	B	D	D
2380 – 000	Pension contrib withheld	B	D	D
2390 – 000	Charity contrib withheld	B	D	D
2410 – 000	Accrued fed income tax	B	D	D
2420 – 000	Accrued state income tax	B	D	D
2430 – 000	Accrued state sales tax	B	D	D
2440 – 000	Accrued local sales tax	B	D	D
2450 – 000	Accrued fed unemp tax	B	D	D
2460 – 000	Accrued state unemp tax	B	D	D
2510 – 000	Deposits received	B	D	D
2520 – 000	Notes and loans payable	B	D	D
2530 – 000	Long term debt	B	D	D
3000 – 000	Common stock	B	D	D
3100 – 000	Paid in capital	B	D	D
3200 – 000	Treasury stock	B	D	D
3300 – 000	Retained earnings	B	D	D
4010 – 000	Sales – merchandise	P	D	P
4031 – 000	Non–inventory item	P	D	N
4032 – 000	Labor	P	D	N
4033 – 000	Travel	P	D	N
4035 – 000	Freight	P	D	N
4050 – 000	Rental Income	P	D	N
4510 – 000	Sales discounts	P	D	P
4520 – 000	Sales retrns & allowances	P	D	P
4910 – 000	Finance charges	P	D	P
4920 – 000	Freight charges	P	D	P
4930 – 000	Miscellaneous charges	P	D	P
4940 – 000	Deposits forfeited	P	D	P
4950 – 000	Other misc income	P	D	P
5010 – 000	Cost of goods sold	P	C	P
5020 – 000	Inventory adjustments	P	C	P
5030 – 000	Purchase discounts	P	C	P
5040 – 000	Cost corrections	P	C	P
6000 – 000	Wage Account	P	C	N
6010 – 000	Advertising	P	C	P
6020 – 000	Auto and truck	P	C	P
6030 – 000	Bad debt expense	P	C	P
6040 – 000	Bank charges and fees	P	C	P

Date 06/01/97 Acme Hardware Co. #0096 Page 0003

PREDEFINED CHART OF ACCOUNTS LIST

Account-#	Description	Fin-stmnt type	Paren code	Compress code
6050 - 000	Cash over or short	P	C	P
6060 - 000	Charitable contributions	P	C	P
6070 - 000	Commissions	P	C	P
6070 - 100	Commissions	P	C	N
6080 - 000	Depreciation	P	C	P
6090 - 000	Insurance	P	C	P
6100 - 000	Interest	P	C	P
6110 - 000	Legal & accounting fees	P	C	P
6120 - 000	Licenses and fees	P	C	P
6130 - 000	Merchant credit card fees	P	C	P
6140 - 000	Miscellaneous	P	C	P
6150 - 000	Office expense	P	C	P
6160 - 000	Rents & utilities	P	C	P
6170 - 000	Repairs and maintenance	P	C	P
6180 - 000	Salaries - administrative	P	C	P
6190 - 000	Salaries - floor sales	P	C	P
6200 - 000	Salaries & Wage exp-Elm	P	C	P
6210 - 000	Salaries - bonuses	P	C	P
6220 - 000	Sales and promotions exp	P	C	P
6230 - 000	Supplies	P	C	P
6240 - 000	Taxes - other	P	C	P
6250 - 000	Taxes - payroll	P	C	P
6260 - 000	Taxes - sales tax	P	C	P
6270 - 000	Telephone	P	C	P
6280 - 000	Travel & entertainment	P	C	P
7110 - 000	Taxes - federal income	P	C	P
7120 - 000	Taxes - state income	P	C	P
8200 - 000	Telephone exp.	P	C	N
9110 - 000	Interest income	P	D	P
9120 - 000	Gain/loss sale of assets	P	D	P
9999 - 000	Transfer/suspense Account	P	D	D

108 Accounts printed

-- End of report --

Date 06/01/97 Acme Hardware Co. #0097 Page 0001

MODIFIED CHART OF ACCOUNTS LIST

Accounts: "First" thru "Last"
Financial statement types: P = profit and loss B = balance sheet
Parenthesis control codes: D = enclose when debit C = enclose when credit
Compression codes: N = no compression D = by date P = by period

Account–#	Description	Fin–stmnt type	Paren code	Compress code
1010 – 000	Checking #1 – Payables	B	C	D
1020 – 000	Checking #2 – Payroll	B	C	D
1040 – 000	Credit card deposits	B	C	D
1050 – 000	Petty cash	B	C	D
1100 – 000	Accts Receivable – Trade	B	C	D
1110 – 000	Accts Recvble – Employee	B	C	D
1200 – 000	Notes receivable	B	C	D
1210 – 000	Interest receivable	B	C	D
1300 – 000	Prepaid expenses	B	C	D
1400 – 000	Inventory	B	C	D
1410 – 000	Services	B	D	N
1600 – 000	Furniture and fixtures	B	C	D
1610 – 000	Office equipment	B	C	D
1620 – 000	Automobiles and trucks	B	C	D
1630 – 000	Building	B	C	D
1640 – 000	Leasehold improvements	B	C	D
1650 – 000	Land	B	C	D
1700 – 000	Accum depr – furn & fixt	B	C	D
1710 – 000	Accum depr – office equip	B	C	D
1720 – 000	Accum depr – auto & truck	B	C	D
1730 – 000	Accum depr – building	B	C	D
1800 – 000	Deposits	B	C	D
1810 – 000	Investments	B	C	D
1910 – 000	Other intangibles	B	C	D
2005 – 000	Uninvoiced Receivings	B	D	N
2025 – 000	Medical Ins. Deduct	B	D	N
2100 – 000	Accounts Payable – Trade	B	D	D
2110 – 000	Notes Payable – Main St.	B	D	N
2200 – 000	Accrued expenses	B	D	D
2310 – 000	Fed income tax withheld	B	D	D
2320 – 000	EIC advances paid	B	D	D
2330 – 000	Emp Social Sec Payable	B	D	D
2335 – 000	Emp Medicare Payable	B	D	D
2340 – 000	Empr Social Sec Payable	B	D	D
2345 – 000	Empr Medicare Payable	B	D	D
2350 – 000	State income tax withheld	B	D	D

Date 06/01/97 Acme Hardware Co. #0097 Page 0002

MODIFIED CHART OF ACCOUNTS LIST

Account–#	Description	Fin–stmnt type	Paren code	Compress code
2360 – 000	Other state tax withheld	B	D	D
2370 – 000	Local income tax withheld	B	D	D
2380 – 000	Pension contrib withheld	B	D	D
2390 – 000	Charity contrib withheld	B	D	D
2410 – 000	Accrued fed income tax	B	D	D
2420 – 000	Accrued state income tax	B	D	D
2430 – 000	Accrued state sales tax	B	D	D
2450 – 000	Accrued fed unemp tax	B	D	D
2460 – 000	Accrued state unemp tax	B	D	D
2510 – 000	Deposits received	B	D	D
2520 – 000	Notes and loans payable	B	D	D
2530 – 000	Long term debt	B	D	D
3000 – 000	Common stock	B	D	D
3100 – 000	Paid in capital	B	D	D
3200 – 000	Treasury stock	B	D	D
3300 – 000	Retained earnings	B	D	D
4000 – 000	Sales – Main St. Store	P	D	P
4020 – 000	Sales – Services	P	D	P
4025 – 000	Income – Mower Repair	P	D	P
4026 – 000	Income – Blower Repair	P	D	P
4030 – 000	Income – Rentals	P	D	P
4010 – 000	Sales – merchandise	P	D	P
4031 – 000	Non–inventory item	P	D	N
4032 – 000	Labor	P	D	N
4033 – 000	Travel	P	D	N
4035 – 000	Freight	P	D	N
4510 – 000	Sales discounts	P	D	P
4520 – 000	Sales retrns & allowances	P	D	P
4910 – 000	Finance charges	P	D	P
4920 – 000	Freight charges	P	D	P
4930 – 000	Miscellaneous charges	P	D	P
4940 – 000	Deposits forfeited	P	D	P
4950 – 000	Other misc income	P	D	P
5010 – 000	Cost of goods sold	P	C	P
5020 – 000	Inventory adjustments	P	C	P
5030 – 000	Purchase discounts	P	C	P
5040 – 000	Cost corrections	P	C	P
6000 – 000	Wage Account	P	C	N
6010 – 000	Advertising	P	C	P
6020 – 000	Auto and truck	P	C	P
6030 – 000	Bad debt expense	P	C	P

Date 06/01/97 Acme Hardware Co. #0097 Page 0003

MODIFIED CHART OF ACCOUNTS LIST

Account–#	Description	Fin–stmnt type	Paren code	Compress code
6040 – 000	Bank charges and fees	P	C	P
6050 – 000	Cash over or short	P	C	P
6060 – 000	Charitable contributions	P	C	P
6070 – 000	Commissions – Store	P	C	P
6070 – 100	Commissions – Repair	P	C	N
6080 – 000	Depreciation	P	C	P
6090 – 000	Insurance	P	C	P
6100 – 000	Interest	P	C	P
6110 – 000	Legal & accounting fees	P	C	P
6120 – 000	Licenses and fees	P	C	P
6130 – 000	Merchant credit card fees	P	C	P
6140 – 000	Miscellaneous	P	C	P
6150 – 000	Office expense	P	C	P
6160 – 000	Rents & utilities	P	C	P
6170 – 000	Repairs and maintenance	P	C	P
6180 – 000	Salaries – administrative	P	C	P
6190 – 000	Salaries – floor sales	P	C	P
6200 – 000	Salaries & Wage exp–Elm	P	C	P
6210 – 000	Salaries – bonuses	P	C	P
6220 – 000	Sales and promotions exp	P	C	P
6230 – 000	Supplies	P	C	P
6240 – 000	Taxes – other	P	C	P
6250 – 000	Taxes – payroll	P	C	P
6260 – 000	Taxes – sales tax	P	C	P
6270 – 000	Telephone	P	C	P
6280 – 000	Travel & entertainment	P	C	P
7110 – 000	Taxes – federal income	P	C	P
7120 – 000	Taxes – state income	P	C	P
8200 – 000	Telephone exp.	P	C	N
9110 – 000	Interest income	P	D	P
9120 – 000	Gain/loss sale of assets	P	D	P
9999 – 000	Transfer/suspense Account	P	D	D

109 Accounts printed

-- End of report --

Date 06/01/97 Acme Hardware Co. #0098 Page 0001

GENERAL JOURNAL TRANSACTION EDIT LIST

Period: 06/01/97 to 06/30/97

Account: 1010–000 Checking #1 – Payables

Trans–date	Debit–amt	Credit–amt	Reference
06/01/97	50,000.00		Cash transfer

Account: 2530–000 Long term debt

Trans–date	Debit–amt	Credit–amt	Reference
06/01/97		50,000.00	Debt to begin business

	Debit–amt	Credit–amt	
Grand totals:	50,000.00	50,000.00	2 Transactions

–– End of report ––

Date 06/01/97 Acme Hardware Co. #0099 Page 0001

GENERAL JOURNAL TRANSACTION REGISTER

Period: 06/01/97 to 06/30/97

Account: 1010−000 Cash #1 − Payables

Trans−date	Debit−amt	Credit−amt	Reference
06/01/97	50,000.00		Cash transfer

Account: 2530−000 Long term debt

Trans−date	Debit−amt	Credit−amt	Reference
06/01/97		50,000.00	Debt to begin business

Grand totals:	50,000.00	50,000.00	2 Transactions

−− End of report −−

Date 06/01/97 Acme Hardware Co. #0100 Page 0001

CHECKING ACCOUNT ADJUSTMENT EDIT LIST

Checking account #: 1 8765–432–19876 4400998877

Adjustment date	Reference Acct–#	Account–description	Payment/DR	Deposit/CR
06/01/97	Set up cash balance			50,000.00
	1010–000	Checking #1 – Payables		
1 Adjustment transaction		Totals:	.00	50,000.00

Date 06/01/97 Acme Hardware Co. #0100 Page 0002

CHECKING ACCOUNT ADJUSTMENT EDIT LIST

---------- G/L account distribution totals ----------

50,000.00 Distributed to 1010–000 Checking #1 – Payables

-- End of report --

Date 06/01/97 | Acme Hardware Co. | #0101 Page 0001

CHECKING ACCOUNT ADJUSTMENT REGISTER

Checking account #: 1 8765−432−19876 4400998877

Adjustment date	Reference Acct−#	Account−description	Payment/DR	Deposit/CR
06/01/97	Set up cash balance			50,000.00
	1010−000	Checking #1 − Payables		
1 Adjustment transaction		Totals:	.00	50,000.00

Date 06/01/97 | Acme Hardware Co. | #0101 Page 0002

CHECKING ACCOUNT ADJUSTMENT REGISTER

---------- G/L account distribution totals ----------

50,000.00 Distributed to 1010−000 Checking #1 − Payables

-- End of report --

Date 06/01/97 Acme Hardware Co. #0102 Page 0001

CHECKBOOK

Checking account #: 1 8765–432–19876 4400998877
Cleared items have "*" next to them

Item	Date	Reference	Amount	Balance
Adjustmnt	06/01/97	Set up cash balance	50,000.00CR	50,000.00

Current checkbook balance: 50,000.00

-- End of report --

Practice Set 3 – ESTABLISH ACCOUNTING CONTROL DATA

Introduction

This practice set asks you to establish accounting invoicing control data. You are asked to do the following:

- ➡ modify accounting control data
- ➡ establish accounting periods
- ➡ modify invoicing control data

Set Transaction Date

Before starting this practice set, enter today's date as **06–01–97.**

Modify Accounting Control Data

Select Setup Functions once again, and type 3 (Modify Accounting Control Data). Set the following defaults:

Default sales acct #	**4000**
Default returns acct #	**4520**

Next, correct the employee name and address (fields 19–22).

Establish Accounting Periods

The accounting periods should be correct; if not, correct them. Select Maintain Accounting Periods. The year should be 1997. If it isn't, enter the start and end dates for all months. If the period is not #6, change it to #6 (field #14).

Modify Invoicing Control Data

You are asked to make several invoicing control data changes as follows:

Next bill ref #	**501**
Next invoice #	**500**
Default payment terms:	**NET 30** **2/10 NET 30** **CASH**
Default shipping methods:	**TRUCK** **FED EX** **UPS GROUND** **US MAIL**

Cust hist class 1 desc	**Products**
Cust hist class 2 desc	**Services**
Cust hist class 3 desc	**Repairs**
Cust hist class 4 desc	**Other**
Fin chg pct – level 1	**1.5**
Level 1 cut–off amt	**3000**
Fin chg pct – level 2	**1.0**

Next, change the code and description for the back room printer invoicing station as follows:

From:	To:
Code 2	(Type your initials)
Back room prnts	(Type your name)

Finally, change the Michigan sales tax as follows:

Code	Description	Rate	Acct #	
MI	Mich. tax	7.0	2430–000	Accrued state sales tax

Answer the following:

What is the purpose of the default sales number?
What happens when you change the next invoice number to 500?
Explain the new settings for the company finance charge. What is meant by level 1 and level 2?
What is the value of having several default payment terms and shipping methods?
Why were the customer history classes changed?

Practice Set 4 – LOAD CUSTOMER & VENDOR FILES

Introduction

This practice set asks you to add customer and vendor files, and establish accounting invoicing control data. You are asked to:

- ➡ add and modify customer records
- ➡ add and modify vendor records
- ➡ print the contents of the customer and vendor master files

Set Transaction Date

Before starting this practice set, enter today's date as **06–01–97.**

Add Customer Master File Information

Select Accounts Receivable to reach Maintain Customer Data. Add the following customers to the file:

Ariel Enterprises	Telephone:	**554–4300**
69 Vacca Ct.	Contact:	**M. J. Thorpe**
East Kalamazoo, MI 12445	Sales Rep:	**PH**
	Cust–type:	**WSL**
	Bal–meth:	**Open item**
	Tax code:	**MI**
	Stat–freq:	**Monthly**
	Fin–chg?	**Yes**
	1st–actv–dat	**06–01–97**

Washington, Mrs. Thomas	Telephone:	**444–7780**
350 Hillcrest Circle	Contact:	**Ann Washington**
Lansing, MI 12335	Sales Rep:	**TJF**
	Cust–type:	**RET**
	Bal–meth:	**Open item**
	Tax code:	**MI**
	Stat–freq:	**Monthly**
	Fin–chg?	**No**
	1st–actv–dat	**06–01–97**

Webber Landscaping	Telephone:	**323–2342**
33 East Lansing Dr.	Contact:	**Marvin Webber**
Winoga Falls, MI 12345	Sales Rep:	**AW**
	Cust–type:	**LAND**
	Bal–meth:	**Open item**
	Tax code:	**MI**
	Stat–freq:	**Monthly**
	Fin–chg?	**Yes**
	1st–actv–dat	**06–01–97**

Change Customer Master File Information

Change the following customer records:

* Change the spelling of Baker in the "Baker, Richard C." record

from	to
Baker	Bakker

* Change the name of the customer contact to Richard Bakker.

* Check all customer records. All open item records should not include a finance charge (answer NO). All balance–forward records should include a finance charge (answer YES). Make any needed corrections.

Print the Contents of the Customer Master File

Print all customer records and answer the following:

How many customers are open–item accounts?
How many customers are balance–forward accounts?

Add Supplier (Vendor) Master File Information

Select Accounts Payable to reach Maintain Vendor Data. Add the following customers to the file:

"Biggies" Hardware	Contact:	**"Biggy" Swanson**
55443 Warehouse Drive	Phone:	**888–BIGY**
Detroit, MI 49123	Comment:	**Check here first**
	First–date	**05–15–97**
	Exp–acct	**2100–000**

Tools Galore	Contact:	**"Kate" Schiepzo**
24355 S. W. Drive	Phone:	**1800412TOOLS**
Gary, IN 47777	Comment:	**Major supplier**
	First–date	**05–05–97**
	Exp–acct	**2100–000**

Change Vendor Master File Information

Change the following vendor information:

Bitznbytes Computer	Change First–date to: Change Exp–acct to:	**05–24–97** **6150–000**
Hanson Manufacturing Co.	Change Exp–acct to:	**2100–000**
Jones Property Management	Change First–date to:	**05–01–97**

Print the Contents of the Vendor Master File

Print all vendor records and answer the following:

How many vendors are outside the state of Michigan?
How many vendors have a 2100 exp–acct?
What is an exp–acct, and why is this field found in the vendor master file?

This completes Practice Set 4.

Date: 06/01/97 Time: 21:15:57 Acme Hardware Co. Report #0103 Page 0001

CUSTOMER LIST

Starting customer: "First"
Ending customer: "Last"
Customer type: "All"
Last sale date: "Earliest"

Cust–name Address	Phone–# Contact Sales–rep	Cust–typ Bal–meth Tax–code	Stmt–freq Fin–chg?	1st–actv–dat Lst–sls–dat Lst–pmt–dat	Lst–fin–chg–dat Lst–fin–chg–amt Fin–chg–YTD	Comment
21st Century Construction	555–7844	WSL	M	6/01/97	(None)	
P.O. Box 4545	Herbert Mardhat	Open item	N	(None)	.00	
670 Mason Street	JAK	MI		(None)	.00	
Ann Arbor, MI 48136						
Allied Plumbing Co.	554–4300	WSL	M	6/01/97	(None)	
555 N. Grand Blvd.	Cathy Sinks	Bal fwd	Y	(None)	.00	
Lansing, MI 48135	JAK	MI		(None)	.00	
Ariel Enterprises	554–4300	WSL	M	6/01/97	(None)	
69 Vacca Ct.	M. J. Thorpe	Open item	N	(None)	.00	
East Kalamazoo, MI 12445	PH	MI		(None)	.00	
Bakker, Richard C.	478–9090	RET	M	6/01/97	(None)	
2554 Broad Street	Richard Bakker	Open item	N	(None)	.00	
Lansing, MI 48135	TJF	MI		(None)	.00	
Elliot Enterprises	779–6010	WSL	M	6/01/97	(None)	
123 Broadway	Paul Elliot	Open item	N	(None)	.00	
Glendale, MI 48133	TJF	MI		(None)	.00	
Harris, Goldberg, & Jones	554–4300	RET	M	6/01/97	(None)	
1 Commerce Square	Michael Jones	Open item	N	(None)	.00	
Northtown, MI 48135	JAK	MI		(None)	.00	
Holcomb Industrial Supply	722–2233	WSL	M	6/01/97	(None)	
2323 Holcomb Way	Jim Ewing	Open item	N	(None)	.00	
Lansing, MI 48135	JAK	MI		(None)	.00	
Neptune Underwater Supply	736–1102	RET	M	6/01/97	(None)	
345 Lewisville Rd.	Sam Knorkle	Bal Fwd	Y	(None)	.00	
Lewisville, MI 48132	TJF	MI		(None)	.00	
Newton, Boyd, & Co.	886–7722	WSL	M	6/01/97	(None)	
1024 Marble Avenue	Bob Newton	Bal fwd	Y	(None)	.00	
Lansing, MI 48135	JAK	MI		(None)	.00	

Date: 06/01/97 Time: 21:16:03 Acme Hardware Co. Report #0103 Page 0002

CUSTOMER LIST

Cust–name / Address	Phone–# / Contact / Sales–rep	Cust–typ / Bal–meth / Tax–code	Stmt–freq / Fin–chg?	1st–actv–dat / Lst–sls–dat / Lst–pmt–dat	Lst–fin–chg–dat / Lst–fin–chg–amt / Fin–chg–YTD	Comment
Washington, Mrs. Thomas	444–7780	RET	M	6/01/97	(None)	
350 Hillcrest Circle	Ann Washington	Open item	N	(None)	.00	
Lansing, MI 12335	TJF	MI		(None)	.00	
Webber Landscaping	323–2342	LAND	M	6/01/97	(None)	
33 East Lansing Dr.	Marvin Webber	Open item	N	(None)	.00	
Winoga Falls, MI 12345	AW	MI		(None)	.00	

11 customers 3 balance forward 8 open item

-- End of report --

Date: 06/01/97 | Acme Hardware Co. | Report #0104 | Page 0001

VENDOR LIST

Starting vendor: "First"
Ending vendor: "Last"

Name	Address-1 Address-2 Address-3	Contact Phone Comment	First-date Exp-acct
"Biggies" Hardware	55443 Warehouse Drive Detroit, MI 49123	"Biggy" Swanson 888-BIGY	05/15/97 2100-000
Acme Office Supplies	456 N. Broadway Lansing, MI 48135	B. Caldwell 999-9765	04/01/97 6230-000
Bitznbytes Computer	15 Amherst St. Ann Arbor, MI 48136	Dave Bitzn 405-569-8956 Computer Supplies	05/24/97 6150-000
Hanson Manufacturing Co.	65 Industrial Circle Chicago, IL 60655	Don Handy 413-669-8560	03/12/97 2100-000
Hill Equipment & Supply	3507 Oak Rd. South Bend, IN 47405	Carl Rawlings 412-968-7650	03/24/97 2100-000
Jones Property Management	11056 E. Commercial Dallas, TX 75330	Robert Rents 214-774-6700 Property Owner	05/01/97 6160-000
NorthWestern Bell	Irving Office 500 S. Central Amherst, MI 48132	 721-1213	03/30/97 6270-000
Reynolds Tool Company	3922 Frontier Pkwy. Kalamazoo, MI 48138	Kate Plierson 512-447-8900 Full-service wholesaler	01/01/97 2100-000
Tools Galore	24355 S.W. Drive Gary, IN 47777	"Kate" Schiepzo 180041 2TOOLS Major supplier	05/05/97 2100-000

9 vendors

-- End of report --

Practice Set 5 – PROCESS CUSTOMER INVOICES

Introduction

This practice set allows you to begin processing transactions, once you ready the inventory master file and add the cost of inventory to the general ledger. You are asked to:

- ➡ modify product records
- ➡ modify general ledger records
- ➡ process several sales transactions
- ➡ print the invoice transaction register
- ➡ print customer invoices
- ➡ post invoice transaction totals
- ➡ print a sales tax report

Set Transaction Date

Before starting this practice set, enter today's date as **06–03–97.**

Change the Product Master File

Several things are wrong with the product master file as it now reads. Some products are classified incorrectly as services, all product returns are posted to account 4010 rather than 4520 and, in one case, a bin location is missing.

* To begin, change the general ledger name for account 4010 from Sales–Merchandise to Sales – Yard.

* Switch to Inventory and change the following product information:

Item #'s	Change to Make
1091, 1100, 1105, 2200, 5770, EQ–DEER	Change Sales acct to 4000 Change Returns acct to 4520
BS–BLOCK, BS–BRACKET, BS–PLYWOOD	Change Hist–class to Products Change Returns acct to 4520
BS–DOORS	Change Hist–class to Products Add bin location K4 Change Returns acct to 4520
EL–WIRE	Change Hist–class to Products Change Sales acct to 4000 Change Returns acct to 4520

* Print the revised item list, showing as much detail as possible for all products.

  How many products are on file?
  Why was it important to change some of the items from Services to Products?
  What is a bin location, and what happens if this information is missing in a very large hardware store?

Post the Value of Inventory

This step is added to remind you that inventory should be added to the books at start–up of a business. To determine what the inventory is worth, do the following:

* Select Inventory Management and display the Inventory Valuation Report.

  Record the total Retail Value and Inventory Value.

* Switch to the General Ledger and select Process General Journal. Add the following transactions for the period 6/01/97 to 6/30/97:

  Account 1400–000. Add the dollar value of inventory to this account. Refer to this as **Beginning inventory.**

  Account 2520–000. Credit the dollar value of inventory to this account. Again refer to this as **Beginning inventory.**

* Post these two transactions to produce the General Journal Transaction Register.

  How does this step affect the company's Balance Sheet?

Process Invoice (Sales) Transactions

In this section you are asked to process the several invoice (sales) transactions.

* Switch to Sales Invoicing, and select Enter Invoices.

* Type your initials for the invoicing station.

Given the following general invoice information, enter invoices 1–5 shown on the next three pages.

General Invoice Information

All bill types will be invoices, with the invoice date assigned at print time. You will deliver to the same address as the billing address. The information provided next is organized as Header information, Line Item information, and Summary information.

Invoice #1

Customer	PO	Terms	Ship Via	Bill Group	Profit Center
Elliott Enterprises	6410	**2% 10, Net 30**	**Truck**	**F1**	**F1**

Sequence	Item	Quantity	Unit Price	Discount
10	1105	5	29.95	0.00
20	5770	5	28.50	0.00
30	**BS–BLOCK**	100	1.59	0.00

Inv disc %	Misc charges	Freight	Sales Tax	Payment
0.00	0.00	85.00 + F1	F1	0.00

Comment	Print Invoice
Thanks Paul!	**No**

Invoice #2

Customer	PO	Terms	Ship Via	Bill Group	Profit Center
Allied Plumbing	23412	**Net 30**	**Truck**	**F1**	**F1**

Sequence	Item	Quantity	Unit Price	Discount
10	1091	50	17.95	0.00
20	2200	3	13.50	0.00
30	**BS–BRACKET**	2	44.95	0.00
40	**EL–WIRE**	10	5.19	0.00

Inv disc %	Misc charges	Freight	Sales Tax	Payment
0.00	0.00	45.00 + F1	F1	0.00

Comment	Print Invoice
Thank you!	**No**

Invoice #3

Customer	PO	Terms	Ship Via	Bill Group	Profit Center
Holcomb Industrial Supply	**12229**	**2% 10, Net 30**	**Truck**	**F1**	**F1**

Sequence	Item	Quantity	Unit Price	Discount
10	**1091**	**150**	**17.95**	**0.00**
20	**BS–BLOCK**	**200**	**1.59**	**0.00**
30	**BS–DOORS**	**3**	**68.00**	**0.00**
40	**BS–PLYWOOD**	**100**	**13.95**	**0.00**
50	**EQ–DEER**	**1**	**87.00**	**0.00**

Inv disc %	Misc charges	Freight	Sales Tax	Payment
0.00	**0.00**	**145.00 + F1**	**F1**	**0.00**

Comment	Print Invoice
Thank you for your business!	**No**

Invoice #4

Customer	PO	Terms	Ship Via	Bill Group	Profit Center
Ariel Enterprises	**556ACS**	**2% 10, Net 30**	**Truck**	**F1**	**F1**

Sequence	Item	Quantity	Unit Price	Discount
10	**1100**	**5**	**25.95**	**0.00**
20	**BS–BLOCK**	**100**	**1.59**	**0.00**
30	**BS–BRACKET**	**1**	**44.95**	**0.00**
40	**BS–DOORS**	**1**	**68.00**	**0.00**
50	**EL–WIRE**	**15**	**5.19**	**0.00**
60	**EQ–DEER**	**2**	**87.00**	**0.00**

Inv disc %	Misc charges	Freight	Sales Tax	Payment
0.00	**0.00**	**145.00 + F1**	**F1**	**0.00**

Comment	Print Invoice
Hope we satisfy your building needs!	**No**

Invoice #5

Customer	PO	Terms	Ship Via	Bill Group	Profit Center
Webber Landscaping	**23423**	**2% 10, Net 30**	**Truck**	**F1**	**F1**

Sequence	Item	Quantity	Unit Price	Discount
10	**1091**	**50**	**17.95**	**0.00**
20	**BS–BLOCK**	**50**	**1.59**	**0.00**
30	**BS–BRACKET**	**1**	**44.95**	**0.00**
40	**EL–WIRE**	**20**	**5.19**	**0.00**

Inv disc %	Misc charges	Freight	Sales Tax	Payment
0.00	**0.00**	**65.00 + F1**	**F1**	**0.00**

Comment	Print Invoice
We appreciate your business!	**No**

View Invoices

Exit entering invoice information, and select View Invoices. Enter a billing reference of 500. Select Ariel Enterprises.

What is the taxable total for this invoice?
What is the billed total?

Print Invoice List

Exit and select Print Invoice List. Do the following:

* Print in order by **customer name,** for all customers and all dates. Print all header lines, all line items, and all bill and report totals.

What is the Total Amount of Invoices?
What is the Total Freight?
What is the Total Sales Tax?
What is the Total Amount Billed?

Print the Invoices

Exit and select Print Invoices. Do the following:

* Enter your initials for the billing station.

* Print in order by **customer name.** Use 06/03/97 as the date. Print all invoices. Add no default comment.

  What is the starting invoice number?
  Where did this number come from?
  Why does the invoice number differ from the bill–ref#?

Post the Printed Invoices

After invoices are printed, select Post Invoices. Use a date of 060397, press F1 for the invoice cut–off number, press F1 for the bill group to post, and use 060397 for the deposit date. Do not print deposit slips since there are no funds to deposit.

More Things to Explore

* Display the Sales Tax Report.

  What is the taxable amount?
  What is the non–taxable amount?
  Why are some funds not taxable?

* Switch over to the General Ledger.

  What new balances are stored in account #s 2430, 4000, 4010 and 4920 ?
  Explain the meaning of these new balances.

* Display account #s 1400 and 5010.

  Explain what happened to each as a result of invoicing.

* Compare these new balances with those shown on the Inventory Transaction Register.

  What does this register tell managers?

* Switch to Inventory Management and display the Inventory Valuation Report.

  How did invoicing change the contents of this report?

This completes Practice Set 5.

Date: 06/03/97 Time: 10:45:31 | Acme Hardware Co. | Report #0105 Page #0001

ITEM LIST

Item # range: "First" to "Last"
Department: "All" Vendor: "All"
Item types: I = Inventory N = Non–inventory S = Service T = Text
"****" indicates that the contra account varies by invoice profit center

Item–#	Description	Bar–code / Subst–item–# / Hist–class / Inv–contra–#	Typ / Txb	Dept / Sls–# / Ret–#	Loc / COG–#	Stk–unit / Pur–unit / Prf–unit	List–price / Stk–qty/Pur	Avg–cost / Last–cost / Min–qty–OH / Max–qty–OH	Qty–on–hand / Qty–commit / Qty–on–ord / Min–ord–qty	Last–rcvd / 1st–rcvd / Last–ord / Last–sale
1091	**Gauge, Hi–Pressure**		I	TOOLS	3D	EACH	17.95	9.72000	500	6/01/97
			Y	4000	5010	100	9.72000	9.720	0	6/01/97
	Hill Equipment & Supply	Products		4520				100	0	5/15/97
		1400–000						500	100	None

Better price: 15.75

Qty–sold:	this prd	0	last prd	0	this yr	0	Last yr	0
Sales:	this prd	.00	last prd	.00	this yr	.00	Last yr	.00
Cost:	this prd	.00	last prd	.00	this yr	.00	Last yr	.00

Item–#	Description	Bar–code / Subst–item–# / Hist–class / Inv–contra–#	Typ / Txb	Dept / Sls–# / Ret–#	Loc / COG–#	Stk–unit / Pur–unit / Prf–unit	List–price / Stk–qty/Pur	Avg–cost / Last–cost / Min–qty–OH / Max–qty–OH	Qty–on–hand / Qty–commit / Qty–on–ord / Min–ord–qty	Last–rcvd / 1st–rcvd / Last–ord / Last–sale
1100	**Drill, Power Hand**		I	TOOLS	E16	EACH	25.95	13.14000	30	6/01/97
			Y	4000	5010			13.140	0	6/01/97
	Hill Equipment & Supply	Products		4520				10	0	5/12/97
		1400–000						30	10	None

Better price: 22.57

Qty–sold:	this prd	0	last prd	0	this yr	0	Last yr	0
Sales:	this prd	.00	last prd	.00	this yr	.00	Last yr	.00
Cost:	this prd	.00	last prd	.00	this yr	.00	Last yr	.00

Item–#	Description	Bar–code / Subst–item–# / Hist–class / Inv–contra–#	Typ / Txb	Dept / Sls–# / Ret–#	Loc / COG–#	Stk–unit / Pur–unit / Prf–unit	List–price / Stk–qty/Pur	Avg–cost / Last–cost / Min–qty–OH / Max–qty–OH	Qty–on–hand / Qty–commit / Qty–on–ord / Min–ord–qty	Last–rcvd / 1st–rcvd / Last–ord / Last–sale
1105	**Drill, Cordless**		I	TOOLS	E17	10	29.95	14.95000	40	6/01/97
			Y	4000	5010			14.950	0	6/01/97
	Hill Equipment & Supply	Products		4520				10	0	5/12/97
		1400–000						40	10	None

Better price: 24.95

Qty–sold:	this prd	0	last prd	0	this yr	0	Last yr	0
Sales:	this prd	.00	last prd	.00	this yr	.00	Last yr	.00
Cost:	this prd	.00	last prd	.00	this yr	.00	Last yr	.00

Date: 06/03/97 Time: 10:45:36 | Acme Hardware Co. | Report #0105 Page #0002

ITEM LIST

Item-#	Description	Bar-code	Typ	Dept	Loc	Stk-unit	List-price	Avg-cost	Qty-on-hand	Last-rcvd
		Subst-item-#	Txb	Sls-#	COG-#	Pur-unit	Stk-qty/Pur	Last-cost	Qty-commit	1st-rcvd
	Vendor	Hist-class		Ret-#		Prf-unit		Min-qty-OH	Qty-on-ord	Last-ord
	Notes	Inv-contra-#						Max-qty-OH	Min-ord-qty	Last-sale
2200	**Hammer, 16 oz. claw**		I	TOOLS	F6	EACH	13.50	7.31000	15	6/01/97
			Y	4000	5010			7.310	0	6/01/97
	Hill Equipment & Supply	Products		4520		EACH		20	0	5/12/97
		1400-000						36	12	None

Better price: 12.60

Alt-price-1: 138.00 (12.00000 EACH per DOZ)

Qty-sold:	this prd	0	last prd	0	this yr	0	Last yr	0
Sales:	this prd	.00	last prd	.00	this yr	.00	Last yr	.00
Cost:	this prd	.00	last prd	.00	this yr	.00	Last yr	.00

Item-#	Description	Bar-code	Typ	Dept	Loc	Stk-unit	List-price	Avg-cost	Qty-on-hand	Last-rcvd
5770	**Chisel, 5 pc set**		I	TOOLS	E8	SET	28.50	18.20000	15	6/01/97
			Y	4000	5010	DOZ	218.40000	18.200	0	6/01/97
	Hill Equipment & Supply	Products		4520				15	0	5/12/97
		1400-000						24	12	None

Better price: 27.75

Qty-sold:	this prd	0	last prd	0	this yr	0	Last yr	0
Sales:	this prd	.00	last prd	.00	this yr	.00	Last yr	.00
Cost:	this prd	.00	last prd	.00	this yr	.00	Last yr	.00

Item-#	Description	Bar-code	Typ	Dept	Loc	Stk-unit	List-price	Avg-cost	Qty-on-hand	Last-rcvd
BS-BLOCK	**Block, Concrete**		I	MATL	K21	EACH	1.59	.99000	500	6/01/97
			Y	4010	5010	DOZ	11.88000	.990	0	6/01/97
	Hanson Manufacturing Co.	Products		4520		EACH		250	0	5/25/97
		1400-000						1,000	144	None

Better price: 1.39 (Cust type: WSL)

Alt-price-1: 15.00 (1.25000 EACH per DOZ)

Qty-sold:	this prd	0	last prd	0	this yr	0	Last yr	0
Sales:	this prd	.00	last prd	.00	this yr	.00	Last yr	.00
Cost:	this prd	.00	last prd	.00	this yr	.00	Last yr	.00

Date: 06/03/97 Time: 10:45:42 Acme Hardware Co. Report #0105 Page #0003

I T E M   L I S T

Item-#	Description	Bar-code	Typ	Dept	Loc	Stk-unit	List-price	Avg-cost	Qty-on-hand	Last-rcvd
		Subst-item-#	Txb	Sls-#	COG-#	Pur-unit	Stk-qty/Pur	Last-cost	Qty-commit	1st-rcvd
	Vendor	Hist-class		Ret-#		Prf-unit		Min-qty-OH	Qty-on-ord	Last-ord
	Notes	Inv-contra-#						Max-qty-OH	Min-ord-qty	Last-sale
BS-BRACKET	**Bracket sets**		I	MATL	K18	SET	44.95	32.00000	5	6/01/97
			Y	4010	5010			32.000	0	6/01/97
	Hill Equipment & Supply	Products		4520				2	0	5/25/97
		1400-000						12	6	None

Better price: 41.50

Qty-sold:	this prd	0	last prd	0	this yr	0	Last yr	0
Sales:	this prd	.00	last prd	.00	this yr	.00	Last yr	.00
Cost:	this prd	.00	last prd	.00	this yr	.00	Last yr	.00

Item-#	Description	Bar-code	Typ	Dept	Loc	Stk-unit	List-price	Avg-cost	Qty-on-hand	Last-rcvd
GS-DOORS	**Utility Door Unit**		I	MATL	K4	EACH	68.00	32.00000	5	6/01/97
			Y	4010	5010			32.000	0	6/01/97
	Hill Equipment & Supply	Products		4520				3	0	6/25/97
		1400-000						12	5	None

Better price: 55.00

Qty-sold:	this prd	0	last prd	0	this yr	0	Last yr	0
Sales:	this prd	.00	last prd	.00	this yr	.00	Last yr	.00
Cost:	this prd	.00	last prd	.00	this yr	.00	Last yr	.00

Item-#	Description	Bar-code	Typ	Dept	Loc	Stk-unit	List-price	Avg-cost	Qty-on-hand	Last-rcvd
BS-PLYWOOD	**Plywood, Exterior**		I	MATL	K6	EACH	13.95	7.00000	100	6/01/97
			Y	4010	5010			7.000	0	6/01/97
	Hanson Manufacturing Co.	Products		4520				60	0	5/05/97
		1400-000						200	36	None

Qty-sold:	this prd	0	last prd	0	this yr	0	Last yr	0
Sales:	this prd	.00	last prd	.00	this yr	.00	Last yr	.00
Cost:	this prd	.00	last prd	.00	this yr	.00	Last yr	.00

Date: 06/03/97 Time: 10:45:48 Acme Hardware Co. Report #0105 Page #0004

ITEM LIST

Item-#	Description	Bar-code	Typ	Dept	Loc	Stk-unit	List-price	Avg-cost	Qty-on-hand	Last-rcvd
		Subst-item-#	Txb	Sls-#	COG-#	Pur-unit	Stk-qty/Pur	Last-cost	Qty-commit	1st-rcvd
	Vendor	Hist-class		Ret-#		Prf-unit		Min-qty-OH	Qty-on-ord	Last-ord
	Notes	Inv-contra-#						Max-qty-OH	Min-ord-qty	Last-sale
EL-WIRE	**Electrical House Wire**		I	MATL	E43	REEL	5.19	2.50000	50	6/01/97
			Y	4000	5010			2.500	0	6/01/97
	Reynolds Tool Company	Products		4520				15	0	5/12/97
		1400-000						50	10	None

Qty-sold:	this prd	0	last prd	0	this yr	0	Last yr	0
Sales:	this prd	.00	last prd	.00	this yr	.00	Last yr	.00
Cost:	this prd	.00	last prd	.00	this yr	.00	Last yr	.00

Item-#	Description	Bar-code	Typ	Dept	Loc	Stk-unit	List-price	Avg-cost	Qty-on-hand	Last-rcvd
EQ-DEER	**Ignition Cable**		I	EQUIP	W6	EACH	87.00	40.00000	15	None
			Y	4000	5010			40.000	0	None
	Hill Equipment & Supply	Products		4520				5	0	None
		1400-000						25	12	None

Qty-sold:	this prd	0	last prd	0	this yr	0	Last yr	0
Sales:	this prd	.00	last prd	.00	this yr	.00	Last yr	.00
Cost:	this prd	.00	last prd	.00	this yr	.00	Last yr	.00

11 items on file

-- End of report --

Date 06/03/97 Acme Hardware Co. #0106 Page 0001

GENERAL JOURNAL TRANASACTION REGISTER

Period: 06/01/97 to 06/30/97

Account: 1400–000 Inventory

Trans–date	Debit–amt	Credit–amt	Reference
06/03/97	8,474.85		Beginning inventory

Account: 2520–000 Notes and Loans payable

Trans–date	Debit–amt	Credit–amt	Reference
06/03/97		8,474.85	Beginning inventory

Grand totals:	8,474.85	8,474.85	2 Transactions

–– End of report ––

Date: 06/03/97 Time: 11:17:07 Acme Hardware Co. Report #0107 Page #0001

INVOICE LIST

Costs shown were current at the time the invoice was entered.
For inventory items, actual costs are exactly determined during posting of invoices.

Bill–ref–#: 502 Invc–date: NONE YET Cust: Allied Plumbing Co. Deliver to: * SAME AS BILL ADDRESS *
Bill–group: ALE Profit–ctr: 000 555 N. Grand Blvd
Bill–type: INVOICE Lansing, MI 48135

Cust–PO–#: 23412 Invc–disc–%: .000
Terms: NET 30 Tax code: MI Mich. tax
Ship–via: TRUCK

Seq#	Type	Quantity Unit	Item/Service/Text		Unit price Unit cost	Line–item–net Line–disc–%	G/L acct Ret–to–inv	Txbl?
10	Inventory	50 EACH	1091	Gauge, Hi–Pressure	17.95 / EACH 9.720 / EACH	897.50	4000–000	Y
20	Inventory	3 EACH	2200	Hammer, 16 oz. claw	13.50 / EACH 7.310 / EACH	40.50	4000–000	Y
30	Inventory	2 SET	BS–BRACKET	Bracket sets	44.95 / SET 32.000 / SET	89.90	4010–000	Y
40	Inventory	10 REEL	EL–WIRE	Electrical House Wire	5.19 / REEL 2.500 / REEL	51.90	4000–000	Y

4 line items

Invoice total	:	1,079.80	Comment:	Thank you!
Invoice disc	:	.00		
Misc charges	:	.00		
Freight	:	45.00	Dist–to:	4920–000 (not taxbl)
Sales tax	:	75.59	Taxable:	1,079.80
Total billed	:	1,200.39		

Date: 06/03/97 Time: 11:17:11 Acme Hardware Co. Report #0107 Page #0002

INVOICE LIST

Bill–ref–#: 504 Invc–date: NONE YET Cust: Ariel Enterprises Deliver to: * SAME AS BILL ADDRESS *
Bill–group: ALE Profit–ctr: 000 69 Vacca Ct.
Bill–type: INVOICE East Kalamazoo, MI 12445

Cust–PO–#: 556ACS Invc–disc–%: .000
Terms: 2/10 NET 30 Tax code: MI Mich. tax
Ship–via: TRUCK

Seq#	Type	Quantity Unit	------------Item/Service/Text------------		Unit price Unit cost	Line–item–net Line–disc–%	G/L acct Ret–to–inv	Txbl?
10	Inventory	5 EACH	1100	Drill, Power Hand	25.95 / EACH 13.140 / EACH	129.75	4000–000	Y
20	Inventory	100 EACH	BS–BLOCK	Block, Concrete	1.59 / EACH .990 / EACH	159.00	4010–000	Y
30	Inventory	1 SET	BS–BRACKET	Bracket sets	44.95 / SET 32.000 / SET	44.95	4010–000	Y
40	Inventory	1 EACH	BS–DOORS	Utility Door Unit	68.00 / EACH 32.000 / EACH	68.00	4010–000	Y
50	Inventory	15 REEL	EL–WIRE	Electrical House Wire	5.19 / REEL 2.500 / REEL	77.85	4000–000	Y
60	Inventory	2 EACH	EQ–DEER	Ignition Cable	87.00 / EACH 40.000 / EACH	174.00	4000–000	Y

6 line items

Invoice total :	653.55		
Invoice disc :	.00		
Misc charges :	.00		
Freight :	145.00	Dist–to:	4920–000 (not taxbl)
Sales tax :	45.75	Taxable:	653.55
Total billed :	844.30		

Comment: Hope we satisfy your building needs!

Date: 06/03/97 Time: 11:17:15 | Acme Hardware Co. | Report #0107 Page #0003

INVOICE LIST

Bill-ref-#: 501 | Invc-date: NONE YET | Cust: Elliott Enterprises | Deliver to: * SAME AS BILL ADDRESS *
Bill-group: ALE | Profit-ctr: 000 | 123 Broadway
Bill-type: INVOICE | Glendale, MI 48133

Cust-PO-#: 6410 | Invc-disc-%: .000
Terms: 2/10 NET 30 | Tax code: MI Mich. tax
Ship-via: TRUCK

Seq#	Type	Quantity Unit	----Item/Service/Text----		Unit price Unit cost	Line-item-net Line-disc-%	G/L acct Ret-to-inv	Txbl?
10	Inventory	5 10	1105	Drill, Cordless	29.95 / 10 14.950 / 10	149.75	4000-000	Y
20	Inventory	5 SET	5770	Chisel, 5 pc set	28.50 / SET 18.200 / SET	142.50	4000-000	Y
30	Inventory	100 EACH	BS-BLOCK	Block, Concrete	1.59 / EACH .990 / EACH	159.00	4010-000	Y

3 line items

Invoice total	:	451.25			Comment: Thanks Paul!
Invoice disc	:	.00			
Misc charges	:	.00			
Freight	:	85.00	Dist-to:	4920-000 (not taxbl)	
Sales tax	:	31.59	Taxable:	451.25	
Total billed	:	567.84			

Date: 06/03/97 Time: 11:17:18 | Acme Hardware Co. | Report #0107 Page #0004

I N V O I C E   L I S T

Bill-ref-#: 503 | Invc-date: NONE YET | Cust: Holcomb Industrial Supply | Deliver to: * SAME AS BILL ADDRESS *
Bill-group: ALE | Profit-ctr: 000 | 2323 Holcomb Way
Bill-type: INVOICE | Lansing, MI 48135

Cust-PO-#: 12229 | Invc-disc-%: .000
Terms: 2/10 NET 30 | Tax code: MI Mich. tax
Ship-via: TRUCK

Seq#	Type	Quantity Unit	Item/Service/Text		Unit price Unit cost	Line-item-net Line-disc-%	G/L acct Ret-to-inv	Txbl?
10	Inventory	150 EACH	1091	Gauge, Hi-Pressure	17.95 / EACH 9.720 / EACH	2,692.50	4000-000	Y
20	Inventory	200 EACH	BS-BLOCK	Block, Concrete	1.59 / EACH .990 / EACH	318.00	4010-000	Y
30	Inventory	3 EACH	BS-DOORS	Utility Door Unit	68.00 / EACH 32.000 / EACH	204.00	4010-000	Y
40	Inventory	100 EACH	BS-PLYWOOD	Plywood, Exterior	13.95 / EACH 7.000 / EACH	1,395.00	4010-000	Y
50	Inventory	1 EACH	EQ-DEER	Ignition Cable	87.00 / EACH 40.000 / EACH	87.00	4000-000	Y

5 line items

Invoice total :	4,696.50		Comment: Thank you for your business!
Invoice disc :	.00		
Misc charges :	.00		
Freight :	145.00	Dist-to:	4920-000 (not taxbl)
Sales tax :	328.76	Taxable:	4,696.50
Total billed :	5,170.26		

Date: 06/03/97 Time: 11:17:21 | Acme Hardware Co. | Report #0107 Page #0005

INVOICE LIST

Bill-ref-#: 505 | Invc-date: NONE YET | Cust: Webber Landscaping | Deliver to: * SAME AS BILL ADDRESS *
Bill-group: ALE | Profit-ctr: 000 | 33 East Lansing Dr.
Bill-type: INVOICE | Winoga Falls, MI 12345

Cust-PO-#: 23423 | Invc-disc-%: .000
Terms: 2/10 NET 30 | Tax code: MI Mich. tax
Ship-via: TRUCK

Seq#	Type	Quantity / Unit	Item/Service/Text		Unit price / Unit cost	Line-item-net / Line-disc-%	G/L acct / Ret-to-inv	Txbl?
10	Inventory	50 EACH	1091	Gauge, Hi-Pressure	17.95 / EACH 9.720 / EACH	897.50	4000-000	Y
20	Inventory	50 EACH	BS-BLOCK	Block, Concrete	1.59 / EACH .990 / EACH	79.50	4010-000	Y
30	Inventory	1 SET	BS-BRACKET	Bracket sets	44.95 / SET 32.000 / SET	44.95	4010-000	Y
40	Inventory	20 REEL	EL-WIRE	Electrical House Wire	5.19 / REEL 2.500 / REEL	103.80	4000-000	Y

4 line items
Invoice total : 1,125.75 — Comment: We appreciate your business!
Invoice disc : .00
Misc charges : .00
Freight : 65.00 — Dist-to: 4920-000 (not taxbl)
Sales tax : 78.80 — Taxable: 1,125.75
Total billed : 1,269.55

Date: 06/03/97 Time: 11:17:24 Acme Hardware Co. Report #0107 Page #0006

INVOICE LIST

5 Invoices with	22 line items	Total amount of Invoices:	8,006.85		
		Freight:	485.00		
		Sales tax:	560.49	Taxable:	8,006.85
		Total amount Billed:	9,052.34		

-- End of report --

SALES INVOICE TO ALLIED PLUMBING CO.

INVOICE

Acme Hardware
123 Main St.
Winoga Falls, MI 12345

Date: 6/03/97 Page: 1
Invoice #: 500

Sold to:

Allied Plumbing Co.
555 N. Grand Blvd
Lansing, MI 48135

Ship to:

Allied Plumbing Co.
555 N. Grand Blvd
Lansing, MI 48135

Ref-#	P.O.-#	Terms	Ship-via
502	23412	NET 30	TRUCK

Item-#	Description	Quantity	Unit	Unit-price	Ext-price
1091	Gauge, Hi-Pressure	50	EACH	17.95	897.50
2200	Hammer, 16 oz. claw	3	EACH	13.50	40.50
BS-BRACKET	Bracket sets	2	SET	44.95	89.90
EL-WIRE	Electrical House Wire	10	REEL	5.19	51.90

Sale total:	1079.80
Misc. charges:	0.00
Sales tax:	75.59
Shipping:	45.00
Invoice total:	1200.39

Thank you!

SALES INVOICE TO ARIEL ENTERPRISES

INVOICE

Acme Hardware
123 Main St.
Winoga Falls, MI 12345

Date: 6/03/97 Page: 1
Invoice #: 501

Sold to:	Ship to:
Ariel Enterprises 69 Vacca Ct. East Kalamazoo, MI 12445	Ariel Enterprises 69 Vacca Ct. East Kalamazoo, MI 12445

Ref-#	P.O.-#	Terms	Ship-via
504	556ACS	2/10 NET 30	TRUCK

Item-#	Description	Quantity	Unit	Unit-price	Ext-price
1100	Drill, Power Hand	5	EACH	25.95	129.75
BS-BLOCK	Block, Concrete	100	EACH	1.59	159.00
BS-BRACKET	Bracket sets	1	SET	44.95	44.95
BS-DOORS	Utility Door Unit	1	EACH	68.00	68.00
EL-WIRE	Electrical House Wire	15	REEL	5.19	77.85
EQ-DEER	Ignition Cable	2	EACH	87.00	174.00

Sale total:	653.55
Misc. charges:	0.00
Sales tax:	45.75
Shipping:	145.00
Invoice total:	844.30

Hope we satisfy your building needs!

SALES INVOICE TO ELLIOTT ENTERPRISES

INVOICE

Acme Hardware
123 Main St.
Winoga Falls, MI 12345

Date: 6/03/97 Page: 1
Invoice #: 502

Sold to:

Elliott Enterprises
123 Broadway
Glendale, MI 48133

Ship to:

Elliott Enterprises
123 Broadway
Glendale, MI 48133

Ref–#	P.O.–#	Terms	Ship–via
501	6410	2/10 NET 30	TRUCK

Item–#	Description	Quantity	Unit	Unit–price	Ext–price
1105	Drill, Cordless	5	10	29.95	149.75
5770	Chisel, 5 pc set	5	SET	28.50	142.50
BS–BLOCK	Block, Concrete	100	EACH	1.59	159.00

	Sale total:	451.25
Thanks Paul!	Misc. charges:	0.00
	Sales tax:	31.59
	Shipping:	85.00
	Invoice total:	567.84

SALES INVOICE TO HOLCOMB INDUSTRIAL SUPPLY

INVOICE

Acme Hardware
123 Main St.
Winoga Falls, MI 12345

Date: 6/03/97 Page: 1
Invoice #: 503

Sold to:

Holcomb Industrial Supply
2323 Holcomb Way
Lansing, MI 48135

Ship to:

Holcomb Industrial Supply
2323 Holcomb Way
Lansing, MI 48135

Ref-#	P.O.-#	Terms	Ship-via
503	12229	2/10 NET 30	TRUCK

Item-#	Description	Quantity	Unit	Unit-price	Ext-price
1091	Gauge, Hi-Pressure	150	EACH	17.95	2,692.50
BS-BLOCK	Block, Concrete	200	EACH	1.59	318.00
BS-DOORS	Utility Door Unit	3	EACH	68.00	204.00
BS-PLYWOOD	Plywood, Exterior	100	EACH	13.95	1,395.00
EQ-DEER	Ignition Cable	1	EACH	87.00	87.00

Sale total:	4,696.50
Misc. charges:	0.00
Sales tax:	328.76
Shipping:	145.00
Invoice total:	5,170.26

Thank you for your business!

SALES INVOICE TO WEBBER LANDSCAPING

INVOICE

Acme Hardware
123 Main St.
Winoga Falls, MI 12345

Date: 6/03/97 Page: 1
Invoice #: 504

Sold to:

Webber Landscaping
33 East Lansing Dr.
Winoga Falls, MI 12345

Ship to:

Webber Landscaping
33 East Lansing Dr.
Winoga Falls, MI 12345

Ref-#	P.O.-#	Terms	Ship-via
505	23423	2/10 NET 30	TRUCK

Item-#	Description	Quantity	Unit	Unit-price	Ext-price
1091	Gauge, Hi-Pressure	50	EACH	17.95	897.50
BS-BLOCK	Block, Concrete	50	EACH	1.59	79.50
BS-BRACKET	Bracket sets	1	SET	44.95	44.95
EL-WIRE	Electrical House Wire	20	REEL	5.19	103.80

Sale total:	1,125.75
Misc. charges:	0.00
Sales tax:	78.80
Shipping:	65.00
Invoice total:	1,269.55

We appreciate your business!

Date 06/03/97 Time 11:22:01 | Acme Hardware Co. | Report #0108 Page #0001

INVENTORY TRANSACTION REGISTER

Current period ending date: 6/30/97

G/L account is shown for up and down adjustments; Profit center is shown for sales and credit memos
List, better, best, and alternate prices are only shown if modified by the transaction
Cost correction is only shown if applicable to the transaction

Date	Type	Doc-#	Trans-qty Unit Running-qty-oh	Unit-cost	Tot-actual-cost New-avg-cost	Comment G/L-acct/Pft-cntr	Price-per-unit
Item: 1091		**Gauge, Hi-Pressure**			Stocking unit:	EACH	
6/03/97	Sale	000500	50 EACH 450 EACH	9.720	486.00 9.72000	From invoice: 000500 000	17.950
6/03/97	Sale	000503	150 EACH 300 EACH	9.720	1,458.00 9.72000	From invoice: 000503 000	17.950
6/03/97	Sale	000504	50 EACH 250 EACH	9.720	486.00 9.72000	From invoice: 000504 000	17.950
Item: 1100		**Drill, Power Hand**			Stocking unit:	EACH	
6/03/97	Sale	000501	5 EACH 25 EACH	13.140	65.70 13.14000	From invoice: 000501 000	25.950
Item: 1105		**Drill, Cordless**			Stocking unit:	10	
6/03/97	Sale	000502	5 10 35 10	14.950	74.75 14.95000	From invoice: 000502 000	29.950
Item: 2200		**Hammer, 16 oz. claw**			Stocking unit:	EACH Alt-unit-1: DOZ	
6/03/97	Sale	000500	3 EACH 12 EACH	7.310	21.93 7.31000	From invoice: 000500 000	13.500
Item: 5770		**Chisel, 5 pc set**			Stocking unit:	SET	
6/03/97	Sale	000502	5 SET 10 SET	18.200	91.00 18.20000	From invoice: 000502 000	28.500

Date 06/03/97 Time 11:22:06 | Acme Hardware Co. | Report #0108 Page #0002

INVENTORY TRANSACTION REGISTER

Date	Type	Doc-#	Trans-qty	Unit	Unit-cost	Tot-actual-cost	Comment	Price-per-unit
			Running-qty-oh			New-avg-cost	G/L-acct/Pft-cntr	
Item: BS-BLOCK		**Block, Concrete**				Stocking unit:	EACH Alt-unit-1: DOZ	
6/03/97	Sale	000502	100	EACH	0.990	99.00	From invoice: 000502	1.590
			400	EACH		0.99000	000	
6/03/97	Sale	000503	200	EACH	0.990	198.00	From invoice: 000503	1.590
			200	EACH		0.99000	000	
6/03/97	Sale	000501	100	EACH	0.990	99.00	From invoice: 000501	1.590
			100	EACH		0.99000	000	
6/03/97	Sale	000504	50	EACH	0.990	49.50	From invoice: 000504	1.590
			50	EACH		0.99000	000	
Item: BS-BRACKET		**Bracket sets**				Stocking unit:	SET	
6/03/97	Sale	000500	2	SET	32.000	64.00	From invoice: 000500	44.950
			3	SET		32.00000	000	
6/03/97	Sale	000501	1	SET	32.000	32.00	From invoice: 000501	44.950
			2	SET		32.00000	000	
6/03/97	Sale	000504	1	SET	32.000	32.00	From invoice: 000504	44.950
			1	SET		32.00000	000	
Item: BS-DOORS		**Utility Door Unit**				Stocking unit:	EACH	
6/03/97	Sale	000503	3	EACH	32.000	96.00	From invoice: 000503	68.000
			2	EACH		32.00000	000	
6/03/97	Sale	000501	1	EACH	32.000	32.00	From invoice: 000501	68.000
			1	EACH		32.00000	000	
Item: BS-PLYWOOD		**Plywood, Exterior**				Stocking unit:	EACH	
6/03/97	Sale	000503	100	EACH	7.000	700.00	From invoice: 000503	13.950
			0	EACH		7.00000	000	

Date 06/03/97 Time 11:22:11 Acme Hardware Co. Report #0108 Page #0003

INVENTORY TRANSACTION REGISTER

Date	Type	Doc-#	Trans-qty / Running-qty-oh	Unit	Unit-cost	Tot-actual-cost / New-avg-cost	Comment / G/L-acct/Pft-cntr	Price-per-unit
Item: EL-WIRE		**Electrical House Wire**				Stocking unit:	REEL	
6/03/97	Sale	000500	10	REEL	2.500	25.00	From invoice: 000500	5.190
			40	REEL		2.50000	000	
6/03/97	Sale	000501	15	REEL	2.500	37.50	From invoice: 000501	5.190
			25	REEL		2.50000	000	
6/03/97	Sale	000504	20	REEL	2.500	50.00	From invoice: 000504	5.190
			5	REEL		2.50000	000	
Item: EQ-DEER		**Ignition Cable**				Stocking unit:	EACH	
6/03/97	Sale	000503	1	EACH	40.000	40.00	From invoice: 000503	87.000
			14	EACH		40.00000	000	
6/03/97	Sale	000501	2	EACH	40.000	80.00	From invoice: 000501	87.000
			12	EACH		40.00000	000	

Grand totals:						
	Receiving entries:	0	Qty received:	0	Cost:	.00
	Credit memo entries:	0	Qty credited:	0	Cost:	.00
	Up adj entries:	0	Qty adjusted:	0	Cost:	.00
	Down adj entries:	0	Qty adjusted:	0	Cost:	.00
	Sale entries:	22	Qty sold:	874	Cost:	4,317.38

-- End of report --

Date 06/03/97 | Acme Hardware Co. | #0109 Page 0001

SALES REGISTER

Customer–name / Trans–type		Trans–dat / Reference	Doc–#	Terms	Apply–to	Trans–amt
Allied Plumbing Co.		06/03/97	500	NET 30		1,200.39
Sale		Ref #: 000502				
Distributions:	4920–000	Freight charges			45.00	
	2430–000	Accrued state sales tax			75.59	
	4000–000	Sales – Main St. Store			989.90	
	4010–000	Sales – Yard			89.90	
Ariel Enterprises		06/03/97	501	2/10 NET 30		844.30
Sale		Ref #: 000504				
Distributions:	4920–000	Freight charges			145.00	
	2430–000	Accrued state sales tax			45.75	
	4000–000	Sales – Main St. Store			381.60	
	4010–000	Sales – Yard			271.95	
Elliott Enterprises		06/03/97	502	2/10 NET 30		567.84
Sale		Ref #: 000501				
Distributions:	4920–000	Freight charges			85.00	
	2430–000	Accrued state sales tax			31.59	
	4000–000	Sales – Main St. Store			292.25	
	4010–000	Sales – Yard			159.00	
Holcomb Industrial Supply		06/03/97	503	2/10 NET 30		5,170.26
Sale		Ref #: 000503				
Distributions:	4920–000	Freight charges			145.00	
	2430–000	Accrued state sales tax			328.76	
	4000–000	Sales – Main St. Store			2,779.50	
	4010–000	Sales – Yard			1,917.00	
Webber Landscaping		06/03/97	504	2/10 NET 30		1,269.55
Sale		Ref #: 000505				
Distributions:	4920–000	Freight charges			65.00	
	2430–000	Accrued state sales tax			78.80	
	4000–000	Sales – Main St. Store			1,001.30	
	4010–000	Sales – Yard			124.45	
5 Sales transactions				Grand total:	9,052.34	

Date 06/03/97 | Acme Hardware Co. | #0109 Page 0002

SALES REGISTER

------------G/L account distribution totals------------

560.49	credited to 2430–000	Accrued state sales tax
5,444.55	credited to 4000–000	Sales – Main St. Store
2,562.30	credited to 4010–000	Sales – Yard
485.00	credited to 4920–000	Freight charges

9,052.34	Total credited	
9,052.34	debited to 1100–000	Accts Receivable – Trade

-- End of report --

Practice Set 6 – PROCESS NON–INVOICED SALES AND DR/CR MEMOS

Introduction

You can assume that the Hardware store represented by this practice set would be required to handle special sales, debit and credit memos, and recurring sales accounts. This practice set asks you to process these special types of sales transactions, and to make special postings to make these types of transactions consistent with sales invoicing transactions. You are asked to:

- ➡ process several non–invoiced sales
- ➡ process a credit memo
- ➡ process a debit memo
- ➡ print an A/R transaction list
- ➡ post A/R transactions
- ➡ view customer accounts
- ➡ add a recurring sale

Set Transaction Date

Before starting this practice set, enter today's date as **06–10–97.**

Process Non–Invoiced Sales

Move to accounts receivable and select Process Sales and DR/CR Memos, followed by Add Trans–actions. Enter the following information for two accounts ... Neptune Underwater Supply, and Newton, Boyd and Co.

Neptune Underwater Supply

Trans	Date	Doc #	$	Terms	Reference	G/L
Sale	6/04/97	S100	25.95	CASH	1100 Qty 1	4000
Sale	6/07/97	S101	28.50	CASH	5770 Qty 1	4000
Sale	6/10/97	S102	44.95	CASH	BS–BRACKET Qty 1	4010
Sale	6/10/97	T101	6.96	CASH	Sales Tax	2430

Newton, Boyd and Company

Trans	Date	Doc #	$	Terms	Reference	G/L
Sale	6/04/97	S103	29.95	NET 30	1105 Qty 1	4000
Sale	6/05/97	S104	68.00	NET 30	BS–DOORS Qty 1	4010
Sale	6/08/97	S105	87.00	NET 30	EQ–DEER Qty 1	4010
Credit	6/10/97	C105	87.00	NET 30	EQ–DEER Qty 1	4010
Sale	6/10/97	S106	25.95	NET 30	EL–WIRE Qty 5	4010
Sale	6/10/97	T102	8.67	NET 30	Sales Tax	2430

Print the Sales Edit List

After you have entered the transactions for the two accounts, exit and select Print Transaction Edit List. After printing the Sales Edit list, answer the following questions:

How much does accounts receivable increase?
How is a credit shown on this list?

Post the Sales and Credit Transactions

Once you are satisfied with the transactions printed on the Sales Edit list, select Post Transactions and print the Sales Register.

* Compare this Sales Register to the one printed for the last practice set.

How do the two registers differ?

View Customer Accounts

Exit and view the Neptune Underwater Supply and the Newton, Boyd and Co. accounts. Compare these to the view of Allied Plumbing.

How do the views differ?

Special Postings

To make non–invoiced transactions consistent with invoiced transactions, changes to inventory and adjustments to sales totals are required.

* Exit Accounts Receivable and select Inventory Management.

* Move to Process Inventory and add the following transactions (use the dates from the Sales Register shown in a previous step):

Item No.	Type	Doc #	Trans–qty	Comment
1100	Sale	S100	1	Neptune Underwater Supply
5770	Sale	S101	1	Neptune Underwater Supply
BS–BRACKET	Sale	S102	1	Neptune Underwater Supply
1105	Sale	S103	1	Newton, Boyd and Co.
BS–DOORS	Sale	S104	1	Newton, Boyd and Co.
EL–WIRE	Sale	S106	5	Newton, Boyd and Co.
EQ–DEER	Sale	S105	1	Newton, Boyd and Co.
EQ–DEER	Adjustment	C105	1	Newton, Boyd and Co.

* After making these postings, print the Inventory Transaction list and, once satisfied, print the Inventory Transaction Register.

Answer the following:

Why is this special posting required?
What happens if it is not completed?

Add a Recurring Sale

Next, we ask you to add a recurring sale. Use a next due date of 6/10/97. You know the following:

21st Century Construction places a monthly order for 50 high pressure gauges. Delivery is requested on the 10th of each month. The unit price is 17.95 (sorry, no price discount). The details of the sale are:

			Post to acct:
50 units @ 17.95	=	**$ 897.50**	**4000**
Sales tax	=	**62.82**	**2430**
Freight	=	**11.65**	**4920**

Total Amount	=	**$ 971.97**	
Terms:		**2/10 NET 30**	
Reference:		**1091 Qty 50**	

To add this type of sale, remember to press F1 from the Process Sales and DR/CR Memos menu to make selection 6 appear.

After entering this sales information, print the Recurring Sales List, and answer the following question:

What '' message is added to this report?**

Activate the Recurring Sale

Continue on to activate the recurring sale. Select Activate Individual. Use a next due date of 7/10/97 and a document # of S107. Once activated,

* Print the Sales Transaction Edit List

* Post the sale, and print the Sales Register.

By how many dollars does Accounts Receivable increase as a result of this transaction?

Special Inventory Posting

As before, a non–invoiced sale requires special postings. Do the following:

* Select Inventory Management to process (add) the 50 units of inventory sold for item 1091. Use the document number RS100. Comment: 21st Century Construction.

* Print the Inventory Transaction Edit List

* Print Inventory Transaction Register

* Compare the processing of a recurring sale to the processing of the same sale using the customer invoicing module.

  What are the advantages of entering a recurring sale? What are the disadvantages?

Special Sales Postings

Besides posting inventory, posting the type of sale to a product account is also necessary.

* Move to the A/R menu once again and print the customer list. Observe how the detailed entries from Non–invoiced Sales differ from the entries for A/R – Process Sales entries.

* Select Accounts Receivable to do maintenance on customer data. Change this year's Product Sales (field #24) for customers Neptune Underwater Supply and Newton, Boyd and Co. to correspond to their Sales This Year (field #22).

* Likewise, change Product Sales for 21st Century Construction. However, in this case, do not include its Freight and Sales Tax in the amount you record.

  IMPORTANT NOTE! Since this is a restricted field, press F2 to gain entrance to the field. If PAS does not allow you to make changes to a restricted field using the F2 key, return to Setup Functions and select Maintain Company Data. Change field 8 from No to Yes. Then return to A/R – Maintain Customer Data and change product sales information for the three accounts.

More Things to Explore

* Log off and change the date to 07/10/97. Log on and move to Process Sales and DR/CR Memos. Display the recurring sales list.

  What information on this report has been changed?

* Print the Inventory Status Report.

  Which inventory items are now out of stock?
  Which inventory items are understocked?
  What is meant by the term understocked?

This completes Practice Set 6.

Date 06/10/97 Acme Hardware Co. #0110 Page 0001

SALES EDIT LIST

Customer-name Trans-type	Trans-dat Reference	Doc-#	Terms	Apply-to	Trans-amt
Neptune Underwater Supply	06/04/97	S100	CASH		25.95
Sale	1100 Qty 1				
Distributions: 4000-000	Sales - Main St. Store			25.95	
Neptune Underwater Supply	06/07/97	S101	CASH		28.50
Sale	5770 Qty 1				
Distributions: 4000-000	Sales - Main St. Store			28.50	
Neptune Underwater Supply	06/10/97	S102	CASH		44.95
Sale	BS-BRACKET Qty 1				
Distributions: 4010-000	Sales - Yard			44.95	
Neptune Underwater Supply	06/10/97	T101	CASH		6.96
Sale	Sales Tax				
Distributions: 2430-000	Accrued state sales tax			6.96	
Newton, Boyd, and Co.	06/04/97	S103	NET 30		29.95
Sale	1105 Qty 1				
Distributions: 4000-000	Sales - Main St. Store			29.95	
Newton, Boyd, and Co.	06/05/97	S104	NET 30		68.00
Sale	BS-DOORS Qty 1				
Distributions: 4010-000	Sales - Yard			68.00	
Newton, Boyd, and Co.	06/08/97	S105	NET 30		87.00
Sale	EQ-DEER Qty 1				
Distributions: 4010-000	Sales - Yard			87.00	
Newton, Boyd, and Co.	06/10/97	C105	NET 30		87.00 CR
CR memo	EQ-DEER Qty 1				
Distributions: 4010-000	Sales - Yard			87.00	
Newton, Boyd, and Co.	06/10/97	S106	NET 30		25.95
Sale	EL-WIRE Qty 5				
Distributions: 4010-000	Sales - Yard			25.95	
Newton, Boyd, and Co.	06/10/97	T102	NET 30		8.67
Sale	Sales Tax				
Distributions: 2430-000	Accrued state sales tax			8.67	

10 Sales transactions Grand total: 238.93

Date 06/10/97	Acme Hardware Co.	#0110 Page 0002

SALES EDIT LIST

------------G/L account distribution totals------------

87.00	credited to 1100–000	Accts Receivable – Trade
15.63	credited to 2430–000	Accrued state sales tax
84.40	credited to 4000–000	Sales – Main St. Store
225.90	credited to 4010–000	Sales – Yard

412.93	Total credited	
325.93	debited to 1100–000	Accts Receivable – Trade
87.00	debited to 4010–000	Sales – Yard

412.93	Total debited	

-- End of report --

Date 06/10/97 Acme Hardware Co. #0111 Page 0001

SALES REGISTER

Customer–name Trans–type	Trans–dat Reference	Doc–#	Terms	Apply–to	Trans–amt
Neptune Underwater Supply	06/04/97	S100	CASH		25.95
Sale	1100 Qty 1				
Distributions: 4000–000	Sales – Main St. Store			25.95	
Neptune Underwater Supply	06/07/97	S101	CASH		28.50
Sale	5770 Qty 1				
Distributions: 4000–000	Sales – Main St. Store			28.50	
Neptune Underwater Supply	06/10/97	S102	CASH		44.95
Sale	BS–BRACKET Qty 1				
Distributions: 4010–000	Sales – Yard			44.95	
Neptune Underwater Supply	06/10/97	T101	CASH		6.96
Sale	Sales Tax				
Distributions: 2430–000	Accrued state sales tax			6.96	
Newton, Boyd, and Co.	06/04/97	S103	NET 30		29.95
Sale	1105 Qty 1				
Distributions: 4000–000	Sales – Main St. Store			29.95	
Newton, Boyd, and Co.	06/05/97	S104	NET 30		68.00
Sale	BS–DOORS Qty 1				
Distributions: 4010–000	Sales – Yard			68.00	
Newton, Boyd, and Co.	06/08/97	S105	NET 30		87.00 CR
Sale	EQ–DEER Qty 1				
Distributions: 4010–000	Sales – Yard			87.00	
Newton, Boyd, and Co.	00/10/97	C105	NET 30		87.00
CR memo	EQ–DEER Qty 1				
Distributions: 4010–000	Sales – Yard			87.00	
Newton, Boyd, and Co.	06/10/97	S106	NET 30		25.95
Sale	EL–WIRE Qty 5				
Distributions: 4010–000	Sales – Yard			25.95	
Newton, Boyd, and Co.	06/10/97	T102	NET 30		8.67
Sale	Sales Tax				
Distributions: 2430–000	Accrued state sales tax			8.67	

10 Sales transactions Grand total: 238.93

Date 06/10/97 Acme Hardware Co. #0111 Page 0002

SALES REGISTER

-----------G/L account distribution totals-----------

87.00	credited to 1100–000	Accts Receivable – Trade
15.63	credited to 2430–000	Accrued state sales tax
84.40	credited to 4000–000	Sales – Main St. Store
225.90	credited to 4010–000	Sales – Yard

412.93	Total credited	
325.93	debited to 1100–000	Accts Receivable – Trade
87.00	debited to 4010–000	Sales – Yard

412.93	Total debited	

-- End of report --

Date 06/10/97 Time: 21:09:30 Acme Hardware Co. Report #0112 Page #0001

INVENTORY TRANSACTION EDIT LIST

Current period ending date: 6/30/97
Item # range: "First" to "Last"

G/L account is shown for up and down adjustments; Profit center is shown for sales and credit memos
List, better, best, and alternate prices are only shown if modified by the transaction
Cost correction is only shown if applicable to the transaction

Date	Type	Doc-#	Trans-qty Unit / Running-qty-oh	Unit-cost	Tot-actual-cost / New-avg-cost	Comment / G/L-acct/Pft-cntr	Price-per-unit
Item: 1100		**Drill, Power Hand**			Stocking unit:	EACH	
6/04/97	Sale	S100	1 EACH	13.140	13.14	Neptune Underwater Supply	25.950
			24 EACH		13.14000	000	
Item: 1105		**Drill, Cordless**			Stocking unit:	10	
6/04/97	Sale	S103	1 10	14.950	14.95	Newton, Boyd and Co.	29.950
			34 10		14.95000	000	
Item: 5770		**Chisel, 5 pc set**			Stocking unit:	SET	
6/07/97	Sale	S101	1 SET	18.200	18.20	Neptune Underwater Supply	28.500
			9 SET		18.20000	000	
Item: BS-BRACKET		**Bracket sets**			Stocking unit:	SET	
6/10/97	Sale	S102	1 SET	32.000	32.00	Neptune Underwater Supply	44.950
			0 SET		32.00000	000	
Item: BS-DOORS		**Utility Door Unit**			Stocking unit:	EACH	
6/05/97	Sale	S104	1 EACH	32.000	32.00	Newton, Boyd and Co.	68.000
			0 EACH		32.00000	000	
Item: EL-WIRE		**Electrical House Wire**			Stocking unit:	REEL	
6/10/97	Sale	S106	5 REEL	2.500	12.50	Newton, Boyd and Co.	5.190
			0 REEL		2.50000	000	

Date 06/10/97 Time: 21:09:35 Acme Hardware Co. Report #0112 Page #0002

INVENTORY TRANSACTION EDIT LIST

Date	Type	Doc-#	Trans-qty Unit Running-qty-oh	Unit-cost	Tot-actual-cost New-avg-cost	Comment G/L-acct/Pft-cntr	Price-per-unit
Item: EQ-DEER		**Ignition Cable**			Stocking unit:	EACH	
6/08/97	Sale	S105	1 EACH	40.000	40.00	Newton, Boyd and Co.	87.000
			11 EACH		40.00000	000	
6/10/97	Up adj	C105	1 EACH	40.000	40.00	Newton, Boyd and Co.	
			12 EACH		40.00000	000	
			(1 EACH	40.000)			

Grand totals:						
	Receiving entries:	0	Qty received:	0	Cost:	.00
	Credit memo entries:	0	Qty credited:	0	Cost:	.00
	Up adj entries:	1	Qty adjusted:	1	Cost:	40.00
	Down adj entries:	0	Qty adjusted:	0	Cost:	.00
	Sale entries:	7	Qty sold:	11	Cost:	162.79

-- End of report --

Date 06/10/97 Time: 21:11:09 Acme Hardware Co. Report #0113 Page #0001

INVENTORY TRANSACTION REGISTER

Current period ending date: 6/30/97

G/L account is shown for up and down adjustments; Profit center is shown for sales and credit memos

List, better, best, and alternate prices are only shown if modified by the transaction

Cost correction is only shown if applicable to the transaction

Date	Type	Doc-#	Trans-qty Unit Running-qty-oh	Unit-cost	Tot-actual-cost New-avg-cost	Comment G/L-acct/Pft-cntr	Price-per-unit
Item: 1100		**Drill, Power Hand**			Stocking unit:	EACH	
6/04/97	Sale	S100	1 EACH	13.140	13.14	Neptune Underwater Supply	25.950
			24 EACH		13.14000	000	
Item: 1105		**Drill, Cordless**			Stocking unit:	10	
6/04/97	Sale	S103	1 10	14.950	14.95	Newton, Boyd and Co.	29.950
			34 10		14.95000	000	
Item: 5770		**Chisel, 5 pc set**			Stocking unit:	SET	
6/07/97	Sale	S101	1 SET	18.200	18.20	Neptune Underwater Supply	28.500
			9 SET		18.20000	000	
Item: BS-BRACKET		**Bracket sets**			Stocking unit:	SET	
6/10/97	Sale	S102	1 SET	32.000	32.00	Neptune Underwater Supply	44.950
			0 SET		32.00000	000	
Item: BS-DOORS		**Utility Door Unit**			Stocking unit:	EACH	
6/05/97	Sale	S104	1 EACH	32.000	32.00	Newton, Boyd and Co.	68.000
			0 EACH		32.00000	000	
Item: EL-WIRE		**Electrical House Wire**			Stocking unit:	REEL	
6/10/97	Sale	S106	5 REEL	2.500	12.50	Newton, Boyd and Co.	5.190
			0 REEL		2.50000	000	

Date 06/10/97 Time: 21:11:14 | Acme Hardware Co. | Report #0113 Page #0002

INVENTORY TRANSACTION REGISTER

Date	Type	Doc-#	Trans-qty Unit / Running-qty-oh	Unit-cost	Tot-actual-cost / New-avg-cost	Comment / G/L-acct/Pft-cntr	Price-per-unit
Item: EQ-DEER		**Ignition Cable**			Stocking unit:	EACH	
6/08/97	Sale	S105	1 EACH	40.000	40.00	Newton, Boyd and Co.	87.000
			11 EACH		40.00000	000	
6/10/97	Up adj	C105	1 EACH	40.000	40.00	Newton, Boyd and Co.	
			12 EACH		40.00000	000	
			(1 EACH	40.000)			

Grand totals:							
	Receiving entries:	0	Qty received:	0	Cost:	.00
	Credit memo entries:	0	Qty credited:	0	Cost:	.00
	Up adj entries:	1	Qty adjusted:	1	Cost:	40.00
	Down adj entries:	0	Qty adjusted:	0	Cost:	.00
	Sale entries:	7	Qty sold:	11	Cost:	162.79

-- End of report --

Date 06/10/97 Acme Hardware Co. #0115 Page #0001

RECURRING SALES LIST

" ** " next to date means the transaction is now due

Customer–name	Next–due–date	Terms		Trans–amt
Frequency	Reference			
21st Century Construction	06/10/97 **	2/10 NET 30		971.97
Monthly				
Distributions: 4000–000	Sales – Main St. Store		897.50	
2430–000	Accrued state sales tax		62.82	
4920–000	Freight charges		11.65	

1 Recurring transaction

Date 06/10/97 Acme Hardware Co. #0115 Page #0002

RECURRING SALES LIST

---------------G/L account distribution totals---------------

62.82	credited to	2430–000 Accrued state sales tax
897.50	credited to	4000–000 Sales – Main St. Store
11.65	credited to	4920–000 Freight charges

971.97	Total credited	
971.97	debited to	1100–000 Accts Receivable – Trade

-- End of report --

Date 06/10/97 Acme Hardware Co. #0116 Page 0001

SALES EDIT LIST

Customer-name Trans-type	Trans-dat Reference	Doc-#	Terms		Apply-to	Trans-amt
21st Century Construction Sale	06/10/97 1091 Qty 50	S107	2/10 NET 30			971.97
Distributions: 4000-000	Sales - Main St. Store			897.50		
2430-000	Accrued state sales tax			62.82		
4920-000	Freight charges			11.65		

1 Sales transaction

Date 06/10/97 Acme Hardware Co. #0116 Page 0002

SALES EDIT LIST

----------------G/L account distribution totals----------------

62.82	credited to	2430-000	Accrued state sales tax
897.50	credited to	4000-000	Sales - Main St. Store
11.65	credited to	4920-000	Freight charges

971.97	Total credited		
971.97	debited to	1100-000	Accts Receivable - Trade

-- End of report --

Date 06/10/97 Acme Hardware Co. #0117 Page 0001

SALES REGISTER

Customer–name Trans–type		Trans–dat Reference	Doc–#	Terms	Apply–to	Trans–amt
21st Century Construction Sale		06/10/97 1091 Qty 50	S107	2/10 NET 30		971.97
Distributions:	4000–000	Sales – Main St. Store		897.50		
	2430–000	Accrued state sales tax		62.82		
	4920–000	Freight charges		11.65		

1 Sales transaction

Date 06/10/97 Acme Hardware Co. #0117 Page 0002

SALES REGISTER

G/L account distribution totals

62.82	credited to	2430–000	Accrued state sales tax
897.50	credited to	4000–000	Sales – Main St. Store
11.65	credited to	4920–000	Freight charges

971.97	Total credited		
971.97	debited to	1100–000	Accts Receivable – Trade

-- End of report --

Date 06/10/97 Time: 21:33:13 Acme Hardware Co. Report #0118 Page #0001

INVENTORY TRANSACTION EDIT LIST

Current period ending date: 6/30/97
Item # range: "First"

G/L account is shown for up and down adjustments; Profit center is shown for sales and credit memos
List, better, best, and alternate prices are only shown if modified by the transaction
Cost correction is only shown if applicable to the transaction

Date	Type	Doc-#	Trans-qty Unit Running-qty-oh	Unit-cost	Tot-actual-cost New-avg-cost	Comment G/L-acct/Pft-cntr	Price-per-unit
Item: 1091		**Gauge, Hi-Pressure**			Stocking unit:	EACH	
6/10/97	Sale	RS100	50 EACH 200 EACH	9.720	486.00 9.72000	21st Century Construction 000	17.950

Grand totals:						
	Receiving entries:	0	Qty received:	0	Cost:	.00
	Credit memo entries:	0	Qty credited:	0	Cost:	.00
	Up adj entries:	0	Qty adjusted:	0	Cost:	.00
	Down adj entries:	0	Qty adjusted:	0	Cost:	.00
	Sale entries:	1	Qty sold:	50	Cost:	486.00

-- End of report --

Date 06/10/97 Time: 21:33:48 | Acme Hardware Co. | Report #0119 Page #0001

INVENTORY TRANSACTION REGISTER

Current period ending date: 6/30/97

G/L account is shown for up and down adjustments; Profit center is shown for sales and credit memos
List, better, best, and alternate prices are only shown if modified by the transaction
Cost correction is only shown if applicable to the transaction

Date	Type	Doc-#	Trans-qty Unit Running-qty-oh	Unit-cost	Tot-actual-cost New-avg-cost	Comment G/L-acct/Pft-cntr	Price-per-unit
Item: 1091		Gauge, Hi-Pressure			Stocking unit:	EACH	
6/10/97	Sale	RS100	50 EACH 200 EACH	9.720	486.00 9.72000	21st Century Construction 000	17.950

Grand totals:						
	Receiving entries:	0	Qty received:	0	Cost:	.00
	Credit memo entries:	0	Qty credited:	0	Cost:	.00
	Up adj entries:	0	Qty adjusted:	0	Cost:	.00
	Down adj entries:	0	Qty adjusted:	0	Cost:	.00
	Sale entries:	1	Qty sold:	50	Cost:	486.00

-- End of report --

Date 06/10/97 Time: 21:35:15 | Acme Hardware Co. | Report #0120 Page #0001

CUSTOMER LIST

Starting customer: "First"
Ending customer: "Last"
Customer type: "All"
Last sale date: "Earliest"

Cust-name Address	Phone-# Contact Sales-rep	Cust-typ Bal-meth Tax-code	Stmt-freq Fin-chg?	1st-actv-dat Lst-sls-dat Lst-pmt-dat	Lst-fin-chg-dat Lst-fin-chg-amt Fin-chg-YTD	Comment
21st Century Construction	555-7844	WSL	M	6/01/97	(None)	
P.O. Box 4545	Herbert Mardhat	Open item	N	6/10/97	.00	
670 Mason Street	JAK	MI		(None)	.00	
Ann Arbor, MI 48136						

Sls-this-prd	Sls-this-yr	Sls-last-prd	Sls-last-yr		Products	Services	Repairs	Other
971.97	971.97	.00	.00	This yr:	.00	.00	.00	.00
				Last yr:	.00	.00	.00	.00

Cust-name Address	Phone-# Contact Sales-rep	Cust-typ Bal-meth Tax-code	Stmt-freq Fin-chg?	1st-actv-dat Lst-sls-dat Lst-pmt-dat	Lst-fin-chg-dat Lst-fin-chg-amt Fin-chg-YTD	Comment
Allied Plumbing Co.	554-4300	WSL	M	6/01/97	(None)	
555 N. Grand Blvd	Cathy Sinks	Bal fwd	Y	6/03/97	.00	
Lansing, MI 48135	JAK	MI		(None)	.00	

Sls-this-prd	Sls-this-yr	Sls-last-prd	Sls-last-yr		Products	Services	Repairs	Other
1,200.39	1,200.39	.00	.00	This yr:	1,079.80	.00	.00	.00
				Last yr:	.00	.00	.00	.00

Cust-name Address	Phone-# Contact Sales-rep	Cust-typ Bal-meth Tax-code	Stmt-freq Fin-chg?	1st-actv-dat Lst-sls-dat Lst-pmt-dat	Lst-fin-chg-dat Lst-fin-chg-amt Fin-chg-YTD	Comment
Ariel Enterprises	554-4300	WSL	M	6/01/97	(None)	
69 Vacca Ct.	M. J. Thorpe	Open item	N	6/03/97	.00	
East Kalamazoo, MI 12445	PH	MI		(None)	.00	

Sls-this-prd	Sls-this-yr	Sls-last-prd	Sls-last-yr		Products	Services	Repairs	Other
844.30	844.30	.00	.00	This yr:	653.55	.00	.00	.00
				Last yr:	.00	.00	.00	.00

Cust-name Address	Phone-# Contact Sales-rep	Cust-typ Bal-meth Tax-code	Stmt-freq Fin-chg?	1st-actv-dat Lst-sls-dat Lst-pmt-dat	Lst-fin-chg-dat Lst-fin-chg-amt Fin-chg-YTD	Comment
Bakker, Richard C.	478-9090	RET	M	6/01/97	(None)	
2554 Broad Street	Richard Baker	Open item	N	(None)	.00	
Lansing, MI 48135	TJF	MI		(None)	.00	

Sls-this-prd	Sls-this-yr	Sls-last-prd	Sls-last-yr		Products	Services	Repairs	Other
.00	.00	.00	.00	This yr:	.00	.00	.00	.00
				Last yr:	.00	.00	.00	.00

Date 06/10/97 Time: 21:35:20 | Acme Hardware Co. | Report #0120 Page #0002

CUSTOMER LIST

Cust-name	Phone-#	Cust-typ	Stmt-freq	1st-actv-dat	Lst-fin-chg-dat	Comment
Address	Contact	Bal-meth	Fin-chg?	Lst-sls-dat	Lst-fin-chg-amt	
	Sales-rep	Tax-code		Lst-pmt-dat	Fin-chg-YTD	
Elliott Enterprises	779-6010	WSL	M	6/01/97	(None)	
123 Broadway	Paul Elliott	Open item	N	6/03/97	.00	
Glendale, MI 48133	TJF	MI		(None)	.00	

Sls-this-prd	Sls-this-yr	Sls-last-prd	Sls-last-yr		Products	Services	Repairs	Other
567.84	567.84	.00	.00	This yr:	451.25	.00	.00	.00
				Last yr:	.00	.00	.00	.00

Harris, Goldberg, & Jones	554-4300	RET	M	6/01/97	(None)	
1 Commerce Square	Michael Jones	Open item	N	(None)	.00	
Northtown, MI 48135	JAK	MI		(None)	.00	

Sls-this-prd	Sls-this-yr	Sls-last-prd	Sls-last-yr		Products	Services	Repairs	Other
.00	.00	.00	.00	This yr:	.00	.00	.00	.00
				Last yr:	.00	.00	.00	.00

Holcomb Industrial Supply	722-2233	WSL	M	6/01/97	(None)	
2323 Holcomb Way	Jim Ewing	Open item	N	6/03/97	.00	
Lansing, MI 48135	JAK	MI		(None)	.00	

Sls-this-prd	Sls-this-yr	Sls-last-prd	Sls-last-yr		Products	Services	Repairs	Other
5,170.26	5,170.26	.00	.00	This yr:	4,696.50	.00	.00	.00
				Last yr:	.00	.00	.00	.00

Neptune Underwater Supply	736-1102	RET	M	6/01/97	(None)	
345 Lewisville Rd.	Sam Knorkle	Bal fwd	Y	6/10/97	.00	
Lewisville, MI 48132	TJF	MI		(None)	.00	

Sls-this-prd	Sls-this-yr	Sls-last-prd	Sls-last-yr		Products	Services	Repairs	Other
106.36	106.36	.00	.00	This yr:	.00	.00	.00	.00
				Last yr:	.00	.00	.00	.00

Newton, Boyd, and Co.	886-7722	WSL	M	6/01/97	(None)	
1024 Marble Avenue	Bob Newton	Bal fwd	Y	6/10/97	.00	
Lansing, MI 48135	JAK	MI		(None)	.00	

Sls-this-prd	Sls-this-yr	Sls-last-prd	Sls-last-yr		Products	Services	Repairs	Other
132.57	132.57	.00	.00	This yr:	.00	.00	.00	.00
				Last yr:	.00	.00	.00	.00

Date 06/10/97 Time: 21:35:26	Acme Hardware Co.	Report #0120 Page #0003

CUSTOMER LIST

Cust-name	Phone-#	Cust-typ	Stmt-freq	1st-actv-dat	Lst-fin-chg-dat	Comment
Address	Contact	Bal-meth	Fin-chg?	Lst-sls-dat	Lst-fin-chg-amt	
	Sales-rep	Tax-code		Lst-pmt-dat	Fin-chg-YTD	
Washington, Mrs. Thomas	444-7780	RET	M	6/01/97	(None)	
350 Hillcrest Circle	Ann Washington	Open item	N	(None)	.00	
Lansing, MI 12335	TJF	MI		(None)	.00	

Sls-this-prd	Sls-this-yr	Sls-last-prd	Sls-last-yr		Products	Services	Repairs	Other
.00	.00	.00	.00	This yr:	.00	.00	.00	.00
				Last yr:	.00	.00	.00	.00

Cust-name	Phone-#	Cust-typ	Stmt-freq	1st-actv-dat	Lst-fin-chg-dat	Comment
Webber Landscaping	323-2342	LAND	M	6/01/97	(None)	
33 East Lansing Dr.	Marvin Webber	Open item	N	6/03/97	.00	
Winoga Falls, MI 12345	AW	MI		(None)	.00	

-- End Sls-this-prd	Sls-this-yr	Sls-last-prd	Sls-last-yr		Products	Services	Repairs	Other
1,269.55	1,269.55	.00	.00	This yr:	1,125.75	.00	.00	.00
				Last yr:	.00	.00	.00	.00

11 customers 3 balance forward 8 open item

Date 07/04/97 Time: 21:47:58 Acme Hardware Co. Report #0121 Page #0001

INVENTORY STATUS REPORT

Item # range: "First" to "Last"

Department: "All" Vendor: "All"

Report includes out of stock items

Inventory–value = Qty–on–hand x Average–cost Retail–value = Qty–on–hand x List–price

Out = Out of stock Understocked = Qty–on–hand is below Minimum–qty–on–hand Overstocked = Qty–on=hand is above Maximum–qty–on–hand

Item–#	Description	Dept Loc	Unit Lst–rcvd	List–prc Lst–sold	Qty–on–hand Qty–commit	Qty–on–ord Min–qty–OH	Avg–cost Max–qty–OH	Inv–value	Ret–value	Stat
1091	Gauge, Hi–Pressure	TOOLS	EACH	17.95	200	0	9.720	1,944.00	3,590.00	
		3D	6/01/97	6/10/97		100	500			
1100	Drill, Power Hand	TOOLS	EACH	25.95	24	0	13.140	315.36	622.80	
		E16	6/01/97	6/04/97		10	30			
1105	Drill, Cordless	TOOLS	10	29.95	34	0	14.950	508.30	1,018.30	
		E17	6/01/97	6/04/97		10	40			
2200	Hammer, 16 oz. claw	TOOLS	EACH	13.50	12	0	7.310	87.72	162.00	Undr
		F6	6/01/97	6/03/97		20	36			
5770	Chisel, 5 pc set	TOOLS	SET	28.50	9	0	18.200	163.80	256.50	Undr
		E8	6/01/97	6/07/97		15	24			
BS–BLOCK	Block, Concrete	MATL	EACH	1.59	50	0	.990	49.50	79.50	Undr
		K21	6/01/97	6/03/97		250	1,000			
BS–BRACKET	Bracket sets	MATL	SET	44.95	0	0	32.000	.00	.00	Out
		K18	6/01/97	6/10/97		2	12			
BS–DOORS	Utility Door Unit	MATL	SET	08.00	0	0	32.000	.00	.00	Out
		K4	6/01/97	6/05/97		3	12			
BS–PLYWOOD	Plywood, Exterior	MATL	EACH	13.95	0	0	7.000	.00	.00	Out
		K6	6/01/97	6/03/97		60	200			
EL–WIRE	Electrical House Wire	MATL	REEL	5.19	0	0	2.500	.00	.00	Out
		E43	6/01/97	6/10/97		15	50			
EQ–DEER	Ignition Cable	EQUIP	EACH	87.00	12	0	40.000	480.00	1,044.00	
		W6		6/08/97		5	25			

Date 07/04/97 Time: 21:48:03 | Acme Hardware Co. | Report #0121 Page #0002

INVENTORY STATUS REPORT

Item-#	Description	Dept	Unit	List-prc	Qty-on-hand	Qty-on-ord	Avg-cost	Inv-value	Ret-value	Stat
		Loc	Lst-rcvd	Lst-sold	Qty-commit	Min qty-OH	Max-qty-OH			
Totals:					341	0		3,548.68	6,773.10	
						490	1,929			

490	is the minimum stock level	– cost of minimum inventory:	$2,737.10	(at avg-cost).	Retail-value:	$5,092.75
1,929	is the maximum stock level	– cost of maximum inventory:	$10,835.16	(at avg-cost).	Retail-value:	$20,291.40
4	items are out of stock	– cost to replenish to minimum:	$617.50	(at last-cost).	Retail-value:	$1,208.75
		cost to replenish to maximum:	$2,293.00	(at last-cost).	Retail-value:	$4,404.90
3	Items are understocked	– cost to replenish to minimum:	$365.68	(at last-cost).	Retail-value:	$597.00
		cost to replenish to maximum:	$1,388.94	(at last-cost).	Retail-value:	$2,262.00
0	items are overstocked	– value in excess of maximum:	$0.00	(at avg-cost).	Retail-value:	$0.00
4	items are stocked ok	– cost to replenish to maximum:	$3,604.54	(at last-cost).	Retail-value:	$6,851.40

11 items printed

-- End of report --

Practice Set 7 – PROCESS CASH RECEIPTS

Introduction

In this practice set, you will be able to take in some money. You are asked to process cash receipts which follow from customer invoicing and special A/R billings, and in so doing:

- ➡ print aged accounts receivable reports
- ➡ enter receipt information into processing
- ➡ print the receipts transaction list and produce a bank statement
- ➡ post cash receipts and print a cash receipts register
- ➡ print an aged A/R report

Set Transaction Date

Before starting this practice set, enter today's date as **06–13–97.**

Print Aged Accounts Receivables Report

To gain a better understanding of the opening A/R balance, print an aged accounts receivable report by doing the following:

* From the A/R menu, select Print A/R Aging Report.
* Use an aging date of 6/13/97.
* Do not include items after this date.
* Print the report for all customers and all sales reps.
* Print both DR and CR accounts.
* Do not print zero balance customers.
* Indicate zero cutoff balance.
* Print a detailed report, not on separate pages.
* Answer NO when asked if you want to age open–item customers like balance–forward customers, and NO for invoice balance only.

Process Payments on Accounts

Move to Process Cash Receipts and select Add Transactions. Add the following receipts information:

Neptune Underwater Supply

Check No.	Receipt Date	Amount Received	Chkg Acct	Reference	Credit A/R	Discount
CASH	6/10/97	$ 106.36	1	R5500	Y	.00

21st Century Construction

Check No.	Receipt Date	Amount Received	Chkg Acct	Bank Number	Credit A/R	Discount
16315	6/13/97	$ 671.97	1	410/310	Y	.00

Reference
First installment *** *Apply the entire amount to the first outstanding invoice.* ***

Newton, Boyd, and Co.

Check No.	Receipt Date	Amount Received	Chkg Acct	Bank Number	Credit A/R	Discount
14310	6/13/97	$ 64.57	1	66/315	Y	.00

Allied Plumbing Co.

Check No.	Receipt Date	Amount Received	Chkg Acct	Bank Number	Credit A/R	Discount
8429	6/13/97	$ 885.39	1	2243/2432	Y	.00

Ariel Enterprises

Check No.	Receipt Date	Amount Received	Chkg Acct	Bank Number	Credit A/R	Discount
16429	6/13/97	$ 827.41	1	2243/2432	Y	16.89

Reference
Discount allowed *** *Apply the entire amount to the first outstanding invoice.* ***

Elliott Enterprises

Check No.	Receipt Date	Amount Received	Chkg Acct	Bank Number	Credit A/R	Discount
16933	6/13/97	$ 467.84	1	66412/410	Y	.00

Reference
Apply to balance *** *Apply the entire amount to the first outstanding invoice.* ***

Holcomb Industrial Supply

Check No.	Receipt Date	Amount Received	Chkg Acct	Bank Number	Credit A/R	Discount
61312	6/13/97	$5,066.85	1	2243/2432	Y	103.41

Reference
Paid in full *** *Apply the entire amount to the first outstanding invoice.* ***

Print Cash Receipts Edit List

Following the entry of these seven transactions, print the Cash Receipts Edit List.

Which G/L account will sales discounts be posted to?

Print the Bank Deposit Slip

Print the bank deposit slip next, using the date 6/13/97.

Why is the check number missing for one amount?

Post Cash Receipt Transactions to the G/L

The final step is to post the cash receipts transactions to the G/L. Use the date 6/13/97.

Explain why this report is needed.

Other Things to Explore

1. Print a second aged receivables report and compare it to the first. Follow the same steps as before, for the date 6/13/97.

   Explain the effects of cash receipts processing on aged accounts receivable balances.

2. Display or print the customer list for all customers, for the earliest sales date.

   How is this list changed by cash receipts processing?
   Which customer(s) did not pay within the 10 day period?
   Which customer(s) have recorded no sales thus far?

3. **Move over to the general ledger and explain the change made by cash receipts processing for the following accounts:**

   1100 1010 4510

   Inspect accounts 4000 and 4010.

   Explain why cash receipts DOES NOT change the totals for these accounts.

This completes Practice Set 7.

Date: 06/13/97 Time: 13:28:24 Acme Hardware Co. Report #0124 Page #0001

AGED ACCOUNTS RECEIVABLE

Aging date: 6/13/97

Document types: S = Sale P = Payment C = CR memo D = Dr memo B = Balance forward F = Finance charge

Customer–name / Sls–rep	Phone–# / Contact	Last–pmt–dat / Bal–meth	Balance	Current	31–60 days	61–90 days	Over 90 days
21st Century Construction	555–7844	None	971.97	971.97	.00	.00	.00
JAK	Herbert Mardhat	OPN–ITM					

Doc–#	Doc–date	Typ	Apply–to	Reference	Doc–amount	Discount	Doc–total	Age	Terms
S107	6/10/97	S		1091 Qty 50	971.97	.00	971.97	3	2/10 NET 30

Customer–name / Sls–rep	Phone–# / Contact	Last–pmt–dat / Bal–meth	Balance	Current	31–60 days	61–90 days	Over 90 days
Allied Plumbing Co.	554–4300	None	1,200.39	1,200.39	.00	.00	.00
JAK	Cathy Sinks	BAL–FWD					

Doc–#	Doc–date	Typ	Apply–to	Reference	Doc–amount	Discount	Doc–total	Age	Terms
500	6/03/97	S		Ref #: 000502	1,200.39	.00	1,200.39	10	NET 30

Customer–name / Sls–rep	Phone–# / Contact	Last–pmt–dat / Bal–meth	Balance	Current	31–60 days	61–90 days	Over 90 days
Ariel Enterprises	554–4300	None	844.30	844.30	.00	.00	.00
PH	M. J. Thorpe	OPN–ITM					

Doc–#	Doc–date	Typ	Apply–to	Reference	Doc–amount	Discount	Doc–total	Age	Terms
501	6/03/97	S	501	Ref #: 000504	844.30	.00	844.30	10	2/10 NET 30

Customer–name / Sls–rep	Phone–# / Contact	Last–pmt–dat / Bal–meth	Balance	Current	31–60 days	61–90 days	Over 90 days
Elliot Enterprises	779–6010	None	567.84	567.84	.00	.00	.00
TJF	Paul Elliot	OPN–ITM					

Doc–#	Doc–date	Typ	Apply–to	Reference	Doc–amount	Discount	Doc–total	Age	Terms
502	6/03/97	S	502	Ref #: 000501	567.84	.00	567.84	10	2/10 NET 30

Customer–name / Sls–rep	Phone–# / Contact	Last–pmt–dat / Bal–meth	Balance	Current	31–60 days	61–90 days	Over 90 days
Holcomb Industrial Supply	722–2233	None	5,170.26	5,170.26	.00	.00	.00
JAK	Jim Ewing	OPN–ITM					

Doc–#	Doc–date	Typ	Apply–to	Reference	Doc–amount	Discount	Doc–total	Age	Terms
503	6/03/97	S	503	Ref #: 000503	5,170.26	.00	5,170.26	10	2/10 NET 30

Customer–name / Sls–rep	Phone–# / Contact	Last–pmt–dat / Bal–meth	Balance	Current	31–60 days	61–90 days	Over 90 days
Neptune Underwater Supply	736–1102	None	106.36	106.36	.00	.00	.00
TJF	Sam Knorkle	BAL–FWD					

Doc–#	Doc–date	Typ	Apply–to	Reference	Doc–amount	Discount	Doc–total	Age	Terms
S100	6/04/97	S		1100 Qty 1	25.95	.00	25.95	9	CASH
S101	6/07/97	S		5770 Qty 1	28.50	.00	28.50	6	CASH
S102	6/10/97	S		BS–BRACKET Qty 1	44.95	.00	44.95	3	CASH
T101	6/10/97	S		Sales Tax	6.96	.00	6.96	3	CASH

Date: 06/13/97 Time: 13:28:29 Acme Hardware Co. Report #0124 Page #0002

AGED ACCOUNTS RECEIVABLE

Aging date: 6/13/97

Document types: S = Sale P = Payment C = CR memo D = Dr memo B = Balance forward F = Finance charge

Customer-name Sls-rep	Phone-# Contact	Last-pmt-dat Bal-meth	Balance	Current	31-60 days	61-90 days	Over 90 days
Newton, Boyd, and Co. JAK	886-7722 Bob Newton	None BAL-FWD	132.57	132.57	.00	.00	.00

Doc-#	Doc-date	Typ	Apply-to	Reference	Doc-amount	Discount	Doc-total	Age	Terms
S103	6/04/97	S		1105 Qty 1	29.95	.00	29.95	9	NET 30
S104	6/05/97	S		BS-DOORS Qty 1	68.00	.00	68.00	8	NET 30
S105	6/08/97	S		EQ-DEER Qty 1	87.00	.00	87.00	5	NET 30
C105	6/10/97	C		EQ-DEER Qty 1	87.00CR	.00	87.00CR	3	NET 30
S106	6/10/97	S		EL-WIRE Qty 5	25.95	.00	25.95	3	NET 30
T102	6/10/97	S		Sales Tax	8.67	.00	8.67	3	NET 30

Customer-name Sls-rep	Phone-# Contact	Last-pmt-dat Bal-meth	Balance	Current	31-60 days	61-90 days	Over 90 days
Webber Landscaping AW	323-2342 Marvin Webber	None OPN-ITN	1,269.55	1,269.55	.00	.00	.00

Doc-#	Doc-date	Typ	Apply-to	Reference	Doc-amount	Discount	Doc-total	Age	Terms
504	6/03/97	S	504	Ref #: 000505	1,269.55	.00	1,269.55	10	2/10 NET 30

Grand totals for 8 customers printed; aging date 6/13/97

DR Lines show totals for customers with debit balances as of the aging date
CR Lines show totals for customers with credit balances as of the aging date

	Balance	Current	31-60 days	61-90 days	Over 90 days
DR bal cust totals:	10,263.24	10,263.24	.00	.00	.00
CR bal cust totals:	.00	.00	.00	.00	.00
Net totals:	10,263.24	10,263.24	.00	.00	.00

-- End of report --

Date 06/13/97 Time 13:43:24 — Acme Hardware Co. — Report #0125 — 0001

CASH RECEIPTS EDIT LIST

Customer-name	Bal-meth	Rect-dat	Check-#	Amount-recd	Cash-acct	Bank-rte-#/Ref	Discount
21st Century Construction	OPEN-ITEM	6/13/97	16315	671.97	1010-000	410/310	

Apply-to	Amt-paid	Discount	Total-applied	Reference
Open	671.97	.00	671.97	First installment
Chk totals:	671.97	.00	671.97	

Customer-name	Bal-meth	Rect-dat	Check-#	Amount-recd	Cash-acct	Bank-rte-#/Ref	Discount
Allied Plumbing Co.	BAL-FORWD	6/13/97	8429	885.39	1010-000	2243/2432	.00
						Total credited:	885.39
Ariel Enterprises	OPEN-ITEM	6/13/97	16429	827.41	1010-000	2243/2432	

Apply-to	Amt-paid	Discount	Total-applied	Reference
501	827.41	16.89	844.30	Discount allowed
Chk totals:	827.41	16.89	844.30	

Customer-name	Bal-meth	Rect-dat	Check-#	Amount-recd	Cash-acct	Bank-rte-#/Ref	Discount
Elliott Enterprises	OPEN-ITEM	6/13/97	16933	467.84	1010-000	66412/410	

Apply-to	Amt-paid	Discount	Total-applied	Reference
502	467.84	.00	467.84	Apply to balance
Chk totals:	467.84	.00	467.84	

Customer-name	Bal-meth	Rect-dat	Check-#	Amount-recd	Cash-acct	Bank-rte-#/Ref	Discount
Holcomb Industrial Supply	OPEN-ITEM	6/13/97	61312	5,066.85	1010-000	2243/2432	

Apply-to	Amt-paid	Discount	Total-applied	Reference
503	5,066.85	103.41	5,170.26	Paid in full
Chk totals:	5,066.85	103.41	5,170.26	

Customer-name	Bal-meth	Rect-dat	Check-#	Amount-recd	Cash-acct	Bank-rte-#/Ref	Discount
Neptune Underwater Supply	BAL-FORWD	6/10/97	*Cash*	106.36	1010-000	R5500	.00
						Total credited:	106.36
Newton, Boyd, and Co.	BAL-FORWD	6/13/97	14310	64.57	1010-000	66/315	.00
						Total credited:	64.57

Date 06/13/97 Time 13:43:29 Acme Hardware Co. Report #0125 0002

CASH RECEIPTS EDIT LIST

Customer–name	Bal–meth	Rect–dat	Check–#	Amount–recd	Cash–acct	Bank–rte–#/Ref	Discount

	Total recd:	8,090.39
	Total disc:	120.30
7 cash receipt transactions	Total credited:	8,210.69

---------- G/L account distribution totals ----------

8,210.69	credited to 1100–000	Accts Receivable – Trade
8,090.39	debited to 1010–000	Checking #1 – Payables
120.30	debited to 4510–000	Sales discounts
8,210.69	Total debited	

-- End of report --

DEPOSIT SLIP

Acme Hardware
123 Main St.
Winoga Falls, MI 12345

8765–432–19876
Acct #: 4400998877

Deposit date: 06/13/97

Bank #	Amount	Check #
* * Cash * *	106.36	
410/310	671.97	16315
2243/2432	885.39	8429
2243/2432	827.41	16429
66412/410	467.84	16933
2243/2432	5,066.85	61312
66/315	64.57	14310
Total deposit:	8,090.39	

Date 06/13/97 Time 13:46:29 Acme Hardware Co. Report #0126 0001

CASH RECEIPTS REGISTER

Customer-name	Bal-meth	Rect-dat	Check-#	Amount-recd	Cash-acct	Bank-rte-#/Ref	Discount
21st Century Construction	OPEN-ITEM	6/13/97	16315	671.97	1010-000	410/310	

Apply-to	Amt-paid	Discount	Total-applied	Reference
Open	671.97	.00	671.97	First installment
Chk totals:	671.97	.00	671.97	

Customer-name	Bal-meth	Rect-dat	Check-#	Amount-recd	Cash-acct	Bank-rte-#/Ref	Discount
Allied Plumbing Co.	BAL-FORWD	6/13/97	8429	885.39	1010-000	2243/2432	.00
						Total credited:	885.39
Ariel Enterprises	OPEN-ITEM	6/13/97	16429	827.41	1010-000	2243/2432	

Apply-to	Amt-paid	Discount	Total-applied	Reference
501	827.41	16.89	844.30	Discount allowed
Chk totals:	827.41	16.89	844.30	

Customer-name	Bal-meth	Rect-dat	Check-#	Amount-recd	Cash-acct	Bank-rte-#/Ref	Discount
Elliott Enterprises	OPEN-ITEM	6/13/97	16933	467.84	1010-000	66412/410	

Apply-to	Amt-paid	Discount	Total-applied	Reference
502	467.84	.00	467.84	Apply to balance
Chk totals:	467.84	.00	467.84	

Customer-name	Bal-meth	Rect-dat	Check-#	Amount-recd	Cash-acct	Bank-rte-#/Ref	Discount
Holcomb Industrial Supply	OPEN-ITEM	6/13/97	61312	5,066.85	1010-000	2243/2432	

Apply-to	Amt-paid	Discount	Total-applied	Reference
503	5,066.85	103.41	5,170.26	Paid in full
Chk totals:	5,066.85	103.41	5,170.26	

Customer-name	Bal-meth	Rect-dat	Check-#	Amount-recd	Cash-acct	Bank-rte-#/Ref	Discount
Neptune Underwater Supply	BAL-FORWD	6/10/97	*Cash*	106.36	1010-000	R5500	.00
						Total credited:	106.36
Newton, Boyd, and Co.	BAL-FORWD	6/13/97	14310	64.57	1010-000	66/315	.00
						Total credited:	64.57

Date 06/13/97 Time 13:46:33 Acme Hardware Co. Report #0126 0002

CASH RECEIPTS REGISTER

Customer-name	Bal-meth	Rect-dat	Check-#	Amount-recd	Cash-acct	Bank-rte-#/Ref	Discount

Total recd: 8,090.39
Total disc: 120.30
----
7 cash receipt transactions Total credited: 8,210.69

--------- G/L account distribution totals ---------

8,210.69	credited to 1100-000	Accts Receivable - Trade
8,090.39	debited to 1010-000	Checking #1 - Payables
120.30	debited to 4510-000	Sales discounts

8,210.69	Total debited	

-- End of report --

Date: 06/13/97 Time: 13:48:33 Acme Hardware Co. Report #0128 Page #0001

AGED ACCOUNTS RECEIVABLE

Aging date: 6/13/97

Document types: S = Sale P = Payment C = CR memo D = Dr memo B = Balance forward F = Finance charge

Customer–name	Phone–#	Last–pmt–dat	Balance	Current	31–60 days	61–90 days	Over 90 days
Sls–rep	Contact	Bal–meth					
21st Century Construction	555–7844	6/13/97	300.00	300.00	.00	.00	.00
JAK	Herbert Mardhat	OPN–ITM					

Doc–#	Doc–date	Typ	Apply–to	Reference	Doc–amount	Discount	Doc–total	Age	Terms
S107	6/10/97	S		1091 Qty 50	971.97	.00	971.97	3	2/10 NET 30
16315	6/13/97	P	Open	First installment	671.97CR	.00	671.97CR	0	2/10 NET 30

Allied Plumbing Co.	554–4300	6/13/97	315.00	315.00	.00	.00	.00
JAK	Cathy Sinks	BAL–FWD					

Doc–#	Doc–date	Typ	Apply–to	Reference	Doc–amount	Discount	Doc–total	Age	Terms
500	6/03/97	S		Ref #: 000502	1,200.39	.00	1,200.39	10	NET 30
8429	6/13/97	P		2243/2432	885.39CR	.00	885.39CR	0	

Elliot Enterprises	779–6010	6/13/97	100.00	100.00	.00	.00	.00
TJF	Paul Elliot	OPN–ITM					

Doc–#	Doc–date	Typ	Apply–to	Reference	Doc–amount	Discount	Doc–total	Age	Terms
502	6/03/97	S	502	Ref #: 000501	567.84	.00	567.84	10	2/10 NET 30
16933	6/13/97	P	502	Apply to balance	467.84CR	.00	467.84CR	0	NET 30

Newton, Boyd, and Co.	886–7722	6/13/97	68.00	68.00	.00	.00	.00
JAK	Bob Newton	BAL–FWD					

Doc–#	Doc–date	Typ	Apply–to	Reference	Doc–amount	Discount	Doc–total	Age	Terms
S103	6/04/97	S		1105 Qty 1	29.95	.00	29.95	9	NET 30
S104	6/05/97	S		BS–DOORS Qty 1	68.00	.00	68.00	8	NET 30
S105	6/08/97	S		EQ–DEER Qty 1	87.00	.00	87.00	5	NET 30
C105	6/10/97	C		EQ–DEER Qty 1	87.00CR	.00	87.00CR	3	NET 30
S106	6/10/97	S		EL–WIRE Qty 5	25.95	.00	25.95	3	NET 30
T102	6/10/97	S		Sales Tax	8.67	.00	8.67	3	NET 30
14310	6/13/97	P		66/315	64.57CR	.00	64.57CR	0	

Webber Landscaping	323–2342	None	1,269.55	1,269.55	.00	.00	.00
AW	Marvin Webber	OPN–ITN					

Doc–#	Doc–date	Typ	Apply–to	Reference	Doc–amount	Discount	Doc–total	Age	Terms
504	6/03/97	S	504	Ref #: 000505	1,269.55	.00	1,269.55	10	2/10 NET 30

Date: 06/13/97 Time: 13:48:39 | Acme Hardware Co. | Report #0128 Page #0002

AGED ACCOUNTS RECEIVABLE

Aging date: 6/13/97

Document types: S = Sale P = Payment C = CR memo D = Dr memo B = Balance forward F = Finance charge

Customer–name	Phone–#	Last–pmt–dat	Balance	Current	31–60 days	61–90 days	Over 90 days
Sls–rep	Contact	Bal–meth					

Grand totals for 5 customers printed; aging date 6/13/97

DR Lines show totals for customers with debit balances as of the aging date
CR Lines show totals for customers with credit balances as of the aging date

	Balance	Current	31–60 days	61–90 days	Over 90 days
DR bal cust totals:	2,052.55	2,052.55	.00	.00	.00
CR bal cust totals:	.00	.00	.00	.00	.00
Net totals:	2,052.55	2,052.55	.00	.00	.00

-- End of report --

Practice Set 8 – PROCESS ACCOUNTS PAYABLE

Introduction

In this practice set, you are required to spend some money. You are asked to process accounts payable for goods ordered and received from company vendors. More specifically, you are asked to:

- record bills that have been received, but previously paid
- add and activate a recurring payable
- print the recurring payables list
- record bills that have been received, but not paid
- process and post disbursements
- print an edit list and vendor checks
- print an aged payables report

Set Transaction Date

Before starting this practice set, enter today's date as **06–15–97.**

Record Bills Received by the Company, but Previously Paid

The company has received the following bills from vendors for goods shipped and received. The dollar amount of $8,474.85 was previously set aside to cover these charges.

Move to accounts payable, select bills payable, and add transactions. Observe that the first entries are balance–forward transactions. **With these amounts, be sure to include the minus sign.**

Hill Equipment & Supply

Trans Type	Date	Amount
Bal Forward	6/01/97	–7154.85

Hanson Manufacturing Co.

Trans Type	Date	Amount
Bal Forward	6/01/97	–1195.00

Reynolds Tool Company

Trans Type	Date	Amount
Bal Forward	6/01/97	–125.00

Next, add the following vendor billing information:

Hill Equipment & Supply

Trans Type	Date	Invoice #	Reference	Amount	Credit A/P?	Distrib Account
Bill	6/01/97	66554	ORD 107 (Doors)	160.00	Y	2100–000

Hill Equipment & Supply

Trans Type	Date	Invoice #	Reference	Amount	Credit A/P?	Distrib Account
Bill	6/01/97	66503	ORD 100 (Hardware)	1374.85	Y	2100–000

Hill Equipment & Supply

Trans Type	Date	Invoice #	Reference	Amount	Credit A/P?	Distrib Account
Bill	6/01/97	66715	ORD 101 (gauges)	4860.00	Y	2100–000

Hill Equipment & Supply

Trans Type	Date	Invoice #	Reference	Amount	Credit A/P?	Distrib Account
Bill	6/01/97	67189	ORD 104 (Cable, brackets)	760.00	Y	2100–000

Hanson Manufacturing

Trans Type	Date	Invoice #	Reference	Amount	Credit A/P?	Distrib Account
Bill	6/01/97	11510	ORD 105 (C. Blocks)	495.00	Y	2100–000

Hanson Manufacturing

Trans Type	Date	Invoice #	Reference	Amount	Credit A/P?	Distrib Account
Bill	6/01/97	11924	ORD 103 (Plywood)	700.00	Y	2100–000

Reynolds Tool Company

Trans Type	Date	Invoice #	Reference	Amount	Credit A/P?	Distrib Account
Bill	6/01/97	69421	ORD 102 (Wire)	125.00	Y	2100–000

Print the Payables Edit List and the Payables Register

After entering the ten transactions described above, print the Payables Edit List and post the transactions. The latter will print the Accounts Payable Register.

How does this processing alter the accounts payable G/L balance? Explain why this occurs.

Add and Activate Recurring Bills

Again begin with Process Bills Payable, but select Process Recurring Bills (press F1). Add the following recurring bills:

Jones Property Management

Trans Type	Frequency	Date	Reference	Amount	Credit A/P?
Bill	Monthly	6/15/97	Lease of property	1000.00	Y

Disbribution Account	
6160–000	Rents and Utilities

Bitznbytes Computer

Trans Type	Frequency	Date	Reference	Amount	Credit A/P?
Bill	Monthly	6/15/97	Lease of equipment	250.00	Y

Disbribution Account	
6150–000	Office Expense

Once these transactions are entered,

* Print the Recurring Bills Payable List.
* Activate the recurring payables. For the next due date, type **07/15/97** for both accounts. Leave the invoice number blank. Distribute the dollar amounts as you did before.
* Print the Recurring Bills Payable List.

Return to Process Bills Payable and add the following transaction:

NorthWestern Bell

Trans Type	Date	Invoice #	Reference	Amount	Credit A/P?	Distribution Account
Bill	6/15/97	(nonc)	Monthly bill	250.00	Y	6270–000 Telephone

Following this:

* Print the Bills Payable Edit List.
* Post the transactions which prints a second Bills Payable Register.

What vendor names appear on this second list?
What does this list tell you about recurring bills, once they become active?

Add Additional Inventory Charges

There are two additional vendor charges we ask you to enter. These represent additions to inventory of two new products. To begin processing, we ask you to add these new items to the master product (items) file.

Add Item Information

Move to Inventory Management and Maintain Item Data. Select Add Item. The details on each of the two new products are as follows:

Product 1

Item number:	**EQ–BLADE**
Description:	**Replacement blade**
Bar code:	(leave blank)
Substitute item #:	(leave blank)
Item Type:	**Inventory**
Department:	**SHOP**
Cust hist class:	**Repairs**
Stocking Unit:	**Each**
Qty on hand:	(leave blank)
Qty committed:	(leave blank)
Qty on order:	**25**
Average cost:	**19.95**
Last cost:	**19.95**
Purchase unit:	(leave blank)
List price:	**29.95**
Discount by:	**No**
Better price:	(leave blank)
Best price:	(leave blank)
Alt sell unit 1:	(leave blank)
Alt sell unit 2:	(leave blank)
Preferred unit:	(leave blank)
Vendor:	**Tools Galore**
Notes:	(leave blank)
Inventory acct #:	**1400–000**
Sales acct #:	**4025**
Cost of goods acct #:	**5010**
Returns acct #:	**4520**
Taxable?	**Yes**
Bin location:	**R52**
Minimum qty on hand:	**5**
Minimum order qty:	**10**
Maximum qty on hand:	**40**

All remaining fields are blank or zero.

Product 2	Item number:	**EQ–FILTER**
	Description:	**Replacement oil filter**
	Bar code:	(leave blank)
	Substitute item #:	(leave blank)
	Item Type:	**Inventory**
	Department:	**SHOP**
	Cust hist class:	**Repairs**
	Stocking Unit:	**Each**
	Qty on hand:	(leave blank)
	Qty committed:	(leave blank)
	Qty on order:	**60**
	Average cost:	**1.25**
	Last cost:	**1.25**
	Purchase unit:	(leave blank)
	List price:	**2.95**
	Discount by:	**No**
	Better price:	(leave blank)
	Best price:	(leave blank)
	Alt sell unit 1:	(leave blank)
	Alt sell unit 2:	(leave blank)
	Preferred unit:	(leave blank)
	Vendor:	**"Biggies" Hardware**
	Notes:	(leave blank)
	Inventory acct #:	**1400–000**
	Sales acct #:	**4025**
	Cost of goods acct #:	**5010**
	Returns acct #:	**4520**
	Taxable?	**Yes**
	Bin location:	**R14**
	Minimum qty on hand:	**12**
	Minimum order qty:	**36**
	Maximum qty on hand:	**72**

All remaining fields are blank or zero.

Print the Item List

Once the two new products are added, print the item list, as follows:

Print in order by:	**Item number**	Report format:	**Full**
Starting item number:	**"First"**	Print price detail?	**Yes**
Ending item number:	**"Last"**	Print sales detail?	**No**
Item type:	**Inventory**	Print single spaced?	**No**
Department:	**SHOP**		
Vendor:	**"All"**		
Last sale date:	**"Earliest"**		

Process Bills Payable

We will assume that the invoices for the new orders are received the same day. Move once again to accounts payable and bills payable. Add the two additional vendor invoices:

Tools Galore

Trans Type	Date	Invoice #	Reference	Amount	Credit A/P?	Distribution Account
Bill	6/15/97	345432	Repair shop	498.75	Y	1400–000 Inventory

"Biggies" Hardware

Trans Type	Date	Invoice #	Reference	Amount	Credit A/P?	Distribution Account
Bill	6/15/97	3434333	Repair shop	75.00	Y	1400–000 Inventory

Print the Bills Payable Edit List and the Bills Payable Register

To complete the processing of these two additional invoices, print the Bills Payable Edit List and, following verification, post the transactions which prints the Bills Payable Register.

Why is it important to add product information to the items file 'before' processing the vendor charges?
Why were these transactions posted to distribution account 1400 instead of 2100, as was the case with the initial set of ten transactions?

View Vendor Accounts

Move to View Vendor Accounts.

* View the Hill Equipment & Supply, the Hanson Manufacturing Co., and the Reynolds Tool Company accounts.

  What is the ending balance for each account?
  What was the effect of posting a balance forward charge to each account?

* View the Jones Property Management account.

  What is the ending balance for this account?
  What was the effect of posting the payable?

Process Disbursements

Now that all payables have been posted, it's finally time to pay some, but not all, vendors.

Print the Aged Payables Summary

Before paying any vendor, print the aged payables summary. Use a cut off date of 6/15/97. Do not print zero balances.

What is the total amount due to vendors by the company?
How many charges are older than 30 days?

Add Transactions

After determining who needs to be paid, add transactions to disburse checks to the following vendors:

Bitznbytes Computer Bill

Trans Type	Prev. Entered?	Date	Check No.	Reference	Amount	Discount
C	Y	6/15/97	N/A	Lease of equipment	250.00	(None)

Check Acct	Debit A/P?	INVOICE #	INV-DATE	INV-AMOUNT
1	Y	Press F2 and type 9999	6/15/97	250

CASH PAID	DISC-TAKEN	INV-AMT-CR
250	0.00	250

Jones Property Management

Trans Type	Prev. Entered?	Date	Check No.	Reference	Amount	Discount
C	N	6/15/97	N/A	Lease of property	1000.00	(None)

Check Acct	Debit A/P?	INVOICE #	INV-DATE	INV-AMOUNT
1	Y	Press F2 and type 9999	6/15/97	1000

CASH PAID	DISC-TAKEN	INV-AMT-CR
1000	0.00	1000

NorthWestern Bell

Trans Type	Prev. Entered?	Date	Check No.	Reference	Amount	Discount
C	N	6/15/97	N/A	May phone bill	250.00	(None)

Check Acct	Debit A/P?	INVOICE #	INV–DATE	INV–AMOUNT
1	Y	Press F2 and type 9999	6/15/97	250

CASH PAID	DISC–TAKEN	INV–AMT–CR
250	0.00	250

In this part of the practice set, checks were not written for all vendors.

What is the significance of this action?

Print Edit List and Checks

After the above check information has been entered, print the Disbursements Edit List. Interpret the totals and the postings.

What is the dollar value of the checks to be printed?
How will this action change the dollar amount in checking account #1?
How will this action change the amount in accounts payable?

Print the checks next. Use checking account #1, and a starting check number of 2100.

Why must checks be printed before they are posted?

Post Disbursements

Following the printing of the vendor checks, post the disbursements.

What are the effects of this action?

Other Things to Explore

1. Print a second aged payables report and compare it to the first. Use a cut off date of 6/15/97.

   Explain the results of disbursements on the aged balances.

2. Move to General Ledger and examine the accounts payable account # 2100–000. Answer the following:

   How did the first set of ten bills payable transactions change the accounts payable "running" balance? (Did it increase it, or decrease it, or did it stay the same. Indicate the dollar amount of the change.)

   How did the next set of three bills payable transactions change the accounts payable "running" balance?

   How did the third set of two bills payable transactions change the accounts payable "running" balance?

   How did the three disbursements change the accounts payable "running" balance?

3. **Explain the changes made by accounts payable processing for these additional general ledger accounts:**

   6150 6160 6270 1400 1010

This completes Practice Set 8.

Date 06/15/97 | Acme Hardware Co. | #0129 Page 0001

BILLS PAYABLE EDIT LIST

Vendor–name / Invoice–#	Trans–type	Trans–date / Reference	Credited–to	Trans–amt / Debited–to
Hanson Manufacturing Co.		**06/01/97**		**1,195.00CR**
	Bal forward	**Balance forward**		
Hanson Manufacturing Co.		06/01/97	A/P	495.00
11510	Bill	ORD 105 (C. Blocks)		
Distributions: 2100–000	Accounts Payable – Trade			495.00
Hanson Manufacturing Co.		06/01/97	A/P	700.00
11924	Bill	ORD 103 (Plywood)		
Distributions: 2100–000	Accounts Payable – Trade			700.00
Hill Equipment & Supply		**06/01/97**		**7,154.85CR**
	Bal forward	**Balance forward**		
Hill Equipment & Supply		06/01/97	A/P	160.00
66554	Bill	ORD 107 (doors)		
Distributions: 2100–000	Accounts Payable – Trade			160.00
Hill Equipment & Supply		06/01/97	A/P	1,374.85
66503	Bill	ORD 100 (Hardware)		
Distributions: 2100–000	Accounts Payable – Trade			1,374.85
Hill Equipment & Supply		06/01/97	A/P	4,860.00
66715	Bill	ORD 101 (Gauges)		
Distributions: 2100–000	Accounts Payable – Trade			4,860.00
Hill Equipment & Supply		06/01/97	A/P	760.00
67189	Bill	ORD 104 (Cable, brackets)		
Distributions: 2100–000	Accounts Payable – Trade			760.00
Reynolds Tool Company		**06/01/97**		**125.00CR**
	Bal forward	**Balance forward**		
Reynolds Tool Company		06/01/97	A/P	125.00
69421	Bill	ORD 102 (Wire)		
Distributions: 2100–000	Accounts Payable – Trade			125.00

10 Bills payable transactions | Grand total: .00

Date 06/15/97 Acme Hardware Co. #0129 Page 0002

BILLS PAYABLE EDIT LIST

------------ G/L account distribution totals ------------

8,474.85	Credited to	2100–000	Accounts Payable – Trade
8,474.85	Debited to	2100–000	Accounts Payable – Trade

-- End of report --

Date 06/15/97 Acme Hardware Co. #0130 Page 0001

BILLS PAYABLE REGISTER

Vendor–name Invoice–#	Trans–type	Trans–date Reference	Credited–to	Trans–amt Debited–to
Hanson Manufacturing Co.	**Bal forward**	**06/01/97** **Balance forward**		**1,195.00CR**
Hanson Manufacturing Co. 11510	Bill	06/01/97 ORD 105 (C. Blocks)	A/P	495.00
Distributions: 2100–000	Accounts Payable – Trade			495.00
Hanson Manufacturing Co. 11924	Bill	06/01/97 ORD 103 (Plywood)	A/P	700.00
Distributions: 2100–000	Accounts Payable – Trade			700.00
Hill Equipment & Supply	**Bal forward**	**06/01/97** **Balance forward**		**7,154.85CR**
Hill Equipment & Supply 66554	Bill	06/01/97 ORD 107 (doors)	A/P	160.00
Distributions: 2100–000	Accounts Payable – Trade			160.00
Hill Equipment & Supply 66503	Bill	06/01/97 ORD 100 (Hardware)	A/P	1,374.85
Distributions: 2100–000	Accounts Payable – Trade			1,374.85
Hill Equipment & Supply 66715	Bill	06/01/97 ORD 101 (Gauges)	A/P	4,860.00
Distributions: 2100–000	Accounts Payable – Trade			4,860.00
Hill Equipment & Supply 67189	Bill	06/01/97 ORD 104 (Cable, brackets)	A/P	760.00
Distributions: 2100–000	Accounts Payable – Trade			760.00
Reynolds Tool Company	**Bal forward**	**06/01/97** **Balance forward**		**125.00CR**
Reynolds Tool Company 69421	Bill	06/01/97 ORD 102 (Wire)	A/P	125.00
Distributions: 2100–000	Accounts Payable – Trade			125.00

10 Bills payable transactions Grand total: .00

Date 06/15/97 Acme Hardware Co. #0130 Page 0002

BILLS PAYABLE REGISTER

------------ G/L account distribution totals ------------

8,474.85	Credited to	2100-000	Accounts Payable - Trade
8,474.85	Debited to	2100-000	Accounts Payable - Trade

-- End of report --

Date 06/15/97 Acme Hardware Co. #0132 Page 0001

RECURRING BILLS PAYABLE LIST

'' next to date means the transaction is now due**

Vendor-name		Nxt-due-date	Credited-to		Trans-amt
Frequency	Trans-type	Reference			
Bitznbytes Computer		07/15/97	A/P		250.00
Monthly	Bill	Lease of equipment			
Distributions: 6150-000	Office expense			250.00	
Jones Property Management		07/15/97	A/P		1,000.00
Monthly	Bill	Lease of property			
Distributions: 6160-000	Rents & utilities			1,000.00	
2 Recurring transactions			Grand total:		1,250.00
			Now due:		.00

Date 06/15/97 Acme Hardware Co. #0132 Page 0002

RECURRING BILLS PAYABLE LIST

------------ G/L account distribution totals ------------

1,250.00	Credited to 2100-000	Accounts Payable - Trade
250.00	Debited to 6150-000	Office expense
1,000.00	Debited to 6160-000	Rents & Utilities

1,250.00	Total debited	

-- End of report --

Date 06/15/97 | Acme Hardware Co. | #0133 Page 0001

BILLS PAYABLE EDIT LIST

Vendor–name		Trans–date	Credited–to	Trans–amt
Invoice–#	Trans–type	Reference		Debited–to
Bitznbytes Computer		06/15/97	A/P	250.00
	Bill	Lease of equipment		
Distributions: 6150–000	Office expense			250.00
Jones Property Management		06/15/97	A/P	1,000.00
	Bill	Lease of property		
Distributions: 6160–000	Rents & utilities			1,000.00
NorthWestern Bell		06/15/97	A/P	250.00
	Bill	Monthly bill		
Distributions: 6270–000	Telephone			250.00
3 Bills payable transactions			Grand total:	1,500.00

Date 06/15/97 | Acme Hardware Co. | #0133 Page 0002

BILLS PAYABLE EDIT LIST

------------ G/L account distribution totals ------------

1,500.00	Credited to	2100–000	Accounts Payable – Trade
250.00	Debited to	6150–000	Office expense
1,000.00	Debited to	6160–000	Rents & utilities
250.00	Debited to	6270–000	Telephone

1,500.00	Total debited		

–– End of report ––

Date 06/15/97 Acme Hardware Co. #0134 Page 0001

BILLS PAYABLE REGISTER

Vendor–name		Trans–date	Credited–to	Trans–amt
Invoice–#	Trans–type	Reference		Debited–to
Bitznbytes Computer		06/15/97	A/P	250.00
	Bill	Lease of equipment		
Distributions: 6150–000	Office expense			250.00
Jones Property Management		06/15/97	A/P	1,000.00
	Bill	Lease of property		
Distributions: 6160–000	Rents & utilities			1,000.00
NorthWestern Bell		06/15/97	A/P	250.00
	Bill	Monthly bill		
Distributions: 6270–000	Telephone			250.00
3 Bills payable transactions			Grand total:	1,500.00

Date 06/15/97 Acme Hardware Co. #0134 Page 0002

BILLS PAYABLE REGISTER

------------ G/L account distribution totals ------------

1,500.00	Credited to 2100–000	Accounts Payable – Trade
250.00	Debited to 6150–000	Office expense
1,000.00	Debited to 6160–000	Rents & utilities
250.00	Debited to 6270–000	Telephone
1,500.00	Total debited	

–– End of report ––

Date 06/15/97 Time: 22:37:00 Acme Hardware Co. #0135 Page #0001

ITEM LIST

Item # range: "First" to "Last"

Department: SHOP Vendor: "All"

Item type: I = Inventory

"****" indicates that the contra account varies by invoice profit center

Item-#	Description	Bar-code	Typ	Dept	Loc	Stk-unit	List-price	Avg-cost	Qty-on-hand	Last-rcvd
		Subst-item-#	Txb	Sls-#	COG-#	Pur-unit	Stk-qty/Pur	Last-cost	Qty-commit	1st-rcvd
	Vendor	Hist-class		Ret-#		Prf-unit		Min-qty-OH	Qty-on-ord	Last-ord
	Notes	Inv-contra-#						Max-qty-OH	Min-ord-qty	Last-sale
EQ-BLADE	Replacement blade		I	SHOP	R52	EACH	29.95	19.95000	0	None
			Y	4025	5010			19.950	0	None
	Tools Galore	Repairs		4520				5	25	None
		1400-000						40	10	None
EQ-FILTER	Replacement oil filter		I	SHOP	R14	EACH	2.95	1.25000	0	None
			Y	4025	5010			1.250	0	None
	"Biggies" Hardware	Repairs		4520				12	60	None
		1400-000						72	36	None

2 items printed

-- End of report --

Date 06/15/97		Acme Hardware Co.		#0136 Page 0001

BILLS PAYABLE EDIT LIST

Vendor–name		Trans–date	Credited–to	Trans–amt
Invoice–#	Trans–type	Reference		Debited–to
"Biggies" Hardware		06/15/97	A/P	75.00
3434333	Bill	Repair shop		
Distributions: 1400–000	Inventory			75.00
Tools Galore		06/15/97	A/P	498.75
345432	Bill	Repair shop		
Distributions: 1400–000	Inventory			498.75
2 Bills payable transactions			Grand total:	573.75

Date 06/15/97		Acme Hardware Co.		#0136 Page 0002

BILLS PAYABLE EDIT LIST

------------ G/L account distribution totals ------------

573.75	Credited to 2100–000	Accounts Payable – Trade
573.75	Debited to 1400–000	Inventory

-- End of report --

Date 06/15/97 Acme Hardware Co. #0137 Page 0001

BILLS PAYABLE REGISTER

Vendor–name		Trans–date	Credited–to	Trans–amt
Invoice–#	Trans–type	Reference	Debited–to	
"Biggies" Hardware		06/15/97	A/P	75.00
3434333	Bill	Repair shop		
Distributions: 1400–000	Inventory		75.00	
Tools Galore		06/15/97	A/P	498.75
345432	Bill	Repair shop		
Distributions: 1400–000	Inventory		498.75	

2 Bills payable transactions Grand total: 573.75

Date 06/15/97 Acme Hardware Co. #0137 Page 0002

BILLS PAYABLE REGISTER

------------ G/L account distribution totals ------------

573.75	Credited to 2100–000	Accounts Payable – Trade
573.75	Debited to 1400–000	Inventory

-- End of report --

Date 06/15/97 Acme Hardware Co. #0138 Page 0001

AGED ACCOUNTS PAYABLE SUMMARY

Starting vendor: "First" Ending vendor: "Last"
Cut off date: 06/15/97

Vendor Contact	Phone	Current	31-60	61-90	Over 90
"Biggies" Hardware					
"Biggy" Swanson	888-BIGY	75.00	.00	.00	.00
Bitznbytes Computer					
Dave Bitzn	405-569-8956	250.00	.00	.00	.00
Jones Property Management					
Robert Rents	214-774-6700	1,000.00	.00	.00	.00
NorthWestern Bell					
	721-1213	250.00	.00	.00	.00
Tools Galore					
"Kate" Schiepzo	180041 2TOOLS	498.75	.00	.00	.00
	Totals:	2,073.75	.00	.00	.00
	Grand total:	2,073.75			

-- End of report --

Date 06/15/97 Acme Hardware Co. #0139 Page 0001

DISBURSEMENTS EDIT LIST

Payee Trans–type	Chk–#	Trans–date Credit–to	Amt–paid Disc–taken	Total–CR Reference	Debit–to
Bitznbytes Computer **Computer check**		06/15/97 Chk acct 1	250.00 .00	250.00 Lease of equipment	A/P

*** Check must be printed for this transaction before posting ***

Payee Trans–type	Chk–#	Trans–date Credit–to	Amt–paid Disc–taken	Total–CR Reference	Debit–to
Jones Property Management **Computer check**		06/15/97 Chk acct 1	1,000.00 .00	1,000.00 Lease of property	A/P

*** Check must be printed for this transaction before posting ***

Payee Trans–type	Chk–#	Trans–date Credit–to	Amt–paid Disc–taken	Total–CR Reference	Debit–to
NorthWestern Bell **Computer check**		06/15/97 Chk acct 1	250.00 .00	250.00 May phone bill	A/P

*** Check must be printed for this transaction before posting ***

3 Transactions

Date 06/15/97 Acme Hardware Co. #0139 Page 0002

DISBURSEMENTS EDIT LIST

	#–of–trans	Amt–paid	Disc–taken	Total–CR
Computer checks:	3	1,500.00	.00	1,500.00
		–––––––	–––––––	–––––––
Grand totals:	3	1,500.00	.00	1,500.00

–––––––––––– G/L account distribution totals ––––––––––––

1,500.00 Credited to 1010–000 Checking #1 – Payables

1,500.00 Debited to 2100–000 Accounts Payable – Trade

*** Check must be printed for this transaction before posting ***

–– End of report ––

PRINTED CHECK AND STUB

VENDOR Bitznbytes Computer CHECK NO. 002100

INVOICE NO.	INVOICE DATE	INVOICE AMOUNT	AMOUNT PAID	DISCOUNT TAKEN	NET CHECK AMOUNT
9999	06/15/97	250.00	250.00	.00	250.00
				Check total	250.00

Acme Hardware Co.
123 Main St.
Winoga Falls, MI 12345

CHECK NO.	CHECK DATE
002100	06/15/97

TWO HUNDRED FIFTY AND 00/100 DOLLARS****************

CHECK AMOUNT
$*****250.00

Pay to the
order of Bitznbytes Computer
15 Amherst St.
Ann Arbor, MI 48136

Authorized Signature

PRINTED CHECK AND STUB

VENDOR Jones Property Management CHECK NO. 002101

INVOICE NO.	INVOICE DATE	INVOICE AMOUNT	AMOUNT PAID	DISCOUNT TAKEN	NET CHECK AMOUNT
9999	06/15/97	1,000.00	1,000.00	.00	1,000.00
				Check total	1,000.00

Acme Hardware Co.
123 Main St.
Winoga Falls, MI 12345

CHECK NO.	CHECK DATE
002101	06/15/97

CHECK AMOUNT
$***1,000.00

ONE THOUSAND AND 00/100 DOLLARS***********************

Pay to the
order of Jones Property Management
11056 E. Commercial
Dallas, TX 75330

Authorized Signature

PRINTED CHECK AND STUB

VENDOR NorthWestern Bell				CHECK NO. 002102	
INVOICE NO.	INVOICE DATE	INVOICE AMOUNT	AMOUNT PAID	DISCOUNT TAKEN	NET CHECK AMOUNT
9999	06/15/97	250.00	250.00	.00	250.00
				Check total	250.00

Acme Hardware Co.
123 Main St.
Winoga Falls, MI 12345

CHECK NO.	CHECK DATE
002102	06/15/97

CHECK AMOUNT
$*****250.00

TWO HUNDRED FIFTY AND 00/100 DOLLARS*****************

Pay to the
order of

NorthWestern Bell
Irving Office
500 S. Central
Amherst, MI 48132

Authorized Signature

Date 06/15/97 Acme Hardware Co. #0140 Page 0001

DISBURSEMENTS REGISTER

Payee Trans–type	Chk–#	Trans–date Credit–to	Amt–paid Disc–taken	Total–CR Reference	Debit–to
Bitznbytes Computer **Computer check**	2100	06/15/97 Chk acct 1	250.00 .00	250.00 Lease of equipment	A/P
Jones Property Management **Computer check**	2101	06/15/97 Chk acct 1	1,000.00 .00	1,000.00 Lease of property	A/P
NorthWestern Bell **Computer check**	2102	06/15/97 Chk acct 1	250.00 .00	250.00 May phone bill	A/P

3 Transactions

Date 06/15/97 Acme Hardware Co. #0140 Page 0002

DISBURSEMENTS REGISTER

	#–of–trans	Amt–paid	Disc–taken	Total–CR
Computer checks:	3	1,500.00	.00	1,500.00
Grand totals:	3	1,500.00	.00	1,500.00

———————— G/L account distribution totals ————————

1,500.00 Credited to 1010–000 Checking #1 – Payables

1,500.00 Debited to 2100–000 Accounts Payable – Trade

-- End of report --

Date 06/15/97 | Acme Hardware Co. | #0141 Page 0001

AGED ACCOUNTS PAYABLE SUMMARY

Starting vendor: "First" Ending vendor: "Last"
Cut off date: 06/15/97

Vendor Contact	Phone	Current	31–60	61–90	Over 90
"Biggies" Hardware					
"Biggy" Swanson	888–BIGY	75.00	.00	.00	.00
Tools Galore					
"Kate" Schiepzo	180041 2TOOLS	498.75	.00	.00	.00
	Totals:	573.75	.00	.00	.00
	Grand total:	573.75			

–– End of report ––

Practice Set 9 – PRODUCE MONTHLY STATEMENTS, RECONCILE CANCELLED CHECKS AND TRANSFER BANK FUNDS

Introduction

In this practice set, you are required to analyze customer payments to determine which customer should receive monthly statements. In addition, you are asked to bring forward customer balances and to purge a customer record. You are then asked to do some clean up work which includes reconciling cancelled checks and transferring cash from account 1 to account 2 in preparation for the processing of the company payroll. You are expected to be able to:

- ➡ determine which customers owe the company money
- ➡ print monthly customer statements
- ➡ compute finance charges
- ➡ purge a customer record
- ➡ reconcile checks
- ➡ make a transfer of funds

Set Transaction Date

Before starting this practice set, enter today's date as **06–25–97.**

Print Aged Accounts Receivable Report

Move to Accounts Receivable and select Print A/R Aging Report. Include all customers with a balance greater than zero, and reflect the following information as you prepare to print the statements:

* Use an aging date of 6/25/97.
* Do not include customers after this date.
* Print the report for all customers and all sales reps.
* Show both DR and CR accounts.
* Do not print zero balance customers.
* Use no cut off balance.
* Print a detailed report.
* Do not print on separate pages.
* Answer Yes (Y) to the question:
  "Age open item customers like bal forward customers?"

After printing the report, answer the following questions:

Which open–item customers did not make full payment of their outstanding invoices within 10 days, and require a monthly statement?

Which balance–forward customers did not make full payment of their outstanding invoices, and require a monthly statement?

Print Customer Statements

Change over to Print Customer Statements and enter the following:

* Use the statement period 6/01/97 to 6/25/97.
* Print for all customers.
* Produce monthly statements (M) for DR accounts only.
* Print finance charges (Y).
* Print document references for bal fwd customers (Y).
* Print open item customers by apply–to number (Y).
* Do not show invoice balance only (N).
* Show fully paid items for open item customers (Y).
* Take the necessary steps to print the monthly statements.

Examine the statements and answer the following questions:

What do the numbers S107 and 16315 refer to on the 21st Century Construction statement?
On the Newton, Boyd and Co. statement, why is the dollar amount $29.95 shown three times on the first line of the detail portion of the statement?

Calculate Finance Charges

A new area for you to explore is the assignment of finance charges to customer accounts. We will assume that no customer shown on the A/R aging report makes a payment from 6/25/97 to 7/10/97. Move to Process Finance Charges and Calculate Finance Charges, and do the following:

* Use a cut off date of 7/10/97.
* Compute finance charges for all statement cycles.
* Do not include payments after the cut off.
* Exclude customers with finance charges already claculated after 6/10/97.

After computing the finance charges, print the Finance Charges Edit List.

Not all customers will be assigned a finance charge. Explain why this occurs.

After determining that the Finance Charges Edit List is correct, post the charges which prints the Finance Charges Journal.

Purge the Customer File

Another new area to explore is the purging of a customer record. Purging of detail can begin after the printing of customer statements. In this section you are asked to purge only one customer account, namely, the Newton, Boyd and Co. account. Select Purge Customer Accounts and do the following:

* For the starting customer, type Newton, Boyd and Co. (or type New and press ENTER).
* For the ending customer, press ENTER for same customer.
* For Thru what Date, type 7/10/97.

* Press F1 for all statement cycles.
* Type Y for purge file.

Go ahead and purge this record, which prints the Customer Accounts Purge Report.

What does the customer total dollar amount represent on this purge report?

To fully demonstrate the consequences of purging a record, print a second (Partial) Aged Accounts Receivable report.

* Use an aging date of 7/10/97.
* Do not include customers after this date.
* Print the report for all Newton, Boyd and Co. only (Starting and Ending customer), for all sales reps.
* Show both DR and CR accounts.
* Do not print zero balance customers.
* Use no cut off balance.
* Print a detailed report.
* Do not print on separate pages.
* Answer No (N) to the question: "Age open item customers like bal forward customers?" and No (N) to "Invc bal only?".

Print the Aged Accounts Receivable Report for this single customer.

Compare this aged report to the one prepared at the beginning of this practice set. How has the Newton, Boyd and Co. account been changed by the purging of the record?
Explain why purging of customer records should be done only AFTER the printing of monthly statements.

Reconcile the Checking Account

Move to Check Reconciliation next and select Reconcile a Checking Account.

* Mark cleared items for checking account #1.
* Use a statement date of 6/25/97.
* Use the earliest check date.
* Clear all items.
* Print the Check Reconciliation.

How can you determine that a check has been cleared?
What is the purpose of check reconciliation?

Next, select Print a Checkbook and do the following:

* Enter checking account #1.
* Answer Yes (Y) to "Purge cleared items?".
* Enter a date of 6/01/97.

Explain the report that is printed.

Repeat the three steps above, namely,

* Enter checking account #1.
* Answer Yes (Y) to "Purge cleared items?".
* Enter a date of 6/01/97.

Explain what happens in processing and how this second report differs from the first.
What is the purpose of the purge cleared items selection?

Transfer Bank Funds

We want you to record the transfer of $15,000 from Checking account #1 to checking account #2, in order to meet the June payroll.

* Use a check # of 2103 and a date of 6/25/97.
* Reference the check "June Payroll."
* Print the edit list.
* Return to Record Checking Acct Transfers
* Answer Yes (Y) to make the transfer.

Post the cash transfer to the G/L using Process Cash Receipts (A/R) and Process Disbursements (A/P) as outlined below. **Complete the following T accounts before starting.**

Payroll Cash	A/P Cash	Cash Transfer

Payroll Cash	A/P Cash	Cash Transfer

* Process/post cash receipts first. Use a deposit date of 6/25/97.
* Print the Cash Receipts Register.

* Process/post disbursements next.
* Print the Disbursements Register.

Why is it necessary to perform these two additional postings to complete the transfer of cash from one account to another?

Other Things to Explore

1. Select one of the accounts shown on the Finance Charges Journal.

   How has finance charges changed the customer accounts detail section of the display?
   How has finance charges changed the customer accounts summary section of the display?

2. From the G/L, view account number 1100 A/R – Trade.

   How have finance charges altered receivables?

3. View account 4910.

   Explain the use of this account.

4. View the Newton, Boyd and Co. customer record.

   How has the purging of this record changed this display?

5. Explore the following G/L accounts. **Indicate whether the account balance has increased, decreased, or stayed the same.**

   1010 1020 9999

   What is the purpose of this last (9999) account?

This completes Practice Set 9.

Date: 06/25/97 Time: 13:52:25	Acme Hardware Co.	Report #0144 Page #0001

AGED ACCOUNTS RECEIVABLE

Selections for this report:

1.	Aging date	**06/25/97**
2.	Include items after aging date?	**N**
3.	Starting customer	**"first"**
4.	Ending customer	**"Last"**
5.	Sales rep	**"All"**
6.	Print DR/CR bal customers	**Both DR and CR accounts**
7.	Print zero bal customers?	**N**
8.	Cut–off balance due	**No cut–off**
9.	Detail or summary	**Detail**
10.	Print on separate pages?	**N**
11.	Age open item customers like bal forward customers?	**Y**

Date: 06/25/97 Time: 13:52:26 Acme Hardware Co. Report #0145 Page #0001

AGED ACCOUNTS RECEIVABLE

Aging date: 6/25/97

Document types: S = Sale P = Payment C = Cr memo D = Dr memo B = Balance forward F = Finance charge

Customer–name Sls–rep	Phone–# Contact	Last–pmt–dat Bal–meth	Balance	Current	31–60 days	61–90 days	Over 90 days
21st Century Construction JAK	555–7844 Herbert Mardhat	6/13/97 OPN–ITM	300.00	300.00	.00	.00	.00

Doc–#	Doc–date	typ	Apply–to	Reference	Doc–amount	Discount	Doc–total	Age	Terms
S107	6/10/97	S		1091 Qty 50	971.97	.00	971.97	15	2/10 NET 30
16315	6/13/97	P	Open	First installment	671.97CR	.00	671.97CR	12	2/10 NET 30

Customer–name Sls–rep	Phone–# Contact	Last–pmt–dat Bal–meth	Balance	Current	31–60 days	61–90 days	Over 90 days
Allied Plumbing Co. JAK	554–4300 Cathy Sinks	6/13/97 BAL–FWD	315.00	315.00	.00	.00	.00

Doc–#	Doc–date	typ	Apply–to	Reference	Doc–amount	Discount	Doc–total	Age	Terms
500	6/03/97	S		Ref #: 000502	1,200.39	.00	1,200.39	22	NET 30
8429	6/13/97	P		2243/2432	885.39CR	.00	885.39CR	12	

Customer–name Sls–rep	Phone–# Contact	Last–pmt–dat Bal–meth	Balance	Current	31–60 days	61–90 days	Over 90 days
Elliot Enterprises TJF	779–6010 Paul Elliott	6/13/97 OPN–ITM	100.00	100.00	.00	.00	.00

Doc–#	Doc–date	typ	Apply–to	Reference	Doc–amount	Discount	Doc–total	Age	Terms
502	6/03/97	S	502	Ref #: 000501	567.84	.00	567.84	22	2/10 NET 30
16933	6/13/97	P	502	Apply to balance	467.84CR	.00	467.84CR	12	NET 30

Customer–name Sls–rep	Phone–# Contact	Last–pmt–dat Bal–meth	Balance	Current	31–60 days	61–90 days	Over 90 days
Newton, Boyd and Co. JAK	886–7722 Bob Newton	6/13/97 BAL–FWD	68.00	68.00	.00	.00	.00

Doc–#	Doc–date	typ	Apply–to	Reference	Doc–amount	Discount	Doc–total	Age	Terms
S103	6/04/97	S		1105 Qty 1	29.95	.00	29.95	21	NET 30
S104	6/05/97	S		BS–DOORS Qty 1	68.00	.00	68.00	20	NET 30
S105	6/08/97	S		EQ–DEER Qty 1	87.00	.00	87.00	17	NET 30
C105	6/10/97	C		EQ–DEER Qty 1	87.00CR	.00	87.00CR	15	NET 30
S106	6/10/97	S		EL–WIRE Qty 5	25.95	.00	25.95	15	NET 30
T102	6/10/97	S		Sales Tax	8.67	.00	8.67	15	NET 30
14310	6/13/97	P		66/315	64.57CR	.00	64.57CR	12	

Customer–name Sls–rep	Phone–# Contact	Last–pmt–dat Bal–meth	Balance	Current	31–60 days	61–90 days	Over 90 days
Webber Landscaping AW	323–2342 Marvin Webber	None OPN–ITM	1,269.55	1,269.55	.00	.00	.00

Doc–#	Doc–date	typ	Apply–to	Reference	Doc–amount	Discount	Doc–total	Age	Terms
504	6/03/97	S	504	Ref #: 000505	1,269.55	.00	1,269.55	22	2/10 NET 30

Date: 06/25/97 Time: 13:52:32 Acme Hardware Co. Report #0145 Page #0002

AGED ACCOUNTS RECEIVABLE

Aging date: 6/25/97

Document types: S = Sale P = Payment C = Cr memo D = Dr memo B = Balance forward F = Finance charge

Customer-name Sls-rep	Phone-# Contact	Last-pmt-dat Bal-meth	Balance	Current	31-60 days	61-90 days	Over 90 days

Grand totals for 5 customers printed; aging date 6/25/97

DR Lines show totals for customers with debit balances as of the aging date
CR Lines show totals for customers with credit balances as of the aging date

	Balance	Current	31-60 days	61-90 days	Over 90 days
DR bal cust totals:	2,052.55	2,052.55	.00	.00	.00
CR bal cust totals:	.00	.00	.00	.00	.00
Net totals:	2,052.55	2,052.55	.00	.00	.00

-- End of report --

PRINTED CUSTOMER STATEMENT

Acme Hardware
123 Main St.
Winoga Falls, MI 12345

Telephone 213–443–1234

STATEMENT

21st Century Construction
P.O. Box 4545
670 Mason Street
Ann Arbor, MI 48136

STATEMENT DATE
6/25/97

DATE	CODE	REF.NO.	CHARGES	CREDITS	BALANCE
6/10/97	I	S107	Applies to:	–OPEN–	971.97
6/13/97	P	16315	Applies to:	–OPEN–	671.97CR
Unapplied open items				Invoice balance:	300.00

TOTAL
300.00

PLEASE RETURN THIS STUB WITH PAYMENT

ACCOUNT NAME
21st Century Construct

STATEMENT DATE
6/25/97

AMOUNT
ENCLOSED $ ____________

REF.NO.	CODE	CHARGES
–OPEN–	I	971.97
	P	671.97CR
Balance:		300.00

TOTAL AMT DUE
300.00

PRINTED CUSTOMER STATEMENT

Acme Hardware
123 Main St.
Winoga Falls, MI 12345

Telephone 213–443–1234

STATEMENT

Allied Plumbing Co.
555 N. Grand Blvd
Lansing, MI 48135

STATEMENT DATE
6/25/97

DATE	CODE	REF.NO.	CHARGES	CREDITS	BALANCE
6/01/97	BF	Balfwd	.00		.00
6/03/97	I	500	1,200.39		1,200.39
			Ref #: 000502		
6/13/97	P	8429		885.39–	315.00
			2243/2432		

TOTAL
315.00

PLEASE RETURN THIS STUB WITH PAYMENT

ACCOUNT NAME
Allied Plumbing Co.

STATEMENT DATE
6/25/97

AMOUNT
ENCLOSED $ ____________

REF.NO.	CODE	CHARGES
Balfwd	BF	.00
500	I	1,200.39
8429	P	885.39CR

TOTAL AMT DUE
315.00

PRINTED CUSTOMER STATEMENT

Acme Hardware
123 Main St.
Winoga Falls, MI 12345

Telephone 213–443–1234

STATEMENT

Elliott Enterprises
123 Broadway
Glendale, MI 48133

STATEMENT DATE
6/25/97

DATE	CODE	REF.NO.	CHARGES	CREDITS	BALANCE
6/03/97	I	502	Applies to:	502	567.84
6/13/97	P	16933	Applies to:	502	467.84CR
Ref #: 000501			Invoice balance:		100.00

TOTAL
100.00

PLEASE RETURN THIS STUB WITH PAYMENT

ACCOUNT NAME
Elliott Enterprises

STATEMENT DATE
6/25/97

AMOUNT ENCLOSED $ ____________

REF.NO.	CODE	CHARGES
502	I	567.84
	P	467.84CR
Balance:		100.00

TOTAL AMT DUE
100.00

PRINTED CUSTOMER STATEMENT

Acme Hardware
123 Main St.
Winoga Falls, MI 12345

Telephone 213–443–1234

STATEMENT

Newton, Boyd and Co.
1024 Marble Avenue
Lansing, MI 48135

STATEMENT DATE: 6/25/97

DATE	CODE	REF.NO.	CHARGES	CREDITS	BALANCE
6/01/97	BF	Balfwd	.00		.00
6/04/97	I	S103	29.95		29.95
			1105 Qty 1		
6/05/97	I	S104	68.00		97.95
			BS–DOORS Qty 1		
6/08/97	I	S105	87.00		184.95
			EQ–DEER Qty 1		
6/10/97	CR	C105		87.00–	97.95
			EQ–DEER Qty 1		
6/10/97	I	S106	25.95		123.90
			EL–WIRE Qty 5		
6/10/97	I	T102	8.67		132.57
			Sales Tax		
6/13/97	P	14310		64.57–	68.00
			66/315		

TOTAL: 68.00

PLEASE RETURN THIS STUB WITH PAYMENT

ACCOUNT NAME: Newton, Boyd and Co.

STATEMENT DATE: 6/25/97

AMOUNT ENCLOSED $ ____________

REF.NO.	CODE	CHARGES
Balfwd	BF	.00
S103	I	29.95
S104	I	68.00
S105	I	87.00
C105	CR	87.00CR
S106	I	25.95
T102	I	8.67
14310	P	64.57CR

TOTAL AMT DUE: 68.00

PRINTED CUSTOMER STATEMENT

Acme Hardware
123 Main St.
Winoga Falls, MI 12345

Telephone 213–443–1234

STATEMENT

Webber Landscaping
33 East Lansing Dr.
Winoga Falls, MI 12345

STATEMENT DATE
6/25/97

DATE	CODE	REF NO.	CHARGES	CREDITS	BALANCE
6/03/97	I	504	Applies to:	504	1,269.55
Ref #: 000505			Invoice balance:		1,269.55

TOTAL
1,269.55

PLEASE RETURN THIS STUB WITH PAYMENT

ACCOUNT NAME
Webber Landscaping

STATEMENT DATE
6/25/97

AMOUNT
ENCLOSED $ ____________

REF.NO.	CODE	CHARGES
504	I	1,269.55
Balance:		1,269.55

TOTAL AMT DUE
1,269.55

Date 06/25/97 Time 14:05:48 Acme Hardware Co. Report #0146 Page 0001

FINANCE CHARGES EDIT LIST

For open items thru 07/10/97

Customer–name		Past–due–amt	Fin–chrg
Allied Plumbing co.		315.00	4.73
Newton, Boyd and Co.		68.00	1.02
	Totals:	383.00	5.75

-- End of report --

Date 06/25/97 Time 14:06:33 | Acme Hardware Co. | Report #0147 Page 0001

FINANCE CHARGES JOURNAL

For open items thru 07/10/97

Customer–name		Past–due–amt	Fin–chrg
Allied Plumbing co.		315.00	4.73
Newton, Boyd and Co.		68.00	1.02
	Totals:	383.00	5.75

–– End of report ––

Date: 06/25/97 Time: 14:08:25 | Acme Hardware Co. | Report #0148 Page 0001

CUSTOMER ACCOUNTS PURGE REPORT

Starting customer: Newton, Boyd and Co.
Ending customer: Newton, Boyd and Co.

Purge cut–off date: 7/10/97

Document types: S = Sale P = payment C = Cr memo D = Dr memo F = finance charge B = balance forward

Customer–name	Address–1	Address–2	Address–3	Phone
Newton, Boyd and Co.	1024 Marble Avenue	Lansing, MI 48135		886–7722

Doc–#	Doc–date	Typ	Apply–to	Doc–amount	Discount	Doc–total	Terms	Reference
S103	6/04/97	S		29.95	.00	29.95	NET 30	1105 Qty 1
S104	6/05/97	S		68.00	.00	68.00	NET 30	BS–DOORS Qty 1
S105	6/08/97	S		87.00	.00	87.00	NET 30	EQ–DEER Qty 1
526079	6/08/97	B		33.38	.00	33.38	NET 30	EQ–DEER Qty 1
C105	6/10/97	C		87.00CR	.00	87.00CR	NET 30	EQ–DEER Qty 1
14310	6/13/97	P		64.57CR	.00	64.57CR		66/315
		Customer totals:		33.38	.00	33.38		
1 Customers		Grand totals:		33.38	.00	33.38		

–– End of report ––

Date: 06/25/97 Time: 14:10:55 | Acme Hardware Co. | Report #0149 Page #0001

AGED ACCOUNTS RECEIVABLE

Selections for this report:

1.	Aging date	**07/10/97**
2.	Include items after aging date?	**N**
3.	Starting customer	**Newton, Boyd and Co.**
4.	Ending customer	**Newton, Boyd and Co.**
5.	Sales rep	**"All"**
6.	Print DR/CR bal customers	**Both DR and CR accounts**
7.	Print zero bal customers?	**N**
8.	Cut–off balance due	**No cut–off**
9.	Detail or summary	**Detail**
10.	Print on separate pages?	**N**
11.	Age open item customers like bal forward customers?	**N** Invc bal only? **N**

Date: 06/25/97 Time: 14:10:56 Acme Hardware Co. Report #0150 Page #0001

AGED ACCOUNTS RECEIVABLE

Aging date: 7/10/97

Document types: S = Sale P = Payment C = Cr memo D = Dr memo B = Balance forward F = Finance charge

Customer–name Sls–rep	Phone–# Contact	Last–pmt–date Bal–meth	Balance	Current	31–60 days	61–90 days	Over 90 days
Newton, Boyd and Co. JAK	886–7722 Bob Newton	6/13/97 BAL–FWD	69.02	35.64	33.38	.00	.00

Doc–#	Doc–date	typ	Apply–to	Reference	Doc–amount	Discount	Doc–total	Age	Terms
526079	6/08/97	B		EQ–DEER Qty 1	33.38	.00	33.38	32	NET 30
S106	6/10/97	S		EL–WIRE Qty 5	25.95	.00	25.95	30	NET 30
T102	6/10/97	S		Sales Tax	8.67	.00	8.67	30	NET 30
9707	7/10/97	F		Finance chgs on 07/10/97	1.02	.00	1.02	0	

Grand totals for 1 customers printed; aging date 7/10/97

DR Lines show totals for customers with debit balances as of the aging date
CR Lines show totals for customers with credit balances as of the aging date

	Balance	Current	31–60 days	61–90 days	Over 90 days
DR bal cust totals:	69.02	35.64	33.38	.00	.00
CR bal cust totals:	.00	.00	.00	.00	.00
Net totals:	69.02	35.64	33.38	.00	.00

-- End of report --

Date 06/25/97 | Acme Hardware Co. | #0151 Page 0001

RECONCILIATION

Checking account #: 1 8765-432-19876 4400998877

Chk-#	Date	Reference	Clr-date	Amount	Balance
			Beginning bank balance:		.00
	06/01/97	Set up cash balance	06/25/97	50,000.00CR	50,000.00
	06/13/97	Deposit	06/25/97	8,090.39CR	58,090.39
2100	06/15/97	Bitznbytes Computer	06/25/97	250.00	57,840.39
2101	06/15/97	Jones Property Management	06/25/97	1,000.00	56,840.39
2102	06/15/97	NorthWestern Bell	06/25/97	250.00	56,590.39
			Ending bank balance:		56,590.39

Total depostis/CR: 58,090.39 Total checks/DR: 1,500.00

-- End of report --

Date 06/25/97 Acme Hardware Co. #0152 Page 0001

CHECKBOOK

Purging cleared items through 06/01/97.

Checking account #: 1 8765-432-19876 4400998877
Cleared items have "*" next to them

Chk-#	Date	Reference	Amount	Balance
Adjustmnt *	06/01/97	Set up cash balance	50,000.00CR	50,000.00
Deposit *	06/13/97		8,090.39CR	58,090.39
CK# 2100*	06/15/97	Bitznbytes Computer	250.00	57,840.39
CK# 2101*	06/15/97	Jones Property Management	1,000.00	56,840.39
CK# 2102*	06/15/97	NorthWestern Bell	250.00	56,590.39

Current checkbook balance: 56,590.39

-- End of report --

Date 06/25/97 Acme Hardware Co. #0153 Page 0001

CHECKBOOK

Purging cleared items through 06/01/97.

Checking account #: 1 8765-432-19876 4400998877
Cleared items have "*" next to them

Chk-#	Date	Reference	Amount	Balance
Balance				50,000.00
Deposit *	06/13/97		8,090.39CR	58,090.39
CK# 2100*	06/15/97	Bitznbytes Computer	250.00	57,840.39
CK# 2101*	06/15/97	Jones Property Management	1,000.00	56,840.39
CK# 2102*	06/15/97	NorthWestern Bell	250.00	56,590.39

Current checkbook balance: 56,590.39

-- End of report --

Date 06/25/97 Acme Hardware Co. #0154 Page 0001

CHECKING ACCOUNT TRANSFER EDIT LIST

Checking accounts: 1 = 8765–432–19876
2 = 9983–321–87651

From	Chk–#	Chk–date	To	Chk–amount	Reference
1	2103	06/25/97	2	15,000.00	June Payroll

1 transfer

–– End of report ––

Date 06/25/97 Time 14:25:05 Acme Hardware Co. Report #0155 0001

CASH RECEIPTS REGISTER

Customer–name	Bal–meth	Rect–date	Check–#	Amount–recd	Cash–acct	Bank–rte–#/Ref	Discount
*Cash transfer		6/25/97	2103	15,000.00	1020–000	June Payroll	

Amt–credited	Acct–#
15,000.00	9999–000 Transfer/suspense Account

Date 06/25/97 Time 14:25:05 Acme Hardware Co. Report #0155 0002

CASH RECEIPTS REGISTER

Customer–name	Bal–meth	Rect–date	Check–#	Amount–recd	Cash–acct	Bank–rte–#/Ref	Discount

Total recd: 15,000.00

Total disc: .00

----

1 cash receipt transactions Total credited: 15,000.00

---------------G/L account distribution totals---------------

15,000.00 credited to 9999–000 Transfer/suspense Account

15,000.00 debited to 1020–000 Checking #2 – Payroll

-- End of report --

Date 06/25/97 Acme Hardware Co. #0156 Page 0001

DISBURSEMENTS REGISTER

Payee Trans-type	Chk-#	Trans-date Credit-to	Amt-paid Disc-taken	Total-CR Reference	Debit-to
*Cash transfer		06/25/97	15,000.00	15,000.00	
Hand wrt check	2103	Chk acct 1	.00	June Payroll	

Distributions: 9999-000 Transfer/suspense Account 15,000.00

1 Transaction

Date 06/25/97 Acme Hardware Co. #0156 Page 0002

DISBURSEMENTS REGISTER

	#-of-trans	Amt-paid	Disc-taken	Total-CR
Hand wrt checks:	1	15,000.00	.00	15,000.00
		-------	-------	-------
Grand totals:	1	15,000.00	.00	15,000.00

---------------G/L account distribution totals---------------

15,000.00 Credited to 1010-000 Checking #1 - Payables

15,000.00 Debited to 9999-000 Transfer/suspense Account

-- End of report --

Practice Set 10 – PROCESS EMPLOYEE PAYROLL

Introduction

This practice set asks you to process the bi–weekly payroll for the Acme Hardware Co. It differs from the material presented in the text in several ways. You are asked to produce the payroll for 6/15/97, and be able to:

- ➡ set up deduction and earning codes
- ➡ set up federal tax codes and tables
- ➡ add employees to the master file
- ➡ process payroll transactions
- ➡ print all payroll reports and summaries

Set Transaction Date

Before starting this practice set, enter today's date as **6–15–97.**

Set Up and Print Deduction / Earning Codes

Move to employee payroll and select Maintain Deduction/Earning Codes.

- * Display all existing codes. How many codes are there?
- * Delete the code for Tips.
- * Change the description of code D1 to **UntFund.**
- * Add code D2. Use the description **F/Peace.**
  Add the type (D – Deduction), and post to G/L 2390.
- * Print all deduction and earning codes.

Set Up and Print Federal / State Codes and Tables

Move to Maintain Tax Codes and Tables.

- * Display all existing codes. Why are three state income tax codes needed?
- * Change the minimum wage to 12.00 for all codes. (Remember this is 1997!)
- * Change maximum social security wages to 82,000.
- * State taxes have been increased for people with higher incomes. Enter new data to line #47 of each state withholding table, using the information shown below.

TABLE	$–AMT	%–AMT	ON–AMT–OVER
MI–H	1,731.00	12.00	32,930
MI–M	3,359.00	12.00	57,400
MI–S	1,668.50	12.00	28,600

Suppose you are asked to explain how the MI–H new amount of $1,731.00 was determined. Explain the calculation by filling in the following equation with data from the MI–H table.

$1,452.70 + (X percent) (Y dollar amount) = $1,731.00

Add Employee Data

Move to Maintain Employee Data.

* Display the employee list. **How many employees are on file?**

Make the following changes to Edward Palmer's record.

* The Hire Date is 06/01/97.
* The Review Date should be 12/01/97.
* Home Department should be 0300.
* Distribute Wages should be set to Y.
* # SWT Exemptions should be set to 4.
* $ SWT Exemptions should be $0.00.
* The State Tax Credit of $64.00 should be $0.00.
* The Added SWT should be $0.00.

Why would an employee ever request that an "Added SWT" be added to his or her payroll record?

Add employees 2,3 and 4 to the file using the following data.

1. Employee–#	**2**
2. Name	**Earnest Wantabee**
3. Street	**25436 Stony Drive**
4. City	**Winoga Falls**
5. St	**MI**
6. Zip	**12345**
7. Soc sec #	**235–23–9999**
8. Birth date	**01/01/97**
9. Marital status	**Single (S)**
10. Hire date	**06/01/97**
11. Last raise	(leave blank)
12. Review date	**12/01/97**
13. Terminate date	(leave blank)
14. Emp type	**Hourly (H)**
15. Pay frequency	**Bi–weekly (B)**
16. Home department	**0200**
17. Wage account #	**6200–000**

18. Salary
19. Regular rate — **16.00**
20. Overtime rate — **(press F1)** 24.00
21. Special rate — **(press F1)** 32.00
22. Vac hours due — **0**

23. Vac hours paid — **0**
24. Sick hours due — **0**
25. Pension plan? — **Y**
26. Distrib wages? — **Y**
27. W–2 Ins premium — **0**

28. Can get tip CR? — **N**
29. State tax codc — **MI–S**
30. City tax code — (leave blank)
31. # FWT exemptions — **1**
32. $ FWT exemptions — **0**

33. # SWT exemptions — **1**
34. $ SWT exemptions — **0**
35. # OST exemptions — **0**
36. $ OST exemptions — **0**
37. # CWT exemptions — **0**

38. $ CWT exemptions — **0**
39. State tax credit — **0**
40. Added FWT — **0**
41. Added SWT — **0**
42. Added CWT — **0**

43. Soc sec exempt? — **N**
44. Medicare exempt? — **N**
45. FUI exempt? — **N**
46. SUI exempt? — **N**
47. # of EIC certs — **0**

Leave vacation and sick leave data blank. Set all remaining fields to zero.

---

1. Employee–# — **3**
2. Name — **Sara Sweetheart**
3. Street — **354 East 54 Street**
4. City — **Winoga Falls**
5. St — **MI**

6. Zip — **12345**
7. Soc sec # — **333–46–4945**
8. Birth date — **01/01/97**
9. Marital status — **Head of Household (H)**

10.	Hire date	**06/01/97**
11.	Last raise	(leave blank)
12.	Review date	**12/01/97**
13.	Terminate date	(leave blank)
14.	Emp type	**Hourly (H)**
15.	Pay frequency	**Bi−weekly (B)**
16.	Home department	**1234**
17.	Wage account #	**6200−000**
18.	Salary	
19.	Regular rate	**16.00**
20.	Overtime rate	**(press F1)** 24.00
21.	Special rate	**(press F1)** 32.00
22.	Vac hours due	**0**
23.	Vac hours paid	**0**
24.	Sick hours due	**0**
25.	Pension plan?	**Y**
26.	Distrib wages?	**Y**
27.	W−2 Ins premium	**0**
28.	Can get tip CR?	**N**
29.	State tax code	**MI−H**
30.	City tax code	(leave blank)
31.	# FWT exemptions	**2**
32.	$ FWT exemptions	**0**
33.	# SWT exemptions	**2**
34.	$ SWT exemptions	**0**
35.	# OST exemptions	**0**
36.	$ OST exemptions	**0**
37.	# CWT exemptions	**0**
38.	$ CWT exemptions	**0**
39.	State tax credit	**0**
40.	Added FWT	**0**
41.	Added SWT	**0**
42.	Added CWT	**0**
43.	Soc sec exempt?	**N**
44.	Medicare exempt?	**N**
45.	FUI exempt?	**N**
46.	SUI exempt?	**N**
47.	# of EIC certs	**0**

Leave vacation and sick leave data blank. Set all remaining fields to zero.

1.	Employee–#	**4**
2.	Name	**Hermann Acme**
3.	Street	**1245 First Street South**
4.	City	**Winoga Falls**
5.	St	**MI**
6.	Zip	**12345**
7.	Soc sec #	**443–55–3838**
8.	Birth date	**01/01/97**
9.	Marital status	**Married (M)**
10.	Hire date	(leave blank)
11.	Last raise	(leave blank)
12.	Review date	(leave blank)
13.	Terminate date	(leave blank)
14.	Emp type	**Salary (S)**
15.	Pay frequency	**Bi–weekly (B)**
16.	Home department	**0100**
17.	Wage account #	**6180–000**
18.	Salary	**5000**
19.	Regular rate	**0.00**
20.	Overtime rate	**0.00**
21.	Special rate	**0.00**
22.	Vac hours due	**0**
23.	Vac hours paid	**0**
24.	Sick hours due	**0**
25.	Pension plan?	**Y**
26.	Distrib wages?	**Y**
27.	W–2 Ins premium	**0**
28.	Can get tip CR?	**N**
29.	State tax code	**MI–M**
30.	City tax code	(leave blank)
31.	# FWT exemptions	**3**
32.	$ FWT exemptions	**0**
33.	# SWT exemptions	**3**
34.	$ SWT exemptions	**0**
35.	# OST exemptions	**0**
36.	$ OST exemptions	**0**
37.	# CWT exemptions	**0**
38.	$ CWT exemptions	**0**
39.	State tax credit	**0**
40.	Added FWT	**0**
41.	Added SWT	**0**
42.	Added CWT	**0**

43. Soc sec exempt? **N**
44. Medicare exempt? **N**
45. FUI exempt? **N**
46. SUI exempt? **N**
47. # of EIC certs **0**

Leave vacation and sick leave data blank. Set all remaining fields to zero.

After entering these new employees,

* Print the Numeric Employee List, showing Detail.

Disengage the Payroll Setup Mode

At this point, you are ready to begin processing the employee payroll for 06/15/97. Before starting, we ask you to check to determine if the payroll is not in setup mode. Move to Setup Functions and examine the last item in Maintain Accounting Control Data (#47). If the payroll is in setup mode (Y), change this field to No (N) by typing the field number and pressing ENTER, followed by the function key F2. (If this fails ... since field #47 is a protected field ... exit and move to the Maintain Company Data display. Change field #8 (Allow Protected Changes) to Yes (Y), and repeat the above instructions.)

What is the value in having the payroll setup mode protected?

Process the 6/15/97 Payroll

Now we can begin processing payroll for the first two weeks in June. Move to Process Payroll Time Transactions to add transactions. Enter the following:

* Pay period starting date (leave blank)
* Pay period ending date **6/15/97**
* Pay employees with pay frequencies **B**
* Number of holiday hours to take **0**

Using the default values for all employees, process all payroll time transactions.

* Print the Payroll Time Edit List.
* Examine this list. **What is the purpose of this report?**

Why is it important to be able to distribute hours?

Calculate the Payroll

Next, move to Calculate Payroll (bi–weekly). Enter a date of 6/15/97.

Explain the purpose of each document that is produced following this step.

Print Payroll Checks

Finally, Print the Payroll Checks.

* Use a beginning check number of 3001, and check date of 6/15/97.
* Print checks for all departments.

Press END and type DONE after the checks are printed to print the Check Register and to post the payroll distributions.

Explain the purpose of the Check Register.

Print Payroll Reports and Summaries

The last part of this practice set asks you to print several reports and summaries, even though payroll data is limited to a single payroll period.

Print the Payroll History report by entering the following:

* Starting date	**(Press F1)**	"Earliest"
* Ending date	**(Press F1)**	"Latest"
* Starting employee	**(Press F1)**	"First"
* Ending employee	**(Press F1)**	"Last"
* By what date?	**P**	Pay period date
* Purge file?	**N**	
* Format	**B**	Brief

Examine this report. **Explain why deductions are shown as .00 for all employees. What is the purpose of this report?**

Print the Quarterly Payroll Report. Enter the following:

* Report format	**B**	Brief	
* Which quarter	**2**	Ending	**063097**

What new information does this report provide, where "new" consists of additional calculations or payroll data presented in a different format?

Select Print Year–end Payroll Reports, followed by Print Year–end Payroll Report. Enter the following:

* Print grand totals only?	**N**	
* Employee to print	**4**	Hermann Acme

What new information does this report provide (following the definition of "new" from the previous question)?

Other Things To Explore

1. The function Generate Payroll does not work with this Practice Set. **Explain why.**

2. Inspect the G/L.

   What accounts are changed by this Practice Set? Complete the following table in answering this question:

Account #	Name

3. Suppose Edward Palmer wants to contribute $100.00 of his pay to the United Fund during the next pay period, but make no further contributions. How would this be handled in processing Edward's next paycheck?

4. Suppose Hermann Acme decides to pay $50.00 to F(ood)/Peace with EACH paycheck, beginning with the next pay period. How would this be handled in processing Hermann's next paycheck?

   How would this be handled in processing Hermann's next paycheck?

This completes Practice Set 10.

Date 06/15/97 Time 13:43:56 — Acme Hardware Co. — Report #0158 Page 0001

DEDUCTION AND EARNING CODE LIST

Starting code: "First" Ending code: "Last"

Ded/Earn types: D=after tax ded B=before tax ded E=earning S=supplemental pay M=meals T=tips X=special tax

Rate basis: P = percent on subject wages W = work units

Type of earnings: 1 = FWT gross 4 = fed unemp gross 5 = state unemp gross 7 = Emp soc sec gross 8 = Emp medicare gross 9 = Empr soc sec gross 10 = Empr medicare gross

SoSc = Social security MdCr = Medicare

Code	Desc	Typ	G/L-acct	G/L-acct-desc	FWT	Emp SoSc	Emp MdCr	Empr SoSc	Empr MdCr	FUI	EIC	SWT	SUI	OST	Suppl-ben	CWT
				Rate-basis Rate	YTD-earn-limit			Current-limit		Wrk-unit-desc			Type-of-earn			
B1	Pension	B	2380−000	Pension contrib withheld	N	N	N	N	N	N	N	N	N	N	N	N
D1	UntFund	D	2390−000	Charity contrib withheld												
D2	F/Peace	D	2390−000	Charity contrib withheld												
EB1	Bonus	E	6210−000	Salaries − bonuses	N	N	N	N	N	N	N	N	N	N	N	N
EC1	Comissn	E	6210−000	Salaries − bonuses	N	N	N	N	N	N	N	N	N	N	N	N
ET1	Travel	E	6280−000	Travel & entertainment	Y	Y	Y	Y	Y	Y	Y	Y	Y	Y	Y	Y
M1	Meals	M			Y	N	N	N	N	N	N	Y	N	N	N	N
S1	Sls com	S	6070−000	Commissions − Store	N	N	N	N	N	N	N	N	N	N	N	N

8 codes on file: 2 after tax ded 1 before tax ded 3 earnings 1 supplement pay 1 meals 0 tips 0 spec tax

−− End of report −−

Date: 06/15/97 Time: 15:23:46 Acme Hardware Co. Report #0159 Page 0001

NUMERIC EMPLOYEE LIST

Starting employee #: "First" Ending employee #: "Last"

Marital statuses: S = single M = Married H = head of household

Employee types: H = hourly S = salary N = non−emp

Pay/Deduct freq: D = daily W = weekly B = bi−wkly S = semi−monthly M = monthly

For deduction/earning codes see deduction/earning code list

Tx−pct−of−gross: 1 = FWT gross 4 = fed unemp gross 5 = state unemp gross

7 = Emp soc sec gross 8 = Emp medicare gross 9 = Empr soc sec gross 10 = Empr medicare gross

Exemption flags: SS? = Social security exempt ? MC? = Medicare exempt ?

Emp#	Name	Street	City	St	Zip	Soc−sec−#	Birth−dt	Mar	Hire−dt
1	**Palmer, Edward W**	225 Vista Boulevard	Orchard City	MI	12511	415−59−6091	01/01/97	M	06/01/97

Lst−rais	Revu−dt	Term−dt	Typ	Frq	Dept	Wage−acct	Salary	Reg−rt	Ovt−rt	Spc−rt	V−due	V−pd	Sk−due	Pen	Dst	Ins−prm
	12/01/97		S	B	0300	6190−000	1,500.00	18.750	28.125	37.500	.00	.00	.00	Y	Y	5.00

Stax	Ctax	#/$−exm−FWT		#/$−exm−SWT		#/$−exm−OST		#/$−exm−CWT		State−crd	AD−FWT	Ad−SWT	Ad−CWT	EIC	SS?	MC?	FUI?	SUI?
MI−M		4	.00	4	.00	0	.00	0	.00						N	N	N	N

Vac−date/Hrs−per−frq/Max−v−hrs	Sick−date/Hrs−per−frq/Max−s−hrs	D−E1/amount/frq	D−E2/amount/frq	D−E3/amount/frq	D−E4/amount/frq
		.00	.00	.00	.00

D−E5/amount/frq	D−E6/amount/frq	YTD−gross	YTD−FWT−gr	YTD−emp−SoSc−gr	YTD−emp−Mdcr−gr	YTD−EMPR−SoSc−gr	YTD−EMPR−Mdcr−gr
.00	.00	.00	.00	.00	.00	.00	.00

YTD−FUI−gr	YTD−othr−tax	YTD−supp−ben−gr	YTD−SUI−gr	YTD−Emp−SoSc	YTD−Emp−Mdcr	YTD−Empr−SoSc	YTD−Empr−Mdcr	YTD−FWT
.00	.00	.00	.00	.00	.00	.00	.00	.00

YTD−EIC	YTD−SWT	YTD−OST	YTD−CWT	TYD−tip−CR	CR−elig
	.00				N

Emp#	Name	Street	City	St	Zip	Soc−sec−#	Birth−dt	Mar	Hire−dt
2	**Earnest Wantabee**	25436 Stony Drive	Winoga Falls	MI	12345	235−23−9999	01/01/97	S	06/01/97

Lst−rais	Revu−dt	Term−dt	Typ	Frq	Dept	Wage−acct	Salary	Reg−rt	Ovt−rt	Spc−rt	V−due	V−pd	Sk−due	Pen	Dst	Ins−prm
	12/01/97		H	B	0200	6200−000		16.000	24.000	32.000	.00	.00	.00	Y	Y	

Stax	Ctax	#/$−exm−FWT		#/$−exm−SWT		#/$−exm−OST		#/$−exm−CWT		State−crd	AD−FWT	Ad−SWT	Ad−CWT	EIC	SS?	MC?	FUI?	SUI?
MI−S		1	.00	1	.00	0	.00	0	.00						N	N	N	N

Vac−date/Hrs−per−frq/Max−v−hrs	Sick−date/Hrs−per−frq/Max−s−hrs	D−E1/amount/frq	D−E2/amount/frq	D−E3/amount/frq	D−E4/amount/frq
		.00	.00	.00	.00

D−E5/amount/frq	D−E6/amount/frq	YTD−gross	YTD−FWT−gr	YTD−emp−SoSc−gr	YTD−emp−Mdcr−gr	YTD−EMPR−SoSc−gr	YTD−EMPR−Mdcr−gr
.00	.00	.00	.00	.00	.00	.00	.00

Date: 06/15/97 Time: 15:23:52 Acme Hardware Co. Report #0159 Page 0002

NUMERIC EMPLOYEE LIST

YTD-FUI-gr	YTD-othr-tax	YTD-supp-ben-gr	YTD-SUI-gr	YTD-Emp-SoSc	YTD-Emp-Mdcr	YTD-Empr-SoSc	YTD-Empr-Mdcr	YTD-FWT
.00	.00	.00	.00	.00	.00	.00	.00	.00

YTD-EIC	YTD-SWT	YTD-OST	YTD-CWT	TYD-tip-CR	CR-elig
	.00				N

Emp#	Name	Street	City	St	Zip	Soc-sec-#	Birth-dt	Mar	Hire-dt
3	**Sara Sweetheart**	354 East 54 Street	Winoga Falls	MI	12345	333-46-4945	01/01/97	H	06/01/97

Lst-rais	Revu-dt	Term-dt	Typ	Frq	Dept	Wage-acct	Salary	Reg-rt	Ovt-rt	Spc-rt	V-due	V-pd	Sk-due	Pen	Dst	Ins-prm
	12/01/97		H	B	1234	6200-000		16.000	24.000	32.000	.00	.00	.00	Y	Y	

Stax	Ctax	#/$-exm-FWT	#/$-exm-SWT	#/$-exm-OST	#/$-exm-CWT	State-crd	AD-FWT	Ad-SWT	Ad-CWT	EIC	SS?	MC?	FUI?	SUI?
MI-H		2 .00	2 .00	0 .00	0 .00						N	N	N	N

Vac-date/Hrs-per-frq/Max-v-hrs	Sick-date/Hrs-per-frq/Max-s-hrs	D-E1/amount/frq	D-E2/amount/frq	D-E3/amount/frq	D-E4/amount/frq
		.00	.00	.00	.00

D-E5/amount/frq	D-E6/amount/frq	YTD-gross	YTD-FWT-gr	YTD-emp-SoSc-gr	YTD-emp-Mdcr-gr	YTD-EMPR-SoSc-gr	YTD-EMPR-Mdcr-gr
.00	.00	.00	.00	.00	.00	.00	.00

YTD-FUI-gr	YTD-othr-tax	YTD-supp-ben-gr	YTD-SUI-gr	YTD-Emp-SoSc	YTD-Emp-Mdcr	YTD-Empr-SoSc	YTD-Empr-Mdcr	YTD-FWT
.00	.00	.00	.00	.00	.00	.00	.00	.00

YTD-EIC	YTD-SWT	YTD-OST	YTD-CWT	TYD-tip-CR	CR-elig
	.00				N

Emp#	Name	Street	City	St	Zip	Soc-sec-#	Birth-dt	Mar	Hire-dt
4	**Hermann Acme**	1245 First Street South	Winoga Falls	MI	12345	443-55-3838	01/01/97	M	

Lst-rais	Revu-dt	Term-dt	Typ	Frq	Dept	Wage-acct	Salary	Reg-rt	Ovt-rt	Spc-rt	V-due	V-pd	Sk-due	Pen	Dst	Ins-prm
			S	B	0100	6180-000	5,000.00	.000	.000	.000	.00	.00	.00	Y	Y	

Stax	Ctax	#/$-exm-FWT	#/$-exm-SWT	#/$-exm-OST	#/$-exm-CWT	State-crd	AD-FWT	Ad-SWT	Ad-CWT	EIC	SS?	MC?	FUI?	SUI?
MI-M		3 .00	3 .00	0 .00	0 .00						N	N	N	N

Vac-date/Hrs-per-frq/Max-v-hrs	Sick-date/Hrs-per-frq/Max-s-hrs	D-E1/amount/frq	D-E2/amount/frq	D-E3/amount/frq	D-E4/amount/frq
		.00	.00	.00	.00

D-E5/amount/frq	D-E6/amount/frq	YTD-gross	YTD-FWT-gr	YTD-emp-SoSc-gr	YTD-emp-Mdcr-gr	YTD-EMPR-SoSc-gr	YTD-EMPR-Mdcr-gr
.00	.00	.00	.00	.00	.00	.00	.00

YTD-FUI-gr	YTD-othr-tax	YTD-supp-ben-gr	YTD-SUI-gr	YTD-Emp-SoSc	YTD-Emp-Mdcr	YTD-Empr-SoSc	YTD-Empr-Mdcr	YTD-FWT
.00	.00	.00	.00	.00	.00	.00	.00	.00

YTD-EIC	YTD-SWT	YTD-OST	YTD-CWT	TYD-tip-CR	CR-elig
	.00				N

Date 06/15/97 Time 16:36:13 Acme Hardware Co. Report #0160 Page 0001

PAYROLL TIME EDIT LIST

For the pay period ending 06/15/97

Employee types: H = hourly S = salary N = non–employee
Pay frequencies: D = daily W = weekly B = bi–weekly S = semi–monthly M = monthly
Distribution types: S = salary % R = regular hours O = overtime hours X = special hours

Dept	Emp#	Name / Soc–sec–#	Typ	Wage–acct	Frq	Salary	Hours: Regular / Overtime	Special / Holiday	Sick / Vac	Temp–ded/earn Desc Type Amt	Accrued: Vacation / Sick–tim	Wks wrk	Work units
0100	4	**Hermann Acme**				5,000.00	80.00	.00	.00		.000	2.00	
		443–55–3838	S	6180–000	B		.00	.00	.00		.000		

Distribution:

Type	Acct–#		Hrs/%	Rate
S	6180–000	Salaries – administrative	100.00	

		Regular / Overtime	Special / Holiday	Sick / Vac		Accrued
1 entries	Department totals:	80.00		.00	Actual:	.000
0 hourly			.00			
1 salary		.00		.00	Actual:	.000
0 non–employee			.00			

Dept	Emp#	Name / Soc–sec–#	Typ	Wage–acct	Frq	Salary	Hours: Regular / Overtime	Special / Holiday	Sick / Vac	Temp–ded/earn Desc Type Amt	Accrued: Vacation / Sick–tim	Wks wrk	Work units
0200	2	**Earnest Wantabee**				.00	80.00	.00	.00		.000	2.00	
		235–23–9999	H	6200–000	B		.00	.00	.00		.000		

Distribution:

Type	Acct–#		Hrs/%	Rate
R	6200–000	Salaries & Wage exp–Elm	80.00	16.000

		Regular / Overtime	Special / Holiday	Sick / Vac		Accrued
1 entries	Department totals:	80.00		.00	Actual:	.000
1 hourly			.00			
0 salary		.00		.00	Actual:	.000
0 non–employee			.00			

Dept	Emp#	Name / Soc–sec–#	Typ	Wage–acct	Frq	Salary	Hours: Regular / Overtime	Special / Holiday	Sick / Vac	Temp–ded/earn Desc Type Amt	Accrued: Vacation / Sick–tim	Wks wrk	Work units
0300	1	**Palmer, Edward W.**				1,500.00	80.00	.00	.00		.000	2.00	
		415–59–6091	S	6190–000	B		.00	.00	.00		.000		

Distribution:

Type	Acct–#		Hrs/%	Rate
S	6190–000	Salaries – floor sales	100.00	

		Regular / Overtime	Special / Holiday	Sick / Vac		Accrued
1 entries	Department totals:	80.00		.00	Actual:	.000
0 hourly			.00			
1 salary		.00		.00	Actual:	.000
0 non–employee			.00			

Date 06/15/97 Time 16:36:18 Acme Hardware Co. Report #0160 Page 0002

PAYROLL TIME EDIT LIST

Dept	Emp#	Name / Soc-sec-#	Typ	Wage-acct	Frq	Salary	Hours: Regular / Overtime	Hours: Special / Holiday	Hours: Sick / Vac	Temp-ded/earn / Desc Type Amt	Accrued: Vacation / Sick-tim	Wks wrk	Work units
1234	3	**Sara Sweetheart**				.00	80.00	.00	.00		.000	2.00	
		333-46-4945	H	6200-000	B		.00	.00	.00		.000		

Distribution:	Type	Acct-#		Hrs/%	Rate
	R	6200-000	Salaries & Wage exp-Elm	80.00	16.000

1 entries	Department totals:	80.00		.00	Actual:	.000
1 hourly			.00			
0 salary		.00		.00	Actual:	.000
0 non-employee			.00			

Grand totals:	320.00		.00	Actual:	.000
		.00			
	.00		.00	Actual:	.000
		.00			

-- End of report --

Date 06/15/97 Time 16:38:40 — Acme Hardware Co. — Report #0161 Page 0001

PAYROLL TIME REGISTER

For the pay period ending 06/15/97

Employee types: H = hourly S = salary N = non−employee
Pay frequencies: D = daily W = weekly B = bi−weekly S = semi−monthly M = monthly
Distribution types: S = salary % R = regular hours O = overtime hours X = special hours

Dept	Emp#	Name / Soc−sec−#	Typ	Wage−acct	Frq	Salary	Hours: Regular / Overtime	Hours: Special / Holiday	Hours: Sick / Vac	Temp−ded/earn (Desc Type Amt)	Accrued: Vacation / Sick−tim	Wks wrk	Work units
0100	4	**Hermann Acme**				5,000.00	80.00	.00	.00		.000	2.00	
		443−55−3838	S	6180−000	B		.00	.00	.00		.000		

Distribution:	Type	Acct−#		Hrs/%	Rate
	S	6180−000	Salaries − administrative	100.00	

	Department totals:					
1 entries		80.00		.00	Actual:	.000
0 hourly			.00			
1 salary		.00		.00	Actual:	.000
0 non−employee			.00			

Dept	Emp#	Name / Soc−sec−#	Typ	Wage−acct	Frq	Salary	Hours: Regular / Overtime	Hours: Special / Holiday	Hours: Sick / Vac	Temp−ded/earn (Desc Type Amt)	Accrued: Vacation / Sick−tim	Wks wrk	Work units
0200	2	**Earnest Wantabee**				.00	80.00	.00	.00		.000	2.00	
		235−23−9999	H	6200−000	B		.00	.00	.00		.000		

Distribution:	Type	Acct−#		Hrs/%	Rate
	R	6200−000	Salaries & Wage exp−Elm	80.00	16.000

	Department totals:					
1 entries		80.00		.00	Actual:	.000
1 hourly			.00			
0 salary		.00		.00	Actual:	.000
0 non−employee			.00			

Dept	Emp#	Name / Soc−sec−#	Typ	Wage−acct	Frq	Salary	Hours: Regular / Overtime	Hours: Special / Holiday	Hours: Sick / Vac	Temp−ded/earn (Desc Type Amt)	Accrued: Vacation / Sick−tim	Wks wrk	Work units
0300	1	**Palmer, Edward W.**				1,500.00	80.00	.00	.00		.000	2.00	
		415−59−6091	S	6190−000	B		.00	.00	.00		.000		

Distribution:	Type	Acct−#		Hrs/%	Rate
	S	6190−000	Salaries − floor sales	100.00	

	Department totals:					
1 entries		80.00		.00	Actual:	.000
0 hourly			.00			
1 salary		.00		.00	Actual:	.000
0 non−employee			.00			

Date 06/15/97 Time 16:38:44 Acme Hardware Co. Report #0161 Page 0002

PAYROLL TIME REGISTER

Dept	Emp#	Name / Soc-sec-#	Typ	Wage-acct	Frq	Salary	Regular / Overtime	Special / Holiday	Sick / Vac	Temp-ded/earn / Desc Type Amt	Accrued Vacation / Sick-tim	Wks wrk	Work units
1234	3	**Sara Sweetheart**				.00	80.00	.00	.00		.000	2.00	
		333-46-4945	H	6200-000	B		.00	.00	.00		.000		

Distribution:

Type	Acct-#		Hrs/%	Rate
R	6200-000	Salaries & Wage exp-Elm	80.00	16.000

1 entries	Department totals:	80.00		.00	Actual:	.000
1 hourly			.00			
0 salary		.00		.00	Actual:	.000
0 non-employee			.00			

Grand totals:	320.00		.00	Actual:	.000
		.00			
	.00		.00	Actual:	.000
		.00			

-- End of report --

Date 06/15/97 Time 16:38:48 Acme Hardware Co. Report #0162 Page 0001

PAYROLL REGISTER

For department: 0100

For the pay period ending 06/15/97

Frequencies used on this run: B

Dept	Emp#	Employee-name		Salary	Reg-pay	Hol-pay	Gross	YTD-gross	Medicare	YTD-mdcr	Oth-ded
		Soc-sec-#	Emp-typ	Wks-wrk	Ovt-pay	Vac-pay	FWT-gross	YTD-FWT-grs	SWT	YTD-SWT	
		Net-pay		Prd-start	Spec-pay	Sick-pay	FWT	YTD-FWT	OST	YTD-OST	
							Soc-sec	YTD-soc-sec	CWT	YTD-CWT	
0100	4	**Hermann Acme**		5,000.00			5,000.00	5,000.00	72.50	72.50	
		443-55-3838	Salary	2.00			5,000.00	5,000.00	450.42	450.42	
		2,971.10					1,165.98	1,165.98			
							310.00	310.00			

Date 06/15/97 Time 16:38:50 Acme Hardware Co. Report #0162 Page 0002

PAYROLL REGISTER

For department: 0100

For the pay period ending 06/15/97

Frequencies used on this run: B

1 checks to be printed

Department totals:

			YTD-in	This-period	YTD-out
Sal-pay:	5,000.00	Gross:	.00	5,000.00	5,000.00
Reg-pay:	.00	FWT-grs:	.00	5,000.00	5,000.00
Ovt-pay:	.00	Soc-sec:	.00	310.00	310.00
Vac-pay:	.00	Medicare:	.00	72.50	72.50
Hol-pay:	.00	FWT:	.00	1,165.98	1,165.98
Sick-pay:	.00	EIC:	.00	.00	.00
Spec-pay:	.00	SWT:	.00	450.42	450.42
		OST:	.00	30.00	30.00
		CWT:	.00	.00	.00
		Spec-tax:	.00	.00	.00
		Oth-ded:		.00	
		Net:		2,971.10	

Department employer liability totals:

	YTD-in	This-period	YTD-out
Soc-sec:	.00	310.00	310.00
Medicare:	.00	72.50	72.50
FUI:	.00	40.00	40.00
SUI:	.00	45.00	45.00
Supp-ben:	.00	.00	.00
EMPR-OST:	.00	.00	.00

Date 06/15/97 Time 16:38:53 | Acme Hardware Co. | Report #0162 Page 0003

PAYROLL REGISTER

For department: 0200
For the pay period ending 06/15/97

Frequencies used on this run: B

Dept	Emp#	Employee-name / Soc-sec-# / Net-pay	Emp-typ	Salary / Wks-wrk / Prd-start	Reg-pay / Ovt-pay / Spec-pay	Hol-pay / Vac-pay / Sick-pay	Gross / FWT-gross / FWT / Soc-sec	YTD-gross / YTD-FWT-grs / YTD-FWT / YTD-soc-sec	Medicare / SWT / OST / CWT	YTD-mdcr / YTD-SWT / YTD-OST / YTD-CWT	Oth-ded
0200	2	**Earnest Wantabee**			1,280.00		1,280.00	1,280.00	18.56	18.56	
		235-23-9999	Hourly	2.00			1,280.00	1,280.00	81.16	81.16	
		873.21					220.03	220.03			
							79.36	79.36			

Date 06/15/97 Time 16:38:55 Acme Hardware Co. Report #0162 Page 0004

PAYROLL REGISTER

For department: 0200
For the pay period ending 06/15/97

Frequencies used on this run: B

1 checks to be printed

Department totals:				YTD-in	This-period	YTD-out
	Sal-pay:	.00	Gross:	.00	1,280.00	1,280.00
	Reg-pay:	1,280.00	FWT-grs:	.00	1,280.00	1,280.00
	Ovt-pay:	.00	Soc-sec:	.00	79.36	79.36
	Vac-pay:	.00	Medicare:	.00	18.56	18.56
	Hol-pay:	.00	FWT:	.00	220.03	220.03
	Sick-pay:	.00	EIC:	.00	.00	.00
	Spec-pay:	.00	SWT:	.00	81.16	81.16
			OST:	.00	7.68	7.68
			CWT:	.00	.00	.00
			Spec-tax:	.00	.00	.00
			Oth-ded:		.00	
			Net:		873.21	
Department employer liability totals:			Soc-sec:	.00	79.36	79.36
			Medicare:	.00	18.56	18.56
			FUI:	.00	10.24	10.24
			SUI:	.00	11.52	11.52
			Supp-ben:	.00	.00	.00
			EMPR-OST:	.00	.00	.00

Date 06/15/97 Time 16:38:58 Acme Hardware Co. Report #0162 Page 0005

PAYROLL REGISTER

For department: 0300

For the pay period ending 06/15/97

Frequencies used on this run: B

Dept	Emp#	Employee-name Soc-sec-# Emp-typ Net-pay	Salary Wks-wrk Prd-start	Reg-pay Ovt-pay Spec-pay	Hol-pay Vac-pay Sick-pay	Gross FWT-gross FWT Soc-sec	YTD-gross YTD-FWT-grs YTD-FWT YTD-soc-sec	Medicare SWT OST CWT	YTD-mdcr YTD-SWT YTD-OST YTD-CWT	Oth-ded
0300	1	**Palmer, Edward W.** 415-59-6091 Salary 1,171.93	1,500.00 2.00			1,500.00 1,500.00 154.90 93.00	1,500.00 1,500.00 154.90 93.00	21.75 49.42	21.75 49.42	

Date 06/15/97 Time 16:38:58 | Acme Hardware Co. | Report #0162 Page 0006

PAYROLL REGISTER

For department: 0300
For the pay period ending 06/15/97

Frequencies used on this run: B

1 checks to be printed

Department totals:

			YTD-in	This-period	YTD-out
Sal-pay:	1,500.00	Gross:	.00	1,500.00	1,500.00
Reg-pay:	.00	FWT-grs:	.00	1,500.00	1,500.00
Ovt-pay:	.00	Soc-sec:	.00	93.00	93.00
Vac-pay:	.00	Medicare:	.00	21.75	21.75
Hol-pay:	.00	FWT:	.00	154.90	154.90
Sick-pay:	.00	EIC:	.00	.00	.00
Spec-pay:	.00	SWT:	.00	49.42	49.42
		OST:	.00	9.00	9.00
		CWT:	.00	.00	.00
		Spec-tax:	.00	.00	.00
		Oth-ded:		.00	
		Net:		1,171.93	

Department employer liability totals:

	YTD-in	This-period	YTD-out
Soc-sec:	.00	93.00	93.00
Medicare:	.00	21.75	21.75
FUI:	.00	12.00	12.00
SUI:	.00	13.50	13.50
Supp-ben:	.00	.00	.00
EMPR-OST:	.00	.00	.00

Date 06/15/97 Time 16:38:59 Acme Hardware Co. Report #0162 Page 0007

PAYROLL REGISTER

For department: 1234

For the pay period ending 06/15/97

Frequencies used on this run: B

Dept	Emp#	Employee-name Soc-sec-# Net-pay	Emp-typ	Salary Wks-wrk Prd-start	Reg-pay Ovt-pay Spec-pay	Hol-pay Vac-pay Sick-pay	Gross FWT-gross FWT Soc-sec	YTD-gross YTD-FWT-grs YTD-FWT YTD-soc-sec	Medicare SWT OST CWT	YTD-mdcr YTD-SWT YTD-OST YTD-CWT	Oth-ded
1234	3	**Sara Sweetheart** 333-46-4945 917.92	Hourly	 2.00	1,280.00		1,280.00 1,280.00 196.88 79.36	1,280.00 1,280.00 196.88 79.36	18.56 59.60	18.56 59.60	

Date 06/15/97 Time 16:38:59 Acme Hardware Co. Report #0162 Page 0008

PAYROLL REGISTER

For department: 1234

For the pay period ending 06/15/97

Frequencies used on this run: B

1 checks to be printed

Department totals:

			YTD-in	This-period	YTD-out
Sal-pay:	.00	Gross:	.00	1,280.00	1,280.00
Reg-pay:	1,280.00	FWT-grs:	.00	1,280.00	1,280.00
Ovt-pay:	.00	Soc-sec:	.00	79.36	79.36
Vac-pay:	.00	Medicare:	.00	18.56	18.56
Hol-pay:	.00	FWT:	.00	196.88	196.88
Sick-pay:	.00	EIC:	.00	.00	.00
Spec-pay:	.00	SWT:	.00	59.60	59.60
		OST:	.00	7.68	7.68
		CWT:	.00	.00	.00
		Spec-tax:	.00	.00	.00
		Oth-ded:		.00	
		Net:		917.92	

Department employer liability totals:

	YTD-in	This-period	YTD-out
Soc-sec:	.00	79.36	79.36
Medicare:	.00	18.56	18.56
FUI:	.00	10.24	10.24
SUI:	.00	11.52	11.52
Supp-ben:	.00	.00	.00
EMPR-OST:	.00	.00	.00

Date 06/15/97 Time 16:39:00 | Acme Hardware Co. | Report #0162 Page 0009

PAYROLL REGISTER

For department: "All"

For the pay period ending 06/15/97

Frequencies used on this run: B

4 checks to be printed

Totals this run:

			YTD-in	This-period	YTD-out
Sal-pay:	6,500.00	Gross:	.00	9,060.00	9,060.00
Reg-pay:	2,560.00	FWT-grs:	.00	9,060.00	9,060.00
Ovt-pay:	.00	Soc-sec:	.00	561.72	561.72
Vac-pay:	.00	Medicare:	.00	131.37	131.37
Hol-pay:	.00	FWT:	.00	1,737.79	1,737.79
Sick-pay:	.00	EIC:	.00	.00	.00
Spec-pay:	.00	SWT:	.00	640.60	640.60
		OST:	.00	54.36	54.36
		CWT:	.00	.00	.00
		Spec-tax:	.00	.00	.00
		Oth-ded:		.00	
		Net:		5,934.16	

Company employer liability totals:

	YTD-in	This-period	YTD-out
Soc-sec:	.00	561.72	561.72
Medicare:	.00	131.37	131.37
FUI:	.00	72.48	72.48
SUI:	.00	81.54	81.54
Supp-ben:	.00	.00	.00
EMPR-OST:	.00	.00	.00

-- End of report --

PAYROLL CHECK

Hermann Acme CHECK NO. 003001

EMPLOYEE NO.	HOURS				EARNINGS				
	REGULAR	OVERTIME	HOLIDAY	SPECIAL	REGULAR	VACATION	SICK		
4	80.00	.00	.00	.00	5,000.00	.00	.00	.00	.00
SOCIAL SECURITY NO.	VACATION	SICK	TOTAL HRS		OVERTIME	HOLIDAY	SPECIAL		GROSS PAY
443–55–3838			80.00						5,000.00

TAXES / WITHHOLDINGS			VOLUNTARY DEDUCTIONS					
FICA	STATE W/H TAX	CITY W/H TAX	CHARITY					TOTAL TAXES W/H
382.50	450.42	.00	.00	.00	.00	.00	.00	2,028.90
FEDRL W/H TAX	OTHER ST. W/h							TOTAL VOL. DED.
1165.98			.00	.00	.00	.00		.00

YEAR–TO–DATE						PAY PERD	NET PAY
GROSS	FICA	FEDRL W/H TAX	STATE W/H TAX	OTHER ST. W/H	CITY W/H TAX		
5,000.00	382.50	1,165.98	450.42		.00	06/15/97	2,971.10

PLEASE DETACH AND RETAIN THIS STUB FOR YOUR RECORDS

Acme Hardware Co.
123 Main St.
Winoga Falls, MI 12345

CHECK DATE	CHECK NO.
06/15/97	003001

CHECK AMOUNT
**2,971.10

TWO THOUSAND NINE HUNDRED SEVENTY–ONE AND*********
10/100 DOLLARS**

PAY
TO THE
ORDER OF

Hermann Acme
1245 First Street South
Winoga Falls MI 12345

Authorized Signature

PAYROLL CHECK

Earnest Wantabee

CHECK NO. 003002

EMPLOYEE NO.	HOURS				EARNINGS				
	REGULAR	OVERTIME	HOLIDAY	SPECIAL	REGULAR	VACATION	SICK		
2	80.00	.00	.00	.00	1,280.00	.00	.00	.00	.00
SOCIAL SECURITY NO.		VACATION	SICK	TOTAL HRS	OVERTIME	HOLIDAY	SPECIAL		GROSS PAY
235–23–9999				80.00					1,280.00

TAXES / WITHHOLDINGS			VOLUNTARY DEDUCTIONS					
FICA	STATE W/H TAX	CITY W/H TAX	CHARITY					TOTAL TAXES W/H
97.92	81.16	.00	.00	.00	.00	.00	.00	406.79
FEDRL W/H TAX	OTHER ST. W/h							TOTAL VOL. DED.
220.03			.00	.00	.00	.00		.00

YEAR–TO–DATE						PAY PERD	NET PAY
GROSS	FICA	FEDRL W/H TAX	STATE W/H TAX	OTHER ST. W/H	CITY W/H TAX		
1,280.00	97.92	220.03	81.16		.00	06/15/97	873.21

Regular rate: 16.000

PLEASE DETACH AND RETAIN THIS STUB FOR YOUR RECORDS

Acme Hardware Co.
123 Main St.
Winoga Falls, MI 12345

CHECK DATE	CHECK NO.
06/15/97	003002

CHECK AMOUNT
****873.21

EIGHT HUNDRED SEVENTY–THREE AND 21/100 DOLLARS****

PAY
TO THE
ORDER OF

Earnest Wantabee
25436 Stony Drive
Winoga Falls MI 12345

Authorized Signature

PAYROLL CHECK

Palmer, Edward W. CHECK NO. 003003

EMPLOYEE	HOURS				EARNINGS				
NO.	REGULAR	OVERTIME	HOLIDAY	SPECIAL	REGULAR	VACATION	SICK		
1	80.00	.00	.00	.00	1,500.00	.00	.00	.00	.00
SOCIAL SECURITY NO.	VACATION	SICK	TOTAL HRS	OVERTIME	HOLIDAY	SPECIAL		GROSS PAY
415–59–6091			80.00					1,500.00

TAXES / WITHHOLDINGS			VOLUNTARY DEDUCTIONS					
FICA	STATE W/H TAX	CITY W/H TAX	CHARITY					TOTAL TAXES W/H
114.75	49.42	.00	.00	.00	.00	.00	.00	328.07
FEDRL W/H TAX	OTHER ST. W/h							TOTAL VOL. DED.
154.90			.00	.00	.00	.00		.00

YEAR–TO–DATE						PAY PERD	NET PAY
GROSS	FICA	FEDRL W/H TAX	STATE W/H TAX	OTHER ST. W/H	CITY W/H TAX		
1,500.00	114.75	154.90	49.42		.00	06/15/97	1,171.93

PLEASE DETACH AND RETAIN THIS STUB FOR YOUR RECORDS

Acme Hardware Co.
123 Main St.
Winoga Falls, MI 12345

CHECK DATE	CHECK NO.
06/15/97	003003

CHECK AMOUNT
**1,171.93

ONE THOUSAND ONE HUNDRED SEVENTY–ONE AND*********
93/100 DOLLARS**

PAY
TO THE
ORDER OF Edward W. Palmer
225 Vista Boulevard
Orchard City MI 12511

Authorized Signature

PAYROLL CHECK

Sara Sweetheart CHECK NO. 003004

EMPLOYEE	HOURS				EARNINGS				
NO.	REGULAR	OVERTIME	HOLIDAY	SPECIAL	REGULAR	VACATION	SICK		
3	80.00	.00	.00	.00	1,280.00	.00	.00	.00	.00
SOCIAL SECURITY NO.	VACATION	SICK	TOTAL HRS		OVERTIME	HOLIDAY	SPECIAL		GROSS PAY
333–46–4945			80.00						1,280.00

TAXES / WITHHOLDINGS			VOLUNTARY DEDUCTIONS					
FICA	STATE W/H TAX	CITY W/H TAX	CHARITY					TOTAL TAXES W/H
97.92	59.60	.00	.00	.00	.00	.00	.00	362.08
FEDRL W/H TAX	OTHER ST. W/h							TOTAL VOL. DED.
196.88			.00	.00	.00	.00		.00

YEAR–TO–DATE						PAY PERD	NET PAY
GROSS	FICA	FEDRL W/H TAX	STATE W/H TAX	OTHER ST. W/H	CITY W/H TAX		
1,280.00	97.92	196.88	59.60		.00	06/15/97	917.92

Regular rate: 16.000

PLEASE DETACH AND RETAIN THIS STUB FOR YOUR RECORDS

Acme Hardware Co.
123 Main St.
Winoga Falls, MI 12345

CHECK DATE	CHECK NO.
06/15/97	003004

CHECK AMOUNT
****917.92

NINE HUNDRED SEVENTEEN AND 92/100 DOLLARS*********

PAY
TO THE
ORDER OF Sara Sweetheart
354 East 54 Street
Winoga Falls MI 12345

Authorized Signature

Date: 06/15/97 Time: 16:45:55 Acme Hardware Co. Report #0163 Page 0001

PAYROLL CHECK REGISTER

For the pay period ending 06/15/97

Check-#	Check-date	Check-amt	Emp-#	Name
3001	06/15/97	2,971.10	4	Hermann Acme
3002	06/15/97	873.21	2	Earnest Wantabee
3003	06/15/97	1,171.93	1	Edward W. Palmer
3004	06/15/97	917.92	3	Sara Sweetheart

4 checks Total: 5,934.16

-- End of report --

Date: 06/15/97 Time: 16:49:36 Acme Hardware Co. Report #0164 Page 0001

PAYROLL HISTORY REPORT

Starting date: "Earliest" Ending date: "Latest"
Starting employee: "First" Ending employee: "Last"
Transaction types: P = payroll check M = manual transaction
For checks dated before 1/01/91 employee FICA tax is shown as social security.

Emp#	Name	Typ	Check#	Chk-date	Prd-date	Gross	Tot-taxes	Deductions	Net pay	Tips
1	Palmer, Edward W.	P	3003	6/15/97	6/15/97	1,500.00	319.07	.00	1,171.93	
		Employee	1	Totals:	1 check	1,500.00	319.07	.00	1,171.93	
2	Earnest Wantabee	P	3002	6/15/97	6/15/97	1,280.00	399.11	.00	873.21	
		Employee	2	Totals:	1 check	1,280.00	399.11	.00	873.21	
3	Sara Sweetheart	P	3004	6/15/97	6/15/97	1,280.00	354.40	.00	917.92	
		Employee	3	Totals:	1 check	1,280.00	354.40	.00	917.92	
4	Hermann Acme	P	3001	6/15/97	6/15/97	5,000.00	1,998.90	.00	2,971.10	
		Employee	4	Totals:	1 check	5,000.00	1,998.90	.00	2,971.10	
	Grand totals:		4 employees		4 checks	9,060.00	3,071.48	.00	5,934.16	

-- End of report --

Date: 06/15/97 Time: 16:51:47 Acme Hardware Co. Report #0165 Page 0001

PAYROLL QUARTERLY REPORT

State: CA head of household Quarter ending: 06/30/97

Company: Acme Hardware Co.
Address: 123 Main St.
Winoga Falls, MI 12345

ID: 213–4495–1
"Grs–wages" = Gross wages for SWT

Soc–sec–no	Name	Grs–wages	Tot–hrs	Wks–wrk
415–59–6091	Edward W. Palmer	1,500.00	80.00	2.00
235–23–9999	Earnest Wantabee	1,280.00	80.00	2.00
333–46–4945	Sara Sweetheart	1,280.00	80.00	2.00
443–55–3838	Hermann Acme	5,000.00	80.00	2.00
	Subtotal this page	9,060.00	320.00	8.00
	Grand total	9,060.00	320.00	8.00

Date: 06/15/97 Time: 16:51:48 Acme Hardware Co. Report #0165 Page 0002

PAYROLL QUARTERLY REPORT

State: CA head of household Quarter ending: 06/30/97

Company: Acme Hardware Co.
Address: 123 Main St.
Winoga Falls, MI 12345

ID: 213−4495−1
"Grs−wages" = Gross wages for SWT

*** State return information ***

Total taxable wages	9,060.00
Income tax withheld	640.60
Other state taxable wages	9,060.00
Other state tax withheld	54.36

*** Unemployment insurance contribution ***

State unemp insurance taxable wages	
9,060.00 X .90%	81.54

*** City income tax withheld *** .00

Date: 06/15/97 Time: 16:51:50 Acme Hardware Co. Report #0165 Page 0003

PAYROLL QUARTERLY REPORT

Quarter ending: 06/30/97

Company: Acme Hardware Co.
Address: 123 Main St.
Winoga Falls, MI 12345

ID: 99–9999999
"Grs–wages" = Gross wages for SWT

*** Federal return information ***

Total taxable wages	9,060.00
Income tax withheld	1,737.79
Taxable social security wages paid	9,060.00
@ 12.40% =	1,123.44
Taxable social security tips	.00
@ 12.40% =	.00
Total social security taxes	1,123.44
Taxable medicare wages paid	9,060.00
@ 2.90% =	262.74
Taxable medicare tips	.00
@ 2.90% =	.00
Total medicare taxes	262.74
Total taxes	3,123.97
EIC paid	.00
Net taxes	3,123.97

*** Unemployment insurance contribution ***

Fed unemp insurance taxable wages	
9,060.00 X .80%	72.48

Date: 06/15/97 Time: 16:54:35 Acme Hardware Co. Report #0166 Page 0001

YEAR-END PAYROLL REPORT

Company: Acme Hardware Co.
Address: 123 Main St.
Winoga Falls, MI 12345

Fed ID: 99-9999999
State: CA head of household State ID: 213-4495-1

Emp-#	Soc-sec-#		-1st-qtr-	-2nd-qtr-	-3rd-qtr-	-4th-qtr-	Year-total
4	443-55-3838	Grs-wages:	.00	5,000.00	.00	.00	5,000.00
Name:	Hermann Acme	FWT-gross:	.00	5,000.00	.00	.00	5,000.00
Addr:	1245 First Street South	FWT-w/h:	.00	1,165.98	.00	.00	1,165.98
	Winoga Falls	Emp-soc-sec-wgs:	.00	5,000.00	.00	.00	5,000.00
	MI 12345	Emp-soc-sec-tips:	.00	.00	.00	.00	.00
		Emp-soc-sec-w/h:	.00	310.00	.00	.00	310.00
		Emp-medicare-wgs:	.00	5,000.00	.00	.00	5,000.00
		Emp-medicare-tips:	.00	.00	.00	.00	.00
		Emp-medicare-w/h:	.00	72.50	.00	.00	72.50
		SWT-gross:	.00	5,000.00	.00	.00	5,000.00
		SWT-w/h:	.00	450.42	.00	.00	450.42
		OST-gross:	.00	5,000.00	.00	.00	5,000.00
		OST-w/h:	.00	30.00	.00	.00	30.00
		CWT-gross:	.00	.00	.00	.00	.00
		CWT-w/h:	.00	.00	.00	.00	.00
		EIC-gross:	.00	.00	.00	.00	.00
		EIC-paid:	.00	.00	.00	.00	.00
		Empr-soc-sec-wgs:	.00	5,000.00	.00	.00	5,000.00
		Empr-soc-sec-tips:	.00	.00	.00	.00	.00
		Empr-soc-sec-tax:	.00	310.00	.00	.00	310.00
		Empr-medicare-wgs:	.00	5,000.00	.00	.00	5,000.00
		Empr-medicare-tip:	.00	.00	.00	.00	.00
		Empr-medicare-tax:	.00	72.50	.00	.00	72.50
		FUI-gross:	.00	5,000.00	.00	.00	5,000.00
		SUI-gross:	.00	5,000.00	.00	.00	5,000.00
		EMPR-OST-gross:	.00	.00	.00	.00	.00
		Supp-ben-grs:	.00	.00	.00	.00	.00
		Reported-tips:	.00	.00	.00	.00	.00
		Fed-tip-cr:	.00	.00	.00	.00	.00
		State-tip-cr:	.00	.00	.00	.00	.00

Earning categories year totals:		
	Reg-pay:	5,000.00
	Ovt-pay:	.00
	Spec-pay:	.00
	Vac-pay:	.00
	Hol-pay:	.00
	Sick-pay:	.00

Practice Set 11 – PROCESS PHYSICAL INVENTORY

Introduction

This practice set asks you to perform a number of tasks associated with the management and control of physical inventory. Initially, you are asked to inspect the on–hand inventory, to add a new product to inventory, and to make a purchase of that item. Following this, you are asked to take a physical count of items and to make an adjustment. You must then determine which items to purchase to replenish inventory. Finally, you are asked to produce a number of important inventory reports and summaries.

In this practice set, you are expected to be able to:

- review the contents of the inventory file
- add a new item to inventory
- change the price of an item
- process a physical count of inventory
- process inventory to determine what items are in need of reorder
- change product information, based on the results of an edit report
- produce a variety of inventory reports and summaries

Set Transaction Date

Before starting this practice set, enter today's date as **6–30–97.**

Review the Contents of Inventory

Move to Inventory Management and select Maintain Item Data.

* Print the inventory item list by
  - item number for all items, departments and vendors
  - earliest sale date
* Print a full report, print price detail, and print sales detail.

Answer the following:

How many units of product 1091 are on hand?
How many concrete blocks were sold this period?
If product 2200 can be purchased for $7.31 and is sold for 13.50, what is the percent markup? Use the formula ... [$7.31 X (1 + percent markup) = $13.50.]

Add a New Item to Inventory

Add product 2300 to stock. The product is expected to have a pricing and sales history similar to product 2200. Use the information for product 2200 shown on the Item List, unless otherwise noted on the next page.

Item	**2300**
Description	**Hammer, Sledge**
Quantity on hand	**0** (press ENTER)
Quantity committed	**0** (press ENTER)
Quantity ordered	**0**
Average cost	**14.62**
Last cost	**14.62**
List price	(same markup as product 2200)
Discount by	(same as product 2200 – No discounts)
Better price	(same markup as product 2200)
Best price	(press ENTER)
Alt sell unit 1	**DOZ** (same markup as product 2200)
Bin loc(ation)	(same as 2200 plus 1)
Entries 33–36	**None** (press ENTER)
Entries 37–48	**0** (press ENTER)

After completing these entries, print a second Item List, but for product 2300 only.

Purchase Items

Next, we ask you to purchase item #2300. Move to Process Purchases and add a transaction. Use your Item List in completing some of the requested information. Enter the following:

Vendor	(Use information shown on the Item List)
Item#	**2300**
Order date	**6/30/97**
Order quantity	(Use maximum quantity suggested)
Cost per EACH	(Use information shown on the Item List)
New item notes	**First order**
Reference	(leave blank)

* Display and review the "full" Transaction Edit List.
* Post the transaction, which prints the Purchase Transaction Register.

Using the Purchase Transaction Register,

How much has the replacement cost of inventory increased?
How much has the retail value of inventory been increased?

* Print the Item List for item 2300.

Compare the new information to the information shown before purchasing.

How has purchasing changed the information shown?
How does posting of the purchase change G/L accounts?

Change Item Prices

Suppose you next want to examine item prices and set a sales price.

* Print the Price List for all products by doing the following:
  - Print by item#.
  - Print for all items, departments and vendors.
  - Do not print sale items only.
  - Print "all" prices, including sale prices.

Which three products have been assigned a price per dozen?

Move to Set Sales Prices.

* Find the item with the **largest** List Gross Profit %. When the display appears for this product, complete the display using the following information:

  Start sale date of **7/01/97**
  End sale date of **7/15/97**
  Set a sale price to arrive at a gross profit of 50%. You can compute this amount or use trial and error until you reach 50%.

* Print another price list, but this time only for items with sales prices. As before, print in order by item#, for all items, departments and vendors, print sales items only (Yes), and print all prices.

What is the value of this revised Price List?

Perform a Physical Count of Inventory

Before determining which items to reorder, you are asked to perform a physical count on the stock on hand.

Move to Process Physical Inventory and select Print Inventory Count sheet.

* Print the sheet in bin location/item number order, for all bin locations, items, departments and vendors.
* Print the quantity on hand.
* Print and generate using a transaction count, a date of 6/30/97, and the default comment – June physical count.

Move to Change Transactions.

* Indicate that 5 concrete blocks are found to be broken and must be removed from inventory.
* Print the Transaction Edit List for item BS–BLOCK. (Check your Item List for bin location.)
* Post this transaction, which prints the Physical Inventory Transaction Register.
  - Use a date of 6/30/97.
  - Post to account 5020.
  - Answer No to "adjust non–counted items to zero?"

The quantity variance is shown as 5–. How is this value computed?
The inventory value variance is shown as 7.95. How is this value computed?
Why is it a good practice to take a physical count before ordering new merchandise?

Order Items for Inventory

Finally, we ask you to determine which items (there are actually quite a few) to order to replenish inventory.

Move to Print Inventory Status Report.

* Print in order by item number, for all items, departments and vendors.
* Print out of stock items.
* Print a full report.

How many items are out of stock?
How many items are understocked?
What is the difference between out of stock and understocked?

Move to Process Purchases and select Print Purchasing Advise Report.

* Print in order by item number, for all items, departments and vendors.
* Print and generate the report.
  - Use a default order date of 6/30/97.
  - Add the default item note – July orders.

On this report, how many of the out of stock items reported on the inventory status report are to be reordered? (_____ out of _____)
How many understocked items are to be reordered? (_____ out of _____)
Compare the two reports. Explain why some out of stock or understocked items are NOT suggested for reorder.

* Print a brief (Purchase) Transaction Edit List. Note the unit–cost problem with item #5770.

Move back to Maintain Item Data and fix the problem shown on the edit list.

Explain what you did.

Move back to Process Purchases.

* Delete the order for item #5770.
* Add a new transaction for item #5770. Order 12 more units (1 DOZ) at a cost of $18.20 per unit. Add the item note – July orders.
* Print a second brief (Purchase) Transaction Edit List.
* Post the 7 transactions, which prints the Purchase Transaction Register.

If you were the purchasing agent for Acme Hardware, how would this last report help you?

Print Valuation and Analysis Reports

The final part of this rather long practice set asks you to prepare the Inventory Valuation Report and the Inventory Analysis Report.

Move to Print Inventory Valuation Report.

* Print by item number for all items, departments and vendors.
* Print the report.

Which member of an organization, such as Acme Hardware, would most likely use this report?

Move to Print Inventory Analysis Report.

* Print for all items, departments and vendors.
* Print in order by rank, where the ranking method is based on sales and the ranking basis is by period.
* Print all rankings and items.

Product 1091 is ranked first. Explain why.
The periods of supply is the predicted amount of time before an item runs out of stock, based on the quantity sold during the current period and the current quantity on hand. Explain how the .1 is computed for concrete blocks.

Other Things to Explore

1. Account 5020 was debited when the 5 concrete blocks were found to be broken. Which G/L account was credited?

2. Suppose your boss asks you to prepare a **brief** report showing the goods that are currently on order. Print this brief report.

3. Suppose next that your boss asks you to prepare a report listing products in inventory ranked based on profitability this period. Print this report.

This completes Practice Set 11.

Date: 06/30/97 Time: 10:27:25 | Acme Hardware Co. | Report #0167 Page #0001

ITEM LIST

Item # range: "First" to "Last"

Department: "All" Vendor: "All"

Item type: I = Inventory

"****" indicates that the contra account varies by invoice profit center

Item-#	Description	Bar-code	Typ	Dept	Loc	Stk-unit	List-price	Avg-cost	Qty-on-hand	Last-rcvd
		Subst-item-#	Txb	Sls-#	COG-#	Pur-unit	Stk-qty-Pur	Last-cost	Qty-commit	1st-rcvd
	Vendor	Hist-class		Ret-#		Prf-unit		Min-qty-OH	Qty-on-ord	Last-ord
	Notes	Inv-contra-#						Max-qty-OH	Min-ord-qty	Last-sale
1091	**Gauge, Hi-Pressure**		I	TOOLS	3D	EACH	17.95	9.72000	200	6/01/97
			Y	4000	5010	100	9.72000	9.720	0	6/01/97
	Hill Equipment & Supply	Products		4520				100	0	5/15/97
		1400-000						500	100	6/10/97
1100	**Drill, Power Hand**		I	TOOLS	E16	EACH	25.95	13.14000	24	6/01/97
			Y	4000	5010			13.140	0	6/01/97
	Hill Equipment & Supply	Products		4520				10	0	5/12/97
		1400-000						30	10	6/04/97
1105	**Drill, Cordless**		I	TOOLS	E17	10	29.95	14.95000	34	6/01/97
			Y	4000	5010			14.950	0	6/01/97
	Hill Equipment & Supply	Products		4520				10	0	5/12/97
		1400-000						40	10	6/04/97

1091 — Better price: 15.75

Qty-sold:	this prd	300	Last prd	0	this yr	300	last yr	0
Sales:	this prd	5,385.00	Last prd	.00	this yr	5,385.00	last yr	.00
Cost:	this prd	2,916.00	Last prd	.00	this yr	2,916.00	last yr	.00

1100 — Better price: 22.57

Qty-sold:	this prd	6	Last prd	0	this yr	6	last yr	0
Sales:	this prd	155.70	Last prd	.00	this yr	155.70	last yr	.00
Cost:	this prd	78.84	Last prd	.00	this yr	78.84	last yr	.00

1105 — Better price: 24.95

Qty-sold:	this prd	6	Last prd	0	this yr	6	last yr	0
Sales:	this prd	179.70	Last prd	.00	this yr	179.70	last yr	.00
Cost:	this prd	89.70	Last prd	.00	this yr	89.70	last yr	.00

Date: 06/30/97 Time: 10:27:31 Acme Hardware Co. Report #0167 Page #0002

ITEM LIST

Item-#	Description	Bar-code	Typ	Dept	Loc	Stk-unit	List-price	Avg-cost	Qty-on-hand	Last-rcvd
		Subst-item-#	Txb	Sls-#	COG-#	Pur-unit	Stk-qty-Pur	Last-cost	Qty-commit	1st-rcvd
	Vendor	Hist-class		Ret-#		Prf-unit		Min-qty-OH	Qty-on-ord	Last-ord
	Notes	Inv-contra-#						Max-qty-OH	Min-ord-qty	Last-sale
2200	**Hammer, 16 oz. claw**		I	TOOLS	F6	EACH	13.50	7.31000	12	6/01/97
			Y	4000	5010			7.310	0	6/01/97
	Hill Equipment & Supply	Products		4520		EACH		20	0	5/12/97
		1400-000						36	12	6/03/97

Better price: 12.60
Alt-price-1: 138.00 (12.00000 EACH per DOZ)

Qty-sold:	this prd	3	Last prd	0	this yr	3	last yr	0
Sales:	this prd	40.50	Last prd	.00	this yr	40.50	last yr	.00
Cost:	this prd	21.93	Last prd	.00	this yr	21.93	last yr	.00

Item-#	Description	Bar-code	Typ	Dept	Loc	Stk-unit	List-price	Avg-cost	Qty-on-hand	Last-rcvd
5770	**Chisel, 5 pc set**		I	TOOLS	E8	SET	28.50	18.20000	9	6/01/97
			Y	4000	5010	DOZ	218.40000	18.200	0	6/01/97
	Hill Equipment & Supply	Products		4520				15	0	5/12/97
		1400-000						24	12	6/07/97

Better price: 27.75

Qty-sold:	this prd	6	Last prd	0	this yr	6	last yr	0
Sales:	this prd	171.00	Last prd	.00	this yr	171.00	last yr	.00
Cost:	this prd	109.20	Last prd	.00	this yr	109.20	last yr	.00

Item-#	Description	Bar-code	Typ	Dept	Loc	Stk-unit	List-price	Avg-cost	Qty-on-hand	Last-rcvd
BS-BLOCK	**Block, Concrete**		I	MATL	K21	EACH	1.59	.99000	50	6/01/97
			Y	4010	5010	DOZ	11.88000	.990	0	6/01/97
	Hanson Manufacturing Co.	Products		4520		EACH		250	0	5/25/97
		1400-000						1,000	144	6/03/97

Better price: 1.39 (Cust type: WSL)
Alt-price-1: 15.00 (1.25000 EACH per DOZ)

Qty-sold:	this prd	450	Last prd	0	this yr	450	last yr	0
Sales:	this prd	715.50	Last prd	.00	this yr	715.50	last yr	.00
Cost:	this prd	445.50	Last prd	.00	this yr	445.50	last yr	.00

Date: 06/30/97 Time: 10:27:37 Acme Hardware Co. Report #0167 Page #0003

ITEM LIST

Item-#	Description	Bar-code	Typ	Dept	Loc	Stk-unit	List-price	Avg-cost	Qty-on-hand	Last-rcvd
		Subst-item-#	Txb	Sls-#	COG-#	Pur-unit	Stk-qty-Pur	Last-cost	Qty-commit	1st-rcvd
	Vendor	Hist-class		Ret-#		Prf-unit		Min-qty-OH	Qty-on-ord	Last-ord
	Notes	Inv-contra-#						Max-qty-OH	Min-ord-qty	Last-sale
BS-BRACKET	**Bracket sets**		I	MATL	K18	SET	44.95	32.00000	0	6/01/97
			Y	4010	5010			32.000	0	6/01/97
	Hill Equipment & Supply	Products		4520				2	0	5/25/97
		1400-000						12	6	6/10/97

Better price: 41.50

Qty-sold:	this prd	5	Last prd	0	this yr	5	last yr	0
Sales:	this prd	224.75	Last prd	.00	this yr	224.75	last yr	.00
Cost:	this prd	160.00	Last prd	.00	this yr	160.00	last yr	.00

Item-#	Description	Bar-code	Typ	Dept	Loc	Stk-unit	List-price	Avg-cost	Qty-on-hand	Last-rcvd
BS-DOORS	**Utility Door Unit**		I	MATL	K4	EACH	68.00	32.00000	0	6/01/97
			Y	4010	5010			32.000	0	6/01/97
	Hill Equipment & Supply	Products		4520				3	0	6/25/97
		1400-000						12	5	6/05/97

Better price: 55.00

Qty-sold:	this prd	5	Last prd	0	this yr	5	last yr	0
Sales:	this prd	340.00	Last prd	.00	this yr	340.00	last yr	.00
Cost:	this prd	160.00	Last prd	.00	this yr	160.00	last yr	.00

Item-#	Description	Bar-code	Typ	Dept	Loc	Stk-unit	List-price	Avg-cost	Qty-on-hand	Last-rcvd
BS-PLYWOOD	**Plywood, Exterior**		I	MATL	K6	EACH	13.95	7.00000	0	6/01/97
			Y	4010	5010			7.000	0	6/01/97
	Hanson Manufacturing Co.	Products		4520				60	0	5/05/97
		1400-000						200	36	6/03/97

Qty-sold:	this prd	100	Last prd	0	this yr	100	last yr	0
Sales:	this prd	1,395.00	Last prd	.00	this yr	1,395.00	last yr	.00
Cost:	this prd	700.00	Last prd	.00	this yr	700.00	last yr	.00

Item-#	Description	Bar-code	Typ	Dept	Loc	Stk-unit	List-price	Avg-cost	Qty-on-hand	Last-rcvd
EL-WIRE	**Electrical House Wire**		I	MATL	E43	REEL	5.19	2.50000	0	6/01/97
			Y	4000	5010			2.500	0	6/01/97
	Reynolds Tool Company	Products		4520				15	0	5/12/97
		1400-000						50	10	6/10/97

Qty-sold:	this prd	50	Last prd	0	this yr	50	last yr	0
Sales:	this prd	259.50	Last prd	.00	this yr	259.50	last yr	.00
Cost:	this prd	125.00	Last prd	.00	this yr	125.00	last yr	.00

Date: 06/30/97 Time: 10:27:43 Acme Hardware Co. Report #0167 Page #0004

ITEM LIST

Item-#	Description	Bar-code	Typ	Dept	Loc	Stk-unit	List-price	Avg-cost	Qty-on-hand	Last-rcvd
		Subst-item-#	Txb	Sls-#	COG-#	Pur-unit	Stk-qty-Pur	Last-cost	Qty-commit	1st-rcvd
	Vendor	Hist-class		Ret-#		Prf-unit		Min-qty-OH	Qty-on-ord	Last-ord
	Notes	Inv-contra-#						Max-qty-OH	Min-ord-qty	Last-sale
EQ-BLADE	**Replacement blade**		I	SHOP	R52	EACH	29.95	19.95000	0	None
			Y	4025	5010			19.950	0	None
	Tools Galore	Repairs		4520				5	25	None
		1400-000						40	10	None

Qty-sold:	this prd	0	Last prd	0	this yr	0	last yr	0
Sales:	this prd	.00	Last prd	.00	this yr	.00	last yr	.00
Cost:	this prd	.00	Last prd	.00	this yr	.00	last yr	.00

Item-#	Description	Bar-code	Typ	Dept	Loc	Stk-unit	List-price	Avg-cost	Qty-on-hand	Last-rcvd
EQ-DEER	**Ignition Cable**		I	EQUIP	W6	EACH	87.00	40.00000	12	None
			Y	4000	5010			40.000	0	None
	Hill Equipment & Supply	Products		4520				5	0	None
		1400-000						25	12	6/08/97

Qty-sold:	this prd	4	Last prd	0	this yr	4	last yr	0
Sales:	this prd	348.00	Last prd	.00	this yr	348.00	last yr	.00
Cost:	this prd	160.00	Last prd	.00	this yr	160.00	last yr	.00

Item-#	Description	Bar-code	Typ	Dept	Loc	Stk-unit	List-price	Avg-cost	Qty-on-hand	Last-rcvd
EQ-FILTER	**Replacement oil filter**		I	SHOP	R14	EACH	2.95	1.25000	0	None
			Y	4025	5010			1.250	0	None
	"Biggies" Hardware	Repairs		4520				12	60	None
		1400-000						72	36	None

Qty-sold:	this prd	0	Last prd	0	this yr	0	last yr	0
Sales:	this prd	.00	Last prd	.00	this yr	.00	last yr	.00
Cost:	this prd	.00	Last prd	.00	this yr	.00	last yr	.00

13 items printed

-- End of report --

Date: 06/30/97 Time: 11:20:26 Acme Hardware Co. Report #0168 Page #0001

ITEM LIST

Item # range: 2300 to 2300
Department: "All" Vendor: "All"
Item type: I = Inventory
"*****" indicates that the contra account varies by invoice profit center

Item-#	Description	Bar-code	Typ	Dept	Loc	Stk-unit	List-price	Avg-cost	Qty-on-hand	Last-rcvd
		Subst-item-#	Txb	Sls-#	COG-#	Pur-unit	Stk-qty-Pur	Last-cost	Qty-commit	1st-rcvd
	Vendor	Hist-class		Ret-#		Prf-unit		Min-qty-OH	Qty-on-ord	Last-ord
	Notes	Inv-contra-#						Max-qty-OH	Min-ord-qty	Last-sale
2300	**Hammer, Sledge**		I	TOOLS	F7	EACH	27.00	14.62000	0	None
			Y	4000	5010			14.620	0	None
	Hill Equipment & Supply	Products		4520		EACH		20	0	None
		1400-000						36	12	None

Better price: 25.20
Alt-price-1: 276.00 (12.00000 EACH per DOZ)

Qty-sold:	this prd	0	Last prd	0	this yr	0	last yr	0
Sales:	this prd	.00	Last prd	.00	this yr	.00	last yr	.00
Cost:	this prd	.00	Last prd	.00	this yr	.00	last yr	.00

1 item printed

-- End of report --

Date: 06/30/97 Time: 11:40:15 Acme Hardware Co. Report #0172 Page 0001

PURCHASE TRANSACTION REGISTER

Suggested–qty = Calculated order quantity based on min/max
Resultant–qty = Qty–on–hand + Qty–on–order – Qty–committed + Order–qty
Extended–cost = Order–qty x Unit–cost
Replacement–cost = Order–qty x Last–cost
Retail–value = Order–qty x List–price

Item–#	Description	Dept	Ord–date Min–qty–OH Max–qty–OH	Order–qty Suggest–qty Result–qty	Unit	Unit–cost Last–cost List–price	Extend–cost Replace–cost Retail–value	Notes Reference
Vendor: Hill Equipment & Supply								
2300	**Hammer, Sledge**	TOOLS	6/30/97	36	EACH	14.620	526.32	First order
			20	36	EACH	14.620	526.32	
			36	36	EACH	27.00	972.00	
	Vendor totals:		1 items	36			526.32	
				36			526.32	
				36			972.00	
	Grand totals:	1 vendors	1 items	36			526.32	
				36			526.32	
				36			972.00	

–– End of report ––

Date: 06/30/97 Time: 11:45:34 Acme Hardware Co. Report #0173 Page #0001

PRICE LIST

Starting item #: "First"
Ending item #: "Last"
Department: "All"
Vendor: "All"
List/better/best and alternate prices with sale prices

Item-#	Description	Dept	Stock Unit	List-price	Better-price Alt-prc-1	Qty/type	Best-price Alt-prc-2	Qty/type
1091	Gauge, Hi-Pressure	TOOLS	EACH	17.95	15.75			
1100	Drill, Power Hand	TOOLS	EACH	25.95	22.57			
1105	Drill, Cordless	TOOLS	10	29.95	24.95			
2200	Hammer, 16 oz. claw	TOOLS	EACH	13.50	12.60			
					138.00 per DOZ			
2300	Hammer, Sledge	TOOLS	EACH	27.00	25.20			
					276.00 per DOZ			
5770	Chisel, 5 pc set	TOOLS	SET	28.50	27.75			
BS-BLOCK	Block, Concrete	MATL	EACH	1.59	1.39	WSL		
					15.00 per DOZ			
BS-BRACKET	Bracket sets	MATL	SET	44.95	41.50			
BS-DOORS	Utility Door Unit	MATL	EACH	68.00	55.00			
BS-PLYWOOD	Plywood, Exterior	MATL	EACH	13.95				
EL-WIRE	Electrical House Wire	MATL	REEL	5.19				
EQ-BLADE	Replacement blade	SHOP	EACH	29.95				
EQ-DEER	Ignition Cable	EQUIP	EACH	87.00				
EQ-FILTER	Replacement oil filter	SHOP	EACH	2.95				

14 items printed

-- End of report --

Date: 06/30/97 Time: 11:54:15 Acme Hardware Co. Report #0174 Page #0001

PRICE LIST

Starting item #: "First"
Ending item #: "Last"
Department: "All"
Vendor: "All"
List/better/best and alternate prices with sale prices

Item–#	Description	Dept	Stock Unit	List–price	Better–price Alt–prc–1	Qty/type	Best–price Alt–prc–2	Qty/type
EQ–FILTER	Replacement oil filter	SHOP	EACH	2.95				
		Sale price:		2.50			From 7/01/97 thru 7/15/97	

1 item printed

–– End of report ––

Date: 06/30/97 | Acme Hardware Co. | Report #0175 | Page 0001

INVENTORY COUNT SHEET

Bin location range: "First" to "Last"
Item # range: "First" to "Last"
Department: "All" Vendor: "All"

Bin	Item-#	Description	Unit Dept	On-hand	Count
3D	**1091**	Gauge, Hi-Pressure	EACH TOOLS	200	________
E16	**1100**	Drill, Power Hand	EACH TOOLS	24	________
E17	**1105**	Drill, Cordless	10 TOOLS	34	________
E43	**EL-WIRE**	Electrical House Wire	REEL MATL	0	________
E8	**5770**	Chisel, 5 pc set	SET TOOLS	9	________
F6	**2200**	Hammer, 16 oz. claw	EACH TOOLS	12	________
F7	**2300**	Hammer, Sledge	EACH TOOLS	0	________
K18	**BS-BRACKET**	Bracket sets	SET MATL	0	________
K21	**BS-BLOCK**	Block, Concrete	EACH MATL	50	________
K4	**BS-DOORS**	Utility Door Unit	EACH MATL	0	________
K6	**BS-PLYWOOD**	Plywood, Exterior	EACH MATL	0	________
R14	**EQ-FILTER**	Replacement oil filter	EACH SHOP	0	________

Date: 06/30/97 Acme Hardware Co. Report #0175 Page 0002

INVENTORY COUNT SHEET

Bin	Item–#	Description	Unit Dept	On–hand	Count
R52	**EQ–BLADE**	Replacement blade	EACH SHOP	0	________
W6	**EQ–DEER**	Ignition Cable	EACH EQUIP	12	________
			Total:	341	

14 items printed

-- End of report --

Date: 06/30/97 Time: 12:01:41 Acme Hardware Co. Report #0176 Page #0001

PHYSICAL INVENTORY TRANSACTION EDIT LIST

Current period ending date: 6/30/97
Bin location range: K21 to K21

Retail-value = Transaction-qty x List-price
Variance-quantity = Transaction-qty - Qty-on-hand
Variance-inventory-value = New-value - Old value
Transactions are printed in location/item number order

Item-number	Description	Type Doc-#	Date	Trans-qty New-qty-OH	Unit	Unit-cost	Total-cost New-avg-cost	List-price Retail-val	---Variance--- Quantity	Inv-value
BS-BLOCK	Block, Concrete	Cnt	6/30/97	45	EACH	.990	44.55	1.59	5-	4.95-
		Phys-count		45	EACH		.99000	71.55		
							Comment: June physical count			

Location K21 totals:	Count entries:	1	Qty counted:	45	Cost:	45.55	Retail:	71.55
			Variance:	5-	Cost:	4.95-	Retail:	7.95-
Grand totals:	Count entries:	1	Qty counted:	45	Cost:	45.55	Retail:	71.55
			Variance:	5-	Cost:	4.95-	Retail:	7.95-

-- End of report --

Date: 06/30/97 Time: 12:03:22 Acme Hardware Co. Report #0177 Page #0001

P H Y S I C A L   I N V E N T O R Y   T R A N S A C T I O N   R E G I S T E R

Current period ending date: 6/30/97 Posting date: 6/30/97
Adjustment account: 5020–000

Retail–value = Transaction–qty x List–price
Variance–quantity = Transaction–qty – Qty–on–hand
Variance–inventory–value = New–value – Old value
Transactions are printed in location/item number order

Item–number	Description	Type Doc–#	Date	Trans–qty New–qty–OH	Unit	Unit–cost	Total–cost New–avg–cost	List–price Retail–val	–––Variance––– Quantity	Inv–value
1091	Gauge, Hi–Pressure	Cnt	6/30/97	***** Item not counted *****			.00	17.95		
		Phys–count		200	EACH		9.72000	.00		
							Comment: June physical count			
Location 3D	totals:	Count entries: 1		Qty counted:		0	Cost: .00		Retail:	.00
				Variance:		0	Cost: .00		Retail:	.00
1100	Drill, Power Hand	Cnt	6/30/97	***** Item not counted *****			.00	25.95		
		Phys–count		24	EACH		13.14000	.00		
							Comment: June physical count			
Location E16	totals:	Count entries: 1		Qty counted:		0	Cost: .00		Retail:	.00
				Variance:		0	Cost: .00		Retail:	.00
1105	Drill, Cordless	Cnt	6/30/97	***** Item not counted *****			.00	29.95		
		Phys–count		34	10		14.95000	.00		
							Comment: June physical count			
Location E17	totals:	Count entries: 1		Qty counted:		0	Cost: .00		Retail:	.00
				Variance:		0	Cost: .00		Retail:	.00
EL–WIRE	Electrical House Wire	Cnt	6/30/97	***** Item not counted *****			.00	5.19		
		Phys–count		0	REEL		2.50000	.00		
							Comment: June physical count			
Location E43	totals:	Count entries: 1		Qty counted:		0	Cost: .00		Retail:	.00
				Variance:		0	Cost: .00		Retail:	.00
5770	Chisel, 5 pc set	Cnt	6/30/97	***** Item not counted *****			.00	28.50		
		Phys count		9	SET		18.20000	.00		
							Comment: June physical count			
Location E8	totals:	Count entries: 1		Qty counted:		0	Cost: .00		Retail:	.00
				Variance:		0	Cost: .00		Retail:	.00

Date: 06/30/97 Time: 12:03:28 Acme Hardware Co. Report #0177 Page #0002

PHYSICAL INVENTORY TRANSACTION REGISTER

Item–number	Description	Type Doc–#	Date	Trans–qty New–qty–OH	Unit	Unit–cost	Total–cost New–avg–cost	List–price Retail–val	–––Variance––– Quantity	 Inv–value
2200	Hammer, 16 oz. claw	Cnt	6/30/97	*** **Item not counted** ***			.00	13.50		
		Phys–count		12	EACH		17.31000	.00		
							Comment: June physical count			
Location F6	totals:	Count entries:	1	Qty counted:		0	Cost:	.00	Retail:	.00
				Variance:		0	Cost:	.00	Retail:	.00
2300	Hammer, Sledge	Cnt	6/30/97	*** **Item not counted** ***			.00	27.00		
		Phys–count		0	EACH		14.62000	.00		
							Comment: June physical count			
Location F7	totals:	Count entries:	1	Qty counted:		0	Cost:	.00	Retail:	.00
				Variance:		0	Cost:	.00	Retail:	.00
BS–BRACKET	Bracket sets	Cnt	6/30/97	*** **Item not counted** ***			.00	44.95		
		Phys–count		0	SET		32.00000	.00		
							Comment: June physical count			
Location K18	totals:	Count entries:	1	Qty counted:		0	Cost:	.00	Retail:	.00
				Variance:		0	Cost:	.00	Retail:	.00
BS–BLOCK	Block, Concrete	Cnt	6/30/97	45	EACH	.990	44.55	1.59	5–	4.95–
		Phys–count		45	EACH		.99000	71.55		
							Comment: June physical count			
Location K21	totals:	Count entries:	1	Qty counted:		45	Cost:	44.55	Retail:	71.55
				Variance:		5–	Cost:	4.95–	Retail:	7.95–
BS–DOORS	Utility Door Unit	Cnt	6/30/97	*** **Item not counted** ***			.00	68.00		
		Phys–count		0	EACH		32.00000	.00		
							Comment: June physical count			
Location K4	totals:	Count entries:	1	Qty counted:		0	Cost:	.00	Retail:	.00
				Variance:		0	Cost:	.00	Retail:	.00
BS–PLYWOOD	Plywood, Exterior	Cnt	6/30/97	*** **Item not counted** ***			.00	13.95		
		Phys–count		0	EACH		7.00000	.00		
							Comment: June physical count			
Location K6	totals:	Count entries:	1	Qty counted:		0	Cost:	.00	Retail:	.00
				Variance:		0	Cost:	.00	Retail:	.00

Date: 06/30/97 Time: 12:03:35 Acme Hardware Co. Report #0177 Page #0003

PHYSICAL INVENTORY TRANSACTION REGISTER

Item–number	Description	Type / Doc–#	Date	Trans–qty / New–qty–OH	Unit	Unit–cost	Total–cost / New–avg–cost	List–price / Retail–val	Variance Quantity	Variance Inv–value
EQ–FILTER	Replacement oil filter	Cnt	6/30/97	*** **Item not counted** ***			.00	2.95		
		Phys–count		0	EACH		1.25000	.00		
							Comment: June physical count			
EQ–BLADE	Replacement blade	Cnt	6/30/97	*** **Item not counted** ***			.00	29.95		
		Phys–count		0	EACH		19.95000	.00		
							Comment: June physical count			
EQ–DEER	Ignition Cable	Cnt	6/30/97	*** **Item not counted** ***			.00	87.00		
		Phys–count		12	EACH		40.00000	.00		
							Comment: June physical count			

Location R14	totals:	Count entries:	1	Qty counted:	0	Cost:	.00	Retail:	.00
				Variance:	0	Cost:	.00	Retail:	.00
Location R52	totals:	Count entries:	1	Qty counted:	0	Cost:	.00	Retail:	.00
				Variance:	0	Cost:	.00	Retail:	.00
Location W6	totals:	Count entries:	1	Qty counted:	0	Cost:	.00	Retail:	.00
				Variance:	0	Cost:	.00	Retail:	.00
Grand totals:		Count entries:	14	Qty counted:	45	Cost:	44.55	Retail:	71.55
				Variance:	5–	Cost:	4.95–	Retail:	7.95–

–– End of report ––

Date: 06/30/97 Time: 12:05:56 Acme Hardware Co. Report #0178 Page #0001

INVENTORY STATUS REPORT

Item # range: "First" to "Last"

Department: "All" Vendor: "All"

Report includes out of stock items

Inventory–value = Qty–on–hand x Average–cost Retail–value = Qty–on–hand x List–price

Out = Out of stock Understocked = Qty–on–hand is below Minimum–qty–on–hand Overstocked = Qty–on–hand is above Maximum–qty–on–hand

Item–#	Description	Dept	Unit	List–prc	Qty–on–hand	Qty–on–ord	Avg–cost	Inv–value	Ret–value	Stat
		Loc	Lst–rcvd	Lst–sold	qty–commit	Min–qty–OH	Max–qty–OH			
1091	Gauge, Hi–Pressure	TOOLS	EACH	17.95	200	0	9.720	1,944.00	3,590.00	
		3D	6/01/97	6/10/97		100	500			
1100	Drill, Power Hand	TOOLS	EACH	25.95	24	0	13.140	315.36	622.80	
		E16	6/01/97	6/04/97		10	30			
1105	Drill, Cordless	TOOLS	10	29.95	34	0	14.950	508.30	1,018.30	
		E17	6/01/97	6/04/97		10	40			
2200	Hammer, 16 oz. claw	TOOLS	EACH	13.50	12	0	7.310	87.72	162.00	Undr
		F6	6/01/97	6/03/97		20	36			
2300	Hammer, Sledge	TOOLS	EACH	27.00	0	36	14.620	.00	.00	Out
		F7				20	36			
5770	Chisel, 5 pc set	TOOLS	SET	28.50	9	0	18.200	163.80	256.50	Undr
		E8	6/01/97	6/07/97		15	24			
BS–BLOCK	Block, Concrete	MATL	EACH	1.59	45	0	.990	44.55	71.55	Undr
		K21	6/01/97	6/03/97		250	1,000			
BS–BRACKET	Bracket sets	MATL	SET	44.95	0	0	32.000	.00	.00	Out
		K18	6/01/97	6/10/97		2	12			
BS–DOORS	Utility Door Unit	MATL	EACH	68.00	0	0	32.000	.00	.00	Out
		K4	6/01/97	6/05/97		3	12			
BS–PLYWOOD	Plywood, Exterior	MATL	EACH	13.95	0	0	7.000	.00	.00	Out
		K6	6/01/97	6/03/97		60	200			
EL–WIRE	Electrical House Wire	MATL	REEL	5.19	0	0	2.500	.00	.00	Out
		E43	6/01/97	6/10/97		15	50			
EQ–BLADE	Replacement blade	SHOP	EACH	29.95	0	25	19.950	.00	.00	Out
		R52				5	40			

Date: 06/30/97 Time: 12:06:01 Acme Hardware Co. Report #0178 Page #0002

INVENTORY STATUS REPORT

Item-#	Description	Dept Loc	Unit Lst-rcvd	List-prc Lst-sold	Qty-on-hand qty-commit	Qty-on-ord Min-qty-OH	Avg-cost Max-qty-OH	Inv-value	Ret-value	Stat
EQ-DEER	Ignition Cable	EQUIP	EACH	87.00	12	0	40.000	480.00	1,044.00	
		W6		6/08/97		5	25			
EQ-FILTER	Replacement oil filter	SHOP	EACH	2.95	0	60	1.250	.00	.00	Out
		R14				12	72			
Totals:					336	121		3,543.73	6,765.15	
						527	2,077			

527 is the minimum stock level	– cost of minimum inventory:	$3,144.25 (at avg–cost).	Retail–value:	$5,817.90
2,077 is the maximum stock level	– cost of maximum inventory:	$12,249.48 (at avg–cost).	Retail–value:	$22,673.80
7 items are out of stock	– cost to replenish to minimum:	$1,024.65 (at last–cost).	Retail–value:	$1,933.90
	cost to replenish to maximum:	$3,707.32 (at last–cost).	Retail–value:	$6,787.30
3 items are understocked	– cost to replenish to minimum:	$370.63 (at last–cost).	Retail–value:	$604.95
	cost to replenish to maximum:	$1,393.89 (at last–cost).	Retail–value:	$2,269.95
0 items are overstocked	– value in excess of maximum:	$0.00 (at avg–cost).	Retail–value:	$0.00
4 items are stocked ok	– cost to replenish to maximum:	$3,604.54 (at last–cost).	Retail–value:	$6,851.40

14 items printed

–– End of report ––

Date: 06/30/97 Time: 12:08:47 | Acme Hardware Co. | Report #0179 Page 0001

PURCHASING ADVICE REPORT

Item # range: "First" to "Last"
Vendor range: "First" to "Last"
Department: "All"
Default notes: July orders Default order date: 6/30/97
Order–cost = Order–qty x Last–cost Retail–value = Order–qty x List–price

Item–#	Description Vendor	Stk–unit Pur–unit Dept	Last–cost Avg–cost List–price	Min–qty–OH Max–qty–OH Min–ord–qty	Qty–on–hand Qty–commit Qty–on–ord	–Qty–sold– This–perod Last–period This–year	–Suggested–Order– Order–cost Retail–val	Order–qty
2200	Hammer, 16 oz. claw	EACH	7.310	20	12	3	175.44	24 EACH
			7.310	36	0	0	324.00	
	Hill Equipment & Supply	TOOLS	13.50	12	0	3		
5770	Chisel, 5 pc set	SET	18.200	15	9	6	.00	0 DOZ
		DOZ	18.200	24	0	0	.00	(15)SET
	Hill Equipment & Supply	TOOLS	28.50	12	0	6		
BS–BLOCK	Block, Concrete	EACH	.990	250	45	450	940.88	80 DOZ
		DOZ	.990	1,000	0	0	1,511.14	(955) EACH
	Hanson Manufacturing Co.	MATL	1.59	144	0	450		
BS–BRACKET	Bracket sets	SET	32.000	2	0	5	384.00	12 SET
			32.000	12	0	0	539.40	
	Hill Equipment & Supply	MATL	44.95	6	0	5	** Out of stock **	
BS–DOORS	Utility Door Unit	EACH	32.000	3	0	5	384.00	12 EACH
			32.000	12	0	0	816.00	
	Hill Equipment & Supply	MATL	68.00	5	0	5	** Out of stock **	
BS–PLYWOOD	Plywood, Exterior	EACH	7.000	60	0	100	1,400.00	200 EACH
			7.000	200	0	0	2,790.00	
	Hanson Manufacturing Co.	MATL	13.95	36	0	100	** Out of stock **	
EL–WIRE	Electrical House Wire	REEL	2.500	15	0	50	125.00	50 REEL
			2.500	50	0	0	259.50	
	Reynolds Tool Company	MATL	5.19	10	0	50	** Out of stock **	
				Totals:	66	619	3,409.32	378
					0	0	6,240.04	970
					0	619		

7 items printed 4 items are out of stock

–– End of report ––

Date: 06/30/97 Time: 12:16:47 Acme Hardware Co. Report #0180 Page 0001

PURCHASE TRANSACTION EDIT LIST

Vendor range: "First" to "Last"
Item # range: "First" to "Last"
Department: "All"

Item–#	Description	Dept	Ord–date	Order–qty	Unit	Unit–cost	Extend–cost	Notes Reference
Vendor: Hanson Manufacturing Co.								
BS–BLOCK	Block, Concrete	MATL	6/30/97	80	DOZ	11.761	940.88	July orders
BS–PLYWOOD	Plywood, Exterior	MATL	6/30/97	200	EACH	7.000	1,400.00	July orders
	Vendor totals:		2 items	280			2,340.88	
Vendor: Hill Equipment & Supply								
2200	Hammer, 16 oz. claw	TOOLS	6/30/97	24	EACH	7.310	175.44	July orders
5770	Chisel, 5 pc set	TOOLS	6/30/97	0	DOZ	3,074.880	.00	July orders
BS–BRACKET	Bracket sets	MATL	6/30/97	12	SET	32.000	384.00	July orders
BS–DOORS	Utility Door Unit	MATL	6/30/97	12	EACH	32.000	384.00	July orders
	Vendor totals:		4 items	48			943.44	
Vendor: Reynolds Tool Company								
EL–WIRE	Electrical House Wire	MATL	6/30/97	50	REEL	2.500	125.00	July orders
	Vendor totals:		1 items	50			125.00	
	Grand totals:	3 vendors	7 items	378			3,409.32	

–– End of report ––

Date: 06/30/97 Time: 12:49:36 Acme Hardware Co. Report #0184 Page 0001

PURCHASE TRANSACTION EDIT LIST

Vendor range: "First" to "Last"
Item # range: "First" to "Last"
Department: "All"

Item-#	Description	Dept	Ord-date	Order-qty	Unit	Unit-cost	Extend-cost	Notes Reference
Vendor: Hanson Manufacturing Co.								
BS-BLOCK	Block, Concrete	MATL	6/30/97	80	DOZ	11.761	940.88	July orders
BS-PLYWOOD	Plywood, Exterior	MATL	6/30/97	200	EACH	7.000	1,400.00	July orders
	Vendor totals:		2 items	280			2,340.88	
Vendor: Hill Equipment & Supply								
2200	Hammer, 16 oz. claw	TOOLS	6/30/97	24	EACH	7.310	175.44	July orders
5770	Chisel, 5 pc set	TOOLS	6/30/97	12	EACH	18.200	218.40	July orders
BS-BRACKET	Bracket sets	MATL	6/30/97	12	SET	32.000	384.00	July orders
BS-DOORS	Utility Door Unit	MATL	6/30/97	12	EACH	32.000	384.00	July orders
	Vendor totals:		4 items	48			943.44	
Vendor: Reynolds Tool Company								
EL-WIRE	Electrical House Wire	MATL	6/30/97	50	REEL	2.500	125.00	July orders
	Vendor totals:		1 items	50			125.00	
	Grand totals:	3 vendors	7 items	378			3,409.32	

-- End of report --

Date: 06/30/97 Time: 12:50:21 Acme Hardware Co. Report #0185 Page 0001

PURCHASE TRANSACTION REGISTER

Suggested–qty = Calculated order quantity based on min/max
Resultant–qty = Qty–on–hand + Qty–on–order – Qty–committed + Order–qty
Extended–cost = Order–qty x Unit–cost
Replacement–cost = Order–qty x Last–cost
Retail–value = Order–qty x List–price

Item–#	Description	Dept	Ord–date Min–qty–OH Max–qty–OH	Order–qty Suggest–qty Result–qty	Unit	Unit–cost Last–cost List–price	Extend–cost Replace–cost Retail–value	Notes Reference
Vendor: Hanson Manufacturing Co.								
BS–BLOCK	Block, Concrete	MATL	6/30/97	80	DOZ	11.761	940.88	July orders
			250	80	DOZ	.990	940.90	
			1,000	995	EACH	1.59	1,511.14	
BS–PLYWOOD	Plywood, Exterior	MATL	6/30/97	200	EACH	7.000	1,400.00	July orders
			60	200	EACH	7.000	1,400.00	
			200	200	EACH	13.95	2,790.00	
	Vendor totals:		2 items	280			2,340.88	
				280			2,340.90	
				1,195			4,301.14	
Vendor: Hill Equipment & Supply								
2200	Hammer, 16 oz. claw	TOOLS	6/30/97	24	EACH	7.310	175.44	July orders
			20	24	EACH	7.310	175.44	
			36	36	EACH	13.50	324.00	
5770	Chisel, 5 pc set	TOOLS	6/30/97	12	EACH	18.200	218.40	July orders
			15	15	EACH	18.200	218.40	
			24	21	SET	28.50	342.00	
BS–BRACKET	Bracket sets	MATL	6/30/97	12	SET	32.000	384.00	July orders
			2	12	SET	32.000	384.00	
			12	12	SET	44.95	539.40	
BS–DOORS	Utility Door Unit	MATL	6/30/97	12	EACH	32.000	384.00	July orders
			3	12	EACH	32.000	384.00	
			12	12	EACH	68.00	816.00	
	Vendor totals:		4 items	60			1,161.84	
				63			1,161.84	
				81			2,021.40	

Date: 06/30/97 Time: 12:50:26 Acme Hardware Co. Report #0185 Page 0002

PURCHASE TRANSACTION REGISTER

Item-#	Description	Dept	Ord-date Min-qty-OH Max-qty-OH	Order-qty Suggest-qty Result-qty	Unit	Unit-cost Last-cost List-price	Extend-cost Replace-cost Retail-value	Notes Reference
Vendor: Reynolds Tool Company								
EL-WIRE	Electrical House Wire	MATL	6/30/97	50	REEL	2.500	125.00	July orders
			15	50	REEL	2.500	125.00	
			50	50	REEL	5.19	259.50	
	Vendor totals:		1 items	50			125.00	
				50			125.00	
				50			259.50	
	Grand totals:	3 vendors	7 items	390			3,627.72	
				393			3,627.74	
				1,326			6,582.04	

-- End of report --

Date: 06/30/97 Time: 12:52:33 Acme Hardware Co. Report #0186 Page #0001

INVENTORY VALUATION REPORT

Starting item #: "First"
Ending item #: "Last"
Department: "All"
Vendor: "All"

Retail-value = Qty-on-hand x List-price
Replacement-value = Qty-on-hand x Last-cost
Inventory-value = Qty-on-hand x Average-cost

Item-#	Description	Dept Loc	Stock Unit	Qty-on-hand Qty-avail	List-price Last-cost	Retail-value Replace-value	Average-cost	Inv-value
1091	Gauge, Hi-Pressure	TOOLS 3D	EACH	200 200	17.95 9.72	3,590.00 1,944.00	9.72000	1,944.00
1100	Drill, Power Hand	TOOLS E16	EACH	24 24	25.95 13.14	622.80 315.36	13.14000	315.36
1105	Drill, Cordless	TOOLS E17	10	34 34	29.95 14.95	1,018.30 508.30	14.95000	508.30
2200	Hammer, 16 oz. claw	TOOLS F6	EACH	12 12	13.50 7.31	162.00 87.72	7.31000	87.72
5770	Chisel, 5 pc set	TOOLS E8	SET	9 9	28.50 18.20	256.50 163.80	18.20000	163.80
BS-BLOCK	Block, Concrete	MATL K21	EACH	45 45	1.59 .99	71.55 44.55	.99000	44.55
EQ-DEER	Ignition Cable	EQUIP W6	EACH	12 12	87.00 40.00	1,044.00 480.00	40.00000	480.00

Retail value: 6,765.15
Replacement value: 3,543.73
Inventory value: 3,543.73

7 items printed

-- End of report --

Date: 06/30/97 Time: 12:55:18 | Acme Hardware Co. | Report #0187 Page 0001

INVENTORY ANALYSIS REPORT

DETAIL BY RANK

Item range: "First" to "Last"
Department: "All"
Vendor: "All"
Ranking is based on sales this period.
Turn rates are based on 30 of 30 days completed for this period and 181 of 365 days completed for this year.
This report includes: All stock levels
All turn rates
All ranks

Dept	Item–Number	Rank		Qty–on–hnd	Qty–commit	Qty–on–ord	Retail–val	Profit–val	Pft–%	Prds	
	Description	Rank–Val	This–prd:	Qty–sold	Disc–amt	Disc–%	Sales	Profit	Pft–%	of	Turn
			This–yr:	Qty–sold	Disc–amt	Disc–%	Sales	Profit	Pft–%	Supply	Rate
TOOLS	**1091**	**1**		200	0	0	3,590	1,646	45.8		
	Gauge, Hi–Pressure	5385		300	0	.0	5,385	2,469	45.8	.7	36.0
				300	0	.0	5,385	2,469	45.8	4.0	6.0
MATL	**BS–PLYWOOD**	**2**		0	0	200	0	0	.0		
	Plywood, Exterior	1395		100	0	.0	1,395	695	49.8	.0	20.0
				100	0	.0	1,395	695	49.8	.0	3.4
MATL	**BS–BLOCK**	**3**		45	0	950	72	27	37.5		
	Block, Concrete	716		450	0	.0	716	270	37.7	.1	21.6
				450	0	.0	716	270	37.7	.6	3.6
EQUIP	**EQ–DEER**	**4**		12	0	0	1,044	564	54.0		
	Ignition Cable	348		4	0	.0	348	188	54.0	3.0	9.6
				4	0	.0	348	188	54.0	17.9	1.6
MATL	**BS–DOORS**	**5**		0	0	12	0	0	.0		
	Utility Door Unit	340		5	0	.0	340	180	52.9	.0	20.0
				5	0	.0	340	180	52.9	.0	3.4
MATL	**EL–WIRE**	**6**		0	0	50	0	0	.0		
	Electrical House Wire	260		50	0	.0	260	135	51.9	.0	40.0
				50	0	.0	260	135	51.9	.0	6.7
MATL	**BS–BRACKET**	**7**		0	0	12	0	0	.0		
	Bracket sets	225		5	0	.0	225	65	28.9	.0	30.0
				5	0	.0	225	65	28.9	.0	5.0
TOOLS	**1105**	**8**		34	0	0	1,018	510	50.1		
	Drill, Cordless	180		6	0	.0	180	90	50.0	5.7	7.2
				6	0	.0	180	90	50.0	33.7	1.2

Date: 06/30/97 Time: 12:55:24 | Acme Hardware Co. | Report #0187 Page 0002

INVENTORY ANALYSIS REPORT

Dept	Item–Number	Rank		Qty–on–hnd	Qty–commit	Qty–on–ord	Retail–val	Profit–val	Pft–%	Prds	
	Description	Rank–Val	This–prd:	Qty–sold	Disc–amt	Disc–%	Sales	Profit	Pft–%	of	Turn
			This–yr:	Qty–sold	Disc–amt	Disc–%	Sales	Profit	Pft–%	Supply	Rate
TOOLS	**5770**	**9**		9	0	12	257	93	36.2		
	Chisel, 5 pc set	171		6	0	.0	171	62	36.3	1.5	4.8
				6	0	.0	171	62	36.3	8.9	.8
TOOLS	**1100**	**10**		24	0	0	623	307	49.3		
	Drill, Power Hand	156		6	0	.0	156	77	49.4	4.0	7.2
				6	0	.0	156	77	49.4	23.8	1.2
TOOLS	**2200**	**11**		12	0	24	162	74	45.7		
	Hammer, 16 oz. claw	41		3	0	.0	41	19	46.3	4.0	1.8
				3	0	.0	41	19	46.3	23.8	.3
TOOLS	**2300**	**12**		0	0	36	0	0	.0		
	Hammer, Sledge	0		0	0	.0	0	0	.0	.0	.0
				0	0	.0	0	0	.0	.0	.0
SHOP	**EQ–BLADE**	**13**		0	0	25	0	0	.0		
	Replacement blade	0		0	0	.0	0	0	.0	.0	.0
				0	0	.0	0	0	.0	.0	.0
SHOP	**EQ–FILTER**	**14**		0	0	60	0	0	.0		
	Replacement oil filter	0		0	0	.0	0	0	.0	.0	.0
				0	0	.0	0	0	.0	.0	.0
Grand totals:				336	0	1,381	6,766	3,221	47.6		
				935	0	.0	9,217	4,250	46.1		19.0
				935	0	.0	9,217	4,250	46.1		3.2

Records Read	14
Records Processed	14
Records Printed	14

–– End of report ––

Date: 06/30/97 Time: 12:59:14 Acme Hardware Co. Report #0188 Page #0001

INVENTORY STATUS REPORT

Item # range: "First" to "Last"

Department: "All" Vendor: "All"

Report includes out of stock items

Inventory–value = Qty–on–hand x Average–cost Retail–value = Qty–on–hand x List–price

Out = Out of stock Understocked = Qty–on–hand is below Minimum–qty–on–hand Overstocked = Qyt–on–hand is above Maximum–qty–on–hand

Item–#	Description	Dept	Unit	List–price	Qty–on–hand	Qty–on–ord	Avg–cost	Inv–value	Ret–value	Stat
1091	Gauge, Hi–Pressure	TOOLS	EACH	17.95	200	0	9.720	1,944.00	3,590.00	
1100	Drill, Power Hand	TOOLS	EACH	25.95	24	0	13.140	315.36	622.80	
1105	Drill, Cordless	TOOLS	10	29.95	34	0	14.950	508.30	1,018.30	
2200	Hammer, 16 oz. claw	TOOLS	EACH	13.50	12	24	7.310	87.72	162.00	Undr
2300	Hammer, Sledge	TOOLS	EACH	27.00	0	36	14.620	.00	.00	Out
5770	Chisel, 5 pc set	TOOLS	SET	28.50	9	12	18.200	163.80	256.50	Undr
BS–BLOCK	Block, Concrete	MATL	EACH	1.59	45	950	.990	44.55	71.55	Undr
BS–BRACKET	Bracket sets	MATL	SET	44.95	0	12	32.000	.00	.00	Out
BS–DOORS	Utility Door Unit	MATL	EACH	68.00	0	12	32.000	.00	.00	Out
BS–PLYWOOD	Plywood, Exterior	MATL	EACH	13.95	0	200	7.000	.00	.00	Out
EL–WIRE	Electrical House Wire	MATL	REEL	5.19	0	50	2.500	.00	.00	Out
EQ–BLADE	Replacement blade	SHOP	EACH	29.95	0	25	19.950	.00	.00	Out
EQ–DEER	Ignition Cable	EQUIP	EACH	87.00	12	0	40.000	480.00	1,044.00	
EQ–FILTER	Replacement oil filter	SHOP	EACH	2.95	0	60	1.250	.00	.00	Out
Totals:					336	1,381		3,543.73	6,765.15	

527 is the minimum stock level	– cost of minimum inventory:	$3,144.25	(at avg–cost).	Retail–value:	$5,817.90
2,077 is the maximum stock level	– cost of maximum inventory:	$12,249.48	(at avg–cost).	Retail–value:	$22,673.80
7 items are out of stock	– cost to replenish to minimum:	$1,024.65	(at last–cost).	Retail–value:	$1,933.90
	cost to replenish to maximum:	$3,707.32	(at last–cost).	Retail–value:	$6,787.30
3 items are understocked	– cost to replenish to minimum:	$370.63	(at last–cost).	Retail–value:	$604.95
	cost to replenish to maximum:	$1,393.89	(at last–cost).	Retail–value:	$2,269.95
0 items are overstocked	– value in excess of maximum:	$0.00	(at avg–cost).	Retail–value:	$0.00
4 items are stocked ok	– cost to replenish to maximum:	$3,604.54	(at last–cost).	Retail–value:	$6,851.40

14 items printed

–– End of report ––

Date: 06/30/97 Time: 13:00:35 Acme Hardware Co. Report #0189 Page 0001

INVENTORY ANALYSIS REPORT

Item range: "First" to "Last" **DETAIL BY RANK**

Department: "All"

Vendor: "All"

Ranking is based on profit this period.

Turn rates are based on 30 of 30 days completed for this period and 181 of 365 days completed for this year.

This report includes: All stock levels

All turn rates

All ranks

Dept	Item–Number	Rank		Qty–on–hnd	Qty–commit	Qty–on–ord	Retail–val	Profit–val	Pft–%	Prds	
	Description	Rank–Val	This–prd:	Qty–sold	Disc–amt	Disc–%	Sales	Profit	Pft–%	of	Turn
			This–yr:	Qty–sold	Disc–amt	Disc–%	Sales	Profit	Pft–%	Supply	Rate
TOOLS	**1091**	**1**		200	0	0	3,590	1,646	45.8		
	Gauge, Hi–Pressure	2469		300	0	.0	5,385	2,469	45.8	.7	36.0
				300	0	.0	5,385	2,469	45.8	4.0	6.0
MATL	**BS–PLYWOOD**	**2**		0	0	200	0	0	.0		
	Plywood, Exterior	695		100	0	.0	1,395	695	49.8	.0	20.0
				100	0	.0	1,395	695	49.8	.0	3.4
MATL	**BS–BLOCK**	**3**		45	0	950	72	27	37.5		
	Block, Concrete	270		450	0	.0	716	270	37.7	.1	21.6
				450	0	.0	716	270	37.7	.6	3.6
EQUIP	**EQ–DEER**	**4**		12	0	0	1,044	564	54.0		
	Ignition Cable	188		4	0	.0	348	188	54.0	3.0	9.6
				4	0	.0	348	188	54.0	17.9	1.6
MATL	**BS–DOORS**	**5**		0	0	12	0	0	.0		
	Utility Door Unit	180		5	0	.0	340	180	52.9	.0	20.0
				5	0	.0	340	180	52.9	.0	3.4
MATL	**EL–WIRE**	**6**		0	0	50	0	0	.0		
	Electrical House Wire	135		50	0	.0	260	135	51.9	.0	40.0
				50	0	.0	260	135	51.9	.0	6.7
TOOLS	**1105**	**7**		34	0	0	1,018	510	50.1		
	Drill, Cordless	90		6	0	.0	180	90	50.0	5.7	7.2
				6	0	.0	180	90	50.0	33.7	1.2
TOOLS	**1100**	**8**		24	0	0	623	307	49.3		
	Drill, Power Hand	77		6	0	.0	156	77	49.4	4.0	7.2
				6	0	.0	156	77	49.4	23.8	1.2

Date: 06/30/97 Time: 13:00:41 Acme Hardware Co. Report #0189 Page 0002

INVENTORY ANALYSIS REPORT

Dept	Item–Number	Rank	Qty–on–hnd	Qty–commit	Qty–on–ord	Retail–val	Profit–val	Pft–%	Prds	
	Description	Rank–Val	This–prd: Qty–sold	Disc–amt	Disc–%	Sales	Profit	Pft–%	of	Turn
			This–yr: Qty–sold	Disc–amt	Disc–%	Sales	Profit	Pft–%	Supply	Rate
MATL	**BS–BRACKET**	**9**	0	0	12	0	0	.0		
	Bracket sets	65	5	0	.0	225	65	28.9	.0	30.0
			5	0	.0	225	65	28.9	.0	5.0
TOOLS	**5770**	**10**	9	0	12	257	93	36.2		
	Chisel, 5 pc set	62	6	0	.0	171	62	36.3	1.5	4.8
			6	0	.0	171	62	36.3	8.9	.8
TOOLS	**2200**	**11**	12	0	24	162	74	45.7		
	Hammer, 16 oz. claw	19	3	0	.0	41	19	46.3	4.0	1.8
			3	0	.0	41	19	46.3	23.8	.3
TOOLS	**2300**	**12**	0	0	36	0	0	.0		
	Hammer, Sledge	0	0	0	.0	0	0	.0	.0	.0
			0	0	.0	0	0	.0	.0	.0
SHOP	**EQ–BLADE**	**13**	0	0	25	0	0	.0		
	Replacement blade	0	0	0	.0	0	0	.0	.0	.0
			0	0	.0	0	0	.0	.0	.0
SHOP	**EQ–FILTER**	**14**	0	0	60	0	0	.0		
	Replacement oil filter	0	0	0	.0	0	0	.0	.0	.0
			0	0	.0	0	0	.0	.0	.0
Grand totals:			336	0	1,381	6,766	3,221	47.6		
			935	0	.0	9,217	4,250	46.1		19.0
			935	0	.0	9,217	4,250	46.1		3.2

Records Read 14

Records Processed 14

Records Printed 14

–– End of report ––

Practice Set 12 – PROCESS GENERAL LEDGER AND PRINT FINANCIAL STATEMENTS

Introduction

This next practice set asks you to review month–end activities for the Acme Hardware Company. You are asked to make final postings to the general ledger, to print the trial balance, to modify financial statement layouts, and to print the company Balance Sheet and Income Statement. You are expected to be able to:

- ➡ process both regular and recurring G/L entries
- ➡ print the trial balance
- ➡ modify financial statement layouts
- ➡ print financial statements

Set transaction date

Before starting this practice set, enter today's date as **6–30–97.**

Process General Journal Entries

Move to the General Ledger and select Process General Journal. For the entries shown below, you must determine whether to DEBIT or CREDIT an account. Add the following six entries:

Account #	**1620–000**	**2520–000**
Trans date	6/1/97	6/1/97
Amount	15000	15000
Reference	1995 Delivery truck	1995 Delivery truck
Account #	**1600–000**	**2520–000**
Trans date	6/1/97	6/1/97
Amount	3200	3200
Reference	Furniture	Furniture
Account #	**1610–000**	**2520–000**
Trans date	6/1/97	6/1/97
Amount	5000	5000
Reference	Cash registers	Cash registers

* Print the Transaction Edit List after entering these entries.
* Post these entries, which prints the General Journal Transaction Register.

How can you tell whether to debit or credit Notes Payable?

Process Recurring G/L Entries

Move to Process General Journal again, but this time select Process Recurring Transactions (press F1, if necessary). Add the following recurring transactions, once again deciding whether to debit or credit the dollar amount:

Account #	**1720–000**	**6080–000**
Frequency	Monthly	Monthly
Next date	6/30/97	6/30/97
Amount	300	300
Reference	1995 Delivery truck	1995 Delivery truck
Account #	**1700–000**	**6080–000**
Frequency	Monthly	Monthly
Next date	6/30/97	6/30/97
Amount	90	90
Reference	Furniture	Furniture
Account #	**1710–000**	**6080–000**
Frequency	Monthly	Monthly
Next date	6/30/97	6/30/97
Amount	110	110
Reference	Cash registers	Cash registers

* Print the Recurring Transaction List.
* Activate these entries using the cut–off and Trans date of 6/30/97, and the Next date of 7/30/97.
* Print the General Journal Transaction Edit List.
* Post the entries, which prints the General Journal Transaction Register.

What is the difference between a recurring and a non–recurring G/L journal entry?
What will happen when the truck is fully depreciated?

View G/L Accounts

Move to View G/L Account Activity and examine account 6080–000 for the month of June.

What is the ending balance of depreciation for the month of June?
What does this tell you about how recurring G/L entries work?

Print the G/L Trial Balance

Print the Trial Balance for all accounts, using a starting date of 6/1/97 and an ending date of 6/30/97. Show all details for all profit centers.

* Examine account 1100.

What does the source document SL0109 refer to?
What other G/L accounts show this same number?

Account #	Account Name

Why do all of these accounts refer to the same number?

* Examine account 1400.

What does the source IM0113 refer to?
What other G/L accounts show this same number?

Account #	Account Name

Explain the relationship between these two accounts.

Prepare Financial–Form Layouts

In this section, you are asked to prepare the layouts needed for printing the Balance Sheet and the Income Statement. Move to Print Financial Statements, and select Financial Statement Layout.

* Change layout #1, the Balance Sheet. The corrected Financial Statement Layout Edit List is shown on the following pages. Modify the existing, stored layout to conform to this list. Once you have made all changes, select Test Layouts to print a sample Balance Sheet.

* Change layout #2, the Income Statement (P&L). The corrected Financial Statement Layout Edit List is also shown on the following pages. Modify the existing, stored layout to conform to this list. Select Test Layouts to print a sample Profit and Loss Statement.

Print Financial Statements

Once you are satisfied with the two layouts, print the Balance Sheet and the Income Statement. Do not show ratios on the Income Statement.

How is the loss on the Income Statement reflected by the Balance Sheet?

Date 06/30/97 Acme Hardware Co. #0198 Page 0001

FINANCIAL STATEMENT LAYOUT EDIT LIST

Starting layout #: 1
Ending layout #: 2

Layout #: 1 Sample Balance Sheet
--Retailer--

Balance sheet

Seq-#	Function code					
0010	TXT	Acme Hardware Co.				
0020	TXT	Balance Sheet				
0030	BL					
0040	DAT					
0050	TXT	ASSETS				
0060	BL					
0070	TXT	CURRENT ASSETS				
0080	BL					
0090	1010-000	Checking #1 - Payables	Prt/Accum	P	Print column 1
0095	1020-000	Checking #2 - Payroll	Prt/Accum	P	Print column 1
0100	1040-000	Credit card deposits	Prt/Accum	A	
0140	1050-000	Petty cash	Prt/Accum	P	Print column 1
0150	SUB2	Cash	Paren ctrl	C	Print column 2
0160	BL				
0170	1100-000	Accts Receivable - Trade	Prt/Accum	P	Print column 1
0180	1110-000	Accts Receivable - Employee	Prt/Accum	P	Print column 1
0190	BL				
0200	1200-000	Notes receivable	Prt/Accum	P	Print column 1
0210	1210-000	Interest receivable	Prt/Accum	P	Print column 1
0220	1300-000	Prepaid exp	Prt/Accum	P	Print column 1
0230	1400-000	Inventory	Prt/Accum	P	Print column 1
0235	1410-000	Services	Prt/Accum	P	Print column 1
0240	SL				Print column 2
0250	SUB3	TOTAL CURRENT ASSETS	Paren ctrl	C	Print column 2
0260	BL				
0270	BL				
0280	TXT	PROPERTY AND EQUIPMENT			
0290	BL				
0300	1600-000	Furniture and fixtures	Prt/Accum	P	Print column 1
0310	1610-000	Office equipment	Prt/Accum	P	Print column 1
0320	1620-000	Automobile and trucks	Prt/Accum	P	Print column 1
0330	1630-000	Buildings	Prt/Accum	P	Print column 1
0340	1640-000	Leasehold improvements	Prt/Accum	P	Print column 1
0350	1650-000	Land	Prt/Accum	P	Print column 1

Date 06/30/97 Acme Hardware Co. #0198 Page 0002

FINANCIAL STATEMENT LAYOUT EDIT LIST

Seq–#	Function code					
0360	SUB2		Total property and equipment	Paren ctrl	C	Print column 2
0370	BL					
0380	1700–000	Accum depr – furn & fixt		Prt/Accum	P	Print column 1
0390	1710–000	Accum depr – office equip		Prt/Accum	P	Print column 1
0400	1720–000	Accum depr – auto & truck		Prt/Accum	P	Print column 1
0410	1730–000	Accum depr – building		Prt/Accum	P	Print column 1
0430	SUB2		Total accum depreciation	Paren ctrl	C	Print column 2
0440	SL					Print column 2
0450	SUB3		NET FIXED ASSETS	Paren ctrl	C	Print column 2
0470	BL					
0480	TXT		OTHER ASSETS			
0490	BL					
0510	1910–000	Other intangibles		Prt/Accum	P	Print column 1
0520	1800–000	Deposits		Prt/Accum	P	Print column 1
0530	1810–000	Investments		Prt/Accum	P	Print column 1
0540	SL					Print column 2
0550	SUB2		TOTAL OTHER ASSETS	Paren ctrl	C	Print column 2
0560	BL					
0570	SUB5		TOTAL ASSETS	Paren ctrl	C	Print column 2
0580	DL					Print column 2
0640	NP					
0650	TXT		LIABILITIES AND STOCKHOLDERS' EQUITY			
0660	BL					
0670	TXT		CURRENT LIABILITIES			
0680	BL					
0690	2100–000	Accounts Payable – Trade		Prt/Accum	P	Print column 1
0700	2005–000	Uninvoiced Receivings		Prt/Accum	P	Print column 1
0705	2110–000	Notes Payable – Main St.		Prt/Accum	P	Print column 1
0710	2200–000	Accrued expenses		Prt/Accum	P	Print column 1
0715	2025–000	Medical Ins. Deduct		Prt/Accum	P	Print column 1
0720	2310–000	Federal income tax withheld		Prt/Accum	P	Print column 1
0730	2320–000	EIC advances paid		Prt/Accum	P	Print column 1
0740	2330–000	Emp Social Sec Payable		Prt/Accum	P	Print column 1
0741	2335–000	Emp Medicare Payable		Prt/Accum	P	Print column 1
0750	2340–000	Empr Social Sec Payable		Prt/Accum	P	Print column 1
0751	2345–000	Empr Medicare Payable		Prt/Accum	P	Print column 1
0760	2450–000	Accrued fed unemp tax		Prt/Accum	P	Print column 1
0770	2350–000	State income tax withheld		Prt/Accum	P	Print column 1
0780	2360–000	Other state tax withheld		Prt/Accum	P	Print column 1
0790	2460–000	Accrued state unemp tax		Prt/Accum	P	Print column 1
0800	2370–000	Local income tax withheld		Prt/Accum	P	Print column 1

Date 06/30/97 Acme Hardware Co. #0198 Page 0003

FINANCIAL STATEMENT LAYOUT EDIT LIST

Seq-#	Function code				
0810	2380-000	Pension contrib withheld	Prt/Accum	A	
0820	2390-000	Charity contrib withheld	Prt/Accum	A	
0830	PAT	Other withholding	Paren ctrl	D	Print column 1
0840	2410-000	Accrued fed income tax	Prt/Accum	P	Print column 1
0850	2420-000	Accrued state income tax	Prt/Accum	P	Print column 1
0860	2430-000	Accrued state sales tax	Prt/Accum	P	Print column 1
0880	2510-000	Deposits received	Prt/Accum	P	Print column 1
0890	2520-000	Notes and loans payable	Prt/Accum	P	Print column 1
0900	SL				Print column 2
0910	SUB3	TOTAL CURRENT LIABILITIES	Paren ctrl	D	Print column 2
0920	BL				
0930	2530-000	Long term debt	Prt/Accum	A	
0940	PAT	LONG TERM DEBT	Paren ctrl	D	Print column 2
0950	SL				Print column 2
0960	SUB4	TOTAL LIABILITIES	Paren ctrl	D	Print column 2
0970	BL				
0980	BL				
0990	TXT	STOCKHOLDERS' EQUITY			
1000	BL				
1010	3000-000	Common stock	Prt/Accum	P	Print column 1
1020	3100-000	Paid in capital	Prt/Accum	P	Print column 1
1030	3200-000	Treasury stock	Prt/Accum	P	Print column 1
1040	3300-000	Retained earnings	Prt/Accum	P	Print column 1
1045	BSNI	Current year income	Prt/Accum	P	Print column 1
1050	SL				Print column 2
1060	SUB2	TOTAL STOCKHOLDERS' EQUITY	Paren ctrl	D	Print column 2
1070	BL				
1080	SUB5	TOTAL LIAB AND EQUITY	Paren ctrl	D	Print column 2
1090	DL				Print column 2
1100	NP				

Date 06/30/97 Acme Hardware Co. #0198 Page 0004

FINANCIAL STATEMENT LAYOUT EDIT LIST

Layout #: 2 Income Statement (P & L)

--Retailer--

Profit and loss statement

Seq–#	Function code			
0010	TXT	Acme Hardware Co.		
0020	TXT	Income Statement		
0030	BL			
0040	DAT			
0041	TXT	SALES		
0042	BL			
0045	SRB			
0047	4000–000	Sales – Main St. Store	Prt/Accum	P
0050	4010–000	Sales – Yard	Prt/Accum	P
0060	4020–000	Sales – services	Prt/Accum	P
0070	BL			
0080	SUB1	Total product sales	Paren ctrl	D
0081	BL			
0082	4025–000	Income – Mower Repair	Prt/Accum	P
0085	4026–000	Income – Blower Repair	Prt/Accum	P
0087	4030–000	Income – Rentals	Prt/Accum	P
0088	4031–000	Non–inventory item	Prt/Accum	P
0089	4032–000	Labor	Prt/Accum	P
0090	4033–000	Travel	Prt/Accum	P
0092	4035–000	Freight	Prt/Accum	P
0095	BL			
0097	SUB1	Rental and Repair Income	Paren ctrl	D
0098	BL			
0100	4510–000	Sales discounts	Prt/Accum	P
0110	4520–000	Sales retrns & allowances	Prt/Accum	P
0120	4910–000	Finance charges	Prt/Accum	P
0130	4920–000	Freight charges	Prt/Accum	A
0140	4930–000	Miscellaneous charges	Prt/Accum	A
0150	4940–000	Deposits forfeited	Prt/Accum	A
0160	4950–000	Other misc income	Prt/Accum	A
0170	PAT	Other income	Paren ctrl	D
0180	BL			
0190	SUB1	Total misc & other sales	Paren ctrl	D
0195	ERB			
0200	BL			
0210	DL			
0220	SUB3	TOTAL SALES	Paren ctrl	D

Date 06/30/97 Acme Hardware Co. #0198 Page 0005

FINANCIAL STATEMENT LAYOUT EDIT LIST

Seq-#	Function code			
0230	BL			
0240	BL			
0245	TXT	COST OF GOODS SOLD		
0246	BL			
0250	5010-000	Cost of goods sold	Prt/Accum	P
0260	5020-000	Inventory adjustments	Prt/Accum	P
0270	5030-000	Purchase discounts	Prt/Accum	P
0280	5040-000	Cost corrections	Prt/Accum	P
0290	BL			
0300	DL			
0310	SUB3	TOTAL COST OF GOODS SOLD	Paren ctrl	C
0320	BL			
0330	BL			
0331	SUB4	GROSS PROFIT ON SALES	Paren ctrl	D
0332	BL			
0333	BL			
0335	TXT	OPERATING EXPENSES		
0336	BL			
0338	6000-000	Wage Account	Prt/Accum	P
0340	6010-000	Advertising	Prt/Accum	P
0350	6020-000	Auto and truck	Prt/Accum	P
0360	6030-000	Bad debt expense paid	Prt/Accum	P
0370	6040-000	Bank charges and fees	Prt/Accum	P
0380	6050-000	Cash over or short	Prt/Accum	P
0390	6060-000	Charitable contributions	Prt/Accum	P
0400	6070-000	Commissions	Prt/Accum	P
0405	6070-100	Commissions - Repair	Prt/Accum	P
0410	6080-000	Depreciation	Prt/Accum	P
0420	6090-000	Insurance	Prt/Accum	P
0430	6100-000	Interest	Prt/Accum	P
0440	6110-000	Legal & accounting fees	Prt/Accum	P
0450	6120-000	Licenses and fees	Prt/Accum	P
0460	6130-000	Merchant credit card fees	Prt/Accum	P
0470	6140-000	Miscellaneous	Prt/Accum	P
0480	6150-000	Office expense	Prt/Accum	P
0490	6160-000	Rent & utilities	Prt/Accum	P
0500	6170-000	Repairs and maintenance	Prt/Accum	P
0510	6180-000	Salaries - administrative	Prt/Accum	P
0520	6190-000	Salaries - floor sales	Prt/Accum	P
0530	6200-000	Salaries - officers	Prt/Accum	P
0540	6210-000	Salaries - bonuses	Prt/Accum	P

Date 06/30/97 Acme Hardware Co. #0198 Page 0006

FINANCIAL STATEMENT LAYOUT EDIT LIST

Seq-#	Function code			
0550	6220-000 Sales and promotions exp		Prt/Accum	P
0560	6230-000 Supplies		Prt/Accum	P
0570	6240-000 Taxes - other		Prt/Accum	P
0580	6250-000 Taxes - payroll		Prt/Accum	P
0590	6260-000 Taxes - sales tax		Prt/Accum	P
0600	6270-000 Telephone		Prt/Accum	P
0605	8200-000 Telephone exp.		Prt/Accum	P
0610	6280-000 Travel & entertainment		Prt/Accum	P
0620	BL			
0630	DL			
0640	SUB3	TOTAL OPERATING EXPENSES	Paren ctrl	C
0650	BL			
0660	BL			
0665	TXT	NON-OPERATING INCOME AND EXPENSES		
0680	BL			
0690	9110-000 Interest income		Prt/Accum	P
0700	9120-000 Gain/loss sale of assets		Prt/Accum	P
0705	9999-000 Transfer/suspense Account		Prt/Accum	P
0710	SL			
0720	SUB1	Other income	Paren ctrl	D
0730	BL			
0740	DL			
0750	SUB5	NET INCOME BEFORE TAXES	Paren ctrl	D
0760	BL			
0770	BL			
0780	7110-000 Taxes - federal income		Prt/Accum	P
0790	7120-000 Taxes - state income		Prt/Accum	P
0800	SL			
0810	SUB1	Federal & state income tax	Paren ctrl	C
0820	BL			
0830	BL			
0840	SUB6	NET INCOME	Paren ctrl	D
0850	DL			
0860	NP			

-- End of report --

Other Things to Explore

1. Examine the Trial Balance once again.

    For account 1020, what does PR0163 refer to?
    List all other accounts in the trial balance that refer to this same source document.

Account #	Account Name

    Given this understanding, what is an important (if not THE main) value in using the computer to process the company payroll?

2. Test the accuracy of the Income Statement and the Balance Sheet, and answer the following questions with YES or NO.

    Are the balances shown for Checking #1 and #2 consistent with the balances shown in Checking accounts 1 and 2?
    Are the amounts shown for Accounts Receivable – Trade and Accounts Payable – Trade consistent with the G/L sales accounts?
    Are total product sales consistent with the G/L sales accounts?
    Are all salaries consistent with the three G/L accounts?
    Is the cost of goods sold consistent with the G/L account?

This completes Practice Set 12.

Date: 06/30/97 | Acme Hardware Co. | #0190 Page 0001

GENERAL JOURNAL TRANSACTION EDIT LIST

Period: 06/01/97 to 06/30/97

Account: **1600−000** **Furniture and fixtures**

Trans−date	Debit−amt	Credit−amt	Reference
06/01/97	3,200.00		Furniture

Account: **1610−000** **Office equipment**

Trans−date	Debit−amt	Credit−amt	Reference
06/01/97	5,000.00		Cash registers

Account: **1620−000** **Automobiles and trucks**

Trans−date	Debit−amt	Credit−amt	Reference
06/01/97	15,000.00		1995 Delivery truck

Account: **2520−000** **Notes and loans payable**

Trans−date	Debit−amt	Credit−amt	Reference
06/01/97		15,000.00	1997 delivery truck
06/01/97		3,200.00	Furniture
06/01/97		5,000.00	Cash registers
Totals:	.00	23,200.00	

Grand totals:	23,200.00	23,200.00	6 Transactions

−− End of report −−

Date: 06/30/97	Acme Hardware Co.	#0191 Page 0001

GENERAL JOURNAL TRANSACTION REGISTER

Period: 06/01/97 to 06/30/97

Account: **1600–000** **Furniture and fixtures**

Trans–date	Debit–amt	Credit–amt	Reference
06/01/97	3,200.00		Furniture

Account: **1610–000** **Office equipment**

Trans–date	Debit–amt	Credit–amt	Reference
06/01/97	5,000.00		Cash registers

Account: **1620–000** **Automobiles and trucks**

Trans–date	Debit–amt	Credit–amt	Reference
06/01/97	15,000.00		1995 Delivery truck

Account: **2520–000** **Notes and loans payable**

Trans–date	Debit–amt	Credit–amt	Reference
06/01/97		15,000.00	1997 delivery truck
06/01/97		3,200.00	Furniture
06/01/97		5,000.00	Cash registers
Totals:	.00	23,200.00	

Grand totals:	23,200.00	23,200.00	6 Transactions

–– End of report ––

Date: 06/30/97 Acme Hardware Co. #0192 Page 0001

RECURRING JOURNAL TRANSACTION LIST

"**" next to date means the transaction is now due

Account: **1700–000** **Accum depr – furn & fixt**

Due–date	Debit–amt	Credit–amt	Reference	Frequency
** 06/30/97		90.00	Furniture	Monthly

Account: **1710–000** **Accum depr – office equip**

Due–date	Debit–amt	Credit–amt	Reference	Frequency
** 06/30/97		110.00	Cash registers	Monthly

Account: **1720–000** **Accum depr – auto & truck**

Due–date	Debit–amt	Credit–amt	Reference	Frequency
** 06/30/97		300.00	1995 Delivery truck	Monthly

Account: **6080–000** **Depreciation**

Due–date	Debit–amt	Credit–amt	Reference	Frequency
** 06/30/97	300.00		1995 Delivery truck	Monthly
** 06/30/97	90.00		Furniture	Monthly
** 06/30/97	110.00		Cash registers	Monthly

Due this prd:	500.00	500.00	6 Transactions

-- End of report --

Date: 06/30/97 Acme Hardware Co. #0193 Page 0001

GENERAL JOURNAL TRANSACTION EDIT LIST

Period: 06/01/97 to 06/30/97

Account: **1700–000** **Accum depr – furn & fixt**

Due–date	Debit–amt	Credit–amt	Reference
06/30/97		90.00	Furniture

Account: **1710–000** **Accum depr – office equip**

Due–date	Debit–amt	Credit–amt	Reference
06/30/97		110.00	Cash registers

Account: **1720–000** **Accum depr – auto & truck**

Due–date	Debit–amt	Credit–amt	Reference
06/30/97		300.00	1995 Delivery truck

Account: **6080–000** **Depreciation**

Due–date	Debit–amt	Credit–amt	Reference
06/30/97	90.00		Furniture
06/30/97	110.00		Cash registers
06/30/97	300.00		1995 Delivery truck
Totals:	500.00	500.00	

Grand totals:	500.00	500.00	6 Transactions

–– End of report ––

Date: 06/30/97 Acme Hardware Co. #0194 Page 0001

GENERAL JOURNAL TRANSACTION REGISTER

Period: 06/01/97 to 06/30/97

Account: **1700–000** **Accum depr – furn & fixt**

Due–date	Debit–amt	Credit–amt	Reference
06/30/97		90.00	Furniture

Account: **1710–000** **Accum depr – office equip**

Due–date	Debit–amt	Credit–amt	Reference
06/30/97		110.00	Cash registers

Account: **1720–000** **Accum depr – auto & truck**

Due–date	Debit–amt	Credit–amt	Reference
06/30/97		300.00	1995 Delivery truck

Account: **6080–000** **Depreciation**

Due–date	Debit–amt	Credit–amt	Reference
06/30/97	90.00		Furniture
06/30/97	110.00		Cash registers
06/30/97	300.00		1995 Delivery truck
Totals:	500.00	500.00	

Grand totals:	500.00	500.00	6 Transactions

-- End of report --

Date: 06/30/97 Acme Hardware Co. #0195 Page 0001

GENERAL LEDGER TRIAL BALANCE

Starting account #: "First" Starting date: 06/01/97
Ending account #: "Last" Ending date: 06/30/97

Acct-#	Description				
	Begin-balance	Total-DR	Total-CR	Net-change	End-balance
1010-000	**Checking #1 - Payables**				
	.00	108,090.39	66,500.00	41,590.39	41,590.39

Dist-date	Source	DR-amount	CR-amount	Reference
06/01/97	CA0100	50,000.00		Set up cash balance
06/01/97	CA0100		50,000.00	Set up cash balance
06/01/97	GJ0098	50,000.00		Cash transfer
06/10/97	CR0126	106.36		Neptune Underwater Supply
06/13/97	CR0126	671.97		21st Century Construction
06/13/97	CR0126	885.39		Allied Plumbing Co.
06/13/97	CR0126	64.57		Newton, Boyd, and Co.
06/13/97	CR0126	827.41		Ariel Enterprises
06/13/97	CR0126	467.84		Elliott Enterprises
06/13/97	CR0126	5,066.85		Holcomb Industrial Supply
06/15/97	DB0140		250.00	Bitznbytes Computer
06/15/97	DB0140		1,000.00	Jones Property Management
06/15/97	DB0140		250.00	NorthWestern Bell
06/25/97	DB0156		15,000.00	*Cash transfer

Acct-#	Description				
1020-000	**Checking #2 - Payroll**				
	.00	15,000.00	5,934.16	9,065.84	9,065.84

Dist-date	Source	DR-amount	CR-amount	Reference
06/15/97	PR0163		2,971.10	Hermann Acme
06/15/97	PR0163		873.21	Earnest Wantabee
06/15/97	PR0163		1,171.93	Palmer, Edward W.
06/15/97	PR0163		917.92	Sara Sweetheart
06/25/97	CR0155	15,000.00		*Cash transfer

Acct-#	Description				
1100-000	**Accts Receivable - Trade**				
	.00	10,350.24	8,297.69	2,052.55	2,052.55

Dist-date	Source	DR-amount	CR-amount	Reference
06/03/97	SL0109	1,200.39		Allied Plumbing Co.
06/03/97	SL0109	844.30		Ariel Enterprises
06/03/97	SL0109	567.84		Elliott Enterprises

Date: 06/30/97 Acme Hardware Co. #0195 Page 0002

GENERAL LEDGER TRIAL BALANCE

Acct-#	Description				
	Begin-balance	Total-DR	Total-CR	Net-change	End-balance

Dist-date	Source	DR-amount	CR-amount	Reference
06/03/97	SL0109	5,170.26		Holcomb Industrial Supply
06/03/97	SL0109	1,269.55		Webber Landscaping
06/04/97	SL0111	25.95		Neptune Underwater Supply
06/04/97	SL0111	29.95		Newton, Boyd, and Co.
06/05/97	SL0111	68.00		Newton, Boyd, and Co.
06/07/97	SL0111	28.50		Neptune Underwater Supply
06/08/97	SL0111	87.00		Newton, Boyd, and Co.
06/10/97	CR0126		106.36	Neptune Underwater Supply
06/10/97	SL0111		87.00	Newton, Boyd, and Co.
06/10/97	SL0111	44.95		Neptune Underwater Supply
06/10/97	SL0111	25.95		Newton, Boyd, and Co.
06/10/97	SL0111	6.96		Neptune Underwater Supply
06/10/97	SL0111	8.67		Newton, Boyd, and Co.
06/10/97	SL0117	971.97		21st Century Construction
06/13/97	CR0126		671.97	21st Century Construction
06/13/97	CR0126		885.39	Allied Plumbing Co.
06/13/97	CR0126		64.57	Newton, Boyd, and Co.
06/13/97	CR0126		844.30	Ariel Enterprises
06/13/97	CR0126		467.84	Elliott Enterprises
06/13/97	CR0126		5,170.26	Holcomb Industrial Supply

1400-000	**Inventory**				
	.00	9,088.60	4,971.12	4,117.48	4,117.48

Dist-date	Source	DR-amount	CR-amount	Reference
06/03/97	GJ0106	8,474.85		Beginning inventory
06/03/97	IM0108		4,317.38	Inventory sales
06/04/97	IM0113		28.09	Inventory sales
06/05/97	IM0113		32.00	Inventory sales
06/07/97	IM0113		18.20	Inventory sales
06/08/97	IM0113		40.00	Inventory sales
06/10/97	IM0113	40.00		Inventory adjustment
06/10/97	IM0113		44.50	Inventory sales
06/10/97	IM0119		486.00	Inventory sales
06/15/97	BP0137	75.00		"Biggies" Hardware
06/15/97	BP0137	498.75		Tools Galore
06/30/97	IM0177		4.95	Physical inventory count

Date: 06/30/97 Acme Hardware Co. #0195 Page 0003

GENERAL LEDGER TRIAL BALANCE

Acct-#	Description				
	Begin-balance	Total-DR	Total-CR	Net-change	End-balance
1600-000	**Furniture and fixtures**				
	.00	3,200.00	.00	3,200.00	3,200.00
	Dist-date	Source	DR-amount	CR-amount	Reference
	06/01/97	GJ0191	3,200.00		Furniture
1610-000	**Office equipment**				
	.00	5,000.00	.00	5,000.00	5,000.00
	Dist-date	Source	DR-amount	CR-amount	Reference
	06/01/97	GJ0191	5,000.00		Cash registers
1620-000	**Automobiles and trucks**				
	.00	15,000.00	.00	15,000.00	15,000.00
	Dist-date	Source	DR-amount	CR-amount	Reference
	06/01/97	GJ0191	15,000.00		1995 Delivery truck
1700-000	**Accum depr - furn & fixt**				
	.00	.00	90.00	90.00CR	90.00CR
	Dist-date	Source	DR-amount	CR-amount	Reference
	06/30/97	GJ0194		90.00	Furniture
1710-000	**Accum depr - office equip**				
	.00	.00	110.00	110.00CR	110.00CR
	Dist-date	Source	DR-amount	CR-amount	Reference
	06/30/97	GJ0194		110.00	Cash registers
1720-000	**Accum depr - auto & truck**				
	.00	.00	300.00	300.00CR	300.00CR
	Dist-date	Source	DR-amount	CR-amount	Reference
	06/30/97	GJ0194		300.00	1995 Delivery truck

Date: 06/30/97 Acme Hardware Co. #0195 Page 0004

GENERAL LEDGER TRIAL BALANCE

Acct-#	Description				
	Begin-balance	Total-DR	Total-CR	Net-change	End-balance
2100-000	**Accounts Payable - Trade**				
	.00	9,974.85	10,548.60	573.75CR	573.75CR

Dist-date	Source	DR-amount	CR-amount	Reference
06/01/97	BP0130		495.00	Hanson Manufacturing Co.
06/01/97	BP0130	495.00		Hanson Manufacturing Co.
06/01/97	BP0130		700.00	Hanson Manufacturing Co.
06/01/97	BP0130	700.00		Hanson Manufacturing Co.
06/01/97	BP0130		1,374.85	Hill Equipment & Supply
06/01/97	BP0130	1,374.85		Hill Equipment & Supply
06/01/97	BP0130		160.00	Hill Equipment & Supply
06/01/97	BP0130	160.00		Hill Equipment & Supply
06/01/97	BP0130		4,860.00	Hill Equipment & Supply
06/01/97	BP0130	4,860.00		Hill Equipment & Supply
06/01/97	BP0130		760.00	Hill Equipment & Supply
06/01/97	BP0130	760.00		Hill Equipment & Supply
06/01/97	BP0130		125.00	Reynolds Tool Company
06/01/97	BP0130	125.00		Reynolds Tool Company
06/15/97	BP0134		250.00	Bitznbytes Computer
06/15/97	BP0134		1,000.00	Jones Property Management
06/15/97	BP0134		250.00	NorthWestern Bell
06/15/97	BP0137		75.00	"Biggies" Hardware
06/15/97	BP0137		498.75	Tools Galore
06/15/97	DB0140	250.00		Bitznbytes Computer
06/15/97	DB0140	1,000.00		Jones Property Management
06/15/97	DB0140	250.00		NorthWestern Bell

Acct-#	Description				
2310-000	**Fed income tax withheld**				
	.00	.00	1,737.79	1,737.79CR	1,737.79CR

Dist-date	Source	DR-amount	CR-amount	Reference
06/15/97	PR0163		1,165.98	Hermann Acme
06/15/97	PR0163		220.03	Earnest Wantabee
06/15/97	PR0163		154.90	Palmer, Edward W.
06/15/97	PR0163		196.88	Sara Sweetheart

Date: 06/30/97 Acme Hardware Co. #0195 Page 0005

GENERAL LEDGER TRIAL BALANCE

Acct-#	Description				
	Begin-balance	Total-DR	Total-CR	Net-change	End-balance
2330-000	**Emp Social Sec Payable**				
	.00	.00	561.72	561.72CR	561.72CR

Dist-date	Source	DR-amount	CR-amount	Reference
06/15/97	PR0163		310.00	Hermann Acme
06/15/97	PR0163		79.36	Earnest Wantabee
06/15/97	PR0163		93.00	Palmer, Edward W.
06/15/97	PR0163		79.36	Sara Sweetheart

Acct-#	Description				
2335-000	**Emp Medicare Payable**				
	.00	.00	131.37	131.37CR	131.37CR

Dist-date	Source	DR-amount	CR-amount	Reference
06/15/97	PR0163		72.50	Hermann Acme
06/15/97	PR0163		18.56	Earnest Wantabee
06/15/97	PR0163		21.75	Palmer, Edward W.
06/15/97	PR0163		18.56	Sara Sweetheart

Acct-#	Description				
2340-000	**Empr Social Sec Payable**				
	.00	.00	561.72	561.72CR	561.72CR

Dist-date	Source	DR-amount	CR-amount	Reference
06/15/97	PR0163		310.00	Hermann Acme
06/15/97	PR0163		79.36	Earnest Wantabee
06/15/97	PR0163		93.00	Palmer, Edward W.
06/15/97	PR0163		79.36	Sara Sweetheart

Acct-#	Description				
2345-000	**Empr Medicare Payable**				
	.00	.00	131.37	131.37CR	131.37CR

Dist-date	Source	DR-amount	CR-amount	Reference
06/15/97	PR0163		72.50	Hermann Acme
06/15/97	PR0163		18.56	Earnest Wantabee
06/15/97	PR0163		21.75	Palmer, Edward W.
06/15/97	PR0163		18.56	Sara Sweetheart

Date: 06/30/97 Acme Hardware Co. #0195 Page 0006

GENERAL LEDGER TRIAL BALANCE

Acct-#	Description				
	Begin-balance	Total-DR	Total-CR	Net-change	End-balance
2350-000	**State income tax withheld**				
	.00	.00	640.60	640.60CR	640.60CR

Dist-date	Source	DR-amount	CR-amount	Reference
06/15/97	PR0163		450.42	Hermann Acme
06/15/97	PR0163		81.16	Earnest Wantabee
06/15/97	PR0163		49.42	Palmer, Edward W.
06/15/97	PR0163		59.60	Sara Sweetheart

2360-000	**Other state tax withheld**				
	.00	.00	54.36	54.36CR	54.36CR

Dist-date	Source	DR-amount	CR-amount	Reference
06/15/97	PR0163		30.00	Hermann Acme
06/15/97	PR0163		7.68	Earnest Wantabee
06/15/97	PR0163		9.00	Palmer, Edward W.
06/15/97	PR0163		7.68	Sara Sweetheart

2430-000	**Accrued state sales tax**				
	.00	.00	638.94	638.94CR	638.94CR

Dist-date	Source	DR-amount	CR-amount	Reference
06/03/97	SL0109		75.59	Allied Plumbing Co.
06/03/97	SL0109		45.75	Ariel Enterprises
06/03/97	SL0109		31.59	Elliott Enterprises
06/03/97	SL0109		328.76	Holcomb Industrial Supply
06/03/97	SL0109		78.80	Webber Landscaping
06/10/97	SL0111		6.96	Neptune Underwater Supply
06/10/97	SL0111		8.67	Newton, Boyd, and Co.
06/10/97	SL0117		62.82	21st Century Construction

2450-000	**Accrued fed unemp tax**				
	.00	.00	72.48	72.48CR	72.48CR

Dist-date	Source	DR-amount	CR-amount	Reference
06/15/97	PR0163		40.00	Hermann Acme
06/15/97	PR0163		10.24	Earnest Wantabee
06/15/97	PR0163		12.00	Palmer, Edward W.

Date: 06/30/97 Acme Hardware Co. #0195 Page 0007

GENERAL LEDGER TRIAL BALANCE

Acct-#	Description				
	Begin-balance	Total-DR	Total-CR	Net-change	End-balance
	Dist-date	Source	DR-amount	CR-amount	Reference
	06/15/97	PR0163		10.24	Sara Sweetheart
2460-000	**Accrued state unemp tax**				
	.00	.00	81.54	81.54CR	81.54CR
	Dist-date	Source	DR-amount	CR-amount	Reference
	06/15/97	PR0163		45.00	Hermann Acme
	06/15/97	PR0163		11.52	Earnest Wantabee
	06/15/97	PR0163		13.50	Palmer, Edward W.
	06/15/97	PR0163		11.52	Sara Sweetheart
2520-000	**Notes and loans payable**				
	.00	.00	31,674.85	31,674.85CR	31,674.85CR
	Dist-date	Source	DR-amount	CR-amount	Reference
	06/01/97	GJ0191		15,000.00	1995 Delivery truck
	06/01/97	GJ0191		3,200.00	Furniture
	06/01/97	GJ0191		5,000.00	Cash registers
	06/03/97	GJ0106		8,474.85	Beginning inventory
2530-000	**Long term debt**				
	.00	.00	50,000.00	50,000.00CR	50,000.00CR
	Dist-date	Source	DR-amount	CR-amount	Reference
	06/01/97	GJ0098		50,000.00	Debt to begin business
4000-000	**Sales - Main St. Store**				
	.00	.00	6,426.45	6,426.45CR	6,426.45CR
	Dist-date	Source	DR-amount	CR-amount	Reference
	06/03/97	SL0109		989.90	Allied Plumbing Co.
	06/03/97	SL0109		381.60	Ariel Enterprises
	06/03/97	SL0109		292.25	Elliott Enterprises
	06/03/97	SL0109		2,779.50	Holcomb Industrial Supply
	06/03/97	SL0109		1,001.30	Webber Landscaping
	06/04/97	SL0111		25.95	Neptune Underwater Supply

Date: 06/30/97 Acme Hardware Co. #0195 Page 0008

GENERAL LEDGER TRIAL BALANCE

Acct-#	Description				
	Begin-balance	Total-DR	Total-CR	Net-change	End-balance

Dist-date	Source	DR-amount	CR-amount	Reference
06/04/97	SL0111		29.95	Newton, Boyd, and Co.
06/07/97	SL0111		28.50	Neptune Underwater Supply
06/10/97	SL0117		897.50	21st Century Construction

4010-000 Sales - Yard

Begin-balance	Total-DR	Total-CR	Net-change	End-balance
.00	87.00	2,788.20	2,701.20CR	2,701.20CR

Dist-date	Source	DR-amount	CR-amount	Reference
06/03/97	SL0109		89.90	Allied Plumbing Co.
06/03/97	SL0109		271.95	Ariel Enterprises
06/03/97	SL0109		159.00	Elliott Enterprises
06/03/97	SL0109		1,917.00	Holcomb Industrial Supply
06/03/97	SL0109		124.45	Webber Landscaping
06/05/97	SL0111		68.00	Newton, Boyd, and Co.
06/08/97	SL0111		87.00	Newton, Boyd, and Co.
06/10/97	SL0111	87.00		Newton, Boyd, and Co.
06/10/97	SL0111		44.95	Neptune Underwater Supply
06/10/97	SL0111		25.95	Newton, Boyd, and Co.

4510-000 Sales discounts

Begin-balance	Total-DR	Total-CR	Net-change	End-balance
.00	120.30	.00	120.30	120.30

Dist-date	Source	DR-amount	CR-amount	Reference
06/13/97	CR0126	16.89		Ariel Enterprises
06/13/97	CR0126	103.41		Holcomb Industrial Supply

4920-000 Freight charges

Begin-balance	Total-DR	Total-CR	Net-change	End-balance
.00	.00	496.65	496.65CR	496.65CR

Dist-date	Source	DR-amount	CR-amount	Reference
06/03/97	SL0109		45.00	Allied Plumbing Co.
06/03/97	SL0109		145.00	Ariel Enterprises
06/03/97	SL0109		85.00	Elliott Enterprises
06/03/97	SL0109		145.00	Holcomb Industrial Supply
06/03/97	SL0109		65.00	Webber Landscaping
06/10/97	SL0117		11.65	21st Century Construction

Date: 06/30/97 Acme Hardware Co. #0195 Page 0009

GENERAL LEDGER TRIAL BALANCE

Acct-#	Description				
	Begin-balance	Total-DR	Total-CR	Net-change	End-balance
5010-000	**Cost of goods sold**				
	.00	4,966.17	.00	4,966.17	4,966.17

Dist-date	Source	DR-amount	CR-amount	Reference
06/03/97	IM0108	4,317.38		Inventory sales
06/04/97	IM0113	28.09		Inventory sales
06/05/97	IM0113	32.00		Inventory sales
06/07/97	IM0113	18.20		Inventory sales
06/08/97	IM0113	40.00		Inventory sales
06/10/97	IM0113	44.50		Inventory sales
06/10/97	IM0119	486.00		Inventory sales

Acct-#	Description				
5020-000	**Inventory adjustments**				
	.00	4.95	40.00	35.05CR	35.05CR

Dist-date	Source	DR-amount	CR-amount	Reference
06/10/97	IM0113		40.00	Inventory adjustment
06/30/97	IM0177	4.95		Physical inventory count

Acct-#	Description				
6080-000	**Depreciation**				
	.00	500.00	.00	500.00	500.00

Dist-date	Source	DR-amount	CR-amount	Reference
06/30/97	GJ0194	90.00		Furniture
06/30/97	GJ0194	110.00		Cash registers
06/30/97	GJ0194	300.00		1995 Delivery truck

Acct-#	Description				
6150-000	**Office expense**				
	.00	250.00	.00	250.00	250.00

Dist-date	Source	DR-amount	CR-amount	Reference
06/15/97	BP0134	250.00		Bitznbytes Computer

Date: 06/30/97 Acme Hardware Co. #0195 Page 0010

GENERAL LEDGER TRIAL BALANCE

Acct-#	Description				
	Begin-balance	Total-DR	Total-CR	Net-change	End-balance
6160-000	**Rents & utilities**				
	.00	1,000.00	.00	1,000.00	1,000.00

Dist-date	Source	DR-amount	CR-amount	Reference
06/15/97	BP0134	1,000.00		Jones Property Management

Acct-#	Description				
6180-000	**Salaries - administrative**				
	.00	5,000.00	.00	5,000.00	5,000.00

Dist-date	Source	DR-amount	CR-amount	Reference
06/15/97	PR0163	5,000.00		Hermann Acme

Acct-#	Description				
6190-000	**Salaries - floor sales**				
	.00	1,500.00	.00	1,500.00	1,500.00

Dist-date	Source	DR-amount	CR-amount	Reference
06/15/97	PR0163	1,500.00		Palmer, Edward W.

Acct-#	Description				
6200-000	**Salaries & Wage exp-Elm**				
	.00	2,560.00	.00	2,560.00	2,560.00

Dist-date	Source	DR-amount	CR-amount	Reference
06/15/97	PR0163	1,280.00		Earnest Wantabee
06/15/97	PR0163	1,280.00		Sara Sweetheart

Acct-#	Description				
6250-000	**Taxes - payroll**				
	.00	847.11	.00	847.11	847.11

Dist-date	Source	DR-amount	CR-amount	Reference
06/15/97	PR0163	467.50		Hermann Acme
06/15/97	PR0163	119.68		Earnest Wantabee
06/15/97	PR0163	140.25		Palmer, Edward W.
06/15/97	PR0163	119.68		Sara Sweetheart

Date: 06/30/97 Acme Hardware Co. #0195 Page 0011

GENERAL LEDGER TRIAL BALANCE

Acct-#	Description				
	Begin-balance	Total-DR	Total-CR	Net-change	End-balance
6270-000	**Telephone**				
	.00	250.00	.00	250.00	250.00

Dist-date	Source	DR-amount	CR-amount	Reference
06/15/97	BP0134	250.00		NorthWestern Bell

Acct-#	Description				
9999-000	**Transfer/suspense Account**				
	.00	15,000.00	15,000.00	.00	.00

Dist-date	Source	DR-amount	CR-amount	Reference
06/25/97	CR0155		15,000.00	*Cash transfer
06/25/97	DB0156	15,000.00		*Cash transfer

Grand totals:					
	.00	207,789.61	207,789.61	.00	.00

-- End of report --

Date: 06/30/97 Acme Hardware Co. #0196 Page 0001

Layout #: 1 Sample balance sheet

Acme Hardware Co.
Balance Sheet

As of 99/99/99

ASSETS

CURRENT ASSETS

Checking #1 – Payables	$ 9,999,999.99	
Checking #2 – Payroll	9,999,999.99	
Petty cash	9,999,999.99	
Cash		$ 9,999,999.99
Accts Receivable – Trade	$ 9,999,999.99	
Accts Recvble – Employee	9,999,999.99	
Notes receivable	9,999,999.99	
Interest receivable	9,999,999.99	
Prepaid expenses	9,999,999.99	
Inventory	9,999,999.99	
Services	9,999,999.99	

TOTAL CURRENT ASSETS		$ 9,999,999.99

PROPERTY AND EQUIPMENT

Furniture and fixtures	$ 9,999,999.99	
Office equipment	9,999,999.99	
Automobiles and trucks	9,999,999.99	
Building	9,999,999.99	
Leasehold improvements	9,999,999.99	
Land	9,999,999.99	
Total property and equipment		$ 9,999,999.99
Accum depr – furn & fixt	$ 9,999,999.99	
Accum depr – office equip	9,999,999.99	
Accum depr – auto & truck	9,999,999.99	
Accum depr – building	9,999,999.99	
Total accum depreciation		$ 9,999,999.99

NET FIXED ASSETS		$ 9,999,999.99

OTHER ASSETS

Other intangibles	$ 9,999,999.99	
Deposits	9,999,999.99	
Investments	9,999,999.99	

TOTAL OTHER ASSETS		$ 9,999,999.99
TOTAL ASSETS		$ 9,999,999.99
		========

LIABILITIES AND STOCKHOLDERS' EQUITY

CURRENT LIABILITIES

Accounts Payable – Trade	$ 9,999,999.99	
Uninvoiced receivings	9,999,999.99	
Notes Payable – Main St.	9,999,999.99	
Accrued expenses	9,999,999.99	
Medical Ins. Deduct	9,999,999.99	
Fed income tax withheld	9,999,999.99	
EIC advances paid	9,999,999.99	
Emp Social Sec Payable	9,999,999.99	
Emp Medicare Payable	9,999,999.99	
Empr Social Sec Payable	9,999,999.99	
Empr Medicare Payable	9,999,999.99	
Accrued fed unemp tax	9,999,999.99	
State income tax withheld	9,999,999.99	
Other state tax withheld	9,999,999.99	
Accrued state unemp tax	9,999,999.99	
Local income tax withheld	9,999,999.99	
Other withholding	9,999,999.99	
Accrued fed income tax	9,999,999.99	
Accrued state income tax	9,999,999.99	
Accrued state sales tax	9,999,999.99	
Deposits received	9,999,999.99	
Notes and loans payable	9,999,999.99	

TOTAL CURRENT LIABILITIES		$ 9,999,999.99
LONG TERM DEBT		$ 9,999,999.99

TOTAL LIABILITIES		$ 9,999,999.99

STOCKHOLDERS' EQUITY

Common stock	$ 9,999,999.99	
Paid in capital	9,999,999.99	
Treasury stock	9,999,999.99	
Retained earnings	9,999,999.99	
Current year income	9,999,999.99	

TOTAL STOCKHOLDERS' EQUITY		$ 9,999,999.99
TOTAL LIAB AND EQUITY		$ 9,999,999.99
		========

-- End of report --

Date: 06/30/97 Acme Hardware Co. #0197 Page 0001

Layout #: 2 Sample profit and loss statement

Acme Hardware Co.
Income Statement

For the period 99/99/99 to 99/99/99

	Current period amount	Year-to-date amount
SALES		
Sales – Main St. Store	$ 9,999,999.99	$ 9,999,999.99
Sales – Yard	9,999,999.99	9,999,999.99
Sales – Services	9,999,999.99	9,999,999.99
Total product sales	$ 9,999,999.99	$ 9,999,999.99
Income – Mower Repair	$ 9,999,999.99	$ 9,999,999.99
Income – Blower Repair	9,999,999.99	9,999,999.99
Income – Rentals	9,999,999.99	9,999,999.99
Non–inventory item	9,999,999.99	9,999,999.99
Labor	9,999,999.99	9,999,999.99
Travel	9,999,999.99	9,999,999.99
Freight	9,999,999.99	9,999,999.99
Rental and Repair Income	$ 9,999,999.99	$ 9,999,999.99
Sales discounts	$ 9,999,999.99	$ 9,999,999.99
Sales retrns & allowances	9,999,999.99	9,999,999.99
Finance charges	9,999,999.99	9,999,999.99
Other income	9,999,999.99	9,999,999.99
Total misc & other sales	$ 9,999,999.99	$ 9,999,999.99
	========	========
TOTAL SALES	$ 9,999,999.99	$ 9,999,999.99
COST OF GOODS SOLD		
Cost of goods sold	$ 9,999,999.99	$ 9,999,999.99
Inventory adjustments	9,999,999.99	9,999,999.99
Purchase discounts	9,999,999.99	9,999,999.99
Cost corrections	9,999,999.99	9,999,999.99

	========	========
TOTAL COST OF GOODS SOLD	$ 9,999,999.99	$ 9,999,999.99
GROSS PROFIT ON SALES	$ 9,999,999.99	$ 9,999,999.99
OPERATING EXPENSES		
Wage Account	$ 9,999,999.99	$ 9,999,999.99
Advertising	9,999,999.99	9,999,999.99
Auto and truck	9,999,999.99	9,999,999.99
Bad debt expense	9,999,999.99	9,999,999.99
Bank charges and fees	9,999,999.99	9,999,999.99
Cash over or short	9,999,999.99	9,999,999.99
Charitable contributions	9,999,999.99	9,999,999.99
Commissions – Store	9,999,999.99	9,999,999.99
Commissions – Repair	9,999,999.99	9,999,999.99
Depreciation	9,999,999.99	9,999,999.99
Insurance	9,999,999.99	9,999,999.99
Interest	9,999,999.99	9,999,999.99
Legal & accounting fees	9,999,999.99	9,999,999.99
Licenses and fees	9,999,999.99	9,999,999.99
Merchant credit card fees	9,999,999.99	9,999,999.99
Miscellaneous	9,999,999.99	9,999,999.99
Office expense	9,999,999.99	9,999,999.99
Rents & utilities	9,999,999.99	9,999,999.99
Repairs and maintenance	9,999,999.99	9,999,999.99
Salaries – administrative	9,999,999.99	9,999,999.99
Salaries – floor sales	9,999,999.99	9,999,999.99
Salaries & Wage exp–Elm	9,999,999.99	9,999,999.99
Salaries – bonuses	9,999,999.99	9,999,999.99
Sales and promotions exp	9,999,999.99	9,999,999.99
Supplies	9,999,999.99	9,999,999.99
Taxes – other	9,999,999.99	9,999,999.99
Taxes – payroll	9,999,999.99	9,999,999.99
Taxes – sales tax	9,999,999.99	9,999,999.99
Telephone	9,999,999.99	9,999,999.99
Telephone exp.	9,999,999.99	9,999,999.99
Travel & entertainment	9,999,999.99	9,999,999.99
	========	========
TOTAL OPERATING EXPENSES	$ 9,999,999.99	$ 9,999,999.99

NON–OPERATING INCOME AND EXPENSES

Interest income	$ 9,999,999.99	$ 9,999,999.99
Gain/loss sale of assets	9,999,999.99	9,999,999.99
Transfer/suspense Account	9,999,999.99	9,999,999.99
	--------	--------
Other income	$ 9,999,999.99	$ 9,999,999.99
	========	========
NET INCOME BEFORE TAXES	$ 9,999,999.99	$ 9,999,999.99
Taxes – federal income	$ 9,999,999.99	$ 9,999,999.99
Taxes – state income	9,999,999.99	9,999,999.99
	--------	--------
Federal & state income tax	$ 9,999,999.99	$ 9,999,999.99
NET INCOME	$ 9,999,999.99	$ 9,999,999.99
	========	========

-- End of report --

Acme Hardware Co.

BALANCE SHEET

As of 06/30/97

ASSETS				
CURRENT ASSETS				
Checking #1 – Payables	$	41,590.39		
Checking #2 – Payroll		9,065.84		
Cash			$	50,656.23
Accts Receivable – Trade	$	2,052.55		
Inventory		4,117.48		

TOTAL CURRENT ASSETS			$	56,826.26
PROPERTY AND EQUIPMENT				
Furniture and fixtures	$	3,200.00		
Office equipment		5,000.00		
Automobiles and trucks		15,000.00		
Total property and equipment			$	23,200.00
Accum depr – furn & fixt	$	(90.00)		
Accum depr – office equip		(110.00)		
Accum depr – auto & truck		(300.00)		
Total accum depreciation			$	(500.00)

NET FIXED ASSETS			$	22,700.00
OTHER ASSETS				

TOTAL OTHER ASSETS			$	.00
TOTAL ASSETS			$	79,526.26
				========

LIABILITIES AND STOCKHOLDERS' EQUITY

CURRENT LIABILITIES

Accounts Payable – Trade	$	573.75		
Fed income tax withheld		1,737.79		
Emp Social Sec Payable		561.72		
Emp Medicare Payable		131.37		
Empr Social Sec Payable		561.72		
Empr Medicare Payable		131.37		
Accrued fed unemp tax		72.48		
State income tax withheld		640.60		
Other state tax withheld		54.36		
Accrued state unemp tax		81.54		
Accrued state sales tax		638.94		
Notes and loans payable		31,674.85		

TOTAL CURRENT LIABILITIES			$	36,860.49
LONG TERM DEBT				50,000.00
				========
TOTAL LIABILITIES			$	86,860.49
STOCKHOLDERS' EQUITY				
Current year income		(7,334.23)		

TOTAL STOCKHOLDERS' EQUITY			$	(7,334.23)

TOTAL LIAB AND EQUITY			$	79,526.26
				========

Acme Hardware Co.
INCOME STATEMENT

For the period: 06/01/97 to 06/30/97

	Current-period Amount	Year-to-date Amount
SALES		
Sales - Main St. Store	$ 6,426.45	$ 6,426.45
Sales - Yard	2,701.20	2,701.20
Total product sales	$ 9,127.65	$ 9,127.65
Rental and Repair Income	$ .00	$ .00
Sales discounts	$ (120.30)	$ (120.30)
Other income	496.65	496.65
Total misc & other sales	$ 376.35	$ 376.35
	=======	=======
TOTAL SALES	$ 9,504.00	$ 9,504.00
COST OF GOODS SOLD		
Cost of goods sold	$ 4,966.17	$ 4,966.17
Inventory adjustments	(35.05)	(35.05)
	=======	=======
TOTAL COST OF GOODS SOLD	$ 4,931.12	$ 4,931.12
GROSS PROFIT ON SALES	$ 4,572.88	$ 4,572.88
OPERATING EXPENSES		
Depreciation	$ 500.00	$ 500.00
Office expense	250.00	250.00
Rents & utilities	1,000.00	1,000.00
Salaries - administrative	5,000.00	5,000.00
Salaries - floor sales	1,500.00	1,500.00
Salaries & Wage exp-Elm	2,560.00	2,560.00
Taxes - payroll	847.11	847.11
Telephone	250.00	250.00
	=======	=======
TOTAL OPERATING EXPENSES	$ 11,907.11	$ 11,907.11

NON–OPERATING INCOME AND EXPENSES

	-------	-------
Other income	$ .00	$ .00
	=======	=======
NET INCOME BEFORE TAXES	$ (7,334.23)	$ (7,334.23)
	-------	-------
Federal & state income tax	$ .00	$ .00
NET INCOME	$ (7,334.23)	$ (7,334.23)
	=======	=======

Practice Set 13 – ANALYZE SALES TAX DATA AND DISPLAY CHART OF ACCOUNTS USING LOTUS 1–2–3 SPREADSHEETS

Introduction

In this practice set, you are asked to follow the same procedure as described in the text for using Lotus 1–2–3 to import data from PAS. You are asked to:

- ➡ export sales tax data from PAS
- ➡ import sales tax data into Lotus 1–2–3
- ➡ parse the data and modify it to produce a sales tax report
- ➡ print the report using Lotus 1–2–3

Print the Sales Tax Report

Before using Lotus, move to Sales Invoicing and select Print Sales Tax Report. Print the report for all tax codes, all dates, and all sales detail. Do not purge the file at this time.

Export Data from PAS

Exit PAS and move to the PAS top–level directory. Type PASFU to access the utilities programs. Make the following selections:

* Sales Invoicing
* Export a file
* Sales tax history file
* The drive where you store Lotus 1–2–3 files (e.g., A, B, C, D and so forth).
* "First" and "last" file key

What is the name of the file you created and saved?

Import Data into Lotus 1–2–3

Switch over to Lotus 1–2–3, and select **/ File Import Text.** TYPE the name of the file you exported above. Once imported, SAVE this file and name it TAX_EXP.

Parse the File

The difficult part lies in parsing the file. Examine the records as they now appear and answer the following:

What information is placed in the first two data columns (not the Lotus column, but the data itself)?
After a space, what information is stored in the next six data columns?
What do the numbers 500 to 504 signify?
What does the letter S signify?

Next, go ahead and parse the file, following the format and the instructions in the text. Use the values V, D, S and L.

* Input the parsed file from range A1..A6.
* Output the new file to range A10..K23.
* Make column width changes as needed.
* Print the data file you started with, along with the parsed file.
* Save the revised file, again as TAX_EXP.

Complete the Lotus 1–2–3 Sales Tax Analysis Statement

Format the Sales Tax Report as you like, and print it.

Other Things to Explore

1. Move back to PAS and select Sales Invoicing followed by Print Sales Tax Report. This time, print and purge the file. After the purge is complete, exit PAS and export the TAXHIS file.

   Explain what happens.
   What is the value of Lotus 1–2–3 in this situation?

2. Move back to PASFU, export YCHART from the G/L, and import YCHART.EXP into Lotus 1–2–3. Parse this file, and construct a report using this account information. Print this report and save the file, naming it ACCOUNTS.

   Of what value is this type of spreadsheet to management?

This completes Practice Set 13.

Date: 06/30/97 Time: 14:14:50 Acme Hardware Co. Report #0199 Page 0001

SALES TAX REPORT

Tax code: All

Starting date: "Earliest"
Ending date: "Latest"

Code	Description	Sale-amt	Taxable-amt	Non-txbl-amt	Sales-tax
MI	Mich. tax	9,052.34	8,006.85	485.00	560.49

Doc-#	Doc-type	Doc-date	Customer-name	Sale-amt	Txbl-amt	Non-txbl	Sls-tax
500	Sale	06/03/97	Allied Plumbing Co.	1,200.39	1,079.80	45.00	75.59
501	Sale	06/03/97	Ariel Enterprises	844.30	653.55	145.00	45.75
502	Sale	06/03/97	Elliott Enterprises	567.84	451.25	85.00	31.59
503	Sale	06/03/97	Holcomb Industrial Supply	5,170.26	4,696.50	145.00	328.76
504	Sale	06/03/97	Webber Landscaping	1,269.55	1,125.75	65.00	78.80

1 tax codes printed

-- End of report --

```
   A       B       C       D       E       F       G       H
1  L>>D>>>>>V>>>>>S>>L>>>>>>>>>>>>>>>>>>>>>>>>SV>>>>>>>SV>>>>>>>SV>>>>>>>SV>>>>>>S
2  MI 970603000500000Allied Plumbing Co.        S00120039+00107980+00004500+0007559+
3  MI 970603000501000Ariel Enterprises          S00084430+00065355+00014500+0004575+
4  MI 970603000502000Elliott Enterprises        S00056784+00045125+00008500+0003159+
5  MI 970603000503000Holcomb Industrial SupplyS00517026+00469650+00014500+0032876+
6  MI 970603000504000Webber Landscaping         S00126955+00112575+00006500+0007880+
```

MI	970603	500	Allied Plumbing Co.	120039	107980	4500	7559
MI	970603	501	Ariel Enterprises	84430	65355	14500	4575
MI	970603	502	Elliott Enterprises	56784	45125	8500	3159
MI	970603	503	Holcomb Industrial Supply	517026	469650	14500	32876
MI	970603	504	Webber Landscaping	126955	112575	6500	7880

ACME HARDWARE COMPANY
SALES TAX SUMMARY
June, 1997

Tax Code	Doc Date (yymmdd)	Doc #	Customer Name	Sale Amount	Taxable	Non–Taxable	Sales Tax
State							
MI	970603	500	Allied Plumbing Co.	1,200.39	1,079.80	45.00	75.59
MI	970603	501	Ariel Enterprises	844.30	653.55	145.00	45.75
MI	970603	502	Elliott Enterprises	567.84	451.25	85.00	31.59
MI	970603	503	Holcomb Industrial Supply	5,170.26	4,696.50	145.00	328.76
MI	970603	504	Webber Landscaping	1,269.55	1,125.75	65.00	78.80
			TOTALS	9,052.34	8,006.85	485.00	560.49

Date: 06/30/97 Time: 15:11:29 Acme Hardware Co. Report #0200 Page 0001

SALES TAX REPORT

Tax code: All

Starting date: "Earliest"
Ending date: "Latest"
Printed records are being purged

Code	Description	Sale-amt	Taxable-amt	Non-txbl-amt	Sales-tax
MI	Mich. tax	9,052.34	8,006.85	485.00	560.49

Doc-#	Doc-type	Doc-date	Customer-name	Sale-amt	Txbl-amt	Non-txbl	Sls-tax
500	Sale	06/03/97	Allied Plumbing Co.	1,200.39	1,079.80	45.00	75.59
501	Sale	06/03/97	Ariel Enterprises	844.30	653.55	145.00	45.75
502	Sale	06/03/97	Elliott Enterprises	567.84	451.25	85.00	31.59
503	Sale	06/03/97	Holcomb Industrial Supply	5,170.26	4,696.50	145.00	328.76
504	Sale	06/03/97	Webber Landscaping	1,269.55	1,125.75	65.00	78.80

1 tax codes printed

-- End of report --

Date: 06/30/97 Acme Hardware Co. Page 1
Time: 5:00 PM

CHART OF ACCOUNTS

Account Code	Description	Account Code	Description
1010–000	Checking #1 – Payables	2430–000	Accrued state sales tax
1020–000	Checking #2 – Payroll	2450–000	Accrued fed unemp tax
1040–000	Credit card deposits	2460–000	Accrued state unemp tax
1050–000	Petty cash	2510–000	Deposits received
1100–000	Accts Receivable – Trade	2520–000	Notes and loans payable
1110–000	Accts Recvble – Employee	2530–000	Long term debt
1200–000	Notes receivable	3000–000	Common stock
1210–000	Interest receivable	3100–000	Paid in capital
1300–000	Prepaid expenses	3200–000	Treasury stock
1400–000	Inventory	3300–000	Retained earnings
1410–000	Services	4000–000	Sales – Main St. Store
1600–000	Furniture and fixtures	4010–000	Sales – Yard
1610–000	Office equipment	4020–000	Sales – Services
1620–000	Automobiles and trucks	4025–000	Income – Mower Repair
1630–000	Building	4026–000	Income – Blower Repair
1640–000	Leasehold improvements	4030–000	Income – Rentals
1650–000	Land	4031–000	Non–inventory item
1700–000	Accum depr – furn & fixt	4032–000	Labor
1710–000	Accum depr – office equip	4033–000	Travel
1720–000	Accum depr – auto & truck	4035–000	Freight
1730–000	Accum depr – building	4510–000	Sales discounts
1800–000	Deposits	4520–000	Sales retrns & allowances
1810–000	Investments	4910–000	Finance charges
1910–000	Other intangibles	4920–000	Freight charges
2005–000	Uninvoiced Receivings	4930–000	Miscellaneous charges
2025–000	Medical Ins. Deduct	4940–000	Deposits forfeited
2100–000	Accounts Payable – Trade	4950–000	Other misc income
2110–000	Notes Payable – Main St.	5010–000	Cost of goods sold
2200–000	Accrued expenses	5020–000	Inventory adjustments
2310–000	Fed income tax withheld	5030–000	Purchase discounts
2320–000	EIC advances paid	5040–000	Cost corrections
2330–000	Emp Social Sec Payable	6000–000	Wage Account
2335–000	Emp Medicare Payable	6010–000	Advertising
2340–000	Empr Social Sec Payable	6020–000	Auto and truck
2345–000	Empr Medicare Payable	6030–000	Bad debt expense
2350–000	State income tax withheld	6040–000	Bank charges and fees
2360–000	Other state tax withheld	6050–000	Cash over or short
2370–000	Local income tax withheld	6060–000	Charitable contributions
2380–000	Pension contrib withheld	6070–000	Commissions – Store
2390–000	Charity contrib withheld	6070–000	Commissions – Repair
2410–000	Accrued fed income tax	6080–000	Depreciation
2420–000	Accrued state income tax	6090–000	Insurance

Date: 06/30/97 Acme Hardware Co. Page 2
Time: 5:00 PM

CHART OF ACCOUNTS

Account Code	Description
6100–000	Interest
6110–000	Legal & accounting fees
6120–000	Licenses and fees
6130–000	Merchant credit card fees
6140–000	Miscellaneous
6150–000	Office expense
6160–000	Rents & utilities
6170–000	Repairs and maintenance
6180–000	Salaries – administrative
6190–000	Salaries – floor sales
6200–000	Salaries & Wage exp–Elm
6210–000	Salaries – bonuses
6220–000	Sales and promotions exp
6230–000	Supplies
6240–000	Taxes – other
6250–000	Taxes – payroll
6260–000	Taxes – sales tax
6270–000	Telephone
6280–000	Travel & entertainment
7110–000	Taxes – federal income
7120–000	Taxes – state income
8200–000	Telephone exp.
9110–000	Interest income
9120–000	Gain/loss sale of assets
9999–000	Transfer/suspense Account

Practice Set 14 – ANALYZE CHECKBOOK INFORMATION AND REVIEW VENDOR TRANSACTIONS USING LOTUS 1–2–3 SPREADSHEETS

Introduction

For this second spreadsheet practice set, you are asked to follow the same procedure as described in the text for using Lotus 1–2–3 to import and parse information from PAS. You are asked to:

- ➡ export checkbook data from PAS
- ➡ import checkbook data into Lotus 1–2–3
- ➡ parse the data and modify it to produce a cash flow report
- ➡ print the report using Lotus 1–2–3

Export Data from PAS

Change to the PAS top–level directory and type PASFU to access the utilities programs. Make the following selections:

* Check Reconciliation
* Export a file
* Checkbook file
* The drive where you normally store Lotus 1–2–3 files (e.g., A, B, C, D and so forth).
* "First" and "last" file key

What is the name of the file you created and saved?

Import Data into Lotus 1–2–3

Switch over to Lotus 1–2–3, and select **/ File Import Text.** TYPE the name of the file you exported above. Once imported, SAVE this file and name it CASH_EXP.

Parse the File

Like the last practice set, the difficult part lies in parsing the file. Examine the records as they now appear and answer the following:

What information is placed in the first data column (not the Lotus column, but the data itself)?
What information is stored in the next six data columns?
Assuming that filler is placed in data columns 8 and 9, what information is placed in data columns 10 to 13?
Assuming that filler is placed in data columns 14 and 16, what do the letters B, C, and R mean in column 17?
What are the contents of the remaining three fields in this file?

Next, go ahead and parse the file, using the values V, D, S and L.

* Input the parsed file from range A1..A12.
* Output the new file to range A14..K26.
* Make column–width changes as needed.
* Print the data file you started with, along with the parsed file.
* Save the revised file, again as CASH_EXP.

Complete the Lotus 1–2–3 Cash Flow Statement

Format the Cash Flow Report as you like, and print it.

Other Things to Explore

1. Move back to PAS and display the checkbook for checking accounts 1 and 2.

   What new information is provided by the Lotus 1–2–3 report that is NOT provided by the display of the check register?
   How might you revise the Lotus 1–2–3 report prepared for this practice set to make it even more valuable to management?

2. Move back to PASFU and export the file VENACT (which stands for Vendor accounts). Import it into Lotus 1–2–3 and save the new file with the name VENDOR. Create and print a report using this vendor information.

   Why would this type of report be important to the management of a company?

This completes Practice Set 14.

```
   A         B         C         D         E         F         G         H
1  LD>>>>>V>>>>>S>>LL>>>>>>>>>>>>>>>>>>>>>>>>V>>>>>>>>SD>>>>>
2  1000000000000000BBalance forward         005000000+000000
3  1970613000000000CDeposit                 000809039+970625
4  1970615002100000RBitznbytes Computer     000025000-970625
5  1970615002101000RJones Property Management000100000-970625
6  1970615002102000RNorthWestern Bell       000025000-970625
7  1970625002103000RJune Payroll            001500000-000000
8  2970615003001000RHermann Acme            000297110-000000
9  2970615003002000REarnest Wantabee        000087321-000000
10 2970615003003000RPalmer, Edward W.       000117193-000000
11 2970615003004000RSara Sweetheart         000091792-000000
12 2970625000000000CDeposit                 001500000-000000
```

1	000000	0000	B	Balance forward	5000000	000000
1	970613	0000	C	Deposit	809039	970625
1	970615	2100	R	Bitznbytes Computer	25000	970625
1	970615	2101	R	Jones Property Management	100000	970625
1	970615	2102	R	NorthWestern Bell	25000	970625
1	970625	2103	R	June Payroll	1500000	000000
2	970615	3001	R	Hermann Acme	297110	000000
2	970615	3002	R	Earnest Wantabee	87321	000000
2	970615	3003	R	Palmer, Edward W.	117193	000000
2	970615	3004	R	Sara Sweetheart	91792	000000
2	970625	0000	C	Deposit	1500000	000000

ACME HARDWARE COMPANY
CASH FLOW STATEMENT
June, 1997

BEGINNING CASH BALANCE:			$50,000.00
Cash inflows:			
Cash receivables		$ 8,090.39	
TOTAL INFLOWS:		8,090.39	
Cash Outflows:			
Equipment lease – Bitznbytes Computer		250.00	
Property lease – Jones Property Management		1,000.00	
Payment on payables – NorthWestern Bell		250.00	
Payroll – Hermann Acme	2,971.10		
– Earnest Wantabee	873.21		
– Palmer, Edward W.	1,171.93		
– Sara Sweetheart	917.92		
Total Payroll		5,934.16	
TOTAL OUTFLOWS:		7,434.16	
Change in cash from current activities:		656.23	
ENDING CASH BALANCE:			$50,656.23

ACME HARDWARE COMPANY
VENDOR TRANSACTION ACTIVITY
June, 1997

Transaction Date	Document Number	Description	Amount
Purchases			
6/01/97	69421	ORD 102 (Wire)	125.00
6/01/97	66554	ORD 107 (Doors)	160.00
6/01/97	66503	ORD 100 (Hardware)	1,374.85
6/01/97	66715	ORD 101 (Gauges)	4,860.00
6/01/97	67189	ORD 104 (Cable, brackets)	760.00
6/01/97	11510	ORD 105 (C. Blocks)	495.00
6/01/97	11924	ORD 103 (Plywood)	700.00

		Total Purchases	8,474.85
Repairs			
6/15/97	345432	Repair shop	498.75
6/15/97	3434333	Repair shop	75.00

		Total Repairs	573.75
Services			
6/15/97	2102	May phone bill	250.00

		Total Services	250.00
Leases			
6/15/97	2101	Lease of property	1,000.00
6/15/97	2100	Lease of equipment	250.00

		Total Leases	1,250.00
		TOTAL VENDOR TRANSACTIONS	10,548.60
			=======

REFERENCE MATERIAL

Setup Functions

Menu Selections

1. **Maintain company data**

   Contains general information about your company, such as company name, address and printer information.

2. **Maintain chart of accounts**

   Used to add, change, delete and print a list of accounts.

3. **Maintain accounting control data**

   Contains information regarding default account numbers, payroll data and check–printing data.

4. **Maintain accounting periods**

   Used to maintain accounting periods and to define accounting year and current period.

5. **Maintain invoicing control data**

   Use this function to add and change control information used for Sales Invoicing functions and initial set–up for Accounts Receivable and Inventory Management.

Setup Functions

Maintain Company Data

1. **Company name (long)**

   Enter the name you want to print at the top of all reports. You are allowed up to 50 characters, including spaces and punctuation. The name will be automatically centered at the top of all reports.

2. **Company name (short)**

   Enter the name you want to appear in the upper right–hand corner of the screen. You are allowed up to 30 characters, including spaces and punctuation. The name will be automatically aligned to the right (right–justified) on all video screens.

3–5. **Address lines 1, 2, 3**

   Enter up to three lines for your company address, with up to 30 characters on each line. (You may skip over one or more lines of the address by pressing ENTER.) This address may be printed on statements, invoices and A/P checks if you choose to do so.

6. **Phone Number**

   Enter your phone number, including area code. You are allowed up to 12 characters. This phone number prints on A/R statements. The usual format is xxx–xxx–xxxx.

7. **Are G/L profit centers used?**

   Answer Y to maintain accounting information by profit center. If you answer Y, you will have two–part G/L account numbers which consist of up to 4 digits for the first part and 3 digits in the second part, in the format 9999–999. The second 3 digits are the "profit center" or "sub–account".

   If you answer N, you will have one–part G/L account numbers which can be up to 4 digits long.

8. **Allow protected changes?**

   Some screens of your software contain information that is normally protected from changes, such as historical data. If you want to be able to access and change these fields, answerY; otherwise, press ENTER for N. In some places where the data is essential to an audit trail or otherwise, change is not allowed, even if you answer Y.

Setup Functions

Maintain Company Data

9. **Use passwords?**

   This setting turns on or shuts off the use of passwords. NOTE: A common mistake with setting up company information is to answer Y to passwords before you or your instructor have set them up. Be sure you have already set up passwords before you enter Y in this field. If passwords are not set up and you answer Y to passwords, you will be stopped from going into the software because you will not have a password to enter.

10. **Printer**

    Enter the name of the printer (device name) to be used, or press F1 to default to the standard printer (LPT1).

11. **Compressed?**

    Enter Y for compressed print (8.5" wide carriage). Answer N for full-sized print (14" carriage). If you answer Y for compressed print, you must also enter a printer type below.

12. **Printer type**

    If you answered Y for compressed print above, enter the number of the printer type from the list displayed on the screen. NOTE: If you answered Y to compressed print, and the printer you have is not listed on the screen, try choosing "Epson" or "IBM compatible". Many printers on the market emulate one of these types of printers.

Setup Functions

Maintain Chart of Accounts – Add Accounts

1. **Account Number**

This is the number of the G/L account. Enter the main account number, up to 4 digits. Then, if you specified in the Company file that you use profit centers, enter the 3–digit sub–account number. You can press ENTER to default to sub–account 000.

2. **Description**

Enter the description of the G/L account, up to 25 characters.

3. **Fin statement type**

Enter the financial statement type, a 1–character code, as follows:

B = applies to balance sheet. [Asset, liability, and equity (or capital) accounts should be coded "B".]

P = applies to profit and loss (or income) statement. (Revenue, cost of goods and expense accounts should be coded "P".)

4. **Paren control code**

This stands for "parentheses control code". It determines when parentheses are printed on financial statements.

Most amounts printed on financial statements are not enclosed in parentheses. However, when an account has a balance which is the opposite of what is normally expected, that amount is usually enclosed in parentheses when it appears on a financial statement.

For example, revenue accounts normally have credit balances, and such amounts are shown on financial statements without parentheses. However, if a particular revenue account has a debit balance (which means revenue less than zero), that amount is enclosed in parentheses.

The two valid entries for this code are:

D = Enclose when the amount is a debit.

C = Enclose when the amount is a credit.

Setup Functions

Maintain Chart of Accounts – Add Accounts

5. **Compression code**

The G/L transactions which accumulate as the year goes by can take up quite a bit of disk space. This function compresses those transactions. ("Compress" means "to make small".)

Enter the 1–character compression code. Allowed entries are:

N = Do not compress transactions for this G/L account.

D = Compress transactions for this G/L account by individual date. The result is a single transaction for each date on which there is any activity for this G/L account.

P = Compress transactions for this G/L account by accounting period. The result is a single transaction for each period in which there is any activity for this G/L account.

When you are adding an account, you can use the UP ARROW to go back to a previous field to change it, then use the DOWN ARROW to move forward to the field you were entering.

After you enter the last field on the screen, "FIELD NUMBER TO CHANGE?" appears. If the data on the screen is correct, press ENTER and the addition is complete. Otherwise, use the ARROWs or enter the number of the field to make changes. Then add another account, using the above procedure, or return to the previous menu by pressing TAB or END.

NOTE: You cannot add an account with a number exactly the same as an account number already on file. If you try to do this, the existing account is displayed along with "FIELD NUMBER TO CHANGE?". If this occurs, press ENTER, then select a different account number to use for the account you want to add.

Setup Functions

Maintain Chart of Accounts – Change Accounts

The Change Accounts function allows you to review and change data in accounts that were entered in Add Accounts.

From the Maintain Chart of Accounts menu, type 2. A screen appears for entry of the number of the account that you want to change or inquire into.

Enter the number, or use F1 to display each account in order. If you enter an account number which is not on file, you see "ACCOUNT NOT ON FILE". Press ENTER to try again with another account number.

Make any desired changes by using the ARROW keys or entering the number of the field you want to change, then entering the new data. Press ENTER at "FIELD NUMBER TO CHANGE?" to save the changes. You can also press F1 to save the changes and display the next account.

When you are through with this function, press END at the "first" field. The Maintain Chart of Accounts menu reappears.

Maintain Chart of Accounts – Delete Accounts

From the Maintain Chart of Accounts menu, type 3. A screen appears for entry of the number of the account that you want to delete. Enter the number, or use F1 to display each account in order.

In answer to "OK TO DELETE ACCOUNT?", make the deletion by typing Y, or type N to bring up an empty screen for entry of another account to delete. You can also press F1 to see the next account without deleting the current account.

When you are through with this function, press END. The Maintain Chart of Accounts menu reappears.

Setup Functions

Maintain Accounting Control Data – Screen 1 of 3

1. **Accts receivable acct #**

   Enter the G/L account used to record A/R transactions. The A/R account will be debited (increased) when sales are made on account, and credited (decreased) when payments are made on account.

2. **Discount allowance acct #**

   Enter the G/L account used to record sales discounts given to customers. The discount allowance account is a contra sales account. When a customer makes an early payment, the discount allowance account will get debited.

3. **Accts payable acct #**

   Enter the G/L account used to record A/P transactions. The A/P account will be credited (increased) when invoices from vendors are posted, and debited (decreased) when payments are made to vendors.

4. **Discounts taken acct #**

   Enter the G/L account used to record purchase discounts taken from vendors. The discounts taken account is credited when early payments are made to vendors.

5. **Check acct transfer acct #**

   Enter the G/L account used to record transfers of funds between checking accounts. The check account transfer account is a suspense account used when transferring funds.

6. **Check acct adjustment acct #**

   Enter the G/L account used to record checking account adjustments, such as bank charges. This is a default account, and a different account number can be entered for each adjustment transaction, if necessary.

7. **Summarize G/L distributions?**

   Answer N to keep full transaction detail in the General Ledger. Otherwise, answer Y. If you answer Y, a single G/L entry is created to summarize each batch of A/R, A/P, Payroll activity, or C/R adjustments instead of several G/L entries. NOTE: G/L distributions created by I/M or S/I are always summarized and are not affected by what you enter for this field. If you answer N, individual entries are created, and cause the size of one of your data files stored on hard disk to increase.

Setup Functions

Maintain Accounting Control Data – Screen 1 of 3

8. **Print company name on stmts?**

   If you are using statements on which your company name and address are preprinted, answer N; otherwise, answer Y to print your company name and address on top of statements.

9. **Default profit center**

   You can enter this field only if you have specified that G/L profit centers are used in the Maintain Company Data function.

   Enter the profit center to be used as a default for Sales Invoicing, Inventory Management and Accounts Receivable processing. Enter up to 3 digits, or press ENTER for profit center 000.

> NOTE: In field numbers 10 through 13 below, the account numbers which you enter are default accounts. Different account numbers can be entered for each item (or adjustment transaction) if necessary. If you are using profit centers, enter only the first part of the G/L account number in these fields. A profit center will be added to the end of the account numbers specified below at posting time.

10. **Default sales acct #**

    Enter the G/L account most frequently used to record sales transactions.

11. **Default cost of goods acct #**

    Enter the G/L account most frequently used to record the cost of the items you sell.

12. **Default returns acct #**

    Enter the G/L account most frequently used to record returns. This can be the same as Default Sales Acct # if you do not record returns separately from sales.

13. **Default adjustment acct #**

    Enter the G/L account most frequently used to record adjustments to your inventory.

Setup Functions

Maintain Accounting Control Data – Screen 1 of 3

NOTE: In the next three "Acct #" fields, if you are using profit centers, enter a 4–digit main account number and a 3–digit sub–account number.

14. Default inventory acct #

Enter the G/L account used to record the value of your inventory items. Your entry should be a balance sheet inventory account.

15. Uninvoiced receivings acct #

Enter the G/L account used to record inventory receipts which have not yet been invoiced. This account will automatically be credited for inventory receivings transactions. Your entry should be a balance sheet liability account, or a "clearing" account.

16. Cost correction acct #

Enter the G/L account used to record cost corrections. Cost corrections occur if an inventory receiving transaction is processed for an item with a negative quantity on hand.

17. Price to 3 decimal places?

Answer Y to enter inventory item prices with 3 decimal places, and for all prices to display and print with 3 decimal places (e.g., $1.355). Answer N for prices to be entered, displayed and printed with 2 decimal places (e.g., $1.36).

18. Stock to 3 decimal places?

Answer Y to enter inventory quantities with 3 decimal places, and for all quantities to display and print with 3 decimal places. Answer N for quantities to be entered, displayed and printed as whole numbers only.

NOTE: In field numbers 17 and 18, if you change from Y to N after you have used the software, decimal figures will continue to be used by the software, even though they do not appear on the screen or reports.

Setup Functions

Maintain Accounting Control Data – Screen 2 of 3

19. Employer name

Enter the employer name, up to 25 characters. This name (and the address entered below) will be printed on the year–end W–2 forms and the Quarterly Payroll Report.

20–22. Employer name

Enter up to three lines for your company address, with up to 25 characters per address line.

23–27. Hours in day/ in week/ in bi–week/ in semi–mon/ in month

This information is used to calculate hourly rates of pay and to track the number of hours salaried employees work. Use the number of hours in the standard work unit, or press F1 for the default.

Day	This amount is used in payroll calculations. The default is 8.00 hours.
Week	The default is 5 times the "hours in day" figure.
Bi–week	The default is 2 times the "hours in week" figure.
Semi–mon	The default is "hours in week" multiplied by 52 and divided by 24.
Month	The default is "hours in week" multiplied by 52 and divided by 12.

28–32. Yearly days/ weeks/ bi–weeks/ semi–mons/ months

Enter the number of working units in a year, or press F1 for the default. This data is used to calculate payroll taxes based on the IRS and state annual withholding tax tables.

Days	The default is 260 days.
Weeks	The default is 52.
Bi–weeks	The default is 26.
Semi–mons	The default is 24.
Months	The default is 12.

Setup Functions

Maintain Accounting Control Data – Screen 2 of 3

33. Overtime pay factor

Enter the overtime pay factor (up to 4 digits including 3 decimal places). This factor is the number by which the employee's regular pay rate is multiplied to compute the overtime pay rate.

34. Special pay factor

Enter the special pay factor (up to 4 digits including 3 decimal places). This factor is the number by which the employee's regular pay rate is multiplied to compute the special pay rate.

35. Distribute wages?

The capability of distributing payroll amounts to G/L accounts remains part of the PAS package no matter what your answer is to this question. Your entry here controls whether or not MANUAL distributions to G/L are made for an employee's regular pay.

Enter a one–letter code as follows:

N = Never manually distribute
A = Always manually distribute
S = Selectively manually distribute

If you answer N, all employee wages for regular hours or salary, overtime hours and special hours will be distributed automatically to the wage account specified for each employee in the Employee file.

If you answer A, you will be asked in both the Process Payroll Time Transactions function and the Process Manual Payroll Transactions function to manually distribute employee regular pay, overtime pay and special pay to the G/L accounts that you specify at that time.

If you answer S, you will be asked to enter manual G/L distributions only for employees specifically designated for manual distribution in the Employee file.

36. Use meals and tips?

Answer Y if either meals (or any non–cash form of compensation) or tips are received by employees.

Setup Functions

Maintain Accounting Control Data – Screen 3 of 3

37. Print A/P check # on

The check number can be printed on the check, on the stub or on both. Enter C for check, S for stub, or B for both check and stub.

38. Print comp name on A/P checks?

Answer Y to print your company name on A/P checks. Answer N to not print it.

39. Print PR check # on

The check number can be printed on the check, on the stub or on both. Enter C for check, S for stub, or B for both check and stub.

40. Print comp name on PR checks?

Answer Y to print your company name on PR checks. Answer N to not print it.

41–43. Checking accounts #1, #2, #3

Up to three checking accounts may be defined. You must make entries to define at least checking account #1. If you are defining two checking accounts, define #1 and #2, leaving #3 undefined.

If you have more than one checking account, define checking account #1 as your main account (the one into which you deposit most of your cash receipts). If you have a special checking account you use mostly for Payroll, define that as checking account #2.

For each checking account you want to use, enter the data as follows:

- ➡ Enter the description of the account, up to 25 characters.
- ➡ Enter the number of the bank account (as assigned by your bank), up to 14 characters. This is NOT a G/L account number. It is the specific account number of this checking account.
- ➡ Enter your G/L account used to record the transactions for this checking account.

44. Payroll checking account

Enter the number of the checking account above which you use for payroll. Enter 1 digit: either checking account 1, 2 or 3.

Setup Functions

Maintain Accounting Control Data – Screen 3 of 3

45. Last PR check # used

Enter the check number of the last payroll check you have used, up to 6 digits.

46. Current payroll year

Enter the current year for which payroll checks are being cut. For example, enter 99 for 1999. This field will be automatically updated to the new year when you run Close Payroll For Calendar Year from the Payroll menu.

47. Payroll is in setup mode?

When first installing PAS, answer Y. After you have completed setting up Payroll, set this field to N.

This field is provided so that you can properly enter information into PAS regarding the amounts you have paid to each employee this calendar year PRIOR to installing the software.

Maintain Accounting Periods

1–13. Accounting periods

Up to 13 accounting periods may be defined. The accounting year must be exactly 365 days long (366 for a leap year).

14. Current period number

The current period number verifies that transaction dates are within the current period when entering general journal transactions. The software gives you a "warning" if you enter a date outside of the current period.

Setup Functions

Maintain Invoicing Control Data – Screen 1 of 2

1. **Next bill ref #**

   Enter a bill reference number, up to 6 digits. This is the number that will be assigned to the next invoice ADDED. This is NOT the invoice number, but is your own internal reference. Each time a new invoice is added, this number is incremented by 1 automatically.

2. **Next invoice #**

   Enter an invoice number, up to 6 digits. This is the number that will be assigned to the next invoice PRINTED. Each time a new invoice is added, this number is incremented by 1 automatically.

3. **Use pre–printed invoices?**

   If you plan to use pre–printed invoices, answer Y. If you wish to print invoices using plain paper, answer N.

4. **Print comp data on invc?**

   If you wish to have your company name and address (as entered using Maintain Company Data) printed on each invoice, answer Y here. If you answer N, the company name and address will not be printed on each invoice. NOTE: If you are printing on plain paper, then this field is set to Y automatically.

5. **Invoice line item format**

   Two line item formats are provided. Enter 1 for the first format and 2 for the second format. The first format includes any line item discount in the extended price. The second format shows the full extended price as well as the line item discount.

6. **Print invoices immed?**

   Answer Y to have the option of printing invoices immediately after you enter them ("point–of–sale" mode). If you print your invoices in batches, answer N.

   Single user note:

   If you answer Y here, define a single invoicing station on the next screen. Then enter the code for this invoicing station when using Enter Invoices in order to print invoices immediately.

Setup Functions

Maintain Invoicing Control Data – Screen 1 of 2

7. **Multiple profit centers?**

   Answer Y if you group your invoices by profit center. Otherwise, answer N. You can enter information in this field only if you specified in Maintain Company Data that you are using profit centers.

8. **Default payment terms**

   Every invoice must be assigned payment terms. These terms are printed on the invoice and are also transferred to A/R and retained with the open item for your reference. You may enter up to four default payment terms here for use in Enter Invoices.

9. **Default shipping methods**

   An invoice may optionally be assigned a shipping method. This method is printed on the invoice as the "ship–via". You may enter up to four default shipping methods here for use in Enter Invoices.

10. **Calc sls tax on misc chgs?**

    Answer Y if miscellaneous charges are taxable; otherwise, answer N. This field is used as a default when entering miscellaneous charges on an invoice.

11. **Calc sls tax on freight?**

    Answer Y if freight charges are taxable; otherwise, answer N.

12. **Dflt misc chgs acct #**

    Enter the G/L account number of the miscellaneous charges account to be used as the default account when miscellaneous charges are entered using Enter Invoices.

13. **Dflt freight acct #**

    Enter the G/L account number of the freight account to be used as the default account when freight charges are entered using Enter Invoices.

Setup Functions

Maintain Invoicing Control Data – Screen 1 of 2

14. Dflt scrap acct #

Enter the number of the G/L account to use as the default "scrap" account. A scrap account is used for a credit memo when the quantity of goods being returned to inventory is smaller than the quantity being credited (for example, faulty merchandise is credited but not returned). The dollar value of the quantity "scrapped" (not returned to inventory) is put into the scrap account.

15–18. Cust hist class desc

History on four different classes of items is automatically kept for each customer. Enter a description of each of the four customer history classes, up to 10 characters. For example, you may wish to use "Products", "Services", "Repairs" and "Other".

19. Fin chg pct – level 1

If two levels of finance charges are used, this field is for the finance charge percentage on amounts up to and including the first level (level 1 cutoff, entered next). You can enter a percentage from 0 to 99.999.

For example, if finance charges are computed at 1.5% on amounts up to $1,000.00 and 1% on amounts over $1,000.00, the finance charge percentage for level 1 would be 1.5.

If there is only one finance charge percentage, enter it here and skip fields 20 and 21.

20. Level 1 cut–off amt

Enter the highest amount in whole dollars (from 0 to 999,999) that the level 1 finance charge percentage in field 19 applies to. If there is only one finance charge percentage, skip this field by pressing ENTER.

21. Fin chg pct – level 2

Enter a number here, from 0 to 99.999, if there is a different finance charge percentage for past–due amounts above the level 1 cut–off amount.

22. No. days for fin charge

Enter the number of days allowed after the Date of the Invoice before finance charges are assessed. You can enter from 0 to 999 days.

Setup Functions

Maintain Invoicing Control Data – Screen 1 of 2

23. **Minimum finance charge**

    This is the minimum finance charge (in dollars and cents) to be charged to a past–due account. Enter 0 to 99.99.

24. **Calc F/C on F/C?**

    This question asks whether you want to include finance charges already past due in the new past due amount on which you are now going to calculate finance charges.

    If you answer Y, they will be included in the past due amount that new finance charges are calculated on.

    If N, previous past due finance charges are excluded when current finance charges are calculated.

25. **Finance charges acct #**

    Enter the number of the finance charges account. All finance charge amounts calculated and posted from the Finance Charges function, or from type "F" documents in the Sales and DR/CR Memos function, will be posted to this account.

26. **Period end date**

    Enter the ending date of the current period. This date is usually the ending date of your current period in the Maintain Accounting Periods function.

27. **Year end date**

    Enter the ending date of the current year. This date is usually the ending date of your fiscal year.

Setup Functions

Maintain Invoicing Control Data – Screen 2 of 2

Entering Invoicing Stations

Up to 5 invoicing stations may be defined. If you wish to define fewer than 5 invoicing stations, press ENTER for each subsequent invoicing station code field to leave it blank.

For each invoicing station that you define, enter the data as follows:

28–32. Code, Description, Nxt–invc–#, Printer

Code

Enter an abbreviation for the invoicing station, up to 3 characters. This code is entered when using Enter Invoices or Print Invoices to specify the invoicing station being used. At least one invoicing station code must be defined if a single–user has indicated they desire to print invoices immediately in the Maintain Invoicing Control Data function.

Description

Enter a description of this invoicing station, up to 15 characters. For example, enter the location of the invoicing station as its description in order to further identify it.

Nxt–invc–#

Enter the starting invoice number to be used when invoices are next printed using this invoicing station. This number is increased automatically by 1 for each invoice printed.

Printer

Enter the name of the printer (device name), up to 15 characters. You may press F1 to default to the standard printer (LPT1).

Setup Functions

Maintain Invoicing Control Data – Screen 2 of 2

Entering Tax Codes

Up to 8 tax codes may be defined. If you wish to define fewer than 8 tax codes, press ENTER for each subsequent tax code field to leave it blank.

For each tax code that you define, enter the data as follows:

33–40. Code, Description, Rate, Acct

Code

Enter an abbreviation for the tax code, up to 3 characters. This abbreviation will be used when you define your customers. At least one tax code must be defined. The first tax code is used as a default when adding new customers and in the Add Invoices function to add new customer data.

Deleting a tax code
To delete a tax code, type spaces over the tax code abbreviation. The first tax code cannot be deleted.

Description

Enter a description of the tax code, up to 10 characters. This description is used on reports.

Rate

Enter the percentage for calculating sales tax for customers with this tax code. Press ENTER for a tax rate of 0%.

Acct

Enter the G/L account number for sales tax accruals calculated for this tax code.

Accounts Receivable

Menu Selections

1. **Maintain customer data**

   Lets you add, change and delete customers, print customer lists and labels, and purge inactive customers.

2. **Process sales and DR/CR memos**

   Allows you to handle regular and recurring transactions. This function is used to enter, change, delete or print an edit list of sales, finance charges, credit memos and debit memos. You can also post these transactions.

3. **Process cash receipts**

   Tracks customer payments and prints deposit slips.

4. **Print A/R aging report**

   Used to print a report showing each customer's account balance in each of four aging periods.

5. **Change apply–to number**

   Used to change the apply–to number for any A/R open item.

6. **View customer accounts**

   Used to view all or part of the account activity for one or more specified customers.

7. **Process finance charges**

   Used to calculate finance charges on overdue items, and post them to the Customer Accounts file; the account balance is posted in the Customer file.

8. **Print customer statements**

   Used to print statements of accounts for customers.

9. **Purge customer accounts**

   Used either to purge fully paid documents from the Customer Accounts file, or to print a report showing which documents are eligible to be purged.

Accounts Receivable

Maintain Customer Data – Add Customers

1–6. Name, Address, Contact, Phone

Enter the customer's business name, address, contact person and phone number.

7. Comment

Enter any additional information or comments you wish to have on file for this customer, up to 25 characters. You may press ENTER to skip this field.

8. Cust type

Enter a code of your choice that identifies the type of customer. Customer type is used to include this customer on reports and mailing labels.

9. Sales rep

Enter the initials of the salesperson for this customer. You can press ENTER to skip this field.

10. Tax Code

Enter the tax code that applies to this customer, or press ENTER to use the first tax code on file.

11. Bal method

Enter the code for the method you use in handling this customer's account. Enter either O for "open item" or B for "balance forward".

12. Statement frequency

Enter the code for how often you want to send this customer a statement of account. Choose from the following, or press ENTER to default to monthly.

W = weekly	M = monthly	O = other
B = bi–weekly	Q = quarterly	

13. Fin chg?

Specify whether this customer will have finance charges on past due items auto–matically calculated by the Calculate Finance Charges function.

Accounts Receivable

Maintain Customer Data – Add Customers

14. First activity date

Enter the date of the customer's first activity with your company, or press ENTER to default to the current date.

15. Last sale date

Enter the date of the last sale for this customer, or press ENTER for "None". This date will be updated automatically each time a sale is processed for the customer.

16. Last payment date

Enter the date of the last payment received from this customer, or press ENTER for "None". This date will be updated automatically when a payment is processed for the customer.

17. Last fin chg date

This field contains the last date finance charges were computed for this customer. It is updated automatically when any finance charge is posted for this customer. You can press ENTER to set this field to "None".

18. Last fin chg amt

This field contains the last finance charge amount that was posted for this customer. It is updated automatically when any finance charge is posted.

19. Fin charges YTD

This field contains the year–to–date finance charges posted for this customer.

20–23. Sales this period, last period, this year and last year

Enter the sales for this customer for this period, last period, this year and last year.

24–27. Class fields

The classes of sales are user–defined in Maintain Invoicing Control Data.

Accounts Receivable

Process Sales and DR/CR Memos – Add Transactions

1. **Customer**

   Enter a full or partial customer name for the transactions. You may press F1 to display the next customer name.

2. **Trans Type**

   Enter the type of transaction, as follows:

S = sale	**F** = finance charge
C = credit memo	**B** = balance forward
D = debit memo	**L** = load A/R open

   The B and L types are used to transfer outstanding accounts receivable items from your former A/R package or manual system to PAS A/R.

3. **Trans date**

   Enter the date of the transaction. Press ENTER for the same date as the previous transaction. For the first transaction you enter, pressing ENTER defaults to the current date.

4. **Document #**

   Enter a document number, up to 6 characters. For example, enter the memo number for a debit or credit memo. Press ENTER to leave this number blank for a balance forward transaction type.

5. **Amount**

   Enter the amount of the sale, credit memo, debit memo, or finance charge (up to 8 digits including 2 decimal places). This amount must include any taxes, shipping charges, miscellaneous charges, etc.

6. **Terms**

   Enter up to 15 characters for a payment terms description or press F1 for the next default payment terms on file in the Invoicing Control file.

7. **Reference**

   Enter any reference for this transaction.

Accounts Receivable

Glossary of Terms

Account

Record of sales/cash received activity.

Accounts Receivable

The area of accounting dealing with sales and monies owed.

Age

The age of an invoice is simply how many days old it is, using the invoice date or the due date as the base (beginning) date.

Balance Forward Method

A method of tracking customer accounts in which customers' accounts are summarized, with payment automatically applied to the oldest item(s).

Customer Account File

The file into which transactions such as sales, debit/credit memos, cash receipts, and finance charges are posted. This file holds any bill that has not been fully paid, and any unused credit or debit memo for all customers.

Open Item Method

A method of tracking customer accounts in which a payment from a customer is matched to the corresponding sale made to the customer.

Receivable

Monies due the company. The two methods of keeping track of customer accounts are the open item method and the balance forward method.

Sales Invoicing

Menu Selections

1. **Enter invoices**

   Lets you add, change, inquire into or delete invoices and credit memos.

2. **Print invoice list**

   Allows you to print a list of invoices that have been entered using "Enter Invoices".

3. **View invoices**

   Used to quickly look at the invoices which have been entered using "Enter Invoices". You can find information you want rapidly; however, you cannot make changes to invoices in this selection. To make changes, use "Enter Invoices".

4. **Print invoices**

   Used to print invoices. If you normally print invoices immediately after they are entered, as specified in the Invoicing Control file, you can still use this function to print them.

5. **Post invoices**

   Used to post invoices to A/R and I/M. When you post, all financial data on the invoices is transferred to A/R and I/M. You must have already printed an invoice before you can post it.

6. **Print sales tax report**

   Used to print a report of the sales tax which has appeared on invoices posted using "Post Invoices". You may print either a summary or a detail report which lists the invoices for each tax code.

7. **Close a sales period**

   Used to clear the period–to–date fields in the Customer file and the Item file.

Sales Invoicing

First Entry Screen – Header Information

1. **Bill ref #**

   This is your OWN reference number for the invoice. It is NOT the invoice number. (The invoice number is assigned when the invoice is posted.) Enter a reference number for this invoice, or press F2 to use the next available bill ref # as specified in the Invoicing Control file.

2. **Bill type**

   Enter the bill type; I for invoice or C for credit memo.

3. **Invoice date**

   Enter the date to assign to this invoice in MMDDYY format. Press ENTER to skip this field if you want the invoice date to be assigned at the time the invoice is printed.

4. **Customer**

   Enter the customer's business name. You may enter all of the customer's name or just a few characters. You can press F1 to scan through the customers on file in order by customer name.

5. **Deliver to**

   Enter the location at which services are performed or to which goods are delivered. You can enter up to 4 lines of characters each for the deliver–to location, or press ENTER to make the deliver–to address the same as the customer's billing address.

6. **P.O. #**

   If there is a customer purchase order, enter the P.O. number.

7. **Terms**

   Enter the terms that apply to this invoice, or press F1 to scroll through the payment terms entered in Maintain Invoicing Control Data. This field may not be left blank.

8. **Ship via**

   Enter the shipping method that applies to this invoice, or press F1 to scroll through the shipping methods entered in Maintain Invoicing Control Data. This field may be left blank.

Accounts Payable

Menu Selections

1. **Maintain vendor data**

   Lets you add, change and delete vendors, and print vendor lists and labels.

2. **Process bills payable**

   Allows you to record bills you owe, plus any debit or credit memos associated with those bills.

3. **Process disbursements**

   Used to record disbursement transactions and, optionally, to print disbursement checks.

4. **View or print vendor accounts**

   Used to view or print all or part of the account activity for one or more specified vendors.

5. **Aged accounts payable summary**

   Used to print the Aged Accounts Payable Summary which shows the aged totals that you owe each of your vendors.

Accounts Payable

Maintain Vendor Data – Add Vendors

1–6. Name, Address, Contact, Phone

Enter the customer's business name, address, contact person, and phone number.

7. First date

Enter the date you started doing business with this vendor, in MMDDYY format. If you do not know this date, use the date you are adding this vendor.

8. Comment

Enter any additional information or comments you wish to have on file for this vendor up to 25 characters. You may press ENTER to skip this field.

9. Default exp acct

Enter the default expense account number. It is an optional entry. If you enter a G/L account number here, you can automatically assign purchases from this vendor to this account at the time you enter the purchases.

Accounts Payable

Process Bills Payable – Add Transactions

1. **Vendor**

   Enter the vendor name for the transaction, or press F1 to display next name.

2. **Trans type**

   Enter the type of transaction, as follows:

   B = Bill (for invoices). The total of the G/L distributions entered for a voucher must always equal the invoice amount.

   C = Credit memo (to back out bills that were posted in error). You can use A/P as the debit account, or specify another account.

   D = Debit memo (to record adjustments to a vendor's account). You can use A/P as the credit account, or specify another account.

   F = Balance forward (to set balances in a vendor's account). Transactions processed as type "F" will not update G/L.

3. **Trans date**

   Enter date of transaction, or press ENTER for same date as previous transaction.

4. **Invoice #**

   Enter an invoice number, up to 8 characters.

5. **Reference**

   Enter any reference for this transaction, up to 25 characters.

6. **Amount**

   Enter the amount of the transaction, up to 8 digits, including 2 decimal places, plus an optional negative sign.

7. **Credit A/P?**

   This question does not appear for balance forward transactions. The question means "Credit this transaction against the accounts payable G/L account?".

Accounts Payable

Glossary of Terms

Accounts Payable

The area of accounting that deals with purchases and disbursements by a company.

Account

A record of financial activity of orders and accounts with vendors.

Aging

The process of determining how old an invoice is. The aging of a vendor invoice is based on either the number of days that have passed since the date of the invoice or the due date of the payment for the invoice.

Payable

Monies owed by a company.

Vendor

A person or business from whom goods and/or services are purchased for use or resale to customers.

Voucher

An internal document issued by a company to track invoices sent in by various vendors. The invoice information is entered as a voucher and the vouchers are selected to be paid.

Check Reconciliation

Menu Selections

1. **Record checking account transfers**

   Lets you record the transfer of funds between PAS checking accounts.

2. **Process checking account adjustments**

   Allows you to record miscellaneous adjustments to accounts, such as interest earned, returned check charges, etc.

3. **Reconcile a checking account**

   Used to reconcile a checking account to its bank statement.

4. **Print a checkbook**

   Used to print a Checkbook Report showing all activity in a checking account. You can also purge cleared items from a checking account.

Check Reconciliation

Glossary of Terms

Adjustment

A transaction posted to Check Reconciliation to reflect changes in your activity or the bank's activity, such as bank service charges.

Beginning Balance

The balance of the checkbook at the beginning of a period.

Clear

To mark an entry as having been recognized and recorded by the bank.

Deposit

The transfer of funds from cash receipts in A/R or a direct deposit of funds into Check Reconciliation.

Ending Balance

The balance of a bank account at the end of reconciliation.

Purge

To permanently remove information from a file. If information has been purged, it cannot be recovered.

Reconciliation

To bring the balance of your checkbook into agreement with the balance shown on your bank statement.

Register

A report listing all checks in date or check number order.

Payroll

Menu Selections

1. **Maintain employee data**

   Lets you add, change, inquire into, or delete employees. You can also print a list of employees or employee labels.

2. **Process payroll time transactions**

   Allows you to add, change, inquire into, delete, or print an edit list of payroll time transactions.

3. **Calculate payroll**

   Used to calculate the employees' earnings, deductions and withholding taxes in preparation for printing payroll checks.

4. **Print payroll checks**

   Used to print the payroll checks.

5. **Process manual payroll transactions**

   Used to add, change, inquire into, delete, print an edit list of, or post manual payroll transactions. Manual payroll transactions include hand–written checks, adjustments to previously printed payroll checks, adjustments to QTD and YTD figures, adjust–ments to distributions, and "non–G/L" checks.

6. **Print payroll history report**

   Allows you to print a report showing the history of payroll transactions for employees who have received computer–printed or manual payroll checks. You can also purge the Payroll History file.

7. **Maintain deduction/earning codes**

   Used to add, change, inquire into, delete, or print a list of deductions and earnings codes that affect an employee's wages.

8. **Maintain tax codes and tables**

   Used to add, change, inquire into, delete, or print a list of the codes and tables used to define your Federal, state, and city tax structures.

Payroll

Menu Selections

9. **Print quarterly payroll report**

   Allows you to compute and print a list of Federal, state, and city taxes and unemployment insurance liabilities for any given quarter.

10. **Print year–end payroll reports**

    Used to enter allocated tips and other auxiliary information for W–2s, and to print W–2s, 1099s and related reports.

11. **Close payroll for calendar year**

    Used to clear YTD totals in the Employee file and QTD and YTD totals in the QTD and YTD History files.

Payroll

Maintain Tax Codes and Tables – Federal

1. **Tax authority**

   Enter F for Federal, S for state, or C for city to designate which tax authority this change/inquiry is for.

2. **Tax code**

   For Federal, no entry is allowed because there is only one tax code for Federal. For state and city tax codes, enter 2 characters to specify the state or city, then enter a one–character code to specify the table.

3. **Description**

   Enter a description of this tax code.

4. **Tax rpt ID#**

   Enter your Federally–assigned employer identification number.

5. **Tax liab acct #**

   Enter the number of the G/L account to which withholding taxes payable are posted. The number you enter must exist in the Chart file.

6. **Suppl earn w/h %**

   For supplemental earnings, you can deduct a fixed percent for withholding tax, or compute the withholding tax at the same rate as regular wages.

7. **Minimum wage**

   Enter the minimum wage.

8–13. **Define exemptions: Employee / Employer**

For each type of pay, specify which tax exemptions apply.

<u>Employee</u>		<u>Employer</u>	
	Fed w/h		Soc–sec
	Soc–scc		Medicare
	Medicare		FUI
			EIC

Payroll

Maintain Tax Codes and Tables – Federal

14–15. Employer/Employee soc sec pct

For each field, enter the share of social security tax for which this person is responsible.

16. Maximum soc sec wages

Enter the maximum annual wage amount on which social security tax can be taken.

17–18. Employer soc sec exp acct/liab acct

Enter the numbers of the accounts that accumulate employer social security tax expenses and the employer portion of social security tax liability.

19. Employee soc sec liab acct

Enter the number of the account that accumulates the amount of the social security tax withheld from employee pay.

20–21. Employer/Employee medicare pct

For each field, enter the share of medicare tax for which this person is responsible.

22. Maximum medicare wages

Enter the maximum annual wage amount on which medicare tax can be taken.

23–24. Employer medicare exp acct/liab acct

Enter the numbers of the accounts that accumulate employer medicare tax expenses and the employer portion of medicare tax liability.

25. Employee medicare liab acct

Enter the number of the account that accumulates the amount of the medicare tax withheld from employee pay.

26. Federal unemployment %

In RealWorld PAS payroll, this employer tax is known as Federal Unemployment Insurance (FUI). This is also known as FUTA (Federal Unemployment Tax Act).

Payroll

Maintain Tax Codes and Tables – Federal

27. **Federal unemp max wages**

Enter the maximum annual wage on which unemployment tax can be taken.

28–29. **FUI expense account # / liability account #**

Enter the numbers of the accounts that accumulate federal unemployment insurance contributions and the amount of the FUI contribution calculated by the software.

30–32. **Exp acct #s for vacation pay, holiday pay, and sick pay**

Enter the numbers of the expense accounts that will be used for the specified pay categories.

For fields 30, 31 and 32, you can enter a special main account number, as well as the special 999 sub–account. Ths special main account number you can use is 0000. If you use this account, the main account number from each employee's wage account will be used to create General Ledger distributions during posting of payroll trans–actions.

34. **Fed w/h allowance amt**

The withholding allowance amount is the amount by which the gross pay is reduced for each exemption the employee claims. Enter the dollar amount of the annual Federal withholding allowance.

35–49. **Federal Tax Tables**

The rest of the entries on this screen are from the data contained in the Tables for Percentage Method of Withholding in the IRS Circular E booklet.

The relevant tables are the Annual Payroll Period Table of Withholding Amounts for single and married persons and the Annual Payroll Period Table of Advance EIC Payments for single–certificate households (Table 7a).

Each of the tables is structured to allow the entry of a tax amount in dollars ($–AMT) plus a percent of income (%–AMT) where the income exceeds a minimum level (ON–AMT–OVER).

Payroll

Maintain Tax Codes and Tables – Federal

For example, if an entry in the table of withholding percentages for single persons shows a tax of $3,052.50 on $21,600.00 and a tax percent of 28% on income greater than $21,600.00, the entries that you would make on the screen are:

$–AMT	%–AMT	ON–AMT–OVER
3052.50	28.00	21600.00

Note that there are certain control accounts that are defined in the Federal tax tables, such as the payroll cash account, and holiday and sick pay accounts.

Payroll

Maintain Employee Data

1. **Employee number**

   Enter the employee number up to four digits. This number is used throughout Payroll to identify the employee.

2. **Employee name**

   The employee name can be entered as Last, First Middle; or as First Middle Last.

3–6. **Street address, City, State, Zip code**

   Enter the employee's address, city, state postal code, and zip code.

7. **Soc sec #**

   Enter the employee's social security number, including hyphens so that it will appear in the correct format.

8. **Birth date**

   Enter the employee's birth date in MMDDYY format.

9. **Marital status**

   Enter the employee's marital status as one of the following:
   S = single
   M = married
   H = head of household for Federal taxes

10. **Hire date**

    Enter the employee's date of hire in MMDDYY format.

11. **Last raise**

    Enter the date of the employee's last raise in MMDDYY format.

12. **Review date**

    Enter the date of the employee's next performance/pay review in MMDDYY format.

Payroll

Maintain Employee Data

14. Emp type

Specify the employee type from among these choices:
H = hourly
S = salaried
N = non–employee

15. Pay frequency

Specify the pay frequency from among these choices:
D = daily (called "miscellaneous" by the IRS)
W = weekly
B = bi–weekly
S = semi–monthly
M = monthly

16. Home department

Enter the number used to identify the department to which this employee is assigned for payroll report purposes.

17. Wage account #

Enter the number of this employee's wage account which will be used as the default account when pay is being distributed to various accounts.

18. Salary

Enter the employee's salary. If not, type "S" to skip this field.

19. Regular rate

If the employee is hourly, enter his regular hourly pay rate.

20. Overtime rate

If the employee is salaried, the overtime rate is automatically calculated. If hourly, press F1 to enter an amount equal to the regular rate multiplied by the overtime factor specified in the Accounting control file.

Payroll

Maintain Employee Data

21. **Special rate**

    The entry for this rate works the same way as the overtime rate.

22. **Vac hours due**

    When you set up your Payroll system, you would normally set this field to zero for each employee.

23. **Vac hours paid**

    Enter the number of vacation hours paid so far this year to this employee.

24. **Sick hours due**

    When you set up your Payroll system, you would normally set this field to zero for each employee.

25. **Pension plan?**

    Specify Y or N to indicate whether or not this employee participates in a pension plan.

26. **Distrib wages?**

    Specify Y if this employee's pay is to be distributed manually to G/L accounts. Otherwise, enter N.

27. **W–2 ins prem**

    If you purchase group term life insurance for an employee and the coverage exceeds an IRS–specified limit, then enter the cost of the coverage in excess of the limit.

28. **Can get tip CR?**

    Answer Y if tip credits are applicable to this employee. Otherwise, enter N. You can make an entry in this field only if the Accounting Control file specifies that meals and tips are used.

Payroll

Maintain Employee Data

29. **State tax code**

    Enter the state tax code that applies to this employee.

30. **City tax code**

    Enter the city tax code that applies to this employee.

31. **# FWT exemptions**

    Enter the number of Federal withholding tax exemptions for this employee.

32. **$ FWT exemption**

    Enter an additional dollar amount, if needed. Otherwise, press ENTER to skip.

33. **# SWT exemptions**

    Enter the number of state withholding tax exemptions for this employee.

34. **$ SWT exemption**

    Enter an additional dollar amount, if needed. Otherwise, press ENTER to skip.

35. **# OST exemptions**

    Enter the number of exemptions for other state tax, for this employee.

36. **$ OST exemption**

    Enter an additional dollar amount, if needed. Otherwise, press ENTER to skip.

37. **# CWT exemptions**

    Enter the number of exemptions for city withholding tax, for this employee.

38. **$ CWT exemption**

    Enter the annual dollar amount of the city withholding tax exemption.

Payroll

Maintain Employee Data

39. **State tax credit**

    Enter the annual dollar amount of the tax credit for which this employee qualifies.

40. **Added FWT**

    Enter the percent of taxable gross pay that is to be taken to increase the employee's federal withholding tax.

41. **Added SWT**

    Enter the percent of taxable gross pay that is to be taken to increase the employee's state withholding tax.

42. **Added CWT**

    Enter the percent of taxable gross pay that is to be taken to increase the employee's city withholding tax.

43. **Soc sec exempt?**

    Answer Y if this employee is exempt from paying social security taxes. Otherwise, answer N.

44. **Medicare exempt?**

    Answer Y if this employee is exempt from paying medicare taxes. Otherwise, answer N.

45. **FUI exempt?**

    Answer Y if this employee is exempt from the FUI tax usually paid by the employer. Otherwise, answer N.

46. **SUI exempt?**

    Answer Y if this employee is exempt from the SUI tax usually paid by the employer. Otherwise, answer N.

Payroll

Maintain Employee Data

47. **# of EIC certs**

Enter the number of earned income credit (EIC) certificates that this employee has in his household. The number may be 0, 1 or 2, depending on whether the employee has filed a W–5 form or whether both the employee and spouse have filed W–5 forms.

48. **Vac due date**

Enter the date on which this employee's vacation is due.

Hrs per pay freq

Enter the number of hours which the employee will accrue during each pay period.

Max vac hrs

Enter the maximum number of vacation hours which the employee is allowed to accrue, or press F1 for unlimited vacation hours.

49. **Sick hours due date**

Enter the date on which this employee's sick hours are due.

Hrs per pay freq

Enter the number of hours which the employee will accrue during each pay period.

Max sick hrs

Enter the maximum number of sick hours which the employee is allowed to accrue, or press F1 for unlimited sick hours.

50–55. **D/E code; Amt/rate/pct; Frequency**

These are the deduction/earnings fields. Enter the deduction/earning code for the employee, then enter the dollar amount and percent of taxable gross of rate per hour of the deduction/earning. All of the deductions require a frequency. Enter any of the valid pay frequencies.

Payroll

Maintain Employee Data

These fields are updated by posting payroll transactions.

56. **YTD gross**

Year–to–date gross wages.

57. **YTD FWT gross**

Year–to–date gross wages on which Federal withholding tax was deducted.

58. **YTD emp soc sec gross**

Year–to–date gross wages on which the employee portion of social security was calculated.

59. **YTD empr soc sec gross**

Year–to–date gross wages on which the employer portion of social security was calculated.

60. **YTD emp medicare gross**

Year–to–date gross wages on which the employee portion of medicare was calculated.

61. **YTD empr medicare gross**

Year–to–date gross wages on which the employer portion of medicare was calculated.

62. **YTD FUI gross**

Year–to–date gross wages on which the employer's contribution to Federal unemployment insurance was calculated.

63. **YTD suppl ben gross**

Year–to–date gross wages on which supplemental benefit contributions have been calculated.

64. **YTD SUI gross**

Year–to–date gross wages on which the employer's contribution to state unemployment insurance was calculated.

Payroll

Maintain Employee Data

65. **YTD emp soc sec**

    Year–to–date social security taxes withheld from the employee's wages.

66. **YTD empr soc sec**

    Year–to–date social security taxes contributed by the employer.

67. **YTD emp medicare**

    Year–to–date medicare taxes withheld from the employee's wages.

68. **YTD empr medicare**

    Year–to–date medicare taxes contributed by the employer.

69. **YTD FWT**

    Year–to–date Federal withholding tax.

70. **YTD EIC**

    Year–to–date earned income credit advance payments.

71. **YTD SWT**

    Year–to–date state withholding tax.

72. **YTD OST**

    Year–to–date other state tax withheld.

73. **YTD CWT**

    Year–to–date city withholding tax.

74. **YTD other taxes**

    Year–to–date other taxes.

75. **YTD tip credit**

    Year–to–date tip credit.

Payroll

Glossary of Terms

Deduction

An amount taken from the wages of an employee by the employer. A deduction is not normally paid to a government agency. Deductions are typically made for voluntary activities such as savings plans, medical insurance, etc. The "frequency" of a deduction refers to how often the deduction is taken.

Earned Income Credit (EIC)

Employers make EIC payments to qualified employees on the government's behalf. The government reimburses employers.

FUI

The abbreviation for Federal Unemployment Insurance.

Payroll

The area of accounting dealing with the wages an employer pays his/her employees.

Payroll Taxes

Those amounts related to payroll wages paid to government agencies. The employer and employee each pay part of the required FICA tax, with the employee's portion being withheld from his/her paycheck. Income taxes are paid entirely by the employee, and are also withheld from his/her paycheck. The employer pays the entire FUI and SUI amounts.

Payroll taxes paid to the Federal (U.S.) government:

Social Security Taxes – FICA
Personal Income Tax – Federal Withholding
Federal Unemployment Insurance – FUI

Payroll taxes paid to state and local governments:

Personal Income Tax – State Withholding
State Unemployment Insurance – SUI

Payroll

Glossary of Terms

SUI

The abbreviation for State Unemployment Insurance.

Supplemental Earning

A special category of earning, such as commissions or bonuses, that is always taxed at the supplemental pay rate specified in Federal and state tables.

Worker's Compensation

A form of insurance that provides for payment to an employee in the event of certain kinds of on–the–job injuries. The premiums are normally paid by the employer to a state or private agency. A few states require the employee to pay part of the workers' compensation premium.

Inventory Management

Menu Selections

1. **Maintain item data**

   Allows you to add, change and delete items, and to print an item list.

2. **Maintain item prices**

   Lets you change prices for items, to set limited–time sale prices, and to purge sale prices. You may also print a list of items and their prices.

3. **Process inventory**

   Used to enter, change or inquire into, delete or print an edit list of receivings and adjustments for your inventory items.

4. **Process purchases**

   Used to print a report showing what needs to be purchased, and to automatically generate purchase transactions. This function also allows you to manually add, change, inquire into, delete, print an edit list of purchase transactions, and post the transactions.

5. **Process physical inventory**

   Used to add, change, inquire into, delete, print an edit list of, or post manual payroll transactions. Manual payroll transactions include hand–written checks, adjustments to previously printed payroll checks, adjustments to QTD and YTD figures, adjust–ments to distributions, and "non–G/L" checks.

6. **Print inventory status report**

   Allows you to print a report showing the history of payroll transactions for employees who have received computer–printed or manual payroll checks. You can also purge the Payroll History file.

7. **Print inventory valuation report**

   Used to add, change, inquire into, delete, or print a list of deductions and earnings codes that affect an employee's wages.

8. **Print inventory analysis report**

   Used to add, change, inquire into, delete, or print a list of the codes and tables used to define your Federal, state, and city tax structures.

Inventory Management

Maintain Item Data

1. **Item number**

   Enter the item number, a unique number, up to 15 alphanumeric characters.

2. **Description**

   Enter the item description.

3. **Bar code**

   A bar code is an alternative method for identifying an item. You can press ENTER to skip this field. If you enter a bar code, it must be different from any other bar code or item number.

4. **Substitute item #**

   Enter the number of a substitute item. The substitute item can be viewed and used in the Add Invoices function.

5. **Item type**

   Enter one of the following codes to specify the item type:

I = Inventory item	Items for which quantities are received and maintained in your inventory.
S = Service item	Items which are not received or maintained in inventory, such as labor.
N = Non–inventory item	Merchandise which may be physically present, but are not received or maintained in inventory, such as "miscellaneous parts".
T = Text item	Used only as predefined comment items or during line item entry in the Add Invoices function; they cannt be received or sold.

6. **Department**

   Enter a code that identifies the department of this item.

Inventory Management

Maintain Item Data

7. **Cust hist class**

   Enter the number of the customer class to update for sales of this item.

8. **Stocking unit**

   Enter the stocking unit for this item. For example, "each"; "box"; "case".

9. **Qty on hand**

   Enter the quantity (in stocking units) which you currently have in your inventory.

10. **Qty committed**

    No entry is allowed in this field; it is automatically updated when inventory items are entered and posted. Quantity committed is the quantity of an item which has been entered on transactions or invoices, but has not yet been posted.

11. **Qty on order**

    Enter the quantity (in stocking units) which you currently have on order with your vendors. An entry is allowed in this field only when you add an item; after that, it is automatically updated.

12. **Average cost or Service cost**

    Enter the average cost per stocking unit of this item.

13. **Last cost**

    Enter the cost per stocking unit of this item at last purchase.

14. **Purchase unit**

    Enter the unit in which you normally purchase this item, if different from the stocking unit. If you enter a purchase unit, it should be a larger unit of measure than the stocking unit. You will then be asked to enter the number of stocking units per purchase unit.

15. **List price**

    Enter the non–discounted selling price for one stocking unit of this item.

Inventory Management

Maintain Item Data

16. Discount by

Enter the code to indicate how prices are automatically discounted in the Add Invoices function. The choices are:

Q = discount by quantity
C = discount by customer type
N = no discounts

17. Better price

Enter the discounted selling price of this item to be used for the minimum quantity or customer type.

18. Best price

Enter the discounted selling price of this item to be used for the minimum quantity or customer type. An entry is allowed only if you also entered "better price".

19–20. Alt sell unit 1/ Alt sell unit 2

If this unit can be sold in units other than the stocking unit, enter the one or two alternate selling units for this item. For example, an item that is normally stocked and sold as "each" might also be sold as a "box" and as a "case".

21. Preferred unit

If you entered an alternate selling unit, enter your preferred selling unit for this item.

22. Vendor

Enter the name of the current vendor or press F1 for the next vendor on file.

23. Notes

Enter any comments you want for this item.

24. Inventory acct # or contra acct #

For an Inventory–type item, enter the G/L account number used to record the balance sheet value of this item.

Inventory Management

Maintain Item Data

Inventory acct # or contra acct # (continued)

For Service and Non–inventory type items, this field is named "Contra account #". Since these types of items are not inventoried, a contra–expense account is specified instead of a balance sheet inventory account.

25. **Sales acct #**

    Enter the G/L account number used to record sales of this item.

26. **Cost of goods acct #**

    Enter the G/L account number used to record the cost of sales for this item.

27. **Returns acct #**

    Enter the G/L account number used to record returns of this item.

28. **Taxable?**

    If this item is taxable, answer Y. Otherwise, answer N.

29. **Bin location**

    Enter the bin or floor location where this item is stored.

30. **Minimum qty on hand**

    Enter the quantity on hand level at which this item should be reordered. You may press ENTER to indicate that there is no specific minimum.

31. **Minimum order qty**

    Enter the minimum quantity to be ordered of this item when new purchases are made. You may press ENTER to indicate that there is no specific minimum.

32. **Maximum qty on hand**

    Enter the maximum quantity that should be on hand for this item. You may press ENTER to indicate that there is no specific maximum.

Inventory Management

Maintain Item Data

33. First receipt date

Enter the earliest date this item was received, or press ENTER for "None". If you enter "None", this date is automatically updated when the first inventory receiving transaction is posted for this item.

34. Last receipt date

Enter the latest date this item was received, or press ENTER for "None". This date is automatically updated when inventory receiving transactions are posted for this item.

35. Last order date

Enter the lastest date this item was ordered from your supplier, or press ENTER for "None". This date is automatically updated when purchase transactions are posted for this item.

36. Last sale date

Enter the latest date this item was sold, or press ENTER for "None".

37–38. Qty sold this prd / Qty sold last prd

Enter the quantity sold of this item for this period or for last period.

39–40. Qty sold this yr / Qty sold last yr

Enter the quantity sold of this item for this year or for last year.

41–42. Sales this prd / Sales last prd

Enter the sales for this item for this period or for last period.

43–44. Sales this year / Sales last year

Enter the sales for this item for this year or for last year.

45–46. Cost this period / Cost last period

Enter the cost of sales for this item for this period or for last period.

Inventory Management

Maintain Item Data

47–48. Cost this year / Cost last year

Enter the cost of sales for this item for this year or for last year.

Maintain Item Prices

1. **Print price list**

   Used to print a list of items and their prices. You may sort the price list by item, department or vendor. You may also see only those items on sale.

2. **Change individual prices**

   Used to change existing prices for an item. You are given the item's current list price and gross profit. When you enter a new price for the item, the gross profit percentage will be automatically recalculated.

3. **Change group prices**

   Used to change existing prices for a group of items. You may select which items to re–price by item number, department or vendor. You may change prices by dollar amount or by a change percentage. Beforc you actually apply the changes, you may print a report showing all items for which prices would be changed.

4. **Set sale prices**

   Used to set specific sales and sale dates for inventory items.

5. **Purge sale prices**

   Used to clear sale prices and dates for a selected group of items.

Inventory Management

Process Inventory

1. **Receivings**

   Process a receiving transaction any time that goods are shipped to your warehouses. This transaction will update the quantity on hand.

2. **Adjustments**

   Process an adjustment transaction to adjust an item's quantity on hand when a physical count reveals that the actual quantity on hand is different.

   You will also process an adjustment to the quantity on hand if the item was received at the wrong price. First, you will do a downward adjustment for the quantity received at the price originally entered (the incorrect price). Then, you will process an upward adjustment for the quantity received at the actual (correct) price. The first step, an offset to the original transaction, reverses the incorrect transaction. The second step inputs the correct information.

3. **Sales**

   Process a sale transaction to record the sale of an item. You may enter your sales through either the Process Inventory function or the Process Invoices function in Sales Invoicing.

4. **Credit Memos**

   Process a credit memo to record the return of an item to inventory. You may enter credit memos through either Sales Invoicing or I/M.

Inventory Management

Glossary of Terms

Average Cost

The average of all costs paid for an item. In RealWorld Software, the average cost is recalculated every time items are added.

Cost

An item's cost is how much the company has spent to acquire that item.

Inventory

The goods or services on hand for sale to customers or for any other use.

Inventory Management

The ability to regulate or keep track of what goes in and out of inventory. This includes knowing the value of inventory at any time.

Inventory Valuation

The method used to calculate a dollar value for your current inventory. Four methods are commonly recognized: LIFO (Last–in first–out); FIFO (first–in first–out); average; standard. PAS uses average valuation.

Item

An identifiable product, material or commodity that can be stocked, sold or used. Data maintained includes cost, price, product category, quantity on hand, and reorder level.

Margin

The difference between the company cost and the customer price. It represents the amount of money the company made on the sale of that item.

Perpetual Inventory

A system that tracks the on–hand amount of inventory items. The term "perpetual" is used to describe the continual updating of inventory amounts, as receivings or sales occur for each item.

Inventory Management

Glossary of Terms

Price

An item's price is what a customer would pay to buy that item.

Replacement Cost

The most current cost of an item. The amount of money the company would pay to replace a specific item.

General ledger

Menu Selections

1. **Maintain chart of accounts**

   Lets you add, change and delete, or print a list of accounts in the Chart of Accounts file.

2. **Process general journal**

   Allows you to add, change, inquire into, delete and print an edit list of general journal transactions.

3. **View G/L account activity**

   Lets you look at all or part of the transaction activity for any specified G/L account.

4. **Print trial balance**

   Used to print the Trial Balance Report for a range of account numbers and dates. This report shows the balance of each selected account.

5. **Print financial statements**

   Used to print financial statements, such as the Profit and Loss (P&L) Statement and Balance Sheet.

6. **Compress G/L transactions**

   Used to summarize several transactions into one transaction, thereby reducing the number of transactions in the file.

7. **Calculate a loan payment**

   Allows you to calculate a loan payment and, optionally, to print an amortization schedule.

8. **Close accounting year**

   Used to close your General Ledger at the end of your accounting year.

General Ledger

Process General Journal

1. **Account #**

   Enter the number of the account to which this transaction will be posted.

2. **Trans date**

   Enter the transaction date in MMDDYY format.

3. **Debit amount / Credit amount**

   Enter the amount of the transaction as either a debit or a credit, but not both.

4. **Reference**

   Enter a description for the entry.

   Running balance

   The running balance displayed under the reference is the total of all debits and credits for all general journal transactions entered but not yet posted.

General Ledger

Add Financial Statement Layouts

Seq

The sequence number is assigned automatically. It begins with 10 and is increased by 10 for each new layout line.

Function code

In this column, enter a code to specify exactly what you want to appear on this line of the financial statement.

Account

Enter a G/L account number. The G/L account description and the amount will be printed on the statement.

Wild cards

You may use an asterisk as one or more digits of the account number to specify that all G/L account numbers which match the other digits are to be included.

Prt/Accum

This means "Print or accumulate?". Enter P if you want the account description and amount of the transaction to print. If you enter A, the account description and amount do not print on the statement. The amount for that account is added to the next amount specified to Print.

Print Column

This means "In what column should the amount print?". Answer one of the following:

1 = Column 1 (leftmost)
2 = Column 2 (middle)
3 = Column 3 (rightmost)

SUBn

You may specify up to 9 subtotal levels on a financial statement. You will be required to enter a description for your subtotal.

General Ledger

Add Financial Statement Layouts

Pat

This code stands for "print accumulated total". Whenever the software sees an account number code which is coded A (for accumulate), the software adds the amount in the G/L account to the PAT amount. If you add a PAT code, it will print a description that you add and the amount that the PAT has accumulated so far.

Paren Ctrl

This has the same function as the parentheses control code in the Chart of Accounts. If the subtotal amount should typically be a debit, enter "C"; if typically a credit, enter "D".

BSNI

The balance sheet net income must be listed on your balance sheet to reflect the profit or loss amount from the P&L Statement.

SRB & ERB

These codes stand for "start ratio basis" and "end ratio basis". You can only use them on P&L Statements. You will use these to show ratios on your statement. Place the SRB code before the first account to be included in the ratio basis. Place the ERB code after the last account to be included. Usually, the SRB goes before the first revenue (sales) account, and ERB goes after the last revenue account.

DAT

This code causes the date of the statement to print. It is similar to a legend.

BL

This code stands for "blank line", and inserts a blank line on the financial statement.

NP

This code stands for "new page", and causes the printer to advance to a new page.

General Ledger

Add Financial Statement Layouts

TXT

You can enter up to 50 characters of text to print on the financial statement.

SL

This code stands for "single line", and is usually used to print a line immediately above a subtotal.

DL

This code stands for "double line", and is usually used to print a double line immediately above a total.

General Ledger

Financial Statement Subtotals

In the following example, the subtotal levels are used to show the relationship between the various asset accounts. The first subtotal level shows total cash in banks, the second shows total cash assets, and the third shows total current assets.

The rules for inserting subtotal levels are highly flexible. The main rules to remember are:

- ➡ You can have up to 9 subtotal levels.
- ➡ After a subtotal is printed, its stored total and the stored totals of all "lower" subtotals are set to zero. In this example, the first subtotal is set to zero after it is printed.

If Petty Cash had been given a subtotal level of 1 instead of 2, the amount of that subtotal would be 100.00 instead of 20,100.00. (Subtotals do not get added together; only the accounts are subtotalled.)

If subtotals had been used later for level 4 and higher levels, they would include the subtotals for levels 1, 2 and 3.

A subtotal level that is the same as or less than the last subtotal level does not include the last subtotal level in its subtotal.

It is sometimes helpful to explain subtotalling using the concept of "buckets". There are 9 subtotal levels (9 buckets). Each time an account prints, the dollar amount in that account is added to each bucket (subtotal level). Once a subtotal/ bucket is printed, the amount in that level is emptied, or zeroed out.

CHART OF ACCOUNTS

Account	Description
1010–000	Cash, First National Bank
1020–000	Cash, First State Bank
SUB1	
1040–000	Petty Cash
SUB2	
1100–000	Accounts Receivable
1200–000	Merchandise Inventory
SUB1	
SUB3	Total Current Assets

General Ledger

Financial Statement Subtotals

The financial statement would print as follows:

Account	Description	Balance
1010–000	Cash, First National Bank	10,000.00
1020–000	Cash, First State Bank	10,000.00
	Subtotal level 1:	20,000.00
1040–000	Petty Cash	100.00
	Subtotal level 2:	20,100.00
1100–000	Accounts Receivable	25,000.00
1200–000	Merchandise Inventory	15,000.00
	Subtotal level 1:	40,000.00
	Total Current Assets	
	Subtotal level 3:	60,100.00

General Ledger

Glossary of Terms

Chart of Accounts

A list of all General Ledger accounts.

Double Entry Bookkeeping

A bookkeeping method used to check the accuracy of information entered into journals and ledgers.

Entries

Record of a completed business event involving money and/or goods and/or services.

Financial Statements

Summarized reports which state how a company is performing financially.

General Journal

The function for entering miscellaneous debit/credit entries into the system.

General Ledger

The area of accounting where records from other areas of the business are brought together for classification and summarization, creating a picture of the overall condition of the company's finances.

General Ledger Account

A specific category under which all financial activity of a certain type is classified.

Journal Number

A two–letter journal code followed by a 4–digit report number that is stored with an entry to identify the exact journal which created the entry.

Profit Center

A part of the company for which revenue and/or expenses (and sometimes profits) can be calculated separately from the total revenue and expenses of the whole company.

General Ledger

Glossary of Terms

Source (of an entry)

The area where the entry originated, or was first entered.

Standard Journal

The function used to enter those entries which routinely occur in every period.

Trial Balance

A trial run used to make sure that total debits equal total credits.

APPENDIX

Appendix A

Computer Requirements

Hardware

Practical Accounting System requires an IBM, Tandy or compatible personal computer with a minimum of 640KB of memory.

A hard disk is required. Diskette drives must support 360KB, 720KB, or 1.2MB.

Either a monochrome or color monitor can be used. If you have an IBM–compatible color display, Practical Accounting System will take advantage of its color capabilities.

A 132–character wide printer is required. This can be either a wide carriage printer or a printer capable of compressed print.

You must have version 3.3 or later of the DOS operating system.

Paper and forms

Most Practical Accounting System reports print on plain paper. Although you can use wider paper, we recommend that you use paper that is 9–1/2" wide and 11" high. This size is readily available, and you can get it with perforated edges, so that the finished page size is 8–1/2" X 11" after the edges are removed.

Besides the many reports which print on plain paper, Practical Accounting System also uses five special pre–printed continuous forms:

1. The invoice (actually optional, since plain paper can be used)
2. The Accounts Receivable customer statement
3. The Accounts Payable check
4. The Payroll check
5. The Payroll W–2 forms

Except for the W–2 form, these forms have been specially designed by RealWorld.

Appendix B

Installation Procedure

Introduction

There is an automated installation procedure on the "Installation Diskette". It will perform all of the steps needed to install the package on your computer.

General instructions

During the installation procedure, you must press the ENTER key after your answer to question. Because you end every answer by pressing ENTER, the word ENTER has been omitted in these instructions. Thus, an instruction to "type 2 and then press ENTER" is written "Type 2."

To end the installation procedure at any time, press ESC.

During this installation procedure, you will be asked to "mount" various diskettes in the diskette drive. If there is already a diskette in that drive, you must remove the existing diskette before inserting a new one.

Always put diskettes back into their protective envelopes after removing them from the diskette drive.

Do not remove the INSTALLATION DISKETTE from drive A until you are prompted to do so by the installation procedure, or until the installation procedure is complete, or until you have ended the procedure, using the ESC key.

Installation steps

Perform the installation as follows:

Step 1

The system "CONFIG.SYS" must contain the line "FILES=50". In order for the software to function properly, the CONFIG.SYS file must reside on the system disk from which you boot your computer. Please verify that this line is present in your CONFIG.SYS file. Use an editor such as the DOS–supplied "EDLIN" if you need to create or modify your CONFIG.SYS file.

Also, you should become familiar with the "BUFFERS" command which is explained in your DOS system manual. Setting BUFFERS in the CONFIG.SYS file may improve the performance of your system.

Please refer to your DOS system manual for information on choosing the correct number of buffers for your system. Keep in mind that increasing the number of buffers reduces available memory.

If you modified the CONFIG.SYS file as noted above, you must reboot your computer before proceeding to Step 2.

On some computers, the hardware "setup" must be modified in order for the computer to use the CONFIG.SYS file on the hard disk.

Step 2

To install PAS, follow these steps:

1. Create a directory on your hard disk. You will be installing PAS into this directory in the remaining steps. For example, to create a directory called PAS on the C: drive, type:

   C: MD C:\PAS

2. Insert the Installation Diskette in drive A, and make A: the default drive by typing A: and pressing ENTER.

3. At the A: prompt, type INSTALL followed by the drive letter you chose in step 1, a back slash, and the directory name you created above. For example:

   A: INSTALL C:\PAS

   Wait a few moments while some files are copied to this directory from the Installation Diskette.

4. From this point on, various information and instructions will display on the screen. Read the information and follow the instructions.

Step 3

You have now completed the installation procedure.

It is suggested that you now load the SAMPLE DATA. The procedure to accomplish this is described in Appendix C, "How to Use the Educational Version."

Appendix C

How to Use the Educational Version

Introduction

This section explains:

How to LOAD your start–up sample data.
How to START the Educational Version.
RESTRICTIONS on the data you can enter in the Educational Version.

Loading the STARTING SET data

The supplied starting set of data provides a start–up position for each of LYONS–GARTEN LAWN AND GARDEN, INC.'s exercises. This gives the user the flexibility of performing one or more of the fourteen Starting Exercises at any time, with the assurance that the data in that exercise's printed reports will exactly match that of the report samples contained in the text.

You should load the starting data AFTER you have used the installation procedure to install the software, and BEFORE you have entered any data into PAS. Loading the starting data destroys any data that may have been entered previously into the data files.

The STARTING SET DATA for each exercise has been loaded onto your 'C' drive in subdirectory TEXTDATA of directory PAS. To load a given exercise's starting data, type the following change directory (cd) command at the C:> prompt:

C:> **CD PAS\TEXTDATA**

At the subsequent prompt, type:

C:\PAS\TEXTDATA> **START? C: PAS**
where ? = a number from 1 to 14,
depending on the exercise that you will be using.

You may load any exercise's start–up data more than once if you choose. However, remember that each time you load another set of data, any data previously entered is destroyed.

Loading the PRACTICE SET data

The supplied practice set of data provides a start–up position for EACH of the practice exercises for ACME HARDWARE CO. As noted with the Starting Exercises, this gives the user the flexibility of performing one or more of the fourteen Practice Exercises at any time, with the assurance that the data in that exercise's printed reports will exactly match that of the report samples contained in the text.

NOTE: Loading the practice data will destroy any of the data that you may have entered previously.

The PRACTICE SET DATA for each exercise has been loaded onto your 'C' drive in subdirectory TEXTDATA of directory PAS. To load a given exercises's starting data, type the following change directory (cd) command at the C:> prompt:

C:> **CD PAS\TEXTDATA**

At the subsequent prompt, type:

C:\PAS\TEXTDATA> **PSTART? C: PAS**
where ? = a number from 1 to 14,
depending on the exercise that you will be using.

You may load any exercise's start–up data more than once if you choose. However, remember that each time you load another set of data, any data previously entered is destroyed.

Starting the system

From the prompt of the drive on which you have loaded the PAS software, change to the PAS directory. For example, if you loaded PAS on drive C, type:

C:> **CD PAS**

At the subsequent prompt, type PAS as follows:

C:PAS> **PAS**

Restriction on the educational version

There is only one restriction on the use of the educational version of PAS. You are only allowed to enter dates from 1/1/97 to 12/31/99.

Appendix D

How to Backup and Restore Data Files

Introduction

Backup

To "backup" means to make a copy of something.

"Backing up" means copying the PAS information from your hard disk onto one or more diskettes.

The reason why you backup your hard disk is that such information can be accidentally erased. Although this is a rare occurrence in a clean and orderly environment, it can be corrected ONLY if proper backups are available.

This appendix explains how to backup your data files.

Restore

To "restore" means to bring back to a former, more desirable condition.

This appendix also explains how to use the automatic procedures to restore your data files. This procedure replaces your data files (the ones you regularly use) with a copy of the data files which you made earlier using the backup function.

When to use the Backup function

Use this function to backup all of your data files AFTER COMPLETING SOME OR ALL OF EACH EXERCISE.

You should understand that if your information is erased, you will have to re–enter everything you entered since the last time you did a backup. The question of how often to backup, therefore, becomes: HOW MUCH INFORMATION ARE YOU WILLING TO RE–ENTER?

Creating Backup diskettes

Before you can backup your data files the very first time, you must create the diskettes that are used to make the backup copies.

You must make three complete sets ("series") of backup diskettes: series A, series B and series C. NOTE: Since the data from the exercises in this text can easily be contained on ONE diskette, you will need only one diskette for EACH of the three "series."

Here's why you use three backup diskettes, instead of just one or two:

The first time you backup, you use series A. For the second backup, you use series B. Then the third time you backup, you use series C. Then for the next backup, you go back to series A. In other words, you rotate the backup sets: A,B,C,A,B,C,A,B,C, etc.

Then, if you ever encounter a situation where you have to "restore" erased information, you always start with the most recent backup series. You may find, however, that the same information is also erased on THAT backup series. (This can occur if you backed up after the information had been erased.) In that case, you go to the previous backup series.

The third backup series (the oldest one at any given time) is a fail–safe. You'll probably never need it. But it's wise to have it, just in case. Since you're only making one backup series at a time (you don't make all three series each time you backup), it takes no longer to do it this way; and it's the "professional" way to do it.

The only extra overhead in having three backup sets is the expense of the diskettes them–selves, and that is a small price to pay to do it right.

All diskettes must be formatted and blank(no files on them) before initial use.

You can backup onto any size diskette which is compatible with your diskette drive A.

Labeling Backup diskettes

Before you use the backup diskettes the very first time, clearly label each diskette for the three "series" as follows:

PAS backup series _____ (A or B or C)

Be sure your diskette labels are easy to read. A mistake made because of a difficult–to–read label could be very costly to you.

Using the Backup function

Follow these steps to back up PAS data files:

1. Remove any diskette which may be in drive A.

2. Change to your PAS top–level directory. For example, if you have installed PAS on your C: drive, type **CD PAS** at the C: prompt and press ENTER. The resulting prompt will be C:\PAS .

3. Get the backup diskette you will be using for this backup. It will be going into drive A (but not yet).

4. Type: **PASBU** and press ENTER. This starts the backup procedure.

If you are using PAS on a network, the next screen cautions you NOT to perform a backup at the same time that another user on the system may be altering the data.

```
Please ensure that no other users are currently using
the Practical Accounting System.  If other users are on the
system, press CTRL/C now, and re-run this batch later.
Press any key to continue . . .
```

The following screen then appears:

```
Practical Accounting Software backup procedure                L-G LAWN AND GARDEN
Backup information

    Your Practical Accounting System data files were last backed up on  99/99/99
    using backup series X.  The oldest set of backup diskettes is series  X.
    You should use series X as your next set of backup diskettes.

                          Backup date        Backup series used

                           99/99/99                 X
                           99/99/99                 X
                           99/99/99                 X

Do you wish to backup Practical Accounting System now?
```

(If this is the first time your data files have ever been backed up on your computer, this screen will be somewhat different than the above, but "DO YOU WISH TO BACKUP PRACTICAL ACCOUNTING SOFTWARE NOW ?" will still appear in the same place, and you should answer as instructed below.)

This screen shows you the last three backups you made and which series was used for each backup. It also tells you which series to use for this backup.

5. To proceed with the backup, answer Y to "DO YOU WISH TO BACKUP PRACTICAL ACCOUNTING SOFTWARE NOW?". Otherwise, answer N and the program will end.

6. Various messages appear on the screen, telling you which diskettes to mount and explaining briefly what is occurring. Follow the instructions exactly.

   MAKE SURE YOU MOUNT THE CORRECT DISKETTE IN THE CORRECT DRIVE.

   The backup procedure puts all of your data onto the backup diskette. NOTE: In the midst of backing up your data, PAS interrupts with instructions to IGNORE an upcoming MS–DOS instruction to "Insert last backup diskette in Drive A:". You should press any key to continue the backup process.

After the backup is completed, you will see the following screen:

```
Practical Accounting System backup procedure                L-G LAWN AND GARDEN

                        PAS backup procedure

    The backup procedure has been completed.  Please be sure to store
    these PAS backup diskettes in a safe location.

    Which diskette series did you use for this backup?

Enter A, B, or C
```

7. Answer "WHICH DISKETTE SERIES DID YOU USE FOR THIS BACKUP?" by entering the letter (A, B, or C) of the series you actually used for the backup just completed.

8. When the "END OF PROCESSING" message appears, the backup is finished.

When to use the Restore function

You normally would use this function only if one or more of your data files were erased. If you do use this restore function, then once it is complete, your data files will be in the same condition they were in at the time you made the backup diskettes.

Using the Restore function

Follow these steps to restore PAS data files:

1. Remove any diskette which may be in drive A.

2. Change to your PAS top–level directory. For example, if you have installed PAS on your C: drive, type **CD PAS** at the C: prompt and press ENTER. The resulting prompt will be C:\PAS .

3. Get the most recent backup diskette. It will be going into drive A (but not yet).

4. Type: **PASRE** and press ENTER. This starts the restore procedure.

   If you are using PAS on a network, the next screen cautions you NOT to perform a restore at the same time that another user on the system may be accessing the data.

```
Please ensure that no other users are currently using
the Practical Accounting System.  If other users are on the
system, press CTRL/C now, and re-run this batch later.
Press any key to continue ...
```

The following screen then appears:

```
Practical Accounting Software restore procedure              L-G LAWN AND GARDEN
Restore information

   Your PAS system was last backed up  99/99/99  using backup series X.
   You should now use series X to restore Practical Accounting Software.

                              Backup date        Backup series used

                               99/99/99                  X
                               99/99/99                  X
                               99/99/99                  X


Do you wish to restore PAS now?
```

This screen shows you the last three backups you made and which series was used for each backup. It also tells you which series to use for this restore.

5. To proceed with the restore, answer Y to "DO YOU WISH TO RESTORE PAS NOW?". Otherwise, answer N and the program will end.

6. Various messages appear on the screen, telling you which diskettes to mount and explaining briefly what is occurring. Follow the instructions exactly.

   MAKE SURE YOU MOUNT THE CORRECT DISKETTE IN THE CORRECT DRIVE.

7. The restore procedure returns all of your previously backed up data from the backup diskette to your computer's hard drive. NOTE: In the seeming midst of restoring your data, PAS interupts with the message, "RESTORE ERROR – Practical Accounting restore procedure unsuccessful." This is NOT the case. All of your data files have been successfully restored. The message is incorrect, and the restore is finished.

   REMEMBER, "RESTORE" PUTS THE DATA FILES BACK INTO THE CONDITION THEY WERE IN WHEN YOU MADE THE BACKUP.

8. The chart on the next page will assist you in keeping track of all backup and restore activity.

Log of Backup & Restore Activity

Backup Series	Backup Date	Backup Time	Comments
A			
B			
C			
A			
B			
C			
A			
B			
C			
A			
B			
C			
A			
B			
C			
A			
B			
C			
A			
B			
C			
A			
B			
C			
A			
B			
C			
A			
B			
C			

Appendix E

How to Export Data Files for Lotus 1–2–3 Use

Introduction

Using the the File Utilities function of PAS, you can export data files in ASCII format for later importing into Lotus 1–2–3.

"ASCII" stands for "American Standard Code for Information Interchange". When you export a file", you are copying records from a data file to an "export" file in ASCII format. This format is used by some popular spreadsheet, word processing, and database systems. Lotus 1–2–3 can "import" ASCII–formatted data files, and then manipulate and display the data in various spreadsheets.

Using this function

Follow these steps to export data files to Lotus 1–2–3:

1. Change to your PAS top–level directory. For example: D:\PAS>

2. Type: **PASFU** and press ENTER. This starts the File Utility program.

   The following screen then appears:

```
Practical Accounting System file utilities                L-G LAWN AND GARDEN

                         Please select
                                1. Sales Invoicing
                                2. Inventory Management
                                3. Accounts Receivable
                                4. Accounts Payable
                                5. Payroll
                                6. General Ledger
                                7. Check Reconciliation
```

3. Select the part of the package from which you wish to export data by typing the appropriate number and pressing ENTER.

   You will see a screen similar to the one shown on the following page:

```
Practical Accounting System file utilities                L-G LAWN AND GARDEN
General Ledger

                  Please select
                         1. Rebuild a file
                         2. Export a file
                         3. Restore from an export file
                         4. Initialize files
                         5. Reset item commitments
```

NOTE: Selection #5 only appears for Inventory Management.

4. Type 2 (Export a File) from the above File Utilities menu, and press ENTER.

   You then see a screen similar to the following one for General Ledger:

```
Practical Accounting System file utilities                L-G LAWN AND GARDEN
Export a file

                  Please select
                         1. Chart of accounts .................... (TCHART)
                         2. Distribution file ......................... (TCDIST)
                         3. General journal file .................. (TGJTRX)
                         4. Financial statement layout file  (LAYOUT)
```

   As the screen shows, there are two names for each file: one in English, the other in "computerese". For example, your computer recognizes the Chart of Accounts file as TCHART.

5. Type the number of the data file you want to export, and press ENTER. The numbers are shown to the left of the file names.

6. Enter your hard disk device letter (usually C or D), or diskette drive A if you want the export file to be on a diskette. NOTE: The export file will havae the same name as the original file, but the extension is ".EXP".

7. Answer N at "Any Change?".

8. Press F1 twice ("First" and "Last") to indicate that you want to export the whole file. As the file is processed, a record count displays and increments by one for each record processed.

9. When the export is complete, press TAB or END. You may export another file through the same procedure, or press TAB or END as needed to exit PAS.